DUMBARTON OAKS STUDIES XLVIII

BOUTTIOS AND LATE ANTIQUE ANTIOCH

DUMBARTON OAKS STUDIES XLVIII

BOUTTIOS AND LATE ANTIQUE ANTIOCH

Reconstructing a Lost Historian

BENJAMIN GARSTAD

DUMBARTON OAKS RESEARCH LIBRARY AND COLLECTION
WASHINGTON, DC

Printed in the United States of America

ISBN 978-0-88402-493-4
LCCN 2021951173

Cataloging-in-Publication data for this book
is on file with the Library of Congress:
https://lccn.loc.gov/2021951173

www.doaks.org/publications

Designed and typeset by Melissa Tandysh

Cover: Marble Roman copy of Eutychides' *Tyche of Antioch*,
Galleria dei Candelabri, Vatican Museums; original dates to the third century BCE.
Photo courtesy Jastrow / Wikimedia Commons.

For Alice, Constance, Hanna, and Georgia

Hør meg, Libanios! Hvorledes kom jeg hit? Med fortrøstning til denne stads innbyggere. Antiokia, som solkongen særlig har kåret til sitte sete, skulle hjelpe meg å gjøre god igjen all den urett og utakknemlighet som så lenge har vært øvet imot de udødelige. Men hvorledes har I møtt meg? Noen med tross, andre med lunkenhet. Hva må jeg ikke oppleve her?

Hear me, Libanius! How did I come hither? With full confidence in the people of this city. Antioch, chosen by the Sun-King for his especial seat, was to help me to repair all the wrong and ingratitude which had so long been shown to the immortals. But how have you met me? Some with defiance, others with lukewarmness. What have I not had to endure here?

—HENRIK IBSEN, *Keiser og Galilæer: Et verdenshistorisk skuespill, Keiser Julian*, Act 3, Scene 1 (Ibsen, *Samlede verker*, 497–98), trans. William Archer (Ibsen, *Emperor and Galilean*, 387).

CONTENTS

FIGURES

TABLE

ACKNOWLEDGMENTS

I vividly recall the evening I drew a copy of Carl Frick's *Chronica Minora* off a shelf in the Dumbarton Oaks library and encountered for the first time the riddles of Picus-Zeus and his traverse from Assyria to Italy and of Alexander's liberation of the Romans. These puzzles have occupied me for half my life now and—who knows?—perhaps determined its course in some way. It is, at any rate, most gratifying, as well as humbling, to draw my scholarly endeavors full circle and publish what I have managed to discover so far in the Dumbarton Oaks Studies series. This would not have been possible without the good graces and hard work of Jan Ziolkowski, Kathleen Sparkes, and Colin Whiting. I am just as grateful to David M. Weeks, copyeditor extraordinaire, who immeasurably improved my writing.

As an undergraduate, my interest in Late Antiquity was fostered by teachers like Barry Baldwin and Robert Schmiel, who did not hold themselves above the perusal of postclassical texts; quite the contrary. In Haijo Westra I found a model not only for the reading of texts, but also for the living of life; I am, however, perhaps most grateful to him for always bearing with my enthusiasms. I could not have asked for a better doctoral supervisor than Karla Pollmann, who did her best to inculcate her exacting standards in me and inadvertently offered me the example of an effort to broaden the horizons of Classics by sheer force of will. Nor can I forget Adrian Gratwick, who often startlingly combined great warmth and kindness with the most uncompromising critical analysis—always to my benefit. Danuta Shanzer has never officially been my teacher, but since first we met, she has been an advocate, a confidant, and a mentor to me; I may happily claim to be her pupil.

Though we have often been apart, Elaine Fulton has been my boon companion throughout the course of our careers; we have trudged together and we

have charged headlong together, but together has always made the march better. Michael Carroll has been the best of colleagues, as well as a constant reminder that the demands of scholarship are absolute, and the rewards of friendship are infinite. Olivier Gengler has brought home to me how lively, engaging, and not least collegial the study of Byzantine chronicles can be. On many occasions and in many ways Sye Van Maanen has offered me the injunction *Sursum corda*, and I have certainly been thankful.

In the course of this lengthy research project, I have accrued many debts of gratitude, large and small, to friends and colleagues throughout the world. It is a great pleasure to recall these friends and register these debts, even if I can never hope to repay them. My sincerest thanks are due to: Francesca Alesse, Ory Amitay, Jacqueline Arthur-Montagne, Liz Baynham, Marianne Bergmann, Henning Börm, Jonas Borsch, Dietrich Boschung, Tommaso Braccini, Stanley Burstein, Laura Carrara, Petr Charvát, Franco De Angelis, Muriel Debié, Christian Thrue Djurslev, Ken Dowden, Boris Dunsch, Agnese Fontana, Jean-Luc Fournet, Christian Gastgeber, Matt Gibbs, Adam Goldwyn, Alain Gowing, Fritz Graf, Fiona Haarer, Jürgen Hammerstaedt, Edward Harris, Gregory Hays, Waldemar Heckel, Michael W. Herren, Sonia Hewitt, John Hilton, Frank Holt, George Huxley, Elizabeth Jeffreys, Corinne Jouanno, Sandy Jung, Walter Kaegi, Anthony Kaldellis, Joel Kalvesmaki, David Konstan, Noel Lenski, Victoria Leonard, Wolf Liebeschuetz, Edvard Lorkovic, Ralph Mathisen, Mischa Meier, Beat Näf, Krzysztof Nawotka, Lea Niccolai, Richard Matthew Pollard, Frances Pownall, Jessica Romney, Catherine Saliou, John Serrati, Eckart Schütrumpf, Kevin Solez, Jacob Stern, Richard Stoneman, Warren Treadgold, Yvona Trnka-Amrhein, Emma Vosper, Pat Wheatley, Craig Williams, Marek Winiarczyk, Michael Winterbottom, Agnieszka Wojciechowska, Ian Wood, John Yardley, and Angela Zielinski Kinney.

My family, my parents, my sisters, Niel Sorensen, Paul Lange, and a great crowd of aunts and uncles and cousins, as well as in-laws, have all reminded me that I am not alone. It has been a salutary discipline and an immense comfort.

There is assuredly a sense in which this project has grown with my family. I started drafting it to the accompaniment of the infant cries of my eldest daughter and I put the finishing touches on it surrounded by the demands and attentions of her and her three sisters. While I have watched these four girls mature in

grace and wit, however, I suspect my work has only increased in tedious length and ungainly bulk. Nevertheless, I have dedicated this book to them in the hope that they have not resented too much the time I have devoted to tracing the shadow of an elusive lost historian while they have been an altogether present reality for me.

While this book is dedicated to my daughters, my greatest debt, as ever, is to my wife for affording me the support, encouragement, inspiration, and time to bring this book to completion. I offer a gratitude that can never be sufficiently expressed to Roxanne, helpmeet indeed.

INTRODUCTION

Bouttios is truly a lost historian. It is not merely that we have no complete work that we can ascribe to him; he has vanished from our picture of ancient historiography. One would search in vain for his entry in all the volumes of Felix Jacoby's *Fragmente der griechischen Historiker*, or even in so exhaustive a reference work as the Pauly-Wissowa *Real-Encyclopädie der classischen Altertumswissenschaft*. If it were not for three citations in the *Chronicle* of John Malalas—each of which has a slightly different spelling of the name—and a couple more even better hidden in the thickets of Jerome's *Chronicle* and the *Chronography* of George the Syncellus, the name of Bouttios would have vanished completely. These few mentions of his name have won Bouttios a narrow place in the attention of modern scholarship, among the sources of Malalas and, with some reservations, in the new *Fragments of the Roman Historians*.[1] The neglect that Bouttios has suffered is unfortunate, however, for students of Late Antiquity no less than for the author's memory. What does remain of Bouttios suggests that he was a remarkable author in his time, on one hand twining together the strands of classical tradition and patristic argument in a manner characteristic of Late Antiquity, and on the other launching out on forays into unprecedented territories of creativity and calumny. And in his own way he exerted a considerable influence; parts at least of the material we can assign to Bouttios found their place in the common stock of Byzantine knowledge about the past, even if they were not associated with his name. Although it may be mysterious and meaningless to us, his account of the gods as ancient human kings, the so-called Picus-Zeus narrative, was the basis of the understanding of the pagan pantheon throughout the Byzantine

1 E. Jeffreys, "Malalas' Sources," 174; Levick and Rich, "Bruttius."

chronicle tradition, as well as in Byzantine encyclopedias.[2] So it seems worthwhile to attempt an examination of Bouttios in detail, to determine just what he contributed to surviving works, the contours of his own writing, and perhaps even what sort of a man he was.

When all the evidence is collected and thoroughly sifted, an intriguing picture of Bouttios, the man and his work, emerges. His name has a slightly different spelling each time he is cited, but sorting out the most probable alternative reveals an individual implicated in the society and history of Antioch. And this is consistent with other signs that Bouttios was Antiochene, not only in terms of residence, but also, we may suggest, in terms of outlook. He wrote in the midst of the fourth century, some time between 330 and 380, but there are also indications that he may have written during Julian the Apostate's stay in Antioch (winter 362/63) and played a part in the city's raillery against the emperor. The interests and tendencies evident in the fragments also show that Bouttios was a Christian, and not merely one of the idle pew-warmers the fourth century must have seen in increasing numbers, but a committed controversialist. His contribution to the ideological disputes of his day consisted not of the more familiar sermon or declamation, but of a work that purported to be history. Not a chronicle, as John Malalas's descriptions of Bouttios might suggest, but a series of largely fictive and often scurrilous vignettes which tend to overturn the standard historical picture with its heroes and notes of praise. Bouttios conveyed his points not so much through argumentation and a command of the facts as with a deft play upon the sentiments of his audience and their habitual reactions to popular fiction. In this he fell below the best standards of historiography, but would hardly have found himself out of step with most disputatious ideologues of any age.

The effort to unearth a lost historian is perhaps at odds with current trends in scholarship. *Quellenforschung*, it is generally acknowledged, had its heyday in the nineteenth century and elicits less interest nowadays. Such an effort might seem to be particularly inconsistent with what has been the prevailing approach to Malalas. The Australian team that prepared an English translation of Malalas and a subsequent volume of studies seems to have been guided by an inclination to read Malalas's *Chronicle* as the integral and unified composition of a single author. As Brian Croke put it, "The chronicle reveals a strong identity for its

2 See below, p. 233 and n. 2.

author. Throughout the work the reader detects the author's sense of purpose and organization of material and cannot but feel that this is no aimless and incoherent chronicle."[3] This approach is by no means unjustified; my own research has shown that Malalas makes the details of his first books speak to the course of events in the last books, and has the contentions of the last explain the narrative of the first.[4] There is a sense, however, in which the view of the inclusive and accommodating chronicler as an integral author has missed a step: that of the careful examination of his sources. This seems especially to be so if we compare the case of Malalas as an author preserving fragments to that of Diodorus Siculus and how his work has been handled over time.

In the none-too-distant past, the *Bibliotheca* or *Library of History* of Diodorus Siculus was treated as little more than a repository of otherwise lost historians. Oswyn Murray referred to it, not without reason, as "a quarry for lost historians—for the work is genuinely a library, a succession of abbreviations of other people's books."[5] The accomplishment and ideas of Diodorus himself were almost entirely neglected in the effort to recover his sources. But Kenneth Sacks's 1990 monograph, which sought to establish Diodorus's own point of view, how it reflected the times in which he lived, and how he imposed it on his sources, marked a turning point in the study of Diodorus.[6] Since then research, such as the work of Iris Sulimani and Charles E. Muntz on the earlier, often mythological books of the *Library*, has followed suit, explicitly rejecting the attempt to ransack Diodorus's work for its sources and endeavoring to come to grips with Diodorus's own project and purposes.[7] As a consequence of this shift in approach and the laudable efforts it has produced we have learned a great deal not only about one of the most ambitious and voluminous historians of antiquity, but also about his sources. Observing how Diodorus manipulated his material and tailored it to his own ends affords us a more refined sensibility in the process of disentangling the remains of lost authors and clearer insight into which ideas belong to them and which to the author who preserved them.

3 Croke, "Malalas, the Man and His Work," 20.

4 Garstad, "Origins of Paganism."

5 Murray, "Greek Historians," 237.

6 Sacks, *Diodorus Siculus*; cf. Sacks, "Diodorus and His Sources."

7 Sulimani, *Diodorus' Mythistory*; Muntz, *Diodorus Siculus*; cf. Yarrow, *Historiography*, 116–18.

If, however, scholarship had from the outset and consistently approached Diodorus with the holistic perspective and the appreciation of the historian's capacity to integrate his sources that characterize current research, it is very possible that we would have missed out on several important studies of his sources. If we had been concentrating all along on how Diodorus's treatment of Egypt fits into the thought evident throughout the *Bibliotheca*, would we have had Murray's perspicacious analysis of Hecataeus of Abdera?[8] If we had only been concerned to see how his Assyrian history answered Diodorus's broader interests, would we have seen collected the most extensive narrative fragments of Ctesias of Cnidos and clarified our impression of an author who gave antiquity a widely read romantic history of the Orient?[9] We could point to a number of other studies that have involved extracting material from Diodorus and attending to the author preserved in the *Bibliotheca* instead of to the preserving author.[10] Each of these studies presumed that Diodorus could be treated as something of an anthologist, and one who allowed us to discuss with some confidence authors from periods and contexts other than his own, with ideas and intentions different from his own. This approach, which may be open to some criticism, did nevertheless make Diodorus an important source not only for the first century BCE, in which he lived and wrote, but also for the thought and literature of several previous epochs.

Such "quarrying" as Diodorus was regularly subjected to in the past may be disparaged as an abuse of the preserving author, but its results are not therefore invalid. Indeed, it may be seen as a positive benefit inasmuch as it serves to extend and expand the value and interest of the preserving author. Yet despite

8 Murray, "Hecataeus of Abdera"; but see also Burton, *Diodorus Siculus, Book I*, whose commentary is less interested in the question of Diodorus's immediate sources than in the evidence he might provide for Egyptian life and lore.

9 As in Lenfant, *Ctésias de Cnide*, and Llewellyn-Jones and Robson, *Ctesias' History*.

10 For instance, T. Brown, *Timaeus of Tauromenium*, and now Baron, *Timaeus of Tauromenium*, on Timaeus of Tauromenium; Rusten, *Dionysius Scytobrachion*, on Dionysius Scytobrachion; Burstein, *Agatharchides of Cnidus*, on Agatharchides of Cnidos; Edelstein and Kidd, *Posidonius*, on Posidonius; Bosworth, "Historical Setting of Megasthenes," on Megasthenes; and Winiarczyk, *Euhemeros von Messene* and Sacred History *of Euhemerus*, on Euhemerus, although Winiarczyk is very careful to designate all of the material he derives from Diodorus *testimonia* rather than *fragmenta*.

a few studies dedicated to Malalas's sources,[11] this stage of research on Malalas seems to have been largely neglected, certainly as compared to the course of work on the *Bibliotheca* of Diodorus. Perhaps this neglect is due to a profound mistrust of the reliability of Malalas, particularly when it comes to the veracity or even the very existence of the authorities he cites. Warren Treadgold has recently advanced the theory that many of the sources cited by Malalas are bogus authors of his own creation, intended to help him pass off his hasty paraphrase of the chronicle of Eustathius of Epiphania as his own composition.[12] There have, however, been even more recent calls to return to the question of Malalas's sources and efforts to flesh out and characterize them. Philip Wood has indicated the need to query the text of Malalas with an eye to identifying several, often anonymous, testimonies for different periods, with their own voices and attitudes.[13] One year's conference of the Tübingen Malalas commentary project and a subsequent volume of proceedings were devoted to the problem of Malalas's sources.[14] In that volume Peter Van Nuffelen introduced his own work, with the avowed methodology of taking Malalas's references to lost historians seriously and rejecting what he calls "a hermeneutics of suspicion"; his method, as he demonstrates, produces results.[15]

The present study is intended as a contribution to this careful reexamination of the sources of John Malalas. I hope to demonstrate that there is some portion of Malalas's material—no matter how thoroughly digested and awkwardly regurgitated it may be—that belongs to Bouttios and responds to the concerns of the fourth century, not the sixth, and that took shape in the contentions of that earlier period, even if it retained some interest for Malalas and his contemporaries. A certain amount of this material can be found in those passages for which Bouttios is cited as a source by name, but these initial passages reveal interests and characteristics that have correspondences in other portions of Malalas's

11 Bourier, *Über die Quellen*; von Stauffenberg, *Kaisergeschichte bei Malalas*; E. Jeffreys, "Malalas' Sources."

12 Treadgold, "Byzantine World Histories" and *Early Byzantine Historians*, 235–56, 311–29. This interpretation has been challenged by Gengler, "Johannes Malalas und seine Quellen"; cf. Carrara and Gengler, "Zu den Quellen der Chronik," 16–18.

13 P. Wood, "Multiple Voices."

14 Carrara, Meier, and Radtki-Jansen, *Die Weltchronik: der Johannes Malalas.*

15 Van Nuffelen, "Malalas and the Chronographic Tradition."

Chronicle, as well as in other works, especially the *Excerpta Latina Barbari*. As with most fragmentary historians, the result offers not so much a complete outline as uneven and disjointed remnants. But these fragments disclose consistent patterns and intentions, and reveal an author who was probably an Antiochene and most likely a Christian, and one who peered into the remote past and revisited the reputations of the most renowned emperors in order to address the pressing concerns of his own day, in the later fourth century. While he spoke of bygone kings, he implicitly established a contrast between Constantine and Julian. He seems to have presented his work as a history, but depended on the tropes and imagery of popular fiction in order to convey partisan and polemical points in a political and ideological debate.

The picture that results from our examination of the work, if not the man, must end up seeming strange and idiosyncratic. There is an account of the gods that corresponds to no known mythography, a series of slanders of the great men of the past as perpetrators of human sacrifice, and an interest in unusual, perhaps fictitious incidents involving the persecution of Christians. There are, nevertheless, indications of some overall sense to it. The figures of pagan religion, whether the traditional gods or the civic *tychai*, are consistently denied the status of divine beings; the pagan rulers, even the best of them, are shown to be criminal and their legitimacy is called into question, but their blood-soaked succession has its redeeming climax in the person of Constantine. There even seems to be a sort of historical equilibrium or contrast between conquest and subjection to eastern peoples under Nebuchadnezzar and liberation and sovereignty for the western peoples under Alexander. And reducing the material we ascribe to Bouttios to some sort of conscious and intentional order responds to Herbert Butterfield's invitation to see the history of "the fourth century of the Christian era," in particular, not in the general and abstract terms of a play of the vast forces of Christianity and Paganism, but rather to "pursue it in its concrete incidence till we discover into what manifold detail it differentiates itself, and learn how various were its workings in actual life, how surprising even its by-play and the side-issues which it raised, how rich its underlying complexity and its implications in human story."[16] Butterfield likewise articulated the inherent interest of this period in particular and all its products: "It is obvious that great and palpable

16 Butterfield, *Whig Interpretation*, 71.

human issues were being raised and decided in these years, and special varieties of human relationship arose, giving life and experience a peculiar intensity. One cannot avoid asking what men were like when they were breaking with an old order of things, changing Gods and putting on new habits and making new adjustments to life. It must be interesting to learn how such a human crisis would present itself in a single soul, in a home, a village, a court."[17] Indeed it must, and so we turn our attention to the fragments of Bouttios.

The first task involved in dealing with the work of a lost historian as an aspect of the "manifold detail" of "such a human crisis" is to determine what evidence remains of his work and to assemble the fragments, and this is tackled in the first four chapters. After an outline of the methodology in the first chapter, we start in the second with those passages in which Bouttios is cited as a source, but it remains to be seen just how much of each of these passages goes back to Bouttios, that is, to decide the extent of each fragment. The distinctive characteristics and apparent interests of these passages associated with Bouttios's name, even their own sources, have clear analogues in other passages in which Bouttios is not named, not only in the *Chronicle* of John Malalas but also in the *Excerpta Latina Barbari*. These passages are also included in the number of Bouttios's fragments. A rationale will be provided in the third chapter for assigning to Bouttios all of the remarkable narratives of virgin sacrifice at city foundations that occur in Malalas, and in the fourth chapter for ascribing to him the parallel accounts of the gods as ancient human kings in Malalas and the *Excerpta*. This task of assembling the fragments is undertaken in the first four chapters. Its results, in the form of a collection of texts and translations, are set out as an appendix at the end of this volume. The translations of the fragments and all translations throughout this book, unless otherwise noted, are my own.

In the fifth chapter we examine these collected fragments in order to sort out what they can tell us about Bouttios the man. The problems to be solved are perhaps more basic than in many other cases. Each of the five attestations of the historian's name, for example, offers a slightly different spelling, and we have to justify our choice among the alternatives as much as determine the correct form.

17 Butterfield, *Whig Interpretation*, 70.

The indisputable dating of Bouttios covers a span of centuries, and our task will be to narrow the window enough to arrive at a meaningful period, although I believe we can actually suggest a remarkably precise pinpoint for the date of his composition, namely Julian's stay in Antioch over the winter of 362–363. The evidence that Bouttios was himself from Antioch is circumstantial, but once the suggestion is made, certain features of the fragments fall into place as consistent with an Antiochene milieu. Our fragments provide only vague hints about other aspects of Bouttios's identity, but they offer relatively strong indications of his ideological bent; he appears to have been a Christian who took his stance seriously enough to engage in antipagan polemics.

The problem of chapter 6, the genre of Bouttios's work, has to be assessed carefully, since Malalas's description of him as a chronographer seems to be misleading. The fragments do not fit consistently into any recognized chronography, but they do have the chronological features of historical notices, such as reign lengths and ages at death. Bouttios's work seems to have taken the form of a history and dealt with historical characters, but it was a largely fictional and partisan contribution to the debate between paganism and Christianity. The accounts of *tyche* sacrifices seem to disclose the overall structure of the work, with a series of macabre but telling atrocities culminating in the romantic heroism of Constantine.

The seventh chapter attempts to place the remains of Bouttios in the context of the debates—as much ideological as political—of the fourth century. These debates often crystallized into a contrast of personalities, especially those of Constantine and Julian, taken to be the champions of Christianity and paganism respectively. The fragments of Bouttios, especially the tyche sacrifice narratives, can be seen to correspond to the praise of Constantine and the blame of Julian that circulated in the fourth century. In form and structure, and even in precise wording, they reflect the rhetoric of human sacrifice and bloodless sacrifice that were attached to both of these figures. Bouttios, moreover, seems to be responding to some of the literary work Julian produced in Antioch. This can be seen not only in his apparent choice of genre, the didactic fiction, which reflects the *Caesars* of Julian and its critical review of emperors, but also in numerous details that assume a more definite meaning when set against certain passages in Julian. The work of Bouttios also appears to exploit invented historical narrative to elaborate or substantiate the political theory articulated by Eusebius of Caesarea that the true ruler was a "friend of God." As the friend of God, according to Eusebius,

Constantine derived the kingly virtues from communion with the Divine and was a king indeed, whereas the pagan rulers who preceded him, being godless, were without kingly virtues and only seemed to be kings, but were in fact tyrants, and as such were led by demons into such characteristically heinous crimes as human sacrifice. This theory, which rendered all the pagan rulers who came before Constantine—as well as any who might come after him—illegitimate, was given vivid narrative substance in the history of Bouttios.

Bouttios took up the cudgels not only against pagan rulers but also against pagan religion. The fragments reveal an assault on two fronts: against the traditional pantheon of the Greeks and Romans on the one hand, and against the cult of the goddess Tyche on the other. The attack on the gods, on their divinity and their character, discussed in chapter 8, is presented as an account of their careers as ancient human kings. The so-called Picus-Zeus narrative is a combination of features commonly found in the euhemeristic accounts of the gods and in the arguments of the Christian apologists against the worship of the Olympians. What is remarkable about the account of the gods ascribed to Bouttios is that whereas the apologists were generally content to cite euhemerizing authorities or even offer sketches of their narratives, this account is a novel and distinct narrative, with the usual basic point about the nature of the "gods." As such, it is itself a contribution to the euhemeristic tradition, the climax, even, of that ancient tradition. Bouttios also tackled the figure of tyche as the personification of an abstract force that was supposed to make its power felt in the lives of men and the course of history, as the popular and revered goddess of luck, and the ubiquitous embodiment of civic pride and prosperity. By insisting that every instance of the tyche cult had its origin in the grisly sacrifice of a helpless victim, Bouttios drained the goddess of her control over human affairs and turned her shrines and images into reminders of the rapacious tyranny of rulers devoted to paganism. Bouttios's approach to this aspect of pagan religion is examined in detail in the ninth chapter.

Chapter 10 is something of an experiment in interpretation and criticism. If Bouttios's history seems to be a sequence of palpably fictitious vignettes which deviate wildly from the received historical record, we may fairly ask how we are to read it. In what sense is this history? One way toward an answer to this question is comparison with another sort of narrative that seems to come about in times of intense political and ideological opposition, namely the conspiracy

theory, or a discourse in what Richard Hofstadter termed "the paranoid style."[18] The abandonment of standard history, but the insistence on evidence, the invention of facts, the stress upon simultaneously appalling and fascinating incidents, the lurid accounts of the victimization of women, and the unmistakable partisan tendency that characterize the fragments of Bouttios all find their analogues in the effusions of the paranoid style. Such narratives, such history, if you will, convey not what has happened, but rather what one's ideological opponents are supposed to be capable of. They constitute not so much a record of events as a denunciation and a dire warning. This comparison is intended to suggest not that ancient literature can be read in modern terms without making ample allowance for their different contexts, but rather that times of ideological polarization, when the stresses of political and social opposition penetrate to the very marrow of individual identity, tend to evoke rather consistent human responses, particularly in regard to the defamation of one's enemies. And it is this consistency that can help us to understand what Bouttios wrote.

18 Hofstadter, *Paranoid Style*, 3–40.

PART I

ASSEMBLING THE FRAGMENTS

1

ASSEMBLING THE FRAGMENTS

It is one thing to call an author a lost historian, and another to call him a fragmentary historian. A lost historian is one whose work has not survived the vicissitudes of chance and circumstance down to the present; citations of his name, in spite of that, alert us to the fact that he wrote and exercised some influence on other writers. A fragmentary historian is one whose work has left some identifiable remains and can in some measure be reconstituted, its contents—in part, if not on the whole—and even its general tendency distinguished in portions of texts that do survive. The history of Bouttios has left traces, however faint at times, in surviving works, and it is up to us to determine which passages in those works can be considered fragments.

This sort of task is relatively easy with a preserving author like Eusebius of Caesarea, who assiduously cited the sources of his material, tended to mark off what came from each, and often quoted them verbatim, or Photius, who paraphrased acknowledged authors one by one.[1] It is rather more difficult when the preserving author is John Malalas, who liberally sprinkled his *Chronicle* with citations of authors he knew only through intermediaries and integrated his sources so that they can only be extricated painstakingly and tentatively, or the

1 Numerous pitfalls, of course, remain in the task of extracting fragments even from either of these authors. Perhaps the best guide to avoiding such hazards in the *Bibliotheca* of Photius, as well as the handiest introduction to the text as a whole, remains Treadgold, *Nature of the* Bibliotheca.

compiler of the *Excerpta Latina Barbari*, who rarely cites authorities, even when his material is obviously derivative. It is in the work of Malalas and the *Excerpta*, nevertheless, that the fragments of Bouttios are to be found. This chapter, as well as the next three, is devoted to demonstrating the process by which these fragments have been identified. In the absence of clear parameters set by the preserving authors, we have tried to discern distinctive features and consistent interests, and to reconstruct coherent narratives. This process has admittedly depended on no small amount of speculation, but no more, I hope, than what reason allows and the evidence demands. We shall begin with an outline of the methodology used to identify fragments in the first four chapters, but first a few qualifications and definitions.

"Fragment" is the conventional term for each of the remains of a lost author like Bouttios, but it may also be inappropriate in his case. As far as we can tell, there is no instance of direct quotation from the work of Bouttios. What we have is material paraphrased from his history, but it is difficult to determine the extent of the paraphrase.[2] On the one hand, John Malalas has more or less thoroughly digested all of his sources to produce a chronicle that is his own, but certain turns of phrase still cluster around citations of Bouttios. Likewise, narrative passages that parallel the Bouttios material in Malalas stand out from the stark chronography of the *Excerpta Latina Barbari*, but they have clearly been adapted to the contents of the *Excerpta* and the purposes of its compiler, as well as his clipped style. On the other hand, the similarities in word and phrase between Malalas and the *Excerpta*, apparent despite the texts' being in two different languages, suggest that Malalas, writing in Bouttios's own Greek, stays recognizably close to their common source. Passages in both Malalas and the *Excerpta* reflect the content of Bouttios's work, but do not necessarily preserve his very words. These passages may not be fragments, strictly speaking, but to consistently speak of "derivative material" or even "remains" would be awkward and tedious. So we shall refer to "fragments" throughout, but it should be understood that this term is used as something of a convenience for those passages indicating the content of a lost history.

2 Most, *Collecting Fragments*, vii, notes that historical fragments, as opposed to poetic or philosophical fragments, are most likely to be paraphrased since they tend to be cited for the information they contain rather than for their precise wording.

It may be said that there are two approaches to the collection of fragments, the "minimal" and the "maximal."[3] The minimal approach limits itself to passages in which the fragmentary author is cited by name and to the immediate context of that citation. The cautious conservatism of this approach rarely leaves the collector of fragments open to charges of making more than what the evidence would allow or constructing a house of cards, but its practitioners can also seem to indulge in a frustrating complacency, content to leave questions unanswered and leads unfollowed. The maximal approach, in contrast, spreads its net more broadly and seeks to identify any material that might possibly be associated with the lost author. This approach may seem adventurous, maybe even reckless, and constantly runs the risk of gathering in material that actually has nothing to do with the lost author, but it is thorough and exhaustive, leaving no stone unturned, and leaving readers free to discard what they consider unwarranted, rather than leaving them wondering what else might have been offered to their judgment. This approach also judiciously assumes that an author—an ancient one, anyway—who uses a source will not always signal that exploitation with an explicit citation, but might include derivative material with no indication of its origin.

The minimal approach has been taken to the fragments of Bouttios (under the name of Bruttius) by Hermann Peter and most recently by Barbara Levick and John Rich.[4] This has resulted in a page or two's worth of fragments which offer a solid foundation for further research, but also raise quite as many questions as they answer. The approach of the present work is decidedly maximal. It is hoped that this can be shown to be not a desperate clutching at straws, but a reasoned and methodical working out of the implications of the secure fragments of Bouttios. New material is added not so much to pad out a disappointingly slender collection of fragments as to explicate the few fragments that are produced by the minimal approach.

For instance, one of the fragments from Malalas (our **F 16.1**) also identified both by Peter and by Levick and Rich (their F 2) has Alexander the Great free the Romans, as well as the Greeks and Egyptians, from a combination of eastern nations—the Assyrians, Persians, Parthians, and Medes—and "restore to them

3 I am indebted to Olivier Gengler for suggesting the term "maximal" for the approach to assembling fragments taken in this book.

4 Peter, *Historicorum Romanorum Reliquiae*, 2:ccviii–ccviiii, 160; Levick and Rich, "Bruttius."

all they had lost." This idiosyncratic involvement of the Romans in Alexander's empire has no explanation in the fragment itself, but it is more fully reiterated, along with an indication that Rome had been made subject to these same eastern powers, by a passage in the *Excerpta* (**F 9**). The *Excerpta*, moreover, includes "all the land of the Romans" among the territories conquered by the famous oriental king Nebuchadnezzar (**F 11**). In neither case does the *Excerpta* cite Bouttios as its source—the *Excerpta* never names Bouttios at all—but both passages not only go over the same peculiar ground, but also provide critical evidence for making sense of a distinctive detail that is identifiable with Bouttios on the basis of a secure citation. These passages are thus justifiable as fragments of Bouttios, and offer exemplary grounds for pursuing the maximal approach. It is reassuring to note, however, that the minimal and the maximal approaches do not result in two radically different assessments of Bouttios and his work, but, as we shall see, agree that he was most likely a later Christian author who wrote in Greek and whose history covered a bewildering diversity of topics.[5]

Methodological Outline

Both the minimal and maximal approach to the collection of fragments must start in the same place, with the citations of the lost author. The next step is to determine just how much of the material surrounding the citation can be associated with the cited source. Even here the minimal approach can be betrayed by its innate conservatism. From Malalas's passage on Alexander (**F 16.1**), for instance, Levick and Rich take the phrases that come before the citation of Bouttios, which occurs in the middle of a sentence, to be a fragment indicating the content of the history of "Bruttius," but not those after the citation, even though the phrases that follow are all participle clauses grammatically dependent on the main verb that comes before the citation.[6] Not only the construction of the sentence but

5 Peter, *Historicorum Romanorum Reliquiae*, 2:ccviiii; Levick and Rich, "Bruttius," 1:593–95.

6 Levick and Rich, "Bruttius," 2:1092 (F 2) provide as much context as Peter, *Historicorum Romanorum Reliquiae*, 2:160 (F 2) did, but mark what they consider the actual fragment in bold type: καὶ εὐθέως ὡς πάρδαλις ἐκεῖθεν ὁρμήσας ὁ Ἀλέξανδρος, ἅμα τοῖς σὺν αὐτῷ στρατηγοῖς παρέλαβε πάσας τὰς χώρας. **καὶ νικήσας τὸν Δαρεῖον, βασιλέα Περσῶν, τὸν Ἀσσαλάμου, παρέλαβεν αὐτὸν καὶ πᾶσαν τὴν βασιλείαν αὐτοῦ καὶ πᾶσαν**

also valuable evidence for the subjects treated by Bouttios are lost by this tendency to trim fragments to their barest possible extent. We take the whole sentence as a fragment of Bouttios, but that is not all. The idiosyncratic phrases and claims that occur in this sentence recur in the paragraph as a whole, and we proceed on the assumption that the paragraph in its entirety reflects the content of Bouttios's history. This is especially likely since Bouttios is the only authority cited by Malalas for his material on Alexander. The alternatives seem to be either that Malalas's peculiar narrative of Alexander is attributable to the one source he cites or that Malalas himself composed this material. Its partial appearance in an independent parallel text, the *Excerpta*, makes the second alternative practically impossible. We can add to the core narrative on Alexander not only passages that repeat its distinctive turns of phrase, but also those that round out and complete its singular account of events. So we proceed on the lookout not only for passages that detail the liberation of the Egyptians, Greeks, and Romans, but also those that relate their subjection in the first place.

In regard to Malalas's previous citation of Bouttios, concerning the conception of Perseus (F 7), Peter and Levick and Rich credit the whole sentence in which the citation occurs to "Bruttius" (their F 1), but do not take its fuller context into account.[7] Bouttios's assertion that "Picus, who is also Zeus" seduced Danae by bribery is presented in deliberate contrast to the version Euripides gave in his drama, that Danae was raped by Zeus after he was transformed into gold and then set adrift in a chest. Euripides' fanciful narration (ἐμυθολόγησεν) is

---

τὴν χώραν Ἀσσυρίων καὶ Μήδων καὶ Πάρθων καὶ Βαβυλωνίων καὶ Περσῶν καὶ πάσας τὰς βασιλείας τῆς γῆς, καθὼς Βόττιος ὁ σοφώτατος συνεγράψατο, ἐλευθερώσας ὁ αὐτὸς Ἀλέξανδρος καὶ τὰς πόλεις καὶ τὰς χώρας καὶ πᾶσαν τὴν γῆν τῶν Ῥωμαίων καὶ Ἑλλήνων καὶ Αἰγυπτίων ἐκ τῆς Ἀσσυρίων καὶ Περσῶν καὶ Πάρθων καὶ Μήδων ὑποταγῆς καὶ δουλείας, ἀποδοὺς Ῥωμαίοις πάντα ἃ ἀπώλεσαν. Van Hoof and Van Neuffelen, *Fragmentary Latin Histories*, 255, claim that "in a strict interpretation, the fragment consists only of the first half of the sentence." Moreover, they include in their translation of this passage a sentence break (after συνεγράψατο) unwarranted by the Greek text. They offer no argument, however, in defense of their dubious claim or their misleading translation.

7 Levick and Rich, "Bruttius," 2:1091 (F 1); cf. Peter, *Historicorum Romanorum Reliquiae*, 2:160 (F 1): ὁ δὲ σοφώτατος Βούττιος, ἱστορικὸς χρονογράφος, ἐξέθετο ὡς ὁ **αὐτὸς Πῖκος ὁ καὶ Ζεὺς οὖσαν ταύτην ἐν κουβουκλείῳ παρακειμένῳ τῇ θαλάσσῃ πολλῷ χρυσῷ πείσας ἠδυνήθη προτρεψάμενος· ἥντινα ἁρπάσας ὡς πάνυ εὐπρεπῆ ἔφθειρεν, καὶ ἐξ αὐτῆς ἔσχεν υἱὸν ὀνόματι Περσέα**, τὸν προειρημένον.

juxtaposed with Bouttios's sober relation of the facts (ἐξέθετο). This contrast of myth and realism, this interpretation of myth in a rationalizing vein, is found not only in the competing versions of Perseus's conception identified with Euripides and Bouttios respectively, but also in the following sentence. The vague "they" of broad literary reference, mythologists like Euripides, write (γράφουσιν) that Perseus was winged, a metaphor used because (διὰ) he was a ferocious child. In fact, the rationalizing tone and the attempt to turn myth into history persist throughout almost the whole account of Perseus (except the interlude with the Ionitans, which is ascribed to Pausanias[8]). The divine gifts Perseus received in myth become a course in necromancy. Medusa has not snakes for hair, but wild and unkempt hair. The sight of her head does not turn men to stone but paralyzes them—petrifies them figuratively, rather than literally. Perseus does not save Andromeda from the sea monster to which she has been consecrated, but drags her from the temple where she is a consecrated priestess and rapes her. His hero's quest becomes a military campaign that culminates in the conquest of Assyria. This interpretation of the Perseus myth in plausible historical terms is consistent with Bouttios's version of Perseus's conception, and the source for the narrative overall is introduced aptly as "Bouttios, the historical chronographer." So we ascribe practically the whole account of Perseus in Malalas to Bouttios and give it as **fragment** 7.

The third and last citation of Bouttios in Malalas concerns the persecution of Christians in the reign of Domitian (**F 27**). Bouttios's treatment of this subject is confirmed by notices in independent sources, the *Chronicle* of Jerome (**F 28**) and George the Syncellus (**F 29**), both of which also include citations. These further attestations of the content of Bouttios's history circumscribe what in Malalas belongs to Bouttios: only those parts of the account of the reign of Domitian that deal with the persecution of the Christians. But once again the other collections of fragments are more cautious than is warranted by the text. Peter and Levick and Rich include no more in their fragments than the sentence in which Bouttios is cited; this states that Domitian persecuted Christians and many fled to Pontus.[9] It actually says that "many *other* Christians" (πολλοὺς δὲ ἄλλους

8 Garstad, "Pausanias of Antioch," 677–78.

9 Levick and Rich, "Bruttius," 2:1094 (F 3f); cf. Peter, *Historicorum Romanorum Reliquiae*, 2:160, n. 3 (F 3): **πολλοὺς δὲ ἄλλους χριστιανοὺς ἐτιμωρήσατο, ὥστε φυγεῖν**

χριστιανοὺς) were punished, and so proceeds naturally from the immediately preceding section that relates the encounter between Domitian and St. John. That section opens with the statement that the Christians were persecuted under Domitian. If Bouttios is Malalas's ultimate source on this persecution, as he appears to be, it is only reasonable to assume that everything he has to say under this heading should be assigned to Bouttios. This is especially so when the construction of the sentence in which Bouttios is cited makes it seem like the conclusion of an account, not one that stands on its own. So our fragment of Bouttios on Domitian and the persecution of the Christians from Malalas (**F 27**) is rather fuller than what is presented by other scholars.

Identifying passages in which Bouttios is cited as a source is the first step in collecting his fragments, but not the last. On the basis of these passages we can expand our collection to include others that are clearly related to them, not merely because they deal with the same subjects but really because they exhibit the same characteristic turns of phrase and odd historical narratives. For instance, we can adduce the first passage in the *Excerpta* on Alexander the Great (**F 9**) as a parallel fragment to the account of Alexander in Malalas, which contains a citation of Bouttios (**F 16.1**), not because they both discuss Alexander, but because they both claim that Alexander freed the Romans, Greeks, and Egyptians from the same motley conglomeration of oriental nations, and they both introduce the whole business by saying that God raised up Alexander to his task. What is distinctive, what is found nowhere else, marks what belongs to Bouttios. Not only parallel but also complementary passages can be assigned to Bouttios. That Alexander freed the Romans from eastern oppressors is an idiosyncratic claim, but it also implies an idiosyncratic narrative, one that among other things has the Romans conquered before they were freed.[10] This narrative, due to the fragmentary state of Bouttios's survival, is in large part lost, but it is also in some part broken up and scattered. The broken pieces can be identified because they reflect this singular narrative and then they can be restored to some semblance of order. So even if there is no citation of Bouttios in the *Excerpta*'s note on Nebuchadnezzar (**F 11**), we cannot neglect its indication that he included Rome in his empire as a

---

ἐξ αὐτῶν πλῆθος ἐπὶ τὸν Πόντον, καθὼς Βώττιος ὁ σοφὸς χρονογράφος συνεγράψατο κατ' αὐτῶν.

10 Garstad, "Alexander the Great's Liberation of Rome."

clue to how the Romans were supposed to have become subject to the easterners in the first place. This is not the only fragment that can be added to the number assigned to our historian in an effort to piece together the idiosyncratic narrative indicated by the passages that explicitly depend on Bouttios.

The passages for which he is cited as a source also connect Bouttios to a series of episodes in which a virgin is sacrificed at the foundation of a city to become the *tyche*, or personified fortune, of the place. Malalas's handling of these strange episodes makes it clear that he has added them to his *Chronicle* without fully understanding their intent or their implications; although not directly ascribed to any source, they obviously represent derivative material. That they are derived from Bouttios is indicated by the citations associated with them. Of the thirteen instances of tyche sacrifice in Malalas, two, quite possibly three, occur in passages that can be assigned to Bouttios on the strength of an explicit citation (FF 7.3, 16.1). Of the remaining ten, one is connected with a citation of Pausanias of Antioch (F 24) and two, maybe three, with citations of Domninos (FF 26, 31). The rest are not linked to any named authority. But an assignment to Bouttios is not merely due to his scraping by with more tyche sacrifice episodes to his name than the others. As we shall see, Domninos is usually taken to be the intermediary between Bouttios and Malalas, and it is also assumed that Domninos mingled material from Pausanias with that from Bouttios. As a consequence, the other citations associated with the tyche sacrifices do not so much establish competing claims to be their source as support the assumption that they belong to Bouttios. Some details of the accounts of tyche sacrifice also reflect the material for which Bouttios is cited and how he is cited. Apart from the two in the account of Perseus, two other tyche sacrifice episodes (FF 6, 24) also feature a contrast between what is said poetically and what is said historically, that is, between the words of poets and those of chroniclers, and Bouttios is instrumental in just such a contrast when he is cited at the opening of the Perseus passage. In the same citation Bouttios is significantly juxtaposed with Euripides, and two instances of tyche sacrifice also bring up Euripides and his poetic version of events (FF 6, 8.2).

One further set of fragments attributable to Bouttios, the so-called Picus-Zeus narrative, gives an account of the gods of Greece and Rome as ancient human kings (FF 1–5). Versions of this account are found in the *Excerpta Latina Barbari* and in the *Chronicle* of John Malalas, and neither is derived from the other. Only a very few narrative passages of this extent and complexity have

been added to the *Excerpta*'s lean chronological spine. For at least one of these, on Alexander the Great, the *Excerpta* clearly shares a source with Malalas. The *Excerpta* compiler, on the whole, made use of only a small number of sources, and it is more probable that he and Malalas had one source in common, rather than two. But the account of the gods is attributable to Bouttios not merely because his influence is evident in the two works that offer the earliest examples of it. This narrative also has compositional similarities to the fragments with citations of Bouttios. In the first place, the passage on Alexander attributed to Bouttios and the Picus-Zeus narrative share at least two sources, namely the *Alexander Romance* and the book of Daniel. In the second, a number of features connect the Picus-Zeus narrative to the account of Perseus ascribed to Bouttios: the story of Perseus opens with the introduction of "Picus, who is also Zeus" as his father; in both there are citations of Euripides, as well as remarkably similar episodes of the rape of a consecrated temple priestess; and Perseus's slaying of Sardanapalus and conquest of Assyria appear in both.

The two earliest versions of this account of the gods obviously share a common origin, but they also exhibit several different features. Determining the extent of what belongs to Bouttios involves more than just identifying the shared material and excluding everything else. The fragments must be recovered by recognizing how a single source has been adapted in different ways to be included in the works that preserve it. In the *Excerpta* the Picus-Zeus narrative has been grafted onto a notice listing the earliest kings of Italy, and so practically all the material irrelevant to Italy has been left out. Malalas, by contrast, tends to cover the intrusive lines of kings descended from Picus-Zeus through their entirety in Assyria, Italy, and Egypt. And so Malalas usually provides sensible beginnings and endings to matters under discussion—but not always. In a few instances, he has broken up the narrative and scattered it throughout his *Chronicle*. The integrity of the narrative, however, is indicated by referring back to the *Excerpta* and can be restored on that basis.

John Malalas and the *Excerpta Latina Barbari*

By far the great bulk of the material that can be assigned to Bouttios is extracted from two sources, the *Chronicle* of John Malalas and the anonymous *Excerpta Latina Barbari*. Neither of these works is especially familiar to the classicist or

the historian and both of them present special problems, particularly in regard to identifying their sources. A few words of introduction, then, might be in order.

The *Chronicle* of John Malalas is a history of the world which begins with the creation of Adam, but its end point is a matter of some dispute. It has long been recognized that while over most of its length the *Chronicle* concentrates on events in Antioch and otherwise gives evidence of an Antiochene perspective, the final chapters (up to the death of Justinian in 565) of Book 18 are reoriented to the point of view of Constantinople.[11] Brian Croke explains this shift as the result of Malalas's issuing two editions of his work about thirty years apart, the first concluding with the agreement of the Endless Peace between the Romans and Persians in 532 and the second after the death of Justinian in 565; he assumes that in the interval between the two editions Malalas decamped from Antioch and took up residence in the imperial capital.[12] Warren Treadgold offers a more complicated reconstruction, positing not one move between Antioch and Constantinople but several over the course of Malalas's career (supposedly reflected in the content of the *Chronicle*), and at least four separate editions by Malalas's own hand, which correspond to the various end points indicated by the witnesses to Malalas's text.[13] Both Croke and Treadgold, nevertheless, agree that Malalas himself was responsible for all the versions of his work that were brought out. An older school of thought, however, put forward a more radical solution to the problem and suggested that the last chapters of Book 18 do not belong to Malalas at all, but rather to a later continuator, even claiming to discern, along with stylistic differences, a doctrinal divide between the Monophysite chronicle as a whole and its Orthodox conclusion.[14] A form of this theory, without its dubious sectarian encumbrances, has been revived recently by Olivier Gengler, who sees Malalas's *Chronicle* coming to a coherent and intentional close with the promulgation of Justinian's edict of 533 "On the Orthodox Faith and against impious heresies" in chapter 78 of Book 18, and attributes the following anticlimactic

11 This shift seems to occur after the conclusion of 18.76.

12 Croke, "Malalas, the Man and His Work," 17–25, with a thorough summary of the previous scholarship.

13 Treadgold, *Early Byzantine Historians*, 236–40, 245.

14 Gelzer, *Sextus Julius Africanus*, 2:129–38; Stein, *Histoire du Bas-Empire*, 2:703; Hunger, *Die hochsprachliche profane Literatur*, 1:320; cf. Croke, "Malalas, the Man and His Work," 21.

chapters to a later continuator, who had no respect for—or understanding of?—the initial purpose and conceptual framework of Malalas's *Chronicle*.[15] Happily, these controversies have practically no bearing on our concerns, as all of the material that can be assigned to Bouttios comes in the first thirteen books of the *Chronicle*, and so well within the portion of the work that can be securely ascribed to Malalas—or in his Antiochene period, if you will. The possibility of a wholesale revision of the entire text accompanying the later editions or redactions cannot be entirely ruled out, but it is most unlikely.[16] It is an Antiochene author, then, with an Antiochene perspective and access to sources in Antioch, who preserved material from Bouttios.

In spite of the impressive number of authors cited throughout the *Chronicle*, scholars have tended to assume that Malalas had access to only a limited number of textual sources (lost and almost completely unknown to us), who mediated his knowledge of the other authorities he cites.[17] Hermann Bourier, the first scholar to seriously address the problem of Malalas's sources, considered most of the material on Perseus and Alexander, for which Bouttios is cited, to be taken from Domninos, an obscure lost historian, whom he took to be one of Malalas's principal direct sources, but the citations themselves to be derived from another of Malalas's immediate sources, the equally mysterious Timotheos.[18] In the first instance, the account of Perseus, Bourier further thought the ultimate source to be Pausanias of Antioch, mediated through Domninos, and the citation not to have originally been of Bouttios at all, but of Ovid (as Müller's text of John of

15 This position was introduced in a paper, "Time, Chronology, and Narrative in John Malalas," presented at the Time Calculation in Late Antiquity: The Chronicon Paschale and Beyond conference, Austrian Academy of Sciences, Vienna, 24 October, 2018, but will be elaborated in the forthcoming Tübingen Commentary on Malalas.

16 Croke, "Malalas, the Man and His Work," 23, for his part avers: "Given that the work had been in circulation for so long it is unlikely that in producing the updated edition Malalas would have modified much of what he had previously written."

17 Bourier, *Über die Quellen*; E. Jeffreys, "Malalas' Sources." This assumption has recently been challenged by Peter Van Nuffelen, "Malalas and the Chronographic Tradition," who proposes that the sources cited by Malalas should be reexamined to test their possible validity and potential usefulness, and further that many of the problems in Malalas's text can be explained as "the result of an unsuccessful integration of material drawn from many texts" (271).

18 Bourier, *Über die Quellen*, 1:13, 14, 20–21; 2:7, 16.

Antioch and the Slavonic Malalas might suggest).[19] The chief difficulty that drove Bourier to accept Ovid as the actual authority cited, that he could find no common thread in the subjects for which Bouttios was cited, is a problem we shall attempt to solve in the course of this and subsequent chapters. Ovid's version of Perseus, moreover, could hardly be contrasted with that of Euripides as more historical. Bourier's efforts to detach the citations from the overall narratives in which they appear also seem perverse. We are asked to believe that Malalas followed one source for the most part, but picked citations out of another source which covered the same material and slipped them into his main source as he saw fit. It is more plausible that the citations had already been integrated into Malalas's source and that the broader narratives in which they occur reflect the content of the works of the authors cited. Bourier does, however, seem to be right in seeing Domninos as the intermediary through whom Malalas knew Pausanias.

Even if Bourier's conclusions in regard to Malalas's sources are not tenable in every detail, his work appears to justify Elizabeth Jeffreys's judgment in regard to Malalas's familiarity with Bouttios, that it is "most unlikely that Malalas knew this author at first hand," and to provide a sensible route of transmission.[20] It appears that Malalas knew of Bouttios, as well as Pausanias, only through Domninos and that he found the material from both Pausanias and Bouttios integrated in Domninos, his immediate source. If Malalas knew Bouttios only at second or third hand, we can explain why he appears unsympathetic to any motives we might impute to Bouttios and why he slots the material derived from Bouttios into often incongruous contexts: charges of human sacrifice, for instance, into generally positive portraits of emperors. It is worth remembering that since Malalas did not know Bouttios directly, while Bouttios's own usage may occasionally be preserved in certain words and phrases, we must assume that what we have identified as fragments are not verbatim excerpts from Bouttios's text but close paraphrases at best, or reworkings which convey some idea of Bouttios's content. That being said, ancient historians were hardly above taking over, word for word, another author's wholesale borrowings from a third author's work.

This reconstruction of the route by which Malalas came to know Bouttios, as well as Pausanias, through the intermediary of Domninos has been challenged

19 Bourier, *Über die Quellen*, 2:44–45.
20 E. Jeffreys, "Malalas' Sources," 174.

recently by Paweł Janiszewski's efforts to give an identity to Domninos.[21] We know nothing about Domninos apart from what ten citations in the *Chronicle* of John Malalas can tell us, but even these citations are uncertain. As with Bouttios, Malalas's text offers three different forms of the historian's name, although they vary even more widely in this case: Domninos (Δομνῖνος), Domnos (Δόμνος), and Dometianos (Δομετιανός)—even if there is general agreement among modern scholars that all of these names refer to a single author.[22] The one consistent feature in all of the material connected with Domninos is an interest in the history of Antioch, especially as it could still be seen in the city's buildings and monuments. Nevertheless, attempts to identify the historian with figures who had the same name and were associated with Antioch—Domnos, bishop of Antioch (441/2–450); Domninos, a Syrian philosopher active in Athens in the middle of the fifth century; and Domninos, bishop of Antioch (545–559)—have little to recommend them beyond the coincidence of names, and the last seems too late to be a source for Malalas.[23] Edwin Patzig's proposal that Nestorianos, also cited by Malalas, was not a separate author but a sectarian epithet applied to Domninos and that the two figures should be identified is even more far-fetched, but has not been conclusively rebutted.[24]

Janiszewski points out that Domninos is last cited by name in regard to the Olympic Games in Antioch in 302, and that he dealt with mythical subjects, "glorified" such pagan figures as Apollonius of Tyana and the emperor Diocletian, and did not adhere to the details of Libanius's speech on Antioch, the *Antiochicos*, delivered at the Antiochene Olympics of 356. From all this he concludes that Domninos was a pagan who wrote shortly after the reign of Diocletian ended in 305, at the outset of the controversies between pagans and Christians that characterized the fourth century.[25] Either aspect of this identification would preclude

21 Janiszewski, *Missing Link*, 282–91.

22 Malalas, praef.; 4.19; 5.37; 8.24; 10.9–10, 51; 11.4; 12.9, 26, 44.

23 E. Jeffreys, "Malalas' Sources," 178; Janiszewski, *Missing Link*, 284–85.

24 Patzig, "Die Abhängigkeit."

25 Janiszewski, *Missing Link*, 282–91. Van Nuffelen, "Malalas and the Chronographic Tradition," 263, does not contradict Janiszewski's suggestion that Domninos was a pagan, but favors a date under Constantius II (337–361) for him on the grounds that Domninos's relation of conflicts between Rome and Persia would reflect the political and military events of that time. But the Persian threat seems to have been a perpetual source of anxiety in Antioch, and so Persian-Roman relations a matter of perennial interest in the city.

the possibility that Domninos served as an intermediary between Malalas and Bouttios, who appears to have written no earlier than the seventh decade of the fourth century and to have been a committed Christian (see below, chapter 5). Although Janiszewski's suggestions present an interesting challenge to the established views on Malalas's sources, there are serious flaws in his arguments on this author, at least, and we are not bound to accept either his dating of Domninos or his designation of the historian as a pagan.

Although Domninos is last cited in regard to Diocletian, Bourier took him to be a source that Malalas used up to Book 14 of his *Chronicle*, and assumed that Domninos's history covered the period up to the middle of the fifth century, at least.[26] Croke and Jeffreys have accepted this assumption, calling attention to the fact that Domninos seems to have been Malalas's source on the remarkable buildings of Antioch and so was probably responsible for the description of the Basilica of Anatolius, constructed in the reign of Theodosius II (408–450), which is the last such digression on the structures of Antioch in Malalas's *Chronicle*.[27] The description of the Basilica of Anatolius is consistent with the material explicitly attributed to Domninos not merely inasmuch as it treats a building in Antioch, but also in its emphasis on the patronage and adornment of the construction.[28] And as long as we accept Bourier's overall argument that Domninos was one of Malalas's few primary sources, we should assume that there is plenty in Malalas's *Chronicle* that was taken from Domninos, but goes without any citation of its source.

Janiszewski further defends his earlier dating of Domninos by insisting that the account of Diocletian he was retailing must have arisen only a short time after his life: "This tendency to glorify the legendary pagan emperor must have emerged a few decades after his death, among those who stayed faithful to the old gods."[29] But the substance of the account puts the lie to this suggestion. Domninos apparently related that Diocletian abdicated as the Olympic Games at Antioch came to a close—three years too early—because he was unwilling to

---

Fragments of an Antiochene history can hardly be dated to one particular reign simply because they show some concern over wars with Persia.

26 Bourier, *Über die Quellen*, 1:9–22; 2:52, 60.

27 Croke, "Malalas, the Man and His Work," 8; E. Jeffreys, "Malalas' Sources," 178.

28 Malalas 14.13.

29 Janiszewski, *Missing Link*, 291.

put off the costume of an Olympic *alytarch* and assume again the robes of state.[30] The imputation of such a motive to the emperor would have been scornfully dismissed shortly after the abdication of Diocletian, when people were familiar with his intention to perpetuate the tetrarchic system, to say nothing of the actual date when the abdication occurred. An account like that of Domninos must have taken a long time to percolate, as not only the events themselves but also living memory receded into the background, and speculation and legend took their place. That what Domninos says does not conform to Libanius's speech, furthermore, is not a compelling argument that he wrote before its composition. We do not know how authoritative the famous rhetor's oration on Antioch was, and a historian might have any number of unspoken reasons for ignoring or contradicting another author.[31] Simply because Domninos does not follow Libanius in lockstep does not prove that he could not have known him because he wrote before him. The accepted, later dating of Domninos, which would accommodate his employing a source who wrote in the 360s, would thus seem to be secure.

As for Domninos's religious or ideological stance, there is nothing to sustain the suggestion that he was a pagan. Janiszewski may point to an interest in myth as a sign of paganism, but what is telling is not *that* Domninos dealt with myth, but *how* he dealt with myth. In the account of Orestes ascribed to Domninos, the hero is presented not only as a matricide prone to bouts of insanity, which is traditional enough, but also as a fugitive and an accomplice to human sacrifice and the subject of a famous statue which caught him in a pose reflecting his craven ingratitude for divine healing.[32] This is hardly the sort of heroic depiction a pagan might offer in the midst of the controversies of the fourth century. The more robust and unchallenged paganism of an earlier day might have countenanced morally ambivalent heroes and happily examined their failings and weaknesses, but facing the intellectual and existential threat posed by Christianity the exponents of traditional culture could little afford to parade the frailties and crimes of their heroes. Domninos can have made no spiritual investment in the figure of Orestes as he depicts him.

30 Malalas 12.44.

31 See Lib., *Or.* 11.

32 Malalas 5.37.

Domninos does describe Apollonius of Tyana making magical talismans for the Antiochenes which successfully warded off scorpions and mosquitoes from their city, and accurately predicting future disasters for Antioch, but this does not necessarily make the historian a pagan.[33] Apollonius is likewise found furnishing effective apotropaic charms and credited with prophetic powers in as undoubtedly Christian a work as the *Patria of Constantinople*.[34] And it is in the no less decidedly Christian *Chronicle* of John Malalas that Domninos's account of Apollonius is preserved, after all. Indeed, we often encounter in Malalas ambiguous, or at least not overtly critical, depictions of the figures lionized by the pagan resistance to Christianity, but they do not necessarily reveal pagan sympathies on the author's part; this is as true of the picture of Apollonius of Tyana as it is of that of the emperor Diocletian.

Domninos may not caricature Diocletian as an inhuman enemy of the Church, and rather focus on his participation in the Olympic Games of Antioch, but we should remember that, as we find it in Malalas, the material that clearly belongs to Domninos is immediately preceded by a notice on Diocletian's persecution of the Christians, which does not downplay the suffering and distress he caused, and this notice may very well be taken from Domninos as well.[35] And perhaps we can detect a hint of hubris in the sentiment Domninos puts into the mouth of Diocletian at his abdication: "I have sloughed off the kingship and worn the visage of deathless Zeus" (ἀπεθέμην τὴν βασιλείαν καὶ ἐφόρεσα σχῆμα τοῦ ἀθανάτου Διός).[36] Altogether, there is nothing in the evidence to persuade us that Domninos was a pagan who would have been constitutionally averse to borrowing material from a Christian author. On the contrary, the more established understanding of Domninos as the intermediary between Bouttios, for one, and John Malalas seems to be confirmed.

The *Excerpta Latina Barbari* is the Latin translation of a now lost Greek world chronicle. For the most part the *Excerpta* is a compendium of patriarchs and kings with a running computation of the age of the world and some brief

33 Malalas 10.51.

34 *Patria Const.* 1.23, 2.79, 103; see Berger, *Accounts of Medieval Constantinople*, 14–15, 102–3, 124–25.

35 Malalas 12.43.

36 Malalas 12.44 (Thurn, *Ioannis Malalae Chronographia*, 239). All translations, unless otherwise noted, are the author's own.

historical notices, followed by a series of the king-lists from which the preceding chronography was compiled. But interspersed throughout this material there are a few relatively lengthy narrative passages: biblical stories or legends extrapolated from the Bible, an account of the pagan gods as ancient kings, and an idiosyncratic version of the history of Alexander the Great. I have argued elsewhere that the combination of elements of a chronography and occasional narrative passages, that is, the composition of the Greek original of the *Excerpta*, was undertaken between 535 and 539, and the finished Greek chronicle was intended as a diplomatic gift for Theudebert, the king of the Austrasian Franks, as an inducement for him to join the Byzantines in their war against the Ostrogoths in Italy.[37] This Greek chronicle was then translated into Latin in the first half of the eighth century as part of the missionary effort to convert the heathens on the Rhine frontier of the Frankish kingdom. In this scenario, the narrative passages were chosen with an eye to cementing the possibly imperfect conversion of the Franks from paganism, especially as they were being called upon to join an Orthodox crusade against the Arian Ostrogoths, and to rousing Theudebert's righteous ardor for military glory. The narrative interludes, apart from the ones on biblical subjects, are our chief interest in the *Excerpta*. They reflect at least one of the passages explicitly associated with Bouttios by Malalas—that on Alexander—and another in Malalas which we think should be assigned to Bouttios—that on the gods. The intentions imputed to the compiler of the *Excerpta* also help to explain a number of the divergences between the narratives in Malalas and the *Excerpta*.

37 Garstad, "Barbarian Interest." Helmut Reimitz, *History, Frankish Identity*, 82, contends that the Greek original behind the *Excerpta Latina Barbari* was composed rather in the last decades of the sixth century, in the context of intensified diplomatic contacts between Byzantium and the Frankish kingdoms and an "image correction" perceptible in the presentation of the Franks from Procopius to Agathias. While I am not persuaded to abandon my earlier proposition, I find nothing unreasonable nor improbable in Reimitz's suggestion. In any case, such a shift in the dating of the composition of the Greek original of the *Excerpta* would have little material bearing on the discussion of the fragments derived from it that follows.

2

CITATIONS OF BOUTTIOS BY NAME AND PARALLEL FRAGMENTS

We may now turn to a detailed examination of the material assigned to Bouttios, explaining why each fragment is supposed to belong to Bouttios and determining its extent. The connections among the various fragments, as they are described in the following discussion, are presented in figure 1. Rather than reproducing the text of each fragment as it is discussed, it is expected that the reader will regularly turn to the end of this volume, where the texts of all the fragments, with translation, are presented together. We shall begin by discussing the fragments according to the order in which the citations of Bouttios occur in the *Chronicle* of John Malalas.

Perseus Material

Malalas's first citation of Bouttios occurs in his description of the career of the mythical hero Perseus. Euripides' "poetic" account of the conception of Perseus, the traditional story of Zeus's transformation into a shower of gold, is contrasted with a rationalizing version he attributes explicitly to Bouttios, which holds that Zeus persuaded Danae with a sum of gold. If this were our only evidence for Bouttios, we might have assumed that he was called into service as an interpreter of myth on this point only. A close reading of the texts and comparison with the other passages associated with Bouttios, however, indicate that Bouttios is responsible not merely for the information in this brief note but for the better

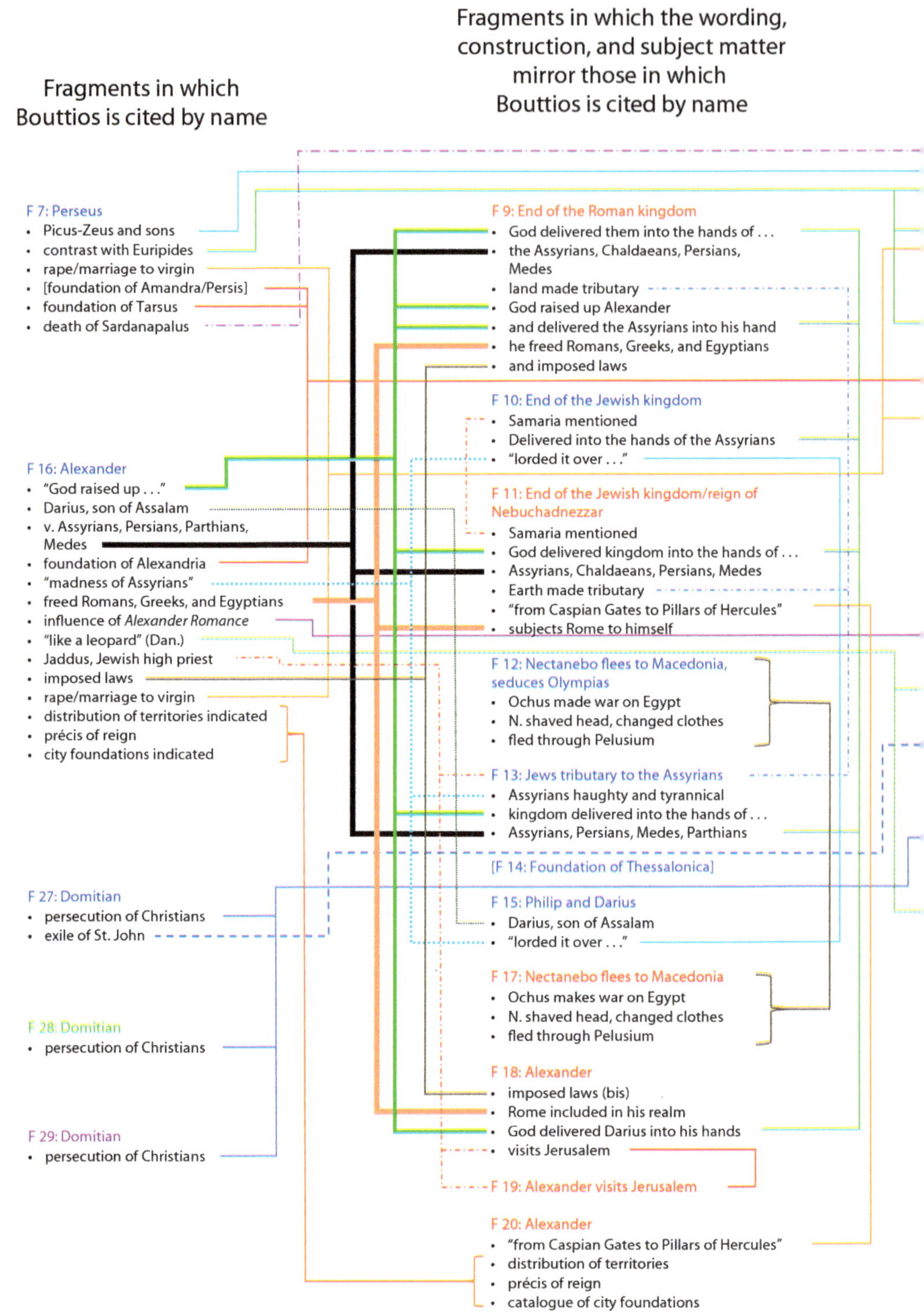

Fragments from Malalas in blue; *Excerpta Latina Barbari* in red; Jerome's *Chronicle* in green; George the Syncellus in purple.

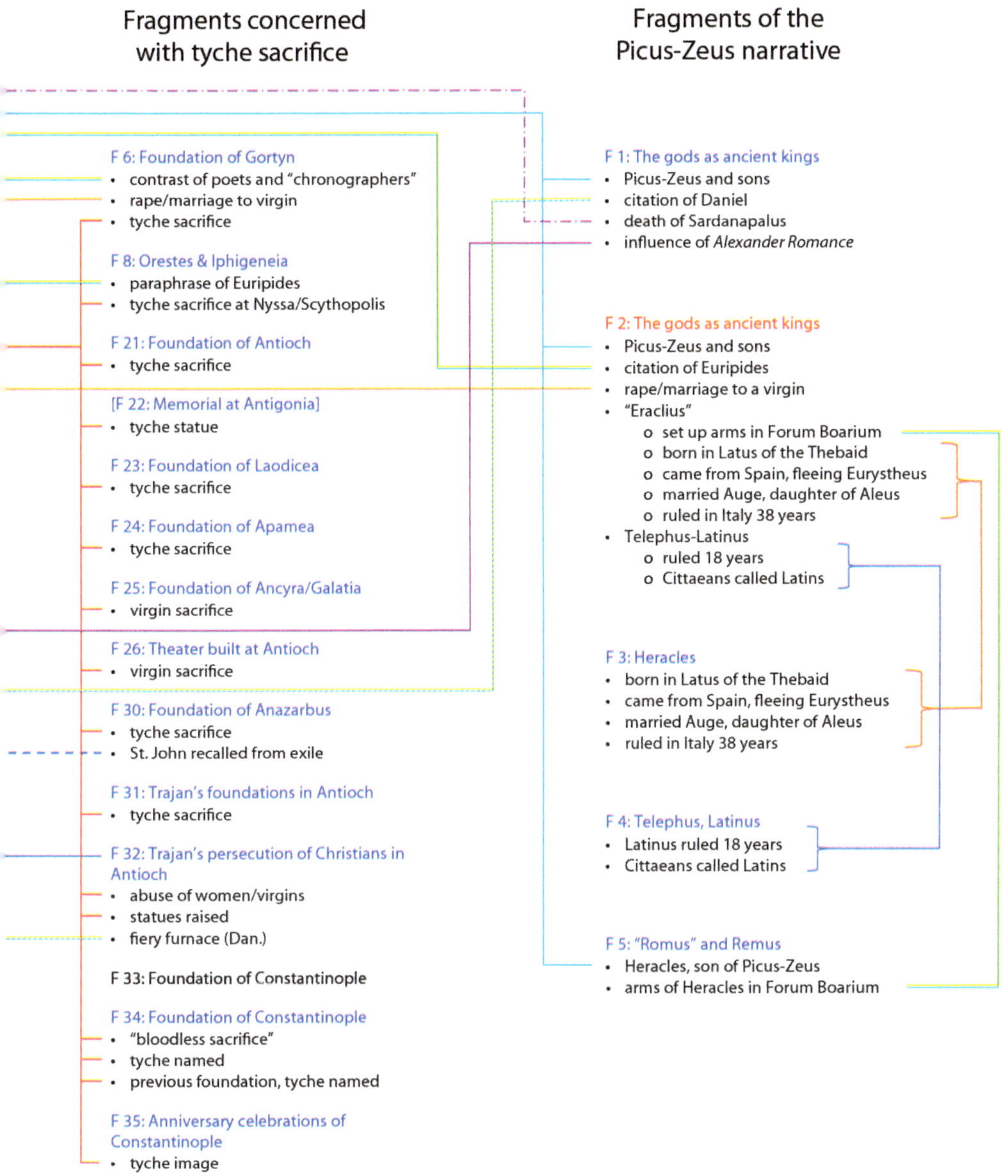

Figure 1. Connections between fragments of Bouttios. Chart by author.

part of Malalas's account of Perseus (F 7). Malalas begins this account by saying that along with Hermes and Heracles, Perseus was also a son of Picus-Zeus; then he offers a précis of Danae's story according to Euripides, followed by Bouttios's version, the sentence ending with the birth of the "aforementioned" (τὸν προειρημένον) Perseus. Francesca D'Alfonso takes this turn of phrase to indicate that Malalas is returning to a previous source,[1] and if this is so Bouttios should be taken as the source for what Malalas says about Perseus from the beginning of this paragraph. It does not even seem as if it was Malalas, or his intermediary source, who established the juxtaposition of Euripides and Bouttios; rather it appears that Bouttios himself set up Euripides as a foil to his own account of Perseus, and what Malalas credits to Euripides is actually derived from Bouttios.[2] The rationalizing tone of the Bouttios version continues throughout most of Malalas's account of Perseus: the hero's winged sandals are read as a metaphor for his fierce nature; the hero himself is an adept in magical arts rather than a semidivine being; Medusa has unruly hair rather than snakes for hair, and the sight of her head paralyzes men, but does not turn them to stone; Perseus does not rescue Andromeda from a sea monster, but abducts her from a temple; and the lone questing hero becomes a general on campaign. All of this is in keeping with the interpretation of the myth of Perseus as garbled history that is ascribed to Bouttios at the opening of the passage.

Later on in his campaigns Perseus is supposed to have founded two cities, Iconium and Tarsus. On the first occasion he performed a sacrifice and named the *tyche* of the city, and on the second he sacrificed an "innocent girl." In Malalas's account of Alexander the Great, for which he cites only Bouttios as an authority, the Macedonian king likewise sacrifices a girl at the founding of Alexandria. I will argue that all of the accounts of tyche sacrifice at city foundations in Malalas are derived from Bouttios, but for the present suffice it to say that this is a common feature in two narratives associated with Bouttios. The ritual killing of virgin girls to achieve political ends such as the founding of cities is, moreover, consistent with Perseus's treatment of Medusa, a virgin girl he

1 D'Alfonso, *Euripide in Giovanni Malala*, 58; cf. Bourier, *Über die Quellen*, 1:13, 2:12; E. Jeffreys, "Malalas' Sources," 198–99. Olivier Gengler sees this phrase rather as a device for organizing the narrative material within the overall chronological framework.

2 D'Alfonso, *Euripide in Giovanni Malala*, 60.

chances upon and kills so that he can make a potent weapon out of her head. These consistencies of theme and subject allow us to infer that these are further aspects of Malalas's account of Perseus that depend upon Bouttios. Indeed, the campaigns of Perseus, the cities he founds along the way, and the conquests he makes with Medusa's severed head account for most of the narrative devoted to Perseus in Malalas.

The final attestation of Bouttios in Malalas, in which he is cited as a source for the exile of St. John to Patmos and Domitian's persecution of the Christians (**FF 27–29**), identifies Bouttios as a Christian himself (as will be discussed at greater length below) and supplies a motive for some of the details and the tone of moral censure found in the account of Perseus. Zeus and Perseus, revered figures in the Greek cultural tradition, are presented as wicked, lustful, and depraved necromancers. Such denigration serves a clear apologetic purpose: if gods and heroes are unworthy, they must be abandoned as objects of worship. Only the visit of Perseus to the Argive Ionitans settled in Syria is incompatible. Here Perseus is a more or less benign character who observes the miraculously efficacious prayers of the—supposedly pagan—Ionitans and founds the Persian religion of fire worship. At any rate, Malalas cites another source in connection with the Ionitans and the fire cult: Pausanias, the early first-century CE author of a work on the establishment, antiquities, and monuments of Antioch and other Seleucid foundations.[3] It would seem that the contrast with Euripides and the account of the birth of Perseus, his magical craft, his campaigns, and his conquests, sexual as well as martial, belong to Bouttios, while the story of the Ionitans and Persian fire worship belong to Pausanias, and that Malalas found them integrated, as he presents them, in his intermediary source, Domninos.

Alexander Material

The next citation of Bouttios comes in the midst of Malalas's account of the career of Alexander the Great, and is indeed the only citation of an authority offered in this entire account (**F 16**). On the narrowest possible reading, Bouttios is said to have written about Alexander's defeat of Darius, "the son of Assalam," and his conquest of the land of the Assyrians, Medes, Parthians, Babylonians,

3 Garstad, "Pausanias of Antioch."

and Persians, and "all the kingdoms of the earth." As we have seen, however, this narrow reading ignores the grammar of the sentence, and we must attribute to Bouttios the assertion not only that Alexander conquered the eastern peoples, but also that he liberated the Romans, Greeks, and Egyptians. There is, moreover, enough in this sentence to indicate that Bouttios is ultimately responsible for much more. The information it contains is found not only in the sentence that mentions Bouttios, but also at the opening of the discussion of Alexander at the head of Malalas's eighth book, and in the sentence following the citation of Bouttios, again after a chronological calculation, suggesting something of a parenthetical arrangement which might allow us to assign everything that comes between these repetitive statements, at least, to the author cited for one very similar to them.

On the basis of Bouttios's being the only source cited for Malalas's treatment of Alexander, and the appearance of phrasing and ideas explicitly connected to Bouttios at the opening and closing of the first paragraph of Malalas's discussion of Alexander, we may begin by assigning this whole paragraph to Bouttios. This lets us identify a number of idiosyncratic features that characterize Bouttios's handling of Alexander's career—as well as his work in general—and distinguish his influence on a number of other passages. Perhaps the most prominent and telling of these is the strange concatenation of eastern peoples, the Assyrians, Persians, Parthians, and Medes, that appears three times in this paragraph. First, as it begins, when it is said that God raised up Alexander against these nations, at the same time disclosing an inclination to indicate divine causation for historical events. Second, in unmistakable connection with the authority of Bouttios, when it is said that Alexander conquered all the territory of these same peoples. And third, immediately thereafter and in equally close proximity to the citation of Bouttios, as Malalas closes this paragraph before a chronological summation, when Alexander is said to have freed the Romans, Greeks, and Egyptians from these peoples. The inclusion of the Romans among the nations liberated by Alexander from eastern oppressors is also an unprecedented and distinctive feature of this narrative.

The paragraph displays further idiosyncratic features. It dwells upon the founding of Alexandria, perhaps unsurprisingly, as this event is recounted in most Alexander histories, but adds the remarkable detail of a virgin sacrifice to inaugurate the city. Making him a practitioner of human sacrifice reveals a

subtle tendency to denigrate Alexander.[4] The founding of Alexandria is described before it is related that Alexander came into conflict with the Persians and other easterners. This course of events is unhistorical—Alexander actually met the Persian army in two major battles before arriving in Egypt—but does follow the one we find in the *Alexander Romance*, in which Alexander first founded his city and then launched his campaign against Darius from Egypt.[5] This suggests that the *Romance* was one of the sources Bouttios exploited; it is also found to lie behind parallel passages in Malalas and the *Excerpta*.[6] According to Malalas, Alexander strangely and unhistorically crossed from Europe to Asia at the Bosporus rather than the Hellespont.[7] Alexander is also said to rush forth "like a leopard" (ὡς πάρδαλις). This may seem like an innocuous simile, but it takes on new significance when it is remembered that Alexander was regularly identified with the "beast like a leopard" (ὡσεὶ πάρδαλις) of the book of Daniel.[8] Such a

4 The negative tone is also evident in the note that Roxane was a prisoner and a virgin when Alexander took her to wife, since this might seem to contradict his famous self-restraint and refusal to take advantage of his female prisoners (Diod. Sic. 17.38.3–7; Curt. 3.12.18–23, 4.10.23–24, 10.5.32; Plut., *Alex.* 21.3–5, *De fort. Alex.* 2.6 [*Mor.* 338D–E], cf. 2.12 [*Mor.* 343A], *De fortuna* 1 [*Mor.* 97D]; Arr., *Anab.* 4.19.6, 20.2; *It. Alex.* 23 [57], 44 [101]; cf. Amm. Marc. 24.4.27); in the route Alexander takes from Europe to Asia, which follows not that of the historical Alexander but that of a *daimon* (?!) who assumed his name and character in the reign of Elagabalus (Cass. Dio 79.18.1–3); and in the encounter with Candace, in which not only is Alexander outwitted and captured by a woman, but the maternal affection Candace has for Alexander in the *Romance* (*Al. Rom.* 3.23.8) is turned into another opportunity for Alexander's rapacious lust.

5 *Al. Rom.* 1.31–33, 34.9–35.1, 41; see Garstad, "Alexander's Circuit," 146–55.

6 The dependence of Bouttios's treatment of Alexander on the *Romance* in general is evident in the ascription of Alexander's true paternity to Nectanebo (F **12**; cf. F **17**); the apparent course of events, which sets the foundation of Alexandria and the administration of Egypt before Alexander meets the Persians in battle (FF **16.1**, **18**); and the inclusion of the story of Alexander's encounter with Candace, the queen of Ethiopia (F **16.3**); see *Al. Rom.* 1.3–7, 31–33; 34.9–35.1, 41, 3.18–23.

7 Alexander's army actually crossed from Sestos to Abydos on the Hellespont, on the other side of the Sea of Marmara from Byzantium and Chrysopolis, and Alexander never seems to have set foot in Byzantium; Arr., *Anab.* 1.11.6; cf. Diod. Sic. 17.17.1; see Instinsky, *Alexander der Grosse am Hellespont*.

8 Dan. 7:6; Hippolytus, *Comm. in Dan.* 4.3 (ed. Bonwetsch, *Kommentar zu Daniel*, 200–202), cf. *De Christ. et Antichr.* 24; Aphrahat, *Demonstrations* 5.18; Jerome, *Comm. in Dan.* 2 (7:6) (Glorie, *Commentariorum in Danielem*, 841–42), cf. *Comm. in Hieremiam*

description of Alexander indicates that Bouttios was one of the many late antique authors whose image of Alexander was informed by the prophecies of Daniel.

The list of eastern peoples defeated by Alexander—the Assyrians, Persians, Parthians, and Medes, with the occasional addition of the Babylonians—is an idiosyncratic feature of Bouttios's treatment of Alexander, not to be found in any other source, and a clear marker of material that belongs to him. It was not uncommon for the Greeks and Romans to conflate and confuse the peoples of the orient, but historical sources usually presented a succession of kingdoms in the east, rather than an agglomerated mass as we have here.[9] Such a concatenation of eastern powers is rare in Malalas; it is essentially limited to the discussion of Alexander and a single passage leading up to it.[10] But it is not found only in Malalas. These peoples are also combined in the *Excerpta*, not in the passage dealing with Alexander in his proper chronological place (FF **18**, **20**), but in reference to Alexander and in more than one passage that makes sense of some of the other distinctive features of the discussion of Alexander in both Malalas and the *Excerpta*.

In the first instance in the *Excerpta*, God is said to have delivered the land of the Romans over to the "Assyrians, Chaldeans, Persians, and Medes," until he raised up Alexander, who freed them along with the Greeks and the Egyptians (F **9**). In the second, the kingdom of Israel "in Judea and Samaria" ends with God handing the land over to the Assyrians, Chaldeans, Persians, and Medes

---

1.95.3 (5.6) (Reiter, *In Hieremiam prophetam*, 53–54); Theodoret, *Comm. in Dan.* (7:6) (Hill, *Commentary on Daniel*, 180–82); see Rowley, *Darius the Mede*, 184–85; Marsch, *Biblische Prophetie*, 72; Barnes, "Constantine and the Christians of Persia," 133. The identification was, moreover, considered appropriate because of the swiftness of Alexander's conquests, which might be alluded to by the adverb εὐθέως.

9 Hdt. 1.95.2, 130.1–2; Dion. Hal., *Ant. Rom.* 1.2.2; Aemilius Sura in Vell. Pat. 1.6.6; Tac., *Hist.* 5.8; Arr., *Anab.* 2.6.7; Plut., *De fort. Rom.* 317F–318A, cf. 326A–C; App., *Praef.* 9, *Pun.* 132 (attributed to Polyb. [38.22]); Aelius Aristid., *Panathenaic Discourse* 335, *Roman Oration* 91; Justin., *Epit.* 1.3.6, 6.17, 8.1, 10.3.6 (et passim); Claud., *Cons. Stil.* 3.159–66; ps.-Ampelius 10.1; Rut. Namat. 83–86.

10 Apart from listing this conglomeration of eastern peoples three times in his treatment of Alexander's reign (8.1 bis, 8.3; F **16.1**, **2**), Malalas speaks of the dominion of the earth being granted to all of these peoples together shortly before his discussion of Alexander, at the close of Book 7 (7.18; F **13**). He also refers (6.13, 17) to famous Persian kings as ruling over the Assyrians, though the Assyrians alone, not the remarkable combination of four peoples.

(F 11). The first passage (F 9) is clearly connected to what is explicitly attributed to Bouttios: with a modicum of variation it relates that Alexander freed the Romans, Greeks, and Egyptians from the Assyrians, Persians, Chaldeans (instead of Parthians), and Medes, as well as explaining—without going into any detail—how the westerners came to be in need of liberation from the easterners in the first place. The second (F 11) deals not with the same subject, but with a very similar one and in remarkably similar terms. In regard to both the Romans and the Jews, according to the *Excerpta*, the Lord God delivered the kingdom of the land (*tradidit dominus deus regnum terrae*) into the hands of the Assyrians, Chaldeans, Persians, and Medes (*in manus Assyriorum et Chaldeorum et Persarum et Midorum*) and the land is made tributary to them (*tributaria facta est eis . . . terra*). The obvious correspondence with what indisputably belongs to Bouttios allows us to assign the first passage to him, and the parallel, almost repetitious phrasing in the discussion of the same subject, the expansion of the empire of the powers of the East and the conquest of the nations of the West—at least as "the West" was conceived in the late Roman Empire—likewise allows us to assign the second to him as well.

Identifying the *Excerpta*'s note on the end of the Israelite kingdom as a fragment of Bouttios is not merely an extension of seeing its note on the end of the Roman kingdom as one of his fragments; it also brings us back to the principal repository of the fragments of Bouttios, the *Chronicle* of John Malalas. Malalas also treats the fall of the Jewish kingdom, and his discussion (F 10) displays a number of parallels with the *Excerpta*'s note on the same event (F 11). He opens his sixth book by relating Nebuchadnezzar's conquest of Jerusalem and the passing of the kingdom from Jerusalem and Samaria. That both of these works should associate the fall of the Jewish kingdom with Nebuchadnezzar is unremarkable, since that king's destruction of Jerusalem and the last remnants of the first Jewish kingdom was a matter of historical record attested in the Bible, but there are striking affinities between the two passages. There is a hint in Malalas of the *Excerpta*'s explicit combination of eastern nations: Nebuchadnezzar, familiar to any attentive reader of the Bible as a Babylonian king, is said to be king of the Assyrians. Both passages insist on a definite end to the kingdom of the Jews (οὐκέτι ἐβασίλευσε / *reges . . . finierunt*). Samaria is mentioned in both passages, although in the *Excerpta* it is inaccurately or anachronistically juxtaposed with the region of Judea, while in Malalas it is set alongside Jerusalem as one of the

two Jewish capital cities no longer to exercise government; Malalas would seem to better preserve the intent of a common source in this instance. Malalas prefers the passive to the *Excerpta*'s active indication of the work of Providence, but they both employ the same image of the kingdom falling into the hands of her enemies (παρεδόθη ἡ βασιλεία . . . εἰς χεῖρας / *tradedit . . . regnum . . . in manus*).[11] Both passages, for what it is worth, also speak of "the whole land" (πᾶσαν τὴν

11 This may seem like just a biblical cliché, but it is apparently one favored by Bouttios. The construction **παρεδόθη ἡ βασιλεία εἰς χεῖρας** also appears in another fragment from Malalas (F **13**) and corresponds to the phrase *tradidit dominus deus regnum in manus*, which is frequently found in those passages from the *Excerpta* that betray the influence of Bouttios (FF **9, 11, 18**). Depicting them as ultimately obedient to God's will is consistent with Bouttios's generally negative view of pagan rulers. The idiom (παραδίδωμι εἰς χεῖρας), with some variation, is commonly found in the Bible to indicate conquest and subjection according to the will of God: Deut. 1:27; Josh. 7:7; Judg. 2:14, 23, 3:10, 13:1; 1 Sam. 18:19; 2 Kings 3:13, 19:10, 21:14; 2 Chron. 25:20, 28:5, 36:17; Ps. 78:61, 106:41 (LXX 77:61, 105:41); Isa. 37:10; Jer. 21:10, 22:25, 32:4, 36, 43, 34:2, 37:17, 38:3, 46:24 (LXX 21:10, 22:25, 39:4, 36, 43, 41:2, 44:17, 45:3, 26:24); Ezek. 11:9, 16:39, 21:31, 23:9, 23:28, 31:11; see Delling, "Alexander der Grosse," 37–38. It is often into the hands of the Assyrians or Babylonians that the Lord delivers his wayward people. The Lord appears as the explicit subject of the active verb so regularly that his agency is implied when the verb is passive.

The passive without a specified agent is also used when the Rabshakeh warns Hezekiah, "Let not thy god in whom thou trustest deceive thee, saying, Jerusalem shall not be delivered into the hands of the king of Assyria" (οὐ μὴ παραδοθῇ Ἱερουσαλὴμ εἰς χεῖρας βασιλέως Ἀσσυρίων); 2 Kings 19:10, cf. Isa. 37:10. This story involves the Assyrians, as does F **10**, and the form of the verb is similar, but the blasphemous boasting of the Rabshakeh and the subsequent destruction of the Assyrian army and deliverance of Jerusalem explicate themes significant to Bouttios.

God accomplishes his purposes against all expectation, undoing the domination of the combined powers of the East (FF **9, 18**) just as he broke the siege of the Assyrians. His chosen instrument, no less than his victim, might be as unaware of his identity and purpose as the Rabshakeh; cf. Smelik, "My Servant Nebuchadnezzar," 129–31, 133. After all, according to Josephus (*AJ* 11.8.5 [333–35]), Alexander was exhorted to invade Asia by a figure in a vision but did not recognize this person until he encountered the high priest of the Jews.

When this idiom appears in the New Testament (Matt. 17:22; 26:45, Mark 9:31, 14:41; Luke 9:44) the verb is παραδίδωμι in the passive, as here, and it is consistently ascribed to Christ, prophesying that the Son of Man will be delivered into the hands of sinful men. The phrase becomes decidedly sinister, and confirms that although the one into whose hands another is delivered may act according to the will of God, he can still be a villain—a sacrificer of virgins, for instance. Cf. Theodoret, *Gr. affect. cur.* 6.30–31.

γῆν / *omnis terra*) being made subject to its conquerors. The accounts of the end of the Jewish kingdom in the *Excerpta* and Malalas are roughly parallel renditions of their common source. If the *Excerpta*'s version can be traced back to Bouttios, so can that of Malalas.

To return to the Alexander passage in Malalas, his *Chronicle* states that Alexander freed the Romans, Greeks, and Egyptians from the combine of oriental powers we have noted (**F 16.1**). The *Excerpta* also recognizes Greece, Egypt, and the land of the Romans, along with Syria and parts of Libya, as the proper dominion of Alexander, to which he gives laws before setting out against his eastern enemies (**F 18**). The Greeks and the Egyptians as the beneficiaries of Alexander's efforts can be explained in terms of the received historical tradition, but the Romans are a distinctive and noteworthy addition to this list. The Romans are even singled out as the people to whom Alexander "returned all they had lost." According to the legendary *Alexander Romance*, Alexander was supposed to have conquered the Romans, but this can only have been the germ of the idea we see articulated here.[12]

We can only make sense of this assertion that the Romans were liberated from the Assyrians, etc., if we take into account the passages in the *Excerpta* that describe both the subjection of the Romans to these easterners at the extinction of the line of Roman kings (**F 9**), a passage which explicitly anticipates Alexander's liberation of the Romans, and the realm of Nebuchadnezzar (Nabuchodonosor) stretching from the Caspian Gates to the Pillars of Hercules and including the land of the Romans (**F 11**), which further alludes to Alexander inasmuch as his kingdom is also supposed to stretch from the Caspian Gates in the east to the Pillars of Hercules in the west (**F 20.1**). These passages must be taken as necessary precursors to the statement that Alexander freed the Romans,

12 *Al. Rom.* (α) 1.26.4–6, (β) 1.29.2–3; see Braccesi, *L'Alessandro occidentale*, 43–88; Garstad, "Rome in the Alexander Romance." Van Hoof and Van Neuffelen, *Fragmentary Latin Histories*, 256, suggest that Rome being freed by Alexander the Great "reads like a garbled reference to a Roman tradition of the succession of world empires." This, however, is just what it cannot be. Whereas the tradition of *translatio imperii* carefully distinguishes the dominant world powers in a series, the passage Malalas credits to Bouttios combines all the great nations of the East together. The actual relation of Bouttios's strange account of past events to the *translatio imperii* tradition is indicated by Garstad, "Alexander the Great's Liberation of Rome," 190–92.

since they adumbrate how the Romans came to be subjugated to this congeries of oriental powers in the first place.[13] And so they are included among the fragments of Bouttios.

The *Excerpta* and Malalas exhibit common ground on a number of other distinctive points concerned with Alexander, and these parallels allow us to identify further fragments of Bouttios. We have already mentioned that in both texts (**FF 9, 16.1**) the Romans, Greeks, and Egyptians are freed from the eastern powers, but—Jeffreys's assertion that "the verbal connections [between Malalas and the *Excerpta*] are not close" notwithstanding[14]—it is worth noting the precise similarity of the statements in the two texts: Alexander is the subject of a verb indicating the work of liberation (ἐλευθερώσας / *liberauit*), which takes as its object the *whole land* (πᾶσαν τὴν γῆν / *omnem terram*) of the Romans, Greeks, and Eyptians (τῶν Ῥωμαίων καὶ Ἑλλήνων καὶ Αἰγυπτίων / *Romanorum et Grecorum et Egyptiorum*), consistently in that order, from slavery (ἐκ τῆς . . . δουλείας / *de servitute*) not merely to the Persians, whom Alexander actually fought, but to the Chaldeans (*Chaldeorum*) or to an equally anachronistic litany of oriental peoples (Ἀσσυρίων καὶ Περσῶν καὶ Πάρθων καὶ Μήδων).[15] Both the *Excerpta* and Malalas also resort to divine intervention as a cause of historical events in these passages, with close verbal similarities: Malalas at the outset of his discussion of Alexander, but the *Excerpta* repeatedly, in this way explaining the subjection of the Romans and the Jews, the rise of Alexander, and the defeat of Darius and the powers of the East.

These references to the providential hand of God are in keeping with the *Excerpta*'s main account of Alexander, which mentions his visit to Jerusalem and the worship he offered there (**F 18**)—this story in particular is repeated in the *Excerpta*'s list of Jewish high priests (**F 19**). The connection between God directing the course of Alexander's career and some mention of his visit to Jerusalem may be implicit, but it is unavoidable when we remember that in the earliest and fullest account of Alexander's visit to Jerusalem in Josephus's *Jewish Antiquities*,

13 See Garstad, "Alexander the Great's Liberation of Rome," 182–87.

14 E. Jeffreys, "Malalas' Sources," 174.

15 **F 9**: *liberauit omnem terram Romanorum et Grecorum et Egyptiorum de servitute Chaldeorum* / **F 16.1**: ἐλευθερώσας ὁ αὐτὸς Ἀλέξανδρος καὶ τὰς πόλεις καὶ τὰς χώρας καὶ πᾶσαν τὴν γῆν τῶν Ῥωμαίων καὶ Ἑλλήνων καὶ Αἰγυπτίων ἐκ τῆς Ἀσσυρίων καὶ Περσῶν καὶ Πάρθων καὶ Μήδων ὑποταγῆς καὶ δουλείας.

Alexander claimed to have seen before setting out on his campaign a vision of a man in the robes that he later recognized as those of the Jewish high priest promising to lead his army and render the Persian Empire up to him.[16] Although there is no mention of Alexander's visiting Jerusalem in Malalas, he does include at least one element from the story, agreeing with the *Excerpta* that Jaddus was the high priest of the Jews in the time of Alexander. This story, moreover, implicitly puts the Jews on an equal footing with the Romans: subjected to the Assyrians, etc., until they were liberated by Alexander. The understanding of Alexander's conquests as the working out of God's providential will is also consistent with the subtle allusion to the prophecies of Daniel in Malalas's account of Alexander.[17]

The *Excerpta* and Malalas exhibit further commonalities in their treatment of Alexander. Both texts identify the father of the Darius defeated by Alexander as Assalamos or Alsamus; perhaps the name is corrupt in each case, but the idiosyncratic patronymic appears in both texts.[18] There is a common concern with Alexander as "the Founder," that is, of Alexandria. The *Excerpta* constantly refers to Alexander as *conditor*, as if the founding of Alexandria were one of the most notable features of his identity—as is only fitting for a work apparently composed in Alexandria[19]—and Malalas provides a more than cursory description of

16 Joseph., *AJ* 11.8.5 (334–35).

17 An allusion to Daniel's prophecy of a beast "like a leopard," identified by the ancient Christian commentators with Alexander, seems to be the import of the phrase that likens Alexander to a leopard (ὡς πάρδαλις); see above, p. 37 and n. 8.

18 Diodorus (17.5.5) is the only one of our standard sources to name the father of Darius III, who, he says, was the son of "Arsanes" (Ἀρσάνου). Badian, "Darius III," 244, assumes that this was actually "Arsames," the name of Darius I's grandfather and a Persian name of the Achaemenid period well attested in our sources; see Kent, "Oldest Old Persian Inscriptions," 209–12; Fitzmyer, "Some Notes"; Whitehead, "Some Distinctive Features." The *Alsami* of the *Excerpta* seems to be a corruption—hardly surprising in this text—of Ἀρσάμου, and perhaps one isolated to the *Excerpta* translation since Ἀρσάμου occurs as the patronymic of Darius in other Byzantine chronicles: Eusebius, *Chronici Canones* ann. Abr. 1670; Agathias, *Hist.* 2.25.8; *Chron. Pasch.* Olymp. 113 (Dindorf, *Chronicon Paschale*, 321); Georg. Sync., 308.8, 318.2; George Hamartolos (George Monachus), 1.19, 6.11. Malalas's "Assalamos" or "Assalames" would appear to be a corruption of Arsames in the Greek tradition, but it is not the only one. Syncellus (308.3, 5) offers Ἀρμουσάμου as an alternate patronymic for Darius, separated by barely a few lines from Ἀρσάμου.

19 On the evidence of the *Excerpta*'s composition in Alexandria, see Garstad, *Apocalypse / Alexandrian World Chronicle*, xx, xxvii–xxviii.

Alexander's establishment of the city, including the detail, found uniquely in this account, of Alexander's offering a virgin girl as a foundation sacrifice. Both texts emphasize the fact that Alexander imposed laws on the territories he conquered, either the "friendly" lands of the West, the defeated Orient, or the whole world.[20] Finally, the *Excerpta* and Malalas both end their accounts of Alexander with some reference to his last will and testament and its distribution of his conquests among his generals, although it is much lengthier and more detailed in the *Excerpta*.

The distinctive elements of Malalas's account of Alexander are the reference to divine causation, the compounded list of oriental powers defeated by Alexander, the founding of Alexandria, the passage into Asia by the Bosporus, the liberation of the Romans along with the Greeks and Egyptians, and Alexander's legislation in his conquered territories. They are distinctive not only in that their selection and composition make for a new narrative, but also in that some of these elements are found in no previous account, only in Malalas (the details of the founding of Alexandria, Alexander's route into Asia) or only in Malalas and the *Excerpta* (the list of Alexander's eastern enemies, Alexander's liberation of the Romans). We can offer no other source for these distinctive elements, and so we are justified in attributing them to Bouttios, the only authority cited by Malalas for his account of Alexander. The *Excerpta* provides more than a corroborating witness to the account of Alexander attributed to Bouttios. If we adduce further passages from the *Excerpta* that contain similar details, we are able to elucidate otherwise inexplicable details in our fragment of Bouttios and compose something of a coherent historical narrative. So along with the description of the career of Alexander in Malalas and its parallels in the *Excerpta*, we should add to our list of the fragments of Bouttios the *Excerpta* passages dealing with the fall of the Roman and Israelite kingdoms and the empire of Nebuchadnezzar.

We have indicated that the *Excerpta* was composed by the addition of a few protracted narrative episodes from other sources to a rather sparse chronography. Almost all of the material on Alexander in the *Excerpta* belongs to such a narrative, and the balance of probability suggests that the added narrative on

20 *ELB* 1.6.6 (F **9**): *et leges posuit mundo*, 1.8.4 (F **18**): *postquam legem poneret in Ellada et omnem Romanorum terram Syriam quoque et Egyptum et partes Lybiae, tunc venit in partes orientales*, 1.8.4 (F **18**): *et legem posuit in omnes civitates eius, et tributarii facti sunt ei sicut proprio regi*. Malalas 8.3 (F **16.2**): καὶ ἐνομοθέτησεν ὁ αὐτὸς Ἀλέξανδρος τὴν χώραν αὐτῶν καὶ ἐβασίλευσεν αὐτῶν.

Alexander came in its entirety from a single source, rather than itself being compiled from a number of sources before being added to the chronography that was the basis of the *Excerpta*. Considering the parallels that we have identified between the accounts of Alexander in Malalas and the *Excerpta*, we should, furthermore, be ready to identify that source as Bouttios—not disregarding the possibility that an intermediary might stand between Bouttios and the *Excerpta* as much as between Bouttios and Malalas. It should be possible, then, to disentangle a narrative of Alexander from the chronographic notices, extract it more or less in toto, and assign these portions of the text to Bouttios.

This procedure receives immediate validation. Apart from the anticipation of Alexander at the end of the Roman royal line already noted, the *Excerpta* begins its disposal of Alexander material with a garbled mention of Nectanebo (F 17). His name has fallen out of the text, but Ochus, the king of the Persians and Medes, is said to have made war on the "last Pharaoh of the kingdom of Egypt," who realized that he would be defeated, shaved his head, changed his clothes, and escaped by way of Pelusium to Macedonia, where he lived out his life as an astrologer. There were traditions of Nectanebo unconnected with Alexander,[21] and we might be disinclined to make this a part of the *Excerpta*'s Alexander narrative, if Nectanebo's destination were not Macedonia and his craft not astrology. But when we turn to Malalas, we see precise parallels for the details of this narrative, as well as an explicit connection to Alexander. In Malalas, the Persians invaded Egypt and Nectanebo discovered by divination that they would be victorious, shaved his head and changed his clothes, escaped through Pelusium, and found refuge until the end of his days in Macedonia, but Malalas adds that it was under these circumstances that Nectanebo seduced Olympias and became the father of Alexander (F 12). This narrative is evidently taken from the *Alexander Romance*, but the *Excerpta* and Malalas also appear to share a common intermediary between themselves and the *Romance*, who selected and compiled specific details offered by the *Romance*.[22] The discussion of the last pharaoh of Egypt in the

21 See Diod. Sic. 16.47.5–51.1; Diog. Laert. 8.8.87; Hogarth, "Nectanebo"; De Meulenaere, "Les monuments du culte"; B. Perry, "Egyptian Legend"; Spalinger, "Date of the Dream"; Ruzicka, *Trouble in the West*, 147–49, 152–53, 161–63, 179–81, 187–88, 190–91, 201–2.

22 This is evident in the fine details that Malalas and the *Excerpta* share: Nectanebo shaved his head, he changed his clothes, and he fled *through* Pelusium (ἔφυγε διὰ τοῦ Πηλουσίου / *fugiit per Piluseum*) to Macedonia.

Excerpta may need to be completed and connected to a fuller sequential narrative by its parallel in Malalas, but it obviously belongs to the account of Alexander that has been added to the chronography, and though separated from the main narrative on Alexander its parallel in Malalas likewise belongs to Alexander's story, and so these are also fragments which should be assigned to Bouttios.

The discovery of a further fragment of Bouttios detached from the core of Malalas's account of Alexander raises the possibility of even more fragments outside of this core passage (F 16.1). The most likely candidates are found in the material intervening between the account of Nectanebo and the beginning of Book 8, but not all of this material can belong to Bouttios. The passage beginning with the remark that the Jews and their high priests paid tribute to the Assyrians (F 13) is consistent with the *Excerpta* passage on the end of the Israelite kingdom (F 11), which also mentions tribute, and with the conflation of the Assyrians, Persians, and other eastern peoples, and makes Alexander's visit to Jerusalem particularly significant inasmuch as he presumably delivered the Jews from subjection to the eastern powers in much the same way as he is supposed to have liberated the Romans. The next statement in Malalas, that the Assyrians and their king Ochus became haughty at this time, that they ruled as tyrants over the whole world, and that "the kingdom was delivered into the hands of the Assyrians, Persians, Medes, and Parthians" (F 13), corresponds to the conflation of eastern peoples (doubly, since Ochus, a Persian, is identified as an Assyrian and a list of oriental nations is also provided) and to the verbal pattern by which conquest is described by Bouttios ("these were delivered into the hands of those"), which we see in the opening of the core passage on Alexander.[23] The haughtiness of the Assyrians (ὑπτιώθησαν) and the tyranny they exercise over the whole earth (ἐτυράννησαν πᾶσαν τὴν γῆν) in this passage also correspond to the madness of the Assyrians which is said to provoke Alexander to attack them (κατὰ τῆς ἀπονοίας τῶν Ἀσσυρίων ὀργισθείς) in the core passage.

It is tempting to include the next passage on Philip (F 14) since it includes the story of a city foundation in which the name of the former village on the site is given, as is the case with Alexandria in the core passage, but this might seem slender grounds for associating the passage with Bouttios, and it must be considered a *fragmentum dubium*, even if this treatment of Philip would provide

23 See above, p. 40, n. 11.

a convenient bridge from Nectanebo to Alexander. Such a purpose is served, in any case, by the subsequent notice of Alexander's succession to Philip and Darius's succession to Ochus, in which Darius is the son of Assalamos, a Mede, and ruler of the Babylonians, and, for good measure, overlord of all (κατεκυρίευσε πάντων), just as in the fragments assigned to Bouttios (F **15**).[24] The last portion of the text before the beginning of Book 8 is definitely not a fragment of Bouttios, depicting as it does the Romans expanding their territory under powerful consuls, when they should, according to Bouttios's reconstruction of the past, be languishing under the yoke of the Assyrians, etc.

After the core passage on Alexander in Malalas (F **16.1**) there is a chronological computation from Adam to the victory of Alexander. It disagrees with the *Excerpta*'s calculation from Adam to the death of Darius by several hundred years. It would appear that each of these texts is following a different chronological system, neither of which depended on their common source for Alexander material.[25] The notice that Jaddus (Addous) was high priest of the Jews at that time may, however, be taken from or at least have found corroboration in Bouttios, since there are similar notices in the *Excerpta* (FF **18**, **19**), detached from the chronological computation there. And even though the high priest is only mentioned as a chronological tag at the end in the *Excerpta*'s story of the visit proper, the earliest surviving account of Alexander's visit to Jerusalem, that of Josephus, gave a prominent place to the high priest. Josephus's version was seminal for all later accounts of this event, and we may reasonably suspect that if we had more of Bouttios's version we might find him appearing there as well.[26]

24 In the passage that ends with the citation of Bouttios (F **16.1**), Alexander's opponent is introduced as Darius the Mede, the son of Assalam. Reference to a Persian king as the ruler of the Babylonians suggests the idiosyncratic combination of oriental peoples apparently characteristic of Bouttios. And in the assessment of Alexander's career most closely associated with the citation of Bouttios (F **16.1**), in defeating Darius Alexander is said to capture "all the kingdoms of the earth" (πάσας τὰς βασιλείας τῆς γῆς) and a similar phrase is used (F **10**) of the "Assyrian" conquest of the kingdom of the Jews (ἐκυρίευσαν αὐτῶν).

25 This is hardly surprising, as Bouttios does not seem to have written a chronicle, as will be discussed below, pp. 162–66.

26 Joseph., *AJ* 11.8.3–7 (313–47). See Tcherikover, *Hellenistic Civilization*, 42–50; Momigliano, "Flavius Josephus"; Delling, "Alexander der Grosse"; Cohen, "Alexander the Great"; Nadich, *Jewish Legends*, 37–44; Bammel, "Der Zeuge des Judentums"; Goldstein,

The passages in Malalas that follow the core treatment of Alexander (**F 16.2**) include specific elements which closely correspond to the parallel passages in the *Excerpta* (**F 18, 20.1**), some of which are not found in the core passage: Alexander defeated a varied assortment of eastern peoples, killed their king Darius, and imposed laws upon them. The parallels in the *Excerpta* suggest that this material in Malalas also depends on Bouttios. The sentence following immediately upon the core passage, in which the Persians raised a statue to Alexander, seems to proceed from the last, since a benefaction (laws and rule) is followed by a show of gratitude (a memorial). In the fragment on Perseus, moreover, there is also a statue which "still stands to the present day" (**F 7.3**). Then there is a sentence indicating that Alexander married Roxane, "the daughter of Darius." This also seems to belong to Bouttios for two reasons: first, Roxane is the daughter of Darius, rather than Oxyartes, in the *Alexander Romance*, which is the source for many of the broad strokes and the details of Bouttios's account of Alexander;[27] and second, Alexander's taking the virgin Roxane, a prisoner, to wife recalls, albeit dimly, Perseus's ravishing the virgin Andromeda and then marrying her.[28] Alexander's defeat of Porus, which is communicated in the next sentence in Malalas, is also mentioned in the *Excerpta*, and so appears to be a fragment of Bouttios. This is followed by a lengthy description of Alexander's capture by Candace and his seduction of her (**F 16.3**). This is more of the legendary material that found a home in the *Alexander Romance*,[29] and while it is inconsistent with the brisk and economical style of the rest of the account of Alexander and there is no

---

"Alexander and the Jews"; Wirth, *Der Weg in die Vergessenheit*, 20–23; Stoneman, "Jewish Traditions"; Jouanno, *Naissance et métamorphoses*, 378–81; Amitay, *From Alexander to Jesus*, 119–20, 127; Jouanno, "Alexandre à Jérusalem."

27 *Al. Rom.* 2.20.11, 22.3, 6, 10–11, 14–16. Our more reliable sources present Roxane as the daughter of the Sogdian satrap Oxyartes, an Iranian nobleman, but not an Achaemenid: Plut., *De fort. Alex.* 1.11 (*Mor.* 332E); Arr., *Anab.* 4.19.5; Curt. 8.4.21–30, 10.3.11; *It. Alex.* 44 (101); cf. Diod. Sic., table of contents, bk. 17.

28 See **F 7.2**. Perseus's marriage to the virgin Andromeda is rather more clearly a subject for condemnation, since she was a consecrated temple priestess and he ravished her (φθείρας αὐτὴν) before they were married. Pointing out Roxane's virginal state before her marriage might seem perfectly innocent, if gratuitous, if not for the possibility of an allusion to the lecherous crime of Perseus.

29 *Al. Rom.* 3.18–23. See Wilmanns, "Alexander und Candace"; Ehlert, "Alexander und die Frauen"; Szalc, "Kandake, Meroe and India."

corroboration for it in the *Excerpta*, it would be unnecessary and inconsistent to suggest that in all other instances Bouttios is the intermediary for the material from the *Alexander Romance* in Malalas, but in this one case Malalas takes his material directly from the *Alexander Romance*. This story of Alexander being bested by a woman and the seemingly disproportionate space given to it, moreover, corroborate the essentially negative tone of the portrayal of Alexander in Malalas, which is most glaringly indicated by his performance of a human sacrifice at the founding of Alexandria. The Candace episode, therefore, can be assigned to Bouttios.

Malalas and the *Excerpta* both provide descriptions of the legacy of Alexander which, in relation to one another, demonstrate parallelism and discrepancy by turns. Malalas tells us that, on the point of death, Alexander ordered that his champions and companions in arms should rule in the places where they found themselves (F 16.4), but that is all he tells us at this point. The *Excerpta* says much the same thing, but follows the statement with a detailed list of the generals of Alexander and the territories they were instructed to govern (F 20.2). The list of Alexander's heirs in the *Excerpta*, as Peter Fraser notes, corresponds almost verbatim to the "Will of Alexander" as it was found in the first texts of the *Alexander Romance*.[30]

In the *Romance* the last will and testament of Alexander is followed by a notice on the length of Alexander's life and reign, on the number of Greek and barbarian nations he subdued, and of the many cities he founded.[31] There is a parallel sentence in both Malalas (F 16.4) and the *Excerpta* (F 20.3), in Malalas immediately after Alexander's order for the distribution of his territories and in

30 *Al. Rom.* (α) 3.33.13–15, 19–24; see P. Fraser, *Cities of Alexander*, 16; cf. Heckel, *Last Days and Testament*, 60–68, 108–9.

31 *Al. Rom.* (α) 3.35a (Kroll, *Historia Alexandri Magni*, 145–46): Οὐ τοσούτους δὲ βασιλεῖς Ἀλέξανδρος πολεμῶν ἐνίκησεν, ὅσους τελευτῶν κατέλειψεν. ἐβίωσε μὲν οὖν Ἀλέξανδρος ἔτη λ′. ἀπὸ ιε′ ἐτῶν ἀρξάμενος πολεμεῖν ἐπολέμησεν ἔτη ζ′, μέχρι κ′ ἐτῶν γεγένεται· τὰ δὲ ἄλλα λ′ ἐν εἰρήνῃ καὶ ἀμεριμνίᾳ καὶ εὐφροσύνῃ ἔζησεν. ὑπέταξεν ἔθνη βαρβάρων κβ′, Ἑλλήνων ι′· ἔκτισε δὲ πόλεις ιγ′, αἵτινες μέχρι τοῦ νῦν κατοικοῦνται καὶ εἰρηνεύονται (Alexander did not fight against and conquer as many kings as he left behind when he died. So, Alexander lived for thirty years. Commencing to make war from his fifteenth year he made war for seven years, until he was twenty years of age; the other thirty he lived in peace and freedom from care and merrymaking. He subdued twenty-two barbarian nations, and ten Greek ones; he founded twenty-two cities, which are inhabited and at peace up to the present).

the *Excerpta* after the list of his heirs and their territories, precisely corresponding to what we find in the *Romance* in terms of subject matter, if not in all of its figures—although this is due to the corrupt state of the A manuscript of the *Romance*. But just as in regard to Alexander's heirs and the distribution of his territories, Malalas indicates a list but does not provide it, while the *Excerpta* does, both Malalas and the *Excerpta* say that Alexander founded cities, but only the *Excerpta* provides us with a list of those cities. This list of Alexandrias, like the list of Alexander's heirs, corresponds to one in the *Alexander Romance*.[32]

Following a chronological computation from Adam, Malalas begins again, describing the division of Alexander's empire into four parts (**F 16.4**). There is no indication of a four-part division in the version of Alexander's will as preserved in the *Excerpta*, and this makes the partition of Alexander's empire into four look suspiciously like the effort of a chronicler, with his long-term perspective, to link one historical period neatly up to the next, rather than that of a historian providing disconnected accounts of various rulers, who had a more biographical interest in the immediate outcome of a man's life. Proceeding from this neat division of Alexander's empire among the four successors who would emerge victorious from the turbulent period after the conqueror's death, Malalas gives a chronology of the Ptolemaic rulers of Egypt which has some parallels with the chronology of the *Excerpta* as it continues after the death of Alexander.[33]

We are on the horns of a dilemma here. We have two accounts of Alexander, in two different texts, with several obvious affinities, affinities that must be due to the two texts' sharing a single source. Some of this material is recognizably from

32 *Al. Rom.* (α) 3.35b (Kroll, *Historia Alexandri Magni*, 146): ἔκτισε δὲ πόλεις ιγ′, αἵτινες μέχρι τοῦ νῦν κατοικοῦνται καὶ εἰρηνεύονται· Ἀλεξάνδρειαν τὴν ἐπὶ Βουκεφάλῳ ἵππῳ, Ἀλεξάνδρειαν τὴν πρὸς Πέρσας, Ἀλεξάνδρειαν τὴν ἐπὶ Πώρῳ, Ἀλεξάνδρειαν τὴν ἐν Σκυθίᾳ, Ἀλεξάνδρειαν τὴν ἐπὶ τοῦ Τίγριδος ποταμοῦ, Ἀλεξάνδρειαν τὴν ἐπὶ Βαβυλῶνος, Ἀλεξάνδρειαν τὴν πρὸς Τρωάδα, Ἀλεξάνδρειαν τὴν ἐπὶ Σούσοις, Ἀλεξάνδρειαν τὴν πρὸς Αἴγυπτον (He founded thirteen cities which are inhabited and at peace up to the present: Alexandria at Bucephalus the horse, Alexandria by the Persians, Alexandria at Porus, Alexandria in Scythia, Alexandria on the River Tigris, Alexandria at Babylon, Alexandria by the Troad, Alexandria at Susa, Alexandria by Egypt). The list in the A MS is obviously incomplete. On the relation of this list to that in the *Excerpta* and the origin and significance of these lists overall, see P. Fraser, *Cities of Alexander*, 10–16, 29 n. 45, 39–41, 46, 170, 204.

33 Malalas 8.6–8.

the same source, but is not presented in the same way in each of the two texts that preserve it. But there is also a crucial discrepancy between the two texts, where they present what appear to be mutually exclusive descriptions of one aspect of Alexander's career, the division of his empire on his death. We might attempt, however, to make sense of this material in the following manner. Where we have parallel statements in Malalas and the *Excerpta* (Alexander divided his empire among his generals, Alexander founded cities) followed by substantiation in the *Excerpta*, we appear to be dealing with material from Bouttios which has been better preserved in the *Excerpta*. If Bouttios is the intermediary between the *Alexander Romance* and both Malalas and the *Excerpta* elsewhere, there are no apparent grounds for believing that he is not the intermediary for this material as well. It is likely that these lists (of Alexander's heirs, of the cities he founded) belong to Bouttios, moreover, since he took a demonstrable interest in accounts of city foundations, including that of the most famous of all Alexandrias, and the list of Alexander's heirs appears to reflect the same concern as the repeated references to the circle of generals and comrades around Alexander in the core passage.[34] It seems as if Malalas—or one of his sources or redactors—included the notice on Alexander's heirs and the summing up of his career, but eliminated the lists as superfluous.

The attribution of the description of the four-part division of Alexander's empire is more ambiguous. On the one hand, not only does it disagree with the "Will of Alexander" as found in the *Excerpta*, but it is also inconsistent with the information we would expect to find in a historian whose chief source on Alexander was the *Romance*, which tells us nothing of the Diadochi, and so the four-part division might seem to belong to some source other than Bouttios. On the other hand, the division of Alexander's empire into four parts after his death is a prominent aspect of the allusions to Alexander in the book of Daniel,[35] which

34 F **16.1**: προτρεψάμενος ὁμόφρονας γενναίους στρατηγούς, F **16.1**: μετὰ τοῦ ἰδίου στρατοῦ καὶ τῶν συμμάχων, F **16.1**: ἅμα τοῖς σὺν αὐτῷ στρατηγοῖς παρέλαβε, F **16.2**: κατεδυνάστευσαν οἱ Μακεδόνες καὶ Ἀλέξανδρος μετὰ τῶν ἅμα αὐτῷ συμμάχων τῆς γῆς, F **16.4**: ὥστε πάντας τοὺς σὺν αὐτῷ ὑπερασπιστὰς καὶ συμμάχους βασιλεύειν. See Garstad, "Alexander's Comrades."

35 Dan. 7:6; 8:5–8, 21–22; 11:2–4.

seems to inform Bouttios's account of Alexander.[36] The indication that the rulers of these four parts are Alexander's "comrades and shield-mates," moreover, rounds off the repeated mentions of his generals and comrades; indeed, it is only this passage that allows us to definitely identify Alexander's συμμάχοι with his companions rather than his allies, since the rulers of his dismembered empire are here called "Macedonians." And finally, there is a nice balance between the references to the toparchy of Macedonia, from which Alexander set out to conquer an empire at the opening of his career, and the four toparchies into which his empire devolves at his death. All of this suggests that the four-part division may belong to Bouttios after all.

It is clear that one has to make a choice between assigning either a rendition of Alexander's Will or the division of his empire among four successors to a single author, but it is equally clear that it is very difficult to decide between the two alternatives, as a case can be made for both. I am personally inclined to assume that it is the list of Alexander's generals and the provinces assigned to them, rather than the four-part division, that represents the content of Bouttios. This is not least because throughout his *Chronicle* Malalas shows an interest in toparchs and toparchies, for the most part in passages that we have no reason to believe have anything to do with Bouttios, and the appearance of these words indicates the overall political trajectory that he perceives in the course of history.[37] But I

36 The simile that likens Alexander to a leopard (F **16.1**) appears to be based on the ancient interpretation of the third beast "like a leopard" of Daniel's vision (7:6) as Alexander; see above, p. 37 and n. 8.

37 For instance, the various kings who led their contingents against Troy under the leadership of Agamemnon are referred to as toparchs (Malalas 5.2, 5), which helps to clarify the relative status of the members and the constitutional arrangements of the Achaean host. The countries swallowed up by the imperial aggrandizement of the Lydian kingdom are called toparchies (6.2), which contributes to an allusive reflection on empire in the context of the conflict between Croesus and Cyrus. Philip and Alexander launched their conquests from the toparchy of Macedonia (7.19, 8.1), and on his death Alexander's empire was broken up into four rival toparchies (8.5). The feuding Successor Kingdoms, despite their imperial ambitions and status, appear again as the realms of kings who are designated toparchs (8.22). Pyrrhus of Epirus, like Alexander, made a bid for empire from the base of his toparchy (8.26), but eventually the great kingdoms of Alexander's heirs dwindled to nothing more than toparchies coterminous with ancestral homelands (8.27, 29). These toparchies were ultimately dissolved by the power of Rome and reduced to provinces (9.11, 13, 16, cf. 10.10) when Octavian, that is, Augustus, became the "sole king"

am not so confident in my conclusions as to refrain from laying out the evidence for the reader's own judgment. So both a version of Alexander's Will (F 20.2) *and* an indication that his empire was inherited by his four Successors (F 16.4) are to be found among the fragments of Bouttios presented at the end of this volume, but only one of them can ultimately be assigned to Bouttios.

If there are parallels between the Ptolemaic chronology in Malalas and the *Excerpta*, these are probably due to another source, even if another one held in common. Our assumption has been that narrative passages from Bouttios have been added to a chronography to form the *Excerpta* as we now have it, and there is no reason to suggest that Bouttios is also responsible for the chronography at this point just because certain parallels can be found in Malalas. Considering their similar genres and purposes, it is most unlikely that the *Excerpta* and Malalas would not share some other sources that provided them both with the same basic chronological information.

Domitian Material

The third and last citation of Bouttios in the text of Malalas comes in the passage on the reign of Domitian. A number of different topics are discussed at some length in the account of this reign—the persecution of the Christians, the affair of the dancer Paris, the emperor's building at Antioch, Apollonius of Tyana's apotropaic talismans at the same city, and the assassination of Domitian—but they are all treated as essentially discrete episodes. Bouttios is cited in regard to the first of these episodes, the persecution of the Christians (F 27).

The physiognomic depiction of the emperor which begins Malalas's account of Domitian's reign does not belong to Bouttios. Malalas includes such descriptions, after all, for practically all of the emperors, and we have no reason to

(μόνος βασιλεὺς). The historical trajectory apparent from Malalas's use of the terms "toparch" and "toparchy" seems to follow that established by Eusebius of Caesarea in the *Tricennalian Oration*, or *Praise of Constantine* (16), according to which the lawless and bloody turmoil of the time when the world was divided into warring toparchies finds its happy consummation in the foundation of the Roman Empire. Eusebius singles out "the evils of Ilium" and the divisions of the Successor Kingdoms as prime examples of what was wrong with the "time of the toparchies," just as Malalas's use of the terms "toparch" and "toparchy" clusters around these same historical periods.

connect Bouttios with any of these other accounts.[38] But the culminating description of Domitian as an "excellent philosopher" may owe something to Bouttios, as such a flattering description is hardly in keeping with most other descriptions of Domitian, but it is consistent with the portrayal of Domitian that follows, in which he takes pains to interview St. John, is impressed with his wisdom, and displays his sympathy and admiration by releasing him.

The first narrative episode begins by stating that there was a persecution of the Christians in Domitian's reign, then describes the emperor's interactions with St. John, ending with the Evangelist's exile to Patmos, and reports the prosecution of other unnamed Christians and their flight to Pontus. Bouttios is cited at the end of the episode in direct relation to the beleaguered Christians fleeing to Pontus, but he appears to be the source for the entire episode. The bald statement that there was a persecution appears to be a heading for a discrete episode, and the citation of Bouttios brings it to a close. All of the action within this episode is socially and geographically isolated, dealing with the Christians in Asia Minor. Bouttios, moreover, is cited by other authors as an authority on the persecution of Christians under Domitian with no mention of Pontus (see below). The other episodes in Malalas's account of the reign of Domitian were most likely taken from sources other than Bouttios.

The persecution of the Christians under Domitian is also noted by Jerome in his translation of the *Chronicle* of Eusebius (**F 28**) and by George the Syncellus in a passage likewise ultimately derived from Eusebius's *Chronicle* (**F 29**). Each of them indicates that this persecution was a subject written on by an authority whom he cites, Jerome a certain Bruttius and George a Brettios (Βρέττιος). Considering the close correspondence of the notices in Jerome and George the Syncellus, as well as the similarity of the names, Bruttius and Brettios seem to be the same individual. The names under which this writer goes are also remarkably similar to that of the other source cited in early references to the persecution under Domitian, that is, Bouttios. It is implausible that two writers with strikingly similar names should have been recognized as authorities on the same subject, the tribulations of the Christians in the time of Domitian. It is rather more likely that Bouttios is one more variant of this author's name and that we are

38 See E. Jeffreys and M. Jeffreys, "Language of Malalas, 3"; Kokoszko, *Descriptions of Personal Appearance*, 84–139.

dealing with the authority of a single writer. The notices of Jerome and George the Syncellus are, therefore, included as fragments of Bouttios; the identification of Bouttios with Bruttius/Brettios and the confusion of the names is discussed at greater length in chapter 5.

Jerome and George may corroborate the information provided by Malalas, that Bouttios discussed the persecution under Domitian, but they do not add anything to it. Both of them mention Flavia Domitilla and her banishment to the island of Pontia in particular; there is none of this in Malalas, but it does correspond to the treatment of the same period in Eusebius's *Ecclesiastical History*.[39] It seems that some later redactor has added the citation of Bouttios, who was known to have written on the persecution under Domitian—but not necessarily on Flavia Domitilla—to an original notice on this incident by Eusebius, which, like his account in the *Ecclesiastical History*, made much of the figure of Flavia Domitilla (see below, chapter 5). These fragments found in Jerome and George the Syncellus, then, should not be taken to indicate any more than that Bouttios treated the persecution of the Christians in the reign of Domitian.

39 Euseb., *HE* 3.18.4.

3

THE TYCHE SACRIFICES

So far, we have started from the citations of Bouttios by name to determine the extent of the material that belongs to him and to work out its ramifications, identifying new fragments on the basis of parallels in narrative, ideas, and distinctive turns of phrase. Our procedure in the present chapter is not really that different, as we turn our attention to the narratives of tyche sacrifice found scattered throughout Malalas's *Chronicle*.[1] (A list of these narratives, with their essential details, is laid out in table 1, and the locations where they are supposed to have occurred are plotted on figure 2.) These odd narratives were clearly not contrived by Malalas himself, but taken by him from another source. Although none of these accounts of virgin sacrifice is directly ascribed to any particular source, more of them are associated with citations of Bouttios than of any other author, and they are better integrated into passages that can be assigned to Bouttios than with material to be associated with any other cited author.

These reports of tyche sacrifice are all so distinct from the received historical record, so consistent with each other in their composition, and so clearly tending to an overall pattern and single conclusion (see below, chapter 6) that they must have a single author. To identify the author of one—or the two or three we can assign to Bouttios—is to identify the author of all of them. It is, however, still necessary to extricate the tyche sacrifice narratives from the broader accounts in

1 Garstad, "Tyche Sacrifices"; Saliou, "Statues d'Antioche"; Saliou, "Les lieux du polythéisme," 62–66; Ogden, *Legend of Seleucus*, 135–38; cf. Wiseman, *Remus*, 124.

Table 1. Narratives of Tyche Sacrifices in Malalas's *Chronicle*

CITY	NAME OF TYCHE / SACRIFICED MAIDEN	SACRIFICING RULER
Gortyna (6)	Callinice	Tauros
Iconium (7.3)	—	Perseus
Tarsus (7.3)	Parthenope	Perseus
Nyssa/Scythopolis (8.4)	Nyssa	Iphigenia
Alexandria (16.1)	Macedonia	Alexander the Great
Antioch (21)	Aimathe	Seleucus Nicator
Laodicea (23)	Agave	Seleucus Nicator
Apamea (24)	Pella	Seleucus Nicator
Galatia (25)	Gregoria	Octavian Augustus
theater of Antioch (26)	Antigone	Tiberius
Anazarbus (30)	Cepara	Zarbus
in Antioch (31)	Calliope	Trajan
Constantinople (34)	Ceroe	Constantine

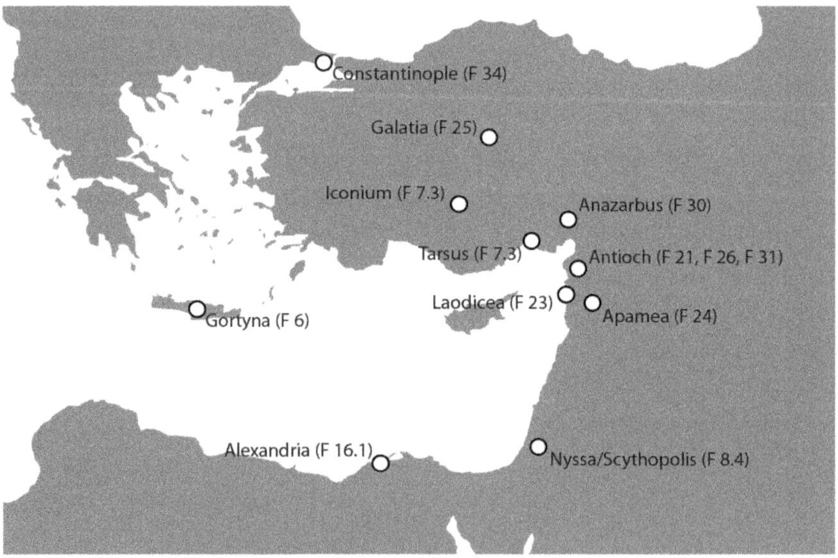

Figure 2. Locations of tyche sacrifices in Malalas. Underlying map by Sémhur / Wikimedia Commons, with modifications by author.

	CITATION OF BOUTTIOS	CITATION OF PAUSANIAS	CITATION OF DOMNINOS
	×		
	×		
			×
	×		
		×	
			×
			?

which we find them embedded, a process that will often leave us trying to determine how much context was required in their original composition and how much was provided by their inclusion in other works.

In Malalas the stories of the sacrifice of a virgin at the founding of a city are attached, seemingly at random, to the accounts of various heroes, kings, and emperors, from the remote past to the much more recent time of Constantine. They demonstrate a consistency and a remarkably peculiar deviation from the received historical record that would suggest a single author, but that author would not seem to be Malalas himself. Rather, they give every appearance of being material that Malalas has taken over from one of his sources, with little understanding and less sympathy. Such a heinous act as human sacrifice is included without comment in what are largely positive depictions of the rulers in question. The Roman senator Zarbos, for instance, applies himself zealously to repairing the damage caused by an earthquake and making the suffering of its victims known to the emperor, in addition to sacrificing an innocent girl at the refoundation of a city, and Trajan is dubbed "the most pious" (ὁ εὐσεβέστατος)

before he sacrifices a maiden.[2] Far from being the author of these sordid fictions, if there is a rhetorical point to them, it is lost on Malalas.

If, moreover, Malalas himself took any particular interest in accounts of virgin sacrifice, we might expect him to deal with the attempted sacrifice of Iphigenia in such a way as to be consistent with the tyche sacrifices, or to discuss the sacrifice of Polyxena more substantially.[3] Likewise, if Malalas himself were responsible for the tyche sacrifice narratives, we would not expect to see, as we do, references to tyche in the abstract, such as "the tyche of the Christians" or victory "through Christ and the tyche" of a Christian emperor,[4] a usage wholly inconsistent with the understanding of a tyche as the concrete product of a wicked ritual.

If Malalas had these stories at second hand, we might also be able to explain why they often appear to be incomplete (i.e., they sometimes fail to include all of the usual elements) in the *Chronicle*.[5] The tyche sacrifice narratives are fractured records which Malalas could assign to some of the reigns he covered, but they are not properly integrated into his *Chronicle* and really belong to one of his sources.

The Authors Cited in Relation to Tyche Sacrifices

Malalas does not identify his source for the accounts of tyche sacrifice. We have already seen, however, that at least two and perhaps three such narratives are included in material that can be assigned to Bouttios, namely the founding of cities by Perseus and Alexander (**FF 7.3, 16.1**). The only other sources associated

2 Malalas 10.53, 11.8; **FF 30, 31**.

3 Malalas 5.6, 10, 13.

4 Malalas 16.17, 18.77.

5 For example, Perseus founds Iconium on the site of the village of Amandra, and names the tyche of the city Persis after himself, but there is no virgin sacrifice to initiate the tyche cult (Malalas 2.11: **F 7.3**); Perseus sacrifices Parthenope at Tarsus, but there is no mention of a tyche (Malalas 2.11: **F 7.3**); likewise, Alexander sacrifices a virgin at the foundation of Alexandria and Augustus does the same at the foundation of Ancyra, but no tyche is mentioned (Malalas 8.1, 9.13: **FF 16.1, 25**); when it was first founded by Phidalia, before Constantine's refoundation, the tyche of Byzantium is supposed to have been called Ceroe, but there is no account, as we would expect, of Phidalia's sacrifice of a virgin named Keroe (Malalas 13.7: **F 34**).

with passages containing tyche sacrifices are Pausanias and Domninos.[6] That these authors are cited is consistent with the interpretation, based on that of Bourier, that Domninos was one of Malalas's principal immediate sources and that Malalas found material from both Pausanias and Bouttios already combined in Domninos.[7]

Pausanias is cited just after the account of the founding of Apamea (**F 24**), which includes a tyche sacrifice, but is cited not so much as an authority for this account in particular as for the numerous other foundations of Seleucus Nicator throughout the East.[8] Malalas also distances the authority of Pausanias from the accounts of Seleucid city foundations he himself endorses and retails, by relating that Pausanias erroneously claimed that Seleucus named Antioch after his father, not his son, as is stated in Malalas's account of the foundation of Antioch (**F 21**).[9] A suspicion that at some point Bouttios's version of this event with its tyche sacrifice may have been set up in deliberate contrast to that of Pausanias—as Bouttios's historical version of the conception of Perseus is contrasted with Euripides' mythological version (**F 7.1**)—is reinforced when Malalas says that Pausanias recorded many other things poetically (πολλά δὲ καὶ ἄλλα ὁ αὐτὸς

6 Pausanias: Malalas 8.18 (**F 24**). Domninos: Malalas 5.37, 10.10 (**F 26**), 11.4 (?).

7 Bourier, *Über die Quellen*, 2:44–45; cf. E. Jeffreys, "Malalas' Sources," 174.

8 Malalas 8.18 (Thurn, *Ioannis Malalae Chronographia*, 154): ἔκτισε δὲ καὶ ἄλλας διαφόρους πόλεις εἰς ἄλλας ἐπαρχίας καὶ εἰς τὰ Περσικὰ μέρη ὁ αὐτὸς Σέλευκος πολλάς, ὧν ὁ ἀριθμός ἐστιν σε′, καθὼς ὁ σοφὸς Παυσανίας ὁ χρονογράφος συνεγράψατο (Seleucus founded various other cities in other provinces and in the Persian lands, very many of them, and their number is seventy-five, as the wise chronographer Pausanias has written).

9 Malalas 8.18 (Thurn, *Ioannis Malalae Chronographia*, 154): ὧντινων πόλεων καὶ τὰ ὀνόματα ἐξέθετο, εἰς ὄνομα ἴδιον καὶ τῶν αὐτοῦ τέκνων, ὡς ἔδοξεν αὐτῷ ὁ Σέλευκος, ὁ δὲ σοφὸς Παυσανίας ἐξέθετο, <ὅτι> εἰς ὄνομα τοῦ ἑαυτοῦ πατρὸς ἔθηκε τὸ ὄνομα τῆς μεγάλης Ἀντιοχείας ὁ αὐτὸς Σέλευκος, ἐπειδὴ καὶ ὁ αὐτοῦ πατὴρ Ἀντίοχος ἐλέγετο. οὐδεὶς δὲ κτίζων πόλιν εἰς ὄνομα τεθνηκότος αὐτὴν καλεῖ· ἔστι γὰρ λῆρος· ἀλλ' εἰς ὄνομα ζῶντος καὶ ἑστῶτος καλεῖ. ἥντινα πόλιν εἰς ὄνομα Ἀντιόχου τοῦ ἰδίου αὐτοῦ υἱοῦ, ὡς προείρηται, ἐκάλεσεν (. . . and he set out the names of these cities, after his own name and those of his children, as seemed good to Seleucus, and the wise Pausanias explained that this Seleucus named Antioch the Great after the name of his father, since his father was also called Antiochus. But no one founds a city and gives it the name of a dead man, for this is nonsense, rather he names it after someone who is still alive and well. He named this city after the name of his own son Antiochus, as has been said already). See Garstad, "Pausanias of Antioch," 687.

σοφώτατος Παυσανίας ποιητικῶς συνεγράψατο).[10] Pausanias, moreover, apparently wrote in the first century CE, earlier than the time when some of the tyche sacrifices are supposed to have occurred, and if there is any trace of ideological intent in his account of the antiquities of Antioch and its environs, it is found in the preservation of Seleucid propaganda rather than the antipagan polemic that informs the tyche sacrifice narratives.[11]

Domninos is cited for the whole account of Orestes and Iphigenia, which includes a tyche sacrifice at Nyssa/Scythopolis (**F 8.4**), and he is indeed most likely the source from which Malalas took this material as a whole.[12] He probably composed the account of Orestes and Iphigenia that we find in Malalas, but he was not the original author of every part of it. He seems to have taken the story of virgin sacrifice from another source in turn. Much the same is true of the citation of Domninos shortly after the note on Tiberius's sacrifice of a maiden while rebuilding the theater of Antioch (**F 26**).[13] Domninos is Malalas's source for Tiberius's activities in Antioch altogether, but Domninos has included the virgin sacrifice story from another source. Domninos is also cited in Malalas's account of Trajan in Antioch, which includes a tyche sacrifice, and he was probably the source for this material overall, although he himself compiled it from different sources and was not ultimately responsible for the account of virgin sacrifice.

The striking aberration of the tyche sacrifice narratives from the historical record, their consistent form and elements, and their tendency to an overall climax indicate that they had a single author in the first place. That author seems to have been Bouttios. Where the descriptions of virgin sacrifice are associated with citations, they are probably best integrated into the identifiably negative tone in the accounts of Perseus and Alexander (**FF 7.3, 16.1**), which are on the whole assigned to Bouttios—although they may also be the most sensational tokens of the disparaging character of these accounts. In these instances, the tyche sacrifice episodes contribute to the denigrating presentation of significant figures in late antique paganism, but wherever they appear they constitute calumnies

10 Malalas 8.18 (Thurn, *Ioannis Malalae Chronographia*, 154).

11 Garstad, "Pausanias of Antioch," 672, 678, 683.

12 Malalas 5.37 (Thurn, *Ioannis Malalae Chronographia*, 111): ταῦτα δὲ ὁ σοφὸς Δομνῖνος συνεγράψατο (The wise Domninos recorded these things).

13 Malalas 10.10 (Thurn, *Ioannis Malalae Chronographia*, 178): ταῦτα δὲ Δομνῖνος ὁ σοφὸς χρονογράφος ἐξέθετο (Domninos the wise chronographer set out these things).

against the pagan rulers who performed the sacrifices and the cults they established. The Christian orientation of Bouttios's history, evident in the fragments on Domitian and St. John (**FF 27–29**), offers us a motive for the denigration of the popular pagan cult of Tyche as the result of human sacrifice. Some of the material connected with the tyche sacrifices, moreover, reflects the attested interests of Bouttios in Euripides and the persecution of Christians.[14] We have, therefore, assigned all of the tyche sacrifice narratives in Malalas to Bouttios, but it remains to be determined in each instance how much of the report's context may also be ascribed to him.

Tyche Sacrifices in the Mythical Period

The first tyche sacrifice in Malalas's *Chronicle* accompanies the founding of Gortyn on Crete by Tauros, the king of the island (**F 6**). A number of features of the account of Tauros are consistent with the more certain fragments of Bouttios. The story opens, as does the story of Perseus, with a contrast between what the poets and the "chronographers" have to say about a certain matter. The rape of Europa by a Cretan king named Tauros, instead of Zeus in the form of a bull (*tauros*), like the seduction of Danae by a bribe of gold rather than by a god transformed into gold, is a rationalization of the deeds credited to Zeus in myth. And as in the treatment of the story of Perseus's conception, the rationalized version is contrasted with Euripides' poetic handling of the same story. Tauros's conduct in regard to Europa and its justification, that he married her because she

14 Euripides is cited for the rape of Europa in the account of Tauros of Crete (**F 6**), which ends with a tyche sacrifice at the founding of Gortyn. Certain parts of Malalas's account of Iphigenia and Orestes, which features a tyche sacrifice (**F 8.4**), reveal striking verbal similarities to Euripides' *Iphigenia among the Taurians*; see Garstad, "Tyche Sacrifices," 134–35. The account of Perseus in Malalas begins with a contrast between Euripides' poetic version and the "historical" version of Bouttios (**F 7.1**); this contrast may have been part of Bouttios's own introduction to this material. The version of the account of the gods in the *Excerpta*, which we assign to Bouttios, also cites Euripides on the career of Heracles (**F 2.3**). Bouttios's interest in the persecution of Christians is evident in the account of the events in the reign of Domitian ascribed to him (**FF 27–29**). The tyche sacrifice Trajan is supposed to have performed at Antioch (**F 31**) seems to have its complement in the account of the Christian women martyred under Trajan in the same city (**F 32**) that follows immediately after it in Malalas's *Chronicle*.

was a virgin, follows a pattern that can also be seen in the stories of Perseus and Andromeda and of Alexander and Roxane, as each of these men marries the woman he has already seized or raped on account of her virginity. There is also, as in the story of Perseus, a connection with the character of Picus-Zeus, who we shall suggest is a creation of Bouttios. Finally, the tradition of the "evil evening" remembered in Tyre might be seen as some local lore Bouttios picked up from his home in the Levant.[15] Not only the appearance of a tyche sacrifice, then, but also a number of other features consistent with the established fragments of Bouttios give us grounds for considering the account of Tauros in its entirety to be a fragment of Bouttios.

A few of the details in the history of Agenor and his offspring within which the Tauros episode is contained may also recall certain details in the Picus-Zeus narrative,[16] but the reminiscences are tenuous, and it is unwarranted for us to claim the whole of the passage on Agenor and his family as a fragment of Bouttios from a connection based primarily on the appearance of a report of tyche sacrifice. The indication of the regnal years of Agenor and his reappearance in the narrative, moreover, provide a neat set of parentheses for something of an interpolation. Everything between these sentences, the account of Tauros, may be assumed to be taken from Bouttios.

At the end of his elaborate account of the adventures of Orestes and Iphigenia, Malalas offers Domninos as an authority for what he has said. There appear to be elements here from both Bouttios and Pausanias, combined by Domninos before being taken over by Malalas (**F 8**). Bouttios would seem to be responsible for the report of a tyche sacrifice that appears in this account, and there is an etymological account of some of the landmarks in the vicinity of Antioch which is

15 For Antioch as the hometown of Bouttios, see below, pp. 145–52.

16 Cadmus sets out on his mission "with a great deal of money and an army" (Malalas 2.7: μετὰ χρημάτων πολλῶν καὶ στρατοῦ). Likewise, Faunus-Hermes leaves Italy for Egypt after having collected "a great supply of gold" (πολὺν χρυσὸν ἐγκολπωσάμενος), and Cronos departed for the West "taking the considerable help of a crowd of well-born men" (λαβὼν πολλὴν βοήθειαν ὄχλου ἀνθρώπων γενναίων). Agenor, furthermore, divides his territory among his three sons, and in the *Excerpta* the Picus-Zeus narrative begins with a reference to the division of territory.

The unity of the account of Agenor and his family is suggested by the fact that both before and after the Tauros episode a son, Syros, is added to the canonical list of Agenor's eponymous sons, perhaps to make an archetypal division among three sons.

reminiscent of Pausanias.[17] But it is not clear just how much of which portions of this narrative should be assigned to Bouttios. The whole of the narrative is probably not from Bouttios. It includes material most likely taken from Pausanias and is therefore a composite. Moreover, the prophecy Orestes receives at Delphi makes no mention of a landfall in Palestine, where the tyche sacrifice takes place, but only of Syria, Orestes' ultimate destination. The account of the founding of Scythopolis in Palestine, including the tyche sacrifice, appears to be an interpolation in the midst of a neat narrative recounting the oracle, which foretells Orestes' journey to Scythia and then to Syria, and its fulfillment. But this interpolated episode, when it was first written, must have required some context. This is certainly provided in the compilation that appears in Malalas. Between the prophecy and the episode in Palestine there is the account of Orestes and Pylades going to Scythia, nearly being sacrificed by Iphigenia, and then making off with her and the golden image of Artemis. For the most part this is a prose summary of Euripides' *Iphigenia among the Taurians*, and there are a number of close verbal similarities with the play.[18] Bouttios's writing was explicitly contrasted with the poetry of Euripides, and it is possible that the rescue of Iphigenia offers us an example of how Bouttios set his work off against the famous tragedian, borrowing liberally, reworking, and introducing new—and scandalous—incidents.

The whole of the passage after the oracle at Delphi and up to Orestes' arrival in Syria has been included among the fragments of Bouttios, but this fragment (**F 8**) should be read with certain qualifications. Not all of this material ultimately belongs to Bouttios, but some of it does. As we have it in Malalas, the passage on Orestes represents a mixture of content from at least two different sources. The combination was probably undertaken by Domninos, whom Malalas names as his source. At least the tyche sacrifice narrative belongs to Bouttios, but this narrative, no matter how spare, needed some explanatory context. How were figures from Greek myth supposed to have appeared in Palestine in the first place? The connection is provided by the common name of the city inaugurated by Iphigenia, Scythopolis, and the sojourn of Iphigenia and Orestes in Scythia. Bouttios may have disposed of all this background in a brief sentence or two,

17 Pausanias of Antioch, FF 9A, 9B, 10 (7, 8); see Garstad, "Pausanias of Antioch," 675, 679, 681, 685, 686.

18 Garstad, "Tyche Sacrifices," 134–35.

but the fact that the Scythian interlude is largely a paraphrase of Euripides' play and that the drama of Euripides has been contrasted with the history of Bouttios to introduce a historicized version of myth must at least raise suspicions. The account of Orestes and Iphigenia in Scythia and their flight to Palestine pursued by Scythians could very well be derived from the work of Bouttios.

Seleucid Foundations

There are two reports of tyche sacrifice, the residue of a third, and even the remote possibility of a fourth in Malalas's account of the career of Seleucus Nicator. In this passage Malalas offers Pausanias as a source for the Seleucid city foundations, and we can assume that Pausanias is indeed the source for most of the material it contains, particularly as it is all so close to his avowed interest in the antiquities of Antioch and its ktistic traditions. Material from Bouttios, however, specifically the tyche sacrifices, appears to have been combined with Pausanias's account, once again probably by Domninos, Malalas's immediate source. It is also possible, though, that Bouttios himself borrowed material from Pausanias in order to give a context—and no small measure of credibility—to his fictitious narratives of virgin sacrifice.

What is most unlikely, however, is that Pausanias first attributed virgin sacrifices to the Seleucid kings at their city foundations and then this allegation was picked up by Bouttios and applied to other rulers. In any age, an accusation of human sacrifice was a grave charge to bring against a ruler, but whereas Bouttios's apparent Christianity provided him with a motive for denigrating pagan rulers, we can discern no reason why Pausanias, who appears to have written not much later than the reign of Augustus (31 BCE–14 CE), would make such a scandalous accusation, especially in a work that seems chiefly concerned with extolling the work of city founding undertaken by these same kings.[19] Bouttios, moreover, seems to have been attributing tyche sacrifices to figures like Perseus and Alexander, who appeared on the scene before the Seleucids and the coverage of Pausanias's work would have begun.

For the most part, the description of the foundation of Antioch (**F 21**) is consistent with Seleucid propaganda and the legends that attached themselves

19 Garstad, "Pausanias of Antioch," 670–71.

to Hellenistic kings, and can be credited to Pausanias.[20] The precise moment of foundation, however, coincides with the sacrifice of a virgin girl. This incident belongs to Bouttios, but it is almost inextricably mixed with Pausanias's account of the episode. The priest Amphion is said to have performed the sacrifice; only here is the officiant of a tyche sacrifice named, and so it seems likely that the presence of a priest at the foundation of Antioch and his name are taken from Pausanias. The hour of the sacrifice is given as sunrise on the twenty-second of May; the other tyche sacrifices, once again, lack such detail, and we may take the precise date and time as belonging to Pausanias, whose focus must have been this very moment. A sunrise sacrifice, moreover, has the ring of authentic Hellenistic tradition, since, as Pierre Chuvin points out, this would be an appropriate time for an offering to Zeus Kasios, a solar deity and the object of special devotion on the part of the Seleucids.[21] The mention of the temple to Zeus Bottios and the name of the architect, Xenarios, may also be taken from Pausanias. The raising of a statue of the victim of the tyche sacrifice, however, and the inauguration of sacrifices to the tyche must be part of Bouttios's account.

Considering the tangled amalgamation of Pausanias and Bouttios in this instance, it may be worth considering the possibility that rather than these two authors' being independent sources combined by Domninos, at certain points Bouttios himself drew on Pausanias. They share, after all, an interest in city foundations and an Antiochene origin. For the sake of clarifying the context, the chapter as a whole has been presented among the fragments, but on the understanding that there is a great deal here that does not belong to Bouttios.

Malalas dwells at some length on the tyche statue of Antigonia, but does not mention a virgin sacrifice (**F 22**). It is possible that this passage reflects an incompletely preserved portion of Bouttios's work. Tyche images were obviously important to an author who offered a series of accounts explaining the origins of several of them. On the other hand, it is probable that a work like Pausanias's on the monuments of Antioch and its environs would also describe a number of tyche statues.[22] For the sake of thoroughness this passage has also been included among the fragments, with the proviso that it must be considered dubious.

20 Garstad, "Pausanias of Antioch," 682–87.

21 Chuvin, "Les fondations syriennes," 103.

22 Garstad, "Pausanias of Antioch," 669–71.

A notice that a tyche sacrifice was performed at the foundation of Laodicea (**F 23**) appears to have been added at the end of an account taken from Pausanias. The initial sacrifice to Zeus and the concomitant miraculous sign involving an eagle are very close to the story of the founding of Antioch. Once again, the whole passage has been presented in order to clarify the context, but only the final note on the tyche sacrifice seems to represent the work of Bouttios.

The passage immediately following in Malalas's text, which describes the founding of Apamea, also appears to preserve material from Bouttios (**F 24**). As it stands, the text indicates that Seleucus inaugurated his new city by performing a sacrifice and renaming "her" (ἥν) Pella, after his hometown in Macedonia. The "her" is usually taken to refer to the city of Apamea, but Seleucus had just given this new name to the village of Pharnace, and it does not seem reasonable that Seleucus should have immediately renamed the city he had only recently named. The city in question, moreover, was known as Apamea, not Pella. The text is almost certainly corrupt and the "her" should refer to a virgin girl, the victim of the sacrifice, mention of whom has fallen out of the text. The original sense can be restored with the addition of only a single word to the manuscript text, in a construction that can be shown to have a parallel among the accounts of tyche sacrifice.[23] We then have a close parallel with the tyche sacrifice in the account of Alexander. Just as the tyche of Alexandria is named after a girl "called by him" Macedonia, the tyche of Apamea is named after a girl "whom he called by the name" of Pella, a place-name, moreover, reminiscent of Macedonia. The description of the tyche sacrifice is followed by the account of another sacrifice, this time of more acceptable victims, a bull and a goat, and, as at the foundations of Antioch and Laodicea, accompanied by a miraculous sign provided by an eagle. It is with this second sacrifice that the material taken from Pausanias must resume. The initial tyche sacrifice would appear to be a garbled fragment of Bouttios.

23 While most accounts of tyche sacrifice indicate this event itself with some form of the verb θυσιάζω taking κόρην as its object, in the story of Zarbus sacrificing a girl at the refoundation of Diocaesarea as Anazarbus (**F 30**) the phrase ποιήσας δὲ θυσίαν κόρην is employed.

Roman Foundations

Malalas also records a tyche sacrifice in the reign of Augustus, when that emperor founded the city of Ancyra and the province of Galatia (**F 25**). Augustus is supposed to have performed this sacrifice on his way from Actium to the assault on Alexandria, and Malalas provides a detailed, if doubtfully authentic, account of his progress through Asia Minor and Antioch, describing his administrative and military activities en route. If we could rely on it, this account would be an unparalleled mine of historical information.[24] The indications, however, are that this narrative is at best misinformed, and more likely fabricated for the most part. For instance, Augustus was not accompanied on this expedition by Agrippa, as Malalas says he was.[25] The tyche sacrifice is likewise a fiction and its details not so much erroneous as invented.

It is tempting to attribute the whole of this account, from Actium to the attack on Alexandria, to Bouttios as a context for the tyche sacrifice at the inauguration of Ancyra and Galatia. We know, after all, that he was willing to play fast and loose with the historical record and there are some vague reminiscences of the expedition of Alexander, which we have credited to him.[26] But if deviation from the standard historical record were a sufficient condition for identifying a fragment of Bouttios, we would be in a position to assign vast swaths of Malalas's

24 Our other, generally more reliable, sources are frustratingly sparse in their descriptions of the movements of Octavian's forces after Actium. Suetonius (*Aug.* 17.3) tells us that Caesar proceeded to Egypt by a roundabout route through Asia and Syria (*Asiae Syriaeque circuitu Aegyptum petit*). Plutarch indicates that (*Ant.* 72.1) Antony and Cleopatra sent ambassadors to Caesar in Asia (εἰς Ἀσίαν), and that (*Ant.* 74.1) at the close of the winter after Actium Caesar advanced against his adversary by way of Syria (διὰ Συρίας), while his generals came through Libya. Josephus (*AJ* 15.10.3 [354]) says that Caesar arrived in Syria in the seventeenth year of Herod's reign. According to Cassius Dio (51.4.1), after the victory at Actium Caesar went over into Asia setting affairs in order and attempting a reconnaissance in pursuit of Antony, but was recalled to Italy; returning from Italy (51.5.2), he hauled his ships over the Isthmus of Corinth and made it back to Asia. It is possible that the route of the gladiators who were being trained at Cyzicus to celebrate the triumph of Antony and Cleopatra, but attempted to reach Egypt to fight for their masters (Cass. Dio 51.7.2–6)—they proceed through Galatia, Cilicia, and Syria—was intended to reflect, or anticipate, the route of their opponent Caesar. See Southern, *Augustus*, 97–99.

25 Croke, "Malalas, the Man and His Work," 7.

26 Augustus (Malalas 9.12), like Alexander, secures his position in Europe and then sets out against eastern enemies, making landfall in Bithynia.

Chronicle to him. Even if they are not preserved in the histories with broader interests, there must have been a number of accounts of Augustus's progress from one end of Asia Minor to the other in circulation among the places he passed through. Royal visits tend to make for long memories. And just as the interest in such records would be local, their information would be parochial. Bouttios could have found a context for his narrative of an incident involving Augustus in just such a history—probably one concentrating on Antioch—and need not have included the whole of Augustus's itinerary in his account of one incident.

The tyche sacrifice is set in the immediate context of the—unhistorical—defeat of Deiotarus, the tetrarch of Galatia. There is an inconsistency between this context as a whole and the tyche sacrifice narrative specifically. Augustus is said to conquer Galatia and defeat Deiotarus, but he is also supposed to have given his new province the name of Galatia on account of the garrison of Gallic troops he left there. The territory Augustus conquered could not have been called Galatia if it was first so called by Augustus after he organized it into a province, and it seems very unlikely that anyone who knew—even imprecisely—of Deiotarus could have been unaware of his own Gallic antecedents, or that his domain was called Galatia well before Augustus arrived in it. We can, therefore, isolate as a fragment of Bouttios only the passage detailing the foundation of Ancyra, the tyche sacrifice, and the establishment of the province of Galatia, which appears to have been inserted into an account of the defeat of Deiotarus, with which it did not agree on all points.

The next virgin sacrifice is attributed to Tiberius, in the midst of a description of his building program at Antioch (**F 26**). Malalas appears to ascribe the passage as a whole to Domninos, who is cited after the mention of the last structure in Antioch credited to Tiberius and before Malalas moves on to the emperor's building projects in Palestine.[27] Bouttios, moreover, appears to be in familiar company, as Domninos seems to be engaged in continuing Pausanias's work of describing the monuments of Antioch beyond the period of Pausanias's coverage. The author of this account even includes immediately before the sacrifice a detail, that the original name of the river Orontes was the Dracon, which seems to have been mentioned by Pausanias.[28] The citation of Domninos, the intermediary

27 Malalas 10.10.

28 Pausanias of Antioch, FF 9, 10 (4); see Garstad, "Pausanias of Antioch," 677–78, 679, 680. It is unlikely that the statement that it was Tiberius who changed the name of the

between Bouttios and Malalas, and the similarities to Pausanias, another of his sources with whom Domninos more than once seems to have mingled material from Bouttios, serve to confirm the suspicion raised by the singular subject matter of the virgin sacrifice that this is a fragment of Bouttios. But there is no reason to attribute to Bouttios any more than the brief statement that Tiberius built the theater in Antioch and sacrificed a girl named Antigone in the process. The innocuous, indeed laudatory description of Tiberius's construction program in Antioch which forms its context is altogether inconsistent with the virgin sacrifice narrative's sinister tone and apparently antipagan intention. It is possible that Bouttios buried his tyche sacrifice narratives in lengthy accounts of other, quite credible foundations so that they might be more readily believed, but it is more likely that Domninos considered a catalog of building projects to be an appropriate place to include material from Bouttios that was ostensibly concerned with foundations and construction.

Another tyche sacrifice occurs in the context of an account of the restoration of Anazarbus by the Roman senator Zarbus (**F 30**). If the brief sentence on the virgin sacrifice probably belongs to Bouttios, it is difficult to tell how much of the rest of the passage does. The report of the tyche sacrifice is followed almost immediately by a notice that St. John returned from Patmos to Ephesus, which seems to offer a conclusion to Bouttios's account of the Evangelist's dealings with Domitian and the persecution of the Christians (**F 27**). This would indicate that material taken from Bouttios is not limited to the human sacrifice story. The imputation of ritual murder, however, is entirely inconsistent with the characterization of Zarbus in the rest of the passage. His solicitous exertions on their behalf relieve the sufferings of the victims of an earthquake, who demonstrate their gratitude by naming their refounded city after him. Zarbus's energetic zeal is capped by his immolation of a girl and the erection of a statue of her to be the tyche of the city. How much of this account belongs to Bouttios will depend on the significance one assigns to the tyche sacrifice in its context. On the one hand, if the sacrifice is read as a denigration of Zarbus, in contrast with the rest of the passage's praise, it can be taken as an isolated intrusion into the account,

river was derived from Pausanias, since Tiberius appears to fall beyond the date of the latest events (in the reign of Augustus) in the fragments attributed to him, though not so far beyond that date that it is impossible that he discussed Tiberius.

but we must then assume that Bouttios wrote of Zarbus's sacrifice without any explanatory context. If, on the other hand, we understand the murder committed by Zarbus as having significance only in the broader context of the restoration of Anazarbus, that is, that in spite of his philanthropy and benefactions Zarbus was capable of an atrocity simply because he was a pagan, the passage as a whole, despite—or perhaps because of—its inconsistency, is integral to the report of tyche sacrifice. This latter reading is more persuasive, and seeing the following sentence as a neat closure to Bouttios's account of St. John, we have included the entire account of the restoration of Anazarbus, along with the notice on St. John, as a fragment of Bouttios.

The next tyche sacrifice, one of the most extensive in Malalas's *Chronicle*, occurs in the context of the visit of Trajan to Antioch (**F 31**). Trajan is said to have undertaken a number of repairs and building projects in the wake of the earthquake that shook the city in December of 115. Only two of these are described in any detail: the building of the so-called Middle Gate and the completion of the theater. According to Malalas, Trajan sacrificed a virgin girl at the first and raised a statue of her at the second. If we allow that some context was required for the tyche sacrifice and the subsequent erection of a tyche image, then the entirety of this paragraph describing Trajan's constructions in Antioch is accounted for as a fragment of Bouttios. The tyche sacrifice is unmistakably derived from Bouttios, but it is not the only part of Malalas's account of Trajan that is indebted to him.

The passage treating together Trajan's building projects and his virgin sacrifice is immediately followed by one on his persecution of the Christians of Antioch (**F 32**).[29] We know from his discussion of St. John and the Christians of Asia Minor (**F 27**) that Bouttios took a sympathetic interest in the persecution of the Christian community and the interaction of its leaders with Roman emperors, which raises the likelihood that this material belongs to Bouttios. The passage in Malalas begins with a brief mention of the martyrdom of Ignatius, the only verifiably historical portion of the narrative of the persecution under Trajan. The reason given for the prosecution of Ignatius, that is, that he abused the emperor, would seem, if we are correct in identifying the Antiochene Christian

29 See Decrept, "Une persécution oubliée"; Meier, "Nero, Traian, und die Christen," 252–63.

criticism of Julian as the context of Bouttios's writing,[30] to be an attempt on our author's part to link himself to a precedent of unimpeachable and saintly heroism in his home city. But what follows bears even more clearly the hallmarks of Bouttios's history.

Trajan is supposed to have martyred five Christian women and, as a response to their hope in the resurrection, mixed their ashes with molten bronze. This bronze was ultimately cast as a series of statues depicting the martyred women. The story smacks of legend and fiction, the chief inspiration and métier of Bouttios, and its essential elements are reducible to a narrative very much like the accounts of tyche sacrifice. Here we also have innocent females done to death by a callous ruler who subsequently raises images, still to be seen, of his victims. The persecution narrative then tells us that Trajan prepared a "fiery furnace" (κάμινον πυρός) into which any Christians might voluntarily throw themselves, and that many took him up on the offer. This is obviously an imitation of the fiery furnace (τὴν κάμινον τοῦ πυρὸς τὴν καιομένην) and the deathless martyrdom of Shadrach, Meshach, and Abednego in the book of Daniel.[31] The fragments of Bouttios are marked elsewhere by significant references and allusions to Daniel, and this should probably be counted among them.[32] The Trajanic persecution narrative ends with a notice that this was the occasion on which St. Drosine and many other virgins were martyred. A remark on the persecution of Christians and the victimization of virgins is certainly consistent with the interests of Bouttios evident in his treatment of Perseus and Andromeda (**F 7.2**) and of Alexander and Roxane (**F 16.2**), to say nothing of the tyche sacrifices generally, as well as his treatment of the persecution under Domitian. We have some warrant, then, for adding the entirety of the persecution narrative to our fragments of Bouttios that discuss Trajan.

30 See below, pp. 140–44, 212–25.

31 Dan. 3:11, 15, 17, 20, 21, 23, 26.

32 Alexander is likened to a leopard (**F 16.1**), and the ancient commentators understood the "beast like a leopard" of Daniel (7:6) to refer to Alexander; see above, p. 37 and n. 8. There is also an explicit reference to Daniel in the account of the gods as Assyrian kings ascribed to Bouttios (**F 1.5**); see below, pp. 100–101.

Constantinople

The last instance of the inauguration of a civic tyche in Malalas's *Chronicle* occurs in the context of his account of the dedication of Constantinople by Constantine in 330 (**F 34**).[33] There is no virgin sacrifice on this occasion, although the name of the new tyche is given, as is usual in the preceding narratives of the establishment of a tyche. Instead, Constantine is said to perform "a bloodless sacrifice to God" before giving the name of Anthousa to the tyche of Constantinople. The inconsistency with Malalas's other accounts of the foundation of cities and the inauguration of their tychai, that is, the absence of a human sacrifice, is not a sign that this one has nothing to do with the other stories recounting the establishment of a civic tyche. On the contrary, the unique character of the origin of Constantinople's tyche indicates that this event serves as the culmination of all of the other tyche sacrifices and provides the rest with a narrative structure. There is the same concern with the founding of cities and the origins of the tyche figure, but in this instance Constantine is presented as overturning the macabre wickedness of his pagan predecessors by offering a "bloodless sacrifice." Just what this "bloodless sacrifice" was supposed to be—perhaps a service of prayers or a celebration of the eucharist—and whether it at all reflects actual events at the dedication of Constantinople is uncertain, but what is clear is that it stands in stark contrast to the bloody sacrifices of maidens that regularly accompanied the foundation of famous cities in Malalas's source.[34] Constantine's inauguration of a civic tyche without a virgin sacrifice is no confusing aberration, but the triumphant climax of a series of horrific tales, and so necessary as a fragment of

33 See Lathoud, "La consécration et la dédicace de Constantinople"; Lathoud, "La consécration et la dédicace de Constantinople (Suite [I])"; Ando, *Matter of the Gods*, 186–95; Agnosini, "Rome in Constantinople," 941.

34 Potter, *Constantine*, 263–65, accepts the report found in Malalas as an essentially historical account of the events of the initial dedication of Constantinople. Frolow, "La dédicace de Constantinople," 83–85; Bardill, *Constantine, Divine Emperor*, 252. Dagron, *Naissance d'une capitale*, 42–43, insists that there must have been some indefinite Christian aspects to the foundation ceremonies at Constantinople in 330, no doubt combined with pagan symbols. The *Parastaseis Syntomoi Chronikai* (56) relates that the *Kyrie eleison* was chanted a hundred times over at the dedication of Constantinople, but this is a late and legendary source to look to for corroboration of a reading of Malalas as a report of historical events. The significance of the "bloodless sacrifice" and perhaps even of the establishment of the civic tyche lies in their relation to previous accounts of city foundation.

Bouttios if we are going to attribute to him all of the tyche sacrifice narratives in Malalas's *Chronicle*.

It is not clear, however, just how much of Malalas's report of the dedication of Constantinople can be assigned to Bouttios. This event is given the lengthiest description, by far, of any in Malalas's account of the reign of Constantine, and includes numerous details on the structures he built in his new city and the ornamentation he applied to them. The mention of specific buildings in a new foundation is consistent with the account of Alexander's establishment of Alexandria, which we have attributed to Bouttios, but the description there is rather brief and goes into nothing like the detail lavished on the buildings of Constantinople. If Malalas visited Constantinople, he is very likely to have had access, moreover, to better sources on Constantine's initial building program than Bouttios did. It is most prudent, therefore, to limit the fragment of Bouttios to those portions of the description of the dedication of Constantinople that show correspondences with the apparent interests and content of Bouttios as attested in already established fragments.

So some indication of the occasion and context is included (**F 33**), although these need not be taken to belong to Bouttios himself. The bloodless sacrifice, as a contrast to the previous bloody ones, and the name of the new tyche, reflecting as it does those same preceding accounts, almost certainly belong to Bouttios. So too the antiquarian account of the city's original establishment by Phidalia with a tyche named Ceroe (**F 34**), which corresponds to Bouttios's concern with stories of the remote past, should be assigned to him.[35] The story of Phidalia might even have originally included a bloody tyche sacrifice as a clear contrast to Constantine's bloodless one, rather than being appended as an erudite but tangential note, as it appears in the present text of Malalas.

The accounts of construction and the descriptions of buildings cannot be securely assigned to Bouttios, but he does seem to be responsible for the detailed report of the procession established by Constantine to mark the anniversary of his foundation (**F 35**).[36] In the first place, the dedication of Constantinople is dated according to the era of Antioch. Such a dating would not only be meaningful to

35 Braccini, *Bisanzio prima di Bisanzio*, 57–60.

36 See Lathoud, "La consécration et la dédicace de Constantinople (Suite [1])," 188–90; Dagron, *Naissance d'une capitale*, 40–41.

Malalas and his first readers in Antioch, but it is also most probably derived from an Antiochene source, as Bouttios seems to have been.[37] The focal point of the procession, and of the description, is an image of Constantine holding the tyche of the city in his right hand. The tyche he holds is said to be named Anthousa, as in the account of the inauguration of Constantinople's tyche, which we have already assigned to Bouttios. The association of rulers and the tychai of the cities they established also seems to have been one of the central concerns of Bouttios all along. Bouttios appears, moreover, to regularly discuss customs and monuments that can be seen "up to the present day," just as it is said that it is possible to watch this procession "up to the present day."[38] There are enough connections between the description of the anniversary celebrations and the account of the establishment of Constantinople's tyche that the whole of the description of the procession should be attributed to the same author, namely Bouttios. And this attribution is confirmed by the further affinities this description exhibits with his other fragments, as we have noted.

It may be unsettling to find a Christian polemicist, as we shall argue Bouttios was, describing a ceremony in which the reigning emperor was obliged to do obeisance to an image of the civic tyche of Constantinople, an act that could easily be construed as idol worship.[39] We should note, though, that while the text says that the emperor is to perform an act of obeisance when he sees the memorial statue of Constantine holding the tyche in his right hand, it does not specify the object of this obeisance. The gesture of reverence may have been directed

37 On Bouttios's identification as a native of Antioch, see below, pp. 145–52.

38 The Persians preserve the ashes of Zoroaster: **F 1.4**. The Assyrians call Thouras Baal: **F 1.5**. The stelae dedicated to Picus-Zeus by the Italian kings remain: **F 3**. The arms of Heracles are shut up in the temple of Picus-Zeus in the Forum Boarium: **F 5**. The Tyrians memorialize the attack of Tauros: **F 6**. The monument of Perseus stands at Amandra/Persis: **F 7.3**. The inscription can be read at Nyssa/Scythopolis: **F 8.4**. Diskoi in Bithynia is called Chrysopolis: **F 16.1**. The cities founded by Alexander are still inhabited: **F 20.3**. The memorials to the women martyred by Trajan stand at the baths of Antioch: **F 32**. The anniversary of the founding of Constantinople is observed: **F 35**.

39 The apparent mixture and juxtaposition of pagan and Christian elements in various accounts of the founding of Constantinople and its commemoration has long troubled modern scholars and prompted, for instance, the explanation of essential Christian triumphalism presented by Lathoud, "La consécration et la dédicace de Constantinople (Suite [1])," 197–201.

toward the tyche, but it is more likely to have been an act of veneration toward the image of Constantine as the late emperor and as the founder of the imperial city. Certainly, if Constantine was depicted holding the tyche in his hand, his own image must have been preponderant and the tyche may have been interpreted as nothing more than a personified emblem of the city he had established. The ceremony would then have been consistent with Eusebius of Caesarea's laudatory assertion that Constantine, unique among mortal rulers, continued to reign and receive the homage of his subjects even after death.[40]

But Bouttios may not have been in a position to dictate the terms of the ceremony accompanying Constantinople's anniversary celebrations. The circumstantial details of the dress uniforms of the military honor guard, the candles, and the precise dispositions of the celebrants in the hippodrome all indicate that this is the description of an actual ceremony. The *Parastaseis Syntomoi Chronikai* seems to corroborate that this ceremony, or one very much like it, was performed up to the time of Theodosius the Great (r. 379–395).[41] Its cessation in the reign of Theodosius, when a number of overtly pagan customs and practices were brought to an end, suggests that some pagan element may also have been perceived in the birthday pageant of Constantinople.[42] It may have been precisely this noxious aspect that led Bouttios to concentrate on the tyche figure and city foundations in his history. The form of the anniversary ceremony appears to have been a fait accompli, and Bouttios did not bother to criticize it or demand its alteration. Instead, he conceded that there was a profoundly important association between

40 Euseb., *VC* 4.67.3.

41 *Parastaseis Syntomoi Chronikai* 5, 56, cf. 38; cf. *Patria Constantinopolis* 2.29, 49, 87 (Berger, *Accounts of Medieval Constantinople*, 68–71, 84–85, 108–11). The accounts in the *Parastaseis* of the anniversary celebrations of Constantinople and the images involved are confused and it is difficult to disentangle the sources used, comprehend how the details of the ceremony were understood and intended to be conveyed, and identify the period—if any—for which they accurately reflect actual events; see Av. Cameron and Herrin, *Constantinople in the Early Eighth Century*, 60–61, 100–103, 130–33, 171–74, 215–18, 242–45. Nevertheless, the note that the city's birthday pageant was celebrated up to the time of Theodosius must have originated somewhere, and it is most likely in the context of an account of these celebrations that at least implicitly acknowledged their pagan aspects and recognized their suppression as the work of Theodosius.

42 Cf. Lathoud, "La consécration et la dédicace de Constantinople (Suite [I])," 191–95, 197–201.

emperors and their city foundations or refurbishments, as well as the tyche figures that served as their emblems. But rather than allowing that this might be a point of contact and potential reconciliation between paganism and—especially a state-sponsored—Christianity, he demonstrated a contrast, a diametrical opposition in this very regard. Constantinople had a tyche, perhaps even something of a tyche cult, but Constantine had established this tyche by means of a "bloodless sacrifice," whereas the pagan emperors who preceded him founded cities and brought their tychai into being through sinister acts of human sacrifice.

4

THE PICUS-ZEUS NARRATIVE

Thus far our survey of the fragments of Bouttios ought to have conveyed at least two general points. First, the *Excerpta Latina Barbari* and John Malalas often present parallel treatments of the same material, which can be associated with Bouttios, or—put another way—offer complementary fragments of Bouttios's work. Second, whether traducing the memory of a traditional hero like Perseus, finding the origin of numerous local cults in a grisly rite of human sacrifice, or deploring the persecution of Christians, the great majority of the fragments of Bouttios betray a marked, if implicit, antipagan intention. These two factors suggest that the idiosyncratic accounts of the pagan gods as ancient human kings, which center on the career of "Picus, who is also Zeus," the earliest versions of which are found in the *Excerpta* and Malalas, belong among the fragments of Bouttios (**FF 1, 2**).[1] A euhemeristic treatment of the gods is not inherently Christian or antipagan; indeed, euhemerism originated early in the Hellenistic era with the apparent purpose of preserving reverence for the gods from the scandal of myth, but by the fourth century it had long since been adopted into the arsenal of Christian apologists' arguments to show that the gods were no gods at all.[2] Certainly, a euhemeristic narrative like the one found in Malalas and the *Excerpta*, which depicts the gods not only as mortals but also as wicked and

1 See Garstad, "Euhemerus and the *Chronicle* of John Malalas."

2 Baumgarten, "Euhemerus' Eternal Gods"; Winiarczyk, Sacred History *of Euhemerus*.

despicable men, bears the hallmarks of Christian polemic rather than the dry and academic hermeneutics of myth.

The passages of protracted narrative in the *Excerpta* are few and far between and in each instance have fairly obviously been grafted from some other source onto the spare chronological frame that forms the spine of the *Excerpta*. The source can usually be identified. In many cases it is the Bible, in a few others the apocryphal *Protevangelium Jacobi* or *Infancy Gospel of James.*[3] The *Excerpta*'s account of Alexander clearly goes back to a source that the compiler of the *Excerpta* shares with Malalas. For the most part this source is more fully and accurately represented in Malalas, not least because in his text it remains in Greek, but some—at times critically important—parts of this source do not appear in Malalas and are preserved only in the *Excerpta*. For instance, the initial subjection of the Romans to the eastern peoples, from which Alexander frees them in both Malalas and the *Excerpta*, is found only in the *Excerpta*.

Much the same is true of the euhemeristic account of the gods. Neither the version in the *Excerpta* nor that in Malalas is the original from which the other was taken. Rather they both depend on a common, lost source. On one hand, the version in Malalas is more complete, sequentially tracing the line of god-kings from their origins, through their various travels, down to their extinction, whereas the *Excerpta*'s version is truncated to merely elaborate on the beginnings of an Italian king-list, and largely eschews any information that has nothing to do with Italy.[4] On the other hand, the *Excerpta* occasionally shows itself to be closer to the original, as when its list of the names of Picus's wife in Assyria, *vocauerunt alii autem Iram Zygiam, et alii Nemesim multiformem*[5] (others called her Hera Zygia, and others Nemesis of many forms), makes sense of a garbled statement on the same matter in Malalas: Ἥραν ὀνόματι, ἣν καὶ ζυγίαν νέμεσιν ἐκάλουν τινὲς[6] (Hera by name, whom some called Zygia Nemesis [matrimonial wrath?]).[7] In this case, as in that of the Alexander material, the *Excerpta* and Malalas share a common source, which is now lost.

3 Old Testament: *ELB* 1.1.2–3, 4.3, 5.1–2, 3; Gospels: *ELB* 2.8.2–9.3; *Protevangelium Jacobi*: *ELB* 2.8.4–9.1. See Garstad, "Barbarian Interest," 26 and n. 77.

4 Garstad, "Excerpta Latina Barbari," 280–84.

5 *ELB* 1.6.1; **F 2.1**.

6 Malalas 1.8; **F 1.1**.

7 See E. Jeffreys, "Malalas' Sources," 202; E. Jeffreys, "John Malalas: A Commentary," 68.

The *Excerpta* was patently compiled from only a small number of sources, and it is easier to believe that its compiler shared one source, rather than two, with Malalas. This becomes decidedly more credible when we consider how the account of the gods and the account of Alexander are essentially concerned with the same things: ancient history and figures prominent in the last resistance of paganism to Christianity. And doubly so when we note that, as we shall demonstrate shortly, the euhemeristic narrative and the story of Alexander themselves have at least one source in common. An account of the gods, moreover, which depicts them as human beings, and rather bad ones at that, has an obvious utility in the antipagan argument in which Bouttios appears to have been engaged. So Bouttios is an eminently plausible candidate for the authorship of the euhemeristic account of the gods found in the *Excerpta* and Malalas, but he is not the only author who has been proposed.

Previous Ascriptions

Previous attempts to identify the author and the date of the original of the distinctive account of the gods in the *Excerpta* and Malalas prove untenable. They tend to rely on late citations, dubious conjectures, the presumption of oddly confused names, and the absence of evidence to refute them. The first such attempt was made by Heinrich Gelzer, and while his proposals do not stand up to examination, they have enjoyed general acceptance for quite some time. Gelzer contended that the "Picus-Zeus narrative" had been in circulation for some time before its first inclusion in texts that have survived, that it could be traced back to the lost *De regibus* of the Roman historian Suetonius (ca. 70–130 CE), that other accounts of early Italian history in late antique chronicles are abbreviated excerpts from this narrative, and that Suetonius's account had entered the Christian chronicle tradition through the work of Sextus Julius Africanus.[8] There are three main points to his argument, and none of them can bear the weight of scrutiny.

First, Gelzer seems to connect the Picus-Zeus narrative to Suetonius because, he insists, the list of kings begins with Picus.[9] This, however, is simply not the case. In both the *Excerpta* and Malalas, Cronos is the first king to rule overall, but also

8 Gelzer, *Sextus Julius Africanus*, 1:239–46.

9 Gelzer, *Sextus Julius Africanus*, 1:243.

specifically first in Assyria and then in Italy. There is, moreover, no reason to associate the appearance of Picus at the head of a king-list with Suetonius. As a matter of fact, we know practically nothing about the *De regibus* apart from what we are told in a few lines of Ausonius (ca. 310–ca. 395) to Paulinus (353/4–431), complimenting him on his verse paraphrase of the history, namely that it mentioned the history of Europe, Asia, and Africa (though it may not have dealt with it in such broad strokes at any length), as well as the names of certain obscure kings:

> His longe iucundissimum poema subdideras, quod de tribus Suetonii libris, quos ille de regibus dedit, in epitomem coegisti tanta eloquentia, solus ut mihi videare assecutus, quod contra rerum naturam est, brevitas ut obscura non esset. In his versibus ego ista collegi:
>
> Europamque Asiamque, duo vel maxima terrae
> membra, quibus Libyam dubie Sallustius addit
> Europae adiunctam, possit cum tertia dici,
> regnatas multis, quos fama oblitterat et quos
> barbara Romanae non tradunt nomina linguae:[10]
> Illibanum Numidamque Avelim Parthumque Vononem
> et Caranum, Pellaea dedit qui nomina regum,
> quique magos docuit mysteria vana Nechepsos,
> et qui regnavit sine nomine, moxque Sesostris . . . [11]

10 Green's punctuation at the end of this line (. . .) seems to suggest that Ausonius has quoted two distinct sets of lines, the first of which ends here, but the royal names that follow seem to be prime examples of the uncouth monikers that give such trouble to Latin speakers, and so I have given the lines as continuous whole.

11 As printed by Green, according to the C and M MSS: *et qui regnavit sine nomine mox Sesoostris*, this line gives the mystifying sense that Sesostris, or Sesoostris, easily the most famous of the kings listed here, ruled soon after Nechepso without a name or a reputation. The variant in the T MS, printed here, offers not only the more usual form of Sesostris's name but also the more acceptable meaning that there was some anonymous king who ruled after Nechepso in Egypt's remote past and then Sesostris came to the throne. Although this requires us to assume that Ausonius broke off his quotation in mid-sentence, the lines he quoted may have been adequate to his purpose of showing Paulinus's handling of awkward foreign names in Latin verse.

> Haec tu quam perite et concinne, quam modulate et dulciter, ita iuxta naturam Romanorum accentuum enuntiasti ut tamen veris et primigeniis vocibus sua fastigia non perirent! Iam quid de eloquentia dicam?[12]
>
> Under the cover of [your letter] you furnished me with an ever so delightful poem, which condensed the three books that Suetonius devoted to the kings into an epitome with such elegance that you alone might seem to me to have attained what is contrary to the nature of things: a concision that would not obscure. Among these verses I have picked out the following:
>
> Europe and Asia, the Earth's two very greatest
> Parts, to which Sallust dubiously added Libya
> Joined to Europe, since it can be called the third part,
> Have been ruled by many, whom Fame forgets and whose
> Barbarous names Roman tongues do not convey:
> Illibanus, Numidian Avelis, Parthian Vonones,
> And Caranus, who granted the Pellaean titles of kings,
> And he who taught the wizards their empty mysteries, Nechepsos,
> And he who ruled without a name, and soon Sesostris . . .
>
> These names you have enunciated so expertly and rhythmically, so melodiously and sweetly, thus according to the natural accent of the Romans, but with their true and original sounds, so that their pitches should not be lost. And now what shall I say of your eloquence?

The intimations of Ausonius are sufficiently vague and capacious so as not to exclude the story of "Picus, who is also Zeus" and his family, but they certainly do not even suggest any of the distinctive features, the combinations of gods or their travels, that would indicate the original of the account in Malalas and the *Excerpta*. Nevertheless, in spite of our essential ignorance of the contents of Suetonius's lost history, it has served brave or reckless scholars as a catchall for

12 Auson., *Ep.* 17, also given as 19 or 23 in other editions (Green, *Ausonii Opera*, 242); with the slight exceptions noted above, I have followed Green's text. See R. Green, *Works of Ausonius*, 215–16, 637–41.

any unattributed work on early Italy,[13] and Gelzer does not appear to have been immune to this tendency.

Second, Gelzer substantiates his case for the early composition and subsequent wide distribution of the Picus-Zeus narrative by demonstrating its parallels in texts dating from the earliest part of the fourth century, most significantly the so-called *Calendar of 354* and a passage in George the Syncellus's late eighth- or early ninth-century *Chronographia*, which is clearly derived from Eusebius's *Chronicle*. Gelzer explains what he considers the omissions and deviations evident in these versions as a result of their having been excerpted from a text more fully preserved in the *Excerpta* and Malalas.[14] These texts are, however, susceptible to quite a different interpretation.

While it is true that the history of earliest Italy in the *Calendar of 354* shares the succession of Picus–Faunus–Latinus, it exhibits none of the characteristic features of the Picus-Zeus narrative, such as the Assyrian origin of the god-kings or the identification of Picus and Zeus.[15] It shows instead every sign of being another version of the standard account of Italian history up to the arrival of Aeneas, which had been articulated in poetry and prose since at least the time of Virgil.[16] Rather than being a truncated excerpt from the Picus-Zeus narrative, the passage in the *Calendar of 354* would seem to indicate one of this narrative's sources. Behind both the account of early Italy in the Calendar and the account of the gods in the *Excerpta* and Malalas must stand a summary history of ancient Italy which included the succession of Saturnus–Picus–Faunus–(Hercules)–Latinus, but numerous sources for such a history were available.

The passage in George the Syncellus adduced by Gelzer, too, is a version of the standard history of early Italy, rather than an excerpt from the Picus-Zeus narrative. It does include the identification of Picus with Zeus and Faunus with Hermes and the reign of Heracles in Italy,[17] but comparison with the Armenian

13 Perhaps most recently for Schmidt, "Zu den Quellen der römischen Mythistorie," 102–4.

14 Gelzer, *Sextus Julius Africanus*, 1:243.

15 MGH AuctAnt 9.143.

16 Virgil, *Aen.* 7.45–49; Ovid, *Met.* 14.320, 449; Just., *Epit.* 43.1.3–10; Serv., *Aen.* 10.76; cf. Arn., *Adv. nat.* 2.71; Lactant., *Div. inst.* 1.22.9; Jer., *Chron. ab Abr.* 840. See Rosivach, "Latinus' Genealogy," 140, n. 3; Moorton, "Genealogy of Latinus," 253–59.

17 Georg. Sync., *Chron.* 322–23.

translation of Eusebius's *Chronicle*, which does not have these items,[18] shows that they are additions to the source shared by Syncellus and the Armenian translation, that is, an early version of the *Chronicle* of Eusebius.[19] These additions could have been made by Syncellus or an intermediary on the basis of the Picus-Zeus narrative, which enjoyed a certain currency in the Byzantine chronicle tradition by his time. There is no textual evidence, at any rate, for the circulation of the Picus-Zeus narrative before the *Excerpta* and John Malalas.

Third, Gelzer was not the first to attribute the Picus-Zeus narrative to Julius Africanus, Martin Routh having included a version in his 1846 edition of the fragments of Africanus, nor the last, as a version has been accepted in recent attempts to identify the fragments of Africanus.[20] But the grounds for this attribution are a set of late citations of dubious value. The earliest of these occurs in the chronicle of Symeon the Logothete, which covers the period up to 948 in its first (more widely distributed) edition and was probably written in the latter half of the tenth century.[21] This chronicle is represented by a family of more than thirty manuscripts marked by variations of greater and lesser significance.[22] Of these manuscripts, one (Vaticanus Graecus 163), ascribed to Leo Grammaticus, contains a marginal note at the outset of its version of the Picus-Zeus narrative which reads: ὥς φησιν Ἀφρικανὸς ὁ σοφώτατος (as the exceeding wise Africanus says).[23] Staffan Wahlgren's 2006 edition of the chronicle of Symeon the Logothete does not include this note in the main text, but consigns it to the apparatus criticus and considers the attribution to Africanus only a possibility.[24] The related, but slightly later—it runs to 963—chronicle of the so-called pseudo-Symeon, represented by a single manuscript (Parisinus Graecus 1712), gives as a heading for its version of the Picus-Zeus narrative a single word: Ἀφρικανοῦ (from Africanus).[25]

18 Euseb., *Arm. Chron.* (Karst, *Die Chronik aus dem Armenischen übersetzt*, 136).

19 See Garstad, "Excerpta Latina Barbari," 281–82.

20 Routh, "Julius Africanus," 2:263–6 (F 12), 408–11; Roberto, "Julius Africanus und die Tradition," 10–11; Wallraff, "Die neue Fragmentensammlung," 56–58.

21 Treadgold, *Middle Byzantine Historians*, 203–17.

22 Wallraff, *Iulius Africanus, Chronographiae*, xliv–xlvi.

23 Wallraff, *Iulius Africanus, Chronographiae*, F 24a, 53, n. 1.

24 Sym. Logoth., *Chron.* 28 (Wahlgren, *Symeonis Magistri et Logothetae Chronicon*, 32).

25 Wallraff, *Iulius Africanus, Chronographiae*, xlvi–xlvii, F 24b, 53, n. 1. On ps.-Symeon, see Treadgold, *Middle Byzantine Historians*, 217–24.

George Cedrenus, whose chronicle continues up to 1057, borrowed his version of the Picus-Zeus narrative from ps.-Symeon, but added a citation of Africanus, ὡς Ἀφρικανός φησι (as Africanus says), to the statement that Cronos had a son named Aphros specifically.[26]

So, it is not until the tenth century that the name of Africanus is associated with the Picus-Zeus narrative, and then only in a unique bit of marginalia and a one-word chapter heading derived from that marginalium, both places where we might expect scribes to intrude their editorializing rather than to preserve source material. And it is not until the eleventh century that we find a citation of Africanus integrated into the text of the passage, but that citation is demonstrably derived from those remote ones of only a century earlier and suspiciously occurs in regard to a character, Aphros/Afrus, whose name is attractively close to that of Africanus himself. If these late citations of Africanus are to be taken as indicating the original author of the Picus-Zeus narrative, we must presume that every reference to Africanus in every surviving version from the preceding four hundred years has somehow fallen out of a number of different textual traditions. It would be dangerous to put too much weight at all on these citations, and in the judgment of Jeffreys the narrative "seems unlikely, in fact, to be connected with Africanus."[27]

Two further objections can be raised to the attribution of the Picus-Zeus narrative to Africanus. If Africanus really did compose the story of "Picus, who is also Zeus," it is perplexing that it was so assiduously neglected by Eusebius, when he openly depended on Africanus in so much else and this story is so admirably suited to his purpose of refuting the pagan tradition as a viable system of religion.[28] And if, at least in the work to which the Picus-Zeus narrative is usually attributed, the chief concern of Africanus was chronology, that is, the assignment of absolute dates to events, as his reputation suggests, it is perhaps more puzzling that wherever the Picus-Zeus narrative appears in the Byzantine chronicle tradition it is given an inconsistent chronological placement from one work

26 George Cedrenus, *Comp. Hist.* 19.2 (Tartaglia, *Georgii Cedreni Historiarum Compendium*, 1:95). Wallraff, *Iulius Africanus, Chronographiae*, xlvi–xlvii, F 24b, 53 n. 1.

27 E. Jeffreys, "John Malalas: A Commentary," 67.

28 On Eusebius's debt to Africanus, particularly in regard to the apologetic purpose of chronography, see Barnes, *Constantine and Eusebius*, 114, 115, 117–19, 129; Kofsky, *Eusebius of Caesarea*, 38, 231, 233.

to the next,[29] as if no definite position in time adhered to the narrative as it was first composed and it had none of the chronological underpinning that would have been a priority for Africanus. There is every possibility that, just as Wallraff defended his inclusion of the Picus-Zeus narrative as a fragment of Africanus by suggesting that it also discusses matters that were evidently of interest to Africanus,[30] Byzantine scribes likewise supposed there were grounds for associating an unattributed narrative to as impressive an authority as Africanus. On the whole, the evidence gathered by Gelzer and his interpretation of it must be discarded if we are to assign a plausible author and date to the Picus-Zeus narrative.

It has been suggested that such an effort is misguided and that the character of "Picus, who is also Zeus" arose in the dim mists of remote antiquity. There was a theory, current in the late nineteenth and early twentieth centuries and popular among the Cambridge Ritualist school, which held that the references to Picus-Zeus represented a folk-belief retaining vestiges of a woodpecker (Latin *picus*) cult associated with the worship of Zeus on Crete.[31] The proponents of this theory were concerned not to explain the whole of the narrative associated with him in detail, but only to make sense of the admittedly odd composite figure of "Picus, who is also Zeus." Perhaps the most prominent among them, J. Rendel Harris, for instance, referred chiefly to the notice in the rather late (ca. 1000) Byzantine encyclopedia, the *Suda*, on the tomb of Zeus, which he does not seem to have understood to result from a literary tradition going back at least to the sixth century, and

29 This is demonstrated by the various biblical synchronisms of different works: *Excerpta Latina Barbari*, in the time of the Judges; Malalas, apparently before the time of Abraham; *Chronicon Paschale*, between the dispersion of the nations and Melchizedek; George Syncellus, in the time of the Judges; George Hamartolos (1.3–8), apparently shortly after Nimrod; Symeon the Logothete (28), apparently after the dispersion of the nations; George Cedrenus, after the death of Phalec (Peleg).

30 Wallraff, "Die neue Fragmentensammlung," 57. It is worth noting that most of the comparanda adduced by Wallraff are discussions of biblical material, not references to the pagan gods. It is by no means implausible that an author like Africanus might have taken an interest in the early history of human society as represented by the Bible and not have been much troubled over the same subject as discussed by the pagan tradition.

31 Cook, "Zeus, Jupiter and the Oak," 412; Harrison, *Themis*, 100–111; Harris, *Boanerges*, 15, 35, 44, 210; Bailey, *P. Ovidi Nasonis Fastorum*, 46; Cook, *Zeus*, 2.1:697. In Harris, *Picus Who Is Also Zeus*, despite the title, a case for the hypothetical cult of Zeus in the guise of a woodpecker is not argued, but the existence of this cult is rather the underlying and rarely stated assumption of the work.

by his own admission Harris had no comprehension of the tradition of a narrative concerned with Picus-Zeus.[32] In spite of the best efforts of Alexander Krappe to bolster it with a bravura display of erudition in comparative mythology, this theory was succinctly and effectively refuted by W. R. Halliday in 1922.[33] He demonstrated that the woodpecker cult itself was a doubtful hypothesis, and one for which the Picus-Zeus narrative and its principals cannot be called into evidence. "Picus, who is also Zeus," said Halliday, striking to the heart of the matter, "is the puppet of the chronographer, not an object of cult nor a factor in religious development."[34] He further identified the bare facts and the fundamental logic that had produced the identification of Picus and Zeus: "If Saturnus is another name for Cronos, it follows that Picus is another name for Zeus."[35]

His astute dismissal of the woodpecker cult hypothesis notwithstanding, the ideas Halliday conveyed concerning the date of the origin and circulation of the Picus-Zeus narrative are not as well considered and prove rather misleading. "Picus, who is also Zeus," he says, "is first mentioned in a fragment of Diodorus."[36] But it is almost certainly the case that Diodorus never mentioned Picus-Zeus or any of the other figures who appear in narratives associated with him. The appearance of "Picus, who is also Zeus" in a fragment of Diodorus is due to the introduction into the Picus-Zeus narrative, perhaps by Malalas, of a note on Zeus's Cretan tomb with a citation of Diodorus, and the association with the note of a portion of the story of Picus-Zeus by the modern editors who have collected the fragments of Diodorus.[37] The inconsistency of Picus-Zeus's burial on Crete with the rest of the narrative, which makes him an Assyrian king who travels to Italy but never visits Greece or the coastlands of the Aegean, as well as its absence from the other early version of the narrative in the *Excerpta*, marks the note on the Cretan tomb, along with the citation of Diodorus, as an intrusion

32 Harris, *Boanerges*, 15, 210, 268. Wiseman, *Remus*, 28–30, gives some indication of the authority Harris could bring in support of his pet theories.

33 Halliday, "Picus-Who-Is-Also-Zeus"; Krappe, "Picus Who Is Also Zeus."

34 Halliday, "Picus-Who-Is-Also-Zeus," 111.

35 Halliday, "Picus-Who-Is-Also-Zeus," 112.

36 Halliday, "Picus-Who-Is-Also-Zeus," 112.

37 Dindorf and Müller, *Diodori Siculi Bibliothecae*, 1:308–11; Vogel, *Diodori Bibliotheca*, 2:v–x, xliii, 121–28 (FF 2, 5); Oldfather, *Diodorus Siculus*, 3:330–45; Cohen-Skalli, *Diodore de Sicile, Fragments, livres VI–X*, 26–34 (FF 1 bis, 4, 6).

into the Picus-Zeus narrative.[38] The report of Zeus's burial on Crete and its attribution to Diodorus could, moreover, be found prepackaged, so to speak, and ready for importation in the *Praeparatio Evangelica* of Eusebius.[39] All in all, it seems that a compiler has made an effort to artificially knit together two euhemeristic accounts of Zeus, not that we are being offered the name of the authentic source of the Picus-Zeus narrative. Halliday performed a considerable service in drawing "Picus, who is also Zeus" and his history back from the nebulous epochs of prehistory, but his assignment of Picus-Zeus to Diodorus produced a date, the first century BCE, that was still too early.

In his exhaustive study of Zeus, A. B. Cook devoted a four-page footnote to the story of "Picus, who is also Zeus" and strove to discover the source of what was to him a strange Byzantine anomaly.[40] Taking such citations as he found more or less at face value, he made his attributions from Africanus, through Diodorus, to C. Sempronius Tuditanus, the Roman annalist who has been identified (not necessarily correctly) with the consul of 129 BCE.[41] But Cook's determinations are of little value. He took the methodologically suspect step of beginning with one of the latest and perhaps most confused versions of the Picus-Zeus narrative, that of Cedrenus, working back through the Byzantine chronicle tradition identifying his sources, and his analysis is cursory and superficial and his conjectures often desperate. We have already dealt with the attributions to Africanus and Diodorus. The ascription to Sempronius is far less probable and altogether without foundation.

Cook noted that in the *Chronicon Paschale* the account of Perseus slaying Sardanapalus and conquering Assyria ends with the statement ἅτινα συνεγράψατο Σεμηρώνιος ὁ Βαβυλώνιος Πέρσης[42] (Semeronios the Babylonian Persian wrote these things). He considered this "Semeronios" to be a garbled form of Sempronius and identified the authority cited in the *Chronicon Paschale* with the Roman author because of his attested interest in the early history of Italy. The few scant fragments we have of Sempronius, however, suggest that he concerned himself for the most part with the period after Romulus, not before Aeneas, and

38 Garstad, "Excerpta Latina Barbari," 301–2; cf. E. Jeffreys, "Malalas' Sources," 177.

39 Euseb., *Praep. evang.* 2.2.48, cf. 35, 52, excerpting Diod. Sic. 3.61.2.

40 Cook, *Zeus*, 2.1:693–97.

41 Cook, *Zeus*, 2.1:696.

42 *Chron. Pasch.* (Dindorf, *Chronicon Paschale*, 1:68). See *FGrHist* 686.

where he delved further back he favored a Greek origin for the early Italians, apparently making no mention of Assyria.[43] If, moreover, Sempronius really had published the original of the remarkably idiosyncratic history of "Picus, who is also Zeus" in the heyday of Republican Rome, we should reasonably expect to find some comment on this outlandish account in one of his many prominent and much better preserved readers.[44]

Perhaps Cook cannot be censured too harshly for allowing his imagination to conjure with the name of Semeronios; he was not the only reputable scholar to do so. Jacob Freudenthal suggested that Semeronios was the confused form of a Samaritan name and wanted to assign the narrative for which he is given as an authority to a Samaritan author, but this is a result of his tendency, more enthusiastic than credible, to see euhemerism as one of the hallmarks of ancient Samaritan historiography.[45] Gelzer numbered Semeronios among the fictitious authorities on ancient wisdom, but thought his name might actually be Assyrian, or intended to mean "the Sumerian."[46] Franz Cumont and Joseph Bidez followed suit and proposed that Semeronios was a corrupt reference to Sumerians,[47] but this is as unlikely as it is optimistic, considering the almost complete absence of Sumer from Greek literature.

The name of Semeronios has a much simpler explanation. The passage for which Semeronios is cited in the *Chronicon Paschale* follows, word for word, a parallel passage in Malalas. Even the citation is the same, except that Malalas names a Membronios instead of Semeronios: ἅτινα συνεγράψατο Μεμβρώνιος ὁ Βαβυλώνιος Πέρσαις.[48] Membronios is just as unique and elusive as Semeronios, being found nowhere else. We are left with a choice of determining which name is a corruption of the other. Semeronios, I would say, may be a conscious attempt to correct the extraordinary Membronios into something at least recognizably

43 Peter, *Historicorum Romanorum Reliquiae*, 1:ccx–ccxii, 142–46; C. Smith, "C. Sempronius Tuditanus," 1:240–42, 2:336–43, 3:222–24.

44 Dionysius of Halicarnassus (*Ant. Rom.* 1.11.13), Pliny the Elder (*HN* 13.84), Plutarch (*Flam.* 14), Aulus Gellius (*NA* 7.4.1), and Macrobius (*Sat.* 1.16.32).

45 Freudenthal, *Alexander Polyhistor*, 101.

46 Gelzer, *Sextus Julius Africanus*, 2:77.

47 Bidez and Cumont, *Les mages hellénisés*, 2:59.

48 Malalas 1.12 (Thurn, *Ioannis Malalae Chronographia*, 13). The phrases are equivalent except for the personal name, if Πέρσαις can be construed as an unusual equivalent of Πέρσης and not the likely more problematic "for Persians" or "in his *Persians*."

oriental, along the lines of the name of Semiramis, and is the less genuine form.[49] Jeffreys considers Membronios an invented source,[50] and considering the double insistence on a suitable ethnicity for him, both Babylonian and Persian, as an apparent guarantee of reliability, she is probably right. Even if Membronios is an authentic source, he may have been cited merely for the fact that the Persians were named after Perseus, hardly a rare or abstruse piece of information, as it is found in Herodotus,[51] rather than for the story of Perseus killing Sardanapalus or any of the other distinctive details of the narrative found in Malalas. Neither Membronios nor Semeronios has much to tell us about the origins and authorship of the Picus-Zeus narrative.

The most incisive and informative analysis of the account of the gods characterized by "Picus, who is also Zeus" and the relation of the two earliest texts in which it is found is offered by Elizabeth Jeffreys, but even this is not without its limitations. She identified "the *Excerpta Barbari* (or more probably, one of its sources)" as a text that contributes to the first book of Malalas's *Chronicle*.[52] In regard to this source, she speaks of the *Excerpta*'s incorporating "a document whose status is unknown, since it is one of the few elements in the *Excerpta* that cannot be assigned to an author or context, and which underlies the Picus Zeus narrative in Malalas."[53] The commendable agnosticism she displays here, however, is not consistently maintained, and elsewhere she repeats, without any justification, Gelzer's negligible proposal that the Picus-Zeus narrative "derives from an antiquarian history of Rome of the 1st cent. A.D."[54] Also, while conceding that a shared source lies behind the accounts in the *Excerpta* and Malalas, Jeffreys exaggerates the compositional role of Malalas, referring to the discrepancies between the version in the *Excerpta* and that in Malalas as distortions

49 Jacoby appears to have taken the opposite view, since he assigned an entry to Semeronios (*FGrHist* 686), but not to Membronios.

50 E. Jeffreys, "Malalas' Sources," 186–87; Jeffreys, "John Malalas: A Commentary," 71.

51 Hdt. 7.61.3, 150.2.

52 E. Jeffreys, "John Malalas: A Commentary," 57; cf. E. Jeffreys, "Malalas' Sources," 202. Jeffreys is not consistently so careful about insisting upon the distinction between the *Excerpta* and a source it shares with Malalas: see "Malalas' Sources," 198, and "Commentary," 66, and it must be borne in mind that she does not intend that the Greek original of the *Excerpta* was itself a source for Malalas.

53 E. Jeffreys, "Malalas' Sources," 198–99, cf. 177.

54 E. Jeffreys, "John Malalas: A Commentary," 67.

on his part.[55] She holds the comparison between the *Excerpta* and Malalas to be "instructive as it demonstrates the extent to which Malalas manipulates his material, both by distorting the contents and by making additions."[56] This is to assume that the compiler of the *Excerpta* made no modifications to his source material, whereas in fact there is every indication that the *Excerpta* version was trimmed to cover mostly Italian affairs and that Malalas preserves a fuller and more faithful version of the original.[57] When she is most careful, then, Jeffreys maintains that the *Excerpta* and Malalas have a common, unknown source for their accounts of the gods, but she occasionally slips into repeating the indefensible notions of her predecessors and speaking as if Malalas were writing on the basis of the *Excerpta* text as we have it.

The most recent conjecture regarding the authorship of the Picus-Zeus narrative, that of Pier Franco Beatrice, has many affinities with that of Jeffreys, but imputes the work of active composition to the author of the *Excerpta* rather than Malalas. Beatrice considers the Greek original of the *Excerpta Latina Barbari* to have been part of a larger whole, identifying it with the "abbreviated chronicle from Adam to Zeno" (χρονικὸν συντομώτατον . . . ἀπὸ Ἀδὰμ ἕως τῶν Ζήνωνος χρόνων) which ended the complete *Theosophy* according to the epitome of the so-called *Tübingen Theosophy.*[58] He proposes Severus of Antioch (ca. 465–538, bp. of Antioch 512–518) as the most likely author of the full *Theosophy*, as he reconstructs it.[59] He presents the author of the *Theosophy* as likewise the author of the account of the gods in the chronicle which he thinks ended it and, following a well-worn trail, says that in composing this account he was "most probably following Diodorus Siculus and Julius Africanus."[60] The practically insurmountable problems with attributing the Picus-Zeus narrative to Diodorus and Africanus have already been discussed, but the inclusion of the story of "Picus, who is also Zeus," along with the *Excerpta* as a whole, in Beatrice's reconstructed *Theosophy* also presents difficulties.

55 E. Jeffreys, "John Malalas: A Commentary," 66, 68–69.

56 E. Jeffreys, "John Malalas: A Commentary," 66.

57 Garstad, "Excerpta Latina Barbari," 280–84.

58 Beatrice, Anonymi Monophysitae Theosophia, xix, lvii–lviii, 3 (for the text of the *Tüb. Theos., epit.* 2).

59 Beatrice, Anonymi Monophysitae Theosophia, xlii–l.

60 Beatrice, Anonymi Monophysitae Theosophia, xxxi.

The aim of the *Theosophy*'s author, according to Beatrice, was to affirm the truth of pagan texts and sages, inasmuch as they testified to Christian truth, and "the continuity of the revelation of divine Wisdom" while still maintaining that the pagan gods are false.[61] The *Excerpta*, containing the Picus-Zeus narrative, which presents the gods as wicked charlatans but offers no overtly redeeming sentiments on pagan oracles or philosophers, hardly seems suitable to this purpose. No chronicle would, unless it explicitly asserted a rather insistent distinction between pagan gods and myth on the one hand and pagan philosophy and sages on the other, and no such distinction is made in the *Excerpta*. Beatrice's suggestion that the Picus-Zeus narrative was first written in the context of the *Excerpta*'s original composition, moreover, leaves unexplained the relation of the *Excerpta* version to the fuller version in Malalas, which has parts that would seem integral to the composition but are missing from the *Excerpta*. Beatrice's admirable attempts to reconstruct an important text are perhaps too ambitious in assigning the *Excerpta* to the lost *Theosophy*, and certainly do not advance our understanding of the authorship of the Picus-Zeus narrative.

The Date of the Picus-Zeus Narrative

If the previous proposals in regard to the authorship and date of the narrative of the gods in the *Excerpta Latina Barbari* and Malalas have proved fragile and unavailing, we may have to begin with a clean slate, but we are not left without recourse. The *Adversus nationes* of Arnobius of Sicca (perhaps written between 302 and 305, or possibly as early as 297 and revised as late as 326[62]) includes a passage that contains certain details remarkable for their similarity to some found in the Picus-Zeus narrative, namely the close association of Picus and Jupiter (Zeus) and the lifespan of 120 years for Picus.[63] This passage comes in the context of Arnobius's efforts to assign a date to Saturn, and so to the origins of pagan religion, and is presented, as is so much of the *Adversus nationes*, as a dispute between a pagan and a Christian.

61 Beatrice, Anonymi Monophysitae Theosophia, xx.

62 Simmons, *Arnobius of Sicca*, 93; Edwards, *Religions*, 33–35; Edwards, "Some Theories."

63 Garstad, "Excerpta Latina Barbari," 274–80.

> Quis Iovem cum fratribus genuit? Genialibus Opis adiunctus Saturnus, ut vos fertis, Caelo atque Hecata procreatus. Quis Picum Fauni patrem, atque avum Latini? Saturnus, ut vos idem vestris scriptis atque auctoribus traditis. Ergo si haec ita sunt, sequitur ut Picus et Iuppiter germanitatis sibi sociati sint iure, utpote uno ex sanguine, unoque ex semine procreati. Consentaneum est ita esse quod dicitur. Ab Iove, et Pico, quot sunt generis usque ad Latinum gradus? Trini, ut indicat series. Vultis Faunus, Latinus, et Picus, annis vixerint vicenis atque centenis? Ultra enim negatur posse hominis vita produci.[64]

> Who fathered Jupiter along with his brothers? Saturn, joined in nuptial relations with Ops, as you say, Saturn, born of Coelus and Hecate. Who fathered Picus, the father of Faunus, and grandfather of Latinus? Saturn, as you yourselves hand down in your writings and authors. Therefore, if these things are so, it follows that Picus and Jupiter are united to each other by the bond of brotherhood, inasmuch as they are born of one blood, and of one seed. It is agreed that what is said is the case. How many generations are there from Jupiter and Picus up to Latinus? Three, as the list shows. Are you willing to agree that Faunus, Latinus, and Picus each lived for one hundred and twenty years (for it is denied that the life of man can be extended beyond this)?

Earlier authors familiar with the Latin or Italian tradition[65] may have thought it obvious that Picus and Jupiter, as sons of Saturn, were brothers, but Arnobius would seem to be the first to have perceived some apologetic significance in this fact and insisted upon it in his argument. Arnobius offers 120 years as the maximum possible lifespan of man as a generous concession to his opponents and as a point of agreement between Christian and pagan traditions. Christians could derive this maximum lifespan from the pronouncement of God after the Flood in Genesis 6:3, and pagans would recognize it from the legend of Arganthonius, the

64 Arnobius, *Adv. nat.* 2.71 (Marchesi, *Arnobii adversus nationes*, 149–50).

65 See above, p. 84 and n. 16.

king of Tartessus, who was said to have lived for 120 years, as long, according to some, as any man could.[66]

In the *Excerpta* and Malalas, Cronos (the Roman Saturn) is also the father of a Picus and a Zeus (the Roman Jupiter), although they are the same person under two different names, not brothers. Malalas says that Picus-Zeus lived to be 120 years old, and while the *Excerpta* does not say how long Picus-Zeus lived, his reign of 80 years is not inconsistent with a lifespan of 120 years (**FF 1.6**, **2.1**). Arnobius does not say that Picus lived for 120 years, only that he could not have lived any longer. The intent and the disposition of numbers and associations are not identical in Arnobius and the Picus-Zeus narrative, but they are remarkably similar. If we do not posit some relation between Arnobius on the one hand and the original of the narrative in the *Excerpta* and Malalas on the other, we must reconcile ourselves to an unsettling coincidence occurring in two, or rather three, late antique texts.

The relation between the passages in question is one of Arnobius's exerting an influence on the Picus-Zeus narrative. Arnobius, for his part, assembles, for a specific argumentative purpose, a number of details from the cultural patrimony he held in common with his audience. While his argument shares these details, in some fashion, with the Picus-Zeus narrative, Arnobius reveals no knowledge of the idiosyncratic account of the gods that characterizes that narrative. Indeed, the point Augustine makes with reference to Leon of Pella, that not only such minor deities as Picus but even the principal ones like Jupiter were actually mortals, would indicate that the identification of Picus and Jupiter was not an implication from Arnobius worked out in the Latin West, and never enjoyed any currency there.[67] Rather, the author of the Picus-Zeus narrative would seem to have taken the points of Arnobius's argument and transformed them into historical details.

The problem with this suggestion is that while Arnobius wrote in Latin, the original Picus-Zeus narrative was written in Greek. At least the earliest evidence for it is found in Greek works, the Greek exemplar of the *Excerpta Latina*

66 See Hdt. 1.163; Anac., frag. 8 (= Strabo 3.2.14); Cic., *Sen.* 19.69; cf. Censorinus, *DN* 17.3–4; Pliny, *HN* 7.(48) 156; Tac., *Dial.* 17.3; SHA, *Claud.* 2.4 (cf. *Tac.* 15.2); Serv., *Aen.* 4.653.

67 August., *De civ. D.* 8.5.

Barbari and Malalas's *Chronicle*.[68] Literary exchange across languages was hardly unheard of in the fourth century, but usually emanated from the Greek East and proceeded to the Latin West. In this instance, however, we can point to a specific conduit by which the ideas of Arnobius might have arrived in Greek-speaking circles. Jerome tells us that Lactantius was a student of Arnobius,[69] presumably in Africa. Lactantius himself went on to teach Latin at Diocletian's eastern capital of Nicomedia. We find at least one of the particulars of Arnobius's discussion of Saturn repeated in the work of his student. Lactantius concurs with Arnobius that there was some agreement, among competent authorities, as he says, that it was usual for the age of 120 years to be reached (*et auctores idonei tradunt ad centum uiginti annos perueniri solere*).[70] Otherwise, though the specific details under discussion make no appearance in his own writings, Lactantius could have carried the ideas of Arnobius east with him—and in this case, ideas are precisely what we are talking about. Lactantius appears to have left Africa before Arnobius began work on the *Adversus nationes*, even before his teacher converted to Christianity.[71] Fixing a date for the gods of myth, however, might very well have been a topic of interest to a not altogether satisfied pagan, especially to one as sensitive to the scandal of myth as Arnobius shows himself to be in the *Adversus nationes*. The ideas of Arnobius, which were later to appear in his apologetic work and which seem to have been borrowed for the Picus-Zeus narrative, may have gestated in his classroom while Lactantius was still a student there. If we are dealing not with the reading of a text, but with ideas conveyed as hearsay in learned conversation and religious disputation, we should not be surprised to find the notions of Arnobius confused or imperfectly reproduced, as they are in the Picus-Zeus narrative.

If we can trace the influence of Arnobius on the Picus-Zeus narrative, we can also propose a terminus post quem for the original of that narrative. To have borrowed ideas from Arnobius, the author of the Picus-Zeus narrative must presumably have written after Lactantius's arrival at Nicomedia. We cannot say exactly when this was, but it would at any rate be sufficiently precise to say by the

68 See below, pp. 160–61.

69 Jer., *De vir. ill.* 80. See Simmons, *Arnobius of Sicca*, 48 and n. 9.

70 Lactant., *Div. inst.* 2.12.23 (Monat, *Lactance, Institutions divines, II*, 178).

71 Simmons, *Arnobius of Sicca*, 50–51.

beginning of the fourth century. Such a date would be corroborated by Jeffreys's suggestion that the abdication of senior emperors in favor of their juniors, a feature of Diocletian's tetrarchic system, may be an analogy for the succession of Cronos by Picus-Zeus.[72] So the Picus-Zeus narrative seems to have been written after the beginning of the fourth century. This is no pinpoint, but it is a refinement of the "any time before the sixth century" based on the dates of the earliest sources in which it is found, the *Excerpta* and Malalas; and while it helps us put paid to a number of earlier suggestions as to the authorship of the Picus-Zeus narrative, like Diodorus and Julius Africanus, it does not exclude Bouttios.

Ascription to Bouttios

If the possible influence of Arnobius allows us to suggest a terminal date for the Picus-Zeus narrative that does not exclude the authorship of Bouttios, it does not confirm that he was the author. The best indications of that remain the fact that a version of the Picus-Zeus narrative and a version of the account of Alexander ascribed to Bouttios were both among the relatively few narrative expansions included in the composition of the Greek original of the *Excerpta Latina Barbari*, and the harmony of this account of the gods with the overall antipagan intention perceptible in the rest of the fragments of Bouttios. Once the proposal has been made, however, it finds some confirmation in the similarity between certain details we find in both early versions of the Picus-Zeus narrative, on the one hand, and material that can be more securely ascribed to Bouttios on the other.

For instance, the account of Perseus in Malalas, which cites Bouttios and which we have largely assigned to Bouttios, opens by referring to the "aforementioned Picus who is also Zeus" and to two of his other sons, Hermes and Heracles, who both find a place in the Picus-Zeus narrative. This reference could result from Malalas's trying to knit together the various parts of his *Chronicle*, but the reference might also have been found in Malalas's source, and indicate that the story of Perseus was a continuation of the story of Picus-Zeus by the

72 E. Jeffreys, "John Malalas: A Commentary," 70.

same author.[73] The mention of not only Picus-Zeus, but also of two of his sons who appear in the Picus-Zeus narrative, makes the latter more likely.[74]

The citation of Euripides also connects the Picus-Zeus narrative to Bouttios. Euripides is cited as a source for the portion of the narrative on Heracles in the *Excerpta*; he is, in fact, the only authority cited in the *Excerpta*'s account of the gods. When Bouttios is cited for the story of Perseus in Malalas, his rationalizing account is explicitly contrasted with Euripides' "mythological" version, suggesting if not that Bouttios's history responded to Euripides point by point, that it was at least marked by some overt interplay with Euripides and we might expect references to Euripides throughout. This is to say nothing of the unmistakable verbal dependence on Euripides' *Iphigenia among the Taurians* found in Malalas's account of Orestes and Iphigenia (**F 8**), which culminates in one of those virgin sacrifices which we have learned to associate with Bouttios.

The narrative of the gods in the *Excerpta* and Malalas's account of Perseus also both include instances of the seduction or rape of a consecrated virgin in a temple. In the *Excerpta* it is Auge raped by Heracles, and in Malalas it is Andromeda raped by Perseus. Both of these cases are consistent with the criticism we find throughout both the Picus-Zeus narrative and the fragments of Bouttios of the pagan gods and heroes and pagan rulers for their lust, incontinence, and depredations against women.

The connections between the *Excerpta*'s version of the Picus-Zeus narrative and the fragments of Bouttios in Malalas, moreover, are in a way stronger indications of shared authorship, because they cannot be explained as due to Malalas's efforts to integrate his various sources. One final point from Malalas's version

73 Levick and Rich, "Bruttius," 3:629, acknowledge how much of our understanding of the identity of Bouttios and the nature of his work depends on which of these alternatives we choose, but cautiously do not make a decision themselves.

74 It is altogether unclear what relation Van Hoof and Van Neuffelen, *Fragmentary Latin Histories*, 254, perceive between the citation of Bouttios in Malalas's account of Perseus and the Picus-Zeus narrative: "As Malalas usually identifies Zeus with Picus, it is likely that he imported this identification in the citation from Bruttius." They do manage, however, to dismiss without argument the possibility that Bouttios was responsible for the Picus-Zeus narrative, both by overstating the case ("all mentions of Picus-Zeus go back to 'Bouttios'") and by implying that it rests on no more than the appearance together of a citation of Bouttios and a reference to "Picus, who is also Zeus" (or "Zeus Picus" as they perversely insist on translating Malalas's phrase) in their abbreviated fragment.

of the Picus-Zeus narrative and his account of Perseus is nevertheless telling. In both of these, Perseus slays Sardanapalus and takes over his kingdom (**F 1.5**, **7.4**). In one the event marks the end of the line of Assyrian kings, and in the other it is the climax of Perseus's military career and the origin of the name of Persians for the people of the East, but it is clearly the same event. The account of Perseus, moreover, notes that Sardanapalus was from his own family, while the Picus-Zeus narrative explains how this was so.

Links between the Picus-Zeus narrative and the fragments of Bouttios are not, however, found only in the account of Perseus, although they are understandably most frequent there, as these are two examples of the rationalization of myth. The ultimate source of much of Malalas's account of Alexander is obviously the *Alexander Romance*.[75] Everything from Alexander's route to extended narrative passages can be traced to the *Romance*, but the *Romance* is not a direct source for Malalas. An intermediary has done the work of selecting and arranging, as well as adjusting and augmenting material from the *Romance*. This can be shown from the fact that the same selections and adjustments can be found in the *Excerpta*'s discussion of Alexander. This intermediary would seem to be the only authority cited for Malalas's account of Alexander, namely Bouttios.

It is also demonstrable that the *Alexander Romance* was an important source for at least a portion of the euhemerizing narrative of the gods found in Malalas.[76] The line of god-kings in Egypt, which begins with Faunus-Hermes, the son of Picus-Zeus, ends with Thoulis, an Egyptian king who conquers the world and consults an oracle only to receive a deflating response (**F 1.10**). The account of Thoulis, in a number of ways, reflects and depends upon the presentation of Alexander in the *Romance*. From the outset, the *Romance* makes Alexander, as the son of Nectanebo, like Thoulis, an Egyptian king. Alexander's consultation of the oracle of Ammon at Siwa was famous and found in a number of historical sources, but whereas the historians reported the oracular responses

75 The dependence of the passage in Malalas on the *Romance* in general is evident in the ascription of Alexander's true paternity to Nectanebo (7.17: **F 12**, cf. **F 17**); the apparent course of events, which sets the foundation of Alexandria before Alexander meets the Persians in battle (8.1: **F 16.1**, cf. **F 18**); and the inclusion of the story of Alexander's encounter with Candace, the queen of Ethiopia (8.3: **F 16.3**). See *Al. Rom.* 1.3–7, 31–33, 34.9–35.1, 41; 3.18–23.

76 Garstad, "Account of Thoulis," 62–66.

Alexander received as overwhelmingly positive and encouraging, the *Romance* has Alexander visit several oracles, or receive oracular information from fantastic sources, almost all of which upbraid him for his reckless ambition or warn him of his impending mortality. These prophecies are remarkably consistent with the oracular consultation that is the centerpiece of the account of Thoulis. The denouement of the story of Thoulis, moreover, owes the *Romance* a debt for its very wording. Thoulis leaves the oracle to be immediately slain "by his own" (ὑπὸ τῶν ἰδίων). This enigmatic phrase becomes clearer with reference to the *Romance*, which has one of its fabulous oracles tell Alexander repeatedly that he will very soon be killed "by his companions," or rather literally "by his own" (ὑπὸ τῶν ἰδίων).[77] The *Romance* reports the plot to poison Alexander as an established fact and imputes to its ringleader Antipater a motive, namely concern over Alexander's growing arrogance (πρὸς ὑπερηφανίαν),[78] which elucidates another obscure aspect of Malalas's account of Thoulis: the ascription to him, without further elaboration, of the quality of arrogance (ἐν ὑπερηφανίᾳ). The structure, details, and very wording of the account of Thoulis depend on the *Alexander Romance*. Two different authors could have exploited the same prominent source, but given the other connections it seems reasonable to assume that we are dealing with two instances of the same author betraying his reliance on the *Alexander Romance*.

One further example from the account of the gods and the account of Alexander in Malalas reveals the exploitation of a common source, once again explicitly and unmistakably in one and implicitly and allusively in the other. In the list of Assyrian kings who followed the departure of Picus-Zeus there is a puzzling reference to "the prophetic voice of Daniel" by way of an explanation of the image and cult of Thouras-Ares, who is identified as Baal (**F 1.5**). The intention of this reference is not altogether clear, although it seems to identify the image the Assyrians raised to Ares with the golden image Nebuchadnezzar set up on the plain of Dura and ordered all of his subjects to worship, which was the occasion of the deliverance of Shadrach, Meshach, and Abednego from the fiery furnace.[79] It is obvious enough, nevertheless, that the text is meant to be better understood

77 *Al. Rom.* 3.17.34, 36; cf. 41.

78 *Al. Rom.* 3.31.2.

79 See Dan. 3.

on the basis of the book of Daniel. Likewise, the account of Alexander says that he "rushed forth like a leopard" (**F 16.1**). No interpretation is imposed on this phrase, but it is most likely to be an allusion to the book of Daniel, in which late antique hermeneutics regularly identified the third beast "like a leopard" of chapter 7 as the kingdom founded by Alexander.[80] Once again, a terse and elliptical text is supposed to make better sense with reference to the book of Daniel. And once again, it seems more reasonable to assume that the same author was making the same kind of use of the same authority than that two different authors were doing much the same thing independently.

The Extent of the Material from Bouttios

If enough circumstantial evidence has been assembled to justify dealing with the two early versions of the Picus-Zeus narrative as fragments of Bouttios, it remains to delineate the extent of those fragments. We have in the *Excerpta Latina Barbari* and Malalas two sources which provide more or less compatible narratives of the gods, although they differ somewhat in extent and content. Malalas provides much more material on the lives of the so-called gods, especially in Assyria and Egypt, while the *Excerpta* concentrates on the activity of the gods in Italy and the West and includes a treatment of Heracles and Latinus, which Malalas separates from the main narrative. The simplistic solution of identifying the material shared by the *Excerpta* and Malalas and putting this forward as the exclusive evidence of their shared source is tempting, but unnecessary.[81] We can, rather, discern why the compiler of the *Excerpta* and Malalas respectively

80 See Hippolytus, *Comm. in Dan.* 4.3 (ed. Bonwetsch, *Kommentar zu Daniel*, 200–202), cf. *De Christ. et Antichr.* 24; Aphrahat, *Demonstrations* 5.18; Jerome, *Comm. in Dan.* 2 (7:6) (Glorie, *Commentariorum in Danielem*, 841–42), cf. *Comm. in Hieremiam* 1.95.3 (5.6) (Reiter, *In Hieremiam prophetam*, 53–54); Theodoret, *Comm. in Dan.* (7:6) (Hill, *Commentary on Daniel*, 180–82); see Rowley, *Darius the Mede*, 184–85; Marsch, *Biblische Prophetie*, 72; Barnes, "Constantine and the Christians of Persia," 133. The identification was, moreover, considered appropriate because of the swiftness of Alexander's conquests, which might be alluded to by the adverb εὐθέως in Malalas.

81 I hesitate to suggest that Jeffreys opted for a simplistic solution, but the careless reader of E. Jeffreys, "John Malalas: A Commentary," 66–67, might very well be left with the impression that the material found in both the *Excerpta* and Malalas represents all we can recover of their common source.

selected and arranged the material from their common source as they did, and thereby arrive at a fuller picture of a more sensibly arranged narrative.

Apparently by the *Excerpta* compiler or translator's own admission there was more to his source on the god-kings than he included in his composition. The introduction to the story of Picus says, concerning Cronus in the West, *de quo multus est sermo et sine interpretatione sunt* (much is said concerning this, and it is not translated).[82] We should look, therefore, for abbreviation in the *Excerpta*, and we do not have to look far. The *Excerpta*'s version of the Picus-Zeus narrative begins by stating that Picus (note that he is not immediately identified with Zeus) ruled in the western regions, which his father Cronus had received in the division of the earth. There seems to be a clumsy attempt to excise any mention of the Assyrian origins of Cronus and Picus. Clumsy because it is quickly conceded that Picus had ruled in Assyria in his youth. But why was the abortive attempt made in the first place? The explanation lies in the situation of the narrative. The story of Picus and his family is placed immediately before a brief account of Aeneas, which follows on from the mention of Latinus, and is itself followed by a list of the Alban kings from Ascanius to Romulus.[83] In Jerome's translation of Eusebius's *Chronological Canons*, at the beginning of the new column listing Latin or Alban kings, there is a brief note indicating that before Aeneas Janus, Saturnus (Cronos in Greek), Picus, and Faunus ruled in Italy.[84] The *Excerpta* compiler's source for the Alban king-list or even the basic chronography he employed must have been prefaced with a short note similar to this one, or more likely to the slightly longer notice on Italy before Aeneas that is preserved in the Armenian translation of Eusebius's *Chronicle* and (with later additions) by George the Syncellus, which begins with Picus and mentions the arrival of Heracles.[85] The naming in this notice of at least three figures (Cronos, Picus, and Faunus) who also definitely appear in the Picus-Zeus narrative (along with Heracles and Latinus, who probably did as well) served as a peg from which to hang the longer, imported

82 **F 2.1**. The awkward shift from singular to plural is characteristic of the *Excerpta* translator's lack of facility.

83 *ELB* 1.6.3–5 (Garstad, *Apocalypse/Alexandrian World Chronicle*, 191–93).

84 Jerome, *Chron.*: *ann. Abr.* 839 (Fotheringham, *Evsebii Pamphili Chronici Canones*, 101).

85 Euseb., *Arm. Chron.* (Karst, *Die Chronik aus dem armenischen Übersetzt*, 136); Georg. Sync., *Chron.* 322–23 (Mosshammer, *Ecloga chronographica*, 200).

narrative. Latinus's relation to Aeneas determined its chronological placement. The version of the Picus-Zeus narrative in the *Excerpta*, then, is intended to elaborate a note on the earliest kings of Italy.[86]

This explains a number of the differences between the versions in the *Excerpta* and in Malalas. The effort to begin the Picus-Zeus narrative with Picus and Cronus in the West is an attempt to accommodate the terms of the notice to which it has been appended. This notice does not discuss the origins of Cronos or stray beyond Italy, so Cronos's career in Assyria, and most of Picus's as well, have been cut from the *Excerpta*'s version. But the account of Cronos in Assyria found in Malalas provides the whole narrative with a proper starting point. The *Excerpta* as good as acknowledges that this starting point was found in its source by admitting that Picus had earlier ruled in Assyria, but confuses matters by not describing Cronos's career there. Our fragment from Malalas, therefore, begins with the first mention of Cronos, and that from the *Excerpta* begins with the obvious introduction of an account of the gods, the "children of Zeus," added from elsewhere, although the *Excerpta* compiler, not Bouttios, is probably responsible for the reference to the division of the earth in which Cronos gained possession of the West.[87]

Faunus would also have been mentioned in the brief notice in the original chronography as one of the kings of Italy, and so the account of Faunus-Hermes is also included in the *Excerpta*. But this account takes Faunus-Hermes to Egypt, as the *Excerpta* testifies. So the presentation of the Picus-Zeus narrative as an elaboration on a list of the early Italian kings was extended beyond the confines of Italy, but no further than was necessary to conclude the story of one of those Italian kings. In the *Excerpta* there is no mention of Egypt after the death of Faunus-Hermes, nor any mention of further kings in Egypt. The material preserved by Malalas, however, maintains that Faunus-Hermes was succeeded on the throne of Egypt by Hephaistos and then his son Helios. The accounts of these two rulers are consistent with the rest of the Picus-Zeus narrative inasmuch as they tell the story of kings taken for gods, the details of whose careers subtly undermine the prestige of the pagan pantheon. The same is true of the account of Thoulis, who is king of Egypt after the intervening reigns of three kings who

86 Garstad, "Excerpta Latina Barbari," 280–84.
87 Garstad, "Excerpta Latina Barbari," 285–87.

are recognizable as Egyptian gods: Sosis (Sothis), Osiris, and Horus. But Thoulis's reign marks an end point, since he is assassinated, apparently without an heir, and the throne reverts to the "tribe of Ham." Mestraim, "of the race of Ham," the eponymous founder of Egypt in the Bible, was supposed to be ruling Egypt when Faunus-Hermes arrived, and the exile from Italy assumed the kingship on his death. The line of god-kings in Egypt is neatly defined as lasting from Faunus-Hermes up to Thoulis, and clearly depicted as a foreign interruption in the native rule of the country and the ethnography of the Bible. Malalas's Egyptian kings from Faunus-Hermes up to and including Thoulis, then, should be included in our fragments of Bouttios's account of the gods, despite the fact that only the first, Faunus-Hermes, also appears in the *Excerpta*.

It is, after all, not difficult to explain why the *Excerpta* compiler did not mention the Egyptian kings after Faunus-Hermes. They have no connection to Italy, and so no place in an account of the gods as an introduction to a list of the kings of Alba Longa. Certainly none of them would have been named in the brief notice on the Italian kings that the Picus-Zeus narrative seems intended to amplify in the *Excerpta*. The criticism of the "gods" in Egypt after Faunus-Hermes, moreover, may have been a bit too subtle for the *Excerpta* compiler's purposes. The tone of the *Excerpta* is rather more condemnatory than that of Malalas, and more explicit in its attempts to denigrate the gods. The notes on the reigns of Hephaistos and Helios as found in Malalas may be primarily intended to make sense of certain details of myth to a literate audience, but offer no overt vilification of the gods. As such, they may have struck the *Excerpta* compiler as altogether beside his purpose.

The Picus-Zeus narrative is manifestly concerned with different, but interconnected, successions of god-kings in various places: Assyria, Italy, and Egypt. The example of Egypt indicates a tendency to trace these lines of rulers through their entire course, with clearly marked beginnings and endings. Cronos is the forefather of all these lines, and he rules in Assyria and Italy. The descendants of Cronos rule in Assyria up until the overthrow of Sardanapalus by Perseus, although Perseus was also supposed to be descended from Cronos. The descriptions of the intervening reigns are all consistent as euhemerizing accounts of the gods under multiple names and attempts to integrate Greco-Roman mythology and the Greek accounts of the legendary history of Assyria in a novel fashion. The death of Sardanapalus marks not only the end of a dynasty but also the last

application of the name "Assyrians" to the people who are thenceforth known as "Persians," after Perseus, as well as the end of Malalas's discussion of Assyria in his first book. He seems to have set the source for this material aside for the time being, although the transition from this source to a standard Assyrian king-list is indicated later on in Malalas's note that the Assyrian king in the time of Abraham, Endelechos, was the first to reign after the demise of the heirs of Perseus and the return of the kingdom to the Assyrians.[88] So we may also include all of the Assyrian material up to Sardanapalus in our fragment of Bouttios.

The conclusion of the Picus-Zeus narrative's treatment of Italian matters is perhaps the most difficult end point to determine, but it is by no means impossible. The problem is that while Malalas and the *Excerpta* each present a discussion of Heracles after the reign of Faunus-Hermes in Italy, they give two substantially different accounts of this figure. In the first book of his *Chronicle*, Malalas interrupts his account of Faunus-Hermes, between his discovery of his brothers' plot and his departure for Egypt, with a description of Heracles as the first philosopher in the regions of the West and an elaborate allegorical interpretation of his club, his lionskin, and the Apples of the Hesperides.[89] This Heracles is not located

88 Malalas 3.6.

89 Malalas 1.14 (Thurn, *Ioannis Malalae Chronographia*, 14–15): τῇ γὰρ Θηβαίᾳ Ἀλκμήνῃ τῇ γυναικὶ Ἀμφιτρύωνος μετὰ ταύτης συνεμίγη, ἀφ' ἧς ἔσχεν ἄλλον υἱὸν ὀνόματι Ἡρακλέα τὸν Ἀλκμήνης, ὅστις ἐκλήθη τριέσπερος. οὗτος κατέδειξεν πρῶτος τὸ φιλοσοφεῖν ἐν τοῖς ἑσπερίοις μέρεσιν τουτέστιν ἐν τοῖς δυτικοῖς. τοῦτον ἀποθεώσαντες οἱ ἐκ τοῦ γένους αὐτοῦ μετὰ τὴν αὐτοῦ τελευτὴν ἐκάλεσαν ἐν τῷ οὐρανῷ ἀστέρα ἐπ' ὀνόματι αὐτοῦ τὸν ἀστέρα Χιτῶνα Ἡρακλέους, ὃν γράφουσιν δορὰν λέοντος φοροῦντα καὶ ῥόπαλον φέροντα τρία μῆλα κρατοῦντα, ἅπερ μῆλα τρία ἀφείλασθαι αὐτὸν ἐμυθολόγησαν τῷ ῥοπάλῳ φονεύσαντα τὸν δράκοντα, τοῦτ' ἔστιν νικήσαντα τὸν ποικίλον τῆς πονηρᾶς ἐπιθυμίας λογισμὸν διὰ τοῦ ῥοπάλου τῆς φιλοσοφίας, ἔχοντα περιβόλαιον τὸ γενναῖον φρόνημα ὡς δορὰν λέοντος, καὶ οὕτως αφειλάμενον τὰ τρία μῆλα, ὅπερ ἐστὶν τὰς τρεῖς ἀρετὰς τὸ μὴ ὀργίζεσθαι, τὸ μὴ φιλαργυρεῖν, τὸ μὴ φιληδονεῖν. διὰ γὰρ τοῦ ῥοπάλου τῆς καρτερικῆς ψυχῆς καὶ τῆς δορᾶς τῆς θρασυτάτου σώφρονος λογισμοῦ ἐνίκησεν τὸ<ν> γήινον τῆς φαύλης ἐπιθυμίας ἀγῶνα φιλοσοφήσας ἄχρι θανάτου, καθὼς Ἡρόδοτος ὁ σοφώτατος συνεγράψατο, ὅς καὶ ἄλλους Ἡρακλεῖς ἱστόρησεν γεγενῆσθαι ἑπτά (For he [Zeus] had relations with the Theban Alcmene, the wife of Amphitryon, and from her he had another son by the name of Heracles of Alcmene, who was called Three-Evenings. This man first offered instruction to philosophize in the dusk lands, that is, in the western regions. Those from his family deified him after his death and called a star in the heaven after his name, the star Shirt of Heracles, whom they depict wearing a lion's hide and carrying a club, winning three apples, which are the very three apples they say in

in Italy, nor, except inasmuch as they are both sons of Picus-Zeus, is he related to Faunus-Hermes. In the *Excerpta* the departure of Faunus-Hermes for Egypt is followed by an overall chronological computation from Adam to the beginning of the reign of Picus-Zeus, which was no doubt an intrusion on the part of the compiler, and then (**F 2.3**) the arrival of Heracles (*Heraclius*) from Spain, his reign in Italy, and finally the reign of his son, "Telephus, who is also called Latinus," in these same parts (*in ipsa provincia*). These two different versions of the life of Heracles are incompatible, and only one can represent the content of the original Picus-Zeus narrative. But it is not a simple choice between the two witnesses. Practically all of the elements included in the passage on Heracles and Telephus and proceeding directly from the Picus-Zeus narrative in the *Excerpta*, with a few discrepancies and variations, are found in Malalas's *Chronicle*; they are just not found in the first book, along with the Picus-Zeus narrative. They are separated from the relation of the Picus-Zeus narrative and included in Malalas's sixth and seventh books (**FF 3, 4, 5**). There Malalas speaks of another Heracles, born many generations later in the region of Thebes but a descendant of the earlier Heracles, the son of Picus-Zeus and Alcmene, as well as his son Telephus, and then his son Latinus.

Malalas's discussion of the "later" Heracles (**F 3**) may be separated from the Picus-Zeus narrative, but it shares a number of details with the notice on *Eraclius* that follows the *Excerpta*'s account of Faunus-Hermes (**F 2.3**), and his indication that this Heracles came from the family of Picus-Zeus suggests some relation to the account of the god-kings. But as with the alternate names of Hera, it is really the fact that the phrasing in one text can make sense of the distortions in the other that confirms that they share a common source. The inexplicable *in Latothibis* of the *Excerpta* becomes comprehensible with Malalas's ἐν Λατῷ τῆς Θηβαΐδος, and his τὴν Αὔγην τὴν Ἀλέου θυγατέρα points us toward the sense

myth that he stole after he slew the dragon with the club, that is, he conquered the ambivalent reckoning of wicked desire through the club of philosophy, having the noble mind for a covering like a lion's hide, and thus he carried off the three apples, which are the three virtues: refraining from wrath, refraining from covetousness, and refraining from the pursuit of pleasure. For by means of the club of a patient spirit and the hide of a confident, moderate reasoning he won out in the earthly contest of mean desire, seeking after wisdom until death, as the exceeding wise Herodotus has written, who recorded that there were also another seven Heracleses.).

of the *Excerpta*'s garbled *ex ipsa neocorum Aleu*. The location of the arms of Heracles in the Forum Boarium is the most obvious link between the *Excerpta*'s relation concerning Heracles and Malalas's report of the discovery of his arms by Romus (that is, Romulus) and Remus (**F 5**), but there are other affinities. Heracles is once again said to come from the family of Picus-Zeus and the founders of Rome set his arms in the shrine of Picus-Zeus, although immediately thereafter they built the Capitol as a great temple to Zeus, plain and simple.[90] The formulae of the foundation of a city where there had previously been a village with another name and noting that an artifact can be seen "up to the present" (ἕως ἄρτι) are also commonly found in the fragments of Bouttios.

If both the *Excerpta* and Malalas preserve material from the same source, but distribute it in different ways, the question becomes one of whether in that source, the Picus-Zeus narrative as it was first composed, the figure of Heracles was originally divided into several individuals and simply taken up that way by Malalas (or his immediate source, Domninos), but afterward combined by the compiler of the *Excerpta*, or the figure of Heracles was originally discussed as a single individual and carried over as such into the *Excerpta*, but later divided by Malalas (or Domninos). Consequently, the question is also one of whether the story of Heracles is integral to the Picus-Zeus narrative's account of early Italy—indeed, provides it with something of a conclusion—or has only tenuous links to the history of Picus-Zeus and Faunus-Hermes.

It is unlikely that the *Excerpta* compiler combined more than one Heracles to produce a single figure. In the first place, he had no need to. He had apparently allowed the placement of the Picus-Zeus narrative in his work to be determined by a single chronological link, that offered by the relation of (Telephus-) Latinus to Aeneas. There was therefore no necessity for him to accommodate one Heracles, the son of Picus-Zeus, who lived shortly after the Flood, and another whose grandson-in-law fought in the Trojan War. The Picus-Zeus narrative, or as much of it as the *Excerpta* compiler selected for inclusion, could stay together because it was appended to a notice on Aeneas and had to adhere only

90 Malalas 7.1b (Thurn, *Ioannis Malalae Chronographia*, 132): καὶ ναὸν μέγαν τῷ Διὶ κτίσαντες ἐκάλεσαν αὐτὸν Καπετώλιον ῥωμαϊστί, ὅ ἐστιν ἡ κεφαλὴ τῆς πόλεως (and establishing a great shrine to Zeus they called it the Capitol in the Roman tongue, which is the head of the city).

to the relation between Aeneas and Latinus, working back from there to find a place for the rest of Cronos's family without much relation to the chronology as a whole.

In the second place, there is a continuity from the account of Faunus-Hermes to that of Heracles and his son. The chronological computation from Adam, which comes after the account of Faunus-Hermes in the *Excerpta*, seems to mark a terminal point in the narrative, and so the cessation of the exploitation of a source, and to exclude the account of Heracles from what has come before. But really this chronological notice is no conclusion, since it refers not to the end of Faunus-Hermes's reign in Italy or in Egypt but to the beginning of Picus-Zeus's reign. Its placement is actually quite perplexing. Moreover, the relation of events up to this point leaves the kingship of Italy vacant. The arrival of Heracles, which is related after the computation, settles the affairs of Italy and continues the rule of Picus-Zeus's descendants in Italy—the text makes a point of noting that Heracles is the son of Zeus—until it is taken up by Aeneas.

Finally, the *Excerpta*'s passage on Heracles and Telephus-Latinus is remarkably compatible with the rest of the Picus-Zeus narrative, as well as the other fragments of Bouttios. It includes a traveling "divinity," a reference to Euripides, the rape of a consecrated virgin, a mythological figure with multiple names, and a reference to a monument that might still be seen. And the combination of the names and identities of Telephus and Latinus in the *Excerpta* is more consistent with the combination of such figures as Picus and Zeus and Faunus and Hermes in the Picus-Zeus narrative than their separation in the later books of Malalas (**F 4**). The presentation of a single figure under the name of Heracles is likewise more consistent with the Picus-Zeus narrative than is the multiplication of such figures.

By contrast, the Heracles who follows on the heels of Faunus-Hermes, or rather interrupts the account of his life, in Malalas's first book is decidedly out of keeping with the overall tone and method perceptible in the Picus-Zeus narrative's historicizing denunciation of the gods. Whereas the material that can reliably be assigned to the Picus-Zeus narrative employs allegory only once, and then to argue that Homer misconstrued in his poetic fashion as the adultery of Ares and Aphrodite an actual historical event in the reign of Helios, king of Egypt (**F 1.9**), the description of Heracles as the first to practice philosophy in the West offers a wholesale allegorical interpretation of his deeds and attributes

as philosophical attainments.[91] And no part of this description does anything to discredit Heracles in the same way that the Picus-Zeus narrative tends to emphasize the misconduct and immorality of the so-called gods. Quite the opposite: it takes the often furious, gluttonous, and libidinous Heracles of myth and presents him as the steadfast victor over the vices of wrath, greed, and sensuality through philosophical virtue. Malalas even attributes this description to a separate authority, Theophilus the chronicler.[92] It is most unlikely that the author of the Picus-Zeus narrative had anything to do with the creation of this Heracles who appears in the first book of Malalas's *Chronicle*.

There is reason to believe, then, that the author of the Picus-Zeus narrative was responsible for neither the depiction of Heracles in Malalas's first book nor the multiplication of figures under the name of Heracles found throughout his *Chronicle*. The *Excerpta* compiler, it follows, did not find more than one Heracles in his source and combine them. Rather, we are left to conclude that Malalas (or perhaps his intermediary, Domninos) found a single Heracles in this same source and divided this one into two figures. Malalas appears to have been more conscious than the *Excerpta* compiler of a broader chronological structure to his work, and wanted to set the so-called gods in a much earlier period than the chronological connection afforded by Latinus and Aeneas would allow. In fact, he set the activity of Cronos and Zeus and their progeny in the time immediately after Noah's Flood, whereas the *Excerpta* sets them much later, in the time of the Judges. This variation in chronological placement was possible because the Picus-Zeus narrative itself had no underlying chronological structure. It was not originally composed as part of a universal chronicle and it offered no fixed points of reference to the chronological frame of such a work. It could therefore be included in a chronicle, in terms of time, at the discretion of the chronicler, as we see in the *Excerpta* and Malalas, but this adaptability had its limits.

The integral Picus-Zeus narrative would appear to have separated Cronos, the first of the line, from Telephus-Latinus by only four generations. (The various relations of the family of Picus-Zeus are laid out in figure 3.) Malalas must have been aware that his chronological placement right after the Flood made Cronos

91 On the rarity of allegory in the fragments of Bouttios, see below, pp. 147–49.

92 Malalas 1.14 (Thurn, *Ioannis Malalae Chronographia*, 15). See Croke, "Byzantine Chronicle Writing," 30; E. Jeffreys, "Malalas' Sources," 194.

Figure 3. Relations of the family of Picus-Zeus. Chart by author.

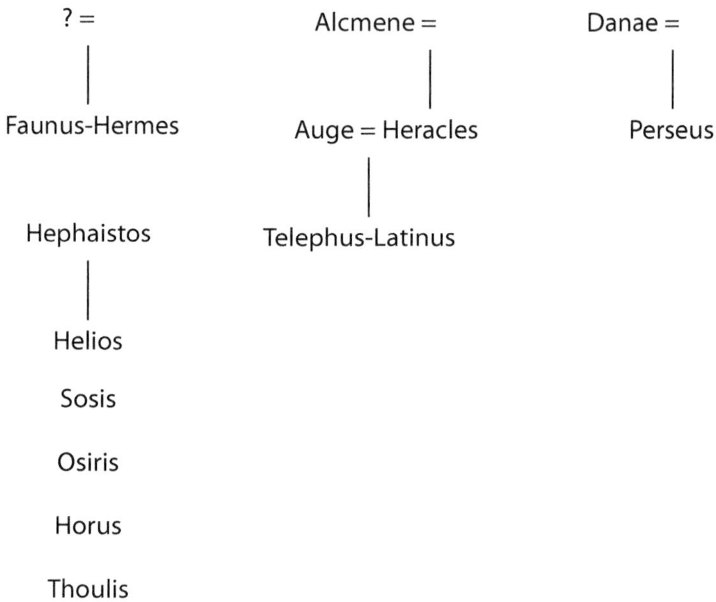

too early to have a descendant in the fourth generation with a son-in-law who had fought in the Trojan War. But with an admirable economy he also seems to have been determined to preserve as much of the material afforded him by his source as he possibly could. The recognition that the relations of Heracles to Picus-Zeus on the one hand and to Latinus and Aeneas on the other were unsustainable in chronological terms, along with the intention of retaining all he could from his source, required Malalas not only to separate and disperse the parts of a single, cohesive narrative which are found together and in continuous succession in the *Excerpta*, but also to divide the person of Heracles.

Malalas gives an account of not one Heracles, but two: Heracles the son of Picus-Zeus and a much later descendant, Heracles the father of Telephus (**FF 3, 4**). There was good precedent for the multiplication of the figure of Heracles. Ever

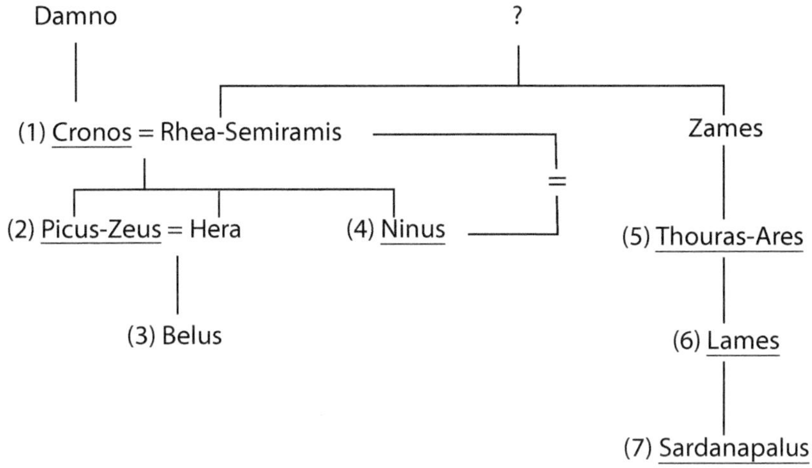

Note: Those who ruled as kings of Assyria are underlined and their order in the succession indicated in parentheses.

since Herodotus, authors puzzled by the chronologically irreconcilable relations of the ubiquitous hero and his syncretistic equivalents in other cultures had turned to the expedient of assuming that there had been more than one person going under the name of Heracles.[93] And Malalas makes it explicitly clear that he was aware of the understanding that there had been more than one Heracles, stating that Herodotus recorded that there were seven others in addition to the son

93 Hdt. 2.43–44, 145–46; Diod. Sic. 3.74.4, 5.76.1–2; Cic., *Nat. D.* 3.42; Plin., *HN* 11.(17) 52; Quint., *Inst.* 7.2.7; Arr., *Anab.* 2.16.1–3, 4.28.2, *Ind.* 5.13, cf. 8.4–7; Paus. 5.25.12, 10.13.8; Aelius Aristid., *Or.* 40.7–12 (ed. Keil); Ampelius 9.12; Arn., *Adv. nat.* 1.36, 4.15; Macrob., *Sat.* 1.20.6; Amm. Marc. 15.9.3, 6, 10.9; Serv., *Aen.* 8.564; August., *De civ. D.* 18.12; see Pease, *Ciceronis De Natura Deorum*, 2:1050–56; A. Lloyd, *Herodotus, Book II*, 2:200–212.

of Picus-Zeus who first practiced philosophy in the West.[94] But this procedure is decidedly inconsistent with the Picus-Zeus narrative's usual tendency to combine, not divide, mythological figures. The division of Heracles is quite obviously the result of Malalas, or perhaps his immediate source, Domninos, attempting to exploit as much as possible of one of his sources on myth while preserving the overall chronological structure of his own work, in which the so-called gods lived many centuries before the Trojan War.

Malalas left his fingerprints, so to speak, on this work of dividing Heracles and the Picus-Zeus narrative. Squeezed between the statement that Zeus had sons with many women, which follows on from the enumeration of the seventy or so brothers of Faunus-Hermes, and the account of Heracles as a philosopher, in the text of Malalas there is a very brief and vague note indicating that Zeus sired someone called "the son of Maias" (υἱὸς Μαιάδος).[95] This looks like a corruption or variation on "the son of Maia," which would be Hermes. Maia, the mother of Hermes, is not mentioned in the account of Faunus-Hermes in either Malalas or the *Excerpta*, and this detail does not appear to belong to the Picus-Zeus narrative, which has come before. But Malalas does later identify Hermes, along with Heracles, as one of the most prominent sons of Zeus. Hermes and Heracles, in addition to Perseus, are listed as the sons of Picus-Zeus in the introduction to Malalas's account of Perseus.[96] Perhaps some understanding of Hermes' importance, along with Heracles', led Malalas to retain the barest mention of Hermes from some source dealing with the sons of Zeus, even if he discarded most of the information about Hermes and almost exclusively adopted information about Heracles. Some such source was introduced at this point to provide details on Heracles, but it was different from and incompatible with the Picus-Zeus narrative. The introduction of such a source that could account for the earlier Heracles would be necessary if what Malalas's source up to this point had to say about Heracles had been transposed to a much later section because of what it conveyed about Heracles' relation to Latinus and Aeneas, leaving the name of a prominent figure but a gap in regard to his life and deeds.

94 Malalas 1.14 (Thurn, *Ioannis Malalae Chronographia*, 15): ὃς καὶ ἄλλους Ἡρακλεῖς ἱστόρησεν γεγενῆσθαι ἑπτά ([he] records that there were also another seven Heracleses).

95 Malalas 1.14 (Thurn, *Ioannis Malalae Chronographia*, 14): ἐγεννήθη τις λεγόμενος <υἱὸς> Μαιάδος (one was born who was called <the son> of Maias).

96 Malalas 2.11; see **F 7.1**.

What is more, the figure of Telephus-Latinus, combined in a manner consistent with the characters of the Picus-Zeus narrative in the *Excerpta*, is separated by Malalas (**F 4**) into two people: Telephus, the son of Heracles, and Latinus, the son and heir of Telephus. This Latinus, however, has a reign of eighteen years, and no reign length at all is indicated for Telephus. But the combined figure of Telephus-Latinus also has a reign of eighteen years in the *Excerpta*. This suggests that while the combined identity of Telephus-Latinus could be pulled apart, his reign went undivided, since the intrusion of new numbers could potentially distort the chronological record, and so was assigned to only one product of the division of his character. This seems to confirm that the combined figure of Telephus-Latinus was the original, and the separate characters of Telephus and Latinus were the products of Malalas's later manipulation.

Altogether, the evidence suggests that the original Picus-Zeus narrative presented a single Heracles, who succeeded Faunus-Hermes in Italy and whose story was integral to the overall account of the so-called gods. The single identity of Heracles and the integrity of the narrative is best reflected in the *Excerpta*. The more complex and perhaps better thought-out chronology of Malalas, or of Domninos, the intermediary who seems to stand between Malalas and Bouttios, and so the Picus-Zeus narrative, demanded that the figure of Heracles be divided. So while Heracles the son of Picus-Zeus was described in terms Malalas (or Domninos) borrowed from some other source, the history of Heracles the father of Telephus, as found in the Picus-Zeus narrative, was apportioned to a much later period. Nevertheless, Malalas adhered closely enough to his source to retain some readings that can correct the garbled text of the *Excerpta* and demonstrate that they are both witnesses to the same source.

Some understanding of the thought and intention that lie behind the arrangement and distribution of the parts of the Picus-Zeus narrative allows us to determine the extent and relation of the fragments. The Picus-Zeus narrative's discussion of early Italy, available to both the *Excerpta* compiler and Malalas, seems to have extended at least as far as Telephus-Latinus. So the fragment from the *Excerpta* includes the material up to this figure. The corresponding passages from Malalas on Heracles and his Italian progeny, along with the mention of his arms in the Forum Boarium (**FF 3, 4, 5**), can be identified as fragments of the same narrative source and treated as a continuation from the reign of Faunus-Hermes in Italy (**F 1.7**). As a consequence, the dissonant account of Heracles in Malalas's first book

can be excluded from the fragment as an ill-fitting intrusion necessitated by the effort to maintain the new chronological relations Malalas imposed upon the narrative, whose chief results were the duplication of the figure of Heracles and the redistribution of previously united material across a span of several centuries and the space of several books in his *Chronicle*. The fragments of Bouttios, then, cover the period in Italy from the arrival of Cronos, through his descendants, until at least the arrival of Aeneas and the death of Telephus-Latinus.

Let the foregoing stand as an explanation of the material presented as fragments at the end of this text. If three meager citations seem to have produced a rather luxurious growth, it is to be hoped that the rationale by which each of these passages has been assigned to Bouttios has been clearly laid out. I would contend that this assignment of a much more extensive list of fragments to Bouttios than those assembled by Peter or Levick and Rich is a reasonable consequence, in the first place, of respecting the grammar of the sentence in which Malalas cites Bouttios in Book 8 of his *Chronicle*. This allows us to associate certain idiosyncratic and therefore distinctive traits, the conglomeration of oriental nations and Alexander's liberation of the Romans, with Bouttios, and then to recognize that these same traits are shared by the *Excerpta Latina Barbari*'s treatment of Alexander. And this is by no means all that Malalas and the *Excerpta* share; they have a number of notions and even passages in common, demonstrably derived from a single shared source. If we allow, moreover, that the citation of authorities in Malalas is meant to cover not merely clauses but whole sections, as is only to be expected, the text renders up a good deal more material.

We have arranged the fragments thus assembled in what appears to be chronological order, although there is always the possibility that some passage originated as an archaeological digression on later events, as the note that Byzantium was founded by Phidalia (**F 34**) seems to have been, and is no longer detectable as such. At any rate, in the absence of biographical details, any impression we have of Bouttios the historian must be based on such indications as we can assemble of what his history contained. And so we turn from the task of collecting the fragments to a discussion of what they have to tell us about their author, his life, and his work.

PART II

BOUTTIOS'S LIFE AND WORK

5

BOUTTIOS'S LIFE

In his rare citations of Bouttios John Malalas tells us two things about him: that he was "exceeding wise" (σοφώτατος) and that he was a chronographer (χρονογράφος). The first of these characterizations is a practically meaningless tag which Malalas liberally applies to a number of authorities he mentions in the course of his *Chronicle*,[1] and is by no means substantiated by the material we can associate with Bouttios. The second is likewise a term Malalas bandies about quite loosely, but it is misleading rather than empty, since it does not appear that what Bouttios wrote was a chronography or a chronicle. If Malalas, the author who cites Bouttios more often than any other, tells us nothing substantial about him, what can we say about him? Everything we can say about Bouttios, the man and his work, must be inferred from the remains of his writing and their setting in surviving works. This is hardly a unique situation when it comes to the fragmentary historians of antiquity. Indeed, it is not exactly rare even in regard to those historians whose work survives completely. So, having assembled his fragments, we must attempt to determine what they tell us about Bouttios and his composition, all the time mindful that we proceed by conjecture and supposition to assemble a picture of a historian—and a history—about whom we know practically nothing definite.

1 See M. Jeffreys, "Language of Malalas, 2," 229.

Name

The uncertainty concerning Bouttios begins with his very name. We have been referring to "Bouttios" all along, but this has been to avoid, or at least postpone, a discussion of the confusion surrounding the historian's name. In each of Malalas's three references to what we have taken, for the very good reasons indicated above, to be a single writer, he goes under a slightly different name. The passage on Perseus refers to "Bouttios" (Βούττιος), that on Alexander to "Bottios" (Βόττιος), and that on Domitian to "Bōttios" (Βώττιος). Although it is possible that three different historians with three such similar names might appear cited in a single work, it is most unlikely, and particularly so when we consider the similarity of traits and interests exhibited by the three different passages in which these names occur. It is much more likely that the various forms of a single name have resulted from not one but two instances of scribal error.

We are dealing with a variation in only a single vowel or diphthong in a rare name which occurs only three times at widely separated intervals in a lengthy text. The vowel sounds in question, moreover, would have struck the ear, and their written forms the eye, as similar and not readily distinguishable. We have every reason, therefore, to believe we are dealing with textual corruption, rather than multiple authors. But saying that the three variations we have are all forms of a single name leaves us with the problem of determining which one is correct and which two are corrupt.

Jeffreys has noted that the historian's "name is suspiciously close to the cult name Zeus Bottios or Bottiaios . . . derived from the village of Bottia on Mount Silpios."[2] Malalas tells us that Antioch was founded on the site of the village of Bottia (Βώττια) and that the first structure erected within the circuit of its walls was a temple to Zeus Bottios (Βωττίος Ζεύς).[3] Libanius offers a variant form of the divine epithet when he says that Alexander the Great founded a shrine to Zeus Bottiaios (Ζεὺς Βοττιαῖος) where Antioch was to be built.[4] These references might suggest that the author's name was somehow linked with that of the village that once stood where Antioch rose and with Zeus's cult title at that

2 E. Jeffreys, "Malalas' Sources," 174.

3 Malalas 8.12. See Downey, *History of Antioch*, 68.

4 Lib., *Or.* 11.76. See Downey, "Libanius' Oration," 662; Downey, *History of Antioch*, 54–55.

city, and so was "Bottios," leaving aside the insoluble—if negligible—problem of whether omega or omicron is to be preferred in the Greek spelling. This seems to be the preference of Jeffreys, since, while she indicates in parentheses the variant "Bouttios," she lists the source cited by Malalas under the name of "Bottios."[5]

The philological principle of *lectio difficilior potior*, however, holds that textual corruption tends to reduce a more complex reading to a simpler one and that the more complex reading should, as a rule, be preferred. The rules of textual criticism, then, suggest that the slightly more complex diphthong of Bouttios should be preferred to the simple vowel of Bottios. But the rules might be ignored when the more complex reading is not corroborated by other occurrences, as the simpler one is in this case. A parallel usage, though, may also be found for the form of Bouttios and connected to the environs of Antioch.

The adjective "Bouttios" (ΒΟΥΤΤΙΟΣ) occurs on several second-century BCE inscriptions from the ruins of a shrine of Asclepius at the site of Longá near the village of Skála in ancient Aetolia (or possibly Locris).[6] It is used, in the singular and plural, to qualify the word ἄρχων and so to designate certain named individuals as magistrates, presumably of the extinct town of Bouttos, a town lost to all record and memory, but in whose territory this shrine appears to have been situated. An obscure epigraphic attestation of "Bouttios" might seem to have little bearing on the question of our author's name—that is until it is remembered that, according to Libanius, when Antiochus III (r. 223–187 BCE) established a new quarter of Antioch on the island in the Orontes adjacent to the old city, he brought in as inhabitants of this neighbourhood Aetolians, Cretans, and

5 E. Jeffreys, "Malalas' Sources," 174. The translation undertaken by Jeffreys and her team (E. Jeffreys, with M. Jeffreys and Scott, et al., *The Chronicle of John Malalas*) gives each of the variant forms as it occurs in the text, though not distinguishing between Βόττιος and Βώττιος.

6 Woodhouse, *Aetolia*, 331–38, 380–84; Lerat, *Les Locriens*, 1:20–23, 76, 93–96, 191–92, 2:85–87, 95–96, 99, 126–28, 154–55; Klaffenbach, *Inscriptiones Graeciae Septentrionalis*, 20–47 (nos. 630–40). The regular forms of the name of the town and the ethnic are Βουττός and Βούττιος, but the variants Βοττός and Βούτιος and Βόττιος also appear, though rarely; Lerat, *Les Locriens*, 1:22–23. With these irregularities in stone-cut inscriptions, the variations in the text of Malalas should be unsurprising. Until the defeat of Aetolia by Rome in 189 BCE the territory in which Bouttos must have lain would have been under Aetolian control, and the question whether the town was properly Aetolian or Locrian is immaterial.

Euboians.[7] Libanius is careful to note that what Antiochus was importing in these settlers was "Hellenic stock" (γένος μὲν Ἑλληνικὸν εἰσάγων) and so to emphasize the irreproachable Greek heritage of the citizenry of the city he is praising.[8]

It is by no means inconceivable that among the Aetolian immigrants there were some from the now obliterated town of Bouttos—some Bouttioi, in fact. Nor, considering the pride with which Libanius recalled six hundred or so years later this injection of Greek blood into the citizen body of his hometown, that the descendants of these settlers retained the name of Bouttios as a commemoration of a vaunted Hellenic pedigree. We can point to similar instances of the ethnic adjective being used as a personal name. The sophist Libanius himself bore a name that associated him with the Syrian town of Libana and Mt. Libanus in the same region, and that in the same fourth-century Antioch where we shall attempt to place Bouttios.[9] Athenaeus is another prominent literary example; others could be adduced. Bouttios then has as good a claim on propriety as Bottios, an even better one if we depend on the *lectio difficilior.* Our options for the author's name, however, are not limited to those offered by Malalas.

Over three hundred years ago now, Richard Bentley asserted that the three different forms of the name attested by Malalas were alike corruptions of "Brouttios" (Βρούττιος) or "Brettios" (Βρέττιος), an authority cited by George the Syncellus and Jerome for the same material.[10] Bentley was referring to a notice in Jerome's translation of the *Canons* of Eusebius's *Chronicle* (**F 28**):

> scribit Bruttius plurimos Christianorum sub Domitiano fecisse martyrium, inter quos et Flauiam Domitillam Flauii Clementis consulis ex

7 Lib., *Or.* 11.119. See Downey, "Libanius' Oration," 665, 682. On the details of this civic expansion project, see Downey, "Strabo on Antioch."

8 Downey, *History of Antioch*, 92–93, is of the opinion that while Libanius wished to suggest that Antiochus sent specially to Greece for immigrants to augment the city's Greek element, the settlers of this new quarter were probably veterans of the king's Roman war and loyal refugees from the Roman conquest of Greece.

9 Steph. Byz., *Ethnica*, s.v. Λίβανα, for whom the correct form of the ethnic is Λιβανίτης. Libanius wore his Syrian heritage on his sleeve; see *Or.* 1.16, *Ep.* 4.13.

10 Bentley, *Works of Richard Bentley*, 2:334 (repr., *Epistola ad Joannem Millium*, 120). Bentley's letter to John Mill was written in 1690.

> sorore neptem in insulam Pontiam relegatam quia se Christianam esse testata sit.[11]
>
> Bruttius writes that very many Christians bore witness [were martyred] under Domitian, among whom also Flavia Domitilla, the niece by his sister of the consul Flavius Clemens, was banished to the island of Pontia because she confessed herself to be a Christian.

A very similar notice is also found, as Bentley says, in the *Chronography* of George the Syncellus (**F 29**), probably much closer to its original, as it is at least in Greek:

> πολλοὶ δὲ Χριστιανῶν ἐμαρτύρησαν κατὰ Δομετιανόν, ὡς ὁ Βρέττιος ἱστορεῖ, ἐν οἷς καὶ Φλαυία Δομετίλλα ἐξαδελφὴ Κλήμεντος Φλαυίου ὑπατικοῦ ὡς Χριστιανὴ εἰς νῆσον Ποντίαν φυγαδεύεται· αὐτός τε Κλήμης ὑπὲρ Χριστοῦ ἀναιρεῖται.[12]
>
> Many Christians bore witness [were martyred] under Domitian, as Brettios records, among whom also Flavia Domitilla, the niece of the consul Flavius Clemens, was banished as a Christian to the island of Pontia; this Clemens himself was killed for the sake of Christ.

These passages confirm that "Bruttius" dealt with the persecution of the Christians under Domitian, as did Malalas's Bouttios (**F 27**), though they do not necessarily cite Bruttius for what follows concerning Flavia Domitilla. As far as the identity of the two cited authors is concerned, in Jerome and George on the one hand and in Malalas on the other, I can only concur with Bentley.[13] It is hardly conceivable that there were two different authors with remarkably similar names

11 Jerome, *Chron.: ann. Abr.* 2112 (Fotheringham, *Evsebii Pamphili Chronici Canones*, 274).

12 Georg. Sync., *Chron.* 650 (Mosshammer, *Ecloga chronographica*, 419).

13 Merrill, *Essays*, 165, remains skeptical: "This man is possibly the same as the Bruttius of Eusebius, but may be another person altogether." Even if such a substantial amount of evidence could not be marshalled in support of his propositions, however, I would, in the main, be inclined to trust Bentley's handling of ancient texts.

who wrote on the same subject and were cited on the same topic in the same literary milieu, the Christian chronicle tradition. Either Bouttios or Bruttius must be a corruption of a single name. But the implications for the identity of the two authorities are much broader than determining whether or not a rho should be included in the spelling of his name.

A citation of Bouttios, even in a slightly different spelling, appearing in what might be considered the two principal witnesses to the lost *Chronological Canons* of Eusebius might be taken to indicate that Eusebius himself cited Bouttios in his *Chronicle*. If this were the case, it would provide crucial evidence for the dating of Bouttios; if he was cited by Eusebius, he must have written at least before the revised version of the *Canons* was prepared in 325/6, and perhaps even the original composition of the *Chronicle* as early as ca. 300. This would further preclude the attribution to Bouttios of any material on events after one of those dates. And this is how the evidence has been handled in the entry on "Bruttius" in one recent reference work.[14] But this terminus ante quem can be fixed only if we are safe in assuming that the citation of Bouttios, or "Bruttius," belongs to Eusebius himself and a version of the *Canons* he himself prepared. This is not a safe assumption. That we have ascribed to Bouttios some treatment of the dedication of Constantinople in 330 (**F 34**) and that we shall attempt to set him in the context of the controversies of the later fourth century are not grounds for doubting that the citation of Bouttios in the *Canons* belongs to Eusebius, but they do raise suspicions. The real reason for doubting that the citation of Bouttios in the *Canons* was included by Eusebius himself is that when he deals with the same matters in the *Ecclesiastical History*, the persecution of the Christians under Domitian and the exile of Flavia Domitilla, he does not mention Bouttios.

On the whole, Jerome's translation is a reliable witness to, even a serviceable substitute for, Eusebius's lost *Canons*, but it is prudent to recall that it is no facsimile and only pushes our evidence back to 380, some forty years after Eusebius's death. There will be a few instances where we have reason to doubt that what we find in Jerome's *Chronicle*, as well as the other witnesses to the text of the lost original, represents what Eusebius actually wrote. The citation of "Bruttius" is one such instance. Eusebius seems to have undertaken his final revisions of both the *Ecclesiastical History* and the *Chronological Canons* at about the same time,

14 Van Nuffelen and Van Hoof, *Clavis Historicorum*, 77–78.

around the Vicennalia of Constantine in 325/6.[15] So whatever material he had access to and whatever authors he was familiar with when he prepared his final version of the one, he also knew when he made his last revisions to the other. In consequence, it is strikingly odd that there is no reference to "Bruttius" associated with the passage in the *Ecclesiastical History* that corresponds to the notices in Jerome's *Chronicle* and in George the Syncellus that do include a citation of Bruttius or Brettios:

> Εἰς τοσοῦτον δὲ ἄρα κατὰ τοὺς δηλουμένους ἡ τῆς ἡμετέρας πίστεως διέλαμπεν διδασκαλία, ὡς καὶ τοὺς ἄποθεν τοῦ καθ' ἡμᾶς λόγου συγγραφεῖς μὴ ἀποκνῆσαι ταῖς αὐτῶν ἱστορίαις τόν τε διωγμὸν καὶ τὰ ἐν αὐτῷ μαρτύρια παραδοῦναι, οἵ γε καὶ τὸν καιρὸν ἐπ' ἀκριβὲς ἐπεσημήναντο, ἐν ἔτει πεντεκαιδεκάτῳ Δομετιανοῦ μετὰ πλείστων ἑτέρων καὶ Φλαυίαν Δομέτιλλαν ἱστορήσαντες, ἐξ ἀδελφῆς γεγονυῖαν Φλαυίου Κλήμεντος, ἑνὸς τῶν τηνικάδε ἐπὶ Ῥώμης ὑπάτων, τῆς εἰς Χριστὸν μαρτυρίας ἕνεκεν εἰς νῆσον Ποντίαν κατὰ τιμωρίαν δεδόσθαι.[16]
>
> The teaching of our faith, then, shone forth in the times being described to such an extent that even some writers from outside of our school of thought did not shrink from transmitting in their histories the persecution and the martyrdoms at that time, and moreover recorded it accurately, relating in historical narrative that in the fifteenth year of Domitian, along with many others, Flavia Domitilla, the niece by his sister of Flavius Clemens, one of the consuls at Rome in this time, on account of her witness for Christ was consigned to the Island of Pontia as a punishment.

The subject matter, the persecution of Christians under Domitian, and the focus of interest on what happened to Flavia Domitilla here, in a work indisputably from the pen of Eusebius in every detail, is the same as in the notices in the witnesses to his *Canons*. So we may safely conclude that Eusebius did include in his *Canons* a notice on Domitian's persecution, mentioning Flavia Domitilla, but

15 Barnes, "Editions."
16 Euseb., *HE* 3.18.4 (Schwartz, *Die Kirchengeschichte*, 232).

not necessarily that this notice had a citation of "Bruttius." The absence of such a citation from the *Ecclesiastical History* alerts us to a problem. And the solution is not that Eusebius was averse to citing named sources in the *Ecclesiastical History*. On the contrary, he cites and quotes both Hegessipus and Tertullian for what immediately follows, an account of the hounding of the descendants of David by Domitian.[17] But in the corresponding notices on the same matters in Jerome's *Chronicle* and George the Syncellus there are no authorities cited.[18] If anything, then, we should expect a named citation in the fuller, more leisurely narrative of the *Ecclesiastical History* and the excision of any citation from the terse and abbreviated notices in the *Canons*. The "Bruttius" of the witnesses to the *Canons* might be identified with one of the several unnamed non-Christian authors Eusebius does bring up as mentioning the events in question. But this is unlikely, since Eusebius cites the anonymous pagans specifically for the incident of Flavia Domitilla's exile, whereas Jerome's "Bruttius" and George the Syncellus's "Brettios" seem to be cited as discussing Domitian's persecution in general.[19]

Some scholars have, nevertheless, taken Bruttius to be one of Eusebius's unnamed pagan sources, or indeed the only actual source to which he refers.[20] Merrill insisted that the several "writers from outside of our school of thought" boil down to a single actual authority, and further that there is one shared authority for the information in the *Canons* and the *Ecclesiastical History*: that is, "Bruttius."[21] Ronald Syme identified the historian with C. Bruttius Praesens, consul under Hadrian, on the basis of nothing more than the coincidence of names

17 Euseb., *HE* 3.19.1–20.7.

18 Jerome, *Chron.*: *ann. Abr.* 2112 (Fotheringham, *Evsebii Pamphili Chronici Canones*, 274): *Domitianus eos qui de genere Dauid erant interfici praecipit ut nullus Iudaeorum regni reliquus foret* (Domitian ordered that those who were from the stirps of David be killed so that none would be left of the kingdom of the Jews). Georg. Sync., *Chron.* 650 (Mosshammer, *Ecloga chronographica*, 419): Δομετιανὸς τοὺς ἀπὸ γένους Δαβὶδ ἀναιρεῖσθαι προσέταξεν, ἵνα μή τις Ἰουδαίων βασιλικοῦ γένους ἀπολειφθῇ (Domitian ordered that those of the line of David be killed, so that no one of the royal line of the Jews might be left).

19 Levick and Rich, "Bruttius," 1:593, 595, 3:631, emphasize the problematic nature of these contradictory pieces of evidence.

20 See von Stauffenberg, *Kaisergeschichte bei Malalas*, 237–38; Keresztes, "The Jews, the Christians," 16.

21 Merrill, *Essays*, 164–65.

and the observation that the career of Praesens would have afforded plenty of material for the writing of history.[22] It could be countered that his career might just as well have offered plenty of incentive for prudent silence. But the identification of "Bruttius" as a non-Christian author and as Eusebius's source for the material discussed in both the *Canons* and the *Ecclesiastical History* does not stand up to scrutiny. Gelzer pointed out the first problem when he noted the obviously Christian character of the material ascribed to Bouttios (under any form of his name) in Malalas. But holding to the single identity of the author cited in the *Canons* and by Malalas, as well as the unnamed authors of the *Ecclesiastical History*, he attempted to overcome the difficulty posed by the supposed identification of Bruttius as a pagan author and the nature of the fragments by suggesting that the chronicle of Bruttius might have been a Christian fabrication, a *pia fraus*, intended to be taken for a pagan work.[23] The simpler answer is that Eusebius was not speaking of "Bruttius"—may not have known of him at all—when he mentioned certain pagan authors who go nameless in the *Ecclesiastical History*.

The next problem is that "Bruttius" does not seem to be cited for the same specific point as Eusebius's anonymous sources are supposed to inform him of, that is, the exile of Flavia Domitilla. The arrangement of the notices in Jerome and George the Syncellus, and particularly the placement of the citation of Bruttius, need not suggest that he was cited for anything more than the occurrence of the persecution in general; indeed, that seems to be what it implies.[24] If Malalas's Bouttios and Jerome's Bruttius are to be identified, moreover, it is remarkable that while Bruttius is cited for much the same material as that for which Bouttios is offered as a source (i.e., the outbreak of a persecution of Christians under Domitian), there is no mention at all in Malalas of Flavia Domitilla, whose exile Eusebius's anonymous sources are meant to corroborate. Nor is it really necessary to try to discover the identity of Eusebius's unnamed sources. We can point to at least two pagan authors who recorded events related to what Eusebius speaks

22 Syme, "Praesens," 288–91.

23 Gelzer, *Sextus Julius Africanus*, 1:282–83; cf. Peter, *Historicorum Romanorum Reliquiae*, 2:ccviiii.

24 Merrill, *Essays*, 164, simply misrepresents matters when he says of Eusebius that "in his *Chronicles* he cites 'Bruttius' as authority for the fact that Domitilla was punished as a Christian." Merrill is followed in this error with a more egregious one by Syme, "Praesens," 289, who says that Malalas cites "Buttios" for the exile of Domitilla.

of, without discussing those precise matters themselves. Suetonius and Cassius Dio both refer to the execution of Flavius Clemens, and Cassius Dio also mentions the exile of his wife, another Flavia Domitilla, to the island of Pandateria.[25] The anonymity of Eusebius's sources may have been intended to conceal the fact that authorities could be found who recorded incidents close to what Eusebius was discussing, but not exactly the events as he related them. There is no reason, then, to believe that Eusebius is referring to "Bruttius" when he speaks of certain unnamed authors outside of the Church as knowing of the exile of Flavia Domitilla in the *Ecclesiastical History*.

We are still left with the problem of why a named authority should be found for the persecution under Domitian in the witnesses to the *Canons* but not in the *Ecclesiastical History*, especially since they were revised at the same time. It is decidedly odd that in regard to much the same events, we should find in one work, renowned for its scrupulous source citation, reference to several authors who are left anonymous, and in the other the citation of a single writer who is named.[26] We would expect the citation of an authoritative source to be carried over from one work to the other. Or rather, as in the case of Hegesippus and Tertullian on the prosecution of the House of David, a citation in the *Ecclesiastical History*, but not necessarily in the *Canons*. The absence of a citation from the *Ecclesiastical History* should make us suspicious of its presence in the witnesses to the *Canons*. The problem dissolves, however, if we posit that Eusebius was not aware of "Bruttius" and that the citation of Bruttius in the material we use to reconstruct his composition of the *Chronicle* is a post-Eusebian interpolation.

The problem boils down to a question of the integrity of the text of the *Canons* in the fourth century. In the main, a comparison of Jerome's translation and George the Syncellus's *Chronicle*, along with the other witnesses to the text, allows us to reconstruct the original *Canons* as Eusebius wrote them with a fair degree of confidence, not only in terms of plan and arrangement, but most often also in terms of detail and wording.[27] But did Jerome translate an immaculate

25 Suet., *Dom.* 15.1; Cass. Dio 67.14.1–2.

26 Merrill, *Essays*, 166, begs the question by opining that the lack of a named citation or quotation in the *Ecclesiastical History* indicates that Eusebius did not have direct access to the text of Bruttius, but depended on an intermediary.

27 Nevertheless, we should not read too much into Mosshammer's enthusiastic suggestion that Jerome may have translated a copy of the *Canons* made in the lifetime of

version of the *Canons*, untouched since it was finished by the hand of Eusebius? There is reason to doubt it, even if there is no direct evidence of manipulation. The very nature of the *Canons* militates against the suggestion that a clean copy reached Jerome forty-odd years after Eusebius's death. The *Canons* was the sort of text that invited regular reworking. Eusebius seems to have recognized this himself. The *Chronicle*, including the *Canons*, was first written before 313, perhaps before 303, or in 311.[28] It is first mentioned in Eusebius's own *Eclogae Propheticae*, which was most likely written around the earlier date.[29] Yet the text of the *Canons* which Jerome translated went down to the Vicennalia of Constantine in 325/6.[30] Eusebius was himself almost certainly responsible for the revision and extension of his work. He would have seen it as a text that had to be updated to remain current and useful. Jerome certainly took this view when he made his translation of the *Canons* in 380/1. He elaborated entries already included among the historical notices in the *Canons*, added new ones, especially to accommodate events in Rome and the West, and brought the chronography down to the year 378 and the Battle of Adrianople.[31] Jerome himself further revised his own translation of the *Canons* before presenting it to the synod of Rome in 382. This is not to say that either Eusebius or Jerome made the specific addition of the citation we are discussing at present, but that both recognized the nature of a work like the *Canons* as open to manipulation. The early history of the text, so far as we can discern it, suggests that the *Canons* was viewed, not least by its author and then its first

---

Eusebius; Mosshammer, Chronicle *of Eusebius*, 67: "The Greek exemplar that Jerome used could not have been far removed from Eusebius' original, and there is a distinct possibility that Jerome's exemplar was copied during Eusebius' lifetime from an archetype residing in Eusebius' great library at Caesarea." There is no evidence for this, and Mosshammer is at pains to demonstrate the proximity and so the reliability of Jerome in regard to the text he was translating.

28 Mosshammer, Chronicle *of Eusebius*, 32–33; Barnes, *Constantine and Eusebius*, 113; Burgess, "Dates and Editions of Eusebius"; Burgess, *Studies*, 21.

29 Mosshammer, Chronicle *of Eusebius*, 32; Burgess, "Dates and Editions of Eusebius," 471, 486–87.

30 Mosshammer, Chronicle *of Eusebius*, 37–38, 67–73; Barnes, *Constantine and Eusebius*, 113.

31 Mosshammer, Chronicle *of Eusebius*, 37–38; Barnes, *Constantine and Eusebius*, 113; Burgess, *Studies*, 23–25; cf. Vessey, "Reinventing History."

translator, as an open text, one that could be revised and augmented without ceasing to go under the name of Eusebius's *Canons*.[32]

Given that practically from its composition the text of the *Canons* was susceptible to addition and expansion, we cannot trust that the version Jerome translated in 380/1 was in every detail the text that left the hand of Eusebius. We do not even know for sure that it was Eusebius who was responsible for the revision that brought the *Canons* down to 325/6; certainly there is no assertion by Eusebius or anyone else that he did so. Some editorial intervention, an added notice or citation, in the interval of over half a century between Eusebius's supposed second edition of the *Canons* and their translation in 380/1 is not only quite likely, it should be expected.[33] This is especially so since Jerome obviously felt free to make the adjustments he deemed necessary in the text he received. He can hardly have been the first to take this attitude toward the *Canons*. At the very least, we must be careful to say that Bruttius does not appear in a text indisputably from the pen of Eusebius, but is rather first attested in a text firmly dated to 382.

The openness of the text of the *Canons* offers a straightforward explanation for the problem of Eusebius's apparent ignorance of "Bruttius," as indicated by the reference to unnamed authors rather than a citation of this author, for the persecution under Domitian in the *Ecclesiastical History*. Eusebius need not have known of Bruttius. He was not necessarily responsible for everything found even in a fourth-century copy of the *Canons*, and an editor or scribe could very well have added the reference to Bruttius to a notice on Domitian's persecution already present in the *Canons*. The addition of the citation as it appears in George the Syncellus (ὡς ὁ Βρέττιος ἱστορεῖ) would not even require any adjustment to the grammar and syntax of the sentence as it already appeared. Eusebius's treatment of the subject in the *Ecclesiastical History* would suggest that he had indeed included such a notice, and the emphasis of the *Canons*' notice on Flavia Domitilla, reflecting the concerns of the *Ecclesiastical History*, further suggests that the notice itself, the reference to events, if not the accompanying citation, is

32 The concept of the "open text" is explored by Konstan, "Alexander Romance."

33 Burgess, *Studies*, 113–34, has plausibly posited the existence of an Antiochene continuation of the *Canons* of Eusebius covering the years 325–350, from which Jerome as well as other later chroniclers drew material. A continuation is not evidence of insertions within the material already present, but it does suggest that the text of the *Canons* was immediately upon its publication open to additions from other parties than the author.

the work of Eusebius. It is once again comparison with the *Ecclesiastical History* that serves to exclude the citation of Bruttius from the notice Eusebius himself wrote. If he had been aware of this authority when he wrote the entry in the *Canons*, he would also have known of him when he prepared the final version of the *Ecclesiastical History*, and we should expect to find the name there as well. We do not, and so we can assume that another hand added the citation of an authority Eusebius did not know.

This addition was not made by Jerome, but had already been made to the Greek version he translated. We can tell this because the citation of Bruttius or Brettios is also found in witnesses to the text of the *Canons* that depend not upon Jerome but on some Greek exemplar they shared with him. This is clear from the *Chronographia* of George the Syncellus. A Syriac epitome of the *Canons* also includes a citation of "BVRTNVS" for the persecution of the Christians under Domitian.[34] A citation of "Brettios" is likewise found in the Armenian translation of Eusebius's *Chronicle*, which is also independent of Jerome and goes back, through the Syriac text, to a Greek exemplar.[35] The numerous appearances of "Bruttius" or "Brettios" in the various witnesses to the text of Eusebius's *Canons* by no means indicate Eusebian authorship of the citation, but merely confirm that the citation was added to the text rather early.[36] The citation of Bruttius belongs to a Greek text of the *Canons* prepared before 380.[37] We cannot

34 Schoene, *Eusebi Chronicorum libri*, 2:214. The citation of Bruttius/Brettios and a reference to the exile of Flavia Domitilla both appear to have fallen out of one of our best witnesses to the Syriac translation of the *Canons* of Eusebius, the *Chronicle* of Dionysius of Tel Mahre (Siegfried and Gelzer, *Eusebii Canonum Epitome*, 57–60).

35 Euseb., *Arm. Chron.* (Karst, *Die Chronik aus dem armenischen Übersetzt*, 218).

36 Van Hoof and Van Neuffelen, *Fragmentary Latin Histories*, 251, insist that the appearance of some form of the name of Bouttios in all the surviving later versions of Eusebius's *Chronicle* is proof positive that he was cited by Eusebius himself, largely ignoring the problem presented by the absence of a citation of Bouttios from the *Ecclesiastical History*. This insistence leads them into the untenable position (252, 255, 256) of denying that two of their three fragments (our **FF 7.1** and **16.1** or parts thereof) represent material from Bouttios at all and maintaining rather that a citation of "Bruttius" drawn from Eusebius was inserted into passages having nothing to do with either author to endow them with a specious authority. What, we are left to wonder, would the citation of a practically unknown author avail in this effort?

37 Van Hoof and Van Neuffelen, *Fragmentary Latin Histories*, 251, dismiss as "implausible" the suggestion that the extant tradition of Eusebius's *Chronicle* might stem

say how long before this date the citation may have been added to the *Canons*, but it was presumably at some point after the revision of the *Ecclesiastical History* in 325/6.

Even if we ascribe the citation of Bruttius or Brettios in the witnesses to the *Canons* to the hand of an interpolator, we are still left with the problem of which form of the name is correct. We may agree with Bentley that Malalas's Bouttios is to be identified with Jerome's Bruttius, but we are not obliged to follow him in assuming that the error lies with Malalas. Bentley had a very low opinion of Malalas's competence and was predisposed to think that whenever a viable alternative was offered, Malalas's version could be discarded as faulty. Considering all of the forms given to the historian's name, Levick and Rich have recently proposed that "these variations are consistent with 'Bruttius' being the original form of the author's name, but we cannot be sure that this was the case."[38] It should be noted, however, that while these same scholars defer to the citation in versions of Eusebius's *Chronicle* as the grounds for reconstructing the form of the name, they take most of the material for the fragments of this "Bruttius" from Malalas.[39] Surely, some consideration should be given to the evidence for Malalas's more extensive exploitation of a source immediately acquainted with the work of "Bouttios" as an indication that he might preserve the correct form of the historian's name, even if the testimony of Jerome is rather earlier. There is, moreover, further evidence in support of Malalas's form without the rho. The Slavonic versions render the name cited by Malalas **Вотиѡ̓съ** (*Votiosu*) or **Вѵтос** (*Vutos*).[40] The Slavonic translation does not derive from our single best Greek manuscript

---

from an interpolated version, as if the popularity and vast proliferation of the *Chronicle* were immediate upon its publication. Nevertheless, they accept that the diverse branches of that tradition represented by the Armenian translation and George the Syncellus relied on a single manuscript which spelled the cited author's name "Brettios."

38 Levick and Rich, "Bruttius," 1:594. It might be suspected that they inclined toward this decidedly Roman form of the name in order to justify the inclusion of this author in a collection of the fragments of Roman historians, but they would seem to be the first to admit the uncertainty that covers the matter and the possibility that we may be dealing with a very different kind of author, who penned a "Christian universal chronicle in Greek," as they would have it (1:595).

39 Levick and Rich, "Bruttius," 2:1090–95.

40 For the former, see Istrin, "Khronika II," 10, 474; for the latter, Istrin, "Khronika X," 17, 36 (repr., *Khronika Ioanna Malaly*, 78, 292).

(Oxford, Baroccianus Graecus 182) and so is to be considered an independent witness to the text of Malalas.[41] As a consequence, we cannot assume that the absent rho is the deficiency of a single manuscript. And, for what it is worth, even one of the manuscripts of Jerome's *Chronicle*, the relatively late, ninth-century manuscript T (Codex Oxoniensis Mertonensis 315), gives the name as "buttius."[42] As we have seen, the epigraphic evidence for the Bouttioi also gives us grounds for favoring the form presented by Malalas, or at least one of the forms preserved in the text of his *Chronicle*. We may say that we have two streams of evidence for the historian's name, each consistent unto itself: one giving the name with a rho, which derives from the citation that intruded into an early copy of the *Canons* and appears in every surviving version and rendition of that work, and one without a rho, represented by the Greek and Slavonic texts of Malalas.

Which of these two streams offers us the more reliable form?[43] On the one hand, the various versions of the *Canons* offer much earlier evidence, but this may merely be evidence for how early the corruption occurred. On the other hand, Malalas, even at second hand, exhibits a more ample familiarity with Bouttios's material, which may have included knowledge of the correct form of his name. To add weight to one side of the scales over the other we might ask whether the form of "Bouttios" or of "Bruttius" is more likely to have been the result of some manipulation, some intentional corruption. And it must be said that the insertion of the rho to make Bruttius would hardly be surprising at the hands of a scribe, the interpolator of the *Canons*, perhaps more familiar with the famous names of Roman history—the Brutus who drove the kings from Rome or Brutus the assassin of Julius Caesar—or even the prominent families of contemporary Rome, than with the parochial niceties of bygone Aetolian nomenclature or Antiochene civic geography.[44] "Bruttius" must have seemed a simple

41 Franklin, "Malalas in Slavonic."

42 Jerome, *Chron.*: *ann. Abr.* 2112 (Fotheringham, *Evsebii Pamphili Chronici Canones*, xv, 274). In this instance an *r* that was present in the exemplar has undoubtedly been omitted. Its probative value simply consists of the demonstration that the letter can fall out of, as well as into, the name.

43 Van Hoof and Van Neuffelen, *Fragmentary Latin Histories*, 251, insist that the various spellings of the author's name are best explained if the original is assumed to have been the Latin "Bruttius" as in Jerome, but they fail to explain how this is so.

44 Merrill, *Essays*, 165, insists that "what was doubtless intended is a transliteration of the Latin *gentilicium* Bruttius," which belonged to a famous family active in the

and sensible correction of the "Bouttios" that the scribe encountered and failed to recognize. Whereas "Bruttius" appears to result from an understandable mistake, the form of "Bouttios" seems an unlikely error to fall into. What reason could Malalas or someone copying out his work have had for erasing the rho, not in one instance, but in every one of three widely separated instances? If we adduce the principle of *lectio difficilior potior* once again, we should stick to the form that cannot be easily explained as an unconscious slip or a purposeful manipulation on the part of the scribe.[45]

One final source of evidence for the historian's name remains to be considered. Bentley referred to the alternatives to Malalas's "Bouttios" found in Jerome, "Bruttius," and George the Syncellus, "Brettios." In examining these alternatives and their sources we have identified two distinct streams of evidence, each preserving different but complementary material and testifying to two different forms of our author's name. These two streams seem to mingle in the early seventh-century *Chronicon Paschale*. Whereas Jerome and Syncellus cite Bruttius or Brettios for the persecution under Domitian, the anonymous author of the *Chronicon Paschale* refers to the authority of one "Brouttios" (Βρούττιος) not only for this event, but also for the demystified version of the story of Perseus. We appear to have material taken from the Malalan stream and a form of the name from the stream of the *Canons* in a single work. The sources of the *Chronicon Paschale* have not been analyzed in detail, but Warren Treadgold has maintained that its author consulted both Malalas and some version of the *Chronicle* of Eusebius, and his assertion is borne out in this particular instance.[46] The citation

imperial administration, but only notes in passing (166 and n. 1) other scholars, including one Englishman consigned to nameless obloquy, who more precisely identified the historian with a Bruttius Praesens, supposed to be a correspondent of Pliny the Younger. Syme, "Praesens," maintains the identification of the historian with Bruttius Praesens and notes (287) the continuing wealth and importance of his family.

45 Von Stauffenberg, *Kaisergeschichte bei Malalas*, 237–38, nevertheless insists that Bruttius must be the correct form of the name.

46 Treadgold, *Early Byzantine Historians*, 343–44. On the basis of one comparison, at least, Treadgold is willing to venture that the *Chronicon Paschale* hews closer to the text of Eusbebius's *Chronicle* than George the Syncellus managed to do. In their discussion of the *Chronicon Paschale*'s sources, Whitby and Whitby, *Chronicon Paschale*, xv–xxii, mention Malalas and Eusebius, but not the latter's *Chronicle*. It seems difficult to believe that with the work he had in hand, the author of the *Chronicon Paschale* neglected

regarding Domitian's persecution, along with the notice it corroborates, is quite clearly taken from the *Canons*, as there is a precise date for the persecution (lacking in Malalas) and none of the supplementary narrative: ἱστορεῖ ὁ Βρούττιος πολλοὺς χριστιανοὺς κατὰ τὸ ιδ' ἔτος Δομετιανοῦ μεμαρτυρηκέναι[47] (Brouttios records that many Christians were martyred in the fourteenth year of Domitian). It is tangentially remarkable that this notice in the *Chronicon Paschale* also seems to confirm that "Brouttios" was understood as an authority on Domitian's persecution in general, and not for the exile of Flavia Domitilla in particular, which is not mentioned in the *Chronicon Paschale*. The passage in the *Chronicon Paschale* on Perseus is taken practically verbatim from Malalas, and "Brouttios" is cited in almost the same terms (cf. **F 7.1**): ὁ δὲ σοφώτατος Βρούττιος ἱστορικὸς καὶ χρονογράφος ἐξέθετο ὡς . . . (The exceeding wise Brouttios, the historian and chronographer, however, set out that . . .).[48] The parallel of the passage to which the third citation of Bouttios is attached in Malalas, the description of Alexander's career, is by comparison drastically foreshortened in the *Chronicon Paschale*, and no authority is cited there.[49] The two passages in which the *Chronicon Paschale* cites "Brouttios" do, nevertheless, confirm that the author of this text had access both to some version of Eusebius's *Canons* with the intrusive citation of Bruttius and to the *Chronicle* of John Malalas.

If the author of the *Chronicon Paschale* had known only Malalas, we might take this as proof that "Brouttios" had also appeared in Malalas's original composition, and become corrupted to Bouttios in the transmission of his text before the Slavonic translation was made. This, however, is not the case. The author of

---

the *Canons*, even if he prepared an independent set of computations which disagreed on certain points with Eusebius. Gastgeber, "Die *Osterchronik*," emphasizes the fidelity of the *Chronicon Paschale* to Malalas and its utility in restoring the latter's often corrupt and lacunose text, which should lead us to pay particular attention to deviations from Malalas in the *Chronicon Paschale*. They may signal material that has fallen out of Malalas and been preserved in the *Chronicon Paschale*, but if we expect the *Chronicon Paschale* to faithfully follow Malalas, such deviations may also indicate intrusions from another source. In this case, the dating of the persecution to Domitian's fourteenth year, which is not found in Malalas, seems to indicate that another source, most likely the *Canons*, was used here in addition to Malalas; cf. Juhász, "Die Indiktionsangaben."

47 *Chron. Pasch.* 218th olympiad (Dindorf, *Chronicon Paschale*, 1:468).

48 *Chron. Pasch.* (Dindorf, *Chronicon Paschale*, 1:69).

49 *Chron. Pasch.* 113th olympiad (Dindorf, *Chronicon Paschale*, 1:321–22).

the *Chronicon Paschale* exploited both the *Canons* of Eusebius and the *Chronicle* of Malalas. He appears to have taken the form of the name of our historian from the *Canons*, but material attributed to Bouttios from Malalas. When he came to the reign of Domitian he took the notice, along with the citation of "Brouttios" (Βρούττιος), the Greek equivalent of Bruttius, from a version of the *Canons*. But he also recognized that there was a parallel passage in Malalas's chronicle, although there was a slight inconsistency there in the spelling of the name cited in connection with this material. He must have assumed, correctly, that the two references were to the same historian, but he further assumed, like Bentley, that the text of the *Canons* as he had it was more reliable. The Βούττιος that we take it he found in Malalas, after all, required only the addition of a single letter to bring it into conformity with the Βρούττιος of the *Canons*. The author of the *Chronicon Paschale* apparently further recognized the author cited in regard to Domitian as the same one cited in regard to Perseus. In preparing or revising his material he emended the citation he had taken from Malalas's discussion of Perseus to agree with the one he took from the *Canons*' notice on Domitian's persecution.[50] With both the *Canons* and Malalas at hand, but no further information that we know of, the author of the *Chronicon Paschale* was faced with a dilemma almost

50 Zuckerman, "Heraclius and the Return of the Holy Cross," 203–4, has proposed that the author of the *Chronicon Paschale* wrote in such haste that he did not have time to find material to fill the carefully noted periods from the point when his copy of Malalas gave out as a source until his own ending of the restoration of the True Cross. He would, no doubt, reject the suggestion of careful revision on the part of the author of the *Chronicon Paschale*, nor, admittedly, would he be the only one. I am dubious of Zuckerman's proposition, not least because overall it seems to accord better with the modern interest in Byzantine historians as sources for contemporary events than with the antiquarian and chronographic interests of Byzantine chroniclers themselves. It would not be impossible, however, to reconcile his proposal that the author of the *Chronicon Paschale* decided on his initial end date of 21 March 629 on account of the coincidence of the Alexandrian date for the creation of the world and the calendar date of the deposition of the Cross, if it were not for his insistence that this coincidence "was what launched the author on his project." I expect, rather, that the author must have been contemplating a project on the scale of the *Chronicon Paschale* for some time and could have worked over the material covering earlier ages with a certain amount of leisure. In general, I assume that even when they depended on previous authors for their treatment of certain historical eras, Byzantine chroniclers were rarely acting simply as copyists but were actively engaged in a process of selecting, editing, and recasting.

identical to the one that presently occupies us: is the "Brouttios" of the *Canons* or the "Bouttios" of Malalas to be preferred as the correct form of author's name? He chose "Brouttios," but we have no reason to believe he chose correctly. The *Chronicon Paschale*, then, may not support the intrusive rho of Bruttius, but it does corroborate the diphthong in Bouttios, as well as the identity of the author cited by Malalas and the one found in the derivatives of Eusebius's *Canons*.

One more proposition in regard to the name of Bouttios remains to be dealt with, namely that it was a figment of Malalas's imagination. Treadgold has argued that the chronicle of John Malalas is merely a hasty and inexpert paraphrase of the now altogether lost chronicle of Eustathius of Epiphania, which Malalas tried to pass off as his own work by introducing citations of a number of fabricated sources. Treadgold has counted "Bottius" among these bogus sources and considered him nothing more than an invention of Malalas.[51] He calls in support of his contention Jeffreys's observation that the historian's name is "suspiciously close to the cult name Zeus Bottios," but if Jeffreys meant to anticipate Treadgold here, she was almost imperceptibly subtle about it.[52] Certain facts also make "Bottius" exceptional among the several sources Treadgold thinks were made up. While all of the other dubious historians are cited for nearly contemporary events and would seem to be early Byzantine historians, Bouttios, as Treadgold himself notes, is cited for events no later than 96 CE and appears to be rather earlier than the rest.[53] Treadgold also suggests that Malalas endeavored to efface all traces of the inspiration of the names of his bogus sources, including Zeus Bottios, but the fact is that Malalas is one of our only two sources for the cult name and the only one who preserves the form closest to the historian's name (as opposed to Libanius's "Bottiaios").[54] Nor did Treadgold take into account the evidence of Jerome's "Bruttius," the *Chronicon Paschale*'s "Brouttios," or George the Syncellus's "Brettios," which may add a degree of confusion to the date and identity of Bouttios, but certainly tend to corroborate his existence as a

51 Treadgold, "Byzantine World Histories," 723–24; cf. Treadgold, *Early Byzantine Historians*, 248–49, 251.

52 Treadgold, "Byzantine World Histories," 725; cf. Treadgold, *Early Byzantine Historians*, 248. See E. Jeffreys, "Malalas' Sources," 174.

53 Treadgold, "Byzantine World Histories," 723–24; cf. Treadgold, *Early Byzantine Historians*, 248.

54 Treadgold, "Byzantine World Histories," 728. See Malalas 8.12.

real, if obscure, source rather than a figment of Malalas's imagination. Moreover, Treadgold's argument further holds that the original form, the wording and arrangement, of Eustathius's chronicle is more accurately preserved in the fragments of the chronicle of John of Antioch.[55] But the remains of John of Antioch do not support Treadgold's reconstruction, at least not in regard to Bouttios, as they differ in substance and content from what we find in Malalas. In those cases where he cites Bouttios, Malalas does not appear simply to have added a citation to a ready-made narrative, but rather covers different topics and offers substantially different material.[56] Whatever one makes of Treadgold's case, it would seem that Bouttios should be removed from his list of possibly fabricated sources and considered an actual author and citations of him reckoned with as such, and Treadgold himself has conceded as much in recently published work.[57]

55 Treadgold, "Byzantine World Histories," 732–40; cf. Treadgold, *Early Byzantine Historians*, 311–29.

56 This can be demonstrated from both of the recent collections of the fragments of John of Antioch—Roberto, *Ioannis Antiocheni Fragmenta* and Mariev, *Ioannis Antiocheni Fragmenta*—but it is most obvious in the more conservative collection of Mariev, which takes into account the century and a half or so of scholarship since Müller, *FHG*, first collected the fragments, including the most intense period of academic investigation of John of Antioch. Roberto (F 13.2–3) treats as a fragment of John of Antioch a narrative of Perseus that is largely similar to that found in Malalas, but includes neither the citation of Bouttios nor any mention of the sacrifice of Parthenope at the foundation of Tarsus. While the absence of a citation of Bouttios might seem to support Treadgold's argument, the similar absence of the virgin sacrifice shows that this argument would beg the question of Malalas's source for the tyche sacrifice narratives. Mariev (F 1), by contrast, offers a completely different text as evidence for the treatment of the mythological period in John's chronicle, a disjointed assemblage of facts and interpretations with no continuous narrative from the *Excerpta Salmasiana*, which is only accidentally similar to Malalas and does not mention Perseus at all, let alone Bouttios. In regard to the other two instances of the citation of Bouttios, Roberto and Mariev are in agreement. John of Antioch's treatment of Alexander (Roberto FF 74–77, Mariev FF 25–29) seems to have differed substantially from that of Malalas in both narrative and detail. The same is true of his discussion of the reign of Domitian (Roberto FF 189–90, Mariev FF 133–34), which does not seem to have included any mention of a persecution of the Christians. Treadgold, "Review of Roberto and Mariev," has been critical of both of the recent editions of the fragments of John of Antioch, especially that of Mariev.

57 Treadgold, "Byzantine Historiography," 533, n. 14.

It would be gratifying to think that we have closed the book on the problem of the name of the historian we are studying and forestalled any further controversy, but that is manifestly not the case. A good argument—the best, in my opinion—can be made that Bouttios was the proper form of his name and all the other versions that appear are corruptions to one degree or another, but a plausible case might also be made that each of those seeming deviations is the genuine form of the name. Likewise, the most cogent interpretation of a number of confusing strands of evidence seems to be that Eusebius did not know of Bouttios and "Bruttius" makes his first appearance in a post-Eusebian version of the *Canons*, added by some editor who reworked the text before it came into the hands of Jerome. We can insist, at least, that Bouttios should be excused from Treadgold's list of bogus sources and dealt with as a real author, and not the invention of a sly and self-serving Malalas. On the whole, the matter of the historian's name calls for a humble admission of agnosticism, rather than an attempt to overcome reasonable skepticism with assertive bluster. "Bouttios" may, nevertheless, remain a useful and convenient cipher, and it is by this name that we shall continue to refer to the object of our attention.

Date

Determining the date of Bouttios is a matter of narrowing the possible interval. The broadest parameters are established by reasonably indisputable facts, but their refinement depends on the conjectures that we have already made in assembling the fragments. The much narrower window we arrive at, and perhaps even something of a pinpoint within it, seems to be confirmed by the context and motivation for Bouttios's writing, which we have yet to discuss.

We can say, in the most conservative terms, that Bouttios must have written at some time between 96 and 565 CE. The terminus post quem is the date given by Eusebius for the persecution of the Christians under Domitian, the latest event for which Bouttios is cited by Malalas or any other author. It makes no real difference in this discussion whether that persecution was real or invented,[58] but if Bouttios dealt with an event whose reality is open to question we might be inclined to place him rather later than sooner after that event. The terminus ante

58 See Merrill, *Essays*, 148–73; Keresztes, "The Jews, the Christians."

quem comes from the last firm date in the final version of Malalas's *Chronicle*, that is, the death of Justinian in 565,[59] and so the earliest utterly indisputable mention of Bouttios. There is no reason, though, to think that the inclusion of Bouttios, material from his work, and citations of his name belongs to the revisions that might have accompanied the additions made to the end of Malalas's work—whether by his own hand or another's—and we are probably justified in reducing the terminus ante quem to 532 or 533, the probable date of the earliest edition of the *Chronicle*.[60]

The four hundred years and more between 96 and 532/3 CE, however, are so broad a period for an author as to be practically meaningless and certainly unhelpful. But we can narrow this interval considerably. First, we have argued that all of the accounts of tyche sacrifice in Malalas are derived from Bouttios and assigned them, along with some portion of the surrounding narrative, to him as fragments. This seems reasonable as Bouttios is the only author (who cannot be excluded on other grounds) cited for the accounts in which tyche sacrifices occur, and tyche sacrifices appear in two of the three narratives for which he is cited. Second, we have included among these accounts of tyche sacrifice the "bloodless sacrifice" performed by Constantine at the dedication of his new capital in 330, which inaugurated the new tyche of the city (**F 34**). This is also reasonable on literary grounds, because without a culmination in Constantine's heroic reversal of the former ritual order the various accounts of tyche sacrifice must remain a largely pointless catalog of pagan atrocities that operated only at the lowest level of slander. The identification of some treatment of the dedication of Constantinople as part of Bouttios's work allows us to move the terminus post quem forward to 330.

The assignment of this fragment, moreover, helps us to settle the question of Eusebius's acquaintance with Bouttios. If Bouttios was writing about the events of 330, he must have been writing after that date and certainly after 325/6, when Eusebius produced the final edition of his *Chronicle*.[61] Eusebius would presumably not have cited an author who had not yet finished his work. The citation of "Bruttius" in Jerome's translation of the *Chronicle*, then, must reflect an addition

59 Croke, "Malalas, the Man and His Work," 21–25.

60 Croke, "Malalas, the Man and His Work," 18–21; see above, pp. 21–23.

61 See above, pp. 122–30.

that had crept into the Greek text after Eusebius finished with it. The anonymous pagans of the *Ecclesiastical History* are a better reflection of Eusebius's sources, or the authorities he wanted to indicate, on the persecution under Domitian. This determination is significant for the dating of Bouttios, since it means that Eusebius's *Chronicle* cannot provide a terminal date for Bouttios.

The identification of Bouttios with Jerome's "Bruttius" also helps us to draw his terminus ante quem much closer to his terminus post quem. Once again, it is unreasonable to posit that there were two different historians with remarkably similar names who wrote on the same matters and were known in the same circles of Christian historiography. The assumption that Bouttios and "Bruttius" are one and the same is much safer. Jerome's citation of "Bruttius" is the earlier, but because it is shared with a number of Greek authors who depend on some text of Eusebius's *Canons* and not on Jerome, we can only say that Jerome was not responsible for the citation of "Bruttius," but found it already in the Greek exemplar he translated. Jerome took up the work of translating the *Chronicle* in 380/1. The revisions he made almost immediately are irrelevant to the question of dating, since if the citation of "Bruttius" was already in his exemplar, it was not among the additions he made to his translation. So we arrive at 380, when we know Jerome to have had his Greek exemplar of the *Canons* in hand, as a date for the earliest citation of Bouttios and thus for a terminus ante quem as well.

I have previously suggested that the inclusion of material from Bouttios in the *Excerpta Latina Barbari* could help us to date him, but have since abandoned this position. The main chronography of the *Excerpta* ends, perhaps quite by accident, at 387, but the latest event mentioned in it is the death of Theophilus of Alexandria in 412, although a list of Roman emperors down to Anastasius (r. 491–518) was also inserted at some point. On the assumption that the *Excerpta* was composed shortly after 412 and that the material from Bouttios was part of the initial composition, I proposed 412 as a rough terminus ante quem for Bouttios.[62] Further investigation has led me to believe that the material from Bouttios was added, with a specific purpose in mind, to a much sparser chronological frame some time between 536 and 539.[63] As a result, the *Excerpta* is rendered a little less helpful than Malalas, who can offer 532, in determining a terminal date for

62 Garstad, "Tyche Sacrifices," 89–93.

63 Garstad, "Barbarian Interest," 25–34, 39–40.

Bouttios. With the determination that the earliest surviving citation of Bouttios is in Jerome's translation of the *Chronicle*, however, we need not turn to either Malalas or the *Excerpta* for Bouttios's terminus ante quem. Jerome reduces this date by a good century and a half.

This leaves the considerably more workable interval of the fifty years between 330 and 380 for the period of Bouttios's activity, but it can be further narrowed. The span of time we have arrived at places Bouttios in the midst of the fourth century, and the controversies of the fourth century between pagans and Christians constitute the context that best explains the remains of Bouttios. The relation of Bouttios to the figures and rhetoric of the fourth century will be discussed in detail below. It will suffice for now to touch upon those points that have a bearing on the problem of dating.

We can, in the first place, corroborate the terminus post quem we determined by assembling the fragments. Bouttios's treatment of Constantine and his predecessors seems to reflect the thought of Eusebius of Caesarea, particularly as expressed in the *Praise of Constantine*, delivered as a panegyric on 25 July 336, the thirtieth anniversary of the emperor's reign.[64] Both Eusebius and Bouttios present Constantine as a uniquely climactic figure, whose new and special relationship with God redeemed the office of kingship and allowed its true form to be realized. Constantine was supposed to be the first true king, after a succession of illegitimate tyrants who had been led into vice, idolatry, and villainy. It may be because Eusebius's work survives intact, while we only have the *disjecta membra* of Bouttios, that we are left with the impression that the latter alludes to the former, but the notion that Bouttios was building on ideas worked out and articulated for the first time by Eusebius is unavoidable, that is, that Bouttios, a relative nonentity, is indebted to the towering authority of Eusebius. If Bouttios refers to Eusebius, he must have been writing after the Tricennalian oration was delivered in 336. This may not move us much farther ahead, but a further consideration might.

The fragments of Bouttios reflect not only praise of Constantine but also Christian attacks on the emperor Julian (r. 361–363), as will be argued at length in chapter 7. Reference to the "bloodless sacrifice" which is pivotal to the narratives of tyche sacrifice in Malalas also crops up in the orations Gregory of Nazianzus wrote immediately after the death of Julian in 363 to celebrate the event and

64 Barnes, *Constantine and Eusebius*, 253–55.

reflect on the apostate emperor's life.[65] Julian was early on accused of abetting and approving rites of human sacrifice, and while accusations of direct involvement seem to have been late in coming, come they did.[66] Stories of Julian's antipathy to the Christianity of his hated "half-uncle" Constantine and of his own successors are often centered, moreover, on the figure of the tyche.[67] All these factors suggest that the various accounts of tyche sacrifice, which we have attributed to Bouttios, were written in response to the reign of Julian, that Julian is the real, if unnamed, target of Bouttios's polemic against pagan kings. If this is so, and a substantial argument will be put forward that it is indeed the case, Bouttios must have written after the commencement of Julian's sole reign in November 361. If we allow time for news of Julian's open profession of paganism on his accession, his simultaneous renunciation of Christianity, and his stance favoring the traditional cult and its adherents to spread throughout the Empire, we might say that he wrote some time after the early months of 362.

If we read the fragments of Bouttios as the remains of a diatribe against Julian—an approach for which we shall argue in chapter 7—we gain some very real help in determining the date *after* which he wrote, but not the date *before* which he wrote. Censure of the Apostate need not have followed hard on the heels of the end of his reign. Indeed, Christian attacks on Julian continued long after his death. Cyril of Alexandria's *Contra Julianum*, a refutation of the emperor's *Contra Galilaeos*, did not appear until some time in the third decade of the fifth century.[68] We are fortunate to have a terminus ante quem provided by other means, the *Chronicle* of Jerome. Nevertheless, there are indications of a certain immediacy in Bouttios's response to Julian.

Bouttios is not reacting to a general impression of Julian or to a demonized memory of the Apostate, but rather to specific points in the position and

65 Greg. Naz., *Or.* 4.4, 52; 5.29.

66 Greg. Naz., *Or.* 4.86, 87, 90, 92; cf. 2.9, 13, 23, 25, 26, 4.93, 94, 5.26, 29, 39; John Chrys., *De Sancto Babyla et Contra Julianum et Gentiles* 14 (79); Socrates Schol., *HE* 3.13.11; Theodoret, *HE* 3.26; Philostorgius, *HE* 7.4; see Shepardson, "Rewriting Julian's Legacy," 109–10; Hilton, "Myth and Narrative Fiction," 42–48. See below, pp. 213–15.

67 See below, pp. 215–17.

68 Malley, *Hellenism and Christianity*, 239–44. Wilken, *John Chrysostom and the Jews*, 129, dates this same work to the fourth decade of the fifth century without discussing the grounds for his dating; he does, however, make it clear (128–30) that the memory of Julian maintained its grip on Christian imaginations long after the Apostate's death.

polemics of the emperor, as articulated in his own writings. Moreover, the works of Julian to which Bouttios is responding are most often those Julian composed during his stay in Antioch from July of 362 until March of 363. We know from Julian himself that he was subjected to a certain amount of satire and raillery by its citizens during his residence in Antioch.[69] None of these verbal assaults is known to survive, but we may have some residue of them in the remains of Bouttios. The correspondences between the fragments of Bouttios and the writings of Julian will be examined in detail below,[70] but at least two points suggest that Bouttios may have written while Julian was resident in Antioch.

First, although Bouttios's wording and his charges against pagan rulers are similar to the rhetoric of the accusations made against Julian, there is no indication that Bouttios mentioned Julian. It would be a wise precaution, if, as seems to be the case, Bouttios wrote under his own name, to let previous pagan kings stand in the place of Julian and let the real target of his polemic go unnamed. Julian himself tells us that the people of Antioch at times masked their sentiments of discontent in veiled language, for example by expressing a preference for "the chi and the kappa," meaning Christ and Constantius.[71] Over the brief span of his reign Julian seems to have been remarkably tolerant of his detractors, but Bouttios may have calculated that this forbearance would not last.[72] Such a precaution, however, might have been necessary not only while the emperor was actually in Antioch, or even up to the time of his death, but also as long as many of the officials he appointed during his stay in Antioch still held power. So while the apparent absence of Julian from the writings of Bouttios might suggest that he wrote during the Apostate's reign or even during his residence in Antioch, they are not sure indications of the time of his writing.

69 Julian, *Mis.* 345D, 355D–356A, 364B; cf. Socrates Schol., *HE* 3.17.4–9; Sozomen, *HE* 5.19.2–3; Malalas 13.19; see Marcone, *Giuliano*, 187–96. On the Antiochene context of certain of Julian's writings, see Festugière, *Antioch païenne et chrétienne*, 63–89.

70 See below, pp. 217–25.

71 Julian, *Mis.* 357A; cf. 360D.

72 For what it is worth, Bowersock, *Julian the Apostate*, 87–93, concluded that the tendency of Julian's reign, and especially its final months, was toward more and more open and harsh persecution of the Christians in the Empire. See also Marcone, *Giuliano*, 182–86, 207–13.

The second point, even if it is a good deal more enigmatic, may also offer greater chronological precision. In the *Misopogon*, his riposte to his critics in Antioch, offered as he was leaving the city, Julian said that the Antiochenes preferred Christ to Zeus, Apollo, and Calliope, saying of Calliope that she "laid bare your contrivance" (ἣ τὸ σόφισμα ὑμῶν ἀπεγύμνωσεν).[73] Zeus, the chief of the old gods, and Apollo, the patron deity of the Seleucid founders of Antioch, whose shrine at Daphne was a battleground for the competing faiths, are quite understandable representatives of the pagan pantheon, but such a minor character as Calliope is an odd addition to their company, even if she had a shrine and cult at Antioch and was considered the patroness, presumably the tyche, of the city.[74] Nor does Julian explain what he means by saying that Calliope revealed the contrivance or fallacy (τὸ σόφισμα) of the Christians of Antioch. Julian's meaning must have been readily apparent to his audience, but we are left to guess at it. It may have been a rejoinder to Bouttios.

Calliope is given by Bouttios as the name of the tyche Trajan established for Antioch through a virgin sacrifice (**F 31**). As the tyche sacrifices seem to have been a distinctive element of Bouttios's polemical history, Julian may have relied on no more than a reference to the figure of Calliope to insist that this particular diatribe against him and his religious party was groundless. Anyone conversant with the history of the city and its cults would know, in the first place, that there was no tradition of virgin sacrifice behind the figure of the tyche, and moreover that there was no reliable record of venerable rulers practicing human sacrifice.[75] Julian may also have been pointing out an inconsistency in Bouttios's accounts of

73 Julian, *Mis.* 357C.

74 Libanius (*Or.* 1.102) confirms that Calliope was considered the patroness of Antioch in Julian's day, as well as that she was among the deities of the city to whom Julian performed public acts of worship (*Or.* 15.79). Calliope appears in this list of gods worshipped by Julian, but Tyche does not, although Julian tells us himself (*Mis.* 346B) that he rendered worship to Tyche at Antioch; presumably this was because Calliope was the proper name of the manifestation of Tyche at Antioch and it would be redundant to list both Calliope and Tyche. See Downey, *History of Antioch*, 216–17, 384.

75 As we shall suggest below (chap. 10), in the context of history in the "paranoid style" it is practically impossible to refute slanderous charges on the basis of an absence of evidence in accepted sources, because the accusers can always retort that the perpetrators of dastardly crimes are adept at covering their tracks. Perhaps this is another reason for Julian's pointing to Calliope in particular, since in the case of this tyche sacrifice narrative

the tyche of Antioch, since he has Seleucus Nicator sacrifice a girl by the name of Aimathe at the foundation of the city (**F 21**), a ritual that would usually establish the civic tyche, but it is not until Trajan sacrifices a virgin at the Middle Gate that the tyche of Antioch appears under her proper name of Calliope (**F 31**).[76] Thus a moment's informed consideration of Calliope and her presentation by Bouttios would reveal the contrivance, the fictional history, of one of his Christian detractors for what it was, so much imposture with the semblance, not the substance, of a historical record. But if this passage in the *Misopogon* is a reference to the slander of Bouttios, his writings must have been in circulation before March 363. Julian is not necessarily referring to Bouttios's accounts of tyche sacrifice in the *Misopogon*, but this is an altogether satisfying way to make sense of the otherwise inexplicable mention of Calliope, and this point should be taken into consideration in the matter of dating Bouttios.

In attempting to assign a date to Bouttios, the closer we move to precision the more we depend on conjecture. That is not to say that our every attempt is so much guesswork, but that the effort is largely based on clues and surmise rather than clear indicators. In the absence of better evidence, we shall have to be content with supposition and tentative assertions. On that basis, supposing, that is, that Bouttios wrote on the dedication of Constantinople and is to be identified with Jerome's "Bruttius," we can narrow the span from the years 96 to 565 down to the more workable interval between 330 and 380 for the time of Bouttios's writing. If we make the not unreasonable assumption (defended at length below) that Bouttios wrote in reaction to the reign of Julian, we can move the initial date up to 362. If we suppose that some time was required for Bouttios to be recognized as an authority worth citing in the Greek exemplar of the *Canons* Jerome had (which must at least marginally predate his translation, begun in 380), we should expect that he wrote closer to 362 than to 380. To say that Bouttios wrote earlier rather than later in this eighteen-year period is to put forward a precision in his dating that would be enviable in the case of many ancient authors, but we can

---

Bouttios seems to have overplayed his hand and reported that Trajan held a bridal procession, a very public event, for the virgin he sacrificed.

76 It is remarkable that while Seleucus sacrifices Aimathe at the foundation of Antioch, she is not said to become thereby the tyche of the city (**F 21**). Perhaps this was an adjustment in the light of the criticism of Julian intended to reconcile two of the accounts of virgin sacrifice at Antioch and the customary name of Antioch's civic tyche.

at least suggest a date of even greater accuracy. If we take the mystifying reference to Calliope in Julian's *Misopogon* to be a rebuttal of Bouttios's accounts of tyche sacrifice, then Bouttios will have been among those Antiochene detractors who poured forth their invective during the emperor's stay in their city. Bouttios would have written, as a consequence, between July 362 and March 363. This precise dating is extremely conjectural, but it accords with all of the evidence we can assemble for the dating of Bouttios, as well as the indications of his proper context and intentions.

Location

We must also depend on conjecture in order to identify a place, as well as a date, for Bouttios, but there are a number of circumstantial reasons that suggest Antioch as the most likely setting for his life and work. The historian's name, itself uncertain, is not a dependable indicator, but two of the forms offered by Malalas point to some connection with Antioch. If we are right in considering Bouttios the genuine form of our author's name and associating it with the epigraphic evidence for this name from Aetolia, then we can trace a line of transmission from Aetolia to Antioch directly, through the Aetolians settled in Antioch by Antiochus III.[77] And if we take "Bottios" to be not a slip of the pen but a variant form of the name—or possibly the correct form?—it has definite Antiochene associations, since Bottia was supposed to be the name of the village originally on the site of Antioch, and Bottios (or Bottiaios) was the epithet of Zeus at one of his temples in Antioch.[78] If, however, the historian was "Brouttios" or "Bruttius" after all, we are still all at sea; a Latin name hardly implies any fixed abode in the later Roman Empire. Nor do the fragments in which Bouttios is cited by name offer much help. Dealing as they do with such themes of universal interest as the heroes of myth, Alexander's career, and the persecution of the Church, they are not of such a nature as to betray some geographical focus or perspective on their author's part. That being said, though, Perseus seems to have been a particularly popular hero in the vicinity of Antioch, and Bouttios's treatment

77 Lib., *Or.* 11.119; see above, pp. 119–20 and 120, n. 7.
78 Malalas 8.12; Lib., *Or.* 11.76; see above, pp. 118–19.

of the persecution of Christians under Domitian, certainly as it is preserved in Malalas, does suggest an eastern orientation, since it mentions the flight of refugees to Pontus.[79]

It is when we turn to the series of tyche sacrifices, which we can ascribe to Bouttios, that we perceive an Antiochene point of view. Many of these, apart from those at such major centers as Alexandria and Constantinople, are said to have occurred at more specific sites in Antioch itself or at smaller centers in the broader region of the city, suggesting an interest in and knowledge of local monuments and history. The reports of these incidents ripple out from Antioch. Three reports of tyche sacrifice are situated in Antioch itself; two others are supposed to occur at Laodicea and Apamea in the Seleucis or Syrian Tetrapolis, which also included Antioch. A further two are said to take place in the adjacent region of Cilicia, at Tarsus and Anazarbus. Within a somewhat wider compass, tyche sacrifices are reported at Nyssa or Scythopolis in Palestine, which was considered part of Syria in the broader sense, whose metropolis was at Antioch, and at Ancyra and the province of Galatia and possibly Iconium in Asia Minor. Further afield, such incidents are said to have taken place at Gortyn on Crete, and of course Alexandria and Constantinople. (The geographical distribution of the sites of reported tyche sacrifice and their concentration in and around Antioch are indicated in figure 2, p. 58 above.) The fragments of Bouttios describing these events, as we have already suggested and will argue at greater length below, have certain affinities with what little we know of—might even be taken as evidence of—the attacks against Julian launched by the Antiochenes on the occasion of the emperor's visit to their city.[80] The rumors of Julian's own participation in rites of human sacrifice, which apparently informed the stories of tyche sacrifice (see p. 214 below), also appear to have circulated predominantly in the Greek east and

79 Van Hoof and Van Neuffelen, *Fragmentary Latin Histories*, 258, obfuscate the significance of this passage by claiming that Malalas offers a garbled version of what we find in the witnesses to Eusebius's *Chronicle*: "exile has become flight, and Ponza [i.e., Pontia] has become Pontus." On the contrary, with no mention of Flavia Domitilla there is no reason to associate the report in Malalas with the island of Pontia, and the plural makes it clear that this is an account of several Christians. Malalas has access to material from Bouttios not indicated by the various versions of Eusebius's *Chronicle*.

80 See Downey, "Julian the Apostate at Antioch."

in the vicinity of Antioch; indeed, some of these gruesome rituals were supposed to have taken place at the palace of Antioch itself.[81]

Finally, we should consider the avenues by which the fragments of Bouttios have been preserved. John Malalas, who was from Antioch and showed a marked interest in the history of his home city and the sources on it, cited Bouttios not once but three times, and seems to have made even more extensive use of his work.[82] Malalas's access to and familiarity with Bouttios further suggest that the writer somehow belonged to Antioch and that his work concentrated on that city. The fragments of Bouttios, moreover, are demonstrably consistent with an Antiochene setting.

The basic historical understanding evident in the fragments of Bouttios might also be said to reflect the exegetical method generally prevalent among the interpreters of the Bible in fourth- and fifth-century Antioch, as opposed to Alexandria. Whereas the Alexandrians tended to employ an allegorical reading of scripture and leap toward the hidden spiritual meaning of the text, following the lead of Origen, the greatest exponent of this method, as a rule the Antiochenes favored a historical and typological approach to understanding the Bible.[83] This

81 Greg. Naz., *Or.* 4.92; Theodoret, *HE* 3.27. As writers in Greek, Gregory and Theodoret are presumably more likely to have had access to stories current in the eastern, Greek portion of the empire.

82 See Croke, "Malalas, the Man and His Work," 6–11.

83 Wallace-Hadrill, *Christian Antioch*, 27–51; see also Burghardt, "On Early Christian Exegesis"; Schäublin, *Untersuchungen zu Methode und Herkunft*; Smalley, *Study of the Bible*, 14–20; Hidal, "Exegesis of the Old Testament"; Hauser and Watson, "Introduction and Overview," 43–47; Edwards, *Religions*, 234–37; Liebeschuetz, *East and West in Late Antiquity*, 408–22; Graves, *Biblical Interpretation*, xix–xxi. The traditional designation of separate Alexandrian and Antiochene schools and the hard-and-fast distinction between their exegetical methods, especially inasmuch as it sees the approach of Antioch as a precursor of the modern historico-critical method, has recently been challenged in favor of an understanding that does not deny certain tendencies identifiable with the two great seats of Christian learning in the East, but views them as the positions of a debate, especially over the principles of hermeneutics, going on within a common tradition; see Guillet, "Les exégètes d'Alexandrie et d'Antioche"; de Lubac, "'Typologie' et 'allégorisme'"; Wiles, "Theodore of Mopsuestia"; Froehlich, *Biblical Interpretation*, 19–23; Young, "Rhetorical Schools"; Wylie, "Exegesis of History," 60, 65; Nassif, "'Spiritual Exegesis'"; Simonetti, *Biblical Interpretation*, 67–77; Trigg, "Eustathius of Antioch's Attack," 220–21; O'Keefe, "Christianizing Malachi"; O'Keefe, "Impassible Suffering?"; Young, *Biblical Exegesis*, 161–213; Clark, *Reading Renunciation*,

entailed an attempt to establish a book or passage within its proper setting and circumstances and its historical context, as well as the actual event that occasioned the writing. It further eschewed any unwarranted allegory, rather preferring a readiness to identify in previous events "types" which prefigured later events, especially ones in the life of Christ. Typology, unlike allegory, insisted on the historical reality of both the previous event (the type), and the event it anticipated. An "insight" (*theoria*) permitted the interpreter to find a meaning in historical events that would have been lost on those unaware of salvation history.

Some such inclination of thought must lie behind the presentation of the gods in the Picus-Zeus narrative attributed to Bouttios, which is thoroughly grounded in a historical reality, albeit a specious one. The gods are not human inventions or emblematic personifications, but historical personages who lived and died at specific times, and as such their divinity can be rejected. Their skulduggery also anticipates the villainy of later pagan rulers. The one point where the narrative of the gods might seem to indulge in allegory, when Homer in his poetic fashion is said to have called "the yearning after fornication" by the name of Aphrodite, in fact affirms the historical approach, since it insists that the allegory in Homer's poem is a garbled recollection of an actual event, Helios's prosecution of a case of adultery (**F 1.9**). This same understanding comes across most clearly in the reconstruction of the origins of the tyche monuments. There is a complete rejection of the—quite correct—notion that the tyche statues in various cities represent the personification of an abstract idea of luck or fortune or of civic identity. Rather, they are taken to be images of the specific victims of specific crimes, crimes which are supposed to have been actual historical events. These monuments are treated much more as forensic evidence than as examples of art or representation. This is due not to a failure or incapacity to think

70–73; Young, "Alexandrian and Antiochene Exegesis"; Mitchell, "Patristic Rhetoric on Allegory"; Fairbairn, "Patristic Exegesis and Theology"; Young, "Traditions of Exegesis"; Torrance, "Barsanuphius, John, and Dorotheos," 67–70; cf. Connor, *Dumbstruck*, 75–101. The affinities with the historical approach discernible in Bouttios's treatment of the past might still be identified as Antiochene. I am immensely grateful to Emma Vosper of the University of Nottingham for providing me with a thorough bibliography on the exegetical method commonly identified with Antioch.

in abstract terms, but to a certain cast of mind, a trained inclination to think in terms of particular historical events, which we might associate with Antioch.[84]

The suggestion of an Antiochene setting for Bouttios also has implications for the account of the gods ascribed to him, implications which are not easy to interpret. The origin of the gods is Assyrian, but in fourth-century discourse the term "Assyrian" was not merely an archaeological designation. Already in the second century Tatian and Lucian (or the author of the *De Dea Syria* attributed to Lucian) had claimed to be "Assyrians" themselves, the former a Christian, it is worth noting, and the latter a pagan.[85] They were not, of course, saying that they had come from the heartland of the ancient state of Assur on the Tigris. The *De Dea Syria* itself makes it clear, when it refers to the Seleucid queen Stratonice as the wife "of the Assyrian king" (τοῦ Ἀσσυρίων βασιλέως), that "Assyrian" is being used throughout as a synonym for "Syrian," as it commonly was.[86] "Syria" was a remarkably imprecise term for the regions of the Levant, Mesopotamia, and into Asia Minor, and its inhabitants could be called, or call themselves, "Syrians." This included the Antiochenes.[87] In the *Misopogon* Julian calls the populace of Antioch "Syrians" and once even refers to their property as "Assyrian."[88] Nor can

84 Elm, *Sons, Fathers*, 401–3 (cf. 412–13), has associated the insistence of Diodore of Tarsus and Theodore of Mopsuestia that any search for the deeper meaning of a text (*theoria*) be firmly grounded in its historical and literal sense with their intellectual and exegetical opposition to Julian the Apostate. If this is so, Bouttios's literal and historical approach may be not only an Antiochene characteristic of his method but also germane to his apparent purpose of writing against Julian (see below, chap. 7).

85 Tatian, *Ad Gr.* 42; Lucian, *Syr. D.* 1; cf. Macrob., *Sat.* 1.17.66; see R. Grant, "Five Apologists," 12; Millar, *Roman Near East*, 227, 245–46, 454–56; Swain, *Hellenism and Empire*, 298–308; Elsner, "Describing Self," 126–27, 142–43; Lightfoot, *Lucian, On the Syrian Goddess*, 205–6, 289; Millar, "Theodoret of Cyrrhus," 120; Andrade, *Syrian Identity*, 293–94. On the disputed authorship of the *De Dea Syria*, see Elsner, "Describing Self," 123–25; Lightfoot, *Lucian, On the Syrian Goddess*, 184–208.

86 Lucian, *Syr. D.* 17, cf. *Scyth.* 9, where Lucian refers to himself as a "Syrian." Some manuscripts of Josephus, *AJ* 13.6.7 (213), likewise refer to the Seleucids as "Assyrian kings" (τῶν Ἀσσυρίων Βασιλέων), a variant of "kings of Syria" (τῶν Συρίας Βασιλέων). See Nöldeke, "ΑΣΣΥΡΙΟΣ ΣΥΡΙΟΣ ΣΥΡΟΣ"; Frye, "Assyria and Syria"; Parpola, "National and Ethnic Identity," 16–18; Rollinger, "Assyrios, Syrios, Syros"; Rollinger, "The Terms 'Assyria' and 'Syria' Again"; Andrade, *Syrian Identity*, 6; cf. Garstad, "Assyrian Hero's Romantic Interlude," 8.

87 See Philostr. of Tyana, *VA* 1.16.1.

88 Julian, *Mis.* 348C, 350B, 365A.

this be taken as an outsider's imposition or a provocative slight, since Libanius, a native of Antioch who made a living off his attainments in Greek culture, was still happy to call himself and his compatriots "Syrians."[89] In the region of ancient Assyria this sort of self-identification even extended to the local Christians' calling themselves *'Athorâyê* and remaining mindful of the deeds of Assyrian as well as Seleucid kings.[90] All of this goes to show that "Assyrian," or its equivalent "Syrian," was an ethnic designation that might be claimed by some Antiochenes. If Bouttios was among them, perhaps identifying himself as an Assyrian on the grounds that he was a resident of Antioch, what might this mean for his claim that the gods were Assyrian?

Tracing the origins of the ruling power of the Romans to one's own nation might have been quite gratifying, but embracing the gods as they are depicted by Bouttios as compatriots would afford a dubious distinction at best. An effort to arrogate divine origins to his own *ethnos* for the glory that offered can hardly lie behind Bouttios's making the gods Assyrians, but there may still be a point of pride at issue. Perhaps the intention was to make up for what was perceived as a deficiency in the textual resources deployed to refute paganism. Eusebius's *Praeparatio Evangelica* included the "theologies" of the Egyptians, Phoenicians, and Greeks, that is, renditions of euhemeristic accounts of the gods as humans associated with each of these nations, but there was no "Syrian theology."[91] This was essentially because the corpus of texts in Greek on the gods and myth, and more importantly Diodorus's *Bibliotheca*, Eusebius's principal source in this regard, had no such work to offer. Yet the "Assyrians," like the Egyptians, were accounted by no less an authority than Iamblichus a "holy people" with special knowledge of the divine.[92] This sentiment is even found in the *Praeparatio evangelica* itself, when Eusebius quotes Porphyry to the effect that the Chaldeans

89 Lib., *Or.* 1 (*De Fortuna/Autobiography*), 16; *Ep.* 4.13, 391.13; *Or.* 64.9. See Nock, "Praises of Antioch," 81.

90 Brock, "Christians in the Sasanian Empire," 16–17; Millar, *Roman Near East*, 494; Swain, *Hellenism and Empire*, 301; Parpola, "National and Ethnic Identity," 22; Becker, "Ancient Near East"; P. Wood, *"We Have No King,"* 82–83, 119–20, 123–24, 125–26, 178–83, 188, 258–59, 260–61; Butts, "Assyrian Christians," 599–601.

91 The "theologies" of the different nations are found throughout the first three books of the *Praeparatio Evangelica*.

92 Iambl., *Myst.* 1.2, 7.4, 9.4; see Millar, "Porphyry," 348.

or Assyrians were among the barbarian peoples, along with the Egyptians, Phoenicians, Lydians, and Hebrews, who had discovered a right path to the gods.[93] It would not do, from the perspective of apologetics, if these hallowed doctrines of the Assyrians did not in the end turn out to be a revelation that the so-called gods were, in fact, merely men. And if a text could not be found to demonstrate this, one could be invented, and a "Syrian" author might claim the authority of a native son for his composition.

The significance of the gods' Assyrian origins may, however, be more a question of the perceived nature of paideia, and a point of ideological, not ethnic pride. In the *Misopogon* Julian uses "Syrian" and "Assyrian" as more or less neutral ethnic designations, but in his anti-Christian diatribe the *Contra Galilaeos* he makes a few rather snide comments at the expense of the Syrians, characterizing them as an effeminate and listless race.[94] The point Julian is trying to make is that distinctive national traits must be produced by different national gods, but it would not be altogether beside his purpose to take aim at the very nature of the broader ethnic group from which the hated religion of his opponents arose. The insult must have cut rather deeply, as it was no doubt intended to, delivered in an attack written in Antioch against the favored creed of the Antiochenes. Perhaps one of them took it hard and attempted a riposte.

The reply, however, is not a slight in kind against Julian's own ethnos; Julian, never above self-deprecation, had already taken the sting out of such an insult by offering it himself, calling the Mysians from whom he traced his own descent boorish and graceless.[95] Rather, the counterblast may have been aimed at what Julian held nearest and dearest, the whole cultural tradition, religious, literary, pedagogical, and political, encompassed by the concept of paideia, which Julian opposed to Christianity. Bouttios's account of the gods contains an answer to Julian's claim that the arts had been the gift of the gods to improve the lives of men.[96] Instead of beneficial contributions to the common good, the arts supposedly cultivated by the "gods" are those of magic, seduction, and murder. In the same way, the broader claim that culture in the highest sense, paideia, was

93 Euseb., *Praep. evang.* 9.10.4.

94 Julian, *Contra Galilaeos* 116A, 138B. For the background of Julian's bigotry, see Isaac, *Invention of Racism*, 335–51.

95 Julian, *Mis.* 348D.

96 Julian, *Contra Galilaeos* 235B–D.

the magnificent gift of the Greeks—and to a much lesser extent the Romans—to mankind is refuted by the assertion that the gods came from Assyria.[97] If the arts and divine knowledge that make up paideia come from the gods, and the gods are not denizens of Greece but wayfarers from Assyria, the claim of the Greeks upon paideia becomes rather tenuous.[98] Bouttios's relation concerning Picus-Zeus and his family not only makes the content of the paideia Julian held so dear sordid in the extreme, it also insists that if it is the proper possession of any ethnos, it belongs not to the Greeks but to the Syrians whom Julian despised.

Ideological Adherence

The citation of Bouttios in regard to a persecution of the Christians under Domitian (**FF 27–29**) would indicate a sympathetic interest in the history of the Church. Such an interest would, in turn, indicate that Bouttios was himself a Christian. This is doubly so if the Domitianic persecution was for the most part a Christian fabrication, as has been suggested.[99] There would have been no actual event for a non-Christian historian to dispassionately note and remark upon, and a Christian historian would have had readier access to the sources that insisted it had in fact happened, as well as an interest in perpetuating the memory of the supposed happening. Nevertheless, some scholars have maintained that Bouttios, or Jerome's "Bruttius," was a pagan.[100] This is without exception because they have considered as complementary the passage in Eusebius's *Ecclesiastical History* that refers to several unnamed pagan writers who mentioned the persecution in which Flavia Domitilla was exiled and the citation of Bruttius for the persecution under Domitian in the Latin and Armenian translations of Eusebius's *Chronicle* (see above). On account of the virtually simultaneous revisions carried out on the *Ecclesiastical History* and the *Chronicle* especially, it is most unlikely that

97 See Liebeschuetz, "View from Antioch," 330–31.

98 On a similar apologetic argument with an ethnic basis in Eusebius's *Praeparatio Evangelica*, see Johnson, "Greek Ethnicity."

99 Merrill, *Essays*, 158–73; B. Jones, *Emperor Domitian*, 114–17; Ulrich, "Euseb, HistEccl III, 14–20"; Riemer, "Domitian"; Timpe, "Domitian als Christenfeind"; cf. Levick and Rich, "Bruttius," 1:593, 3:631; but see Keresztes, "The Jews, the Christians," 15–28.

100 Merrill, *Essays*, 164–65; von Stauffenberg, *Kaisergeschichte bei Malalas*, 237–38; Keresztes, "The Jews, the Christians," 16.

"Bruttius" can be identified with these anonymous pagan sources, and the citation of "Bruttius" in the *Chronicle* translations should not be assigned to Eusebius at all.[101] An attested interest in the persecution of Christians, and especially in what may very well have been a largely fictitious persecution, must stand as the best indication that Bouttios was a Christian. But it is not the only one.

The other two fragments from Malalas in which Bouttios is named as a source (**FF 7** and **16**) also disclose a Christian intention. The first, on Perseus, is not merely a rationalization of the hero's myth, although that is how it presents itself. It is fundamentally an attack on the character and conduct of Perseus. It is hard to say what interest a pagan would have had in depicting a hero as guilty of so many crimes and moral failings, but a Christian writer would have an obvious motive in redirecting popular reverence away from the figures of traditional myth and fortifying the faithful in their rejection of the old cult. This would be especially true of an Antiochene Christian, who must have been aware that in the neighboring region of Cilicia Perseus had long been revered as an ancestral hero and city founder.[102] A Christian of the fourth century, when the Mithraic cult still retained some vitality and was something of a rival to Christianity, would have had an added inducement to attack Perseus, if there is anything to David Ulansey's proposal that Mithraism identified Perseus with Mithras as the ruler and mover of the heavens.[103] If Perseus were considered in some circles a universal religious figure, rather than the hero of a variety of local cults, that would go

101 See above, pp. 120–30.

102 Ziegler, "Der Perseus-Mythos im Prestigedenken"; Ogden, *Perseus*, 119–21; Garstad, "Perseus and the Foundation of Tarsus."

103 Ulansey, "Mithras and Perseus"; Ulansey, *Origins of the Mithraic Mysteries*, 25–45, 93–94. Compelling as it may be, Ulansey's admittedly hypothetical and speculative thesis does not seem to have garnered much support, or even interest, among scholars. Swerdlow's review, "On the Cosmical Mysteries of Mithras," for instance, offers Ulansey's book as a cautionary tale about pushing astrological interpretations too far, but might itself be taken as a cautionary tale about dismissing uncomfortable evidence rather than attempting to account for it. Edwards, *Religions*, 112–17, characterizes Mithraism in the reign of Constantine as a religion on the wane, but it is hard to tell whether a valid generalization would hold true in all places, or in all minds, and Mithraism may have been perceived as a competitor with Christianity even if, on the whole, it was not; cf. Walsh, *Cult of Mithras*.

a long way to explaining why he warranted so much and such negative attention from Bouttios.

It is also possible that Julian's own writings may have invited a Christian treatment of Perseus. There is a passage in Cyril of Alexandria's *Against Julian* that preserves an excerpt from Julian's own *Against the Galilaeans*, in which Julian asks, "Of what kingdom shall I tell you, that of Perseus, or Aeacus, or Minos of Crete?" and then proceeds to describe at some length the strength and virtue of Minos's kingdom.[104] Minos is described very much as a figure of history, rather than myth, subduing pirates and driving back barbarians, extending his frontiers far and wide, ruling not only islands but coastlands as well, and establishing laws for his subjects. Julian's discussion of him seems to owe something to the *Archaeology* of Thucydides.[105] Cyril counters that what Minos's record really exhibits is an imperialistic lust for domination, and he recalls the ill regard for Minos of Homer and Callimachus, as well as the shameful love affairs of his daughters.[106] What is said of Perseus, he avers, he will pass over as so much stuff and nonsense, a sheer pack of lies.[107] But this dismissive assertion suggests that Julian did actually discuss Perseus, even if Cyril did not see fit to preserve that discussion. Presumably this treatment of Perseus would have been similar to the discussion of Minos: the presentation of a character of myth in historical terms, his accomplishments appropriate to a political history rather than an epic quest. Bouttios's account of Perseus, then, might be a send-up of Julian's, still rationalizing and historicizing, but a defamatory rather than a laudatory treatment of the hero.

A pagan, once again, would have no cause to charge Alexander with an atrocity like human sacrifice, as the second fragment (**F 16.1**) does, especially at a time when Alexander was being adopted as an emblematic patron of the pagan cause against Christianity. But that very association between Alexander and the formerly prominent institutions of the Empire would provide a Christian with

104 Julian, *Contra Galilaeos* 190C (cf. PG 76:789D–792A).

105 See Thuc. 1.4, 8.2–3.

106 Cyril Alex., *Contra Julianum* (PG 76:792A–D). Minos's bad reputation, despite being a king and a lawgiver, is confirmed by Plut., *Thes.* 16.3; see Hawes, *Rationalizing Myth in Antiquity*, 162.

107 Cyril Alex., *Contra Julianum* (PG 76:792C): παρείσθω δὲ τὰ Περσέως, μύθους ἔχοντα καὶ λήρου μεστὰ, καὶ ψευδοεπείας ὑπερβολήν.

a reason to denigrate the famous king. As early as Clement of Alexandria, who defined Alexander by the single attribute of conceit (τῦφος), Christian writers had taken a dim view of the Macedonian conqueror.[108] By Late Antiquity the figure of Alexander seems to have been set up as something of a rival to Jesus Christ; as Ory Amitay puts it, "Alexander served for a while as one of the rallying points for the polytheistic resistance to the advent of Christianity."[109] This role for Alexander is perhaps seen most clearly, on the pagan side at any rate, in the so-called contorniate medallions, which displayed images of Alexander along with those of characters from classical myth and Roman emperors, especially images that somehow reflected the story of Christ.[110] It is to such ornaments as these that John Chrysostom was no doubt referring when he warned his catechumens against wearing amulets that depicted Alexander, deriding as he did those who placed their hopes for salvation in the picture of a Greek king rather than the cross.[111] John Chrysostom also set up a pivotal contrast between the deification of Alexander the Great, enrolled by the Roman senate as the "thirteenth god" according to him, and the divinity of Christ, which he said was evident throughout the world in spite of human resistance.[112] Julian the Apostate, the bête noire of the Christians, despite himself having an ambivalent attitude toward Alexander, was closely associated with the Macedonian king in Christian rhetoric; the Church historian Socrates Scholasticus went so far as to claim that Julian considered himself the reincarnation of Alexander and on the basis of this presumption embarked on his own disastrous Persian expedition.[113] In the *Oracle of Ba'albek* (an early sixth-century text with antecedents in the late fourth century) Alexander is named, along with Herod and Seleucus, as one of the kings who will rise up against the Son of God and carry out bloody persecutions.[114] There

108 Clem. Alex., *Paed.* 1.7 (55.1). See Klein, "Zur Beurteilung Alexanders des Großen"; Djurslev, *Alexander the Great*.

109 Amitay, *From Alexander to Jesus*, 140, and 140–44 for full discussion.

110 Alföldi, *Die Kontorniaten*; Stoneman, "Latin Alexander," 181–82; Stoneman, *Alexander the Great*, 12, 200, 218; Dahmen, *Legend of Alexander the Great*, 37–38, 152–54.

111 John Chrysostom, *Ad illuminandos catechesis* 2.5; cf. SHA, *Tyr. Trig.* 14.3–6.

112 John Chrysostom, *Hom. 26 in II Cor.* 4–5.

113 Socrates Schol., *HE* 3.21.6–8. See Soraci, "La figura di Alessandro Magno"; R. Smith, *Julian's Gods*, 12–13. On Socrates' treatment of Julian in general, see Urbainczyk, *Socrates of Constantinople*, 156–9.

114 *Oracle of Baalbek*, 13 (line 61).

is even evidence that Alexander continued to receive worship, and so stand in direct competition to Christ, throughout the fourth century and later. Procopius of Caesarea records that up to his own day at Augila in Libya there were shrines to Ammon and Alexander of Macedon, where sacrifices were performed until the emperor Justinian (r. 527–565) abolished the cult.[115] The decidedly negative presentation of Perseus and Alexander in the fragments of Bouttios thus offers some indication that their author was a Christian.

Gelzer was so persuaded of the essentially Christian character of the remains of Bouttios that he proposed that if the historian was to be identified with the unnamed pagan sources of Eusebius, his writings must actually have been the work of a Christian author who falsely presented them as the product of a pagan's pen.[116] Levick and Rich, the scholars who have most recently undertaken an examination of the fragments of "Bruttius" or Bouttios, likewise incline to the view that it is "altogether more probable" that those fragments represent the composition of a Christian author.[117] Working from those examples in which Bouttios is named, it is possible to proceed to discern a Christian intention in the other fragments we have attributed to Bouttios: the presentation of the gods as not only long-dead mortals but also scoundrels and malefactors, the imputation of unspeakable and barbarous crimes to the honored—but pagan—rulers of the past, and the ultimate heroization of Constantine. When the fragments are considered in this light, we are no doubt best advised to speak of the ideological adherence rather than simply the religion of their author, since his was clearly no accidental allegiance of perfunctory observance, but an active commitment to the advancement of the cause he espoused.

We are now in a position to offer a brief description of Bouttios as he can be reconstructed on the basis of the fragments of his work. There is some reason for selecting Bouttios as the historian's name, out of all the alternatives presented to us, but the other options cannot be categorically dismissed. He seems to have

115 Procop., *Aed.* 6.2.14–20.

116 Gelzer, *Sextus Julius Africanus*, 1:282–3; cf. Peter, *Historicorum Romanorum Reliquiae*, 2:ccviiii.

117 Levick and Rich, "Bruttius," 1:594–95, 3:631.

written some time between 330 and 380, although there are also indications that he wrote while Julian was resident in Antioch from July 362 until March 363. He himself appears to have been Antiochene, and far from being merely an accident of birth, his intellectual milieu informed the subjects he chose and how he handled them. Bouttios was also a Christian; this seems more definite than most of what we can say about him, and again he did not simply happen to be a Christian, but rather his ideological adherence determined the sort of work he wrote. That work, its genre and its structure, will be the subject of the next chapter.

6

BOUTTIOS'S WORK

The chief question in regard to Bouttios's work seems to be one of genre, and on the face of it the question appears quite straightforward. He wrote about the events of the past, so he must have written a history. Even when the characters of myth come up in the fragments, they are discussed as historical personages. And Malalas calls him a chronographer. But much of what remains of Bouttios is incompatible with a chronography. His treatments of the gods and of Alexander are inconsistently slotted into the chronological structures of the *Excerpta* and Malalas. His remarkably short duration for the Assyrian kingdom is irreconcilably at odds with the canonical determinations of chronography. He seems to treat the past not as a succession of connected events but in terms of tectonic shifts denominated by outsized personalities, Nebuchadnezzar and Alexander, and broad abstractions like servitude and liberty. And he regularly employs the recognized tricks and turns of fiction.

Indeed, the work of Bouttios gives every indication of having been a self-conscious and purposeful fiction. In this it has a number of affinities with a contemporary piece of writing, the *Caesars* of Julian. And the anti-Christian *Tendenz* of Julian's work is reflected in the antipagan slant of Bouttios. His work, nevertheless, had the form of history and may even have been intended to be taken seriously as a history. So the questions raised by the fragments of Bouttios, including that of how fictional material relates to historical form, are answered not so much by defining the genre of his work as by identifying his polemical or didactic purpose and the import of the ingredients of his composition. Bouttios exploits the

characteristic ingredients of fiction not merely to garnish a record of the past, but also to guide the responses of his readers and to give structure and direction to his work as a whole. On the basis of their reading in the novels and in literature generally, Bouttios's audience would have known how to react to stories of virgin sacrifice and to recognize a hero who put a stop to them. Bouttios's work may have passed for a history, but it was a tendentious history meant to steer the sentiments of its audience in regard to a lively contemporary debate, and to that end drew on devices familiar from fiction.

First, however, we might address the question of the language in which Bouttios wrote. Hermann Peter included him under the name of "Bruttius" in his collection of the fragments of the Roman historians, and although this inclusion, as well as the form of the name, might suggest that Peter took him for a Roman—whatever that might mean in respect to a person in the later Roman Empire—he perhaps prudently did not broach the question of the historian's ethnicity or language.[1] In going over the same ground with the benefit of more than a century's worth of scholarship, Levick and Rich have seen things rather differently, stating that the balance of probability indicates that the Christian chronography, as they understand the work, of "Bruttius" was "no doubt written in Greek."[2] In fact, they go so far as to concede that Peter may have erred in counting "Bruttius" among the Roman historians in the first place: "A Christian universal chronicle in Greek would hardly fit our criteria for inclusion in the present collection. However, in view of the uncertainty over the authorship and character of the work, we have retained it rather than relegating it to the Appendix."[3]

Peter Van Nuffelen has nevertheless aired the suspicion that "he may have written in Latin."[4] There is nothing to support this suspicion, however, but acquiescence to Syme's rather dubious identification of the historian with C. Bruttius Praesens or an identification with some other Bruttius—Levick and Rich raise the possibility of a freedman of the noble Bruttii—along with the altogether

1 Peter, *Historicorum Romanorum Reliquiae*, 2:ccviii–ccviiii.

2 Levick and Rich, "Bruttius," 1:594–95.

3 Levick and Rich, "Bruttius," 1:595.

4 Van Nuffelen and Van Hoof, *Clavis Historicorum*, 77. They say, however, in Van Hoof and Van Nuffelen, *Fragmentary Latin Histories*, 253, "The language in which Bruttius wrote cannot be determined."

dangerous supposition that someone with a Latin name must have written in Latin.[5] The evidence is against this supposition's having any merit. All of the writers we know to have exploited Bouttios—the interpolator of an early version of the *Canons* of Eusebius, the compiler of the Greek original of the *Excerpta Latina Barbari*, and John Malalas (or rather one of his immediate sources)—themselves wrote in Greek, and so were much more likely to employ sources in Greek. In the passage on Perseus (**F 7.1**), Bouttios's treatment is contrasted with that of a, we may say *another*, Greek author, Euripides; such a contrast is more likely to be made, either by Bouttios himself or by someone who picked him up, between two authors writing in the same language. How likely is it that a Latin author would have put it about that Alexander the Great freed the Romans from the domination of the Assyrians, Persians, Parthians, and Medes (**F 16.1**), when Livy spoke in disparaging terms of those "Greeklings" who imagined that Alexander would have bested the Romans if he had met them in battle?[6] Judging by what Malalas conveys of it, Bouttios's discussion of the persecution under Domitian (**F 27**) concentrated not on Flavia Domitilla and the Roman court, but on events in the eastern, Greek-speaking parts of the empire, where many Christian refugees are said to have fled to Pontus.[7] And when we turn to the fragments that are not explicitly attributed, especially on the tyche sacrifices, they once again show the greatest familiarity with the cities and monuments of the Greek East. Raising a question concerning the language of Bouttios is an extension of an argument concerning the correct form of his name, and offers us little insight into his work.

5 Syme, "Praesens," 288–91. As mentioned above (pp. 124–25), Syme's identification rests on nothing more than the coincidence of names and the likelihood that C. Bruttius Praesens's position would have afforded him the sort of insider information that might make rich fodder for a history; Levick and Rich, "Bruttius," 1:594, rightly reject it. Levick and Rich, "Bruttius," 1:595, may throw out the possibility of a freedman to account for a Christian chronographer writing under the name of Bruttius, but they also assume he would have been writing in Greek.

6 Livy 9.17–19. See Morello, "Livy's Alexander Digression"; Diana Spencer, *Roman Alexander*, 41–53; Braccesi, *L'Alessandro occidentale*, 52–54, 201–13; Garstad, "Rome in the *Alexander Romance*," 485–87.

7 Van Hoof and Van Neuffelen, *Fragmentary Latin Histories*, 258, unsucessfully attempt to negate this evidence by claiming, with no justification, that "Pontus" is a confused form of "Ponza," or "Pontia." See above, p. 146, n. 79.

Bouttios's Work a Chronography?

Levick and Rich consider Bouttios, or "Bruttius" as they call him, most likely to have been not only a Christian but also the author of a Christian chronography.[8] This assumption is only natural. Malalas does call Bouttios a "chronographer" (χρονογράφος) twice, but too much should not be read into this, as Malalas is quite liberal in his use of the term, applying it to authors like Tatian, Clement of Alexandria, and even Moses, who provide chronological information even if that was not the chief purpose of their works.[9] In general terms, chronography was among the genres of history writing, along with ecclesiastical history and hagiography, at which the Christian historians of Late Antiquity excelled and which they made their own proper preserve.[10] The fragments of Bouttios in particular are found in works with an overtly chronographic structure and intent, the *Excerpta Latina Barbari* and the *Chronicle* of John Malalas, where they are fixed to some point in a chronography. It is those very chronographic placements, however, that tell against Bouttios's work itself having been a chronography.

If Bouttios had written a chronography we would expect the dates of the events and the figures he discusses to be carried over from his own work to the chronicles that borrowed his material. But this is not what we find. Where we can check, Bouttios's fragments are assigned very different relative or absolute dates in the *Excerpta* and in Malalas. The account of the gods that we have assigned to Bouttios is synchronized in the *Excerpta* and in Malalas respectively with different biblical dates which are separated by centuries. The *Excerpta* sets Picus-Zeus in the time of the Judges, but Malalas inserts the account of Picus-Zeus in the first generation after the Tower of Babel and the Dispersion of the Nations.[11] Likewise, the *Excerpta* calculates 5,137 years from Adam to the death of Alexander, while Malalas counts 5,557 years from Adam to the (not precisely defined) "victory" of Alexander (ἕως τῆς Ἀλεξάνδρου τοῦ Μακεδόνος νίκης).[12] In both cases we would expect consistent chronological placement for episodes

8 Levick and Rich, "Bruttius," 1:594–95.

9 Papademetriou, "Οἱ ʽΣοφοὶ Χρονογράφοι.'"

10 Momigliano, "Pagan and Christian Historiography."

11 *ELB* 1.6.1 (Garstad, *Apocalypse/Alexandrian World Chronicle*, 187); Malalas 1.8 (Thurn, *Ioannis Malalae Chronographia*, 9). See **FF 1.1** and **2.1**.

12 *ELB* 1.8.4 (Garstad, *Apocalypse/Alexandrian World Chronicle*, 217); Malalas 8.2 (Thurn, *Ioannis Malalae Chronographia*, 147). See **FF 16.1** and **20.1**.

taken from a chronology. What we have suggests that the treatments of Picus-Zeus and the other god-kings and of Alexander did not have a predetermined chronological position, and the compilers who borrowed them felt free to place them in time as they saw fit. In short, they were not taken from a chronography.

The foreshortened Assyrian chronology we find in the fragments of Bouttios also indicates that the preparation of a chronography was far from his chief concern. The Picus-Zeus narrative presents an Assyrian kingdom that lasts barely three generations from its foundation by Cronos until the overthrow of Sardanapalus by Perseus, the son of Picus-Zeus and grandson of Cronos (**F 1**; cf. 7.4). (The succession of Assyrian kings from Cronos to Sardanapalus and their relation to the family of Picus-Zeus is set out in figure 3, above.) This truncated time span is wildly, no doubt purposefully, out of step with the prevailing conception of the duration of the Assyrian kingdom, which was generally held to be one of the longest lasting of the world's realms. Diodorus ends his account of the Assyrians, taken from Ctesias of Cnidos, by saying that their kingdom endured for thirty generations and more than 1,300 years up to its fall under Sardanapalus.[13] Eusebius echoed this recognition of longevity, calculating that altogether from the first year of Ninus to the last year of Sardanapalus the Assyrian kingdom had lasted for 1,240 years.[14] Bouttios's reconfiguration of the duration of the Assyrian kingdom up to its fall under Sardanapalus is not a minor deviation from these authoritative determinations, but a rejection of them.

Bouttios's very brief Assyrian chronology may have been idiosyncratic, but it was neither indefensible nor necessarily without purpose. Appian, who says that the time of the Assyrians, Medes, and Persians together does not amount to 900 years, suggests that there was some elasticity in the calculation of the length of the ancient eastern kingdoms.[15] But the drastic foreshortening of the Assyrian Empire may have come from a far more influential historian. Herodotus—writing before the widespread acceptance of Ctesias's fictional history of Assyria and the establishment of the lengthy Assyrian king-lists—can also give at least the impression of a very short duration for the Assyrian kingdom. Herodotus

13 Diod. Sic. 2.28.8 = Ctesias, F 1b (Lenfant, *Ctésias de Cnide*, 62). See Boncquet, "Ctesias' Assyrian King-List." Cf. Justin., *Epit.* 1.2.13.

14 Jerome, *Chron.*: *ann. Abr.* 1197 (Fotheringham, *Evsebii Pamphili Chronici Canones*, 142). Cf. August., *De civ. D.* 4.6, 12.11, 18.21; Oros. 1.4.1, 12.2, 19.1, 2.3.2.

15 App., *Pref.* 9 (34).

says that Semiramis lived a mere five generations before Nitocris, another notable queen of Babylon, who took measures against the rising power of the Medes and whose son faced the attack of Cyrus the Persian.[16] He does not identify her as such—indeed, he has very little to say about her—but later readers whose knowledge of Assyria was based on the accounts of Ctesias would have recognized Semiramis as the wife of Ninus, reputed to be the founder of the Assyrian Empire.[17] Herodotus does say elsewhere that the Assyrians held the rule of Upper Asia for 520 years—already a span much shorter than Ctesias's 1,300 years—but this passage is detached from his discussion of Semiramis and Nitocris and might have been missed by the inattentive reader.[18] No less an authority than Herodotus, then, when read selectively, could appear to give the kingdom of the Assyrians a duration of not more than five or six generations, even if this was not his intention. This may have provided Bouttios with some warrant for his list of just seven kings of Assyria from Cronos to Sardanapalus.

An abbreviated Assyrian chronology is also in accord with a point often made in Christian apologetics. The apologists took exception to the stupendously long spans of time indicated by the histories of the Egyptians and Babylonians, as well as Plato's conception of the past, not least because of their disagreement with the date of Creation and the age of the world established on the basis of the Bible.[19] An Assyrian king-list comprising only a handful of rulers with reigns of unremarkable length would go some way to obviate such objectionable chronologies. If nothing else, it implies that the extrabiblical histories with their extended chronological durations are not necessarily reliable, that there were alternatives that did not stagger the imagination or challenge credulity.

There may have been some basis and an apologetic purpose to Bouttios's truncated Assyrian chronology, but what has to be recognized here is that it must have stood on its own, and could hardly have been reconciled with the usual chronological systems and integrated into a broader chronology. Certainly there is no relation between Bouttios's Assyrian chronology and the one carefully

16 Hdt. 1.184, 185.1, 188.1.

17 See Rollinger, "Assyria in Classical Sources."

18 Hdt. 1.95.2; cf. Diod. Sic. 2.32.2. See Drews, "Fall of Astyages," 6–7, 10.

19 Theoph., *Ad Aut.* 3.16; Julius Africanus, *Chron.* F 15 (Wallraff, *Iulius Africanus, Chronographiae*, 24–25) = Georg. Sync., *Chron.* 32–33; Lactant., *Div. inst.* 7.14 (cf. Cic., *Div.* 1.[19] 36); August., *De civ. D.* 12.11. See Edwards, *Religions*, 228–29.

established by Eusebius, and Bouttios stands apart from any recognizable system of Christian chronology. There may have been dates and indications of the passage of time (ages, reign lengths, regnal years), which gave the appearance of a history to the work of Bouttios, but the indications are that these were never connected into an overall system of chronology. Bouttios, despite being called a "chronographer" by Malalas, does not seem to have followed in the footsteps of Julius Africanus and Eusebius and written a chronography.

Indeed, there are signs that chronological precision may actually have been detrimental to Bouttios's purpose. The fragments seem to indicate that rather than building up a coherent succession of reigns and kingdoms, Bouttios sought to depict the past in terms of broad contrasts, between East and West, between slavery and freedom.[20] On the one hand, the motley conglomeration of eastern peoples—Assyrians, Babylonians, Chaldeans, Medes, Persians, and Parthians—are portrayed as conquerors, who subjugate (unhistorically) the Romans and (more or less historically) the Jews, as well as the Greeks and the Egyptians, and render the whole world tributary to themselves. These oriental peoples and their subjection of the world are represented in the person of Nebuchadnezzar, who is said to have conquered Egypt and Judea and the land of the Romans. And the domination of the easterners lasts until, on the other hand, Alexander arises to free the Romans, Greeks, and Egyptians from their slavery to the oriental powers. The Jews also seem to share in this liberation, inasmuch as they go from being a conquered people burdened with tribute payments to apparently enjoying friendly relations with Alexander.

The personification of the contrast in the figures of Nebuchadnezzar the conqueror and Alexander the liberator seems most evident in the description of their realms in the same, equally universal terms: stretching from the Caspian Gates to the Pillars of Hercules (**FF 11, 20.1**). Nor is such a presentation of history without significant precedents. In the preamble to his *Histories* Herodotus spoke of relations between the Greek West and the barbarian East as a series of conflicts, with each side having the upper hand in turn.[21] The visions of the book of Daniel, in which Nebuchadnezzar and Alexander figure prominently, may not necessarily set up a contrast in its succession of kingdoms, but they do

20 See Garstad, "Alexander the Great's Liberation of Rome."

21 Hdt. 1.1–5; cf. Curt. 4.14.21.

describe history in similarly broad strokes.[22] The *Alexander Romance* depicts Alexander as the liberator of Greece and Egypt from the Persians and other eastern peoples.[23] Alexander's liberation of the Romans and Jews might be seen as an extrapolation of this role in the *Romance*. There even appears to be an echo of this blunt presentation of history in terms of a personalized contrast along geographical and ethnic lines in the *De aetatibus mundi et hominis* of Fulgentius, in which Alexander's Macedonian kingdom seems to arise in immediate succession to the Babylonian kingdom of Nebuchadnezzar and make war upon it.[24] Just how Alexander's depiction as a liberator is to be reconciled with Bouttios's essentially negative portrayal of him must remain an open question for the present. It is clear, however, that a proper chronography, one that presented history not conceptually but chronologically, could hardly accommodate the vision of the past that seems to be reflected in the fragments of Bouttios.

Bouttios's Work as Didactic Fiction

What sort of work, then, did he write?[25] We must answer that question on the basis of the remnants of the work itself. That being said, it is practically impossible to determine the extent to which what Domninos selected from Bouttios and what from that Malalas took over from Domninos, or what in the *Excerpta*

22 Dan. 2:31–45, 7:2–18, 8:3–25.

23 In the *Romance*, Egypt seems to fall under Persian sway after it is invaded by a horde of "all the great peoples of the East" (1.2.2), but when Alexander comes to the country the Egyptians recognize him as the son of their last king, Nectanebo, and the rightful king of Egypt (1.34.3–6). Alexander's liberation of Greece is largely implicit in the earliest version of the *Romance*, the α recension; he refuses the Persian envoys their demand of the tribute usually paid by Macedon (1.23.2–4) and Darius chides him for not remaining content under his rule (1.40.3). The later β recension, however, has Alexander rallying the Greeks and Macedonians to his standard by calling on them to free themselves from slavery to the Persians (1.25.1).

24 Fulg., *De aetat.* 10. See Garstad, "Alexander the Great's Liberation of Rome," 193–98. Hays, "A World without Letters," is primarily concerned with a stylistic examination of Fulgentius's *De aetatibus*, but provides a solid introduction to the work and manages to collect the most important bibliography on its study.

25 Van Hoof and Van Nuffelen, *Fragmentary Latin Histories*, 13, 250, 253, deny that "Bruttius" as they call him wrote a history, but they do not venture to speculate as to what sort of work he did write.

Latina Barbari was borrowed from Bouttios, and what we can identify as such, reflects the actual composition of Bouttios. It is possible that great swaths of material have been lost beyond all hope of recovery and that all together they, or even a different assortment of them, would have given an entirely different complexion to our impression of Bouttios's work, perhaps revealing what we take to have been his principal and defining interests as nothing more than minor and peripheral topics in his writing. However, we have to handle what we have and not allow an unavoidable ignorance to lead us to paralysis of inquiry. The fragments we possess, moreover, disclose sufficient hints of a pattern to encourage us to attempt at least a tentative reconstruction.

The fragments of Bouttios we do have offer an account of the gods presented as ancient kings and a survey of various other rulers throughout history. This material suggests a comparison with the *Aegyptiaca* of Manetho, which began with the rule of the gods over Egypt and proceeded to catalog the kings of Egypt through numerous dynasties.[26] Unlike Manetho's history of Egypt, however, Bouttios's work does not seem to have been a national or ethnic history. There may be some significance to the Assyrian origins of his so-called gods,[27] but they travel widely and establish themselves in various countries, and while there is some concentration on Antioch, the monarchs Bouttios discusses are mythical heroes, Macedonian kings, and Roman emperors. Nor do I think it safe to assume that Bouttios made anything like Manetho's effort at comprehensiveness; the kings he dealt with seem to have been a selection. The fragments of Bouttios, moreover, do not merely describe in cursory fashion the reigns of a number of kings, they present all of their subjects from Cronos onward, with the signal exception of Constantine, in a more or less unflattering light. They may be accomplished rulers, victorious generals, great conquerors, and city founders, but they are also unmasked as heinous criminals, guilty of wanton seduction, witchcraft, and mercenary deceit, but most often of human sacrifice. The reader must have recognized here the characteristic devices of the novel. So the work of Bouttios seems to have been not only something of a historical miscellany

26 See Redford, *Pharaonic King-Lists*, 203–332; Verbrugghe and Wickersham, *Berossos and Manetho*, 95–120; Dillery, "First Egyptian Narrative History"; Dillery, *Clio's Other Sons*, 84–117.

27 See above, pp. 149–52.

beginning with the time of the gods and treating certain famous kings, it was also a reflection on the virtues and vices of those kings. It did not merely satisfy curiosity about the past, it invited the reader to cast judgment on the figures of the past. What is more, it advertised its resemblance to works of fiction.

The picture that begins to form, of a history of kings beginning with a treatment of the gods, a narrative meditation on kingship which employs the techniques of fiction and provokes moral praise and blame, must at first seem to be that of an odd and idiosyncratic composition, but I think we can point to a useful comparandum in the *Caesars* of the emperor Julian.[28] In terms of subject matter, gods and kings, or more precisely deified kings, and of method, playing on the sentiments by means of dramatic narrative, Bouttios's work has a great deal in common with the *Caesars*, even if in terms of overt genre they differ, one purporting to be a myth and the other a history. We shall discuss the proposal that Bouttios wrote in response to the writings of Julian, and especially those writings composed during his stay in Antioch, at greater length below.[29] For now we shall employ a comparison with the *Caesars* to ascertain the kind of work Bouttios was writing. Such a comparison reveals both similarities and differences, none of which seem to be accidental.

Julian opens the *Caesars* by saying that although he has no talent for entertaining composition, he has prepared a story, a myth, as appropriate to the festival of the Cronia, that is, the Roman Saturnalia.[30] Bouttios's work may not have been such a self-confessed fiction, but in a treatment of the remote time of the gods and the recurrence of virgin sacrifice as often as in a racy novel, his readers must have recognized undisguised affinities with the realms of fiction.[31] And if

28 Hilton, "Myth and Narrative Fiction," offers a detailed and incisive analysis of the place of myth and fiction not only in the writings of Julian, but also in those of his opponents and detractors.

29 See below, pp. 217–25.

30 Julian, *Caes.* 306A–B.

31 Plato (*Resp.* 382C–D) held that among the several rhetorical uses of fiction or falsity (τὸ ψεῦδος), in the case of mythology, an ignorance of the remote past (περὶ τῶν παλαιῶν) prevents us from knowing the truth of the matter and we render fiction useful by making it conform as much as possible to the truth; see P. Green, "'These fragments,'" 58. He furthermore implied (*Resp.* 499C) that the events of "time past without limit" (ἐν τῷ ἀπείρῳ τῷ παρεληλυθότι χρόνῳ), like those in the present in some foreign locale far beyond our acquaintance, could only be recaptured through an exercise of the

Bouttios had assumed at least the pretense of writing history, an open confession of engaging in writing fiction, in myth-making, would have been out of place in the genre. Herodotus, after all, did not admit that he was piecing together an origin story for Cyrus from stray bits of Greek myth, even if his audience must have seen it quite plainly![32] Julian's story is not merely an entertainment, however; he claims that it is a myth with serious intent and a lesson to impart, and refers to the example of Plato.[33] There is likewise an ethical concern to the work of Bouttios, a message about the character of the pagan gods and kings, and an engrossing history which must have been meant to make this pill easier to swallow or perhaps more convincing. Bouttios's accounts of a time when the gods ruled among men might also respond to the example of Plato, who set at least one of his purposive myths in an Egypt ruled by the gods as kings and considered the remote past a suitable subject for fiction.[34]

The myth of the *Caesars* relates that Romulus once invited the gods and the Roman emperors, the Caesars from whom the composition takes its usual title, to a banquet in the heavenly realms. The guests are described as they arrive, and a lengthy succession of emperors is preceded by an elaborate report of the couches prepared for Cronos and Zeus and their wives.[35] Even if Julian's reverence and careful distinction between gods and deified emperors are understandably absent, nevertheless Bouttios's narrative of a list of kings likewise begins with an account of the gods, and with Cronos and Zeus specifically. Also like Julian's *Caesars*, Bouttios's survey of kings seems to have comprised mostly Roman emperors, but was capacious enough to include Alexander and certain Seleucid kings, just as Alexander found a place among the Roman emperors in Julian's *Caesars*.[36] The banquet of the *Caesars* turns into a contest before the gods to determine the best of the deceased rulers, who are judged with regard to both their actions and the guiding principles of their lives. This moral adjudication of historical personages

---

imagination, such as the fiction of his imagined polity. The gods, moreover, often figure as characters in Plato's myths. The frequency of incidents of virgin sacrifice in the ancient novels will be discussed below.

32 Hdt. 1.107–30.

33 Julian, *Caes.* 306C.

34 Pl., *Phdr.* 274C–275B; *Resp.* 499C.

35 Julian, *Caes.* 307B–308B.

36 Julian, *Caes.* 316A–D, etc.

is the explicit purpose of Julian's work and is there undertaken ostensibly by the gods, and it runs through Bouttios's work too, even if he offers only a muted invitation to his readers to judge the kings of the past for themselves. If the commentators are correct that when Julian says Probus "suffered at the hands of impious men" (πεπονθὼς ὑπὸ τῶν ἀθέων) he means that the emperor was assassinated by Christians, then Bouttios and Julian both seem to have found this sort of writing congenial to scurrilous and largely unfounded accusations against their ideological opponents.[37] Also, Constantine is the most recent ruler dealt with in both Julian's *Caesars* and (apparently) Bouttios's history, although the special attention Bouttios gives Constantine is quite different from the unenviable treatment he receives at the hands of Julian. Finally, the *Caesars* discloses Julian's engagement in the contemporary debate between pagans and Christians, especially when it depicts Jesus in the company of Pleasure (*Tryphe*) and Incontinence (*Asotia*), and baptism and repentance as an easy solution to licentiousness.[38] Just so, the fragments of Bouttios may suggest an antiquarian history, but their attacks on the pagan gods and denigration of all kings and emperors apart from the first Christian one indicate an involvement in the religious and ideological arguments that were a pervasive part of late antique discourse.

The differences between Bouttios's history and Julian's *Caesars* are not so much like dissimilarities arising from fundamentally different forms and purposes as intentional contradictions. These differences begin with the setting and cast of characters of each work. Whereas the *Caesars* is set in heaven and peopled with supernal deities and deified emperors, Bouttios's subjects, so-called gods, heroes, and ancient monarchs, are all now-dead kings and their careers are situated firmly on the earth. A mundane history is opposed to a heavenly myth, and the details of the history confront those of the myth. Julian has Cronos and Zeus reclining side by side on the height of Olympus,[39] but according to Bouttios

37 Julian, *Caes.* 314A–B; Lacombrade, *L'empereur Julien. Oeuvres completes* 2.2, 13; Baldwin, "*Caesares* of Julian," 464. Bowersock, "Emperor Julian," 266, is skeptical of this interpretation, preferring to see a confusion of the emperor Probus with another Probus, the governor of Lower Pannonia, who was compelled to execute the bishop Irenaeus in the time of Diocletian, though it is hard to see in what sense the governor "suffered" more than irritation or inconvenience in this situation.

38 Julian, *Caes.* 336A–B.

39 Julian, *Caes.* 307B–308A.

these two were incapable of sharing not one but two earthly kingdoms, the son displacing the father first in Assyria and then in Italy. The parade of emperors in the *Caesars* is depicted with vague and allusive descriptions of each of them as they appear, while the carefully assembled—if hardly dependable—details, such as dates, locations, and specific deeds, in their precision are there to affirm the historical nature of Bouttios's discourse, and seem to corroborate its veracity. Alexander is the only foreign king to appear among the *Caesars*' Roman emperors, but Bouttios also discusses Seleucus. This is consistent with Bouttios's interest in city foundations and their sinister implications, as well as his parochial concentration on the environs of Antioch, but it may also be a defensive insistence on the significance of Antioch's founder along with the universal rulers of the *Caesars*, especially in light of Julian's derisive treatment of the first Seleucid kings as the source of the Antiochenes' sybaritic ways in his *Misopogon*.[40]

Julian's *Caesars* was an occasional piece, written ostensibly for the Cronia, but that is not to say that it was intended as some bit of ephemera; on the contrary it is considered, well researched, and substantial.[41] Much the same seems to have been true of Bouttios's work. The occasion for his writing was not a festival, but quite possibly the visit of Julian to Antioch. Nevertheless, his work appears to have been likewise relatively brief and meant to make a point, not really to entertain and not necessarily to inform. If Bouttios's work is like the *Caesars*, that does not mean that it was a satire, though; at any rate, Barry Baldwin has maintained that it is misleading to classify the *Caesars* itself as a satire.[42] The most instructive category to apply to the *Caesars* is the one explicitly offered by the work itself, that of Platonic myth, a fiction, we might say, made up of recognizable elements with an instructive purpose.[43] Bouttios's work might also fall into this category, even if it took the form of a history and even retained the intention of history. Of all the

40 Julian, *Mis.* 347A–348B.

41 Bowersock, "Emperor Julian," is less impressed than Baldwin, "*Caesares* of Julian," with Julian's composition, repeatedly insisting on the emperor's ignorance of many points of Roman history and his inconsistencies with contemporary Latin historians, but I think this may be a failure to appreciate Julian's choice of genre and intention. Cf. Lacombrade, *L'empereur Julien. Oeuvres completes* 2.2, 6–13; Elm, *Sons, Fathers*, 285–86.

42 Baldwin, "*Caesares* of Julian," 449–50; but see Gallardo, "*Simposios*"; Bowersock, "Emperor Julian," 159. Cf. Lacombrade, *L'empereur Julien. Oeuvres completes* 2.2, 3–4.

43 On Platonic myth, see Detienne, *Creation of Mythology*, 82–102; Gill, "Plato on Falsehood"; Brisson, *Plato the Myth Maker*; Murray, "What Is a *Muthos* for Plato?"; Rowe,

Platonic myths, the fragments of Bouttios indicate a composition most like the Atlantis myth found in the *Timaeus* and the *Critias*, the Platonic myth that itself has the form and presentation closest to history, so much so that it has often—perhaps most often—been taken for a history.[44] We might even detect the possibility of the influence of Plato's story of Atlantis in the most distinctive notions of Bouttios.[45] At any rate, what Bouttios wrote would seem to have presented itself as a history, one that plumbed the depths of the primordial past, and referred to certain obscure sources (even priestly Egyptian ones on occasion), but allowed the author to freely engage in the invention of narratives and details.

"Myth, History, and Dialectic"; Morgan, *Myth and Philosophy*, 132–289; Brisson, *How Philosophers Saved Myths*, 15–28; Partenie, *Plato, Selected Myths*.

44 Pl., *Ti.* 20D–27B, *Criti.* 108E–121C. See Gill, "Genre of the Atlantis Story"; Vidal-Naquet, *Atlantis Story*; Gill, *Plato's Atlantis Story*.

45 Perhaps Bouttios was inspired to speak of Alexander's "freeing" the Romans, Greeks, and Egyptians from slavery (δουλείας) to the Assyrians, etc., by the passage in Plato's *Timaeus* (24E–25D) that describes the war of ancient Athens against the power of Atlantis. The kings of Atlantis were supposed to have ruled the territory along the Ocean shore and within the straits of Gibraltar up to the borders of Egypt and Etruria (25B; cf. *Criti.* 114C), and their assault was intended to "enslave" (δουλοῦσθαι) all the lands within the straits (25B). These would include the very nations mentioned by Bouttios, the Romans, Greeks, and Egyptians; and Greece and Egypt are, in fact, named as the targets of the invasion by Plato's Egyptian narrator (τόν τε παρ' ὑμῖν καὶ τὸν παρ' ἡμῖν). But the stalwart Athenians defeated the invaders and "freed all those within the boundaries of Heracles" (25C: τοὺς δ' ἄλλους, ὅσοι κατοικοῦμεν ἐντὸς ὅρων Ἡρακλείων, ἀφθόνως ἅπαντας ἠλευθέρωσεν). **F 11** indicates that the Romans were included in all the country that Nebuchadnezzar, the "Assyrian" king, subjected from the Caspian Gates to the boundaries of Heracles (*usque in Eracliae finibus*). The intention of the kings of Atlantis to conquer all the lands within the "boundaries of Heracles" is apparently accomplished by Nebuchadnezzar. If a Platonic allusion were intended, the reader would not be too surprised to find the conquering power emanating from the East rather than the West. Atlantis, after all, with its arbitrary rule of kings (*Criti.* 119C), ostentatious wealth, elephants (*Criti.* 114E), and war chariots (*Criti.* 119A), to say nothing of its purpose of invading Greece (*Ti.* 24C), is depicted in decidedly oriental if not specifically Persian terms; cf. Gill, "Genre of the Atlantis Story," 294–95, 298; Vidal-Naquet, *Atlantis Story*, 24–32; Gill, *Plato's Atlantis Story*, 20, 27–28, 119. While Bouttios's odd conception of Alexander's mission does demand an explanation, it would not be prudent to insist on a definitive allusion to the *Timaeus*; such a discussion of the enslavement and liberation of the peoples *within the boundaries of Heracles* in markedly similar terms is nevertheless at least suggestive, and deepens the ambiguous character of Bouttios's Alexander.

Bouttios deals with far more of what might really pass for history than any Platonic myth, perhaps to give his work a more plausible appearance of being a history, perhaps because he earnestly wished to write history, but not least because he treats figures and events from far more recent periods. While this is unlike any myth in the Platonic corpus, there is a parallel for it in the *Caesars*. Julian covers, in a decidedly mythological fashion, emperors up to his own lifetime, just as Bouttios ends with the nearly contemporary reign of Constantine. Bouttios's work assumed the form of history, while Julian's *Caesars* assumed the form of the Olympian banquet in the first book of the *Iliad* or Lucian's *Dialogues of the Dead*. But fundamentally it was a fiction with a message, a Platonic myth, just as the *Caesars* was, and a contribution to the debate between pagans and Christians which forms the background to both works. Both Bouttios and Julian in the *Caesars* address the nature of the gods and the legacy of the great kings of the past, particularly Constantine, in palatable fictions which afforded them a degree of latitude with the facts and allowed them to concentrate on the—definitely opposing—points they were trying to make. Julian's *Caesars*, set as it is in the halls of Olympus and bringing together a number of deified emperors, is an obvious fiction, but Bouttios's work is different not merely because it hides its fiction under the—often rather thin—cloak of history. His accounts of tyche sacrifice are inventions, and they borrow from the realms of fiction to add vivid color to Bouttios's work and to tendentiously coax along his audience's reactions.[46] But these stories of virgin sacrifice also seem to be offered as plausible explanations of the origins of the ancient monuments and revered cults of Antioch and other cities. As such they do more than shape a didactic fiction, they also contribute to a real attempt at writing history.

The pretense of a history was convincing. Or, as I suspect we ought rather to say, an odd but earnest specimen of historiography which happily drew on the elements of fiction was received as a reliable historical record. Malalas gives no indication of recognizing the affinities between what was related in Bouttios's history and what happens in the novels, or of doubting the veracity of his reports, and though the waters are a good deal murkier in this case, there is no hint that his intermediary Domninos did either. Perhaps they were not familiar with the figures and commonplaces of ancient fiction. But perhaps, because the events

46 See Hilton, "Myth and Narrative Fiction," 43–44.

of the ancient novel were not essentially unbelievable, or even implausible, and the only willing suspension of disbelief the genre demanded of the reader was in regard to so many exciting and consequential events' occurring at such an unrelenting pace, the characteristic events of fiction could occur in a history without anyone batting an eye, let alone insisting on a knowing wink. In the same way that the novel borrowed from history for its settings and characters, history could borrow feasible, even likely events from the novel without surrendering itself entirely to the realm of fiction. There is no reason to think that anyone—at least anyone not privy to its first appearance—would have balked at crediting Bouttios's history just because it was occasionally reminiscent of what was to be found in the novels, especially after his history had assumed the patina of age and authority by Malalas's day.

If Bouttios's historical discourse disguises an instructive fiction, however, its most fictional and inventive aspect was also its most tendentiously instructive, namely, the accounts of virgin sacrifice inaugurating the tyche cults of various cities. Such an origin had never before been imputed to the tyche figure that graced practically every city in the Roman East, nor had such a heinous accusation been leveled against so many and such distinguished rulers of the past. But these outlandish narratives seem to disclose not only the tendency but also the overall form and arrangement of Bouttios's work.

The Significance of Human Sacrifice

We have already noted instances of tyche sacrifice at the founding of a city or the dedication of a building project as one of the identifying features of the fragments of Bouttios in the *Chronicle* of John Malalas. These singular reports not only distinguish a narrative as belonging to Bouttios, they are also key to understanding the overall structure of his work. Before we attempt to reconstruct that structure, however, we have to step back and determine the significance of these incidents of human sacrifice for the author and his audience. Malalas records these events like any other in the reign of a king or emperor and provides no commentary, no prompting as to how the reader is supposed to react. I suspect that Malalas and Domninos before him have taken over this sort of presentation from their ultimate source; Bouttios also probably delivered the bare "facts" and expected his audience to make of them what they would. Not that he left the

reader's response to chance. A report of human sacrifice, as we shall see, could be expected to elicit a predictable reaction. The lack of comment is not an indication of neutrality in regard to the significance of human sacrifice or a deferential determination not to sway the opinion of the audience; rather, it is part of an effective rhetorical strategy. The imputation of human sacrifice to a historical figure is already an attempt to sway opinion; not dictating a response compels the reader to own his reaction as a genuine product of his assumptions and prejudices, not simply the view of the reporter. The writer does not abandon the guise of a historian for that of a controversialist and the reader is afforded the dignity of drawing his own—thoroughly manipulated and predetermined—conclusions, which are reinforced because they are his own. We may now proceed to determine just what sort of reaction to reports of virgin sacrifice Bouttios might have expected from his readers on the basis of the cultural context they shared.

Human Sacrifice

Human sacrifice is perhaps a particularly appropriate subject for a "fictional history." The Greeks and Romans were simultaneously fascinated and horrified by the concept of human sacrifice, and they gave it generous treatment in their literature, but there is no unambiguous evidence that they ever actually practiced it. As Albert Henrichs put it,

> Stories of human sacrifice never tell us what the Greeks actually did; their relevance lies in telling us what the Greeks thought. Throughout antiquity, the reality of human sacrifice and its powerful hold on the imagination did not lie in its actual occurrence, but in the pretence—or even possibility—that it once occurred. . . . Like few other acts of violence, human sacrifice blurs the boundaries between imagination and reality, between myth and history. Liminal by definition, human sacrifice provokes extreme and anxious reactions in most people. Outwardly disparaged, it is secretly relished and vicariously performed.[47]

47 Henrichs, "Demythologizing the Past," 228. See also Hughes, *Human Sacrifice*; Bonnechere, *Le sacrifice humain*; Rives, "Human Sacrifice"; Bonnechere, "La Notion d' 'Acte Collectif.'"

So what do the tyche sacrifice stories tell us about the thought of one Greek, (we presume) an Antiochene, a Christian, a subject of Rome in the last century of its secure hegemony over the Mediterranean, and the reaction he sought to provoke in his readers?

Bouttios's human sacrifices seem primarily intended to elicit the requisite sense of horror. Stephen King in *Danse Macabre*, an ardent fan and past master's protracted but unfailingly engaging reflection on the various manifestations of the genre, says that a horror story is effective when it touches a nerve, when the fantasy it presents puts a finger on some very real anxiety. But to tingle spines, rather than elicit bemused smirks, the story's presentation must also be consistent—up to a point—with the audience's "set of reality," their perception of the world-as-it-is.[48] In a day when the atrocities of the Diocletianic persecution were just passing out of living memory, the return to the throne of a pagan, one set on disturbing the Peace of the Church, and the prospect of a long reign for the still young Julian the Apostate must have caused some palpable distress among much of the empire's Christian population.[49] The specter of kings and emperors coldly surveying the sacrifice of virgins at city foundings would have recalled the image of innocent women martyred under the supervision of imperial officials, acting under the emperor's auspices. And such recollections of recent virgin martyrs did not merely spark anxiety; rather, along with the flurry of propagandistic rumors about the outrages upon women by the tyrants Constantine faced down, as well as the regular appearance of abused women in the annals of sinister emperors and of episodes of human sacrifice in the adventures of the ancient novel, they also served to render accounts of emperors sacrificing virgins readily plausible—even if the suggestion that the well-known and eminently civilized rulers of the Hellenistic and Roman periods engaged in human sacrifice may strike us as faintly ridiculous. The function, if not the form, of the horror story seems to be a constant over time, and so we may read the tyche sacrifice narratives as a sequence of low-key and allusive, but effective, terror tales.

48 King, *Danse Macabre*, 113–24, 142–83.

49 Julian came to the throne at the age of thirty. On not only Julian's reign as the context for Bouttios's writings, but also a muted criticism of the emperor as the bent of their substance, see below, chapter 7.

We shall indicate shortly some passages from ancient novels which demonstrate a similar effort to provoke horror in the reader. These are descriptions of human sacrifice, and the horror they elicit seems particularly acute, as it is distinct from the common fear of crime and violence. Human sacrifice, unlike murder, for instance, is more than merely a contravention of social norms and expectations, for the deliberate rituals that bring about death reveal an opposed and antagonistic group with its own obscene and hideous norms. In a murder some motive overcomes basic human decency; human sacrifice denies and overturns it. The rules of society are not frightfully broken or interrupted, they are horrifically reinvented.

These are fairly general observations, however. The horror evoked by the tyche sacrifices must have a direction and a target. The reader's visceral response is meant to persuade him to accept an argument that might otherwise meet with some doubt and hesitation. Because human sacrifice was horrific, and because it inverted accepted social norms, it belonged to the "other" and the outsider. As generally understood by the Greeks and Romans, human sacrifice was practiced by barbarians on the remote periphery of the world,[50] or by their own ancestors in the remote past when they apparently had more in common with barbarians.[51] But it remained repugnant, even in these liminal settings, and so

50 See Balsdon, *Romans and Aliens*, 245–48; Rives, "Human Sacrifice," 67–70. See also Origen, *De princip.* 2.9.5, *C. Cels.* 5.27. As the Greeks and Romans became increasingly familiar with the lands of the Mediterranean, the people to whom they imputed human sacrifice became increasingly farther removed from the center of Graeco-Roman civilization. For instance, the practice was associated with Ethiopia in Late Antiquity; see Heliodorus, *Aeth.* 9.1, 10.7; Procop., *Bell.* 1.19.36; as well as an anonymous sixth-century sermon: Datema, "New Evidence."

51 The numerous Greek examples are as old as Homer, who has Achilles kill twelve Trojan princes on the pyre of Patroclus (*Il.* 18.333–37; 21.26–33; 23.19–23, 175–76, 240–42), and also include Iphigenia at Aulis (see Euripides, *Iphigenia at Aulis*), Polyxena at the tomb of Achilles (see Euripides, *Troades*, *Hecuba*), Macaria before the battle against Eurystheus (see Euripides, *Heraclidae*), Athamas's planned sacrifice of Phrixos (who is replaced by the golden ram), and the daughter of Erechtheus and Praxithea; see Ducrey, *Le traitement des prisonniers*, 205–6; Vermeule and Chapman, "A Protoattic Human Sacrifice?"; Burkert, *Homo Necans*, 114, and n. 27, 148, and n. 58; Buck, "Mycenaean Human Sacrifice"; Hughes, *Human Sacrifice*, 73–74. When the Greeks of the literate period heard the exceptional reports of their contemporary compatriots performing human sacrifice, they considered such incidents egregious aberrations, as in the stories of the priest

human sacrifice was the one item of the otherwise venerated *mos maiorum* that was extirpated by Roman law and Roman legions wherever it was encountered,[52] and some mythographers insisted that the gods of a civilized people would at no time accept a human sacrificial victim.[53] Within the civilized world human sacrifice was supposed to be performed by a different kind of outsider, enemies of the order of the state, especially the Roman state, conspirators such as Tarquin the Proud and Catiline;[54] those enemies of the order of nature and the gods, the magicians;[55] and rulers who were enemies of their own subjects, the most egregiously tyrannical of emperors.[56] To ascribe the practice of human sacrifice to the leaders of Greek and Roman polities, the men at the very heart of the civilized world, and especially in the recent past, is therefore to suggest a radical inversion of the prejudices concerning civilization and barbarity, insider and outsider. It is to suggest that there is something barbarous and flawed about the revered pagan

---

Zoilus at Orchomenos and the three Persian princes before the battle of Salamis; Plutarch, *Quaest. Graec.* 38 (299E–F); *Themistocles* 13.2–3; see Burkert, *Homo Necans*, 175; Henrichs, "Demythologizing the Past," 229–35. The Romans believed that their custom of casting effigies into the Tiber on the Ides of May replaced an ancient rite, abolished by Hercules, in which actual men were thrown into the river: Dion. Hal., *Ant. Rom.* 1.38.2–3; Ov., *Fast.* 6.621–34; Varro, *Ling. Lat.*, 7.44; Plut., *Quaest. Rom.* 32 (272B–C). See also Porph., *Abst.* 2.54–57; Huxley, "Fulgentius on the Cretan Hecatomphonia."

52 See Pomponius Mela 3.18; Pliny, *HN* 30.(4) 13; Suet., *Div. Claud.* 25.5; Plut., *Quaest. Rom.* 83 (283F–284C); Tert., *Apol.* 9.2–6; cf. Caes., *B. Gall.* 6.16; Tac., *Hist.* 4.54; August., *De civ. D.* 7.26.

53 The substitution of an animal for a human victim appears as early as the *Cypria*; Proclus, *Chr.* 104 (ed. Allen); see M. Davies, *Greek Epic Cycle*, 44. Most famously, however, Euripides in his *Iphigenia among the Taurians* and perhaps *Iphigenia at Aulis* (though the latter may be the work of an interpolator) adapted the myth of Iphigenia at Aulis so that the girl was snatched away at the last minute to be the consecrated servant, rather than the sacrificial victim, of Artemis, and replaced by a deer. Plato, *Resp.* 3.391B, insists that Homer's report of Achilles offering live captives on the pyre of Patroclus must be considered a lie.

54 Sall., *Cat.* 22; Plut., *Publicola*, 4.1, *Cic.* 10.3; Cass. Dio 37.30.3. See Marasco, "Sacrifici umani"; Rives, "Human Sacrifice," 70–74.

55 Cic., *In Vatinium* (6)14; Pliny, *HN* 30.19–20; Justin Martyr, *Apol.* 1.18; Cass. Dio 69.11.2–3; Philostr. of Tyana, *VA* 8.5, 7.10, 12–15; Porph., *Abst.* 2.51; Euseb., *HE* 7.10.4; Pauli, *Sententiae*, 5.23.16; Lib., *Decl.* 41; *Clem. Rec.* 2.13; *Clem. Hom.* 2.26, 29, 30. See MacMullen, *Enemies of the Roman Order*, 95–127; Rives, "Human Sacrifice," 78–79.

56 Cass. Dio 74.16.5 on Didius Julianus; SHA, *Comm.* 9.6, *Heliogab.* 8.1–2.

kings and emperors, and that the societies over which they presided were somehow outside the civilization they were traditionally supposed to define.

It is no doubt significant in this regard that the two emperors against whom the Roman Senate of the fourth century gauged their successors in its customary commendations, Augustus and Trajan,[57] appear in Bouttios as perpetrators of virgin sacrifice (**FF 25, 31**). This charge can be seen as an exaggeration or perhaps a reversal of Constantine's attested habit of demeaning his most famous and well-regarded predecessors, Augustus and Trajan among them, with belittling, if humorous, epithets.[58] This allegation of human sacrifice is, moreover, consistent

57 Eutr. 8.5.3; see Van Dam, *Rome and Constantinople*, 19–20. In general, the historians and panegyricists of Late Antiquity held up Augustus and Trajan in particular as examples of good emperors. Bouttios may depict Trajan as the greater criminal, inasmuch as he was supposed to be guilty of not only a virgin sacrifice but also a persecution of the Christians, but Trajan enjoyed, if anything, a better reputation than Augustus; contrast, for instance, the assessment Aurelius Victor (*Caes.* 1.1–7) makes of these two rulers. Augustus: Flor., *Epit.* 2.(14) 3.5–6, (34) 12.61–66; *Pan. Lat.* 2.11.6, 7.11.2; Symmachus, *Or.* 1.11; Auson., *Caes.* (23).50–53; Them., *Or.* 8.115C, 10.132B–C; Eutr. 7.8–10; Sid. Apoll., *Carm.* 7.92–95; Corippus, *In laud. Iustini* 3.27, 4.138; cf. *Pan. Lat.* 2.33.3, 3.9.2, 6.13.4, 7.13.4, 12.10.1; Claud., *IV Cons. Hon.* (8).641–42, *Gild.* (15).49–52, *In Eutr. I* (18).218, *VI Cons. Hon.* (28).116–18; Them., *Or.* 5.63D, 10.130B, 11.145B, 13.173B–C; Aur. Vict., *Caes.* 1.1–7; see Portmann, *Geschichte*, 339. Trajan: Flor., *Epit.* 1.(1) *praef.* 8; *Pan. Lat.* 2.4.5, 11.6; Aur. Vict., *Caes.* 13.1–11; SHA, *Alex. Sev.* 10.2, 13.2, 26.11, 39.1, 48.6, 65.5; Amm. Marc. 16.1.4, 24.3.9, 30.9.1; Them., *Or.* 8.115C, 13.166B, 17.215A; Eutr. 8.2–5; Claud., *IV Cons. Hon.* (8).18–20, 315–20, *Cons. Stil.* (21).193, *VI Cons. Hon.* (28).333–38; Sid. Apoll., *Carm.* 5.317–19, 560–61, 7.114–18; Prisc., *De laude Anastasii* 49; Venantius Fortunatus, *Carm.* 6.2.81–82; cf. *Pan. Lat.* 2.16.1; Auson., *Grat. act.* (21).17 (76), *Caes.* (23).98–101; Them., *Or.* 5.63D, 11.145B, 13.173C, 19.229C; see Syme, *Emperors and Biography*, 89–112; Linder, "Ecclesia and Synagoga," 1029–30; Brennan, "Image of the Frankish Kings," 4; Portmann, *Geschichte*, 342; Halfmann, "Kaiser Trajan," 581–84; Whittaker, *Frontiers of the Roman Empire*, 36; I. Wood, "Incest, Law and the Bible," 296; Greatrex, "Roman Frontiers," 146; Meier, "Nero, Traian und die Christen," 257 and n. 65; Lippold, "Ideal of the Ruler," 363. Trajan's good reputation, despite being traduced by Bouttios, seems to have continued more or less unabated in Byzantium; see Popović, "Zum Bild des römischen Kaisers Trajan." Theodoret (*Gr. affect. cur.* 9.34), however, notes that whereas these two emperors—the same ones held up as models by the Senate—Augustus and Trajan, failed to compel the Persians to submit to the majesty of Roman law, they willingly revered the Gospels and the Kingdom of the Crucified.

58 According to the Anonymus post Dionem or Dio Continuatus, 15 (*FHG* 4:199), Constantine referred to Augustus as the ornament of Fortune (κόσμον τύχης) and Trajan

with one martyr's vociferous denunciation of the decree against the churches of the persecuting emperors Diocletian and Galerius as "unhallowed and utterly impious" (ἀνοσίαν καὶ ἀσεβεστάτην) and an apt rejoinder to Porphyry's charge that Christianity itself represented "barbarian daring" (τὸ βάρβαρον τόλμημα).[59] If the great rulers of the past indulged in human sacrifice, then the monarchy, and potentially the whole *oikoumene*, are erring and barbarous until they are redeemed by Constantine, who establishes a tyche without recourse to human sacrifice. Such ideas, as we shall see, are consistent with the rhetoric of Constantine's reign.

There is a further indictment of the sacrificing rulers in a notable difference between the tyche sacrifices and many of the accounts of human sacrifice famous in antiquity. In some of the most memorable instances of human sacrifice in myth (especially Iphigenia at Aulis) and history (the sons of the Carthaginian nobility), as well as in the Old Testament (Abraham offering Isaac, Jephthah's daughter, the king of Moab's son), the victim is a close relation of the ruler who performs the sacrifice.[60] The narration of these sacrifices consequently expresses the emotional conflict, the anguished resignation, and the immense grief of the sacrificer, to say nothing of his unquestionable commitment to the cause that calls for such a sacrifice.[61] These narratives also emphasize some external compulsion or necessity (the becalmed fleet, the demands of the divine, a thoughtless vow, an

---

as wall creeper (βοτάνην τοίχου); see Van Dam, *Roman Revolution*, 88. The author of the *Epitome de Caesaribus* (41.13) diagnosed this habit as a symptom of Constantine's being eager for praise (*laudis avidus*) and explained his epithet for Trajan (*herbam parietariam*) as a result of his name's appearing on so many buildings. Ammianus Marcellinus (27.3.7) also recalls this jocular name for Trajan (*herbam parietinam*), but does not ascribe it to Constantine specifically.

59 Martyr's denunciation: Euseb., *HE* 8.5.1; cf. Lactant., *De mort. persec.* 13.2; Potter, *Constantine*, 92. Poryphyry's charge: Euseb., *HE* 6.19.7.

60 See Loraux, *Tragic Ways of Killing a Woman*, 37 and n. 18. On the Carthaginian practice of sacrificing the sons of the best families to Cronos/Saturn, see Ps.-Plato, *Minos* 315B–C; Diod. Sic. 20.14.4–7; Curt. 4.3.23; Atkinson, *Commentary on Q. Curtius Rufus, 3 and 4*, 307; S. Brown, *Late Carthaginian Child Sacrifice*. The biblical examples are taken from Gen. 22:1–19, Judg. 11:30–40, 2 Kings 3:26–27; see Sypherd, *Jephthah and His Daughter*.

61 The recognition of the grief of Agamemnon, for one, is strikingly seen in Pliny's description, *HN* 35.36 (73), of a painting of the sacrifice of Iphigenia by Timanthes, in which the artist, having exhausted every evocation of grief, depicted Agamemnon veiled; see Woodford, *Trojan War in Ancient Art*, 37.

ominous siege) that makes the sacrifice all but unavoidable. In contrast, the victims of the tyche sacrifices are not royal princesses. Cepara, sacrificed by Zarbos at Anazarbos, is described as a "country girl," and Calliope, sacrificed by Trajan, is a girl from Antioch.[62] Nor is there so much as a suggestion of any emotional involvement on the part of the sacrificers. The tyche sacrifices, moreover, seem to serve not necessity but the aggrandizing ambition and political purposes of rulers. These cool, detached killings of hapless subjects, compared with the stories of a sorrowful king slaying his nearest and dearest, would inevitably stress the tyranny and abuse of power on the part of the practitioners of human sacrifice.

The charge of human sacrifice is of particular interest coming from the pen of a Christian author. The simultaneous fascination and revulsion that human sacrifice elicited were, if anything, more powerful in the imagination of the Christian than of his polytheist neighbor. Whereas the practice of human sacrifice was anathema to the Hebrew scriptures and the Christians who inherited them, the idea of it was central to the Christian doctrine of redemption and salvation, as well as to the rhetoric of the Christian life.[63] Thus human sacrifice may have been an attractive topic for a Christian author, but the Christian attitude toward human sacrifice was unambiguous. Clement of Alexandria, Eusebius, and Athanasius, among others, characterized the practice as one of the gross errors of profane religion which led to the proliferation of bloodshed.[64]

The Christians, moreover, were not unfamiliar with the accusation of human sacrifice. They had been the victims of such slander, especially in the second century, when they had been accused of infant sacrifice, ritual murder, cannibalism, and other outrageous crimes.[65] But the slander was not so objectionable to them that they hesitated to turn it against their accusers. Human sacrifice, suggested the Christian apologists, was an inevitable and widespread trait of paganism, and they could trot out examples from Greco-Roman literary culture to

62 Malalas 10.53 (**F 30**), 11.9 (**F 31**).

63 See, for example, Rom. 12:1, 1 Cor. 5:7, Eph. 5:2, Heb. 10:10; *Martyrdom of Polycarp* 14.2; cf. Heyman, *Power of Sacrifice*.

64 Clem. Al., *Protr.* 3.42; Euseb., *LC* 13.6–8; Athanasius, *Contra Gentes* 25 *(Adversus Gentes* 1.25); see Meijering, *Athanasius: Contra Gentes*, 83–86.

65 See Dölger, "'*Sacramentum infanticidii*'"; Henrichs, "Pagan Ritual"; Rives, "Human Sacrifice."

prove the point.[66] The charge of human sacrifice was also specifically directed against the persecuting emperors. Dionysius, the bishop of Alexandria (248–ca. 264), according to Eusebius, reported that under the influence of Egyptian magicians the emperor Valerian turned against the Christians and indulged in gruesome child sacrifice in order to win divine favor.[67] Maxentius, the rival of Constantine, was supposed to have sacrificed pregnant women and babies for magical purposes.[68] Bouttios's sweeping accusation of human sacrifice against famous and revered pagan rulers is consistent with this polemic. Nor was this the last time Christians would tar others with the same brush that had painted them, as is evident from the popularity of the blood libel against the Jews in the Middle Ages and later.

Human sacrifice in the tyche narratives, then, is a device used to evoke a horror that could be molded into indignation and outrage against Bouttios's chosen subjects, or targets: pagan rulers, ancient and modern. When accused of human sacrifice these kings and emperors are seen no longer as the protectors and arbiters of civilization, but as barbarous potentates who stand at the heart of society and cast doubt on its claims to civilization. The chosen victims of these rulers show them to be tyrants, since unlike the protagonists of Greek myth and the Old Testament they are killing not their own daughters at grave personal expense, but the daughters of strangers. And in accusing the emperors of human sacrifice, the Christians were turning a calumny that had been fixed on themselves against their erstwhile persecutors.

Virgin Sacrifice

The victims of the tyche sacrifices are maidens not merely because tyche is a feminine word grammatically and the concept is personified as a woman iconographically. *Virgo* was one of the titles of the goddess Fortuna, the Roman equivalent of *Tyche*.[69] Popular wisdom, exemplified in the novels, held that the

66 See Clem. Al., *Protr.* 3.42; Euseb., *LC* 13.6–8; Greg. Naz., *Or.* 4.70; N. Davies, *Human Sacrifice*, 115–30.

67 Euseb., *HE* 7.10.4.

68 Euseb., *HE* 8.14.5, *LC* 1.36.1.

69 Plutarch, *Quaest. Rom.* 74 (281D), *De fort. Rom.* 10 (322F–323A) reports *Fortuna Virgo* as παρθένος Τύχη, and παρθένος is used of a number of the victims of tyche sacrifice.

proper victim of human sacrifice is a virgin, just as the correct animal should be "undefiled" and never have been "brought under the yoke." In Achilles Tatius's novel, Leucippe is selected as a sacrificial victim because of her virginity, and Heliodorus describes the elaborate test of virginity to which the Ethiopians subject their sacrificial victims.[70] Moreover, the topic of virgin sacrifice is, like that of human sacrifice, a means of manipulating the sentiments of the reader, and of indicating the tyranny of the sacrificer.

It is perhaps worth noting that in the Greek and Roman imagination the victims of human sacrifice were not exclusively female. From the earliest literary instances in the *Iliad* to charges against magicians under the empire there were numerous examples of males as the victims of ritual killing, quite possibly equaling female victims in number and distribution.[71] Of course, the victims of the tyche sacrifices are all female because they are supposed to be depicted in the statues of various civic tychai, which are consistently female. But there was also a certain romantic—potentially pornographic—appeal in a female sacrificial victim, or a woman in danger, at any rate.[72] Martin Kilmer's analysis of the Kleophrades Painter's depiction of the rape of Cassandra—in which the victim is likewise a

On *Fortuna Virgo*, see Champeaux, *Fortuna*, 1:268–74. On the distinction between the Roman *Fortuna* and the Greek *Tyche*, see Latte, *Römische Religionsgeschichte*, 176–83.

70 Achilles Tatius 3.12; Heliodorus, *Aeth.* 9.1, 25; 10.7–9.

71 Examples of male sacrificial victims, or prospective victims, include Heracles at the altar of Busiris, Orestes and Pylades in *Iphigenia among the Taurians*, the twelve Trojan youths in the *Iliad*, the Lydian youths in the story of Croesus (Hdt. 1.86.2), the three Persian princes in Plutarch's account of Themistocles, and Theagenes in the final book of Heliodorus's *Aethiopica*. There are also examples from other cultures of which the Greeks and Romans would have been aware: Isaac, the king of Moab's son, and the infant sons of the Carthaginian nobility. Boys or youthful males seem to predominate as the victims of sacrifices for magical purposes.

72 The appeal of a "damsel in distress" in some horrific situation hardly requires explanation; it remains constant to the present day. There is a suggestion (Eur., *Hec.* 267–73) in a case of maiden sacrifice, that of Polyxena, that it is preferable for the victim to have good looks. It is also possible that the sacrifice of Polyxena is eroticized by the exposure of her breasts (Eur., *Hec.* 557–65), but it might also suggest her *andreia*, as she exposes the region in which a mortal blow would be dealt to a warrior; see Loraux, *Tragic Ways of Killing a Woman*, 57–61. The male victims of human sacrifice may have held the same appeal to the more catholic sexual appetites of certain circles in the Graeco-Roman world. In one of the fragments of the novelist Iamblichus's *Babyloniaca* (Extract 2), a character opines that fear and bonds make a prisoner, a male slave, more attractive, and C. Williams,

virgin, the sexual aspect of the situation is obvious, her vulnerability is accentuated, and her role as a prophetess and the setting at the cult statue of Athena, a virgin goddess, imply a perversion of religious ritual—suggests, despite the gulf of time, that even if the tyche sacrifices are supposed to be sexually exciting, in the context of Greco-Roman society they are intended to elicit not sadistic lust but eroticized sympathy for the victim as a beautiful woman.[73] We shall explore the significance and function of this romantic element at greater length below.

The immense dramatic potential of virgin sacrifice was by no means lost on the tragedians of Athens.[74] The sacrifice of Iphigenia was the most prominent but not the only virgin sacrifice dealt with on the tragic stage. A distinction may be made in these treatments. As described by Aeschylus, the death of Iphigenia under compulsion and constraint (she is "seized, hoisted, and gagged" over the altar) is like a murder, which ought to bring shame on those responsible for it, namely her father and the other kings. Euripides' sacrificial heroines, in contrast, go willingly to their deaths, with an acquiescence appropriate to a sacrificial victim, and consequently achieve a noble death and win "glory" (*kleos* or *eukleia*). The glory of the female victim easily outshines that of her aristocratic male sacrificers.[75] In the tragic virgin sacrifices of both Aeschylus and Euripides, however, our sympathies are supposed to rest with the victim, and her sacrificer is supposed to be vilified. Just so, in the tyche sacrifices our sympathies belong with the virgin girls, and our feelings are directed against the rulers who sacrifice them.

Roman Homosexuality, 104–7, notes that little distinction was made between women and freeborn young men as victims of rape in wartime.

73 "Rape of Cassandra" by the Kleophrades Painter = Kilmer, R321; Naples 2422; see Kilmer, "Sexual Violence," 273–75; Kilmer, *Greek Erotica*, 157–59. Closer to the fourth century, spells of erotic magic prescribe that a model of the object of the magician's amorous attentions should be made as a bound figurine in clay, menaced with a sword by a figurine of Ares, and pierced with a number of bronze needles, but the manipulation of circumstances depicted as restraint and violence in these apparently sadistic ritual images is supposed to be realized as acquiescence, not force or compulsion; see Graf, *Magic in the Ancient World*, 136–44. By analogy with modern slasher films, the endangered female may elicit more than sympathy; Clover, *Men, Women, and Chain Saws*, 5, explores "the possibility that male viewers are quite prepared to identify not just with screen females, but with screen females in the horror-film world, screen females in fear and pain."

74 See Loraux, *Tragic Ways of Killing a Woman*, 31–48.

75 See Loraux, *Tragic Ways of Killing a Woman*, 42–48.

The ritual killing of virgins by vicious rulers was not, however, relegated to the mythical past. Domitian buried alive a reputedly defiled vestal virgin (possibly in 92 CE).[76] Pliny protests her innocence, but even if there was some truth to the charge, her guilt must have paled beside Domitian's own vices. In 213 Caracalla himself corrupted one of the vestal virgins and then proceeded to bury her alive, along with two of her colleagues.[77] These monstrous acts were committed by notoriously despotic emperors, but by Roman emperors of the none too distant past nonetheless. They must have both inspired and lent weight to the charges Bouttios apparently leveled against all pagan rulers, irrespective of their reputation for good or bad. These stories should also remind us of the deep sense of outrage with which Greco-Roman society reacted to the violation of respectable women, particularly of virgins, and especially by abusive rulers. An exclusive reading in the myths of Ovid and Nonnus, in which rape is often as playful as it is frequent, might anesthetize us to the disturbed reaction of the ancients to rape as a rule. Rape or murder made heroines of the victims, and tyrants of the perpetrators, from the son of Tarquin and Appius Claudius to the rivals of Constantine.[78]

Virginity was an important subject of Christian discourse when Bouttios wrote, and this can hardly have failed to have some impact on how the virgin victims of the tyche sacrifices were viewed. As Averil Cameron has said, the general theme of virginity "as a subject of treatises and exhortations achieved its greatest success precisely in the fourth century, especially in the second half, when scarcely any major Christian figure neglected to write about it."[79] In addition to the "treatises and exhortations," as Cameron herself makes clear, virginity was also a central topic in many of the apocryphal *Acts* of the apostles, composed

76 Pliny, *Ep.* 4.11; Suet., *Domit.* 8.3–4; Cass. Dio 60.3.4(3^2). On the execution of vestal virgins see Balsdon, *Roman Women*, 238–42.

77 Cass. Dio 78.16.1–3.

78 On the rape of Lucretia by Sextus Tarquinius, see Livy 1.57–60; Dion. Hal., *Ant. Rom.* 4.64–85. On the attempted rape of Verginia by Appius Claudius, see Livy 3.44–58; Diod. Sic. 12.24; Dion. Hal., *Ant. Rom.* 12.28–49. On the seductions and adulteries of Maxentius, see Euseb., *HE* 8.14.2, 17, *VC* 1.33–34, and of Maximin see *HE* 8.14.14–16; cf. *LC* 7.7.

79 Av. Cameron, *Christianity and the Rhetoric of Empire*, 171. For discussions of the early Christian discourse on virginity, see Av. Cameron, "Virginity as Metaphor," 181–205, and *Christianity and the Rhetoric of Empire*, 171–88; K. Cooper, *Virgin and the Bride*. On the fourth-century institutionalization of virginity and the integration of virgins into the structures of the Church, see Elm, *Virgins of God*; Brakke, *Athanasius and Asceticism*.

in the second and third centuries. In the apocryphal *Acts* we often find that a new female convert must maintain her continence in opposition to powerful members of the Roman government and the civic elite.[80] In the *Acts of Andrew*, after her healing and conversion Maximilla denies intercourse to her husband, Aegeastes, the proconsul at Patras.[81] Even more strikingly, Thecla, according to the *Acts of Paul and Thecla*, perseveres in her virginity, despite proposals from eligible men prominent in the city and the importuning and threats of Roman governors in favor of a marriage. As a result of her refusal Thecla is sentenced—not once, but twice—to death, and is saved only by miraculous means.[82] Thecla, it is worth noting, was also mentioned in Gregory of Nazianzus's sermons against Julian,[83] further suggesting some affinity with the tyche sacrifices, which were, we shall suggest, also connected to Julian.

On Kate Cooper's reading, these confrontations between virgins and rulers serve to dramatize an ethical conflict between the celebration of a sexuality that ensured the continuity of the city in its families and institutions on the one hand, and the renunciation of sexuality as part of a challenge to the established social order on the other. A more superficial but no less compelling reading suggests that the *Acts* pursue the same topic as the tyche sacrifice narratives: an opposition between rulers and virgins, in which the virgins are the imperiled heroines. The close connection between Christian virgin martyrs and the tyche sacrifices seems almost explicit in that Trajan's tyche sacrifice at Antioch is followed almost immediately by an account of the execution of five Christian women for their faith, and the mention of the martyrdom of St. Drosine and other virgins.[84] We do not need to suggest that Bouttios is participating in a subversive or antiauthoritarian discourse—the praise of virginity had, after all, become the authoritative social norm by his time—only that he alluded to the popular *Acts* in characterizing pagan rulers as the villains of his piece.

The imagination of antiquity expected the victims of human sacrifice to be virgins, but Bouttios uses this expectation, as well as the necessity that they

80 See K. Cooper, *Virgin and the Bride*, 45–67. Cf. Aubin, "Reversing Romance?"

81 *Passion of Andrew* 14, 16, 17, 23, 36–37, 46; see MacDonald, *Acts of Andrew*.

82 *Acts of Paul and Thecla* 20–21, 27.

83 Greg. Naz., *Or.* 4.69.

84 Malalas 11.10 (**F 32**).

should be female, to expand the referential field of his tyche sacrifice narratives. The virgin victims allude to the sacrificial heroines of tragedy, the vestal victims of the despotism of Domitian and Caracalla, and the virgin martyrs of the apocryphal *Acts*, as well as exploiting the appealing image of a female sacrificial victim. All of this makes the victim the object of our sympathies, and makes the ruler who sacrifices her out to be not a legitimate ruler at all, but a tyrant.

Foundation Sacrifices

Associated as they are with new cities and new buildings, the tyche sacrifices also serve as foundation sacrifices. There is widespread anthropological evidence for sacrifices, even of humans and virgins in particular, being offered in conjunction with laying a foundation stone or inaugurating a new construction,[85] but no indisputable evidence for human foundation sacrifices among the Greeks in any period.[86] Human foundation sacrifice was practiced at a very early period in the Near East, but was largely replaced by the offering of substitute figures.[87] The Greeks did adopt, at a much later time, the Near Eastern custom of depositing valuables as a foundation sacrifice.[88] The Greeks also made animal sacrifices at the founding of buildings, especially temples, well into the historical period.[89] Animal sacrifices are also associated with the inauguration of new cities in legend and history: Aeneas was supposed to have sacrificed a sow and her litter to Juno at the future site of Alba Longa, and Cadmus sacrificed a cow at the site of

85 See Sartori, "Über das Bauopfer"; Burkert, *Homo Necans*, 39 and n. 17; Tierney, *Highest Altar*, 21 and n. 18, 201, 372; N. Davies, *Human Sacrifice*, 21–22, 43, 277–78; Wiseman, *Remus*, 117–25. The price that Hiel of Bethel paid to refound Jericho, that is, the lives of his two sons (1 Kings 16:34; cf. Josh. 6:26), may be a biblical example of foundation sacrifice.

86 The young woman found buried, along with a man and four horses, in the tenth-century "Heroon" at Lefkandi on Euboia might be construed as a foundation sacrifice (the pit in which she was interred is close to a central supporting post), but it is equally possible that she was offered as a burial sacrifice for her male companion or that she was buried separately after a natural death. See Popham, "Hero of Lefkandi"; Hughes, *Human Sacrifice*, 46–47; Henrichs, "Demythologizing the Past," 228.

87 Müller-Karpe, *Handbuch der Vorgeschichte*, 2:336, 351, 361.

88 Burkert, *Orientalizing Revolution*, 53–55.

89 Nilsson, *Geschichte der griechischen Religion*, 1:404, and n. 10; Burkert, *Orientalizing Revolution*, 54–55.

Thebes.[90] Arrian indicates that Alexander made sacrifices at the foundations of Alexandria ad Aegyptum and Alexandria Eschate.[91]

A recollection of practice in the remote past or extrapolation from the well-attested practice of animal sacrifice is hardly necessary to explain the idea of human foundation sacrifice in the tyche narratives. The folk belief that it was necessary to somehow secure a human life within a new construction in order to ensure its durability persisted in Greece and the Balkans at least until the end of the nineteenth century. In addition to applying the blood of a sacrificed animal to the cornerstone, in nineteenth-century Greece builders would try to set the foundation stone over a man's shadow or measure a man's shadow or his person and bury the measure under the foundation stone. In Bulgaria and Romania builders measured a man's shadow with a string and built the string into the wall of a new edifice. Certain people practiced the profession of supplying builders with such strings. Wherever these practices were known, the person whose shadow was thus manipulated was expected to die within a set period of time. His shadow represented his soul, and his life and vigor were transferred to the new building.[92] The same idea is found in the folklore motif of "the walled-up wife," pervasive throughout Greece and the Balkans.[93] In the folk tales that contain this motif a master builder must wall up his wife in the bridge, monastery, or fortress he is building in order to secure its stability. This folk belief seems to contain the best explanation of why Bouttios should suggest, and perhaps expect his readers to believe, that the initiation of a tyche image and cult, which was supposed to personify the city and ensure its prosperity and perpetuation (as the man whose shadow had been stolen or the immured wife was to do for the new construction), in almost every case necessitated a human sacrifice. I assume here that these examples from folklore and folk practice preserve memories of ritual and belief from a period when foundation sacrifices were actually performed (although with an animal substituted for a human victim). But it is also possible, of course, that this folk belief arose from fictions of human sacrifice like those of Bouttios.

90 Virgil, *Aen.* 8.42–85; Nonnus, *Dion.* 4.305–6, 311–55, 5.1–34.

91 Arr., *Anab.* 3.1.5, 4.4.1.

92 Frazer, *Golden Bough*, 3:89–91.

93 See Dundes, *Walled-Up Wife.*

The tyche sacrifices as foundation sacrifices may also have been a means of denigrating the building projects of pagan emperors. Some treatment of the subject's building activity is a standard part of the *basilikos logos*, the formal, rhetorical encomium of a ruler.[94] The building projects of Constantine, almost entirely churches, are lavishly praised by Eusebius in this style.[95] Julian's Christian detractors were quick to point out that on this same count his efforts were a dismal failure. An earthquake wrecked the martyrium he tried to build.[96] Bouttios, as we shall see, seems to make much of the contrast between Constantine and Julian. But Constantine's building program, particularly as it was praised by Eusebius, might itself be open to criticism since the churches he built accommodated only a special group of citizens, and not the general public.[97] Bouttios nullifies the achievement of pagan emperors by suggesting that their building projects, no matter how broad their appeal, are contaminated by human sacrifice. It is relevant in this regard that Tiberius sacrificed a girl in connection with his construction of a theater in Antioch, which was completed by Trajan, who also carried out a tyche sacrifice at Antioch.[98] The theater, a frequent target of criticism by churchmen,[99] was doubly damnable as an imperial building project if it was also founded on human blood.

Human Sacrifice and the *Tyche* Cult

It remains to be seen why sacrifices of the type we have described should be connected with the tyche cult. Analogies from the ancient Mediterranean are not as

94 See Av. Cameron and Hall, *Eusebius,* Life of Constantine, 31–32.

95 Euseb., *LC* 9.14–17; *VC* 2.45.2–46, 3.1.4, 25.1–43.4, 47.4–53.4, 4.58–60. See Krautheimer, "Ecclesiastical Building Policy."

96 Greg. Naz., *Or.* 4.24–26.

97 Julian, *Mis.* 346C, professed to feel the pressure to celebrate those festivals that might be enjoyed by all citizens, not only particularly religious polytheists.

98 Malalas 10.10 (**F 26**), 11.9 (**F 31**).

99 See Tertullian, *De Spectaculis*; Novatian, *De Spectaculis*; John Chrysostom, *Contra ludos et theatra* (PG 56, 263–70); Jürgens, *Pompa diaboli*; Schnusenberg, *Church and Theatre*, 1–53. Gregory of Nazianzus exploited the ambivalent and evocative image of the theatre in his invectives against Julian; see Elm, "Gregory of Nazianzus' Life of Julian," 177–78; Elm, *Sons, Fathers*, 350–53. Bloodshed and death were not, in actuality, altogether foreign to the theatre; Martial, *Spect.* 9 (7), remarks on an actual execution which took place in the context of a mime.

forthcoming as in the cases of human sacrifice and virgin sacrifice, but a broader comparative approach may help us toward an explanation of Bouttios's narratives. In the first place, it is possible that the fourth-century imagination associated the tyche with the moon, and moon worship in turn with virgin sacrifice. Sallustius, a member of Julian's circle who wrote during his reign, says that the power of fortune (*tyche*) resides in the moon, or perhaps extends as far as the moon.[100] Macrobius straightforwardly equates *Tyche* (he uses the Greek term, rather than the Latin *Fortuna*) with the moon.[101] In Heliodorus's novel, the Ethiopians intend to sacrifice the virgin Charicleia to the moon.[102] According to the rumor reported by Theodoret, Julian sacrificed a woman in a temple at Carrhae,[103] and Carrhae was famous for its temple of the Moon.[104] This association of the tyche cult with the moon, and of moon worship with virgin sacrifice, can only have been an initial inspiration for the tyche sacrifice narratives, however, because Bouttios's virgins are not, of course, sacrificed *to* the tyche; rather, by being sacrificed they become tychai.

In the Andes, from Incan until modern times, human sacrifices have apparently been made in order to procure luck or good fortune, what the Greeks might have called tyche, for the person who performs or patronizes the sacrifice.[105] The sacrificial victim becomes a divinity in this process, and himself bestows the luck

100 Sallustius 9: ἐν σελήνῃ δὲ τὴν δύναμιν ἔχει, ἐπειδὴ ὑπὲρ σελήνην οὐδὲ ἕν ἐκ τύχης ἂν γένοιτο; see Nock, *Sallustius, Concerning the Gods*, lxxv, 20–21.

101 Macrob., *Sat.* 1.19.17: Δαίμονα Τύχην Ἔρωτα Ἀνάγκην, *et duo priores solem ac lunam intellegi volunt, . . . luna* Τύχη, *quia corporum praesul est quae fortuitorum varietate iactatnur* (Godhead, Chance, Desire, Necessity: and the first two they wish to be understood as the sun and the moon, . . . the moon is Chance because she directs the steps of bodies, which are cast about by all sorts of different accidents).

102 Heliodorus, *Aeth.* 10.4; cf. 6.

103 Theodoret, *HE* 3.26.

104 Herodian, 4.13.3, says that the temple of the Moon goddess at Carrhae—perhaps something of a misunderstanding on Herodian's part, since while the Greek moon goddess Selene was female, the Mesopotamian moon deity Sin was a male god—was the principal cult center of that region, and the fame of the temple can only have increased when Caracalla was assassinated on his way to sacrifice there (Herodian, 4.13.3–8). *SHA, Carac.* 6.6, 7.1, notes that Caracalla was assassinated on his way from Edessa to Carrhae to worship the moon god, and includes some arcana on the moon cult. Cf. Lib., *Or.* 30.7, 8. See T. Green, *City of the Moon God*, 27.

105 Tierney, *Highest Altar*, 333, 336, 361–63.

on his sacrificers and other devotees in perpetuity.[106] In certain instances there is an insistence that the victim must be a young woman, since she is supposed to be married to the god or spirit to whom she is offered.[107] Grisly reports of a similar nature from India indicate that such beliefs and practices are not necessarily isolated to South America.[108]

It is a long way from the Andes to Antioch, but the parallels we find are instructive, and many of the details of South American ritual would hardly be foreign to the ancient Mediterranean. It is clear that Bouttios envisages the tyche sacrifices as situations remarkably similar to the Andean sacrifices: the virgin is sacrificed in order to produce good luck, indeed, *the* good luck of the city personified, and the victim is deified, with the full apparatus of cult including a cult statue and sacrifices. Bouttios also presents the tyche sacrifice as, in a way, a marriage. Trajan celebrates a bridal procession for Calliope as part of her tyche sacrifice.[109] The understanding of virgin sacrifice as a kind of "marriage to death" or defloration—we have already noted the affinities between rape and the tyche sacrifices—was by no means uncommon in antiquity.[110] The tyche sacrifice as marriage, moreover, might be intended to explain a potential iconographic anomaly: the girls are sacrificed as virgins to become tychai, but as Bouttios and his readers would have been very well aware, the civic tyche was depicted as a matron, rather than a maiden. This makes perfect sense, however, if the sacrifice were also something of a marriage ceremony, and the virgin was supposed to become a matron, a possessor and dispenser of goods, the mistress of a civic household, and as such fulfill her role as tyche.

106 Tierney, *Highest Altar*, 33–41, 320.

107 Tierney, *Highest Altar*, 346–51, 358.

108 A. Perry, "Killing for 'Mother' Kali."

109 Malalas 11.9 (**F 31**). Calliope's bridal procession may have been supposed to be analogous to the Boeotian Daedala ceremony, in which the Daedala, a wooden image dressed as a bride, was led to an altar in a ceremony imitating the marriage rites, sacrifices were performed, and then everything, image, altar, and sacrificial animals, were destroyed by fire; Paus. 9.3.1–8; cf. Plut., *De Daedalis Plataeensibus* 6–7 (Bernardakis, *Plutarchi Chaeronensis Moralia*, 7:46–48) = Euseb., *Praep. evang.* 3.1.6–7; see Burkert, *Greek Religion*, 135.

110 See Loraux, *Tragic Ways of Killing a Woman*, 37–42; Fowler, "Virgil on Killing Virgins"; Rehm, *Marriage to Death*.

No exact parallel to the tyche sacrifices and their rationale is obvious in the Greco-Roman world, but the case of Antinous is close. According to Cassius Dio, the truth concerning the death of Hadrian's "beloved" in 130 was that the youth had been offered as a sacrifice to satisfy Hadrian's appetite for magic spells and divination. As a result, Hadrian built a city named after him at the place where he died and established a cult in his honor, with his sacred images distributed throughout the Roman world.[111] The points of comparison are evident: a youth is sacrificed by a ruler; the victim becomes divine, or at least an object of worship, after death; if not married in death, he does become conjoined with Hadrian's godhead through his sacrifice; and his sacrifice is associated with a city foundation (and like many of the cities founded with tyche sacrifices, Antinoopolis was established on the site of a previous village). There was also some association of the tyche and Antinous inasmuch as a tyche figure was represented on the reverse of some coins depicting Antinous on the obverse.[112] The example of Antinous would have suited the polemic of Bouttios, since Christian authors especially considered Hadrian's relationship with the youth and his public and unmeasured grief for him an irredeemable blot on the emperor's reputation.[113] Gregory of Nazianzus seems to refer to the cult of Antinous as an aspect of the ridiculous paganism of Julian the Apostate, in particular when he speaks in sarcastic tones of the singular venerability of the honors rendered to the Nile by the Egyptians through hermaphrodites (αἱ παρ' Αἰγυπτίοις δι' ἀνδρογύνων τιμαὶ τοῦ Νείλου).[114] Perhaps it is due to the chances of survival, but perhaps it is because of this very open and vociferous criticism that we find no mention of Antinous in the fragments of Bouttios. In the same way that there is no explicit condemnation

111 Cass. Dio 69.11.2–4; cf. *SHA, Hadrian* 14.5–6; Aur. Vict., *Caes.* 14.7–9. On the death and deification of Antinous, see Lambert, *Beloved and God*, esp. 128–54, 177–97; Boatwright, *Hadrian and the City of Rome*, 239–60; Vout, "Biography as Fantasy"; Galimberti, *Adriano e l'ideologia*, 139–44; Calandra, "Villa Adriana," 47; Galli, "La *paideia* di Adriano," 57; C. Jones, *New Heroes in Antiquity*, 75–83. On the foundation of Antinoopolis, see Bell, "Antinoopolis"; Lambert, *Beloved and God*, 198–208; Boatwright, *Hadrian and the Cities*, 190–96; Galimberti, *Adriano e l'ideologia*, 152, 182; Calandra, "La città e il nome."

112 Specifically, the coins of Philadelphia in Mysia; see Blum, "Numismatique d'Antinoos," 49, pl. 3, no. 14.

113 See Hermann, "Antinous infelix," 155–67; Chadwick, *Early Christian Thought*, 11; Guyot, "Antinous als Eunuch"; Nadig, "Antinoos—Ein Paradigma."

114 Greg. Naz., *Or.* 5.32 (Bernardi, *Grégoire de Nazianze, Discours 4–5*, 360).

of virgin sacrifice, so that the reader must make his own judgments, a clear reference to Antinous might have given the game away as a tendentious hatchet job, whereas implicit allusion to the case of Antinous nudges along the reader's reaction to what appears to be a historical report.

Overall Composition

The foregoing has suggested that Bouttios's making villains of the perpetrators of human sacrifice and his direction of the reader's sympathies toward the victim lend a romantic aspect to the accounts of tyche sacrifice. Virgin sacrifice, however, properly belongs to romance insofar as, at the climax of the narrative, the actual sacrifice of the heroine is averted in the nick of time by the arrival of the hero. But in each instance of the tyche sacrifice there is no rescue, and the emphasis seems to be on the grisly rite and not the maiden's vulnerability. This might seem to suggest that the tyche sacrifices are intended merely as an attack on the origins of the tyche cult, appealing to the ancient appreciation for the macabre,[115] and that they cannot properly be described as romantic. Unless, that is, Constantine's "bloodless sacrifice" and the new tyche of Constantinople are seen to constitute the climax of Bouttios's history of tyche sacrifices. The previous tyche sacrifices allow the audience to realize the peril facing the heroine at the climax because they have already seen a number of maidens fall victim to the same danger under similar circumstances, with no hero to rescue them. Constantine's act of romantic heroism lies in that, shunning human sacrifice, or pagan blood sacrifice of any kind, he rescues Anthousa (if Constantinople's tyche, like the previous ones, was supposed to be named after an actual girl[116]) or any

115 Strabo 7.3.9, quoting Ephorus (*FGrHist* 70 F 42), notes in regard to accounts of Scythian cannibalism that terrible and strange phenomena produce a vivid effect and so tend to be favored by writers. Strabo and Ephorus may attest to a taste for the macabre among many in antiquity, but Laws, *Frighteners*, has suggested that it is a persistent human trait, which is perhaps more likely to manifest itself in those societies that are actually most placid and untroubled by real violence and gore.

116 No girl named Anthousa is mentioned in Malalas. "Anthousa" is the Greek equivalent of *Flora*, the "sacred name" of Rome; see Lathoud, "La consécration et la dédicace de Constantinople (Suite [I])," 180–87; Alföldi, *Conversion of Constantine*, 114; Dagron, *Naissance d'une capitale*, 44, 45; Ando, *Matter of the Gods*, 189–92. It is possible that no actual girl was described as being present at the inauguration of Constantinople's tyche,

prospective victim, and, by introducing a new way to establish tychai, all potential victims in future. And so the tyche sacrifices, despite their obvious affinities with the "penny dreadfuls," are more than a simple catalog of terrors. They prepare the audience for the climactic heroism of Constantine.

A number of episodes in the ancient novels follow a similar pattern. The heroine is about to be sacrificed or ritually killed, the audience is made to realize the danger she is in, and the hero arrives to rescue her in the nick of time. These incidents in the novels probably have their antecedents in the myths of Theseus and the Minotaur, and Perseus and Andromeda, but the monsters of the myths add another element to the basic narrative, which is not found in the at least historically plausible accounts of Bouttios. In the novel a pronounced erotic aspect is also found in the pattern of these incidents. In the *Ephesiaca* of Xenophon of Ephesus, Anthia, the virginal heroine, is captured by bandits and about to be sacrificed to Ares, her peril is realized through a detailed description of the sacrificial rite, at the last minute she is rescued by the hero Perilaus, and this rescue leads to repeated proposals of marriage, which constitute the erotic aspect.[117] There is a similar narrative in both ps.-Lucian's *Onos* and the *Metamorphoses* of Apuleius.[118] A maiden (Charite in Apuleius) is captured by bandits, and after an escape attempt they plan to sew her up in the belly of the ass, admittedly not a sacrifice but a death deliberated to the point of ritual. The danger she faces is brought home to the reader through the suicide of the old crone who was guarding her, the bandits' callous treatment of that woman's corpse, and the sadistic debate over the most appropriate method of killing the girl. But she is rescued by her fiancé, and a wedding follows. In Achilles Tatius's novel, Leucippe is snatched away to serve as a virgin sacrifice, and her peril is realized not only in the detailed description of the exotic sacrificial rite with its libations and Egyptian chanting but also in the apparent performance of the sacrifice itself, leaping entrails and

---

but this does not seem altogether consistent with the literal-mindedness displayed in the rest of the tyche sacrifice narratives.

117 Xenophon of Ephesus 2.13.

118 Ps.-Lucian, *Onos* 22–26; Apuleius, *Met.* 4.23–27, 6.25–7.13. Apuleius makes it clear that his bandits, like those in Xenophon, are devotees of Ares; see *Met.* 4.22, 7.5, 11. Lucius, the sometime ass, moreover, shows that virginity is important to the erotic aspect of the narrative by demonstrating a great concern for the maiden's chastity, when he suspects her of being a slattern when he sees her recognize her fiancé; *Met.* 7.11.

all, although the hero and the reader later discover that this was a sham.[119] The erotic aspect of this situation is only articulated later when Cleitophon refers to the dangers they have overcome, including human sacrifice and ritual murder, as an inducement to premature sexual union, which Leucippe demurely refuses.[120] The deliverance of Theagenes and Charicleia just as they are about to be sacrificed by the Ethiopians forms the protracted and much anticipated climax of Heliodorus's *Aethiopica*. It is true that in this case Charicleia is not rescued by Theagenes, but then it would be thoroughly inappropriate for such an active and resourceful heroine to turn helpless in the end. And the climactic sacrifice of the *Aethiopica* becomes a prelude to the wedding of the hero and heroine, the most satisfying erotic outcome possible in the ancient novel.

The pattern can be found not only in the narrative of the novels, but in their descriptions of visual effects as well. Achilles Tatius describes two pictures by the same artist, one of Andromeda and one of Prometheus.[121] These two pictures are united by the similar peril of their subjects: bound to rocks, menaced by beasts, and saved by Argive heroes. They are both depicted at the timely moment of salvation by Perseus and Heracles respectively. There is an erotic element in the depiction of Andromeda only. "Lovely fear" (εὔμορφος φόβος) accentuates her beauty—Prometheus's expression, by contrast, conveys only pain—and she is dressed in a wedding garment to be married to Hades. The erotic undertones of Andromeda's situation, moreover, may have been generally understood. The *Imagines* of Philostratus of Lemnos include Eros as the divine helper of Perseus, and say that the beauty of Andromeda was perfected by her mixed emotions of fear and joy at the moment of her rescue.[122] And Heliodorus mentions a painting of Andromeda, depicted nude and only just rescued by Perseus, in the bedroom of the Ethiopian king and queen, while other scenes decorate less intimate parts of the palace, which catches the eye of the queen during sexual congress, and so may have been intended as erotic art.[123]

119 Achilles Tatius 3.12, 15.

120 Achilles Tatius 4.1.

121 Achilles Tatius 3.6–8. See Harlan, "Description of Paintings," 107–22; Bartsch, *Decoding the Ancient Novel*, 46, 49, 54–62.

122 Philostratus, *Imag.* 1.29. See Bartsch, *Decoding the Ancient Novel*, 54, 71.

123 Heliodorus, *Aeth.* 4.8. See Bartsch, *Decoding the Ancient Novel*, 48.

The most effective means of having the audience realize the danger facing the heroine is for numerous doomed victims, like the tyche sacrifices, to suffer the very fate that threatens her before her final salvation. There are no examples of such previous victims in the ancient novel, but this device is present in the very bedrock of Greco-Roman literature. In the *Odyssey*, the audience knows what terrors await the hero in the cave of the Cyclops because they first witness the death of Odysseus's companions at the hands of Polyphemus, before Odysseus, who is explicitly reserved for the last, manages to save himself.[124] As he himself relates the story to the Phaeacians, Odysseus, as well as his listeners, knows what fate he can expect as soon as Polyphemus snatches up two of his crewmen, slaughters them, and gulps them down; the first instance is emphasized with gruesome detail, but the sense of impending doom and the urgency of escape only build as the Cyclops makes two more meals of two men each.[125] Polyphemus menaces Odysseus by offering him a grim boon of hospitality:

> οὖτιν ἐγὼ πύματον ἔδομαι μετὰ οἷς ἑτάροισι,
> τοὺς δ' ἄλλους πρόσθεν· τὸ δέ τοι ξεινήιον ἔσται.[126]

> I shall eat No Man last of all his companions
> and the others beforehand; this will be your guest-gift!

But this is no kind of a hospitable concession, but rather a dire threat intended to make Odysseus anticipate with dread his own end as he witnesses the horrible deaths of his companions.

An even more apposite example of previous victims underscoring the peril facing the chief protagonist may be found in Pausanias's story of the ghost at

124 *Od.* 9.216–479.

125 *Od.* 9.287–98, 310–12, 343–44.

126 *Od.* 9.369–70. This passage, and the "gift" of the Polyphemus in particular, was recognized in the Christian rhetorical response to the reign of Julian the Apostate, the context that we have suggested for the writings of Bouttios. In his second posthumous invective against the emperor, Gregory of Nazianzus (*Or.* 5.39) tacitly admits that he and Basil of Caesarea went untouched by the persecutions of Julian's reign, but explains this by pretending to assume that Julian had paid them the same courtesy the Cyclops paid to Odysseus, reserving them as the last victims of his persecution, perhaps intending them for thank-offerings to the demons on his victorious return from Persia; see Elm, *Sons, Fathers*, 465–66.

Temesa.[127] According to Pausanias, one of the crew of Odysseus raped a girl at Temesa and was consequently stoned to death by the locals. His ghost (*daimon* is the word used in Greek) was indiscriminately killing the people of Temesa, until they built a temple to him and began to offer him the most beautiful virgin as a wife every year.[128] This arrangement continued until the boxer Euthymus arrived some time in the fifth century BCE, fought the ghost and drove him into the sea, and married the virgin intended for the ghost. Pausanias also describes a picture of the ghost that evokes his baleful character: black in color, frightful in appearance, and garbed in a wolfskin. As in the tyche sacrifices, this story contains the killing in a formal religious context of virgin victims who are supposed to be married through the ritual, numerous previous victims since the legendary past, and ultimate salvation by a hero. These examples from Homer and Pausanias show that Greek and Roman writers were aware of a device commonly used to evoke horror, and one apparently used by Bouttios. By recalling a story like that found in Pausanias, moreover, Bouttios implies that the tyche, rather than being a benevolent or even capricious power, is a dark and malicious spirit, like the ghost, and even seems to echo Eusebius's assertion that demons are the real instigators and recipients of blood sacrifice, including human sacrifice.[129]

When the tyche sacrifice narratives are read together, Constantine's initiation of Constantinople's tyche without a virgin sacrifice becomes not merely one more incident but the heroic climax, on the model of the rescues in the novel, of a grisly history of foundations accompanied by human sacrifice. Such a climactic

127 Paus. 6.6.7–11. The story is also found in Strabo 6.1.5 and Aelian, *VH* 8.18, although without the element of virgin sacrifice (the Temesans are said, rather, to pay a tribute to the ghost). See Frazer, *Pausanias' Description*, 4:23–24; Fontenrose, *Python*, 101–5; Fontenrose, "Hero as Athlete," 79–83; Visintin, *La vergine e l'eroe*; Felton, *Haunted Greece and Rome*, 26–27; Currie, "Euthymos of Locri."

128 In presenting the story of Euthymus of Locri as a model for Bouttios, the interpretation of Visintin, *La vergine e l'eroe*, 79–81, 131–33, 148–53, that the offering of a maiden was understood as a virgin sacrifice, is clearly preferable to Currie's interpretation, "Euthymos of Locri," 30–33, of the offering of a maiden as a prenuptial defloration ritual, and Visintin's reading is adopted here. The settling of this debate, however, is more critical to questions of the precedents and origins, as well as the realia, of the cult of Euthymos, than to the influence of the stories about him, which could obviously be understood in terms of a heroic intervention to bring about the end of a long-standing ritual of human sacrifice.

129 Euseb., *LC* 2.5, 7.6.

abolition of human sacrifice has further affinities with the novel, inasmuch as at the climax of Heliodorus's *Aethiopica* the Ethiopian priest Sisimithres sees the events of the romance as conspiring to convince the Ethiopians to give up their ancestral practice of human sacrifice.[130] The tyche sacrifices that precede the foundation of Constantinople are not only examples of the pagan wickedness abolished by Constantine, they also give a vivid impression of the dangers from which Constantine has rescued an imperiled heroine, be it a girl by the name of Anthousa or innocent maidenhood generally. Bouttios does not, however, fully exploit the erotic aspect of the rescue from virgin sacrifice found in the novels. There is no marriage following the rescue. The sympathies of Bouttios's readers are directed toward a lovely victim, but, as is appropriate for an emperor, the benefits of Constantine's heroism are enjoyed not by himself alone but by his people as a whole.

Our reconstruction of Bouttios's work as a rather romantic history, depicting Constantine as a hero in the mold of a character in an adventure story and extolling him as the culmination of a long line of kings and emperors, is not inconsistent with some presentations of Constantine in his own lifetime, nor with the legends that later grew up around his person. Praxagoras of Athens, an author known to us only from the *Bibliotheca* of Photius, wrote a history of Constantine in two books at some time between the foundation of Constantinople and the emperor's death.[131] Photius's summary suggests that Praxagoras's history portrayed the opponents of Constantine as cruel tyrants and Constantine himself as the deliverer of the people of the Roman Empire. This unsurprising propaganda was colored, however, with fabulous and heroic tints: the first incident in the *Bibliotheca* entry relates that Maximin (Maximian) set Constantine to fight a fierce lion, which he slew and thus escaped the plot against him.[132] Lactantius also reports that Galerius induced the young Constantine to fight a wild beast, but Lactantius is an unlikely source for the pagan Praxagoras, and the incident

130 Heliodorus, *Aeth.* 10.39; see Hunter, "*Aithiopika* of Heliodorus," 58–59; Winkler, "Mendacity of Kalasiris," 344–48.

131 Phot., *Bibl.* 62 (= *FGrHist* 219). See Moreau, "Zum Problem," 236–42; Millar, "P. Herennius Dexippus," 15; Winkelmann, "Historiography," 14–15, 34–35, 41; Janiszewski, *Missing Link*, 161–64, 263–65, 352–71; Smith, "Lost Historian"; Van Dam, *Roman Revolution*, 161.

132 Phot., *Bibl.* 62 (*FGrHist* 219 T 1.2).

probably has some basis in fact, although its emphasis speaks to the nature of the Athenian's work.[133] This briefly related interlude reveals in Praxagoras a flair for the dramatic, as well as a determination to bestow on Constantine the virtues not only of a great emperor but also of a storybook hero. Although he was a pagan, Praxagoras concluded his history by stating that Constantine outdid all the emperors before him in all virtue, nobility, and good fortune.[134] A similar sentiment seems to underlie the composition of Bouttios, and Praxagoras and Bouttios appear to have expressed the same idea in much the same fashion. Indeed, the oeuvre of Praxagoras as a whole bears some comparison with the content and interests of Bouttios. In addition to the history of Constantine, Praxagoras also wrote two books about the kings of Athens and six books on Alexander of Macedon.[135] The treatment of antiquarian lore and the careers of Alexander and Constantine in romantic terms, even if not in a single work, certainly reflects what we can piece together of Bouttios's writing and suggests that it may not have been out of place among the histories composed in the fourth century.

The legendary material concerning Constantine is diffuse and difficult to date, and while the core of it was probably set down in the early fifth century on the basis of earlier material, its composition continued for many centuries thereafter.[136] Some of these legends associate Constantine with human sacrifice, though not exactly as Bouttios does. Rather, he is depicted as both very nearly the perpetrator and very nearly the victim of human sacrifice. According to a story found in the *Acts of Sylvester* and various Byzantine lives, before his conversion Constantine suffered from leprosy and a number of his pagan priests urged him to bathe in the blood of infants as a cure. The children were duly gathered up, but Constantine was so put out by the crying of their mothers that he sent them home. That night he received a vision of Saints Peter and Paul instructing him to seek help from Pope Sylvester. Sylvester eventually baptized Constantine, who was healed of his leprosy and undertook the Christianization

133 Lactant., *De mort. pers.* 24.4; see Janiszewski, *Missing Link*, 365.

134 Phot., *Bibl.* 62 (*FGrHist* 219 T 1.8); cf. Bleckmann, "Pagane Visionen Konstantins."

135 Phot., *Bibl.* 62 (*FGrHist* 219 T 1.10).

136 Levison, "Konstantinische Schenkung"; Halkin, *Bibliotheca Hagiographica Graeca*, 1:121–25, 2:239–41 (361–69, 1628–34); Aiello, "Costantino, la lebbra"; Lieu and Montserrat, *From Constantine to Julian*, 99–106; Lieu, "From History to Legend," 139; Lieu, "Constantine in Legendary Literature," 299.

of his empire.[137] Constantine may seem a less sympathetic character in this story than in Bouttios's account, since he does entertain the thought of slaughtering infants for his own ends, but it is nevertheless Constantine who ultimately prevents the killing of the children. More importantly, the sacrifice of innocent children is presented as emblematic of Constantine's pagan precedents. Bouttios may be more skillful in showing Constantine to be a blameless agent of change in the rule of the Roman Empire, but the legend's depiction of change in the person and conduct of Constantine himself conveys the same message about the horrible rituals of paganism undone by the conversion of Constantine. Another legend relates that Constantine was captured in war by the Persians, who intended to sacrifice him in a religious ceremony. Constantine's soldiers, however, were led by traitors into the Persian camp and rescued their emperor just as he was about to be sacrificed.[138] Constantine does not fill the role of the hero in this story, but it may still be seen that the figure of Constantine attracted novelistic treatments including such tried and true elements as the imminent threat of ritual sacrifice and rescue in the nick of time.

In the legend that comes closest in its mechanics to our reconstruction of the overall composition of Bouttios, Constantine does not figure as the hero, but the contemporary pope Sylvester, whom the legends often associate with Constantine, does. The story goes that in the vicinity of Rome there dwelt in a deep cavern a dragon with lethal breath and horrible appetites. Every month the deceitful pagan priests would descend into this cave with certain virgins, perform their unspeakable mysteries, and leave the girls behind with a meal for the dragon. This went on until Sylvester went down into the cave, overcame the dragon by a means revealed to him in a vision of St. Peter, restrained it and locked it behind a door until Doomsday, and put an end to the monster's exactions upon

137 *Actus Silvestri* 1.4–10 (Mombritius, *Sanctuarium seu Vitae Sanctorum*, 2:510.32–513.34; De Leo, *Ricerche sui falsi medioevali 1*, 161–69); see Burch, *Myth and Constantine*, 62–65; Kazhdan, "'Constantin imaginaire,'" 239; Lieu and Montserrat, *From Constantine to Julian*, 119–22; Lieu, "From History to Legend," 137–38; Lieu, "Constantine in Legendary Literature," 299–300.

138 Kazhdan, "'Constantin imaginaire,'" 234; Lieu and Montserrat, *From Constantine to Julian*, 113–15; see Lieu, "From History to Legend," 167–68; Lieu, "Constantine in Legendary Literature," 313–17.

the virgin daughters of Rome.[139] Here, as in the fragments of Bouttios, we have the regular performance of a ritual akin to virgin sacrifice. The introduction of a monstrous dragon may make the story somewhat more fantastic, but also returns the whole narrative to its roots in myths of heroes saving damsels in distress. The priests who officiate over the sacrifice to the dragon and their mysteries make it clear that the monstrous antagonist represents the whole complex of pagan religion, just as Bouttios uses virgin sacrifice to signify the pagan past of the rulership of the Roman Empire. And it is a Christian hero, a contemporary and associate of Constantine, who brings the long and lamentable history of offering the ministrations of virgins to diabolical powers to an end. With the legends, as with the history of Praxagoras of Athens, we have near contemporary material consistent with our reconstruction of Bouttios's history as an often romantic depiction of Constantine as a climactic hero who brought the grisly rites of paganism to an end.

Bouttios was dubbed a chronographer by Malalas, but he did not write a chronicle. Rather, chronographic precision would have been detrimental to his attempts to recast the timeline of Assyrian history, and ill adapted to his presentation of the past in terms of broad contrasts and vivid episodes. His work took the form of a history, but it reveals the characteristics of a Platonic myth, a purposive fiction along the lines of Julian's *Caesars*. Indeed, it is possible that Bouttios wrote in response to Julian, and offers us a rare glimpse of the sort of mockery the apostate emperor complains he was subjected to by the Antiochenes. Bouttios also seems to have exploited the predispositions of his audience in regard to virgin sacrifice in order to direct their sympathies against the pagan heroes and rulers he discussed, and to incline them to see Constantine as the heroic culmination of a long line of dastardly tyrants. He may have written a history, but it was a partisan history which borrowed freely from the realm of fiction for inspiration, for techniques, and for narrative patterns.

139 *Actus Silvestri* 2.12 (Mombritius, *Sanctuarium seu Vitae Sanctorum*, 2:529.5–530.21; De Leo, *Ricerche sui falsi medioevali 1*, 214–18); see Burch, *Myth and Constantine*, 50–62; Lieu, "From History to Legend," 137, 156.

PART III

WRITING HISTORY, WRITING PROPAGANDA

7

POLEMICAL HISTORY

It is a commonplace among historians that the conversion of Constantine marks a watershed in the Christianization of the Roman Empire. Ever after—with one brief hiatus—the Roman monarchy in all its various permutations would go hand in hand with a state-sponsored church. The reign of Julian the Apostate, that brief hiatus, must seem like an aberration in the course of history or a pitifully quixotic attempt to turn the tide. But history's course is very rarely evident to the man caught in its stream. We can say with the confidence of hindsight that after Julian a pagan would never again occupy the imperial throne. For his contemporaries, however, there was nothing to assure that such a possibility was precluded. Along with the hopes of the pagans, the Apostate's reign must have raised some distressing prospects for Christians, especially those who welcomed an alliance between Christ and Caesar. Such apprehensions would only have been reinforced by the nomination of Julian's friend and fellow pagan, Sallustius, and his son as successors to Jovian (both of which invitations to the purple were declined)[1] and by what were perceived and presented by Christian authors as the pagan aspects of the regime of the usurper Eugenius in Rome (392–394).[2] The Christianization of

1 Zos. 3.36.2; see Marcone, *Giuliano*, 119.

2 Paulinus, *Vit. Ambr.* 26, 31; Rufinus, *HE* 11.33; Sozomen, *HE* 7.22, 24; Theodoret, *HE* 5.25 (24); August., *De civ. D.* 5.26.1; cf. Socrates Schol., *HE* 5.25; Eunapius, *Hist.* FF 58–60 (Blockley, *Fragmentary Classicizing Historians*, 2:83–91); Zos. 4.54–59. See Bloch, "Pagan Revival," 199–201; Chuvin, *Chronicle of the Last Pagans*, 69–71; Hedrick, *History and Silence*, 39–54; Van Dam, *Roman Revolution*, 348–49. Al. Cameron, *Last Pagans of Rome*,

the Roman Empire, at least to all appearances, depended on a Christian emperor, and there was no Act of Settlement to prevent the vicissitudes of death, succession, or usurpation from bringing a pagan to the throne.

So the prevailing climate of the later fourth century was not one of Christian triumphalism, but one of contention and anxiety.[3] The Christians and the pagans

---

74–131, presents the promotion of paganism imputed to Eugenius and the pagan activity attributed to his courtiers as so much artificial rhetorical contrivance on the part of their Christian reporters, and as no evidence for an actual pagan revival in Rome; but even baseless rhetoric, deployed effectively—Cameron's smoke without fire—would have been sufficient to stoke the fears we are discussing.

3 Mayer, "Re-Theorizing Religious Conflict," has done much to uncover many of the biases and prejudices that underlie the academic study of religious conflict in early Christianity and Late Antiquity and to provide a critique of current theoretical approaches, particularly as occasioned by what she calls "the neuroscientific turn." Much recent revisionist scholarship has presented the religious or ideological opposition of Late Antiquity as a product of the Christian perspective, with little active engagement by the pagan side; see P. Brown, *Power and Persuasion*, 127–29; Hedrick, *History and Silence*, 47–54. Drake, "Fourth-Century Christianity," 360, has also indicated his doubts about this "war scenario." There may very well be a great deal of truth in this interpretation, but as we are discussing a Christian author and his writings, the concept of opposition remains significant, even if it reflects a specific contemporary approach to society rather than a broader social reality.

Cannadine, *Undivided Past*, 15–25, in pursuing a broader thesis insisting that humanity has historically been more cohesive and congenial than many ideologues have liked to assert, notes the shift in scholarship on Late Antiquity from a dominant narrative of the fall of paganism and the rise of Christianity to a more nuanced understanding that stresses variety within both traditions, interaction, and peaceful coexistence. This shift has to a great extent been a result of greater scholarly emphasis on the day-to-day reality of the man in the street rather than the rhetorical postures assumed by controversialists. Bouttios, however, must be counted among these polarizing controversialists.

Watts, *Final Pagan Generation*, depicts the "final pagan generation" of his title, the men born early in the fourth century who supposedly worked under the assumption that the world of state-sponsored paganism and institutional order in which they grew up would continue indefinitely, as far more interested in career advancement and the deployment of influence than in what he calls "confessional conflict"—although the pagans had nothing like the Christian confessions—and lays much of the blame for the violence of the last decades of the fourth century at the feet of the next generation, who could imagine and work toward a transformed world (4). The vivid and evocative picture he presents depends to a great extent on a careful selection of representative figures. In intellectual terms the battle lines had already been drawn by the Christian apologists in the third

were opposed as two parties on a more or less equal footing, and the sympathies of the ruling emperor could tip the balance one way or the other, but who would be emperor and for how long nobody knew. This opposition, perhaps more often than not, manifested itself in rhetoric rather than violence.[4] This is the context in which we can make the most sense of the fragments of Bouttios. He neither wrote history for history's sake nor was he engaged in disinterested antiquarianism. Instead, he turned to the past as one more battlefield on which to wage an ongoing war of persuasion and partisan commitment. He was a polemicist who exploited the authority of history, and a historian who was ideologically invested in his version of the events of the past.

The partisan animosity to which Bouttios contributed had an essentially ideological basis. The parties did not disagree over points of policy; they were divided in regard to worldviews and questions of ultimate value. The Christians no longer pleaded for some accommodation in an essentially alien realm, but rather had come to view the dominion of the *oikoumene* as the Church's destiny, while the pagans insisted that the continued order of the world depended on the maintenance of traditional cult and custom. The political dimension of the opposition lay in the fact that the support of the emperor offered inestimable assistance to one side or the other. So each side wanted power in the hands of an adherent of its own ideology. Both parties pursued this goal rather indirectly, because neither was in a position to select the next emperor, much less do anything about

---

century and before, and Eusebius of Caesarea, who belonged to the generation preceding the one of which Watts writes, had already forcefully conceived of the potential of a Christian Empire at the opening of the fourth century.

4 Even Peter Brown, who insisted that the late Roman upper classes would have been scandalized by the suggestion that the designation as pagan or Christian was the paramount distinction in their society, conceded that the rhetoric of intolerance belonged to the theorists or "chattering classes" on both sides, the philosophers and apologists, while actual incidents of violence were moderated by the serene, self-assured, even courteous exercise of power expected of the ruling class made up of magistrates, bishops, and governors; Brown, *Authority and the Sacred*, 29–54, esp. 38 and 47. Once again, Bouttios most certainly belonged to the chattering classes and we should not be surprised to find vehement and polarizing messages embedded in what survives of his writing. As far as actual violence prompted by ideology is concerned, though, Bremmer, "Religious Violence and Its Roots," offers a series of theses, informed by global comparanda and contemporary evidence, that should challenge and guide future research on religious violence in antiquity.

the incumbent one. We are not privy to backroom negotiations and only rarely to public demonstrations, so our evidence for the efforts of both sides is largely rhetorical. And much of this rhetoric is of a historical nature, for very good reasons. It might be dangerous to dwell on the allegiances that were supposed to disqualify a current candidate from the imperial office, or on generalities that might be applied to men who had a good chance of coming to the throne. But there was an established tradition of discussing the virtues and vices of past emperors. The personalities of these now departed rulers could represent the ideologies they had followed, their reigns suggesting the fitness of one ideology or the other to predominate, and they could be praised or disparaged accordingly.

Constantine and Julian were the emperors especially prominent in the rhetorical contest between Christianity and paganism, each side taking one for its champion and the other for its bête noire.[5] Eusebius of Caesarea, particularly in his *Praise of Constantine* and *Life of Constantine*, presented the first Christian emperor and his reign as no less than the culmination of world history and the process of salvation.[6] The pagan historian Eunapius, by contrast, vilified Constantine as a tyrant and the instigator of a dangerous innovation, while he found in Julian, the man and the ruler, a paragon of every virtue.[7] And on the death of the Apostate, Gregory of Nazianzus delivered a Christian riposte in his two *Orations against Julian*, in which the genuine sigh of relief undoubtedly breathed by his party is nearly choked by a stream of vituperation, innuendo, and slander against the recently deceased emperor.[8] But the contrast between Constantine and Julian was made not only on the level of formal rhetoric and literature, but also on that of popular legend. One such story is of particular interest

5 See Marcone, *Giuliano*, 247–54.

6 See Drake, In Praise of Constantine; Av. Cameron and Hall, *Eusebius,* Life of Constantine; Av. Cameron, "Form and Meaning." Lenski, *Constantine and the Cities*, 1–6, traces some of the permutations that the presentation of Constantine has undergone since antiquity.

7 See Blockley, *Fragmentary Classicizing Historians*, 1:2, 3, 7, 19–23, 88–89. See Bleckmann, "*Constantinus tyrannus.*"

8 Greg. Naz., *Or.* 4 and 5. See Elm, "Hellenism and Historiography"; Elm, "Gregory of Nazianzus' Life of Julian"; Elm, *Sons, Fathers,* 336–477. Another contemporary Christian effort to vilify Julian on his death is to be found in the *Hymns against Julian* of Ephraem the Syrian, who mentions in his meditations having seen the coffin of the deceased emperor; see Griffith, "Ephraem the Syrian's Hymns 'Against Julian.'"

because it juxtaposes the two emperors in relation to a tyche figure. According to the *Suda*, Constantine set up a statue of the tyche of the city in a prominent place in Constantinople, but marked her forehead with a cross. Julian was so incensed at this sanctifying mark that he buried the statue in a ditch.[9] This opposition of Constantine and Julian in regard to their treatment of a tyche seems to be one of many indications that the fragments of Bouttios, in which the tyche plays such a prominent part, should be read as praise of Constantine and blame of Julian. There are, moreover, remarkable similarities in diction and content between the material we have ascribed to Bouttios on the one hand and the rhetoric concerning Constantine and Julian on the other.

Constantine and Julian

The last few fragments of Bouttios (**FF 33–35**) are consistent with the other accounts of tyche sacrifice in that they deal with the inauguration of a tyche figure at the foundation of a city, but as we have already noted, this last scenario is climactically distinct. Constantine's sacrifice was a bloodless one and it overturned that custom of virgin sacrifice that had marked the tyche cult up to his own day. The bloodless sacrifice is not only significant in the context of the other fragments of Bouttios, it also plays a part in Eusebius's acclamation of Constantine. In the *Life of Constantine* the emperor's prayers and thanksgiving to God, as well as his banquet with the bishops, are described as "sacrifices without fire or smoke"

9 *Suda*, s.v. Μίλιον (M 1064) (Adler, *Suidae Lexicon*, 3:395); cf. *Parastaseis Syntomoi Chronikai* 38; see Dagron, *Naissance d'une capitale*, 41, 309 n. 1; Av. Cameron and Herrin, *Constantinople in the Early Eighth Century*, 217–18; Kazhdan, "'Constantin imaginaire,'" 250; cf. Ando, *Matter of the Gods*, 189. This seems to be a legend intended to explain some material remains rather than an account of actual events, because the story makes Constantine responsible for setting up the statue in the first place and engraving a cross on its head, but we know that rather than crafting new monuments and marking them, it was common practice for Christians to sanctify relics of the pagan past with the sign of the cross; see Hjort, "Augustus Christianus"; Kristensen, "Embodied Images," 229–31; Sauer, "Disabling Demonic Images," 23. The legend betrays some awareness of Julian's polemic against the Christians, which includes (*Contra Galilaeos* 194C) the accusation that rather than the relics of the gods they revered the cross, and even drew its sign upon their foreheads.

or acceptable sacrifices.[10] The rituals performed by the bishops assembled before Constantine at Jerusalem in 335 are called "bloodless sacrifices."[11] And in a letter to the Persian king, quoted by Eusebius, Constantine contrasts his own prayers to God with the blood and stench of sacrifice.[12] The rhetoric of bloodless sacrifice is even more important in the *Praise of Constantine*. The emperor is presented as rejecting ancient usage and celebrating his Tricennalia not with bloody sacrifices to ghouls, demons, and false gods, but with the devotion of his "kingly soul" and his mind to the Supreme God as a sacrifice "without fire and the shedding of blood."[13] Christ alone, says Eusebius, teaches his followers to offer "bloodless and rational sacrifices" (ἀναίμους δὲ καὶ λογικὰς θυσίας) through their prayers and the silent contemplation of God. These "bloodless sacrifices," offered on altars in churches throughout the world, have displaced gory animal sacrifice, as well as the cruel, mad practice of human sacrifice.[14]

It is not simply the phrase "bloodless sacrifice" in Bouttios's writing that recalls the rhetoric of Eusebius. Human sacrifice also figures prominently in the *Praise of Constantine* as a characteristic trait of the pagan wickedness which the Christianity espoused by Constantine has dispelled. Ancient pagan rulers, deceived by demons, those "spiritual barbarians," are said to have offered their own people as sacrifices to the gods and made war against the champions of truth.[15] A catalog of human sacrifice is offered as an indication of the evils and miseries of the world that prompted the merciful Incarnation of the Logos.[16] And the Crucifixion and the Resurrection of the Savior serve as an apotropaic aversion of the human sacrifices that used to be performed.[17] In Eusebius's encomium of Constantine, as in the tyche sacrifice fragments of Bouttios, human sacrifice is habitually performed by pagan rulers, and Constantine puts a stop to it, as a special boon of Christianity.

10 Euseb., *VC* 1.48, 3.15.1. Constantine's celebration of "bloodless sacrifice" must be seen in the context of his outlawing of bloody sacrifice, a matter that has been contested but seems confirmed by the testimony of Eusebius; see Barnes, "Constantine's Prohibition."

11 Euseb., *VC* 4.45.2.

12 Euseb., *VC* 4.10.1.

13 Euseb., *LC* 2.5, 3.1.

14 Euseb., *LC* 16.9–10.

15 Euseb., *LC* 7.5–6.

16 Euseb., *LC* 13.6b–8; cf. 13.15–16. See Drake, In Praise of Constantine, 176–77.

17 Euseb., *LC* 15.11–13. See Drake, In Praise of Constantine, 178–79.

That the tyche cults begin with virgin sacrifices, moreover, recalls other aspects of the rhetoric of Eusebius. Maxentius, Constantine's rival, is said to have regularly violated the chaste women of Rome, while Constantine enacted laws to improve the legal position of consecrated virgins, for whom he had the utmost respect.[18] Constantine's reign brought an end to the mistreatment of virgins quite as much as to the practice of human sacrifice. What is a rhetorical device in Eusebius is presented as historical fact by Bouttios.

Just as Constantine enjoys a uniquely climactic place in Bouttios's history as a ruler who established the tyche of his newly founded city without the bloody sacrifice of a virgin, he is presented in Eusebius's biography as uniquely superior to his predecessors and an innovator who overturned the evil of his rivals.[19] He is the only emperor to whom God revealed the true religion and whom God made his herald, alone among emperors he received baptism, and alone among mortals he reigned after his death.[20] In contrast to his rivals, who are depicted as tyrants and persecutors of the Church,[21] Constantine's conduct vouchsafes his legitimacy and he protects Christians. Maxentius in particular is shown as a tyrant of the deepest dye. In addition to his rape of chaste women, he engages in sorcery to preserve his throne, and even rips open pregnant women and investigates the entrails of newborn babies.[22] The rulers who engage in tyche sacrifice, with their violation of chaste women, concomitant persecution of Christians (as by Trajan), and ritual killing of innocent victims, reflect the rivals of Constantine as Eusebius presents them. Constantine is singularly superior, moreover, not only to previous

18 Euseb., *VC* 1.33–34 (cf. *HE* 8.14.2), 4.26.3. See Av. Cameron and Hall, *Eusebius,* Life of Constantine, 321–23.

19 Damgaard, "Propaganda against Propaganda," 128–29, asserts that one of the ways Eusebius does this is by jettisoning the usual comparisons with his imperial Roman predecessors and insisting that Constantine can find his equal only in Moses.

20 Euseb., *VC* 1.4; 4.62.4, 67.3.

21 Euseb., *VC* 1.5.1, 12.2, 2.1.2, 18, 3.1–3, 12.2; cf. *LC* 7.12. See Av. Cameron and Hall, *Eusebius,* Life of Constantine, 37–38, 42; Van Dam, *Roman Revolution*, 274; Lenski, *Constantine and the Cities*, 32–42.

22 Euseb., *VC* 1.27.1, 36.1, 37.2; *HE* 8.14.5. On the depiction of Maxentius as a tyrant and Constantine as a legitimate ruler in panegyrists other than Eusebius, see Warmington, "Aspects of Constantinian Propaganda," 379, 381.

Roman emperors, but also to kings throughout history, such as Alexander,[23] whom Bouttios has performing a virgin sacrifice.

If the rhetoric of bloodless sacrifice associated with the inauguration of the tyche of Constantinople recalls Eusebius's praise of Constantine, it is equally—or perhaps even more—reminiscent of the Christian condemnation of Julian. Gregory of Nazianzus's wording is remarkably similar to Bouttios's expression for the sacrifice that instituted the tyche of the new capital: θυσίαν ἀναίμακτον. Gregory characterizes his *Oration against Julian* itself as a "sacrifice of praise" (θυσίαν αἰνέσεως) and a "bloodless offering of words" (τὴν ἀναίμακτον τῶν λόγων τιμὴν).[24] He says that Julian's secret sacrifices undid the Christian rites and "cleansed" the emperor of the "bloodless sacrifice" (τῆς ἀναιμάκτου θυσίας) of the Christians.[25] The blood sacrifices of the pagans, according to Gregory, polluted the Christian altars of "bloodless sacrifice" (ἀναιμάκτου θυσίας).[26]

It is possible that a fairly wide contemporary audience, even if they were unfamiliar with the writings of Gregory, would take the mention of bloodless sacrifice to refer somehow to Julian. Julian's policy of reinvigorating the rites of blood sacrifice scandalized not only the Christians but also some of his pagan supporters, who objected to animal sacrifice on philosophical grounds and preferred some form of "bloodless sacrifice."[27] Julian's sacrifices must have struck a great many people with no vested ideological interests as remarkable, perhaps grotesque, since long disuse had made animal sacrifice largely unfamiliar. At the very least they would have provided a vivid and public contrast between the conduct of Christian and pagan emperors, a contrast accentuated by the stress that the proponents of paganism laid on the role of traditional ritual in the

23 Euseb., *VC* 1.7.1–2, 8.1; 4.74–75.

24 Greg. Naz., *Or.* 4.4. The first phrase is borrowed from Ps. 50:23 (LXX 49:23).

25 Greg. Naz., *Or.* 4.52.

26 Greg. Naz., *Or.* 5.29.

27 See Bradbury, "Julian's Pagan Revival"; Elm, *Sons, Fathers*, 284 and n. 64; and Eckhardt, "'Bloodless Sacrifice'"; but also Harl, "Sacrifice and Pagan Belief," for a rather different interpretation of the vitality of sacrifice in Late Antiquity; cf. Edwards, *Religions*, 200–221; Lenski, *Constantine and the Cities*, 231–34. Stroumsa, *End of Sacrifice*, places the end of sacrifice in the context of a broader religious revolution. Heyman, *Power of Sacrifice*, offers a discussion of the conflict of pagans and Christians in regard to the rhetoric of sacrifice.

maintenance of civilization[28] and one that quite possibly would have favored the Christian party in terms of popular perception.

Not only the language of bloodless sacrifice, but also the theme of human sacrifice, and virgin sacrifice specifically, is found in the rhetoric and the rumors that appeared in response to Julian's reign. Gregory pretends to assume that Julian would admire literary examples of human sacrifice and lists several of them.[29] John Chrysostom holds Julian responsible for reintroducing necromancy and infant sacrifice, suppressed since the advent of Christ.[30] A number of the outrages committed by the pagans are implicitly or explicitly presented by the Christians as human sacrifice.[31] Socrates, the ecclesiastical historian, claims that under Julian certain "philosophers" ritually killed infants for the purpose of divination and cannibalism.[32] Once again in his *Oration against Julian*, Gregory says that in a church in Alexandria the blood of sacrificial animals mingled with the blood of murdered Christians.[33] Gregory relates another highly relevant incident in lurid detail. In the Syrian town of Arethusa the mob is said to have seized consecrated virgins, publicly stripped them, and ripped them open and eviscerated them before cannibalizing them and feeding them to pigs.[34] The deaths of these virgins are recounted in terms similar to the human sacrifice in the fragments of the novelist Lollianus.[35] So here we have, as in Trajan's tyche sacrifice

28 Sallustius 16; Julian, *Ep.* 89b (*Fragment of a Letter to a Priest*), 297A–B, 302A–B, *Contra Galilaeos* 305D–306B, 343C–D, 356C, *Mis.* 361D–363D; Liban., *Or.* 30.33; Zos. 2.6–7, 4.18, 5.5.8–6.3, 41.1–3.

29 Greg. Naz., *Or.* 4.70.

30 John Chrysostom, *De Sancto Babyla et Contra Julianum et Gentiles* 14 (79) ; see Shepardson, "Rewriting Julian's Legacy," 109–10.

31 Cf. Philostorgius, *HE* 7.4.

32 Socrates Schol., *HE* 3.13.11.

33 Greg. Naz., *Or.* 4.86; cf. 5.26, 39.

34 Greg. Naz., *Or.* 4.87; cf. 5.29. It is perhaps on account of a special animus against virgins on the part of Julian that in the later fifth-century *Buzandaran Patmut'iwnk'* or pseudo-P'awstos Buzand, the history of fourth-century Armenia formerly attributed to "Faustus of Byzantium" (4.10), it is St. Thecla, outstanding not only for her witness to Christ but also for the maintenance of her virginity, who convenes the assembly of saints and martyrs who determine to do away with Julian (here under the title of "Valens" used indiscriminately of the Roman emperor) for his crimes; see N. Baynes, "Death of Julian," 23–25, 29; Garsoïan, *Epic Histories*, 130–32, 279–80, 412–13.

35 Lollianus, B1 recto; see Winkler, "Lollianos and the Desperadoes," 166–75.

(**FF 31, 32**), human sacrifice, the violation and killing of virgins, and the martyrdom of Christians combined. Gregory is not, however, able to fix the blame for these atrocities directly upon Julian, although he does consider him their instigator and satisfied observer.[36] Even when Gregory reports bodies hidden in the Orontes or in the cisterns of the palace at Antioch, the bodies of youths and maidens (παρθένοι) killed for purposes of necromancy or divination or sacrifice, and the bodies of martyrs, he goes no further than to say that Julian ordered the concealment of the crimes of others, not the killings themselves.[37]

It is Theodoret, writing some time later but probably preserving earlier material, who makes Julian himself a ritual murderer in a macabre story. On his march against Persia Julian is said to have visited the temple at Carrhae, and when he left had the doors sealed and guarded until his return. When news of his death reached the city the temple was opened, and inside was discovered the body of a woman hung up by the hair, her arms stretched out and her belly ripped open, supposedly in order to divine the outcome of the Persian campaign.[38] Such a charge was not altogether uncommon in the fourth century. We have already seen that Eusebius accused Maxentius of ripping open pregnant

36 Greg. Naz., *Or.* 4.90, cf. 93, 94.

37 Greg. Naz., *Or.* 4.92, cf. 2.9, 13, 23, 25, 26.

38 Theodoret, *HE* 3.26; on Julian at Carrhae, see T. Green, *City of the Moon God*, 50–51, cf. 115; Fowden, *Empire to Commonwealth*, 62. A remarkably similar story is told of Julian in the later (ca. 500) Syriac *Julian Romance*, according to which Julian and the magician Magnus, his friend and counselor in wickedness (probably based on the real theurgist Maximus of Ephesus), take Magnus's pregnant daughter Kuzu into a temple of idols, strip her, hang her by a cord, rip open her belly, and remove the child she has carried for nine months; and having practiced rituals of divination, raised demons, and extracted promises of support for Julian from them, they replaced the fetus, took Kuzu down from the rope by which she was hanging, and placed her on the altar, after which Julian sacrificed her to Satan; see Gollancz, *Julian the Apostate*, 260–61; Drijvers, "Religious Conflict"; Hilton, "Myth and Narrative Fiction," 46–47. The recent text and translation of the *Julian Romance* presented by Sokoloff, *Julian Romance*, translates a different manuscript, which does not include this episode. The composition of the lurid scene we do find in Gollancz's translation seems to borrow freely from the rumor aired by Theodoret in particular, and to be based more generally on Julian's reputation as a practitioner of human sacrifice. I am very grateful to Professor John Hilton of the University of KwaZulu-Natal for pointing this passage out to me and for providing me with a full rendition of it.

women.[39] Ammianus Marcellinus criticized Valens for pardoning the tribune Numerius after he was convicted on his own confession of cutting open the womb of a woman and removing her fetus for purposes of necromancy.[40] But in Theodoret's story of Julian's sacrifice at Carrhae we have a clear parallel to Bouttios's tyche sacrifices: a pitiable woman done to death by a pagan ruler—a tyrant to his enemies—in a self-serving sacrificial ritual.

An attack on pagan rulers that focused on the figure of the tyche, like Bouttios's history, would most likely have been recognized as an attack on the emperor Julian. Tyche, both as a goddess and as a concept, recurs significantly in writings from and discussions of the reign of Julian, by the emperor himself, his supporters, and his opponents. It seems likely that the *genius publicus*, which as Ammianus says appeared to Julian to urge him to assume the title of Augustus and again as a premonition of his death, took the form of the tyche since the specter bore a cornucopia.[41] Once again according to Ammianus, Julian commended the outcome of his bid for the throne to Fortuna.[42] The words of the historian seem to reflect the sentiments of Julian. The emperor wrote his uncle and namesake that if it had come to battle with Constantius he had intended to entrust everything to Tyche and the gods and await their decision.[43] Christians also seemed willing to attribute Julian's success to tyche, but saw it as a travesty. Gregory of Nazianzus insisted that in spite of the fact that Julian had seized power, the empire was not the "spoils of fortune" (ἅρπαγμα τύχης) but the gift of proper succession.[44] Gregory also bemoaned the fact that Julian's career, and God's patience with him, gave people cause to doubt the government of some cosmic rulership (κυβέρνησις) or the principle of requital (ἀνταπόδοσις), and to suspect that "Chance" (τὸ αὐτόματον) ruled the world.[45]

In his *Letter to Themistius*, Julian identified Tyche as the capricious force that rules the lives of men, especially statesmen, testing and undoing both those to

39 Euseb., *HE* 8.14.5; *VC* 1.36.1.
40 Amm. Marc. 29.17.
41 Amm. Marc. 20.5.10, 25.2.3.
42 Amm. Marc. 21.5.13; see Athanassiadi-Fowden, *Julian and Hellenism*, 77.
43 Julian, *Ep.* 28 (*Letter to His Uncle*).
44 Greg. Naz., *Or.* 4.46; see Setton, *Christian Attitude towards the Emperor*, 107.
45 Greg. Naz., *Or.* 5.24.

whom she is hostile and those whom she favors.[46] Julian demonstrates this principle in his *Caesars* when he has Tyche abandon Pompey and favor Octavian.[47] Tyche also appears in Sallustius's Neoplatonist primer *On the Gods and the Universe*—a work probably endorsed by Julian[48]—as the power of the gods to order various unforeseen events for the good in the sublunar world.[49] Libanius was an enthusiastic supporter of Julian, and he related the story of his own life as a series of interventions on the part of Tyche and credited the goddess with the professional success that meant so much to him.[50]

But Julian did not merely give intellectual assent to tyche as a concept, he publicly worshipped her as a goddess, and these acts of worship were often the setting and context for his quarrels with Christians. It was while Julian was sacrificing in the Tychaion of Constantinople that Maris, the bishop of Chalcedon, openly berated him as an impious and godless apostate; when Julian retorted that his god could not heal the bishop's blindness, Maris thanked God for the blindness that kept him from seeing one so fallen from piety.[51] Julian's devotion to the Tyche cult offended the Christians when he publicly sacrificed to a tyche image in the basilica of Constantinople.[52] And the emperor was offended in turn, according to Gregory, when the citizens of Caesarea in Cappadocia offered some insult to the tyche statue

46 Julian, *Ep.* 6 (*Letter to Themistius*), 256C–257D; see Athanassiadi-Fowden, *Julian and Hellenism*, 90–91, 95.

47 Julian, *Caes.* 323B, 330A; see Athanassiadi-Fowden, *Julian and Hellenism*, 200.

48 See Nock, *Sallustius, Concerning the Gods*, xcvi–civ; Bowersock, *Julian the Apostate*, 86, 125; Athanassiadi-Fowden, *Julian and Hellenism*, 154, 159; Marcone, *Giuliano*, 118–23.

49 Sallustius 9; see Nock, *Sallustius, Concerning the Gods*, lxxv, 20–21; Athanassiadi-Fowden, *Julian and Hellenism*, 157–58. The panegyrist Claudius Mamertinus, 23.6, praises Julian by saying that before his ascension fortune and fear, rather than the principles of astronomy, governed the lives of men (*Prorsus terra marique non ratione coelesti, sed casu ac temere vivebatur*). Mamertinus seems to present *casus*, if not *fortuna*, as a malevolent, or at best ambiguous, force which is not the best possible ruling principle of the world. We do not know, however, to what extent Mamertinus was familiar with Julian's public or private philosophy, particularly in regard to Tyche.

50 Lib., *Or.* 1, esp 1.155. See Liebeschuetz, "Libanius and Late Antique Autobiography," 269–72, and below, pp. 273–74.

51 Sozomen, *HE* 5.4.8–9. Bishop Maris's exchange with Julian might profitably be compared to Perseus's fatal encounter with the blind Cepheus (**F 7.5**).

52 Socrates Schol., *HE* 3.11.4.

or shrine in that city.[53] Julian inaugurated the last year of his reign with a visit to the temple of Tyche, and the sudden death of one of the priests on this occasion was taken as an ill omen for the emperor himself.[54] Julian himself mentions his visit to the Tyche shrine in Antioch.[55] It was on such a visit, says Theodoret, that the future emperor Valentinian accompanied Julian and proved his faith. At the gates of the temple of Tyche he was sprinkled with water, and struck the temple servant responsible for this, saying he was defiled, not cleansed. As a consequence, Theodoret continues, he was exiled, but gained two kingdoms: the Roman Empire and the kingdom of heaven.[56] As in the story of the tyche statue at Constantinople from the *Suda*, the figure of the Tyche is once again the focus of a contest between Christianity and paganism, specifically the paganism espoused by Julian.

Bouttios's Fragments and the Writings of Julian

Bouttios's history is perhaps more than another example of the Christian attack on Julian's rule. It can also be read as a response to Julian's writings. The accounts of tyche sacrifice especially are most obviously a counterpart to Julian's *Caesars* (see also above, chapter 6). Julian introduces this account of a banquet during which the ascended emperors were examined to find the worthiest as a "myth," but one that conveys a worthwhile message.[57] Bouttios's history with its palpable fiction of human sacrifices performed by famous kings—even if they were sincerely put forward as plausible explanations of real monuments—likewise seems to be a purposeful myth. As an examination of the virtues and vices of rulers the tyche narratives are also comparable to the *Caesars*. Julian casts his net widely so as to include Alexander of Macedon in the company of the Caesars,[58] just as Bouttios treats not only Alexander but also Seleucus and certain mythical kings

53 Greg. Naz., *Or.* 4.92, 18.34; Sozomen, *HE* 5.4.1–5. The incident was not unheard of in Antioch; see Lib., *Or.* 16.14. See Fatti, "Il principe, la *Tyche*, i cristiani"; Elm, *Sons, Fathers*, 149 and n. 12.

54 Amm. Marc. 23.1.6.

55 Julian, *Mis.* 346B (cf. Amm Marc. 23.1.6); see Athanassiadi-Fowden, *Julian and Hellenism*, 200.

56 Theodoret, *HE* 3.16; cf. Philostorgius, *HE* 7.7, 8.5.

57 Julian, *Caes.* 306A–C. And as Pack, "Notes on the *Caesars*," suggests, it was a message in keeping with Julian's philosophy as a whole.

58 Julian, *Caes.* 316A–D.

along with several Roman emperors. The opposition of Constantine and Julian is implicit in the *Caesars*, as in Bouttios. Julian condemns the folly of Constantine and has him consigned to punishment, while he awards the prize to Marcus Aurelius, after whom he had modeled himself.[59]

It may seem odd, then, that Marcus Aurelius is not one of the emperors to whom Bouttios attaches a charge of human sacrifice. And it would appear that he avoided doing so, rather than simply that the evidence for the charge does not survive, since Malalas reports on Marcus's construction projects in Antioch, that he rebuilt the Centenarium Baths and built the Nymphaeum called the Ocean—an outstanding opportunity for imputing a tyche sacrifice to Marcus, if Bouttios wanted one—but there is no hint that the emperor performed any sort of sacrifice at the dedication of these buildings.[60] And it is not as if Bouttios was averse to casting aspersions against emperors with the most sterling reputations, as he does in regard to Augustus (**F 25**) and Trajan (**F 31**).[61] Perhaps a direct assault on Marcus Aurelius would have been altogether too obvious: to attack Julian's model might have meant shedding any pretense of offering a historical record and making it clear that Bouttios's work was really a diatribe directed against the emperor. There is no indication that Bouttios mentioned Julian by name, and so that he was willing to show his hand in such a blatant way.

It also has to be borne in mind that how one wants to be seen—in terms of which models, for instance—does not necessarily determine how one, even an emperor, is seen, especially by his detractors, who will impose other, less flattering models than those of one's own choosing. A sympathetic member of Julian's court like Eutropius might have taken up the emperor's comparison of himself and Marcus Aurelius, but Julian's critics and even his more distant admirers preferred to link Julian to Alexander the Great, a figure of more dubious repute.[62] Julian himself may have had an unalloyed adulation for Marcus Aurelius, but his regard for Alexander was at best lukewarm. Nevertheless, the figure of Julian attracted an at times unenviable association with Alexander.[63]

59 Julian, *Caes.* 335–36.

60 Malalas 11.30.

61 See above, pp. 179–80.

62 Eutr. 10.16.3; see Van Dam, *Rome and Constantinople*, 35.

63 N. Baynes, "Review of Otto Seeck, *Geschichte des Untergangs*," 759–60; Athanassiadi-Fowden, *Julian and Hellenism*, 192–93, 199–200, 224–25; R. Smith, *Julian's Gods*, 12–13, 168;

Julian's own attitude toward Alexander was ambivalent. On the one hand, he conceded that Alexander's victory over the Persians was a magnificent achievement of unrivaled generalship that still redounded to the glory of Macedon.[64] On the other hand, he held the conqueror up to scorn for his moral failings, his weakness for drink and susceptibility to wrath, and his deficiency as compared to philosophers like Socrates and Aristotle, to say nothing of his own imperial model, Marcus Aurelius.[65] Contemporaries sympathetic to Julian tended to concur in offering a measured comparison of Julian and Alexander and according the latter only a qualified respect.[66] Ammianus Marcellinus, for example, allowed that Julian took Alexander as an example of regal generosity, of chaste and respectful treatment of female prisoners, and even of time management, dividing his nights between rest, dealing with state matters, and the cultivation of the Muses, although he said that Julian, unlike Alexander, required no artificial means to keep himself awake.[67] In an optimistic tone as Julian set out for the East, Libanius could claim that recollection of the deeds of Alexander, as well as other triumphs over the perennial oriental foe at Troy or Salamis, was set aside as everyone

---

Lane Fox, "Itinerary of Alexander," 248–52; den Hengst, *Emperors and Historiography*, 81–83; R. Smith, "Casting of Julian."

64 Julian, *Or.* 1 (*Panegyric on Constantius*), 17C–D; *Or.* 2 (*On the Kingship*), 73A–B, 95B; *Or.* 3 (*Panegyric on Eusebia*), 107B–C; *To Themistius* 253A; *Caes.* 316A–D, 322B–325C (cf. 320C–322A), 327B; *Ep.* 60 (*To the Alexandrians*).378C; *Ep.* 111 (*To the Alexandrians*), 433B–C; *Ep.* 198 (*For the Argives*), 407D; *Contra Galilaeos* 218 B–C.

65 Julian, *Or.* 1 (*Panegyric on Constantius*), 41C, 45D–46B; *Or.* 2 (*On the Kingship*), 96B–C; *Or.* 6 (*To the Uneducated Cynics*), 20 (203B); *Or.* 7 (*To the Cynic Heracleius*), 211D; *Or.* 8 (*To Sallust*), 250D–251C; *To Themistius* 257A–B, 264C–265B; *Caes.* 318C, 319D, 330A–331C; *Ep.* 82 (*To Nilus*), 446A. There is some debate over the dating of the *Epistle to Themistius*, one of the key texts on Alexander in Julian's corpus, which may have a crucial bearing on the question of the development of Julian's thought in regard to Alexander; see Barnes and Vander Spoel, "Julian and Themistius"; Bradbury, "Date of Julian's *Letter to Themistius*." See also Elm, *Sons, Fathers*, 85.

66 On the cultivation of Julian's postmortem reputation by both proponents and detractors, see Marcone, *Giuliano*, 247–54.

67 Amm. Marc. 16.5.4, 24.4.27, 25.4.15; see Szidat, "*Alexandrum Imitatus*"; cf. Soraci, "La figura di Alessandro Magno." At least in regard to Alexander's reputation for generosity, Ammianus may have taken his cue from Julian himself, who used Alexander as a rhetorical model of openhandedness: *Or.* 1 (*Panegyric on Contantius*), 43C; *Or.* 2 (*On the Kingship*), 86B.

awaited news of Julian's Persian expedition.[68] And after the emperor's death he could say that unlike Julian, Alexander was a man not above reproach.[69] But even Libanius might suggest that Alexander represented something of a preoccupation for Julian. He said that Alexander was "dear to him [Julian] and would not allow him to sleep" (τοῦ φίλου τε αὐτῷ καὶ οὐκ ἐῶντος καθεύδειν), likening Julian's admiration for Alexander to Themistocles' fixation on the repute of Miltiades.[70] And he assumed that when he was on campaign in Mesopotamia, Julian's head was full of plans to march through Arbela so that his victory should be celebrated along with Alexander's there, and to pass through all the territories of the Persian Empire, ending up, like Alexander, in Hyrcania and on the banks of the rivers of India.[71]

For Julian's Christian critics, however, the Apostate was utterly, perhaps maniacally, obsessed with Alexander. As soon as news of his death arrived back in the Empire, Gregory of Nazianzus offered as the greatest proof of Julian's madness (κακοδαιμονία) that in his wounded state he had tried to throw himself into the river and, with his body missing, be thought to have disappeared and become a god.[72] Without actually mentioning Alexander, Gregory alleged that Julian was employing the same device Alexander was supposed by some to have unsuccessfully attempted—to his discredit—in the same vicinity, and in the same way that his wife prevented Alexander from doing away with himself, the court eunuchs intervened to stop Julian.[73] In the next generation the Church historian Socrates went so far as to state that, deluded by the divinations of Maximus, Julian believed he was destined to outdo the achievements of Alexander of Macedon or even that he was the reincarnation of Alexander, and so turned a deaf ear to the peaceful overtures of the king of Persia.[74] In the much later *Passion of St. Artemius*, Julian is said to have imitated Alexander and made a point of pitching his camp at Issus, a site

68 Lib., *Or.* 15.2.

69 Lib., *Or.* 17.32.

70 Lib., *Or.* 17.17. Libanius's reference to two Athenian generals alludes to an anecdote related by Plutarch, *Them.* 3.3–4.

71 Lib., *Or.* 18.260–61.

72 Greg. Naz., *Or.* 5.14 (681A); see Elm, *Sons, Fathers,* 418, 455.

73 Arr., *Anab.* 7.27.3; *Al. Rom.* (α) 3.32.4–7; *Epitoma Rerum Gestarum Alexandri et Liber de Morte Eius* (*Epit. Mett.*) 101–2; see Baynham, "'Joining the Gods.'"

74 Socrates Schol., *HE* 3.21.6–8.

made famous by Alexander's victory over Darius, and that he expected "through his gods who are no gods" to have a lengthy reign and become a new Alexander.[75] It is this abusive but not implausible association of Julian and Alexander, the imputation to Julian of an obsessive fascination with Alexander, that seems to have determined the pattern and the apparent prominence of Bouttios's account of Alexander as a cryptic dig at Julian, while Julian's real and sincere attachment to Marcus Aurelius seems to have made no difference to Bouttios.

Julian's more overtly theological works have a counterpart in Bouttios's own treatment of the gods, the Picus-Zeus narrative (**FF 1, 2**). Julian considered the heavenly bodies to be visible gods, albeit a lower order of gods and the images of the invisible gods, but gods nevertheless, whose divinity was evident in the unchanging regularity and harmony of their motions.[76] This may very well explain Bouttios's concentration on god-kings who bear the names of planets; he usually notes that these men were named after the planets. Bouttios also discusses so-called gods made manifest to men, but far from dilating on their perfection, he recounts their sordid and immoral lives as evidence of the true nature of pagan gods. He insists that inasmuch as there are "gods" with the names of planets, they are mortal men, while Julian's planetary gods are imperishable.[77] Julian, moreover, accords a central and commanding place to Helios, in a figurative sense in the intelligible and intellectual realms and perceptibly among the visible gods, and identifies him with Zeus.[78] Bouttios, in what appears to be a deliberate inversion, relegates Helios to a minor role as a lesser king of one of the cadet branches of Cronos's dynasty, and Helios is not included in the *Excerpta*'s ample list of gods identified with Picus-Zeus (**FF 1.9, 2.1**).

75 *S. Artemii Passio* 24, 69 (PG 1273A–B, 1317A).

76 Julian, *Or.* 4 (*Hymn to King Helios*), 138D, 140A, 141B, 148C; *Or.* 5 (*Hymn to the Mother of the Gods*), 166A; *Ep.* 89b (*Fragment of a Letter to a Priest*), 293B, *Contra Galilaeos* 65B–C, 69C–D.

77 Julian, *Ep.* 89b (*Fragment of a Letter to a Priest*), 295A.

78 Julian, *Or.* 4 (*Hymn to King Helios*), 143B, 146C, 149D, 150D, 151A–B, 156D; *Or.* 7 (*To Heracleios the Cynic*), 231B–234C; cf. *Ep.* 79; identification of Helios with Zeus: *Or.* 4.135D–136A, 143D, 144B, 149B; *Ep.* 111 434B–D; *Contra Galilaeos* 200A. See Elm, *Sons, Fathers,* 286–99. Sallustius's remarks on the planetary gods (6–8) might suggest that Julian's views were remarkably idiosyncratic. Be that as it may, according to Libanius (*Or.* 12.80–82), Julian's devotion to the sun god was realized in his daily rituals.

The most aggressively polemical of Julian's own works, his anti-Christian *Against the Galileans*, also seems to receive a rejoinder from Bouttios. Julian insists that the different nations each had different national gods subject to the creator god, and it is ludicrous for the Christians to suggest that the national god of the Jews was himself the creator god.[79] He believes his contention is demonstrated by the different characters of nations—a proof by stereotype, if you will—and makes mention of the humanity, civilization, and bellicosity that typify the Greeks and Romans, the intelligence and expertise of the Egyptians, and the odd combination of unfitness for war, effeminacy, sagacity, rashness, vanity, and docility that marks the Syrians.[80] Julian's ideas are refuted by the traveling gods of the Picus-Zeus narrative who visit all of these nations and become their gods, but are all the same, rather than distinct national gods. And while Julian points out the arts and sciences that originated among the gentiles, many at the instigation of the gods, of which the Jews can claim none,[81] Bouttios makes the so-called gods principally responsible for the cultivation of false worship, immorality, and sorcery, including the necromancy with which Julian equates the Christian habit of "groveling among the tombs" (i.e., the cult of the martyrs).[82]

Julian also derides the Christians for turning to the god of a nation that had been subjected to the Assyrians, Medes, Persians, and Romans in turn, while the Romans enjoy sovereignty.[83] The list of empires by which the Jews were conquered

79 Julian, *Contra Galilaeos* 99E, 100, 106, 115–16, 131, 143A–B, 148B–C. On the *Contra Galilaeos* in general, see Marcone, *Giuliano*, 220–26.

80 Julian, *Contra Galilaeos* 116A.

81 Julian, *Contra Galilaeos* 176A–B, 178A–B, 235B–D. The sneering sentiments noted here are only one side of Julian's ambivalent attitude toward the Jews and Judaism, at once dismissive of their assertions of superiority and exclusivity, as well as any Christian claim to participate in their antiquity and piety, but also willing to recognize the divinity of their god and pursue a largely pro-Jewish (or anti-Christian) public policy; see Adler, "Emperor Julian and the Jews"; Vogt, *Kaiser Julian und das Judentum*; Simon, *Verus Israel*, 139–44; Blanchetière, "Julien Philhellène, Philosémite, Antichrétien"; Gager, *Origins of Anti-Semitism*, 94–97; Millar, "Jews of the Graeco-Roman Diaspora," 105–8; R. Smith, *Julian's Gods*, 7, 189–207, 216–17; Marcone, *Giuliano*, 214–19.

82 Julian, *Contra Galilaeos* 339E–340A.

83 Julian, *Contra Galilaeos* 210A, 213A, 218A–B; cf. *Ep.* 111 (*To the Alexandrians*), 433A–B.

is itself suggestive, as is Julian's pointed contrast between the liberty (ἐλεύθερον εἶναι) of the Greeks and Romans and the slavery (τὸ δουλεύειν) of the Jews. But Bouttios's otherwise mystifying fabrication that the Romans themselves were subject to these eastern powers begins to make sense as a rebuttal to Julian: the subjection of the Jews does not make them inferior to the Romans if the Romans shared this servitude. Julian further belittles the Jews because they can boast of no such general as Alexander,[84] while Bouttios has Alexander act at the prompting of the Jewish God and by his power, and even acknowledge him at Jerusalem.

In other regards, Bouttios seems to intend a deliberate contrast with the ideas of Julian. The emperor considered erotic fiction inappropriate reading for himself and his priests,[85] and so Bouttios may have considered it particularly piquant to borrow the recurrent motif of human sacrifice from a genre Julian despised in order to compose an attack on him. It appears that in his response to the Cynic Heraclius, Julian also attempted to rehabilitate Euripides as a pious mythographer,[86] so it may be more jousting on the part of Bouttios that he exploits Euripides to such a great extent in his own antipagan mythography.

If Bouttios wrote in response to the writings of Julian, we may ask whether this response was the result of lengthy reflection in the context of an argument between men of letters, fought over the span of many years, or a hasty and immediate rejoinder. It is clear that Julian was embroiled in a lively rhetorical exchange with the citizenry during his stay in Antioch. A number of the works we have identified as targets for the history of Bouttios, for instance, the *Caesars*, the *Hymn to King Helios*, and the *Letter to a Priest*, were probably written at Antioch.[87] Certainly the *Misopogon* was expressly composed as a reply to the jibes and raillery of the Antiochenes, something of a Parthian shot as the emperor prepared to leave the city.[88] The *Misopogon*, however, reminds us that

84 Julian, *Contra Galilaeos* 218B; cf. *Ep.* 111 (*To the Alexandrians*), 433C.

85 Julian, *Ep.* 89b (*Fragment of a Letter to a Priest*), 301B–C.

86 Julian, *Ep.* 7 (*Letter to the Cynic Heracleius*), 214–21; see Athanassiadi-Fowden, *Julian and Hellenism*, 135.

87 Pack, "Notes on the *Caesars*," 152 and n. 4; Lacombrade, *L'empereur Julien: Oeuvres complètes* 2.2, 27–30, 75–76; Baldwin, "*Caesares* of Julian," 450–51; R. Smith, *Julian's Gods*, 8, 125; Van Dam, *Roman Revolution*, 1–3; Elm, *Sons, Fathers*, 272.

88 See Gleason, "Festive Satire"; P. Brown, *Power and Persuasion*, 59; Marcone, *Giuliano*, 187–96.

to all appearances we have only one side of the exchange between Julian and his critics in Antioch. The mockery of Julian's beard and the anapestic verse he says was written against him are lost to us.[89] But Bouttios's idiosyncratic history may have found a place among the satires, insolence, and ridicule to which Julian says he was subjected.[90] It is difficult to imagine that the emperor's ingenuity and literary industriousness outstripped that of an entire city—and one as literate as Antioch, at that—and that Julian assailed the Antiochenes from many different angles while they were content merely to poke fun at his beard.

If, however, to return to a point discussed above, we assume that Bouttios wrote his polemical history while Julian was still in Antioch, we might make sense of an enigmatic passage in the *Misopogon*. Julian says that the Antiochenes preferred Christ to Zeus, Apollo, and Calliope, and says of Calliope that it was she "who laid bare your contrivance" (ἣ τὸ σόφισμα ὑμῶν ἀπεγύμνωσεν).[91] Now, Calliope was identified by Bouttios as the tyche of Antioch established by Trajan (**F 31**), and while we may never know for sure how she managed to expose the contrivance or fallacy (τὸ σόφισμα) of the Christians, it seems likely that what Julian refers to is Bouttios's writing itself. To anyone familiar with history, his work was recognizable as an invention and a slander against the tyche Calliope—the explication of whose true character might be said to have "revealed" this contrivance—and it may have been composed in the context of the rhetorical attacks against himself to which Julian is responding in this work. Julian, then, could be replying to Bouttios in the same way that Bouttios replied to Julian.

The suggestion that Bouttios wrote while Julian was still in Antioch is supported by the fact that Bouttios does not seem to have mentioned Julian by name, even though the emperor seems to have been the target of his rhetoric.[92] Perhaps Bouttios wanted to consign Julian to the same sort of *damnatio memoriae* to which Eusebius relegated the rivals of Constantine[93] or the poet of the *Carmen*

89 Julian, *Mis.* 345D, 355D–356A, 364B; cf. Socrates Schol., *HE* 3.17.4–9; Sozomen *HE* 5.19.2–3; Malalas 13.19.

90 Julian, *Mis.* 344A–B.

91 Julian, *Mis.* 357C.

92 Certainly, neither of our chief sources for Bouttios's fragments in their accounts of the reign of Julian connect him with the tyche cult or any of the other telltale signs of Bouttios; see *ELB* 2.10.5; Malalas 13.18–25.

93 Euseb., *VC* 1.47.1, 56.2; 2.49–51; cf. 1.10.3.

contra paganos his unnamed and still unknown target,[94] but it is just as likely that he wanted to avoid the consequences of a direct attack on the emperor, particularly as he seems to have published his work not anonymously but under his own name. Julian himself, moreover, tells us that the Antiochenes were sometimes cryptic in their criticism of him, as when they expressed their preference for Christ and Constantius in a riddling reference to "the chi and the kappa."[95]

The "Friend of God" Political Theory

The stories that contrast Constantine and Julian in regard to the tyche figure and the application of the rhetoric of sacrifice, bloodless or otherwise, to both of them indicate that the real concern of Bouttios's history is the fourth-century contest for the throne between paganism and Christianity. These indicators alone, however, might suggest that Bouttios needlessly belabored his point by including accounts of ancient kings from the mythical past through Alexander to the emperors of Rome. Why not simply contrast Constantine with the pagan rivals he had defeated or the persecuting emperors who had not yet passed out of living memory, as Eusebius had done? The answer is provided by Eusebius himself and goes to the very heart of Bouttios's intention. In the *Praise of Constantine*, Eusebius identifies Constantine as the "friend of God" possessed of the virtues of the kingdom of heaven. This presentation of Eusebius's hero will hardly be surprising, but the consequences he draws from it are revolutionary, if seldom noted. If Constantine is the friend of God, none of his predecessors was; rather they were godless, vice-ridden slaves to deceptive demons. And inasmuch as they lack the kingly virtues derived from contact with the Divine, they are not truly kings, but only seem to be. All pagan kings, therefore, are declared illegitimate and their tyranny is revealed by their slaughter of the godly as sacrifices to their false gods. Students of Eusebius's political theory have largely neglected this proposition

94 See Mommsen, "Carmen codicis Parisini 8084"; Manganaro, "La reazione pagana a Roma"; Manganaro, "Il poemetto anonimo contra paganos"; Matthews, "Historical Setting of the 'Carmen contra paganos'"; Cracco Ruggini, *Il paganesimo romano tra religione e politica*, 3–143; Croke and Harries, *Religious Confilict in Fourth-Century Rome*, 80–83; Grünewald, "Der letzte Kampf des Heidentums," 474–81; Hedrick, *History and Silence*, 60–63, 270, n. 89.

95 Julian, *Mis.* 357A; cf. 360D.

and its startling ramifications,[96] but it seems Bouttios did not. What Eusebius asserted in generalities, Bouttios purported to demonstrate with concrete historical examples. His accounts of ancient kings follow the pattern Eusebius laid out for the depravity of godless, idolatrous rulers and show that every pagan king, on account of his paganism, was an unfit, indeed an invalid king.

Eusebius begins his discussion of kingship in a familiarly positive vein. The Ideas of lawful rule (ἔννομος ἀρχή), kingly authority (βασιλικὴ ἐξουσία), and even autocratic power (αὐτοκρατορικὴ δύναμις) are revealed to men by God through the Logos.[97] But Eusebius imposes an important but little-noticed limitation on the divine inspiration of these political ideas. The friend of God (ὁ τῷ θεῷ φίλος), that is, Constantine, partakes of the heavenly kingdom because he has received the—decidedly Platonic—virtues of that kingdom through contact with their ultimate Ideals.[98] As a consequence he bears the title of king in truth (ἀληθεῖ λόγῳ) because of the kingly virtues in his soul. The man whose soul is given over to every kind of vice, however, may seem to rule by "tyrannical force" (νομίζεται ποτε τυραννικῇ βίᾳ κρατεῖν), but he will never be a king in truth.[99] So far this might seem to be a fairly traditional discourse on the character appropriate to a king and on self-control as a prerequisite to the control of the state, but the concept of virtue validating kingship is pursued and its application is, in fact, quite specific. The vicious ruler is not simply morally depraved, he is a slave to demons and he has formed in his soul, in addition to vices in the place of virtues, "myriads of falsely described images of demons" (μυρίας ἐψευδογραφημήνας

96 See, however, Setton, *Christian Attitude towards the Emperor*, 50; Drake, In Praise of Constantine, 161–62; cf. Av. Cameron, "Eusebius of Caesarea and the Rethinking of History," esp. 84–85; Warmington, "Eusebius of Caesarea and the Governance of Constantine," 270. Johnson, *Ethnicity and Argument*, 194, notes that in the *Praise of Constantine* Eusebius cultivates an image of Constantine as one who can be called a friend of God, and associates this terminology with Eusebius's discussion of the Hebrew patriarchs in the *Praeparatio Evangelica* (cf. 101–10). Edwards, *Religions*, viii, does not refer to this theory in particular, but his general observation concerning the developments in the reign of Constantine is apt: "Indeed, we shall often have reason to observe that Christianity was more revolutionary in its expectations than any sovereign could afford to be in his acts."

97 Euseb., *LC* 4.1.

98 Euseb., *LC* 5.1.

99 Euseb., *LC* 5.2.

δαιμόνων εἰκόνας); in short, he is an idolater.[100] Eusebius is not really dealing in universal questions of virtue and vice and their relation to kingship, he is addressing the religious contentions in the Roman Empire of the fourth century, especially in regard to their political implications.

Eusebius explicates the ways of these seeming rulers, the godless kings, and their relations with the demons. The great project of the "invisible barbarians," the demons, has been the promotion of polytheism which draws men away from the True God.[101] The minions of the demons in this enterprise to subject the human race to polytheism are "those who seemed to rule at that time" (τότε κρατεῖν νομιζόμενοι).[102] These are the vicious rulers of the past who were contrasted with the friend of God, but they are no more true kings than any one of the gods whose worship is encouraged by the demons is a true god; such a one is only "thought to be a god" (ἐνομίσθη θεός).[103] So abject is the slavery of these apparent rulers to the demons that they offer their kith and kin (ὁμοφύλων καὶ συγγενῶν φόνους) in sacrifice to their gods.[104] The victims of these tyrants include the martyrs of the True God and virgins who preferred death to defilement.[105] Eusebius sums up the history of the godly under pagan rulers as a battle between the soldiers of the High King and the ranks of polytheism, and returns to the theme of human sacrifice by decrying the demons and their hordes of followers continually rejoicing in libations of human blood.[106] But he strikes a triumphant note when God relieves his beleaguered forces by raising up Constantine to defeat the visible and invisible barbarians.[107] And in this victorious progress it is Constantine's campaign against idolatry that Eusebius elaborates at great length, and that ends with the cessation of human sacrifice.[108]

Eusebius's view of Constantine's pagan predecessors and the Roman Empire in general is regularly taken to be quite positive. It is usually characterized by

100 Euseb., *LC* 5.3.
101 Euseb., *LC* 7.2.
102 Euseb., *LC* 7.6.
103 Euseb., *LC* 7.3.
104 Euseb., *LC* 7.6.
105 Euseb., *LC* 7.7.
106 Euseb., *LC* 7.8.
107 Euseb., *LC* 7.12–14.
108 Euseb., *LC* 8, esp. 9.

drawing attention to the passages in which he notes the synchronicity of the Incarnation and the rise of the Roman Empire under Augustus.[109] Rome paved the way for the spread of the Gospel by establishing peace and unity throughout the world in which the evangelists would have to travel, and establishing the principle of monarchy which corresponds to monotheism in the place of a multitude of governments and a multitude of gods.[110] Eusebius does not acknowledge any inconsistencies with his earlier writing or dwell upon his new idea's radical implications, but in propounding a political theory on the basis of the concept of the friend of God Eusebius invalidates the rule of all pagan kings, including Augustus and any other emperors who might have been considered virtuous or innocuous. Their idolatry is the evidence of the vices that pollute their souls. On account of these vices, they are divorced from God and his kingdom. This separation from God prevents them from being kings "in truth"; they only seem to be kings. Their idolatry also makes these rulers subject to demons and, metaphorically at least, perpetrators of the awful crime of human sacrifice. Every pagan king has been a vicious tyrant, and Constantine is the first valid ruler of the Roman Empire, the first ruler of any gentile kingdom who does not rule illegitimately as a tyrant.

109 Cranz, "Kingdom and Polity," 55–56; Markus, "Roman Empire," 343–44; Dvornik, *Early Christian and Byzantine Political Philosophy*, 2:611–16; Paschoud, *Cinq études sur Zosime*, 9–10; Hollerich, "Religion and Politics," 314; Martin, *Inventing Superstition*, 217–22; Johnson, *Ethnicity and Argument*, 154; Oakley, *Kingship*, 73; Iricinschi, "Good Hebrew, Bad Hebrew," 78–80. Eusebius's thought in this regard was anticipated by Melito of Sardis; see Euseb., *HE* 4.26.7–8; R. Grant, "Five Apologists," 5, 7. Kannengiesser, "Eusebius of Caesarea, Origenist," 453, however, perceives a direct debt to Origen (*C. Cels.* 2.30). Cf. Theodoret of Cyrus, *Gr. affect. cur.* 10.54. On the presentation of Augustus in general in early Christian literature, see Klein, "Das Bild des Augustus."

110 Euseb., *Dem. evang.* 3.7.30–35, *Praep. evang.* 1.4.2–5, *CI* 2:1–4 (Ziegler, *Der Jesajakommentar*, 14–15), 11:15 (Ziegler, *Der Jesajakommentar*, 91–92), 19:4 (Ziegler, *Der Jesajakommentar*, 126–127), *LC* 16.2–7, 17.12; see Wallace-Hadrill, *Christian Antioch*, 53; Johnson, *Ethnicity and Argument*, 174–80, 185, 187–91, 196–97; Morlet, *La Démonstration Évangélique*, 268, 465–70. Dvornik, *Early Christian and Byzantine Political Philosophy*, notes the influence of these ideas of Eusebius's on later Christian writers; 2:627, 681, 684, 697–98, 724–28. In his invective against Julian (*Or.* 4.37), Gregory of Nazianzus certainly insists that Constantius recognized that the affairs of Rome had grown and prospered along with those of the Christians.

Bouttios, like Eusebius, presents Constantine as a culminating figure who brings an end to the evil of his predecessors at the climax of the narrative, but that is not all. Bouttios's characterization of the pagan rulers who preceded Constantine follows the lines laid out by Eusebius. He describes in detail how these kings, no matter what their other accomplishments, engage in human sacrifice, kill virgins (as well as martyrs on occasion), and promote the cause of idolatry and polytheism. There is a perverse sort of syllogistic reasoning at work for both of these authors. No gentile ruler before Constantine was a friend of God, one who is not a friend of God is godless and overwhelmed with vice, and all godless rulers are guilty of human sacrifice, so all the kings who came before Constantine can be said to have immolated human beings. Eusebius established this in principle and generalized accordingly, so Bouttios could confidently assert that any example he cared to select from the kings before Constantine had been guilty of the crime of human sacrifice. He did not need to demonstrate this in every case; a few telling examples would have sufficed to bear out Eusebius's contention that all pagan rulers had practiced human sacrifice. The tyche cults of various cities are simply supposed to indicate the identity of the victims. But Eusebius's political ideas in the *Praise of Constantine* do not merely permit Bouttios logical grounds for imputing acts of human sacrifice to past rulers.

The tyche sacrifices committed by different rulers are the evidence of their tyranny and godlessness. Their abuse of women made them the colleagues of recognized tyrants and their rule was invalidated in traditional terms as tyranny.[111] They are, moreover, not friends of God and so according to Eusebius's political theory can never do more than seem to be kings. Bouttios's work demonstrates with the vivid examples of history Eusebius's principle: no pagan ruler has done more than "seem to rule by tyrannical force." No pagan has been a king in truth, and no pagan can be. Pagans are excluded from any but seeming kingship. In the late fourth century this was more than a disinterested and retrospective historical judgment. It declared the rule of the emperor Julian invalid and, in theory, excluded any pagan candidate from taking the throne. By implication Bouttios pushes Eusebius's theory into ideological territory that many contemporary Christians would have balked at entering. Gregory of Nazianzus decried the reign of Julian in terms of bitterest vituperation, but he did not say that Julian's

111 See above, pp. 180–82, 185, 187.

paganism disqualified him from the throne, only that he who possesses the kingdom does not necessarily hold the full measure of the honor of the office.[112] Even Juventinus and Maximinus, two Christian guardsmen whose criticism of Julian at a drinking party was reported to the emperor, protested before him that the only thing about his rule to which they objected was the sacrificial aspersion of foodstuffs for sale in the marketplace of Antioch.[113] They were willing to accept a pagan as their sovereign, but spoke out against those impositions and outrages that showed him to be an enemy of their faith. For Bouttios, as for Eusebius before him, this position was untenable: one could not be both a pagan and a lawful sovereign, of Christians or anyone else.

112 Greg. Naz., *Or.* 4.46; see Setton, *Christian Attitude towards the Emperor*, 107.

113 Theodoret, *HE* 3.15; cf. John Chrysostom, *In Ss. Mm. Juventinum et Maximinum* (PG 50:571–78); Mayer and Neil, *Saint John Chrysostom: The Cult of the Saints*, 89–99.

8

THE ATTACK ON THE PAGAN PANTHEON

The rhetorical strife of the fourth century was not primarily political. The theoretical assertions and practical loyalties offered in the realm of politics were gambits in a broader ideological contest which pitted irreconcilable religious beliefs and practices and all-encompassing worldviews against one another. Political persuasion was not the isolated game it had once been. In his exhortation to his fellow citizens to appease the anger of Julian, Libanius, in addition to making points on such time-honored chestnuts as seemly civic government, good order, and ostentatious contrition, ultimately insisted that the gentlemen of Antioch would be reconciled to the emperor only by a wholehearted adherence to paganism. Or, to employ the orator's own supercilious turn of phrase, by abandoning forever the superstition of their wives, scullery maids, and other females of negligible cultural and intellectual attainments in favor of subjection to the gods of whom Homer and Hesiod had taught them since boyhood.[1] The contemporary responses from the pulpits of the churches and the pens of the apologists-turned-polemicists, in the form of calls for conversion to Christianity, could of course be multiplied. But just as Libanius sees religion at the heart of a political disagreement between the civic leaders of Antioch and their emperor, Bouttios presents paganism as something more than merely a disqualifying handicap in aspirants to the throne, or even to a reputation as a good ruler. Paganism, as he tells it, is itself the very wickedness that made bad emperors bad and had its origin in the

1 Lib., *Or.* 16.45–49.

greed, lust, and ambition of disreputable rulers, as well as being the seed that bore such terrible fruit.

The most direct assault on pagan religion in the fragments of Bouttios is the account of the gods as ancient human kings. In a way this was nothing new. Christian apologists had long asserted that the so-called gods were dead kings who had come to be worshipped in the primeval past. The account of Picus-Zeus and his dynasty is remarkable because it does not merely make the assertion, as previous writers had done, coupled with some reference to an authority, but endeavors to substantiate the claim with an account of the gods as historical figures—an account, moreover, that is new and different from anything that had appeared before, and so a part of the euhemeristic tradition. Indeed, at nearly every point the narrative can be seen as a combination of the philosophical complaints against the traditional presentation of the gods and the apologetic arguments of the Christians, who borrowed so much from their pagan predecessors in the critique of myth. Bouttios's account also differs from the treatment of the gods in the Christian apologetic tradition by making no mention of demons, whereas previous writers had regularly explained the origins and current vitality of pagan cults with reference to malign spiritual forces. These two significant exceptions duly noted, the history of the gods presented by Bouttios is infused with the material usually found in apologetic attacks on the gods. Much is made of the shameful conduct of the mortal gods, particularly their philandering and their practice of magic. Bouttios also adopts the apologetic tactic of insisting that central elements of Greek culture were borrowed from barbarian nations. Another characteristic feature of his account of the gods, a concentration on those gods who gave their names to the planets, or rather took their names from the planets, also seems to have some connection with the apologetic criticism of the worship of the "visible gods" in the heavens. One of the most characteristic traits of this account of the gods, the identification of two (or more) traditionally different deities as one personality, may also aid an apologetic purpose. This groundbreaking combination of tested polemical content and a novel narrative presentation was destined to be the most influential part of Bouttios's work as a whole. Even if his name was not attached to any of them, some rendition of the account of the gods authored by Bouttios was the means by which the heathen gods were regularly fitted into the scheme of history perennially articulated by

the Byzantine chronicle tradition, as well as the encyclopedic tradition as represented by the monumental *Suda*.[2]

Bouttios and the Euhemeristic Tradition

The account of the gods relates the births, reigns, and deaths of a number of ancient kings, as well as how some of them came to be taken for gods. In short, it insists that they were not gods at all, but mortal men now deceased. It was not uncommon for Christian authors taking aim at the pagan pantheon to claim that their adversaries, or rather the pagans to whom they were appealing, rendered worship to dead men. Far from it, this was probably the most commonly exploited argumentative gambit in the apologetic arsenal. We find it as early as Justin Martyr and repeated in most authors up to the fourth century and beyond who addressed themselves to the phenomenon of paganism.[3] But most Christian

2 That is to say, if we are correct in attributing the account of the gods found in the *Excerpta Latina Barbari* and Malalas to Bouttios, then his work can be seen to have had a pervasive influence on how the gods of myth and primeval history were understood in Byzantium. A cursory list of instances in which some form of the Picus-Zeus narrative occurs in Byzantine literature—with no claim to exhaustiveness—would include *Chronicon Paschale* (Dindorf, *Chronicon Paschale*, 1:64–68); John of Nikiu 5–15 (Charles, *Chronicle of John, Bishop of Nikiu*, 16–20); George Syncellus 322–23, 450 (Mosshammer, *Ecloga chronographica*, 200, 284); George Hamartolos (George Monachus) 1.3–9 (de Boor, *Georgii Monachi Chronicon*, 1:11–15); Symeon the Logothete, *Chron.* 28.2–5, 32.4, 36.7 (Wahlgren, *Symeonis Magistri et Logothetae Chronicon*, 32–33, 36–37, 45); *Suda*: Αἴγυπτος (Αι 77), Ἥφαιστος (Η 661), Θοῦλις (Θ 415), Θούρρας (Θ 417), Ἰώ (Ι 453), Μέδουσα (Μ 406), Μεταλλεῖς (Μ 704), Πῆκος (Π 1500), Φαῦνος (Φ 148) (Adler, *Suidae Lexicon*, 2:161, 598, 646, 721–22; 3:346, 370; 4:124, 707); George Cedrenus, *Comp. hist.* 19–21 (Tartaglia, *Georgii Cedreni Historiarum Compendium*, 1:95–100); Constantine Manasses, *Comp. chron.* 535–60 (PG 127:240B–241B); Michael Glykas, *Annales* 2:129–30 (PG 158:253B–256A); Joel the Chronograph, *Chron. comp.* 4 (PG 139:225B). Through translations of Greek chronicles this account of the gods even penetrated into the medieval Slavonic and Ethiopic traditions; see Mango, "Byzantine Chronography."

3 Justin, *Apol.* 1.24.2; Theoph., *Ad Aut.* 1.9, 10; Athenagoras, *Leg. pro Christ.* 30.3; *Didache* 6.3 (cf. Clem. Rome, 2 Clement 3); Clem. Al., *Protr.* 2.26.7, 29.1, 30.3–7, 37.4, 4.49.3, 55.2–3; Tert., *Ad nat.* 2.13.1–3, *Apol.* 10.4; Min. Fel., *Oct.* 21.8; Commodian, *Instr.* 1.6.10, 12, 16; Origen, *C. Cels.* 3.43; Cyprian, *De idolorum vanitate* 1–2; Lactant., *Div. inst.* 1.11.44–49, 17.5; *Clem. Rec.* 10.24, 25; *Clem. Hom.* 5.23, 6.21, 10.9.1–2; Euseb., *Praep. evang.*

writers who claimed that the gods were really dead men did that and little more. They made the provocative statement, and might defend it by addressing the mythical accounts of the gods' suffering and misdeeds or by citing a reputable authority who could verify the claim. These authorities—Euhemerus, Alexander's letter to his mother relating the confidential information of an Egyptian priest (Leon of Pella), or Thallus, as well as other names that circulated among the apologists—offered narratives of the lives and deeds of the gods, but the apologists who referred to them did not; rather they made assertions and supported them with citations, not narratives.[4] Even Lactantius and Eusebius, who provide extensive accounts of the gods as ancient kings, largely quote or paraphrase these accounts from their respective authorities, Ennius's translation of Euhemerus and the various versions in Diodorus Siculus, but do not themselves compose their own narratives.[5] What Bouttios does, therefore, is quite remarkable.

Bouttios wrote a history of the gods, and those authorities that appear in his work are there to support subsidiary points, rather than the main one. It is the reverse of the usual Christian apologetic procedure. He prepared his own account of the gods to bear out the contention that they were mortals, which remains his clear, if unspoken, point. Bouttios did not engage in overt apologetics or explicit argumentation. Rather he was ostensibly writing a history, in which the facts supposedly spoke for themselves. The selection—or fabrication—of those facts and their distribution by the author might lead ineluctably to conclusions he had determined beforehand, but the author was still in a position to maintain that he was not engaged in polemic, but simply making a record of the past. The argument might be all the more persuasive for being implicit, presented in the form of a historical narrative. People might be more inclined to believe what—they think, at least—they have discovered for themselves, rather than what is dictated to them. At any rate, whether the polemical purpose of this account of the gods

3.10.21; Athanasius, *Contra Gentes* 10–11; Firm. Mat., *Err. prof. rel.* 7.6, 16.3; August., *De civ. D.* 7.33, 8.26; Prudent., *C. Symm.* 1.157–58, *Perist.* 5.35–36; see Camelot, *Athanase d'Alexandrie, Contre les Païens*, 82–85.

4 Athenagoras, *Leg. pro Christ.* 28; Theoph., *Ad Aut.* 3.29; Tert., *Ad nat.* 2.12.26–29, *Apol.* 10.7–8; Min. Fel., *Oct.* 21.1–6; Cyprian, *De idolorum vanitate* 3; Arn., *Adv. nat.* 4.29; August., *De civ. D.* 6.7, 27, 8.5, 26, 27.

5 Lactant., *Div. inst.* 1.11, 14; Euseb., *Praep. evang.* 1.9.20–10.42 (Philo of Byblos), 2.1 (Diodorus Siculus on Egypt), 2.2.36–51 (Dionysius Scytobrachion), 2.2.52–62 (Euhemerus).

was obvious to its first audience or not, it certainly came to be taken for history, as it insinuated itself in one way or another into most Byzantine chronicles.[6]

When we say that Bouttios wrote a history of the gods, we mean that he prepared a plausible account of the remote—perhaps indeterminate—past on the basis of the somewhat limited source material at his disposal: the genealogies and stories of divine activity contained in the mythological tradition. The result may be a speculative reconstruction, having a great deal in common with science fiction, but the important point was that it appeared to be history. Dionysius of Halicarnassus spoke of rendering the deeds of Heracles into a record of the past "in a scheme of history" (ἐν ἱστορίας σχήματι), and Plutarch expressed his intention to rationalize the myth of Theseus and give it the "look of history" (ἱστορίας ὄψιν).[7] The carefully recorded ages and reign lengths that Bouttios assigns to his god-kings, although seemingly altogether arbitrary, seem to be part of such an effort. They may also owe something to the efforts of Clement of Alexandria and Eusebius to fit the gods into a chronology and make them historical figures, primarily in order to nullify their divinity rather than to give their myths the semblance of history, even if they did also have that coincidental effect.

Such a treatment, as articulated by Dionysius and Plutarch, which simply trimmed away the implausible and irrational, might have sufficed for those working on heroes, who were originally human anyway. But accounts of the gods called for a more thoroughgoing reworking. Euhemerus of Messene seems to have been among the first writers to discuss Zeus and the other Olympians as if they were historical figures, and his name has been appropriately attached to this approach to the gods ever since. His *Hiera Anagraphe* or *Sacred History* is anchored in traditional knowledge about the gods, but it is not an allegorical interpretation of a single text or story, nor an archaeological examination of

6 See above, p. 233 and n. 2.

7 Dion. Hal., *Ant. Rom.* 1.41.1; Plut., *Thes.* 1.3. See Graf, *Greek Mythology*, 124; Wiseman, "Lying Historians," 128–31; Fox, *Roman Historical Myths*, 79; Preston, "Roman Questions, Greek Answers," 116; Pelling, *Plutarch and History*, 171–95; C. Cooper, "Irrational Myth." Strabo (1.2.35) uses the same phrase as Dionysius for those prose writers who consciously relate marvels and embellish their writings with myth, although they present them in the form of history (ἐν ἱστορίας σχήματι); see Gyselinck and Demoen, "Author and Narrator." On this rationalizing approach to myth in general and several of its more notable exponents, see Hawes, *Rationalizing Myth in Antiquity*.

the available evidence (as in Thucydides' preface to his history). Rather it is an innovative and imaginative narrative—perhaps a history, since at no point does it concede its fictional nature—of the gods, which accounts for many aspects of their mythic identities and current cults. As such, it is very similar to Bouttios's history of Picus-Zeus and his family. In detail, however, the accounts of the gods offered by Euhemerus and Bouttios have very little in common. The Zeus of Euhemerus, for instance, holds court on Mount Olympus and is not identified with Picus, whereas Bouttios's "Picus, who is also Zeus" rules over Assyria and then Italy, but apparently not Greece, and Olympus is not mentioned in relation to him, as far as we can see. Further examples of telling discrepancies could be added at length.[8]

Nevertheless, these discrepancies do not mean that Bouttios has nothing to do with Euhemerus. On the contrary, they may very well indicate that he stands within the euhemeristic tradition. If we seek to identify such a tradition, we do not find a succession of authors preserving the details of Euhemerus's *Sacred History* point by point. Rather, we can discern a number of writers who composed treatments of the remote past that share the premise that the gods were once mortal men, but differ in regard to the setting, relations and relative prominence of the characters, and progress of the narrative that is supposed to convey that theory.[9] Indeed, the details of each narrative are so distinct from one to the next that it is hard to believe they are not the result of a conscious effort at novelty and distinctiveness. For instance, Dionysius Scytobrachion, writing about a generation after Euhemerus, also presented the gods as ancient human kings

8 See Garstad, "Euhemerus and the *Chronicle* of John Malalas," 906–7.

9 Evidence for the euhemeristic tradition, that is, accounts of the gods that might be described as historical romances characterized by novelty, may be found in the fragments of Deinarchus of Delos (*FGrHist* 399 F 1 = Euseb., *Chron.*: ann. Abr. 712/20; Georg. Sync., *Chron.* 307; Malalas 2.15), presuming that a chronological discrepancy can be resolved (see Dion. Hal., *De Dinarch.* 1); Phylarchus (*FGrHist* 81 F 78 = Plut., *De Is. et Os.* 29 [362B]); the so-called Phrygian literature (Cic., *Nat. D.* 3.42) which sometimes circulated under the name of Thymoetes, a contemporary of Orpheus (Diod. Sic. 3.67.5), see Rives, "Phrygian Tales"; and especially Dionysius Scytobrachion (*FGrHist* 32 = Diod. Sic. 3.56–74); as well as in the historians Castor of Rhodes (*FGrHist* 250 F 1 = Euseb., *Chron.* 15) and Thallus (*FGrHist* 256 F 2 = Theoph., *Ad Aut.* 3.29). Winiarczyk, *Euhemeros von Messene*, 139–43, simply notes that these romancers were influenced by Euhemerus, whereas it seems more likely that he was the originator of this tradition.

but told a very different story about them, setting much of the action in Africa and making Dionysus, not Zeus, the most important of these legendary kings.[10] It would seem that the expectation of the euhemeristic tradition was that each author who contributed to it would compose a novel narrative on the understanding that the gods were once mortal rulers. This would emphasize the theoretical basis of all of the narratives, namely the original humanity of the gods, and tacitly concede the speculative and fictional nature of the narrative in which it was presented. In this case, Bouttios's account of the gods—not despite its discrepancies with Euhemerus's *Sacred History* but because of them—accords very well with the euhemeristic tradition. Indeed, the Picus-Zeus narrative seems to be the last product of the euhemeristic tradition so conceived. After a long period of Christian writers citing the authors of the euhemeristic tradition to bolster their contention that the gods were dead kings, one of their number composed his own contribution to that tradition, an account of the gods as kings, novel in its detail and arrangement, to substantiate the polemical denial of divinity to the pagan gods. As we shall see, both the polemical purpose and the inheritance from apologetic literature color Bouttios's euhemeristic composition.

Demons, or the Lack Thereof

First, though, we may note an element of the apologetic explanation of the gods that is conspicuous by its absence from Bouttios's account of the gods. A number of apologists had combined the euhemeristic claim that the gods were once men with the notion that idolatry, the worship of those deceased men, was encouraged by demons.[11] In order to turn men from God and arrogate his worship to themselves, the demons inspired men to set up images of their dead kings and offer them sacrifice, and fortified their superstition with occasional manifestations of their power. Certain passages in the Septuagint indicated that sacrifices made to

10 *FGrHist* 32 = Diod. Sic. 3.56–74; see Rusten, *Dionysius Scytobrachion*, 102–12.

11 Justin, *Apol.* 1.5.2, 21.6; Tatian, *Ad Gr.* 8.1–2, 9.1; Clem. Al., *Protr.* 2.39.1–41.4, 4.55.2–56.1, *Strom.* 6.(3) 31.5; Tert., *Apol.* 22.6–12, 23.2, 6, 8–11; Origen, *C. Cels.* 8.3–5; *Clem.*, *Rec.* 1.30–31, 4.13, 19, 30; Athanasius, *De Incarn.* 11, *Vita Ant.* 94.2; August., *De civ. D.* 7.18, 33; Theodoret, *Gr. affect. cur.* 3.59–70, 10.2. See Nock, *Conversion*, 221–22; Dodds, *Pagan and Christian*, 117 and n. 3; Armstrong, *Cambridge History of Later Greek and Early Medieval Philosophy*, 165; Andrade, *Syrian Identity*, 272–73.

false gods were actually offered to demons or demonic forces (δαιμονίοις), but these passages only corroborated a fuller description of the relation between the gods and the demons which came to be accepted in the Christian tradition.[12]

Justin Martyr, in the second century, was the first Christian writer to clearly articulate this understanding of the gods as, in some way, demons:

> τὴν μὲν τῶν ἀνθρώπων καὶ τῶν ὑπὸ τὸν οὐρανὸν πρόνοιαν ἀγγέλοις οὓς ἐπὶ τούτοις ἔταξε παρέδωκεν. οἱ δ' ἄγγελοι, παραβάντες τήνδε τὴν τάξιν, γυναικῶν μίξεσιν ἡττήθησαν καὶ παῖδας ἐτέκνωσαν, οἵ εἰσιν οἱ λεγόμενοι δαίμονες. καὶ προσέτι λοιπὸν τὸ ἀνθρώπειον γένος ἑαυτοῖς ἐδούλωσαν, τὰ μὲν διὰ μαγικῶν στροφῶν, τὰ δὲ διὰ φόβων καὶ τιμωριῶν ὧν ἐπέφερον, τὰ δὲ διὰ διδαχῆς θυμάτων καὶ θυμιαμάτων καὶ σπονδῶν, ὧν ἐνδεεῖς γεγόνασι μετὰ τὸ πάθεσιν ἐπιθυμιῶν δουλωθῆναι. καὶ εἰς ἀνθρώπους φόνους πολέμους μοιχείας ἀκολασίας καὶ πᾶσαν κακίαν ἔσπειραν. ὅθεν καὶ ποιηταὶ καὶ μυθολόγοι, ἀγνοοῦντες τοὺς ἀγγέλους καὶ τοῦς ἐξ αὐτῶν γεννηθέντας δαίμονας ταῦτα πρᾶξαι εἰς ἄρρενας καὶ θηλείας καὶ πόλεις καὶ ἔθνη ἅπερ συνέγραψαν, εἰς αὐτὸν τὸν θεὸν καὶ τοὺς ὡς ἀπ' αὐτοῦ σπορᾷ γενομένους υἱοὺς καὶ τῶν λεχθέντων ἐκείνου ἀδελφῶν καὶ τέκνων ὁμοίως τῶν ἀπ' ἐκείνων ἀνήνεγκαν.[13]

> [God] gave the administration of mortals and affairs below heaven to the angels whom he set over them. But the angels transgressed this order and were overcome by coupling with women and begat children, who are those called demons. And what is more, they enslaved the rest of the human race to themselves, through magical transformations, but also through fear and the punishments they inflicted, and through the teaching of sacrifices and incense offerings and libations, which they came to need after they were enslaved to the passions of lust. And they planted murders, wars, adulteries, licentiousness, and every evil in men. Wherefore both poets and mythologists, not knowing that the angels

12 Deut. 32:17, Ps. 105:37. See Sullivan, "Watchers Traditions," 97.

13 Justin, *Apol.* 2.4(5).2b–5 (Minns and Parvis, *Justin, Philosopher and Martyr*, 282–84). Cf. Chadwick, *Early Christian Thought*, 44. On the composition of Justin's *Second Apology* and its relation to the rest of his corpus, see Parvis, "Justin, Philosopher and Martyr."

> and the demons born from them did these things to men and women and cities and nations, which they have written about, ascribe them to god himself and to the sons born as if from his seed and those called his brothers and their offspring likewise.

In this understanding Justin is clearly indebted to the *Book of the Watchers*, an early elaboration on the account of the "sons of God" and the "daughters of men" in Genesis 6:1–4, which tells how the angels set over human affairs quite literally fell for human women, produced the Giants by their unnatural mixing, and taught men forbidden knowledge.[14] But the identification of the pagan gods with these fallen angels and demons is Justin's own novel addition to the Watchers tradition.[15]

By the beginning of the fourth century, on the basis of a considerable accumulated precedent in the apologetic literature to which he was heir, Lactantius could combine demonology and euhemerism to assert that the demons inaugurated the worship of dead kings and assumed their names:

> Hi sunt qui fingere imagines et simulacra docuerunt, qui, ut hominum mentes a cultu veri Dei averterent, effictos mortuorum regum vultus et ornatos exquisita pulchritudine statui consecrarique fecerunt et illorum sibi nomina quasi personas aliquas induerunt. Sed eos magi et hi quos vere maleficos vulgus appellat, cum artes suas exsecrabiles exercent, veris suis nominibus cient, illis caelestibus quae in litteris sanctis leguntur.[16]

> These [demons] are those who taught [men] to make images and statues; who, that they might turn the minds of men from the worship of the True God, have the visages of dead kings made and decorated with cunning beauty set up and consecrated and take their names to themselves, like so many masks. But the magicians and those whom the common people rightly call evildoers, when they practice their accursed

14 See Reed, *Fallen Angels*, 161–74; Chesnutt, "Descent of the Watchers"; cf. Korteweg, "Justin Martyr."

15 Chesnutt, "Descent of the Watchers," 171–73; Edwards, *Religions*, 21–22.

16 Lactant., *Div. inst.* 2.16.3–4 (Monat, *Lactance, Institutions divines*, 2, 194–96).

> arts, invoke them by their true names, those heavenly names which are read in sacred scripture.

Demons appear in the earliest and most influential Christian explanations of pagan religion and were still current in the interpretations of the fourth century, but there is no suggestion in the fragments of Bouttios that the demons abetted Picus-Zeus, Faunus-Hermes, and their ilk in their efforts to be considered gods.

The prevalence of demons in so many other Christian explanations of the pagan gods indicates that this absence is intentional and tells us something about the author and his work. We must beware, however, that we do not misinterpret Bouttios's eschewing the mention of demons as a sign of acute materialism or rationalism. The efficacy of some forms of magic (even if others are dismissed as charlatanry and sleight of hand) shows that Bouttios's materialism was not all that thoroughgoing and left some room for the supernatural. As for rationalism, the most rational and intelligent minds of Late Antiquity, pagan and Christian, Porphyry and Augustine prominent among them, found a place for demons, angels, and other spiritual beings in their scheme of the world and accepted the influence of these beings and their activities.[17] The absence of demons has more to do with the genre in which Bouttios chose to write.

Bouttios wrote, or purported to write, a history, which included an account of the origin of the pagan gods in historical terms. Those terms, as understood in antiquity, did not limit the historian to archival material, physical data, and verifiable assertions, but they did allow only a peripheral place to the supernatural. Recourse to demonic activity to explain the cults of the gods would have given the game away, and revealed Bouttios's account as not a history so much as a polemical piece deeply indebted to the apologetic tradition. The historical version of events, which had no place for demons, moreover seems consistent with the perspective evident in the accounts of tyche sacrifice, which could not see the Tyche figures as personifications of abstract ideas, but insisted that they must have resulted from a series of specific atrocities committed against specific people

17 Dodds, *Pagan and Christian*, 37–68. In addition to surveying the place of demons, or *daimones*, in the worldviews of antiquity, Martin, *Inventing Superstition*, points out the perils of imputing such modern categories as "superstition" and "the supernatural" to the intellectual circles and general society of the ancient Mediterranean.

at specific points in time. What is more, it seems consistent with the literal and historical tendencies that predominated in the biblical interpretation associated with Antioch, our putative setting for Bouttios, as we have already discussed.[18] The exclusion of demonic activity also accommodates the attitude of the "paranoid style" or conspiracy theory, with which we shall propose that the work of Bouttios has telling affinities,[19] because it insists on imputing human intention to practically all the events of history, and charging the human instigators of historical events with a moral responsibility that can only be lessened if they are supposed to have acted under the compulsion of demons.

The exclusion of demons from its record of events and from its explanatory model allowed the Picus-Zeus narrative to be accepted as a history, and so to find a place in the euhemeristic tradition, which offered a series of mutually distinct and altogether plausible accounts of the gods as ancient human kings.[20] On this one point the account of Picus-Zeus and his family stands apart from the usual explanation of the origin and activity of the so-called gods propounded by Christian apologists up to the fourth century and beyond. It was clearly more important to Bouttios that his work should be taken for a history than that he nail his ideological colors to the mast. Perhaps it was also essential to his project: the same audience who would ignore an obvious apologist or polemicist as another tired old hack might attend to the plain facts proffered by a historian—or a partisan writer who purported to be one. For the rest, however, many of the details of the Picus-Zeus narrative can be identified as points that had been raised in both the earlier critique of the presentation of the gods in myth by pagan philosophers—as well as the accounts of the gods in the euhemeristic tradition—and the attack on the gods of the paideia in Christian apologetics, which borrowed so much from this earlier material. These points did not tend to be objectionable to historiography because they either upbraided the mythographers for depicting the gods in scandalously anthropomorphic terms or set out to demonstrate that the so-called gods were, in fact, human beings.

18 See above, pp. 147–49 and 147–48, n. 83.

19 See below, chapter 10.

20 I hesitate to add "mundane" or "down-to-earth" to the adjective "plausible" as descriptors of these accounts, since they also tend to impute to the primeval kings such stupendous and gargantuan achievements as worldwide rule, repeated travels over the face of the whole earth, and the inducement of mankind to take them for gods.

Divine Misdeeds

One of the most decidedly human aspects of the gods depicted by Bouttios—apart from their mortality—is their propensity for immoral and discreditable behavior, which Bouttios duly emphasizes. Their conduct is marked and their characters blackened by violence, tyranny, consanguineous usurpations, deceit, wanton seduction of women, jugglery, sorcery, and the arrogation of divinity, as well as less substantial but unsurprising vices like arrogance. In ascribing this roster of crimes to the gods, Bouttios not only borrowed a page from the apologists but also echoed some of the very earliest criticism of myth. At the turn of the fifth century BCE, Xenophanes of Colophon drew attention to the fact that the most revered purveyors of myth, Homer and Hesiod, depicted the gods committing misdeeds that would make men blush, such as theft, adultery, and lying.[21] Plato enthusiastically adopted this critique, noting that no divinity worthy of the name would conduct himself as the gods do in the old poets, and dismissed traditional myth as an unacceptable source of information on the gods.[22]

The response to the exposition of this "scandal of myth" in the pagan philosophical tradition was most often to apply elaborate allegorical interpretations to the myths, conceding that their literal sense was untenable and mining them for hidden meanings.[23] The Christian apologists, however, were quite happy to retain the surface meaning of the myths, in all their shameful and repugnant excess, as a testimony to the conduct of the gods the pagans deemed worthy of worship. They regularly included, with as much relish as disgust, catalogs itemizing the bad behavior of the so-called gods, from parricide to pederasty and from incest to money-grubbing.[24] Surely no sensible, decent person could consider beings who did such things worthy of reverence and emulation, and certainly

21 Sext. Emp., *Math.* 9.193 (= Diels-Kranz, *Die Fragmente der Vorsokratiker*, no. 21 F 11). See Lesher, *Xenophanes of Colophon*, 22–23, 82–85, 114–19.

22 Pl., *Resp.* 376E–392D; see Naddaff, *Exiling the Poets*, 11–36.

23 Brisson, *How Philosophers Saved Myths*, 5–106.

24 Aristides, *Apol.* 9; Justin, *Apol.* 1.21.4–5, 25.1–3; Tatian, *Ad Gr.* 8; Athenagoras, *Leg. pro Christ.* 20.2–3, 21, 29.2, 32.1; Theoph., *Ad Aut.* 1.9, 3.15; Clem. Al., *Protr.* 2.30.1; Tert., *Ad nat.* 2.13.10–21, *Apol.* 11.11–14, 21.8; Min. Fel., *Oct.* 24; Origen, *C. Cels.* 1.17, 4.48; Commodian, *Instr.* 1.6.16–26; Arn., *Adv. nat.* 3.8–11, 4.27–28, 32–36; Lactant., *Div. inst.* 1.10, 17.6–17; Euseb., *Praep. evang.* 2.4.1–4; *Clem. Rec.* 10.20–23; *Clem. Hom.* 4.15.2–16.4, 5.11.3–15.3; Athanasius, *Contra Gentes* 11, 12, 15; Firm. Mat., *Err. prof. rel.* 12; August., *De civ. D.* 7.27; Prudent., *C. Symm.* 1.159–63; Theodoret, *Gr. affect. cur.* 3.30, 37, 96, 98, 7.5, 8, 8.12–18.

not endow them with divinity. This must have appeared to be a particularly effective argument, since it depended not only on the pagans' own treasured texts and revered authorities but also on the reactions of their own philosophers. The pagan audience of the apologists was no more likely to disown Plato than Homer. And this is the argument on which Bouttios depends, and which he implicitly repeats, when he notes their misdeeds in his account of the gods. The significant difference is that rather than offering a list of references to traditional mythology, Bouttios presents these crimes as historical actions. While the verses of poets might be interpreted away, matters of historical record—even a fabricated one—were harder to discount.

Gods as Culture Heroes

If they were such disreputable men, why would anyone consider them to be gods? Bouttios seems to address this question when he attributes different inventions and other benefactions to some of the so-called gods, and the practice of impressive arts to others. Cronos was the first to invent kingship—though it is hardly defined as a benefaction: "ruling and prevailing over other men"—and Faunus-Hermes invented gold smelting. Picus-Zeus astounded people with conjuring and the mystic arts, and Faunus-Hermes did the same with philosophy and prophecy. Perhaps the clearest case is that of Hephaistos, who is said to have been the first to introduce chastity laws to the Egyptians and to have begun forging weapons for them; as a consequence, his people deified him as a lawgiver and a benefactor.

There was a long tradition of curiosity about the inventors of various aspects of culture, and such an explanation of the process of god-making had a considerable pedigree.[25] In the fifth century BCE Prodicus of Ceos proposed that people had once deified individuals like Demeter and Dionysus who made contributions to the improvement of the life of man.[26] Other authorities on the origin of the gods and their cult, Hecataeus of Abdera, Dionysus Scytobrachion, and Diodorus Siculus, agreed that the *euergetai* of the past received divine honors

25 See Kleingünther, *ΠΡΩΤΟΣ ΕΥΡΕΤΗΣ*; Cole, *Democritus*, 5, 48–50.

26 Henrichs, "Two Doxographical Notes," 107–23; Henrichs, "Sophists and Hellenistic Religion."

because of their benefactions.[27] Such theorizing was also reinforced by the prominent place of *euergesia* in the rhetoric of Hellenistic royal propaganda.[28]

Even some of the Christian apologists were willing to concede that their arts and contributions to civilization had understandably led to the deification of culture heroes, no matter how improper such deification was in principle.[29] There was no consensus on this matter, however, and other apologists recognized that some gods had been deified for their supposed benefactions, but sharply criticized this consecration of inventors in the place of God.[30] Athanasius of Alexandria strenuously contested inventions and benefactions as a reason for bestowing divine honors, insisting that such ingenuity was evidence of the cultivation of human nature rather than of any sort of divinity.[31] Depicting a figure from primeval history as an inventor, then, suggested some grounds for deification, but did not ultimately commit the historian to ascribing divinity.

The attribution to them of technical discoveries and advances in culture might seem like a commendation of the so-called gods, but in order to understand the intended impression on the audience, any mention of inventions must be seen not only in its Greek context, where it is overwhelmingly positive, but also in its biblical or Judeo-Christian context, where it is dubious at best, if not altogether negative. Genesis 4:17–22 lists the "fathers" or inventors of various arts and crafts, husbandry, musical instruments, and the forging of bronze and iron, in the first ages of man.[32] All of these inventors are descendants of the wicked

27 Hecataeus of Abdera: *FGrHist* 264 F 25 (= Diod. Sic. 1.13.1–3); see Murray, "Hecataeus of Abdera," 160. Dionysius Scytobrachion: *FGrHist* 32 FF 7, 8 (= Diod. Sic. 3.56.5, 72.4, 73.3, 5–6); see Rusten, *Dionysius Scytobrachion*, 102–12. Diodorus Siculus: see Sacks, *Diodorus Siculus*, 61–82; Sulimani, *Diodorus' Mythistory*, 64–73.

28 Murray, "Hecataeus of Abdera," 159–61; Sacks, *Diodorus Siculus*, 69–70; Samuel, "Ptolemies and the Ideology of Kingship," 190–91; Winiarczyk, *Euhemeros von Messene*, 48–50.

29 Athenagoras, *Leg. pro Christ.* 30.2; Clem. Al., *Protr.* 2.26.7; Lactant., *Div. inst.* 1.15.2–7; *Clem. Rec.* 4.30.1; August., *De civ. D.* 18.2, 3, 6, 8, 12, 15, *Enarrationes in Psalmos* 93.3; Theodoret, *Gr. affect. cur.* 2.97. See Chadwick, *Early Christian Thought*, 38.

30 Tert., *Apol.* 11.6–9; Arn., *Adv. nat.* 3.20–22; Lactant., *Div. inst.* 1.18.1–2, 18–25, 7.14.

31 Athanasius, *Contra Gentes* 18; see Camelot, *Athanase d'Alexandrie, Contre les Païens*, 27, 108–9; Meijering, *Athanasius: Contra Gentes*, 67–69.

32 At least one early reader made the connection between some version of Bouttios's account of the gods and this passage from Genesis. John of Nikiu, who largely delivers a garbled and abbreviated rendition of the mythical history also found in Malalas, interrupts

and accursed Cain, and the descendants of the righteous Seth are not credited with any inventions. The negative implications of this list of inventions are compounded by the passage that immediately follows it (Gen. 4:23–24), a vainglorious boast on the part of Lamech, the father of the inventors, about his capacity to do violence to his fellow man.[33] The extrabiblical Jewish literature that the Christians inherited along with the Bible likewise took a dim view of inventions and technical knowledge. Perhaps most significantly, the *Book of the Watchers*, as preserved in the *Book of Enoch*, claims that many arts, including the manufacture of arms and armor, were introduced by the fallen angels as part of the illicit knowledge they conveyed to man.[34]

---

the succession from Hephaistos, an ironsmith and the first to forge weapons of war, to his son Helios with a somewhat garbled account of the family of Lamech and of "Tôbêl," who worked brass and iron before the Flood (Charles, *Chronicle of John, Bishop of Nikiu*, 11), although just how he intended his reader to feel about Tubal-cain's work as a smith is unclear, since he seems to make his craft the result of divine inspiration, "for he had received wisdom from God—Praise be to Him" (19).

33 See Gowen, "Cainite and Sethite Genealogies"; Gabriel, "Die Kainitengenealogie"; J. Miller, "Descendents of Cain"; Klemm, "Kain und die Kainiten"; cf. Enslin, "Cain and Prometheus." Skinner, *Commentary on Genesis*, 115–24, insists that the underlying text, if not its context in Genesis, is neutral (115): "It has commonly been held that the passage involves a pessimistic estimate of human civilization, as a record of progressive degeneracy and increasing alienation from God. That is probably true of the compiler who placed the section after the account of the Fall, and incorporated the Song of Lamech, which could hardly fail to strike the Hebrew mind as an exhibition of human depravity. In itself, however, the genealogy contains no moral judgment on the facts recorded." The standard modern commentaries seem to agree that the development of human arts and technology are to be viewed in a positive light, even as a blessing. Hamilton, *Book of Genesis*, 236–41, is perhaps most effusive (239): "This point may provide another illustration of the grace of God at work in this fallen line. They [the descendants of Cain] too have an important and wholesome contribution to make to God's world." Cf. Westermann, *Genesis 1–11*, 321–37, at 334: "Technology as such is regarded positively." Even Gage, *Gospel of Genesis*, 58–61, 112, sees the problem as being not with technology itself, but that because of the Cainites' impiety their skills (similar to those required to build the Tabernacle) serve no useful purpose; they rather serve the earthly city, which is a parody of the heavenly city, the Edenic Zion. But I suspect this interpretation may reveal an unconscious prejudice in favor of technological advancement on the part of the commentators, one that was not necessarily shared by their forebears.

34 1 *Enoch* 7.1, 8.1, 3. See Fröhlich, "Mesopotamian Elements," 13, 18; Corley, "Enochic Watchers Traditions," 59–60; L. Baynes, "Watchers Traditions," 155, 158–59.

Bouttios may allow that "gods" were responsible for some inventions and advances in civilization, but the biblical view of such supposed benefits would make the—biblically literate, at any rate—reader wary about seeing this as altogether commendable.[35] When the ascription of inventions is combined with the accusation of evil living, as in the cases of Picus-Zeus and Faunus-Hermes especially, there is a suggestion that no amount of contribution to human welfare is the whole story of a life or reign, and it cannot compensate for reprehensible behavior. This is consistent with the ambivalent presentation in the fragments of Bouttios generally of famous kings as both great conquerors or builders on the one hand, and perpetrators of virgin sacrifice on the other, a presentation that is ultimately negative.

Deified Kings

Hephaistos's role as a benefactor as the explicit grounds for his deification notwithstanding, most of the gods in Bouttios seem to have been deified simply because they were kings. All of the men and women who were taken for gods according to Bouttios were rulers or at least members of a royal family, and there seems to have been a common assumption in antiquity that royalty was an attribute necessary for candidates aspiring to divinity. Hecataeus of Abdera, or the Egyptian archaeology based on Hecataeus, claimed that Osiris and Isis ruled as kings of Egypt.[36] Euhemerus presented Zeus as a ruler of the whole world who exploited his position to establish an enduring cult for himself and his family.[37] Euhemerus's successors, especially Dionysius Scytobrachion, in explaining the gods of myth as deified men likewise rendered those men as kings.[38] Even Euhemerus's critics indicate the tendency of his work in this regard, as when Plutarch

35 Cf. August., *De civ. D.* 22.24, and the ambiguous praise that Augustine offers those arts discovered and cultivated by human genius, some of which serve the vices and bring harm (*nonne humano ingenio tot tantaeque artes sunt inventae et exercitae . . .*).

36 Diod. Sic. 1.13.1, 13.5, 15.3, 17.3, 21.2–3, 22.1, 25.7, 26.1–2. Murray, "Hecataeus of Abdera," 149–50, holds that Diodorus's account of the career of Osiris was taken not from Hecataeus of Abdera, but rather from a later source which was itself based on Hecataeus; cf. Burton, *Diodorus Siculus, Book 1*, 16–17, 88.

37 Diod. Sic. 5.46.3, 6.1.6, 8, 9; Lactant., *Div. inst.* 1.11, 14. See Garstad, "Deification in Euhemerus of Messene."

38 Diod. Sic. 3.56.3, 60.1, 61.2, 68.1, 72.6, 73.1, 4, 8.

decries his impious reduction of the gods to "the names of generals, admirals, and kings."[39]

The Christian apologists also tend to suppose that those mortals who were deified had been kings, and their kingship, sometimes characterized as "tyranny," is often given as one of the chief reasons for their deification.[40] So Athenagoras opined that if some thoroughly disreputable characters received divine honors, it should come as no surprise if some others should be called gods by their subjects on account of their rule or tyranny (τὶ θαυμαστὸν τοὺς μὲν ἐπὶ ἀρχῇ καὶ τυραννίδι ὑπὸ τῶν κατ' αὐτοὺς κληθῆναι θεούς), and

> οἷς μὲν οὖν ἢ [αὐτοὶ] οἱ ἀρχόμενοι τιμῆς μετεδίδοσαν ἢ αὐτοὶ οἱ ἄρχοντες, οἱ μὲν φόβῳ, οἱ δὲ καὶ αἰδοῖ μετεῖχον τοῦ <τοῦ θεοῦ> ὀνόματος.[41]
>
> Thus, either those who were ruled—some on account of fear and others on account of respect—rendered some portion of honor or those who ruled partook of the name of god.

Some two centuries later, but in remarkably similar terms, Athanasius decried those who dared to elevate to the status of gods their rulers or their sons, either on account of reverence for those who ruled them or on account of fear of their tyranny (ἐτόλμησαν τοὺς παρ' αὐτῶν ἄρχοντας ἢ καὶ τοὺς τούτων παῖδας εἰς θεοὺς ἀναθεῖναι, ἢ διὰ τιμὴν τῶν ἀρξάντων ἢ διὰ φόβον τῆς αὐτῶν τυραννίδος).[42] The assumption that it was kings who were deified can only have been bolstered by the explanation of the origins of idolatry in the *Wisdom of Solomon*, which traced idols back to images of deceased loved ones and absent kings,

39 Plut., *De Is. et Os.* 23 (*Mor.* 360A).

40 Athenagoras, *Leg. pro. Christ.* 28.1–3, 30.1–2; Commodian, *Instr.* 1.6.16; Cyprian, *De idolorum vanitate* 1; Lactant., *Div. inst.* 1.15.2–7, 2.16.3; *Clem. Hom.* 5.23.1; Athanasius, *Contra Gentes* 9; Firm. Mat., *Err. prof. rel.* 6.1; August., *De civ. D.* 7.18; Prudent., *C. Symm.* 1.145–58. The historicizing "theologies" of various nations quoted by Eusebius in the first two books of the *Praeparatio evangelica* also present the "gods" as kings.

41 Athenagoras, *Leg. pro Christ.* 30.1, 2 (Marcovich, *Athenagoras: Legatio pro Christianis*, 96–97.

42 Athanasius, *Contra Gentes* 9 (Thomson, *Athanasius: Contra Gentes and De Incarnatione*, 24). See Meijering, *Athanasius: Contra Gentes*, 45–46.

which came to be worshipped by "men enslaved to circumstance or tyranny" (ἢ συμφορᾷ ἢ τυραννίδι δουλεύσαντες ἄνθρωποι).[43]

But kingship in itself was hardly innocent grounds for illicit deification, especially from the biblical perspective. In sacred history the royal office was at best a mixed blessing and at worst a despiteful imposition on God by his wayward people which was bound to end badly.[44] Royal sovereignty's sheen is further tarnished in Bouttios's account of the gods by being abetted as a means of acquiring divine status by wanton seduction, in the case of Picus-Zeus, and crass bribery in that of Faunus-Hermes. The one is accounted a god by the women he debauched, and the other because he can provide men with gold. This may owe something to the tradition of the Watchers, who were supposed to have seduced women and offered to enrich humanity with illicit knowledge.[45] The presentation of the recipients of deification as kings is also, once again, in keeping with the rest of the fragments of Bouttios with their generally negative depiction of the pagan kings who preceded Constantine as wicked men who abused their power, especially to introduce religious error.

43 Wisd. 14:12–21; see Gilbert, *La critique des dieux*, 126–31, 138–57; Strait, "Wisdom of Solomon."

44 Deut. 17:14–20; 1 Sam. 8:4–22. In addition to the warnings about the implications of kingship in these two passages, the book of Judges (chap. 9) offers the story of Abimelech, and particularly Jotham's parable of the trees within it (9:7–21), as a reflection on the evils of kingship; see Moore, *Commentary on Judges*, 229–30, 237–70. Abimelech's father Gideon had refused the rule offered him by the men of Israel (8:22–23), saying, "I will not rule over you, neither shall my son rule over you: the Lord shall rule over you." But Abimelech conspired with the men of Shechem to kill his seventy brothers and become king. His bid for a crown, though, ended in a falling-out with the Shechemites, rebellion, slaughter, and Abimelech's shameful death at the hands of a woman (cf. Alexander's capture by the Ethiopian queen Candace in **F 16.3**). The seventy sons of Picus-Zeus as opposed to their lone stepbrother, Faunus-Hermes, and the neat inversion of murderous intent, indicate that the author of the Picus-Zeus narrative was not only aware of this biblical story but also made explicit allusion to it; see Garstad, "Joseph as a Model for Faunus-Hermes," 504–5. We have some reason to conclude, therefore, that he was an exponent of the Bible's negative views of kingship.

45 1 *Enoch* 7.1.

Magical Practices

In some cases, however, it is clear that kingly power alone is not the reason for the deification of Bouttios's gods; they also dazzle their subjects with magic. Picus-Zeus used his magic to seduce women who in turn made him a god, and Faunus-Hermes deceived the Egyptians into considering him a god through his magic arts, among other skills. It was not unknown in pagan retellings of myth for the gods or demigods to practice magic. Diodorus Siculus, for instance, tells us that the second person who went under the name of Heracles, one of the Idaean Dactyls, was a γόης, a wizard, who performed initiation rituals and established the Olympic Games.[46] The term γόης had had pejorative connotations as early as Plato and Demosthenes, but there is no suggestion in Diodorus that this Heracles was wicked or deceitful.[47] There was also a tradition that at least one of the most ancient kings practiced magic, or had even been the inventor of magic. As far back as Pompeius Trogus, Zoroaster, who fought a war against the Assyrian conqueror Ninus, was supposed to have been an adept at sorcery or the first to practice this art.[48] Once again, no judgment is cast upon Zoroaster because he was a magician, only ever surprise that as such he still lost his war against Ninus.

But for Christians, of course, the practice of magic was no less damnable than the appropriation of divine honors.[49] Justin Martyr, however, the first Christian author to associate the practice of magic with an attempt to be considered a god, referred not to an example from the primeval past but to a much more recent one, that of Simon Magus, who appears in the book of Acts and whose cult Justin knew as a contemporary.[50] It is no surprise, then, that the Clementine

46 Diod. Sic. 3.74.4, 5.64.4, 7.

47 Pl., *Symp.* 203D, *Soph.* 235A; Dem. 318.1 (*De cor.* 276), 374.20 (*De fals. Leg.* 109). Nor did Neoplatonism's enthusiasm for theurgy mean unqualified acceptance of magicians; Porphyry (*Abst.* 2.45) distinguishes between the polluted magician (γόης) and the pure holy man (θεῖος ἀνὴρ). On the contrast between magic and theurgy, see also R. Smith, *Julian's Gods*, 103, 105.

48 Just., *Epit.* 1.1.4–10; Arn., *Adv. nat.* 1.5.2; August., *De civ. D.* 21.4; Oros. 1.4.1–3. Diodorus Siculus (2.6.1–4) knew of Ninus's Bactrian war but gave the Bactrian king the name of Oxyartes, possibly borrowed from Alexander the Great's opponent in Bactria, the father of Roxane.

49 See, for instance, Acts 8:18–22, 13:6–13, 19:19.

50 Justin, *Apol.* 1.26.1–3. See Acts 8:9–24; Tuzlak, "Magician and the Heretic," 417–19, 422.

literature, in which Simon Magus figures prominently as the opponent of Peter, not only indicates Simon's efforts to be taken for a god, but also in its explanations of the origins of the pagan pantheon insists that the men who came to be worshipped as gods were magicians, as well as kings, and that magic aided the process whereby they were taken for gods.[51] The gods of Bouttios are, moreover, remarkably consistent with the caricature of the magician put forth by Eusebius when he sought to rebut the pagan charge that Jesus was nothing more than a sorcerer, that is, a dabbler in loathsome and unhallowed rites, only out for filthy lucre, the gratification of his lusts through the seduction of women, and a showy fame.[52] Pursuing a similar argument, Athanasius insisted that none of the ancient kings and tyrants among the barbarians who practiced magic—a description in which the gods of Bouttios might be recognizable—could claim an influence comparable to that of the Christ.[53] Although there was some precedent in the pagan tradition for Bouttios's claim that the gods or at least the most ancient kings practiced magic, a more or less morally neutral magic, the exploitation of magic in an effort to attain godhead, to say nothing of its use for purposes of philandering and money-grubbing, reveals it as the magic vilified in no uncertain terms by the Church.[54]

Peripheral Settings

Another aspect of Bouttios's account of the gods that seems to arise from a combination of euhemerism and apologetics is the location of the gods' origin and activity. All of Bouttios's gods originate outside of the Hellenic world, none reside in Greece, and those in Italy are there only temporarily (Picus-Zeus ends his life

51 Simon Magus's efforts to be reckoned a god: *Clem. Rec.* 2.9.2, 6, 3.63.2, 8, cf. 2.6.9, 10.2, 12.1, 2, 5. Magic as an aid to false deification: *Clem. Rec.* 4.27.2–4, 30.2, 10.25.3; *Clem. Hom.* 5.23.4, 6.20.2.

52 Euseb., *Dem. evang.* 3.6.1–6. See Morlet, *La Démonstration Évangélique*, 267, 274–76.

53 Athanasius, *De incarn.* 50.

54 Many of these elements are combined earlier in Paul's warning to Timothy about the dangerous men "in the last days" (2 Tim. 3:1–9), who will be, among other things, "lovers of money" (φιλάργυροι) and "arrogant" (ὑπερήφανοι)—"arrogance" (ὑπερηφανία) is twice used to characterize Faunus-Hermes' rule over the Egyptians—and will seduce corruptible women, and they are likened to the Egyptian magicians, Jannes and Jambres.

there and Faunus-Hermes departs in middle age), and yet these kings who come from and are most active on the periphery of the Hellenic world are supposed to be the originators of the Greco-Roman pantheon.[55] To make the central and fundamental figures of Greek culture outsiders and barbarians is not merely a trait apparently derived from euhemerism, but must also be a dig at the smug pride of the Greeks in the excellence of their own heritage and their snobbery at anything with a hint of barbarity about it, like the Christian religion.

The euhemeristic narratives are ambivalent on this point of the relation of the gods, the deified mortals, to the Greek world; while they may involve Greece, they also tend to have eccentric settings. Euhemerus himself had Zeus come from Crete and hold court on Mount Olympus, but then establish his own great temple on the far-off island of Panchaea.[56] Dionysius Scytobrachion had his gods come from the farthest shores of Africa, and Crete was the only part of Greece he involved in his narrative, and that only at its edges.[57]

Having the gods come from and concentrate their activity in barbarian lands, however, corresponds closely to a common Christian apologetic theme. The apologists met the complaint of the pagans that Christianity was a despicable faith, barbarous in its discourse and its teaching, by retorting that the Greeks had long been in the habit of borrowing not only their philosophy, but also their arts and indeed all the elements that made up their culture from their barbarian inventors.[58] It is on this note that Tatian, who saw his conversion to Christianity

55 R. Scott, "Malalas' View of the Classical Past," 148–49, referring to his version of the Picus-Zeus narrative, has said, "Malalas treats the Olympian gods in a rationalised, perhaps euhemerised, way as historical figures in the distant past, where, however, they have nothing to do with Greece. Rather they are the early kings or emperors of the major powers that have controlled the world since history began." He understands the historicized gods' avoidance of Greece, however, as evidence of the general dehellenization of the past that is found in the work of Byzantine chroniclers, as well as reinforcing the almost exclusive emphasis on events occurring under monarchical, rather than democratic or republican, governments that has been seen to characterize the chronicles of Malalas and his successors (150). See also Liebeschuetz, "View from Antioch," 330–31.

56 Diod. Sic. 5.46.3, 6.1.6, 10; Lactant., *Div. inst.* 1.11.33, 35, 63, 22.21.

57 Diod. Sic. 3.56.1–3.

58 Justin, *Apol.* 1.44.8–10, 59.1–60.11, cf. 2.13; Tatian, *Ad Gr.* 1.1–3, 40.1–2; Theoph., *Ad Aut.* 2.38; Clem. Al., *Strom.* 1.(15) 66–(16) 80, cf. 6.(2) 4–27; Greg. Naz., *Or.* 4.100–109; Theodoret, *Gr. affect. cur.* 1.12–25. See Droge, *Homer or Moses?*; Johnson, "Greek Ethnicity," 105–8; P. Wood, "*We Have No King*," 41–44; Elm, *Sons, Fathers*, 393–96; Johnson, "Hellenism

as an abandonment of his pursuit of Greek learning and identified himself as an Assyrian outsider, begins his *Address to the Greeks*.[59] What began as a plea for an honest hearing, though, became more and more a cutting attempt to deflate the haughtiness of the Greeks, especially as *Hellen*, that is, "a Greek," came to be the most common term for a pagan. Bouttios's barbarian gods represent not merely a novel and varied narrative of divine origins, but also an effort to rob the Greeks of their gods, the cornerstone of their culture.

Planetary Gods

Some pagans would have been largely untroubled at seeing any one nation deprived of a special claim on the gods, since they could point out that in their visible manifestation the gods were present to all mankind as the heavenly bodies who bore their names and were supposed to share in their identities. It is therefore remarkable that the gods of whom Bouttios gives an account represent not only the principal gods of myth, but also quite explicitly the planetary gods. From perhaps the time of the early Pythagoreans and certainly before the composition of the pseudo-Platonic *Epinomis*, thanks to a translation of Babylonian astronomical nomenclature, the five planets known to antiquity, in addition to the sun and the moon, had borne the names of the gods they still have today, though first in their Greek rather than Latin forms.[60] Bouttios notes in the cases of Cronos, Picus-Zeus, Aphrodite, Ares, and Faunus-Hermes that they were named, or given an additional name, after the appropriate planet. These five "wandering stars," along with Helios, account for six of antiquity's seven planets. Helios's name is not said to be related to the heavenly body, but this seems more likely because the identification was unmistakable—*helios* was, after all, the common name of the sun in Greek—than because he was meant to be excluded from the scheme. The absence of Selene, the Moon, might be explained as a result of her relatively

---

and Its Discontents," 443–44; Andrade, *Syrian Identity*, 270, 285, 336–37; cf. Ridings, *Attic Moses*, on the specifically philosophical aspects of what he calls the "dependency theme."

59 Tatian, *Ad Gr.* 42.1.

60 Cumont, "Les noms des planètes," 7–13. The names of the seven planets were also patent in quotidian speech as they were given to the days of the week, in spite of Christian efforts to adjust the usage to a nomenclature without any pagan or astrological associations; see Pietri, "Les temps de la semaine"; Anderson, "Christianizing the Planetary Week."

minor role in myth and cult, or some mention of her may have fallen out of the fragments as they have come down to us.

The fact that the so-called gods, and especially the most prominent of them, are named after the planets is hardly insignificant, for the heavenly bodies had long been important to explanations of the origins of religion and the gods. Since Plato wrote the *Cratylus*, at least, the idea had been in circulation that the sun, moon, earth, stars, and heaven were the only gods known to the first ancestors of the Greeks, and this idea remained current among the Christian authors of Late Antiquity.[61] Aristotle likewise maintained that the tradition of the divinity of the heavenly bodies was handed down from the remotest epochs of human history and had even survived the periodic cataclysms that had wiped out successive civilizations.[62] Theophrastus traced the custom of sacrifice back to the earliest offerings of first fruits and simple grasses to the visible heavenly gods.[63]

The concept of the primeval reverence for the heavenly bodies also had a place in those interpretations that explained the gods as historical figures. The excerpt from Diodorus Siculus, Book 6, in the *Praeparatio Evangelica* of Eusebius, which includes a précis of Euhemerus's *Hiera Anagraphe*, is introduced with a distinction between the eternal and unchanging gods of the heavens and those gods who had once been active on the earth; this *theologia dipertita* probably belongs to Diodorus, but Euhemerus still recognized, and had the gods

61 Pl., *Cra.* 397C–D; Euseb., *Praep. evang.* 1.9.12; Theodoret, *Gr. affect. cur.* 2.27; see Nilsson, "Origin of Belief among the Greeks." At least on a symbolic level, the importance of the planetary gods continued throughout pagan antiquity. For instance, Praet, "Pythagoreanism and the Planetary Deities," demonstrates that an emphasis on each of the planetary gods in a sequence of significance provided the compositional structure for Philostratus's *Vita Apollonii*.

62 Arist., *Metaph.* 12.8 (1074b). See Johansen, "Myth and Logos in Aristotle."

63 Theophr. F 584A (*Pietas*) (= Porph., *Abst.* 2.5.1–2 [135]); see Fortenbaugh, *Theophrastus of Eresus*, 2:404–7; cf. Fortenbaugh, *Quellen zur Ethik Theophrasts*, 262–74. Obbink, "Origin of Greek Sacrifice," demonstrates that for Theophrastus in *On Piety* "the development of sacrificial forms entailed religious and cultural degeneration" (285), and if the inverse trajectories of ritual sophistication or complication and religious rectitude are indeed operative in this work, the reverence of the heavenly bodies with the simplest rites and offerings is consistent with the contentions of other philosophers that the worship of the heavenly bodies was mankind's earliest cult.

of his *Sacred Record* recognize, the heavenly gods.[64] According to Euhemerus, Uranus, the first of the line of world-rulers, was not only an adept observer of the heavens but also the first to make sacrifices to the heavenly gods, and his grandson Zeus raised an altar to him on the mountain where he used to observe the heavens and make these sacrifices.[65] Dionysius Scytobrachion likewise made two of his mortal gods, Atlas and Hesperus, accomplished astronomers, and said that the latter was caught up by strong winds while observing the stars and that the brightest star, the Evening Star, was named after him.[66] The first gods of the Egyptians, according to Diodorus, were the sun and the moon, named Osiris and Isis by them, and the deified primeval royal couple of Egypt shared their names with these planetary deities.[67] The euhemeristic tradition, then, prepared readers to expect some explanation of the relation between the gods of myth and the planets who shared their names, even to assume that the men who came to be considered gods practiced some sort of cult of the heavenly bodies.

The Christian apologetic tradition also drew a connection between the worship of the heavenly bodies and the origins of pagan religion. For Clement of Alexandria the worship of the sun, moon, and stars was a concession God made to the benighted heathen to prevent them from falling into a thoroughgoing atheism, an idea for which he thought he found some scriptural warrant in Deuteronomy 4:19.[68] The worship of the heavenly bodies was preferable, at any rate, to the worship of graven images, and the nations were supposed to

64 Euseb., *Praep. evang.* 2.2.53–54 = Diod. Sic. 6.1.2–3. Most scholars assign the *theologia dipertita* to Diodorus, rather than Euhemerus himself; see P. Fraser, *Ptolemaic Alexandria*, 1:291; Cole, *Democritus*, 156–57, n. 29; Sacks, *Diodorus Siculus*, 70–71, n. 78; Baumgarten, "Euhemerus' Eternal Gods," 91–103; Winiarczyk, *Euhemeros von Messene*, 28–29. Roubekas, *An Ancient Theory of Religion*, esp. 19–22, in contrast to the apparent majority of previous scholars, but with good reason, considers the worship of the heavenly bodies to have been an integral and defining component of any construct that can be called euhemerism. Cf. Garstad, "Deification in Euhemerus of Messene," 155–57.

65 Diod. Sic. 5.44.5–6, 6.1.8, 10; Lactant., *Div. inst.* 1.11.63.

66 Diod. Sic. 3.60.2–3.

67 Diod. Sic. 1.11, 13.2.

68 Clem. Al., *Strom.* 6.(14) 110–11; cf. Philo, *Congr.* 50–51, *Dec.* 53, 66; Justin, *Dial.* 55.1; Origen, *Comm. in Joh.* 2:27; see Chadwick, *Early Christian Thought*, 38; Armstrong, *Cambridge History of Later Greek and Early Medieval Philosophy*, 149, 165; A. Scott, *Origen and the Life of the Stars*, 72, and n. 66, 106, and n. 18.

proceed from the worship of what they saw in the heavens to the worship of God. In what is perhaps a negative presentation of this same idea, Athanasius said that bestowing the honor due to God on the sun, moon, and stars was man's first misstep away from God, and so presumably the least erroneous form of paganism.[69] Nevertheless, all Christian writers firmly rejected the worship of the heavenly bodies and the identification of the planets as gods.[70]

Bouttios's history of the gods may assume some primeval cult of the planets which preceded idolatry and the gods of myth, as articulated by Clement, since the names of the planets are supposed to have preceded the births of Cronos and his progeny; and if not explicitly said to have been worshipped, the planets were sufficiently revered to have their names given to the favored children of royal birth. Before the appearance of Cronos in his first book, Malalas accounts for the names of the planets by saying that they were named by Seth and his offspring and the names inscribed on a stone slab that survived the Flood, for all of which he cites the authority of Josephus.[71] Josephus does mention the astronomical discoveries of Seth's descendants and the inscribed stone, but not the naming of the planets.[72] There is no reason to believe that this information belongs to Bouttios, but his account does presume that the planets had already been named and received some reverence.[73] Perhaps he provided some account of this, or perhaps he expected his readers to assume a situation like that suggested

69 Athanasius, *Contra Gentes* 9; see Camelot, *Athanase d'Alexandrie, Contre les Païens*, 74–75. Meijering, *Athanasius: Contra Gentes*, 43, understands Athanasius as presenting worship of the heavenly bodies to be the least mistaken form of "idolatry," although the cult of the heavenly bodies does not necessarily involve the adoration of graven images.

70 *Apostolic Constitutions* 5.12.1–4; Aristides, *Apol.* 6; Tatian, *Ad Gr.* 9.1–2; Theoph., *Ad Aut.* 2.35; Clem. Al., *Protr.* 5.66.2; Origen, *C. Cels.* 5.7, 11; Commodian, *Instr.* 1.7, 8; Lactant., *Div. inst.* 2.5.6, 25; Euseb., *Praep. evang.* 1.9.7–19; Athanasius, *Contra Gentes* 27; August., *De civ. D.* 7.15, *Enarrationes in Pslamos* 93.3; cf. Philo, *Decal.* (12) 53; see Camelot, *Athanase d'Alexandrie, Contre les Païens*, 136–37; A. Scott, *Origen and the Life of the Stars*, 104–5, 132–33.

71 Malalas 1.1, 5.

72 Joseph., *AJ* 1.2.3 (69–71).

73 It is worth noting, though, that in the same way that the fragment of Bouttios clearly indicates that the other "gods" were named after the planets, but not Helios after the sun, the first chapter of Malalas, Book 1, makes a distinction between the planets on the one hand and the sun and the moon on the other: while the planets are named by Seth, the sun and the moon are named by God himself.

by Clement and Athanasius. In any case, the reason for the "gods'" being given the names of planets is what is most important. By demonstrating that the connection between the planets, in their perfect and unchanging form and motion the most divine elements of the visible, material world, on the one hand, and the gods of myth and cult on the other is ultimately based on the arbitrary decision of certain parents to name their children after the planets, rather than any real identity between the two, Bouttios undermined the unity of pagan religion and deprived its gods of a celestial abode and the perfection they had borrowed from the heavenly bodies.

Double Names

The names of the gods not only indicate their relation to the planets, but also provide one of the most distinctive features of Bouttios's account. The gods, certainly the most prominent ones, the ones discussed at greatest length, have not just one name but two, that is, double names. So, it is "Picus, who is also Zeus" and "Faunus, who is also Hermes," as well as "Semiramis, also called Rhea" and "Hera, whom some call Zygia Nemesis." There is also "Thouras, whom his father called Ares" after the planet. A double name is also given to a hero in the case of Telephus-Latinus. In the fragments from Malalas the gods truly have double names, each individual having no more than two names, but in the fragment from the *Excerpta Latina Barbari* a whole series of names is applied to Picus and Hera, at least. So the former is also known as Serapis, Olympian Zeus, Pluto of Hades, Chthonian Poseidon, and Ninus, and the latter also as Semiramis, Rhea, Nemesis, and Hecate. At this point, the compiler of the *Excerpta* seems to have confused some of the details and conflated some of the characters in his source, while Malalas better preserves that same source. The more complex narrative and the distinction of Rhea and Hera and Picus and Ninus found in Malalas allow the account of the gods to maintain a consistency with both Greek myth and the largely fictional Greek versions of Assyrian history.[74] But there are also indications that although Malalas and the *Excerpta* are working from the same multiplication of names, the *Excerpta* retains a more accurate list of some of the figures

74 Garstad, "Excerpta Latina Barbari," 288–91.

identified with Hera: the sensible Hera Zygia and Nemesis Multiforma in the *Excerpta* have been reduced to the unparalleled "Zygia Nemesis" in Malalas.[75]

When our two witnesses to the lost original show each other to be by turns more accurate or unreliable than each other in preserving material, we may seem to be in the enviable position of being able to pick and choose the version more suitable for our purposes, but really we are reminded that neither witness depends on the other, and their mutual independence prompts us to be particularly careful in determining which best represents the original. In this case, the multiple identifications found in the *Excerpta* are not necessarily editorial extensions of the double names found in Malalas, but may very well have been part of the original source. The multiple identifications of Picus and Semiramis in the *Excerpta* appear to have the same purpose as the double names attested in Malalas, that is, to demonstrate that a single historical figure accounts for more than one traditional deity. The Picus-Zeus narrative, moreover, would puzzlingly not have a place and therefore an explanation for such important gods as Hades, Poseidon, and Serapis if we did not accept the *Excerpta*'s identification of them with Picus-Zeus as part of the original. And it is hard to imagine as unenterprising a writer as the compiler of the *Excerpta* conjuring the rather abstruse epithets applied to the gods in these identifications (Pluto Aidoneus or Chthonian Poseidon), or perhaps the gods themselves, out of thin air, or even out of a supplementary source. The *Excerpta*, nevertheless, seems to have confused some characters (namely Ninus with Picus and Semiramis-Rhea with Hera) who were distinct in the original, along with preserving the fuller lists of identifications. But the question of what purpose the double names and multiple identifications were intended to serve still requires a bit more of our attention.

The gods might go under innumerable epithets used essentially as other names, and there were mythological examples of individuals with two names, like Paris/Alexander and Neoptolemus/Pyrrhus.[76] But the double names of Bouttios's gods, especially Picus-Zeus and Faunus-Hermes, in which one element belongs to a distinctly Roman deity and the other to a Greek one, reflect the double names borne by common people in the Hellenistic and Roman periods who participated

75 Garstad, "Excerpta Latina Barbari," 296.

76 See Kirk, *Iliad: A Commentary*, 1, 266–67; M. Lloyd, "Paris/Alexandros in Homer and Euripides."

in two different ethnic or cultural milieux. We find not only instances of individuals with two names, often from two different languages, but also examples of the very formula of construction (A. ὁ καὶ B.) most commonly used in the fragments from Malalas. Double names are found in both cuneiform and Greek documents from Seleucid Babylonia, where one is usually a native Babylonian name and the other is recognizably Greek.[77] There are numerous examples of double names in the papyri of Roman Egypt and on the inscriptions of Roman Syria and Asia Minor, most often a native name and a Greek rendering of that name; among these double names, a fair number are constructed as A. ὁ καὶ B., to the extent that this can be identified as a common formula.[78] Double names, a Jewish and a Greek name, were also used among the Hellenistic Jews, especially those who had extensive dealings with the Macedonian overlords of their region.[79] As something of a consequence, there are several instances of double names in the Greek New Testament, and even a unique example of the double name formula A. ὁ καὶ B., used when the Apostle Paul is referred to by both his original name of Saul and his new name (Σαῦλος δέ, ὁ καὶ Παῦλος).[80] Their very names suggest, then, as the narratives of their careers confirm, that the gods of Bouttios's account were active and established themselves in the midst of more than one nation, that is, among different *ethnoi*.

Such multiple cultural contacts indicated by nomenclature are consistent with the earliest explanations of the gods as historical characters. Euhemerus himself told of Zeus traveling five times around the world and acquiring the various epithets by which he was known in different places from the names of the local rulers he visited, his hosts and his coadjutors in the establishment of his cult

77 Sherwin-White, "Aristeas Ardibelteios," esp. 213.

78 Lambertz, "Zur Ausbreitung des Supernomen"; Calderini, "Ricerche sul doppio nome," esp. 229–35; Calderini, "Ricerche sul doppio nome II"; Leclerq, "Note concernant les noms doubles"; Quaegebeur, "Les appellations grecques," 466–67; van Minnen, "A Change of Names"; Horak, "Πινουτίων μουσικός," esp. 105; Quaegebeur, "Greco-Egyptian Double Names"; Williams, "From Jerusalem to the Ends of the Earth."

79 Tcherikover, *Hellenistic Civilization*, 346–47; Hengel, *Jews, Greeks and Barbarians*, 86.

80 Acts 13:9. See Harrer, "Saul Who Also Is Called Paul"; Blass and Debrunner, *Greek Grammar of the New Testament*, 140 (§ 268.1); Leclerq, "Note de grammaire sur les doubles noms," 366.

in their lands.[81] But whereas Euhemerus had Zeus pay brief visits to foreign lands, Bouttios has the gods make lengthy sojourns in their adopted countries and set down roots there. The travels of the gods and their residence outside of Greece, upon which their dual names insist, may be intended to play into the denial of Greece's proprietary claims over the gods and the deflation of Greek cultural superiority, an aspect of Bouttios's account on which we have already remarked.

An insistence on the international character of the gods may have abetted one argument inherited from the apologists, but it ran counter to another old apologetic argument, namely that the pagans themselves disagree about the gods and that each nation and city worships its own gods and does not acknowledge those of others.[82] Bouttios certainly insists that the same set of very human characters lies behind the gods of a number of different nations, the Assyrians, Romans, Egyptians, and—as is evident from their names—the Greeks. Perhaps Bouttios was willing to sacrifice or ignore the argument from the welter of diverse and mutually exclusive pagan cults because of the ease afforded by the identification of different gods and especially the gods of different nations. The story of one god as a historical character, which amounts to exposing him as a human, might account for several deities, particularly if readers were supposed to assume that the combinations noted by Bouttios were not the only ones, as seems to be suggested by the *Excerpta* in the cases of Picus and Hera. Bouttios's approach is also more consistent with contemporary paganism.

Some religious segregation appears to have marked the paganism of the second century, when Justin introduced the argument of disagreement over the gods and their cults among the pagans to the Christian apologetic arsenal, but in Late Antiquity, particularly as the fourth century progressed, unifying trends and rampant syncretism became the order of the day. Orosius shows that an awareness of this trend could be made to serve the purposes of Christian historiography when he insists that "now" (before 418) in debate even pagans say that they

81 Diod. Sic. 6.1.10 (= Euseb., *Praep. evang.* 2.2.61); Lactant., *Div. inst.* 1.22.21–23. See Garstad, "Belus in the *Sacred History*."

82 Justin, *Apol.* 1.24.1; Athenagoras, *Leg. pro Christ.* 14, cf. 1.1; Clem. Al., *Protr.* 2.39.5–9; Tert., *Apol.* 24.7–10; Cyprian, *De idolorum vanitate* 3; Athanasius, *Contra Gentes* 23, *De incarn.* 46. See Camelot, *Athanase d'Alexandrie, Contre les Païens*, 124–27; Meijering, *Athanasius: Contra Gentes*, 79–82.

do not revere many gods, but the many servitors of one supreme god.[83] The syncretism of which he speaks is evident in Julian's *Hymn to King Helios*, where the emperor identifies the object of his adoration with Zeus, Hades, Serapis, Apollo, Athena, Hermes, and Ares.[84] Somewhat later examples of a comparable but more concentrated and comprehensive solar syncretism, in which a number of gods are presented as manifestations or articulations of the sun and its powers, can be found in the works of Macrobius, Martianus Capella, and Nonnus of Panopolis.[85] The religious adherence of these later authors may be open to question, as has been stressed in recent arguments, but Julian's loyalties are not in doubt.[86] If these later writers are supposed to have taken an antiquarian interest in a solar syncretism, which they were happy to record but did not necessarily endorse, then Julian's *Hymn*—in which the syncretism is a matter of lively, if not fervent, interest—is as good a guide as any to the date at which this syncretism really flourished. It is also telling that solar syncretism found the majority of its surviving exponents and most articulate expositions among authors of dubious allegiance, who were if not pagans, then Christians deeply engrossed in the classical heritage. Might Christian scholars in particular have found a syncretism that identified one god with a number of others especially congenial as tending towards monotheism or, as Bouttios seems to have done, lining up the targets of antipagan argument for easier dispatch? If, moreover, we suppose those later

83 Oros. 6.1.3 (Arnaud-Lindet, *Orose, Histoires*, 162): *unde etiam nunc pagani, quos iam declarata veritas de contumacia magis quam de ignorantia convincit, cum a nobis discutiuntur, non se plures deos sequi sed sub uno deo magno plures ministros venerari fatentur.*

84 Julian, *Or.* 4 (*Hymn to King Helios*), 135D–137C, 143D, 144B, 149B–D, 150C–D. Fauth, *Helios Megistos*, 145–64; Smith, *Julian's Gods*, 158, 165.

85 Macrob., *Sat.* 1.17–23; Mart. Cap. 1.13, 2.190–93; Nonnus, *Dion.* 40.392–409. See Nock, "A Vision of Mandulis Aion," 100–103; Courcelle, *Les lettres grecques en Occident*, 16–21; Courcelle, *Late Latin Writers and their Greek Sources*, 26–32; Flamant, *Macrobe et le Néo-Platonisme latin*, 652–77; Shanzer, *A Philosophical and Literary Commentary*, 135–37; Chuvin, *Mythologie et géographie dionysiaques*, 228–39; Fauth, *Helios Megistos*, 165–83; Liebeschuetz, "Use of Pagan Mythology," 78–79; Liebeschuetz, "Significance of the Speech of Praetextatus." The solar syncretism of the fourth and fifth centuries seems to be anticipated in Statius, *Thebaid* 1.717–20, who wonders whether he should address Apollo, the god to whom he is devoting a hymn, as Titan, Osiris, or Mithras; see Nock, *Conversion*, 137.

86 Cameron, *Last Pagans of Rome*, 265–72.

writers who offer examples of solar syncretism not to reveal current belief, but to preserve recondite expositions of religious and mythological lore with a unifying tendency from an earlier day, then those combinations, which the double names of Picus-Zeus and Faunus-Hermes insist upon, may have been Bouttios's way of assuming a similarly erudite posture and suggesting that he too shared similarly arcane insights into the identity of the gods.

What Bouttios has to say about the gods of the pagans presents itself as a history, but it is a polemic, an attack on the divinity of the gods and the reverence in which they were held. The historical form is no accident, though; it allows the points of the attack to be delivered implicitly and as facts, and so we may presume to more devastating effect. They may seem blunt and inept as we read them in Malalas and the *Excerpta*, but there is a subtlety to the various assaults in Bouttios's presentation of the gods, and a little reflection reveals each of them to have impressive precedents. The characterization of the gods corresponds at every point, from their mortality to their being given the names of planets, to the various strands of the Greco-Roman handling of the inheritance of myth and polytheism, including the philosophical identification of the scandal of myth, the tradition of euhemeristic narratives, and the acerbic criticism of Christian apologetics. Far from an eccentric and erroneous account of the gods, the Picus-Zeus narrative can be seen as the culmination of a society's centuries-long effort to come to terms with the pantheon handed down to it.

9

THE ATTACK ON THE FIGURE AND CULT OF TYCHE

The account of the gods we have attributed to Bouttios deals directly with the principals of pagan religion, but it is not the only treatment of paganism found in the fragments. The recurrent descriptions of the inauguration of tyche images and cults indicates a sustained interest on the part of Bouttios in the figure of the tyche and the veneration she received. Indeed, the accounts of tyche sacrifices appear to have been central to the import and the structure of Bouttios's work. This impression may result from the fact that the idiosyncratic narratives of civic foundation including the distinctive detail of virgin sacrifice make these fragments readily identifiable as belonging to Bouttios. Less sensational material embedded in Malalas or the *Excerpta Latina Barbari* that does not recognizably diverge from the standard historical record, but was nevertheless derived from Bouttios, may go unnoticed and so uncollected. If it were added to our list of fragments, such material might give us a very different conception of the composition and emphasis of Bouttios's history. Having acknowledged the caution that the form of Bouttios's work might surprise us if we had it complete, however, we can turn to tackle the thrust and objective of what perhaps constitutes the most prominent and consistent set of fragments we have identified, especially because they seem to disclose a perceptible pattern.

That pattern was based on how the audience was expected—we might say trained—to react to reports of human sacrifice, no matter whether they were encountered in the mythical tradition, the historical record, or the fiction of the novels. We have discussed at length the significance of human sacrifice in

antiquity and how its perpetrators were viewed.[1] To accuse the venerable rulers of the past of sacrificing virgins was to attack their reputations and to suggest there was something deeply flawed about them as a whole. That flaw was a benighted adherence to paganism. Constantine could be depicted as redeeming the office of emperor by his novel inauguration of a civic tyche without human sacrifice. The revolutionary nature of Constantine's rule is depicted not in terms of private decision or public policy, visions or edicts, but rather in the vivid and evocative terms of romantic heroism: by his timely intervention Constantine put a stop to the grisly rituals of human sacrifice.

But the repeated charges that pagan rulers performed virgin sacrifice to establish the tyche cults are not merely assaults on the memory of those rulers. The suggestion that every instance of a widespread cult originated with an act of human sacrifice must be read as an attack on that cult, denigrating its origins and consequently denying its current validity. Yet it is the founders of the cult, the perpetrators of human sacrifice, not the objects of the cult, the tychai, the sacrificial victims, who are really being attacked. Likewise, in the Picus-Zeus narrative the so-called gods are implicitly criticized as much for initiating their own cults as for being the unworthy objects of a misplaced worship. A fictional etiology is imposed on the tyche which reconfigures her significance and deprives her of divinity, but does not attempt to displace her entirely or consign her to the oblivion of primeval history. The attention to the figure of the tyche and the determined but nuanced attack on the tyche cult can be explained with reference to the role of the figure and cult of tyche in the history of Christian encounters with the pagan world, the place of the goddess Tyche in Graeco-Roman thought and literature, and the prominence of the concept and the person of tyche in Late Antiquity.

The Christians and the Goddess Tyche

An opposition to the tyche cult, to the very notion of tyche as fortune or luck, was a consistent feature of Christian sentiment for generations and was ingrained in the Christians of the fourth century.[2] The Christian antipathy to the tyche may have been inherited from the Jewish scriptures. In the Septuagint translation of

1 See above, pp. 174–93.

2 See Anwander, "'Schicksal'-Wörter in Antike und Christentum," 316–22.

Isaiah 65:11 the names of the heathen gods to whom the Israelites offer illicit sacrifices, Gad and Meni, are rendered as *daimonion* and *tyche*. In any case, the imperial tyche, or personal tyche of the ruler—and we should note that each example of tyche sacrifice is directed by a ruler—was an old nemesis of the Christians. Polycarp was enjoined by the proconsul at Smyrna to swear by the tyche of Caesar, and on account of his refusal he was martyred.[3] Clement of Alexandria disparagingly notes that the Romans considered Tyche the greatest divinity, and that the pagans deify tyche along with a number of abstract concepts and natural substances.[4] But Clement, it should be noted, also uses tyche in the sense of fortune neutrally, and says that this fortune is assigned by God.[5] Clement's ambivalence in regard to the tyche paved the way for the sort of accommodation and qualified acceptance of the tyche into the rhetoric and iconography of the Christian empire at a later date, which we shall observe shortly. Origen confirms that the Christians do not swear by the tyche of the emperor, because it is either an expression with no substantial reality or a demon.[6] Eusebius, writing on behalf of Constantine, argued that tyche was just a word and that it was unreasonable to assume that tyche was the power that governed the world.[7] It is evident, therefore, that on the whole the pagan conception, to say nothing of the cult, of tyche was considered antithetical to the Christian understanding of the world and the codes of conduct it fostered.

Christian opposition to tyche, however, was not directed against a peripheral figure in the thought and culture of the pagan world. Tyche was popular as a concept and as a goddess throughout antiquity.[8] Although the word does not occur in Homer, tyche appears as a divinity in our earliest literary evidence for Greek religion, and as an influential power in the classics of the fifth century BCE. Hesiod lists Tyche as one of the Oceanids, and the *Homeric Hymn to Demeter* counts Tyche among the playmates of Persephone.[9] To these perfunctory appearances

3 *Martyrdom of Polycarp* 9.2, 10.1.

4 Clem., *Protrep.* 4.51.1, 10.102.4.

5 Clem., *Quis div. salv.* 26.3.

6 Origen, *C. Cels.* 8.65.

7 Eusebius, *Const. ad coet. sanct.* (*Oration of Constantine to the Saints*) 6.

8 See Nilsson, *Geschichte der griechischen Religion*, 2:190–207; Dohrn, *Die Tyche von Antiochia*; Ferguson, *Religions of the Roman Empire*, 77–87; Shelton, "Imperial Tyches"; Ferguson, *Among the Gods*, 166–68; Turcan, *Cults of the Roman Empire*, 25, 295; Becchi, "TYXH: Storia di un Nome."

9 Hes., *Theog.* 360; *Hom. Hymn Dem.* 420; see West, *Hesiod, Theogony*, 267.

can be added the rather more telling sentiments of Pindar, who addresses one of his odes to Tyche as the power who oversees and controls the uncertain fortunes of men, and a fragment that might belong to Archilochus, which says that it is Tyche and Moira (Fate) who give all things to men.[10]

These early references to Tyche demonstrate the antiquity of the figure of Luck or Fortune and the role of controlling men's lives imputed to her, but from a mythological point of view they lack something. Along with later material that mentions the tyche, they do not tell stories about her, nor present her as an actor in divine dramas or relating on a personal level to human beings. For the polemicist, this made her a particularly tough nut to crack. The usual apologetic attacks against paganism, which tended to concentrate on the "scandal of myth," as we have observed above, were not effective against the figure of the tyche. As a cult without a mythology to speak of, the tyche cult was impervious to attacks based on the immorality or imperfection of the god in question, or on the possibility that he might really be a man or a demon, whether they were launched from the disgusted piety of philosophically minded polytheist theologians or the tested Christian polemical arsenal. Bouttios overcame this particular obstacle by turning to the methods of fiction and his own fertile imagination, and by creating an embarrassing mythology, or rather history, for the tyche cult where none had existed before, which traced the tyche back to all that his society considered barbaric and tyrannical.

At least one passage in a revered author might have allowed a polemicist to knock over the whole pagan pantheon with one well-aimed blow at Tyche. Euripides has one of his more sympathetic characters, faced with an apparent divine indifference to the plight of suffering mortals, entertain the idea that the gods do not exist at all and heedless chance, tyche, rules the lives of men.

> ὦ Ζεῦ, τί λέξω; πότερά σ' ἀνθρώπους ὁρᾶν;
> ἢ δόξαν ἄλλως τήνδε κεκτῆσθαι μάτην,
> ψευδῆ, δοκοῦντας δαιμόνων εἶναι γένος,
> τύχην δὲ πάντα τὰν βροτοῖς ἐπισκοπεῖν;[11]

10 Pind., *Ol.* 12; Archil. F 16 (West, *Delectus ex Iambis et Elegis*, 31) (= Stob. 1.6.3); see Jaeger, *Paideia*, 1:124–25.

11 Eur., *Hec.* 488–91 (Murray, *Euripidis Fabulae*, 1:n.p.).

O Zeus, what shall I say? That you watch over men?
Or that you hold this honor in vain, for no good reason,
While men falsely believe that there is a race of divine beings,
Chance (*tyche*) oversees all that comes to mortals.

To be sure, the reversals in the life of the protagonist of the tragedy from which these lines are taken, Hecuba, at first a queen surrounded by her numerous progeny and then a slave woman bereft of the last of her children, offered one of the most poignant and persuasive examples of the workings of fortune in the life of men.[12] This passage does not merely accentuate the power of tyche, though; it also calls into question the very existence of the gods, certainly as potent and worshipful beings.[13] If there is any validity to these musings, the system of pagan religion is reduced to a single figure, the tyche. Such a distillation is consistent with the practice and amenable to the purposes of Bouttios, who often betrays a familiarity with Euripides. Athenagoras, a Christian apologist of an earlier day, quoted a similar set of lines from a lost and unidentifiable play of Euripides, which queried whether fortune (τύχα) or a divine power (δαίμων) governs mortal affairs, to insist that the rule of the "prince of matter" (ὁ τῆς ὕλης ἄρχων), Satan, was inconsistent with the benevolence of God.[14] We can only wonder whether it was the lines from the *Hecuba* that inspired Bouttios to categorically dismiss the divinity of the Olympian pantheon and then turn to the sustained exposition of Tyche as a plethora of—ironically unlucky!—sacrificial victims, rather than a goddess in control of the world.

It was in the time of the Diadochi, when mighty kings rose and fell with distressing rapidity and an impressive precipitousness and the world must have seemed uncertain and self-determination impossible, that the tyche cult came into its own. As Simon Swain has aptly put it, the meaning of tyche underwent

12 See Abrahamson, "Euripides' Tragedy of Hecuba"; Segal, "Golden Armor and Servile Robes"; Foley, *Euripides: Hecuba*, 74.

13 The line that specifically questions the existence of the gods, 490, was deleted by Nauck, but there is an ancient *scholion* on it. At the very least, it was almost certainly part of the text of the play known in the fourth century CE. On tyche in the *Hecuba*, see Kastely, "Violence and Rhetoric," 1043. On the impiety and atheism espoused by Euripides' characters in general, see Lefkowitz, "'Impiety' and 'Atheism' in Euripides' Dramas."

14 Athenagoras, *Leg. pro Christ.* 25.1; Euripides, fr. 901 (ed. Nauck).

a change "in Hellenistic times from simply what happens to the power which directs this."[15] The plots of New Comedy often depend on the chances and changes of life, rather than human decision, and Menander makes frequent mention of tyche, even giving the goddess Tyche a speaking part in one of his plays, the *Shield*.[16] In the Hellenistic period practically every city maintained an image and public worship of its personified civic identity, good fortune, and protective deity. Each civic tyche was also identified with a universal goddess, Tyche (the Roman Fortuna), "Chance" or "Luck," who oversaw the seemingly random happenstances that determined the success or failure of the lives of great and small alike. This Tyche might often be viewed as a capricious and malevolent force, opposed or indifferent to goodness, justice, and individual happiness. She is regularly presented in this way in the novels and in epitaphs.[17] It is perhaps unsurprising then that Bouttios, who seems to have been influenced by the novels, also took a dim view of tyche. Tyche, nevertheless, continued to be persistently popular in Late Antiquity, as a willful and personified explanation of causation in life and literature, as an embodiment of civic pride, and as an object of cultic devotion. The temples of other gods might be torn down, but the *tychaion* often managed to remain standing. In this way, the tyche cult was a significant competitor with Christianity.

In the foregoing we have, for the most part, traced the development of Tyche as the universal goddess of luck or fortune, whereas Bouttios seems to have dealt exclusively with the individual tyche figures of certain cities. We have made some effort to distinguish the two by referring to the former as Tyche and the latter as tyche. But the distinction is quite possibly misleading. It was not merely that the civic deity and the universal goddess shared the same name and that the several examples of the one were supposed to be the avatars of the other, each in a specific locality. The civic tyche looked after the fortunes and prosperity of a particular

15 Swain, "Plutarch: Chance, Providence, and History," 273.

16 Men., *Aspis* 97–148; cf. 411; *Georgos* fr. 2 (= Stob., *Ecl.* 4.41.28); *Dys.* 800–804; *Theophor.* fr. 1, ll. 7–8 (= Stob., *Ecl.* 4.42.3); *Kithar.* 40; *Pk.* 131–33, 137, fr. 335 (= Aul. Gell. 2.23.15), fr. 417 (= Stob., *Ecl.* 1.6.1a), fr. 740, ll. 10–15 (= [Plut.] *Cons. ad Apoll.* 103C); see Vogt-Spira, *Dramaturgie des Zufalls.*

17 Ferguson, *Religions of the Roman Empire*, 80–82; Hägg, *Novel in Antiquity*, 11, 12, 13, 26, 49, 74, 86, 87, 89, 114, 119, 131, 174, 228; cf. Jouanno, "Du roman grec au roman byzantin."

place in the same way that the goddess Tyche supervised the overall ups and downs of mortal existence throughout the sublunary world. Consequently, the manifestation of Tyche belonging to an individual city was seen as a familiar and apprehensible means of approach to the universal and divine power of Luck—not only for purposes of worship and appeal, but also as an avenue of assault. Except in the most generalized and theoretical terms it was hard for any writer, perhaps particularly a historian, to come to grips with the deified abstraction and the personification of fortune that was the universal goddess Tyche. He could, however, point to the image of her instantiation in any given city and offer an account of how this particular tyche, her image, and her cult had come about. And the accounts of these several individual tyche figures could not help but taint the universal goddess of whom they were supposed to be so many aspects. It was through the civic tychai that Bouttios sought to fix the unstoried and thus immaculate goddess Tyche with his barbs of denigration and nullification.

Tyche and History

The prominence of tyche in all her manifestations in the culture of the Hellenistic era was also evident in the intellectual life of the period, not least in historiography.[18] Tyche was perceived as a factor in historical causation, the source of fortuitous conjunctions of events, and the very mistress of the course of history. Demetrius of Phalerum wrote a treatise on fortune (Περὶ τῆς Τύχης) in which he referred to the career of Alexander and the conquest of the Persian Empire as an instance of the mutability of the fortunes of kingdoms and the role of tyche in history, insisting that every political and material success is enjoyed on loan from Tyche, a debt that might be called in at any moment.[19] Polybius would recall these reflections in regard to the fall of the Macedonian kingdom and credit Demetrius with an inspired prescience.[20] The fragmentary survival of the work of Hieronymus of Cardia makes it difficult to determine the place that tyche held in it, but while Jane Hornblower has seen it as relatively circumscribed, though not altogether eradicable in the context of Hellenistic historiography, Sacks has

18 Chesnut, *First Christian Histories*, 7–17.
19 *FGrHist* 228 F 1 (= Polyb. 29.21.1–6).
20 Polyb. 29.21.7–9.

traced the meditation in Diodorus on the role of fortune and its astonishing reversals in history, occasioned by the life of Eumenes, back to Hieronymus.[21] The remaining work of Duris of Samos is also fragmentary, but those fragments have suggested to the one critic who devoted a full-length study to them that Duris, in a mood of moral indignation, quite self-consciously rejected the burgeoning cult of Tyche; but those same fragments are apparently susceptible to quite another interpretation—as Hornblower says, "There was a tendency in this historian [Duris] . . . to institutionalize the unpredictability of life under the name of the goddess Tyche."[22] Whether Tyche's power was accepted or rejected, Duris makes it clear that she was a force to be reckoned with in the writing of history in his day. Polybius took as his theme the broad sweep of history moving toward a consummation under the guiding hand of Tyche, who purposefully and benevolently ushered Rome to the supremacy of the world.[23]

The importance ascribed to tyche continued unabated among the Greek historians of the imperial period. Even Sallust, a Latin historian, considered the fate of nations subject to the whim of Fortune (Fortuna).[24] As for Diodorus, according to Sacks, "τύχη is the most prevalent and variable force found in the *Bibliotheke* . . . it ranges from a rhetorical device to a true goddess," determining the course of events and providing a touchstone for the character of historical personalities, even if it is often hard to tell whether the sentiments on fortune found in the *Bibliotheca* belong to Diodorus or his sources.[25] Plutarch was well aware of the historical significance imputed to tyche, but he reacted against it. Perhaps appropriately for one who was more a biographer than a historian, Plutarch established a rhetorical contest between Fortune (τύχη) and Virtue

21 Diod. Sic. 18.59.4–60.1; see Sacks, *Diodorus Siculus*, 40–41. Hornblower, for her part, sees this digression as an editorial intrusion on the part of Diodorus; see Hornblower, *Hieronymus of Cardia*, 35, 61–62, 106, 108, 155, n. 210, 180, 197, 203–4. On Hieronymus of Cardia, see also T. Brown, "Hieronymus of Cardia"; Simpson, "Abbreviation of Hieronymus in Diodorus"; Hadley, "Hieronymus of Cardia"; Roisman, "Hieronymus of Cardia."

22 Duris of Samos, *FGrHist* 76. Kebric, *In the Shadow of Macedon*, 25, 30–31; Hornblower, *Hieronymus of Cardia*, 235.

23 Polyb. 1.4.1–5; cf. 36.17.1–6. On the role of tyche in Polybius, see Walbank, *Historical Commentary on Polybius*, 1:16–26; Walbank, *Polybius*, 58–65; Sacks, *Polybius on the Writing of History*, 15, 131, 136–40, 168, 191, 212.

24 Sall., *Cat.* 8.1, 51.25, *Iug.* 102.9.

25 Sacks, *Diodorus Siculus*, 38 and 36–41, 53–54, 81, 103, n. 87, 120, 132–37.

(ἀρετή) over the credit for history's most impressive achievements. In this way he examined the career of Alexander and the rise of Rome and offered an explanation that tended to favor the causal and determining role of virtue and character, without altogether denying the part played by fortune.[26] Plutarch bucked the historiographic trends of his day, but his work, better preserved than that of his opponents, remains a testament to the importance of tyche in the historical tradition, and there is no evidence that Plutarch succeeded in stemming the tide that held tyche paramount in historical events. For Dio Cassius, who claims to have been encouraged in his work as a historian by the goddess Tyche and to have written as a devotee of Tyche, she went from being a factor in the events of history to acting as the patroness of the writing of it.[27] Bouttios, as a historian—or the author of a work that purported to be a history—cannot have been blind to the importance his predecessors attached to tyche, and it is remarkable that he treated the career of Alexander, a recurring lodestone for historians' reflections on tyche, with some striking reference to the foundation of the tyche cult of Alexandria (**F 16.1**).

The role assigned to tyche was one of the most problematic aspects of the historiographic tradition inherited by the Christians, and they attempted to address it through various circumlocutions.[28] As tyche was not merely an abstract concept but also a divine or daemonic power with a widespread and popular cult, it was considered inappropriate to grant this goddess a determining sway over historical events. Eusebius, influential here as in so much of the development of a Christian historiography, denied the importance of fortune in the sense of the mutability of material condition, of success and failure, in human life, especially when compared to the condition and constancy of the soul, and, balking at the word tyche, with all of its connotations, applied the term τὰ συμβεβηκότα

26 The principal works of Plutarch concerned with tyche are the *De fortuna Romanorum*, *De fortuna Alexandri*, and *De fortuna*. On these works and tyche in Plutarch generally, see Powell, "Sources of Plutarch's *Alexander*," 235–37; Wardman, "Plutarch and Alexander"; Buriks, "Source of Plutarch's ΠΕΡΙ ΤΥΧΗΣ"; Swain, "Plutarch: Chance, Providence, and History"; Swain, "Plutarch's *De Fortuna Romanorum*"; Hershbell, "Plutarch's Concept of History," 232–33, 241–43; Whitmarsh, "Alexander's Hellenism"; Asirvatham, "Classicism and *Romanitas*"; Di Serio, "La dimensione mitica di Alessandro."

27 Cass. Dio 73(72).23.2–4. See Millar, *Study of Cassius Dio*, 28–30, 119, 179–80.

28 Chesnut, *First Christian Histories*, 255–56; Chesnut, "Eusebius, Augustine, Orosius," 706.

(accidents) to the unintended but determinative conjunctures of events that occurred in history.[29] Socrates Scholasticus did use the term tyche, although rarely, and more often spoke of καιρός (the opportune moment), a word with a good New Testament pedigree.[30] Sozomen borrowed Socrates' use of the word *kairos* as a solution for the problem of Fortune.[31] Later Christian historians like Theodoret and Evagrius followed suit in avoiding the word tyche, but did not ignore unexpected occurrences and unforeseen concurrences or the mutability of human life, even its tragic quality.[32]

In light of this Christian historiographic reaction against the term and significance of tyche, the stress laid upon the figure of tyche in the fragments of Bouttios can hardly be accidental. The history of Bouttios denies tyche a role in determining the course of human events, but whereas other Christian historians avoided the problem of tyche by employing euphemism and synonym, Bouttios tackled it head-on. The presentation of the tychai as the hapless victims of human sacrifice and their images and cults as memorials to these macabre and scandalous rites drained these erstwhile goddesses of all divinity and any power to influence the course of history. The fragments of Bouttios do indicate the role of God in history, delivering one nation into the hands of another or raising up Alexander, but they do not suggest that the author offered a direct juxtaposition of providence and tyche, an explicit declaration that the hand of God and not tyche directed the course of history. But no such programmatic assertion was necessary. The pagan historiographic tradition had laid such stress on the role of tyche that once she was negated, even silence would insist upon an alternative, another divine power responsible for historical causation. If, moreover, as

29 Chesnut, *First Christian Histories*, 39–45.

30 Chesnut, *First Christian Histories*, 188–92.

31 Chesnut, *First Christian Histories*, 206.

32 Chesnut, *First Christian Histories*, 212–14, 216–22. The role of chance or a divine Tyche in the course of events continued to bedevil historians after the fifth century, and a certain interpretation of the prominence of tyche in the work of Procopius of Caesarea is one of the struts holding up Anthony Kaldellis's argument that he was, in fact, a pagan who could reveal his true sentiments only with sly caution; see Kaldellis, *Procopius of Caesarea*, 165–221; cf. Kaldellis, "Historical and Religious Views of Agathias." Whitby, "Religious Views of Procopius and Agathias," 83–87, remains unconvinced by Kaldellis's case and demonstrates, chiefly with reference to Theophylact Simocatta, that an avowedly Christian historian might still evince a concern with "the unpredictable mutability of fortune."

we shall suggest, Bouttios's work reflects the paranoid or conspiracist thinking outlined by Hofstadter, we should expect to see tyche negated as a factor in historical causation, since the imputation of conspiracy precludes the operation of chance, a relation that was also recognized in antiquity.[33]

Tyche in Late Antiquity

The importance of the tyche figure was not diminished in Late Antiquity; if anything, it grew in stature and significance. When Libanius turned to write his autobiography it received the apt title *Concerning Fortune* (Περὶ Τύχης), since he makes mention of the goddess throughout and sees her as intervening in his life to bestow good fortune as well as bad, to protect him from harm, to crown him with success, to make disappointments turn out in his own best interests, and to avenge him on his enemies.[34] In one particularly piquant passage Libanius grants Tyche a voice and has her remind him that it is she who is responsible for the fame and professional reputation he valued so highly; because of her the scribes cannot keep up with the demand for his work, and he ends with a prayer that she may continue to bless him.[35] Rafaella Cribiore has noted that Tyche appears only rarely in Libanius's vast corpus apart from the autobiography, and so sees the goddess's appearance there as a rhetorical device intended to unify the composition of this work in particular.[36] Few people have delved as deeply as Cribiore into Libanius's relations with the gods, but we might, nevertheless, hesitate to agree with her on this point. Libanius seems to be coming to terms with a lifelong companion rather than decorating his prose with his repeated references to Tyche. Nor should we be too quick to accept this one point in Wolfgang Liebeschuetz's perceptive analysis of Libanius's autobiography: that Libanius chose Tyche as the

33 Roisman, *Rhetoric of Conspiracy*, 4; for examples see also Roisman's index, under "Conspiracy: . . . and chance."

34 Tempting as it is to get away with a quick *passim*, we can be more specific while still indicating the ubiquity of references to Tyche: Lib., *Or.* 1.12, 18, 20, 23, 24–25, 26–27, 35, 60, 67, 73, 78–79, 83–84, 86, 87, 88, 93, 95, 117, 128, 133, 134, 136, 137, 145, 150, 152, 155, 158, 174, 175, 176, 186, 188, 190, 194, 195, 210, 217, 225, 227, 230, 232, 253, 266, 270, 279, 283. See Norman, *Libanius, Autobiography*, 1:11–16.

35 Lib., *Or.* 1.155.

36 Cribiore, *Libanius the Sophist*, 39, 41–42, 51–53, 61, 71.

deity who stood for the providential regard in which the gods to whom he was devoted held him because she would be palatable to an audience of Christians as well as pagans.[37] Rather, there is a hint of the controversialist's stance on the part of the pagan stalwart when he extols Tyche as capable of calming the raging of the sea.[38] How many readers in the late fourth century, I wonder, would have seen this without recalling the Gospel story of Jesus calming the storm upon the sea?[39] If Tyche could be opposed to Christ, there was some necessity in addressing the claims of her divinity and cult, as Bouttios undertook to do.

The epigrammatist Palladas was no enthusiastic worshipper of Tyche, but in a mood of dejected resignation he acknowledged her capricious control over the affairs of men:

> Παίγνιόν ἐστι Τύχης μερόπων βίος, οἰκτρός, ἀλήτης,
> πλούτου καὶ πενίης μεσσόθι ῥεμβόμενος.
> καὶ τοὺς μὲν κατάγουσα πάλιν σφαιρηδὸν ἀείρει,
> τοὺς δ' ἀπὸ τῶν νεφελῶν εἰς ἀΐδην κατάγει.[40]
>
> A game of Chance is the life of mortals, pitiable, vagrant,
> Rolling between pelf and penury.
> Some, whom she hurled down, she tosses up again like a ball,
> And others she throws down from the clouds to hell.

While he observed the destruction of the temples of the Olympian gods with detached irony, Palladas seems to have taken a gleeful satisfaction in observing the misfortune of Fortune when the shrine of Tyche was converted into a tavern and, as he puts it, Lady Luck became a serving wench.[41] And it is with palpable

37 Liebeschuetz, "Libanius and Late Antique Autobiography," 269–72, on Tyche in Libanius's autobiographical *Oration* 1.

38 Lib., *Or.* 1.210; cf. 18.

39 Matt. 8:26; Mark 4:39; Luke 8:24.

40 *Anth. Pal.* 10.80; ed. (Pontani, *Antologia Palatina*, 3:444); cf. 10.62, 65, 87, 96. On Palladas's fraught relationship with Tyche overall, see Bowra, "Palladas on Tyche."

41 On the downfall of the shrines of Heracles, Eros, and the other Olympians, see *Anth. Pal.* 9.441, 528, 773. And on the conversion of the Tychaion, see 9.180–83. It has generally been assumed that this was the Tyche shrine of Alexandria, which was still a recognizable landmark, apparently adorned with statuary, in 602; see Theophylact Simocatta,

relief that Palladas celebrates his escape from the vicissitudes of Hope (Ἐλπίς) and Fortune (Τύχη).[42] This, I suspect, was intended as an anticipatory speech from beyond the grave, an expression of the relief Palladas expected to feel once he was dead,[43] but Maurice Bowra sees it as a realization that his belief in the omnipotence of Tyche had been misguided all along:

> The religious strife of 391 discredited in his eyes the formidable figure of Tyche, in whose merciless omnipotence he had, despite all his scepticism, believed. The visible evidence of her ruin made him realize how foolish his belief in her had been. Once he was freed from this, he seems to have settled into a quiet mood and sought the φάρμακον ἡσυχίης which he had always to some degree admired (10.46). We cannot doubt that in his own twisted way he passed through a crisis of the spirit and at the end of it found himself rid both of troubling elements in himself and of the supernatural power which had challenged and provoked them.[44]

If Bowra is right in his interpretation, the sort of pagan represented by Palladas might have been quite receptive to the denigration of the fierce and fickle goddess who had ruined his life as a sacrificial victim no less than as a barmaid!

Tyche also seems to have enjoyed a certain prestige in the circle of Julian the Apostate, as we have already discussed in another context.[45] She appears to have been particularly prominent in thoughts on the chancy game of politics in which the short-lived emperor was embroiled whether he wanted to be or not.

8.13.10. Wilkinson, "Palladas and the Foundation of Constantinople," 181–85, however, situates the converted Tychaion in Constantinople, although this does not perceptibly modify the attitude to Tyche being expressed.

42 *Anth. Pal.* 9.172; cf. 9.49, 134, 135 (not ascribed to Palladas).

43 Cf. *Anth. Pal.* 10.65.5–6, in which Palladas describes the grave as a haven after the perilous and uncertain voyage of life captained by Tyche. In *Anth. Pal.* 9.172.2 he also claims to have reached the harbor, and so slipped out of the power of Tyche and Elpis.

44 Bowra, "Palladas on Tyche," 128. If Wilkinson, "Palladas and the Age of Constantine," is correct in redating Palladas's career to the time of Constantine, his epigrams might offer not so much a belated context for Bouttios's handling of Tyche as some precedent for it; cf. Barnes, *Constantine: Dynasty, Religion and Power*, 13–16; Edwards, *Religions*, 306–8.

45 See above, pp. 215–17.

Julian related to his uncle that in the event of a battle with Constantius he would have placed the whole matter in the hands of Tyche and the gods.[46] Likewise, Ammianus reports that the *genius publicus*—surely a tyche figure, since she bore a cornucopia—manifested herself to Julian and encouraged him to begin his rising against his cousin and that he entrusted the success of his venture to Fortuna.[47] Ammianus later says that Julian saw an apparition of the same *genius publicus*, veiled and departing, again shortly before his death.[48] Julian himself recognized the involvement of Tyche in political matters, since he spoke of her doling out an insecure happiness to men and of actual, rather than theoretical, rulers being especially subject to her caprice. Returning to a theme of Plutarch's, Julian also saw more rulers and conquerors, and Alexander in particular, undone and enslaved by the favor of Tyche than by her enmity.[49] Tyche's role in politics, according to Julian, could also be seen in the desertion of Pompey and in Octavian's grateful acknowledgment of her support.[50] Tyche has a more general sphere of influence in the *On the Gods and the Universe* of Sallustius, where she is presented as the benign influence of the gods which directs unforeseen events to good effect in the world beneath the sphere of the moon.[51]

The tyche was a prominent feature not merely of the intellectual discourse of Late Antiquity, however. The figure of the tyche was also a conspicuous component of the visible environment.[52] It is significant in this regard that, where we can check his information against other literary sources and artifacts, Bouttios gives the proper names for the civic tyche of each city in which he situates one of his tyche sacrifices.[53] For Bouttios and his audience, the images to which he refers and the names—if not the stories—attached to them were recognizable aspects of the urban landscape of Antioch and the neighboring cities. Bouttios was dealing not—or not only—with tyche in general, but with specific instances of the figure

46 Julian, *Ep.* 28 (*Letter to His Uncle*).

47 Amm. Marc. 20.5.10, 21.5.13; see Athanassiadi-Fowden, *Julian and Hellenism*, 77.

48 Amm. Marc. 25.2.3.

49 Julian, *Ep.* 6 (*Letter to Themistius*), 256C–257D; see Athanassiadi-Fowden, *Julian and Hellenism*, 90–91, 95.

50 Julian, *Caes.* 323B, 330A; see Athanassiadi-Fowden, *Julian and Hellenism*, 200.

51 Sallustius 9; see Nock, *Sallustius, Concerning the Gods*, lxxv, 20–21; Athanassiadi-Fowden, *Julian and Hellenism*, 157–58.

52 See, e.g., Bowersock, *Mosaics as History*, 8–9, 22–23, 82–84.

53 Moffatt, "A Record of Public Buildings and Monuments," 105–7.

of tyche, specific images in specific locations and the particular cults, even sentiments, associated with them.

Bouttios's approach to these tyche monuments can be compared and contrasted with Libanius's treatment of the temples and idols around Antioch. Cribiore has applied Pierre Nora's concept of *lieux de mémoire*, or memory sites, to the situation of the waning paganism of the fourth century and the study of Libanius's oration *On the Temples* in particular.[54] She suggests that from texts like Homer, prayers, rituals, and especially the imposing temples, "pagans might at times experience the illusion that memories were securely preserved, and that history had slowed down."[55] But those for whom the monuments of the pagan past were so meaningful, she shows, were compelled to pursue an ambivalent argument in their efforts to preserve those monuments. In his appeal to the emperor Theodosius to halt the destruction of the shrines and images around Antioch by bands of monks, Libanius gives us an excellent example of this argument. On the one hand, Libanius painted a nostalgic picture of the temples as the very heart of rural and urban communities alike, the "soul of the countryside" and the "eyes of the city," and the scenes of innocent conviviality, as well as crediting the sacrifices performed at them with the preservation and success of the state.[56] Perhaps expecting these submissions to fall on deaf ears no matter how sincerely he intended them, Libanius insisted, on the other hand, that the temples had been "deactivated" and no longer housed the pagan gods, but could be usefully repurposed, as tax offices, for instance.[57] A statue, likewise, should be preserved for the aesthetic pleasure it offered, since it no longer received sacrifice.[58] One senses a certain desperation in this latter gambit, but Libanius probably reckoned it the most persuasive argument at his disposal.

Bouttios's accounts of tyche sacrifice would appear to reject both these lines of argument. Libanius's bucolic idyll of peasants gathering to feast on a fresh roast is replaced with the gruesome spectacle of a helpless girl immolated in the presence of a callous despot. And far from allowing them to be deactivated or

54 Cribiore, *Libanius the Sophist*, 222–28. See Nora, "Between Memory and History"; Ho Tai, "Remembered Realms."

55 Cribiore, *Libanius the Sophist*, 223.

56 Lib., *Or.* 30.9, 17–19, 31–35, 42.

57 Lib., *Or.* 30.42–43.

58 Lib., *Or.* 30.22–23.

repurposed for secular uses, Bouttios reactivated the tyche statues for the purpose of memorializing pagan atrocities. Bouttios was no less interested in the preservation of the tyche images as sites of memory than were his pagan contemporaries, but this was because he intended that the memory that would crystallize about them should be one of his own construction. Or perhaps we should say that Bouttios recognized the inevitability of the preservation of the tyche images and strove to see that they conveyed a new and distinctly antipagan message.

Bouttios seems to have been quite astute in not advocating the obliteration of the tyche images, but attempting to reorient them (or the memories they preserved), since the figure of the tyche had been absorbed into the rhetoric and iconography of Christian Roman imperial propaganda. Despite the fact that Constantinople was deliberately founded as a Christian city,[59] Constantine did in fact raise an image of the civic tyche in his new capital,[60] and celebrated the city's dedication with an issue of coins and medallions representing Constantinople in the guise of her tyche: a winged woman wearing a turreted crown, bearing a cornucopia, and resting her foot on a ship.[61] Even Bouttios might have conceded that the gilded image of the civic tyche, Anthousa, held by a statue of Constantine, received the veneration of the emperor in the course of the capital city's anniversary celebrations (**F 35**).[62] It is, however, unclear what form the worship, if any, of this tyche took. Nevertheless, tyche figures became more common in official Roman iconography in the fourth century than they had been in the

59 See Eusebius, *VC* 3.48.2; see Lathoud, "La consécration et la dédicace de Constantinople (Suite [I])," 195–201; Alföldi, *Conversion of Constantine*, 110.

60 *Parastaseis Syntomoi Chronikai* 34; *Patria Constantinopolis* 2.29 (Preger, *Scriptores Originum Constantinopolitanarum*, 2:166; Berger, *Accounts of Medieval Constantinople*, 68–71); see Lathoud, "La consécration et la dédicace de Constantinople (Suite [I])," 180–87; Alföldi, *Conversion of Constantine*, 111; Dagron, *Naissance d'une capitale*, esp. 43–45, but also 37, 40–42, 307, 373–74 (cf. 26, 32, n. 2, 52, n. 7, 315, 368); Av. Cameron and Herrin, *Constantinople in the Early Eighth Century*, 208; Ando, *Matter of the Gods*, 189–92; Agnosini, "Rome in Constantinople," 941.

61 Alföldi, "On the Foundation of Constantinople," 16; Alföldi, *Conversion of Constantine*, 111–12.

62 It is not clear whether it was the image of Constantine or that of Anthousa, or both, that was supposed to receive the emperor's veneration, but taking their relative sizes into account the proper object would seem to have been the statue of Constantine, while the tyche of his foundation may be considered nothing more than an attribute of his own figure; see above, pp. 76–77.

past, and they remained on the Christian coinage of the time.[63] By the reign of Justinian (527–565) a law stipulated that the tyche of the emperor is exempt from the laws, since God subjected the laws to her, and sent her down to men as a living law.[64] And in the reign of Maurice (582–602) the "godly and heavenly tyche" of the emperor was part of the oath formula that made contracts binding.[65] Such was the change in Christian usage since Polycarp's martyrdom in Smyrna some five centuries before! So Bouttios had to pursue the precarious goal of denigrating the traditional tyche cults while at the same time sanctifying the tyche as it had been adopted into the system of Christian empire. This involved presenting Constantine's inauguration of the tyche of Constantinople as a unique departure from the virgin sacrifices that had marked the founding of previous tyche cults.

Whereas Bouttios's attack on the pagan pantheon had recognizable precedents, his approach to the tyche cult was novel. This novelty was necessary because of the elusive character of the tyche, at once an abstract concept, the deified personification of a city's identity and prosperity, and a popular goddess of fortune in general. In each of these guises she was cherished by the opposition and vilified by the Christians. But how could a Christian polemicist turn the devotee's love to hatred and derision? Bouttios's first step was to essentially negate the abstract concept of luck inherent in the term tyche by dealing exclusively in the concrete realities of history. And he demanded of history an explanation of the ubiquitous images of the civic tychai, avatars and emanations of the great goddess Tyche. When no such explanation was forthcoming—the only one possible, that of deified abstracts, having been precluded—he invented one and imposed it on history. Bouttios's invented etiology for the tyche was neither implausible nor unattractive. It adhered to the tropes of popular fiction and made sense of the details of familiar monuments, and it appealed to a taste for the macabre and an ambiguous or even resentful attitude toward the goddess of Chance that was perhaps pervasive even among her adherents. Tyche was nullified as a power controlling the destinies of men and the course of history, her divinity denied and her worship proven pointless, but Bouttios's stories of virgin sacrifice did not neutralize the tyche figure. The monuments depicting beautiful women became

63 Toynbee, "Roma and Constantinopolis," 135–44; Shelton, "Imperial Tyches," 29, 32.

64 Justinian, *Corpus Juris Civilis*, *Nov.* 105.2.4.

65 Bagnall and Worp, *Chronological Systems of Byzantine Egypt*, 52, 54.

reminders of the savage cruelty and bloodthirsty superstition of the godless rulers who preceded the Christian regime of Constantine. As with most polemical writing, Bouttios's account of the tyche cult's origins was probably more effective in bolstering the prejudices of those already persuaded to his perspective than in convincing his opponents or even the undecided. But his arguments and gambits, nevertheless, give us some insight into how his side thought the war of words should be waged.

10

THE TYCHE SACRIFICES AND THE PARANOID STYLE

If Bouttios's accounts of the origins of various tyche cults solved a problem of historical causation, inasmuch as they discounted tyche as a factor in the unfolding of events, they presented the reader with what is perhaps a more serious historiographical problem of veracity and credibility. And it is in terms of the writing of history that the work of Bouttios asks to be judged, since, even if he wrote a palpable fiction, Bouttios gave it the form of a history and he may even have plumed himself on being a historian. An imaginative reconstruction of the remote past is understandable. The paucity of the sources and the need to ask them questions they were never intended to answer in order to compel them to render up historical information made a certain degree of creativity unavoidable, and there was ample precedent for such ingenuity in the euhemeristic tradition. But Bouttios includes invented material in what purports to be a record of far more recent rulers whose reigns were well attested by readily accessible sources. Even if we grant that he had no conception of our distinction between the historic and the prehistoric, we should still be surprised if his treatments of the times of Picus-Zeus on the one hand, and Alexander and Trajan on the other, are equally the product of his imagination. He even seems to taunt his reader with the patent falsity of many of his claims by drawing so often on fictional sources for his narrative. Do we have here an author without sense, or without scruple?

If a remarkable dependence on invention and a willingness to play fast and loose with the facts make Bouttios fall short of the best standards of history writing, they by no means mark him off as egregious among historians in the ancient

world. In the rather persuasive presentation of Emilio Gabba, although our canon of classics may mislead our perception, Thucydides and Polybius set a standard for critical historiography that was rarely emulated, let alone achieved, in the treatment of the past that characterized the Hellenistic era and afterward. Rather, most historians, with a few remarkable exceptions, abandoned rigorous methodology and the political and military concerns of the city-state and concentrated on providing a wider audience with diverting entertainment touched by the luster of antiquity. Ancient critics identified, and Gabba has elucidated, a distinct genre of "false history," which "along with the exotic, the portentous, [and] the abnormal, jumbled up myths, heroic legends, genuine historical and geographical data, [and] scientific information." The novel, "with its close links with local history and its proliferation of fantastic and exciting episodes"—prominent features in the fragments of Bouttios—is supposed to have developed out of the same Hellenistic milieu.[1] Bouttios is certainly writing this kind of history, but with him "false history" returns to the political forum without having divested itself of any of the baggage it had accumulated through generations of indulging in the fabulous and the frivolous. Bouttios seems to give us history seasoned to the palate of a popular rather than a professional readership employed in the interest of political and ideological polemic. If we are not to dismiss the fragments of his history as so much mendacity, perhaps we can turn to a genre with more modern associations in order to discern the purposes and value behind Bouttios's disposal of his material.

Taken altogether and each in its context, the fragments of Bouttios begin to read like snippets of a conspiracy theory. It should hardly be surprising that a historian of the fourth century would give voice to rumor and suspicion regarding the dark deeds of the powers that be. The canonical orators, whose corpus remained the basis of a good rhetorical education in Late Antiquity, appealed to a cast of mind among Athenian jurors that was inclined to detect conspiracies behind the private and public conduct of their fellow citizens, as well as in the sphere of international relations.[2] Tacitus and Cassius Dio—to say nothing of Suetonius—were not above retailing gossip and innuendo as simple fact and imputing hidden motives and sinister designs to the great and the good

1 Sext. Emp., *Math.* 1.252–62; Gabba, "True History and False History," 53–54.

2 Roisman, *Rhetoric of Conspiracy.*

who peopled their histories.[3] And in a period later than Bouttios, in his *Secret History*, Procopius laid the blame for plague, famine, and death on a cataclysmic scale at the feet of Justinian and Theodora and their diabolically intentional misgovernment.[4] The inclusion of unsubstantiated reports and impressions was part and parcel of the historian's craft in antiquity, but it tended to remain at the margins of the historical narrative. Bouttios, in contrast, sets the shocking, the scandalous, and the dubious at the center of his history, just as we find such material at the onion's heart of any good conspiracy theory.

The most obvious affinity between Bouttios's tyche sacrifice narratives and conspiracy theory, or as Richard Hofstadter aptly termed it in his classic essay, "the paranoid style,"[5] is the deviation from consensus, in this case the consensus

3 E.g., Tac., *Ann.* 1.5, 4.10–11, instances in which Tacitus explicitly relies on rumor and even makes a show of denying its trustworthiness. See Ryberg, "Tacitus' Art of Innuendo"; von Fritz, "Tacitus, Agricola, Domitian," esp. 77; Syme, *Tacitus*, 1:315–16, 401–2; Millar, *Study of Cassius Dio*, 121–22, 149; Shatzman, "Tacitean Rumours"; Allison, "Dissimulatio: Tiberius or Tacitus?"; Rubiés, "Nero in Tacitus," 35, 38–39; M. Grant, *Greek and Roman Historians*, 40–41; Moscovich, "Cassius Dio's Palace Sources"; Chong-Gossard, "Who Slept with Whom in the Roman Empire?"; Gleason, "Identity Theft," 35. Suetonius's scandalmongering hatchet jobs might be more charitably described as rhetorical masterpieces in the genre of invective; see Barton, "The *inventio* of Nero."

4 Kaldellis, *Prokopios, Secret History*, viii, trenchantly observes, "*The Secret History* is a unique historical document. No previous author had yet exposed the crimes of a regime by combining institutional, legal, and military analysis with personal attacks and salacious rumor quite as Prokopios does here. In this dense, behind-the-scenes pamphlet, he artfully combines the roles that today are divided among tabloid reporters, investigative journalists, public intellectuals, and "disgruntled" administration insiders. Its effect on Justinian's reputation has been devastating." Cf. Pazdernik, "'Our Most Pious Consort'"; A. Brown, "Justinian, Procopius, and Deception."

5 Hofstadter, *Paranoid Style*. I wrote this examination of the evidence for Bouttios's work in the light of Hofstadter's analysis of the paranoid attitude and its characterization of the enemy before I became aware of H. A. Drake's excellent essay, "Fourth-Century Christianity," and my ideas developed quite independently of his. Drake, it must also be noted, is concerned not so much with the rhetoric of the paranoid style, and the scandalous accusations and the diabolical phantasmagoria it constructs, as with the circumstances favorable to the activation and activity of the paranoid element, the ascendancy of extremists within a mass movement, and the unchecked recourse to coercion in dealing with an ideological enemy. The one other extended attempt at applying Hofstadter's analysis to the ancient world of which I am aware is Eli Sagan's disappointingly tendentious and doctrinaire *The Honey and the Hemlock*, which actually turns out to be a fine

of historians on the events of the past. It is a characteristic of the culture of conspiracists to assume that any widely held belief is wrong, its general acceptance the result of a successful conspiracy of lies and misinformation, and to embrace commonly rejected and marginalized forms of knowledge.[6] This pattern of thought does not seem foreign to Bouttios, who does not simply add false reports to the historical record, but goes so far as to invert it by attributing the worst of deeds to emperors who were in rhetoric and history usually considered the best.[7] Another significant point of comparison with the paranoid style is the irrefutability of the bogus historical claims. The conspiracist's failure to produce evidence to substantiate his theory demonstrates not an inherent fault in the theory but rather its essential validity: the conspirators have proceeded with such devilish cunning under the cloak of secrecy that they have managed to almost completely cover their tracks.[8] The very fact that no one can provide proof is itself taken as proof. If the tyche sacrifices, by a presumed analogy with Theodoret's sealed chamber at Carrhae, were supposed to have been performed in secret,[9] it

---

example of the "partisan history" discussed below. See also Wooten, "Nature of Form in Demosthenes' *De corona*," 325, n. 28.

6 Barkun, *Culture of Conspiracy*, 24–29; Aaronovitch, *Voodoo Histories*, 105–6, 227–28. As Aaronovitch, *Voodoo Histories*, 106, puts it: revisionist history "was (and is) less an alternative way of studying than an adoption of deliberately alternative opinions about the past." Thompson, *Counterknowledge*, 9–10 (cf. 79), points out that the adoption of views and opinions rejected by intellectual orthodoxy is characteristic not only of conspiracy theories and revisionist history, but of all kinds of what he (borrowing a word from Stav Sherez) aptly terms "counterknowledge," from homeopathy to Afrocentrism and satanic ritual abuse scares, and knits together the adherents of these outlandish theories.

7 See above, pp. 179–80 and n. 57. If Marcus Aurelius was left out of this list and not directly attacked by Bouttios, this seems to have been intentional; see above, p. 218.

8 Given the inherent resistance of conspiracy theories to refutation on the basis of readily available facts and explanations, one can only wonder how effective Dunning, *Conspiracies Declassified*, expected his work, a cursory rehearsal of the official lines and the "nothing to see here" responses of accused perpetrators, would be.

9 The question remains, however, whether Bouttios conceived of the tyche sacrifices as public rituals performed openly or as clandestine rites. If secret, this would be consistent with comparable rumors about emperors, e.g., Hadrian and the death of Antinous (Cass. Dio 69.11.2–4) or Julian at Carrhae (Theodoret, *HE* 3.26), and perhaps Domitian and the burial alive of a vestal virgin (Pliny, *Ep.* 4.11; Suet., *Domit.* 8.3–4; Cass. Dio 60.3.4[3^2]), and would explain, as we have said, why these sacrifices were not part of the broader historical record. Noxious rituals, human sacrifice in particular, could be understood as both

would be impossible for their authenticity to be gainsaid with reference to any of the usual historical authorities; indeed, their absence from the consensus historical record would be explained.

It is also remarkable how often modern conspiracy theories are connected to reports of human sacrifice.[10] Rituals are the mark of a structured and established society, but human sacrifice is a cruel and deplorable ritual. So the imputation of a bloody sacrificial ritual at the heart of a conspiracy indicates at once how pervasive and tenacious the conspirators' organization is, preserving ancient rituals and performing them with due solemnity, and how malevolent are its purposes.[11] Those who make efforts to counteract perceived subversion, as David Bromley has said in regard to the Satanism scare in the United States with all of its attendant fear of ritual abuse and human sacrifice, will regularly attribute a past, including an origin and operation throughout history, to the subversive forces they imagine themselves to be battling in order "to mobilize apprehension about the crisis-dominated present."[12] In Bouttios's history the tyche sacrifices

---

secret and central to a deplorable religion. Josephus (*Ap.* 2.8 [91–98]) refutes the story related by Apion that every year the Jews kidnapped a Greek and feasted him for a year in the inner sanctum of their temple before sacrificing and cannibalizing him, vowing their enduring misanthropy; see Rives, "Human Sacrifice," 70–72. But there is reason to believe that Bouttios conceived of the tyche sacrifices, like other, actual foundation ceremonies, as public celebrations. Other literary instances of virgin sacrifice in tragedy (e.g., Iphigeneia) or the novel (e.g., Charicleia) are supposed to have taken place in front of large crowds. Bouttios himself includes a wedding procession, usually a decidedly public ceremony (but Dido and Aeneas's covert "wedding" should offer a note of caution here; see Virgil, *Aen.* 4.160–72), in at least one instance of tyche sacrifice (**F 31**). As public rituals they would carry an indictment not only of pagan rulers, but also of the wider pagan society as the consenting audience of these events.

10 Barkun, *Culture of Conspiracy*, 1, begins his examination of conspiracy theories by recounting the story of a heavily armed conspiracist who broke into the Bohemian Grove in California fully expecting to interrupt a human sacrifice. The evangelist and conspiracist Texe Marrs proposes to explain the mysterious circumstances of the 2001 death of congressional intern Chandra Levy by suggesting that she was sacrificed to Satan; see Cowan, *Bearing False Witness?*, 90–91. It has also been conjectured that far from dying in a car accident, Princess Diana of Wales was sacrificed in Paris; see McConnachie and Tudge, *Rough Guide to Conspiracy Theories*, 62–63, 108. See also Bromley, "Satanism Scare in the United States," 50.

11 Frankfurter, *Evil Incarnate*, 124–29.

12 Bromley, "Satanism Scare in the United States," 56.

are a measure of the tyranny and barbarity of the rulers involved, but their regular repetition makes virgin sacrifice seem like a recognized custom integral to the institution of pagan kingship and lends a sense of urgency to the censure of a pagan ruler.

The accounts of innocent maidens being immolated by nefarious kings, even if they may seem more perfunctory than spine-tingling as presented by Malalas, are surely examples of what Hofstadter termed "pornography for Puritans,"[13] the lurid descriptions of cruelty and sexuality that often color conspiracist reports of the enemy. David Brion Davis speaks of the "fascinating appeal" that "themes of brutal sadism and sexual immorality" held for the authors and the audiences of countersubversive rhetoric in nineteenth-century America. But they were not merely mesmerizing, he suggests; they could "serve the double purpose of vicariously fulfilling repressed desires, and of releasing the tension and guilt arising from rapid social change."[14] Subversive elements in society were supposed to be responsible not only for specific instances of immorality, but also for the breakdown of morality in society generally: prostitution, divorce, and a licentiousness to be observed around every corner. Thus, for Davis the pornographic element of conspiracy theories, redolent with cruelty and sensuality, is both a projection of illicit desire and a fixing of blame for moral failure in society. Some of this may be true of Bouttios, especially the latter aspect. We can easily imagine a Christian of the fourth century observing with considerable disappointment that official recognition of the Church and even Christian government had not succeeded in bringing about wholesale moral reform. Connecting social evil to the continuing evil conduct of certain individual rulers like Julian would be convenient. But the "damsel in distress" device in Bouttios's writing, rather than being a vicarious acting out of some unpleasant subconscious desires, seems to serve the author's deliberate purpose of orienting his readers' sympathies and sentiments against seemingly innocuous and otherwise admired or even beloved emperors and in favor of, if not an abstract political principle, then concrete examples of wronged womanhood.

13 Hofstadter, *Paranoid Style*, 21, was referring specifically to Protestant, nativist images of Roman Catholics, but these represent only one instance of a common feature of history in the paranoid style.

14 D. Davis, "Some Themes of Counter-Subversion," 217–21.

The device does not seem to have been chosen at random. Audiences seem perennially quick to believe even the most far-fetched stories that include the systematic brutalization of women. In the lead-up to the Spanish-American War, for instance, bellicose passions were inflamed in the States by a report in the yellow press of officials of the Spanish government imposing upon the modesty no less than the rights of decent women. Cries of indignation resounded as far as the halls of Congress—and circulation soared!—after Richard Harding Davis reported in the *New York Journal* that Clemencia Arango and two other women suspected of conveying documents for Cuban insurrectionists had been strip-searched aboard the American steamer *Olivette* in Havana harbor.[15] Perhaps more incendiary than the story itself was the accompanying illustration by as prominent an artistic luminary as Frederic Remington, which took advantage of an ambiguity in the story. Remington's depiction of the incident showed a pitiable woman, naked and mortified, but still shapely, surrounded by three leering dons.[16] The furor did not altogether abate even once the aggrieved lady herself appeared to insist that she had been searched by a matron only, with all the proprieties observed. It is doubtful whether the incident could have sparked the same indignation and contributed a lurid and memorable image to the case for war against Spain if it could not have suggested that, under the pretext of a police inspection, a pack of villains had gratified their rapacious gaze at the expense of a lady's shame, if not her virtue. This suggestion turned out to be fiction, just how calculated a fiction we cannot say for sure, but certainly an effective one. The same trip to Cuba that produced Davis's scoop also supposedly elicited William Randolph Hearst's famous response to Remington's request to return home as there was no war to cover: "Please remain. You furnish the pictures, and I'll furnish the war."[17]

There are other examples of the sentiments of author and audience conspiring to direct outrage at dubious accounts of violated womanhood against

15 Rea, *Facts and Fakes about Cuba*, 229–32; Wisan, *Cuban Crisis*, 191–92, 459; C. Brown, *Correspondents' War*, 80–82, 103; O'Toole, *Spanish War*, 81–82; Lubow, *Reporter Who Would Be King*, 142–44; Campbell, *Year That Defined American Journalism*, 141–42; David R. Spencer, *Yellow Journalism*, 134–35, 196–97; B. Miller, *From Liberation to Conquest*, 37–39.

16 D. Allen, *Frederic Remington and the Spanish-American War*, 11, 22, 24; Samuels and Samuels, *Frederic Remington*, 248–50; Hassrick and Speidel, *Frederic Remington*, 2:644 (no. 2264).

17 O'Toole, *Spanish War*, 82; Campbell, *Year That Defined American Journalism*, 8–10.

particular targets. A peculiarly modern phenomenon, analogous to the age-old rumors of human sacrifice inasmuch as it involves cold-blooded and ritualistic killing, is the "snuff film," a commercial movie in which the actual killing of a victim is supposed to be filmed. In the snuff film, the star or rather victim of which is usually assumed to be a nubile woman, the director's cues and the blocking and staging of the scene substitute for the deliberate performance of a sacrificial rite. Since the specter of snuff films first entered the broader public consciousness in the 1970s, there have been persistent press reports of their production and distribution despite the complete lack of evidence to substantiate these reports, and rumors of their existence have been ubiquitous at the fringes of popular culture. And it has remarkably been those groups that most loudly decry the production and distribution of such depraved films, be they feminist critics of pornography or religious fundamentalists warning against the excesses of the entertainment industry, that have been quickest to uncritically assume their reality, and indeed seem to have had the most invested in it.[18] The absence of evidence that might have reassured anyone in the 1990s unwilling to believe that the movie business could sink so low, even if it did not allay the suspicions—or assumptions—of those who used snuff films as a byword for the depravity of filmmaking, seems less certain in a world where everyone has a production studio in his pocket and practically infinite means of surreptitious distribution, to say nothing of a thoroughly blurred line between soulless profit-seeking and pleasure-seeking. Nevertheless, analogy would suggest that it is quite possible that Bouttios could have anticipated an audience all too willing to take his lurid stories at face value and accept in turn their political and ideological implications, just so long as he included evil befalling a beautiful woman.[19]

18 Kerekes and Slater, *Killing for Culture*, 223–46. The intrepid and consuming efforts of Yavon Svoray, for example, to lay his hands on a snuff film and expose its production and consumption, recounted in his gripping narrative *Gods of Death*, prove not so much the existence of such films as the apparent impossibility of acquiring verifiable proof that they exist.

19 I am grateful to my colleague Sandy Jung of the Psychology Department at MacEwan University for confirming, on the basis of her impressive and hard-won expertise, that snuff films do indeed belong to the realm of urban legends, but also for pointing out that what is truly outrageous about both the tyche sacrifice narratives and the rumors of snuff films is that these extravagant fictions are necessary to incite a furious

Hofstadter warned his readers against being "misled by the fantastic conclusions that are so characteristic of [the paranoid] political style into imagining that it is not, so to speak, argued out along factual lines." On the contrary, he identified a pedantic, even obsessive accumulation of evidence "to prove that the unbelievable is the only thing that can be believed" as one of the characteristic features of the paranoid style.[20] This trait can certainly be seen in Bouttios. His careful identification of tyche cults in the environs of Antioch and throughout the eastern Mediterranean, his discovery of the names attached to the tyche figures in various locations, and his collection and collocation of antiquarian lore from different sources all suggest a scholarly commitment, and not necessarily one that falls below the general standard of antiquity. Livy, for instance, validated the events of the early history of Rome, which he relates in the first books of his history, with reference to monuments still to be seen in his own day.[21] Gabba has explained the process that resulted in these references: explanations based on the legendary history of early Rome were at first attached to monuments whose significance had been forgotten or become unclear, but by the time Livy set about writing the monuments were so closely connected to the legendary incidents that had been used to explain them that the monuments themselves could be used to verify the legends as historical events.[22] Ignorance and misunderstanding are one thing, but T. P. Wiseman has offered a telling example of the tendentious interpretation of Roman monuments and their use and misuse for purposes of vilification in the writing of Republican history, suggesting that the *lemnisci*, or ribbons, of the wreath on a statue of one of the Claudii were willfully misinterpreted as the strands of a royal diadem in order to invent, and simultaneously to find proof for, the story of a member of that distinguished family trying to seize control of Italy through his clients.[23] Bouttios's accounts of maiden sacrifice were

indignation that is largely insensible to the quotidian and low-key violence all too many women endure.

20 Hofstadter, *Paranoid Style*, 35–36. Aaronovitch, *Voodoo Histories*, 338–39, likewise provides a caution against assuming that the poor and the ignorant espouse conspiracy theories; rather they "originate and are largely circulated among the educated and the middle class."

21 Livy 1.25.14, 26.13–15, 36.5, 48.6–7; 2.10.12, 13.5, 11, 14.9, 40.12, 41.10–11.

22 Gabba, "True History and False History," 61.

23 Wiseman, "Monuments and the Roman Annalists," 90–95. Wiseman's discussion is based on Suet., *Tib.* 2.2: *Claudius Drusus statua sibi diademata ad Appi Forum posita*

likewise substantiated—quite literally—by the civic tyche images to be found in every city in the Roman East. While Bouttios's narratives purported to explain the "actual" origin of these statues, accounting for their every detail, the statues themselves stood as evidence of the truth of his charges against ancient kings.

It is possible that Bouttios, like Livy, could have depended on explanations of the origin of the tyche statues circulating in the form of local lore, rather than inventing his scurrilous stories himself. But as Hofstadter notes, "In his extravagant passion for facts the paranoid occasionally manufactures them."[24] With the loss of much of Bouttios's material and literary world it is impossible to tell precisely to what extent this might be so in his case. Neither the collection of facts nor their invention, however, is the distinctive characteristic of the paranoid style. Rather, the hallmark of this manner of thought and discourse is a "curious leap in imagination." "The plausibility the paranoid style has for those who find it plausible lies, in good measure, in this appearance of the most careful, conscientious, and seemingly coherent application to detail, the laborious accumulation of what can be taken as convincing evidence for the most fantastic conclusions, the careful preparation for the big leap from the undeniable to the unbelievable."[25] Bouttios indicated statues his readers might still see and recorded their proper names in order to convince his audience that each one was raised as a memorial to the victim of a heinous act of tyranny and barbarism, from which they were expected to conclude that such was the essence of kingship divorced from Christian faith.

There is one important distinction to be noted between the paranoid style of Bouttios and its more recent manifestations. Hofstadter identified "a vast and sinister conspiracy, a gigantic and yet subtle machinery of influence set in motion to undermine and destroy a way of life" as "the central image" of the American paranoid style. A gigantic conspiracy is "the motive force"—rather than an incidental feature—of historical events.[26] The idea of a "vast conspiracy" at work presumes the coordination of political, economic, and social agencies, the very forces which under a more or less democratic system of popular sovereignty do,

---

Italiam per clientelas occupare temptavit (Claudius Drusus, once his crowned statue was set up at Appii Forum, tried to seize Italy through his clients.).

24 Hofstadter, *Paranoid Style*, 37.

25 Hofstadter, *Paranoid Style*, 37–38.

26 Hofstadter, *Paranoid Style*, 29.

in fact, produce change and consensus, though without the rationality and calculation imputed to them by the conspiracist.[27] Such an immense web of power and influence need not be presumed under an autocracy. The character of the autocratic ruler matters, certainly in theory and to a very great extent in practice, far more than any sinister concert of forces. Hofstadter's phrase "paranoid style" is, therefore, preferable to "conspiracy theory" in the context of the Roman Empire. But the subjects of an autocracy should not be considered any less prone to paranoia than the citizens of a democracy. The focus on an individual ruler makes it easier to impute intention to the enemy. While the modern conspiracist's habit of uncovering a malign and overarching will behind the foibles and chances of human history is indeed paranoid and bad historiography to boot, the intentions and decisions of the Roman emperor really were supposed to direct the affairs of state. And if the conspiracist's discovery of the signs of his enemy everywhere at work seem obsessive and far-fetched today, through the display of his images and the publication of his edicts the emperor cultivated the impression of his own ubiquity throughout the empire and the notion that he himself was operative in the whole apparatus of the state.[28]

27 The presumption of a vast network of power and influence at work to achieve its ends perhaps naturally arouses in the conspiracy theorist a suspicion of even legitimate power structures, including—or especially—the government. So I can only imagine that it was either a keen sense of irony or a staggering obtuseness that led a government insider like Cass Sunstein, *Conspiracy Theories*, 1–32, to conclude his musings on the phenomenon of conspiracy theories by deliberating on the possibility of effective government action to counteract conspiracy theories!

28 See, for instance, Fronto, *Ep. ad M. Caes.* 4.12.6; Greg. Naz., *Or.* 4.80. One of the most impressive testimonies to the ubiquity of the imperial image is offered by Severian of Gabala (*De mundi creatione* 5.6; PG 56:489D), who wrote about 400 in the region of Antioch: ἐννόησον πόσοι εἰσὶν ἄρχοντες ἀνὰ πᾶσαν τὴν γῆν. καὶ ἐπειδὴ βασιλεὺς πᾶσιν οὐ πάρεστι, δεῖ παραστῆναι τὸν χαρακτῆρα τοῦ βασιλέως ἐν δικαστηρίοις, ἐν ἀγοραῖς, ἐν συλλόγοις, ἐν θεάτροις. ἐν παντὶ οὖν τόπῳ, ἐν ᾧ πράττει ἄρχων, δεῖ παρεῖναι, ἵνα βεβαιῶται τὰ γινόμενα (Think how many magistrates there are throughout the whole world. And since the emperor is not present with every one, it is necessary for the likeness of the emperor to be set up in law courts, in assemblies, and in theaters. In every place, therefore, in which a magistrate conducts business, it must be present for what is done to be established.). See Swift, "Imagines in Imperial Portraiture"; Grabar, *L'empereur dans l'art byzantin*, 4–8; Stuart, "How Were Imperial Portraits Distributed?"; Grabar, *Christian Iconography*, 64; Pekáry, *Das römische Kaiserbildnis*, 42–65; Kiilerich, "Sculpture in the Round," 93–94; Gleason, "Identity Theft," 38–39; Kiilerich, "Defacement and Replacement," 67; cf. Elm, "Gregory's

In such a situation it might even be possible for critics to preserve a belief in the ruler's good character despite adverse laws and bad government by allowing the imagination to surround the autocrat with wicked counselors who had abused his magnanimity. This is how the Christian apologists before Constantine had reconciled persecution by the government and loyalty to the emperor.[29] This strategy failed in the fourth century after Eusebius adulated Constantine in terms that contrasted him with his predecessors and introduced the "friend of God" political theory. It was no longer possible for Christians to assume that an emperor, though a pagan, was still devoted to the law and order and the peace and stability that constituted good government. This led Bouttios to insist that pagan rulers were not just incapable of being good, but necessarily bad, and to offer a record of the misdeeds they had perforce committed.

Bouttios's denigration of pagan emperors must be seen in the broader context of the fourth-century conflict between paganism and Christianity. It is not simply that the Christians had had a taste of power and were loath to lose it. Under Constantine they had developed a political theory that asserted that the order of the world depended on a willing partnership between God and the emperor, and dire consequences threatened if any other situation prevailed. It

Women," 179–82. The image of the emperor appeared on coins and in statuary, both that which pertained to the imperial cult and that which decorated public places, and the presence of the emperor's image was necessary to the transaction of much public business; see Zanker, "Prinzipat und Herrscherbild"; Price, *Rituals and Power*, 170–206; Kiilerich, *Late Fourth Century Classicism*, 82–83; Prusac, "*Presence* and the Image Controversies," 43. The laws of the empire were framed as personal directives from the emperor himself. Not only were historical events dated with reference to the reign of the emperor, but so also were the contents of such mundane documents as contracts and tax receipts.

29 Euseb., *HE* 4.26.9, 7.30.20; see Aland, "Relation between Church and State," 124; R. Grant, "Five Apologists," 7; Kofsky, *Eusebius of Caesarea*, 44, 221; Andrade, *Syrian Identity*, 284. Later, Gregory of Nazianzus (*Or.* 5.16) would blame the heresy of Constantius and his persecution of the Orthodox on the stupidity of his subordinates and the emperor's own unsuspecting nature. This same tactic was also adopted by the pagan critics of the legislation of Christian emperors, especially laws directed against pagan practice. Libanius also blames the courtiers of Constantius II for the misguided decision to outlaw sacrifices (*Or.* 30.7) and holds the wicked counselors of Theodosius, not the emperor himself, responsible for the demolition of the temples (*Or.* 30.46–49). In a similar vein Ammianus Marcellinus (14.1.10, 29.3.2) censures the ruler's closest advisors for failing to curb his anger, and so allowing unworthy conduct; see P. Brown, *Power and Persuasion*, 66.

was no longer sufficient to strike the compromise of being in the world but not of the world; the world and all of its powers must belong to God through his followers. If it might once have been possible for Christianity to be compartmentalized as the philosophy or religion of a man who in other respects was very much like his neighbor, it was now clearly an all-encompassing and uncompromising ideology which informed his political opinions, even if those were limited to a desire to see a member of his own party in power. Adherents of traditional polytheism also came to see that they had been dealt willy-nilly into a game with all-or-nothing stakes. The last persecuting emperors aimed not at quelling a tiny deviant cult but at eradicating a widespread menace, Julian did his best to bolster the temple cult by imitating the Church, and the disasters that beset the Empire were blamed on the abandonment of the old gods.[30] Paganism was no longer the status quo to which Christianity must accommodate itself, and Christianity had ceased to be one religion among many circulating throughout the Mediterranean. Instead these ideologies were two increasingly polarized worldviews which demanded absolute commitment from their followers and offered them a clearly delineated stance in a conflict depicted with vibrantly apocalyptic colors.[31] It is just such an ideological impasse which Hofstadter identified as the occasion for the recurring waves of the paranoid style: "The paranoid disposition is mobilized into action chiefly by social conflicts that involve ultimate schemes of values and that bring fundamental fears and hatreds, rather than negotiable interests, into political action."[32] This seems an apt description of the fourth-century standoff between paganism and Christianity, especially in its rhetorical and philosophical aspects.

History offers plenty of examples of a climate of political and ideological polarization producing extravagant accusations of antisocial, even diabolical,

30 Drake, "Fourth-Century Christianity," 367, sees the reign of Julian as a trigger for the ascendancy of the militant and extremist elements in Christianity, the representatives of the paranoid style in his interpretation of the religious and political climate of the fourth century.

31 MacMullen, *Christianizing the Roman Empire*, 19, would lay the lion's share of the blame for this polarization at the feet of the Christians.

32 Hofstadter, *Paranoid Style*, 39. Bromley, "Satanism: The New Cult Scare," 64–69, working perhaps on a more domestic than world-historical scale, interprets the fear of satanic subversion as a socially constructed metaphor for the tension of demands made by family and economy brought to the point of crisis.

crimes. It hardly need be said that in the course of the seventeenth century the views of Englishmen on state policy and procedure were inextricably involved with their most deeply held religious commitments, and this situation led to often unbridgeable oppositions and bloody civil strife, but the effusions of this conflict can still prove remarkable.[33] For instance, after the death of Oliver Cromwell occurred on the seventh anniversary of his victory at Worcester the story was put about, purportedly on the authority of sources close to the Lord Protector, that on the morning of the battle he had sold his soul to the devil in exchange for victory and seven years of power and success.[34] There are as many parallels between this imputation of a wicked ritual that demonstrates incontrovertibly the unalloyed evil of the villain and Bouttios's treatment of the pagan emperors as there are between the contexts of political and religious division that produced them. Whether the audience takes the story for truth depends not upon whether the incident actually took place, but upon one's feelings about Cromwell. To the sober historian it may seem merely absurd, but to a supporter the charge is infuriating, as the very antithesis of Cromwell's proper conduct as a devout Christian. To a political, ideological opponent, however, this diabolical transaction is perfectly consistent with his every speech and action throughout his career. A Royalist like the man who invented this story out of whole cloth would no doubt have considered it not only possible but probable that a man who took up arms against his king and overturned the decorous rites of his Church would have no qualms about selling his soul to the devil.

The wild stories about Cromwell, like Bouttios's accounts of virgin sacrifice, also seem to have required their physical substantiation. It has been postulated that the so-called Cerne Abbas Giant, a hill figure in rural Dorset, though long thought to be of prehistoric or Roman provenance, was in fact created under

33 In examining the partisan historiography of late seventeenth-century England, Knights, "Tory Interpretation," offers a number of what might be taken as interesting parallels to the polemical history writing of the fourth century, particularly in relation to the assumption of conspiracies motivating history, the significance of religion in debates, and the self-conscious use of fiction in writing history. One of Knights's most provocative suggestions must be that the awareness of instances of fiction in the historical debate led to a greater historiographic acuity in terms of offering proofs and scrutinizing sources.

34 Anonymous, *True and Faithful Narrative*; A. Smith, "Image of Cromwell," 36; A. Fraser, *Cromwell*, 387; Carlyle, *On Heroes*, 182, 372; N. Davis, *Oliver Cromwell*, 44–45.

the auspices of Denzil Holles (1599–1680), a leading Parliamentarian and opponent of Oliver Cromwell, as a satire against the Lord Protector.[35] The giant was supposedly intended as a symbol of monstrous depredations and the ungainly exercise of tyrannical power. Unlike the tyche statues, this particular relic had to be manufactured for its polemical purpose, but its form and medium depended on other figures of undoubted antiquity to such a degree that it has long been taken for one of them. This need not have been unintentional. The apparent age of the figure, which was assumed even by some locals as early as the next century,[36] must have offered the double advantage of lending authority to the criticism of Cromwell as well as providing a plausible claim to innocence in the event of prosecution. It is surely more than coincidental that Bouttios likewise concentrates on ancient kings and does not seem to have leveled a direct charge at Julian.

The history writing that tends to be produced at such times of intense and diametric opposition is what Benedetto Croce criticized as *storie di tendenza o di partito*, partisan histories. They are not really historiography at all, but an "effusion of sentiments dressed up in the imagery of the past," and Croce looked forward to the day when "cultured people will disdain the play of optimism and depression which such works produce by making use of the images of the past."[37] The bitter partisan loyalties and antipathies that motivated Bouttios, his attempt to evoke an emotional response by employing novelistic techniques, and his exploitation of history as little more than antiquarian color and argumentative fodder in a contemporary fight all seem to characterize his own work as an example of the party history. Croce was surely right in judging partisan history the predominant form of writing about the past since antiquity, but his hope for its eventual diminution seems unlikely to be fulfilled any time soon. In Croce's own Italy the inveterate conflicts between Left and Right since World War II have produced a popular culture of *dietrologia*, "behindology," which assumes that behind every deed and misdeed there is a hidden motive, and devotes itself to

35 Vale, "Churchwardens and the Other God"; Betty, "Cerne Giant Revisited."

36 Evans, "Eighteenth-Century Descriptions."

37 Croce, *La storia come pensiero e come azione*, 173–81, at 181; Croce, *History as the Story of Liberty*, 181–202, at 186.

uncovering the malign but secret influence of greed, ambition, and, of course, one's political rivals in interconnected webs of crime and corruption.[38]

Such efforts to sway feeling by means of a fabricated record of events is hardly isolated to a single country and can be practiced on a vast scale. Willi Münzenberg, the director of a worldwide publishing consortium and of the activities of the Comintern in western Europe, was famously willing to play fast and loose with sources and facts to achieve the ends of his propaganda, denigrating his opponents and bolstering his own position.[39] Those in the know may have been disappointed or appalled, but they did not contradict, since that would have been to give succor to an enemy they loathed quite as much as Münzenberg did. Some of Münzenberg's urgency and unscrupulousness might be excused by the fact that he was orchestrating a fight against the fascism of Hitler, but it must be remembered that he did so in the service of the no less totalitarian and blood-soaked communism of Stalin. Münzenberg's case shows that ideological polarization and partisan commitment can make one's grasp on the truth tenuous. This is no less obvious in the case of Bouttios, who did not hesitate to assign the most unspeakable crimes to those on the other side of a gulf of loyalties. But if Bouttios's efforts have been all but forgotten, Münzenberg's have left us with a dismal and frightening legacy. In the words of William Pfaff, "The manipulation of information,

38 T. Jones, *Dark Heart of Italy*, 26–29. Paul Ginsborg's *History of Contemporary Italy* provides the historical background of this adversarial culture of tension, indicating instances of—mainly right-wing—plots (333–35, 349, 363, 423) and in one case reporting, if not indulging in, conspiracism (381). The extent to which *dietrologia* has entered the popular Italian discourse is perhaps best indicated by the fact that Carlo Ginzburg, *Judge and the Historian*, 64–65, found it necessary to insist, in the face of the pejorative connotations of any suggestion of conspiracy or *dietrologia* that have become prevalent, that such dismissiveness can prevent the imputation of conspiracies from being recognized as a wholesome, even necessary skepticism that is not content with appearances on the surface. One of the interesting products of *dietrologia* is Giuseppe Genna's novel *Nel nome di Ishmael*, in which the intrigues and misdeeds of the world's political and financial power brokers are punctuated by human sacrifices. Umberto Eco's *Il Cimitero di Praga* is likewise concerned with conspiracies and conspiracism, but manages to demonstrate the essential basis of much conspiracist thought in literary invention, as well as the incestuous crossbreeding of these inventions. Eco's last novel, *Numero Zero*, is also absorbed with later manifestations of the obsession with plots, conspiracies, and the dark forces behind events, though they are handled with a somewhat lighter touch.

39 Koch, *Double Lives*, 122–23, 131–33, 143–46; Pfaff, *Bullet's Song*, 214.

concealment of facts, and invention of virtual realities, with the source of these distortions dissimulated, characterize the political practice of most contemporary governments, possibly democratic governments more than others."[40]

Perhaps more chilling than such a distorted presentation of the facts is John Gray's suggestion that not a partisan writing of history or propaganda masquerading as journalism, but an equally tendentious and blinkered understanding of history led to Great Britain's involvement in the last invasion of Iraq. While it may appear that Tony Blair was unscrupulously mendacious in the days leading up to the outbreak of war, in fact, Gray proposes, in his unwavering devotion to a neoconservative vision of the future he had managed to disentangle himself from the common conceptions of honesty and deception. "For him truth is whatever serves the cause" and "deception is justified if it advances human progress."[41] The partisan historian like Bouttios, no less than the partisan journalist or the partisan politician, is complicit to some degree in this conception of truth, which expresses itself in a rhetoric insisting upon what the enemy is capable of and not necessarily relating what he has done.

Histories of this kind, in addition to their uneasy relation to the truth, fly in the face of what Aristotle declared to be the proper role of history. Whereas poetry deals in universals, history deals in particulars, and while history relates what has happened, poetry sets out to describe the kinds of things that might happen.[42] Bouttios and historians of his ilk, however, whether we term them paranoid or partisan, do not so much report what has happened as determine the character of their subjects and then recount their commission of deeds considered appropriate to the depravity and malice already assigned to them.[43] This approach was not unknown to Late Antiquity. Orosius complains that hostility often prevents

40 Pfaff, *Bullet's Song*, 191.

41 Gray, *Black Mass*, 103–4; cf. Thompson, *Counterknowledge*, 12, 126–27.

42 Arist., *Poet.* (9) 1451A–B. See Else, *Aristotle's Poetics*, 301–14; Ste. Croix, "Aristotle on History and Poetry."

43 It is one thing to judge and interpret a historical figure's actions according to "a preconceived notion of his character," as Pearson determined had been done by Herodotus, and to a lesser extent by Thucydides; it is quite another to fix character and then invent actions that demonstrate that character; Pearson, "Credulity and Scepticism," 349–55; Pearson, "Thucydides as Reporter and Critic," 53 (for quote) and n. 33. The comparatively unbridled perspective of the modern conspiracist, as Aaronovitch, *Voodoo Histories*, 340–41, says, is that "'they' are capable of almost anything."

people from allowing that their enemies might do or say anything that is not depraved, shameful, or self-destructive.[44] This may seem like a hopelessly inept way of treating the past, but it turns out to be taking to extremes the procedure of other ancient historians of unquestionable competence who had been willing to defy the dictates of Aristotle. Thucydides admitted that rather than offering verbatim transcripts he had composed the speeches in his history as seemed fitting for the various occasions and speakers.[45] Commenting on a possibly apocryphal anecdote concerning Alexander, Arrian asserted that the story in question was worth including in his history whether it happened or not because it was consistent with what Alexander would have done and said.[46] Bouttios appears excessive in this method of imputing to historical figures conduct that is thought to be consistent with their understood characters not only because he invents deeds and not merely words for them, but also because he ascribes spurious actions to them for the sake of fixing blame rather than praise.[47] Inappropriate praise, after all, is only a matter of taste and principle, while inappropriate blame is a matter of law.

In our examination of the fragments of Bouttios in comparison with modern conspiracy theory we have often used Hofstadter's term "paranoid" of the style of historiography to which they both belong, but the word should not be taken to mean that we can blithely dismiss the material and its author as irrational or pathological.[48] On the contrary, as Gordon S. Wood has said of the conspiracist tendencies of the eighteenth century, "The belief in plots was not a symptom of

44 Oros., *Hist.* 4.6.36.

45 Thuc. 1.22.1. See Gomme, *Historical Commentary on Thucydides*, 1:139–48; and Pearson, "Thucydides as Reporter and Critic," on how Thucydides' stated method of presenting *logoi* is related to his largely implicit and somewhat inconsistent method of reconstructing *erga*.

46 Arr., *Anab.* 2.12.8.

47 Nevertheless, Quintilian (*Inst.* 4.2.89) allowed considerable latitude to the rhetorician in the composition of false *expositiones*, just so long as they were consistent with the person and the circumstances involved in the fiction; see Barton, "The *inventio* of Nero," 50–51.

48 Nor is it really helpful for Sunstein, *Conspiracy Theories*, 1–12, to try to explain conspiracy theories with reference to "crippled epistemologies." This can only make his final suggestion, that those who undertake to refute conspiracy theories are well advised to "affirm" those who hold them (31), seem particularly condescending.

disturbed minds but a rational attempt to explain human phenomena in terms of human intentions and to maintain moral coherence in the affairs of men."[49] Bouttios may have fallen short of the ideal of the disinterested historian, but he was not therefore a mischievous purveyor of falsehoods for the perverse pleasure of it or a stranger to the bright paths of reason. What he wrote was written in earnest and with clear intention. But where does its historical value lie?

We turn to Bouttios not for information on the ancient kings he wrote about[50] but for evidence of the intensity and the substance of the ideological debate of the times in which he lived. In Bouttios's accounts of virgin sacrifice we see an example of Luise White's insight from a different historical context that "people do not speak with truth, with a concept of the accurate description of what they saw, to say what they mean, but they construct and repeat stories that carry the values and meanings that most forcibly get their points across."[51] Understanding Bouttios's interests and motives does not give us grounds for dismissing his work or continuing to ignore the difficult passages he contributes

49 G. Wood, "Conspiracy and the Paranoid Style," 429. Wood (420) further diagnoses the conspiracist perspective as eminently consistent with the Enlightenment: "Earlier, men had sought to decipher the concealed or partially revealed will of God; now they sought to understand the concealed or partially exposed wills of human beings. That, in a nutshell, was what being enlightened was all about." Addressing the situation of a latter day—and only peripherally the realms of fiction—King, *Danse Macabre*, 331–36, has insisted that far from being the preserve of the insane, paranoia and conspiracism are the responses of sane people to an insane world.

50 It is notable, nevertheless, that so astute a judge of history as Lord Acton accepted Malalas's testimony in regard to Trajan's sacrifice of Calliope, no less, as fact; Acton, *Essays*, 3:416. Bosch, *Die kleinasiatischen Münzen*, 258, n. 194, likewise thought that where there was so much smoke there must be some fire, and suggested that these episodes occur so regularly in accounts of city foundation that they must be based on actual practice continued until the time of Seleucus I. But the regular occurrence of these human sacrifices is found in only one, late text, and is there supposed to continue long after the reign of Seleucus. W. Smith, *Religion of the Semites*, 159, n. 1, did not think the accounts in Malalas of human sacrifice at city foundations were historical, but he did consider them evidence of much older traditions of expiatory sacrifices at the breaking of new fields and the harvest, as well as city foundations. These failures to recognize Bouttios's stories as purposive fictions are a testament to their plausibility and accord with an audience's expectations, rather than to the gullibility of the famous scholars who made them.

51 White, *Speaking with Vampires*, 30; cf. White, "Between Gluckman and Foucault," 88.

to Malalas's *Chronicle* or the *Excerpta Latina Barbari*; rather this process grants us an opportunity to take stock of a new source of information on the literary world and the political discourse of the fourth century. Once again, I think White points the way forward with her appeal "for an expansion of historical epistemologies . . . to include rumor and gossip, to embrace the fantastic and the scandalous, to use stories of bloodsucking firemen and well-known stupefiers to find the very stuff of history, the categories and constructs with which people make their worlds and articulate and debate their understandings of those worlds."[52] Nevertheless, even if we are able to gain some real insight from Bouttios's fragments, the final verdict on his historiography seems to be passed in the words of Czar Nicholas II, an erstwhile enthusiast and promoter of such a landmark in conspiracy theory as *The Protocols of the Elders of Zion*, who was eventually constrained to say of that calumnious screed: "It is impossible to defend something sacred by dirty methods."[53]

52 White, *Speaking with Vampires*, 54–55.

53 Quoted in Levy, introduction to Segel, *A Lie and a Libel*, 16.

APPENDIX

APPENDIX

THE FRAGMENTS

Text and Translation

The following translations are the author's own.

---

1 ⁓ Malalas 1.8–2.3a (Thurn, *Ioannis Malalae Chronographia*, 9–19)

1 ἐκ δὲ τῆς αὐτῆς φυλῆς τοῦ Σὴμ τῆς κρατησάσης τὴν Συρίαν καὶ τὴν Περσίδα καὶ τὰ λοιπὰ μέρη τῆς ἀνατολῆς τοῦ α′ υἱοῦ Νῶε ἐγεννήθη καὶ ἀνεφάνη ἄνθρωπος γιγαντογενὴς ὀνόματι Κρόνος, ἐπικληθεὶς ὑπὸ Δαμνῶ τοῦ ἰδίου αὐτοῦ πατρὸς εἰς τὴν ἐπωνυμίαν τοῦ πλανήτου ἀστέρος. ἐγένετο δὲ δυνατὸς οὗτος, ὅστις πρῶτος κατέδειξεν τὸ βασιλεύειν ἤτοι ἄρχειν καὶ κρατεῖν τῶν ἄλλων ἀνθρώπων. καὶ ἐβασίλευσεν αὐτὸς Ἀσσυρίας ἔτη πολλὰ καὶ ὑπέταξεν πᾶσαν τὴν γῆν Περσίδος ἀπὸ τῆς Ἀσσυρίας ἀρξάμενος. ἦν δὲ φόβον ἔχων πρὸς πάντας ὡς πικρὸς καὶ πολέμιος καὶ ἀναιρῶν πάντας.

Οὗτος εἶχεν γυναῖκα τὴν Σεμίραμιν τὴν καὶ Ῥέαν καλουμένην παρὰ Ἀσσυρίοις διὰ τὸ αὐτὴν εἶναι ὑπερήφανον καὶ ἀλαζόνα. ἦν δὲ καὶ αὕτη ἐκ τῆς αὐτῆς φυλῆς ‹τοῦ Σήμ, υἱοῦ Νῶε›. ἔσχεν δὲ ὁ Κρόνος υἱὸν ὀνόματι Πῖκον, ὅστις ἀπὸ τῶν γονέων ἐκλήθη Ζεὺς εἰς ὄνομα καὶ αὐτὸς τοῦ πλανήτου ἀστέρος. ἔσχεν δὲ καὶ ἄλλον υἱὸν ὁ αὐτὸς Κρόνος, ὀνόματι Νίνον καὶ θυγατέρα δὲ ἔσχεν ὀνόματι Ἥραν. ἔλαβεν δὲ γυναῖκα Πῖκος ὁ καὶ Ζεὺς τὴν ἰδίαν αὐτοῦ ἀδελφὴν τὴν Ἥραν ὀνόματι, ἣν καὶ ζυγίην νέμεσιν ἐκάλουν τινὲς ὡς εὐχαριστοῦντες αὐτῇ ὡς ἀγαθῇ καὶ δικαίᾳ καὶ πάντα θελούσῃ. ἐξ ἧς ἔσχεν ὁ Πῖκος υἱόν, ὃν καὶ ὠνόμασεν Βῆλον διὰ τὸ ὀξύτατον εἶναι τὸν παῖδα.

2 (9) ὁ δὲ προπάτωρ Κρόνος ἐάσας τὸν ἑαυτοῦ υἱὸν Πῖκον ἐν τῇ Ἀσσυρίᾳ καὶ τὴν ἑαυτοῦ γυναῖκα Ῥέαν τὴν Σεμίραμιν μετὰ Πίκου τοῦ καὶ Διὸς υἱοῦ αὐτοῦ καὶ λαβὼν πολλὴν βοήθειαν ὄχλου ἀνθρώπων γενναίων ἀπῆλθεν ἐπὶ τὴν δύσιν ἀβασίλευτον οὖσαν, μὴ κρατουμένην ὑπό τινος κελεύοντος, καὶ ἐκράτησε τῶν δυτικῶν μερῶν ἀφανὴς ἐκ τῆς Ἀσσυρίας γενόμενος. καὶ ἔμεινεν κρατῶν

1 From the tribe of Shem, the first son of Noah, which held sway over Syria and Persia and the rest of the regions of the East, a man of giant breed by the name of Cronos was born and appeared, who was named by Damno, his own father, after the name of the planet. This man became powerful; he was the first of all to invent kingship, that is ruling and prevailing over other men. And he was king of Assyria for many years and he subjected the whole land of Persia, ruling from Assyria. He held fear over all since he was bitter and warlike and did away with all.

This man had a wife called by the Assyrians Semiramis and Rhea because she was arrogant and boastful. She was also from the tribe <of Shem, the son of Noah>. Cronos had a son by the name of Picus, who was called Zeus by his parents after the name of the planet. And this Cronos had another son by the name of Ninus and he had a daughter by the name of Hera. Picus, who is also Zeus, took to wife his own sister, Hera by name, whom some called "matrimonial wrath" since they were thankful to her as good and just and well-disposed in regard to all things. By her Picus had a son, whom he named Belus because the child was particularly sharp.

2 The forefather Cronos left his son Picus in Assyria and his wife Rhea-Semiramis together with his son Picus, who is also Zeus, and taking the large force of a crowd of highborn men he went off to the West, which was without a king, nor was it ruled by anyone issuing commands, and he held sway over the western regions when he disappeared from Assyria. And he remained ruling

καὶ βασιλεύων τῆς δύσεως πάσης ἔτη πολλὰ καὶ ἔσχεν ἐκεῖ γυναῖκα ὀνόματι Φιλύραν, ἐξ ἧς ἔσχεν υἱὸν ὀνόματι Ἄφρον, ᾧτινι ἔδωκε τὴν πρὸς Λιβύην γῆν· καὶ ἐκράτει τῶν ἐκεῖ βασιλεύων ὁ Ἄφρος, ὅστις ἐγάμησε τὴν Ἀστυνόμην ἐκ τῆς Λακερίας νήσου καὶ ἐγέννησε θυγατέρα, ἣν ἐκάλεσεν Ἀφροδίτην εἰς ὄνομα καὶ αὐτὴν τοῦ πλανήτου ἀστέρος τῆς οὐρανίας Ἀφροδίτης, φιλόσοφον γενομένην, ἥτις ἐγαμήθη Ἀδωνίδῃ τῷ υἱῷ τοῦ Κινύρου Ἀθηναίῳ, καὶ αὐτῷ φιλοσόφῳ, ἐκ τῆς οἰκείας αὐτοῦ θυγατρός.

[[οὗτος] ὅστις Κίνυρος τοῦτο δεδρακὼς οἷα τὴν φύσιν ἐνυβρίσας συλλαβηθεὶς ἐν τοῖς ὄρεσιν αὐτὸν ἐναπέθετο. ἀνετράφη δὲ ὑπὸ τῶν καλουμένων ὀρειόνων νυμφῶν. λίαν δὲ γεγονὼς ὡραῖος ἠράσθη αὐτῷ ἡ Ἀφροδίτη. χολάνοντος δὲ Ἄρεως τοῦτον ἐπάταξεν. ἦν γὰρ ἀντεραστὴς Ἀφροδίτης οὗτος. ἥντινα Ἀφροδίτην φασὶ συγκατελθεῖν τῷ Ἀδωνίδῃ τῷ Ἅιδῃ οὐχ ὡς τεθνηξομένη, ἀλλ' ὡς τούτῳ μάλα ἐρῶσα καὶ ἀναστήσουσα. καὶ τινα λοιπὰ περὶ αὐτοῦ ἱστοροῦσιν, ἃ καὶ καλοῦσιν μυστήρια.] λέγονται δὲ ὁμοῦ πεφιλοσοφηκέναι μέχρις θανάτου.

ἔσχεν δὲ ἐκ τῆς αὐτῆς Φιλύρας ὁ Κρόνος καὶ ἄλλον υἱὸν λεγόμενον Χείρωνα φιλόσοφον καὶ αὐτόν.

3 (10) μετὰ δὲ τὸ βασιλεῦσαι τὸν Πῖκον τὸν καὶ Δία τῆς Ἀσσυρίας ἔτη λ′ ἐάσας καὶ αὐτὸς τὴν ἑαυτοῦ μητέρα καὶ τὴν Ἥραν τὴν ἑαυτοῦ ἀδελφὴν καὶ γυναῖκα καὶ ποιήσας τὸν ἑαυτοῦ υἱὸν Βῆλον βασιλέα τῆς Ἀσσυρίας ἀπῆλθεν ἐπὶ τὴν δύσιν πρὸς τὸν ἑαυτοῦ πατέρα τὸν Κρόνον. ὁ δὲ Βῆλος ἐβασίλευσε τῶν Ἀσσυρίων ἔτη β′ καὶ ἐτελεύτα, ὅντινα οἱ Πέρσαι ἀπεθέωσαν. ὁ δὲ Κρόνος ἑωρακὼς τὸν ἴδιον αὐτοῦ υἱὸν Πῖκον τὸν Δία ἐλθόντα πρὸς αὐτὸν ἐν τῇ δύσει παρεχώρησεν αὐτῷ τὴν βασιλείαν τῆς δύσεως. ἦν γὰρ ἀδύνατος καὶ ταλαιπωρήσας ‹ὁ› αὐτὸς Κρόνος καὶ ἐβασίλευσε τῆς δύσεως ἤτοι τῆς Ἰταλίας ὁ Πῖκος ὁ καὶ Ζεὺς ἄλλα ἔτη ξβ′. τῆς δὲ Ἀσσυρίας μετὰ τὸν Βῆλον ἐβασίλευσεν Νίνος ὁ ἄλλος υἱὸς Κρόνου, ὅστις καὶ τὴν ἑαυτοῦ μητέρα τὴν Σεμίραμιν ἔλαβεν γυναῖκα, ἐξ οὗ νόμος Πέρσαις γαμεῖν τὰς ἑαυτῶν μητέρας καὶ τὰς ἀδελφάς· διὰ τοῦτο καὶ τὸν Πῖκον λαβεῖν τὴν ἑαυτοῦ ἀδελφὴν τὴν Ἥραν γυναῖκα, καθὼς καὶ ὁ σοφώτατος Ὅμηρος ἐκτίθεται οὕτως· Ἥραν δὲ προσέειπε κασιγνήτην ἄλοχόν ‹τε›. καὶ τελευτᾷ ὁ Κρόνος.

4 (11) ὁ δὲ Νίνος ἐπικρατὴς γενόμενος τῆς Ἀσσυρίας κτίζει τὴν Νινευὴ πόλιν Ἀσσυρίων καὶ βασιλεύει πρῶτος ἐν αὐτῇ, ἔχων τὴν Σεμίραμιν τὴν Ῥέαν τὴν ἑαυτοῦ γυναῖκα καὶ μητέρα μεθ' ἑαυτοῦ. ἐξ αὐτοῦ οὖν τοῦ γένους ἐγεννήθη ὁ Ζωροάστριος ἀστρονόμος Περσῶν ὁ περιβόητος, ὅστις μέλλων τελευτᾶν ηὔχετο

and reigning over all of the West for many years and he had there a wife by the name of Philyra, by whom he had a son by the name of Aphros, to whom he gave the land facing Libya. And Aphros ruled there, reigning as king, and he married Astynome from the island of Laceria and begat a daughter, whom he called Aphrodite after the name and the person of the planet of heavenly Aphrodite. She became a philosopher and was married to Adonis, an Athenian, himself a philosopher, the son of Cinyrus, by his own blood daughter.

[After this Cinyrus did this thing, offering an insult to nature, he seized him and exposed him in the mountains. But he was brought up by those called the mountain nymphs. When he had come into the bloom of youth Aphrodite fell madly in love with him. But Ares was enraged and struck him. For he was a rival in love for Aphrodite. They say that this Aphrodite went down to Hades with Adonis, not as one who has died, but as one who loved him deeply and would raise him up. They narrate certain other things about him as well, which they call mysteries.] And they are said to have practiced philosophy together until death.

Cronos had by this Philyra also another son called Cheiron, who was also a philosopher.

3 After Picus, who is also Zeus, ruled Assyria for thirty years he left his mother and Hera, his sister and wife, and making his son Belus king of Assyria he went off to the West, to his father Cronos. Belus ruled the Assyrians for two years and he died; the Persians deified him. After Cronos had seen his own son Picus, who is Zeus, coming against him in the West he yielded the kingship of the West to him. For Cronos was weak and in distress, and Picus, who is also Zeus, reigned over the West, that is Italy, for another sixty-two years. After Belus, Ninus, the other son of Cronos, ruled Assyria, who took to wife his own mother Semiramis, from which [it became] a custom for the Persians to marry their own mothers and sisters; because Picus also took his own sister Hera to wife, just as the exceeding wise Homer sets it out in this way: "he addressed Hera, his sister and bedfellow both." And Cronos died.

4 When Ninus became master of Assyria he founded Nineveh, the city of the Assyrians, and was the first to reign in it, keeping Semiramis, who is Rhea, his wife and mother, with him. So, from his family was born Zoroaster, the famous astronomer of the Persians, who, when he was about to die prayed that he be

ὑπὸ πυρὸς ἀναλωθῆναι οὐρανίου, εἰπὼν τοῖς Πέρσαις, ὅτι ἐὰν καύσει με τὸ πῦρ, ἐκ τῶν καιομένων μου ὀστέων ἐπάρατε καὶ φυλάξατε καὶ οὐκ ἐκλείψει τὸ βασίλειον ἐκ τῆς ὑμῶν χώρας ὅσον χρόνον φυλάττετε τὰ ἐμὰ ὀστᾶ. καὶ εὐξάμενος τὸν Ὠρίωνα ὑπὸ πυρὸς ἀνηλώθη ἀερίου. καὶ ἐποίησαν οἱ Πέρσαι, ὡς εἶπεν αὐτοῖς, καὶ ἔχουσιν φυλάττοντες τὸ λείψανον αὐτοῦ τεφρωθὲν ἕως νῦν.

5 (12) μετὰ δὲ Νίνον ἐβασίλευσεν Ἀσσυρίων Θούρας ὀνόματι, ὅντινα μετεκάλεσεν ὁ τούτου πατὴρ Ζάμης, ὁ τῆς Ῥέας ἀδελφός, εἰς ὄνομα τοῦ πλανήτου ἀστέρος Ἄρεα. οὗτος ἐγένετο πικρὸς πολεμιστής, ὅστις ἐπολέμησεν ἐπὶ τὰ ἀρκτῷα μέρη. ἐπελθὼν Καυκάσῳ τινὶ καὶ αὐτῷ δυνατῷ ἀνθρώπῳ γιγαντογενεῖ καὶ πολεμικωτάτῳ, καταχθέντι ἐκ τῆς φυλῆς τοῦ Ἰάφεθ, τοῦ υἱοῦ Νῶε, καὶ πολεμήσας τὸν αὐτὸν Καύκασον ἐνίκησεν αὐτὸν καὶ ἔλαβεν τὴν αὐτοῦ χώραν. καὶ ἐλθὼν ἐν τῇ Θρᾴκῃ ἐκεῖ τελευτήσας κεῖται. ᾧτινι Ἄρεϊ ἀνέστησαν πρώτην στήλην οἱ Ἀσσύριοι καὶ ὡς θεὸν προσεκύνουν αὐτόν, ὃν καὶ ἕως νῦν καλοῦσι περσιστὶ τὸν βάαλ θεόν, ὅ ἐστιν ἑρμηνευόμενον Ἄρης πολέμων θεός. τούτου μνημονεύει ‹ἡ› προφητικὴ φωνὴ τοῦ Δανιὴλ καὶ τῶν γ′ παίδων, ὅτι ἠναγκάζοντο προσκυνεῖν αὐτῷ. καὶ μετὰ τὴν τελευτὴν Ἄρεως ἐβασίλευσεν ὁ Λάμης καὶ μετὰ Λάμην ἐβασίλευσεν Ἀσσυρίων Σαρδανάπαλος ὁ μέγας, ὅντινα Περσεὺς ὁ Δανάης ἐφονευσεν καὶ ἀφείλατο τὴν βασιλείαν ἀπὸ Ἀσσυρίων. καὶ βασιλεύσας αὐτῶν εἰς τὸ ἴδιον αὐτοῦ ὄνομα ἐπεκάλεσεν αὐτοὺς Πέρσας. ἅτινα συνεγράψατο Μεμβρώνιος Βαβυλώνιος Πέρσαις.

6 (13) ὁ δὲ ἀδελφὸς τοῦ Νίνου Πῖκος ὁ καὶ Ζεὺς βασιλεύων τῆς Ἰταλίας ἐπέμενεν. ἐν δὲ τοῖς αὐτοῖς χρόνοις οὔτε πόλις οὔτε διοίκησις τις ἦν ἐν τῇ δύσει, ἀλλ᾽ ἁπλῶς οἰκεῖτο πᾶσα ἡ γῆ ἐκείνη ἀπὸ τῶν μετοικησάντων ἐκεῖ ἐκ τῆς φυλῆς τοῦ Ἰάφεθ, τοῦ υἱοῦ Νῶε. ἔζησεν δὲ Πίκος ὁ καὶ Ζεὺς ἔτη ρκ′ κρατῶν τὴν δύσιν καὶ βασιλεύων αὐτῆς καὶ ἔσχεν υἱοὺς πολλοὺς καὶ θυγατέρας ἀπὸ τῶν εὐπρεπων γυναικῶν (ὑπενόθευεν γὰρ αὐτάς· ἦν γὰρ καὶ μυστικὸς καὶ φαντασίας τινὰς ποιῶν καὶ ἐκπλήττων αὐτάς)· αἵτινες γυναῖκες καὶ ὡς θεὸν εἶχον αὐτὸν φθειρόμεναι ὑπ᾽ αὐτοῦ, ὡς δεικνύοντα αὐταῖς φαντασίας τινὰς μηχανικῶς. ἔσχεν δὲ ὁ αὐτὸς Πίκος ὁ καὶ Ζεὺς υἱὸν ὀνόματι Φαῦνον, ὃν καὶ Ἑρμῆν ἐκάλεσεν εἰς ὄνομα τοῦ πλανήτου ἀστερος. [μέλλων δὲ τελευτᾶν, ὁ αὐτὸς Πῖκος ὁ καὶ Ζεὺς ἐκέλευσε τὸ λείψανον αὐτοῦ ταφῆναι ἐν τῇ Κρήτῃ νήσῳ. καὶ κτίσαντες αὐτῷ ναὸν οἱ αὐτοῦ παῖδες ἔθηκαν αὐτὸν ἐν τῇ Κρήτῃ νήσῳ ἐν μνήματι, ὅπερ μνῆμαι ἦν ἐν τῇ αὐτῇ Κρήτῃ, κεῖται <δ'> ἕως τοῦ παρόντος, ἐν ᾧ ἐπιγέγραπτο «ἐνθάδε κεῖται θανὼν Πῖκος ὁ καὶ Ζεύς, ὃν καὶ Δίαν

consumed by the heavenly fire, saying to the Persians, "If once the fire burns me you extract my bones from what has been burnt and preserve them, the kingdom will not depart from your country for as long as you preserve my bones." And after he had prayed to Orion he was consumed by the aerial fire. And the Persians did just as he told them, and they keep his remains taken from the ash, preserving them, up to the present.

5 After Ninus a man by the name of Thouras reigned over the Assyrians, whom his father Zames, the brother of Rhea, renamed Ares after the name of the planet. He became a harsh warrior, and he went to war against the northern regions. He advanced upon a certain Caucasus, a powerful man himself, giant-born and most warlike, descended from the tribe of Japheth, the son of Noah, and he made war on this Caucasus and conquered him and seized his country. And he went to Thrace and died there and was laid out. To this Ares the Assyrians raised the first monument and they did obeisance to him as a god, whom even up to the present they, in the Persian tongue, call the god Baal, which is interpreted as Ares, god of wars. The prophetic voice of Daniel and the Three Children recalls this, inasmuch as they were compelled to do obeisance to him. And after the death of Ares Lames reigned and after Lames Sardanapalus the Great ruled the Assyrians, whom Perseus the son of Danae slew and took the kingdom away from the Assyrians. And having become their king he nicknamed them Persians after his own name. Membronios, the Babylonian Persian, has written about this.

6 The brother of Ninus, Picus, who is also Zeus, continued to rule as king of Italy. In those times there was neither city nor any government administration in the West, rather that whole country was simply inhabited by those who had come to settle there from the tribe of Japheth, the son of Noah. Picus, who is also Zeus, lived 120 years subduing the West and reigning over it, and he had many sons and daughters by comely women (for he seduced them; for he was also a mystic, and he performed certain spectacles and astounded them). These women also considered him a god, since they were corrupted by him, as he displayed spectacles for them ingeniously [*or* by mechanical means]. And Picus, who is also Zeus, had a son by the name of Faunus, whom he also called Hermes after the name of the planet. [When he was about to die, Picus, who is also Zeus, ordered that his remains be buried on the island of Crete. And his children built a shrine to him and placed him there on the island of Crete in a monument, which monument was on this same Crete and stands there to the present day, on which is inscribed: "Here lies the

καλοῦσιν». περὶ οὗ συνεγράψατο Διόδωρος ὁ σοφώτατος χρονογράφος, ὃς καὶ ἐν τῇ ἐκθέσει τοῦ συγγράμματος αὐτοῦ τοῦ περὶ θεῶν εἶπεν, ὅτι Ζεύς, ὁ τοῦ Κρόνου υἱός, ἐν τῇ Κρήτῃ κεῖται.]

7 (14) μετὰ δὲ τὴν τελευτὴν Πίκου τοῦ καὶ Διὸς ἐβασίλευσεν ὁ αὐτοῦ υἱὸς Φαῦνος ὁ καὶ Ἑρμῆς τῆς Ἰταλίας ἔτη λε′, ὃς ἦν ἀνὴρ πανοῦργος καὶ μαθηματικός, ὅστις ἐφηῦρεν τὸ μέταλλον τοῦ χρυσοῦ ἐν τῇ δύσει πρῶτος καὶ τὸ χωνεύειν, γνοὺς δέ, ὅτι διαφθονοῦνται αὐτῷ οἱ ἀδελφοὶ αὐτοῦ οἱ ἀπὸ τῶν γυναικῶν, ὧν ἔσχεν Πίκος ὁ καὶ Ζεὺς ὁ αὐτοῦ πατήρ· ἐβούλοντο γὰρ αὐτὸν φονεῦσαι· ἦσαν γὰρ πολλοὶ ὡσεὶ περὶ ἑβδομήκοντα. μετὰ γὰρ πολλῶν συμμιγόμενος γυναικῶν ἐτεκνοποίησεν ὁ Ζεύς. . . .

ὁ οὖν Ἑρμῆς γνοὺς τὴν κατ' αὐτοῦ σκευὴν τῶν ἀδελφῶν ἀνεχώρησεν πολὺν χρυσὸν ἐγκολπωσάμενος εἰς ὑπερβολὴν καὶ ἀπέρχεται εἰς τὴν Αἴγυπτον πρὸς τὴν φυλὴν τοῦ Χάμ, υἱοῦ Νῶε, οἵτινες ἐδέξαντο αὐτὸν ἐν τιμῇ, καὶ διέτριβεν ἐκεῖ ὑπερηφανῶν παντὰς καὶ φορῶν στολὴν χρυσῆν. καὶ ἐφιλοσόφει παρὰ τοῖς Αἰγυπτίοις λέγων αὐτοῖς μαντείας. ἦν γὰρ φύσει σφόδρα λογικός. καὶ προσεκύνουν αὐτῷ λέγοντες θεὸν ‹τὸν› Ἑρμῆν ὡς λέγοντα τὰ μέλλοντα καὶ διακονοῦντα αὐτοῖς ἐκ τοῦ θεοῦ ἐκ τῶν μελλόντων τὴν ἀπόκρισιν καὶ παρέχοντα αὐτοῖς χρήματα, ὅντινα καὶ πλουτοδότην ἐκάλουν ὡς τὸν χρυσὸν θεὸν νομίζοντες.

8 (15) ὅτε οὖν ὁ αὐτὸς Ἑρμῆς εἰς τὴν Αἴγυπτον ἦλθεν, ἐβασίλευσε τῶν Αἰγυπτίων τότε ἐκ τοῦ γένους τοῦ Χὰμ ὁ Μεστραΐμ. οὗτινος τελευτήσαντος ἐποίησαν οἱ Αἰγυπτίοι τὸν Ἑρμῆν βασιλέα. καὶ ἐβασίλευσεν τῶν Αἰγυπτίων ἔτη λθ′ ἐν ὑπερηφανίᾳ. καὶ μετ' αὐτὸν ἐβασίλευσε ‹τῶν› Αἰγυπτίων ὁ Ἥφαιστος ἡμέρας ͵αχπ′, ὡς γίνεσθαι ἔτη δ′ ἥμισυ καὶ ἡμέρας λη′. οὐκ ᾔδεισαν γὰρ τότε μετρῆσαι ἐνιαυτοὺς οἱ Αἰγύπτιοι, ἀλλὰ τὴν περίοδον τῆς ἡμέρας ἐνιαυτοὺς ἐκάλουν. τὸν δὲ αὐτὸν Ἥφαιστον ‹θεὸν› ἔλεγον. ἦν γὰρ καὶ πολεμιστὴς καὶ μυστικός. ὅστις ἐξελθὼν εἰς πόλεμον συνέπεσεν σὺν τῷ ἵππῳ αὐτοῦ καὶ πληγεὶς ἔμεινεν χωλεύων. ὁ δὲ αὐτὸς Ἥφαιστος νόμον ἔθηκεν τὰς Αἰγυπτίων γυναῖκας μονανδρεῖν καὶ σωφρόνως διάγειν, τὰς δὲ ἐπὶ μοιχείᾳ εὑρισκομένας τιμωρεῖσθαι. καὶ ηὐχαρίστησαν αὐτῷ οἱ Αἰγύπτιοι, διότι πρῶτον νόμον σωφροσύνης ‹τοῦτον› ἐδέξαντο. ὁ δὲ αὐτὸς Ἥφαιστος ἀπὸ μυστικῆς τινος εὐχῆς τὴν ὀξυλάβην ἐδέξατο ἐκ τοῦ ἀέρος εἰς τὸ κατασκευάζειν ἐκ σιδήρου ὅπλα. ὅθεν καὶ ἐπικρατὴς ηὑρέθη εἰς τοὺς πολέμους. ἀπεθέωσαν οὖν αὐτὸν ὡς σωφροσύνην νομοθετήσαντα καὶ

dead Picus, who is also Zeus, whom they also call Dia." About this Diodorus, the exceeding wise chronographer, has written, who also in the exposition of his writing about the gods said that Zeus, the son of Cronos, is buried on Crete.]

7 After the death of Picus, who is also Zeus, his son Faunus, who is also Hermes, ruled as king over Italy for thirty-five years. He was a cunning [*and/or* wicked] and learned man [*or* an astrologer]. He discovered gold in the West and was the first to smelt it. And he learned that his brothers, by those women his father Picus, who is also Zeus, had had, held a grudge against him, since they were plotting to murder him. There were many of them, about seventy; for Zeus had relations with many women and produced children. . . .

So, when Hermes learned of his brothers' preparations against him, he withdrew. Filling his purse with a great supply of gold for the trip, he went off to Egypt, to the tribe of Ham, the son of Noah. They received him with honor, and he stayed there conducting himself with arrogance to all and wearing a golden robe. And he practiced philosophy among the Egyptians and spoke prophecies to them. For he was by nature very rational. And they worshipped him, saying that Hermes was a god, since he told them things that were going to happen, and provided them with an answer from the god of what was about to occur, and distributed money to them. And they called him "giver of wealth," since they considered him the golden god.

8 When Hermes came to Egypt, Mestraim, of the race of Ham, reigned over the Egyptians. When he died the Egyptians made Hermes king. And he reigned over the Egyptians for thirty-nine years in arrogance. And after him Hephaistos ruled the Egyptians for 1,680 days, which comes to four and a half years and 38 days. For at that time the Egyptians did not know how to measure years, but called the cycle of the day a year. They said this Hephaistos was a god. For he was both a warrior and a mystic. Once when he went out to war he fell with his horse and he remained crippled and limping. This Hephaistos decreed a law that the women of the Egyptians were to have one husband and live chastely, and women found in adultery were to be punished. And the Egyptians were grateful to him, because this was the first law on chastity they had received. This Hephaistos, through a certain mystical prayer, obtained a pair of tongs out of the air for the making of weapons out of iron. And for this reason, he proved to be overwhelmingly mighty in his wars. So, they deified him as a lawgiver who bestowed chastity and an inventor

τροφὴν ἀνθρώποις διὰ κατασκευῆς ὅπλων εὑρηκότα καὶ ἐν τοῖς πολέμοις δύναμιν καὶ σωτηρίαν ποιήσαντα· πρὸ γὰρ αὐτοῦ ῥοπάλοις καὶ λίθοις ἐπολέμουν.

9 (2.2) μετὰ καὶ τὴν τελευτὴν Ἡφαίστου ἐβασίλευσεν Αἰγυπτίων ὁ υἱὸς αὐτοῦ ὀνόματι Ἥλιος ἡμέρας ͵δυοζʹ, ὡς εἶναι ἔτη ιβʹ καὶ ἡμέρας ϟζʹ. οὐ γὰρ ᾔδεισαν οἱ Αἰγύπτιοι τοτε ἢ ἄλλοι τινὲς ἀριθμὸν ‹ἐνιαυτῶν› ψηφίσαι, ἀλλ᾽ οἱ μὲν τὰς περιόδους τῆς σελήνης ἐψήφιζον εἰς ἐνιαυτούς, οἱ δὲ τὰς περιόδους τῶν ἡμερῶν εἰς ἔτη ἐψήφιζον· οἱ γὰρ τῶν ιβʹ μηνῶν ἀριθμοὶ μετὰ ταῦτα ἐπενοήθησαν, ἐξότε ἐπωνομάσθη τὸ ὑποτελεῖς εἶναι τοὺς ἀνθρώπους τοῖς βασιλεῦσιν. ὁ δὲ αὐτὸς Ἥλιος, ὁ υἱὸς Ἡφαίστου, ἦν φιλότιμος δυνατός· ὅστις ἐδιδάχθη ὑπό τινος, ὡς γυνή τις Αἰγυτία τῶν ἐν εὐπορίᾳ καὶ ἀξίᾳ οὐσῶν παρ᾽ αὐτοῖς ἐρῶσά τινος ἐμοιχεύετο ὑπ᾽ αὐτοῦ. καὶ ἀκοῦσας ὁ Ἥλιος ἐζήτησεν αὐτὴν πιάσαι διὰ τὴν τοῦ πατρὸς αὐτοῦ Ἡφαίστου νομοθεσίαν, ἵνα μὴ λυθῇ· καὶ λαβὼν στρατιώτας ἐκ τοῦ ἰδίου στρατοῦ, μαθὼν τὸν καιρὸν τῆς μοιχείας αὐτῆς γίνεσθαι νυκτῶν, ἐπιρρίψας αὐτῇ τοῦ ἀνδρὸς αὐτῆς μὴ ὄντος αὐτόθι εὗρεν αὐτὴν μετὰ ἄλλου καθεύδουσαν τοῦ ἐρωμένου παρ᾽ αὐτῆς. ἥντινα εὐθέως καταγαγὼν ἐπόμπευσεν ἐν πάσῃ τῇ χώρᾳ τῆς Αἰγύπτου· κἀκεῖνον δὲ τὸν μοιχὸν ἀνεῖλον, καὶ εὐχαριστήθη. περὶ οὗ ἱστορεῖ ποιητικῶς Ὅμηρος ὁ ποιητής, ὡς ὁ Ἥλιος, φησίν, ἤλεγξεν τὴν Ἀφροδίτην συμμιγνυμένην νυκτὸς Ἄρεϊ· Ἀφροδίτην δὲ ἐκάλεσεν τὴν ἐπιθυμίαν τῆς πορνείας ἀπὸ τοῦ Ἡλίου βασιλέως ἐλεγχθεῖσαν. τὸ δὲ ἀληθές, ὡς προγέγραπται, Παλαίφατος ὁ σοφώτατος χρονογράφος συνεγράψατο.

10 (2) μετὰ δὲ τὴν τελευτὴν Ἡλίου βασιλέως, υἱοῦ Ἡφαίστου, ἐβασίλευσεν τῶν Αἰγυπτίων Σῶσις, καὶ μετὰ τὴν βασιλείαν αὐτοῦ ἐβασίλευσεν Ὄσιρις, καὶ μετὰ Ὄσιριν ἐβασίλευσεν Ὧρος, καὶ μετὰ Ὧρον ἐβασίλευσεν Θοῦλις, ὃς παρέλαβεν μετὰ δυνάμεως πολλῆς πᾶσαν τὴν γῆν ἕως τοῦ Ὠκεανοῦ. καὶ ἐν τῷ ὑποστρέφειν ἦλθεν ἐπὶ τὴν Ἀφρικὴν χώραν εἰς τὸ μαντεῖον ἐν ὑπερηφανίᾳ· καὶ θυσιάσας ἐπυνθάνετο λέγων· φράσον μοι, πυρισθενές, ἀψευδές, μάκαρ, ὁ τὸν αἰθέριον μετεκλίνων δρόμον, τίς πρὸ τῆς ἐμῆς βασιλείας ἠδυνήθη ὑποτάξαι τὰ πάντα, ἢ τίς μετ᾽ ἐμέ; καὶ ἐδόθη αὐτῷ χρησμὸς οὗτος· πρῶτα θεός, μετέπειτα λόγος καὶ πνεῦμα σὺν αὐτοῖς· σύμφυτα δὲ πάντα καὶ εἰς ἓν ἰόντα, οὗ κράτος αἰώνιον. ὠκέσι ποσὶ βάδιζε, θνητέ, ἄδηλον διανύων βίον. καὶ εὐθέως ἐξελθὼν ἐκ τοῦ μαντείου, συσκευασθεὶς ὑπὸ τῶν ἰδίων [εὐθέως] ἐσφάγη ἐν τῇ Ἀφρικῇ. ταῦτα δὲ παλαιὰ καὶ ἀρχαῖα βασίλεια τῶν Αἰγυπτίων Μανέθων συνεγράψατο· ἐν οἷς συγγράμμασιν αὐτοῦ ἐμφέρεται ἄλλως λέγεσθαι τὰς ἐπωνυμίας τῶν

who found sustenance for men by making arms and one who produced power and safety in war; for before his time they made war with clubs and rocks.

9 And after the death of Hephaistos, his son, by the name of Helios, ruled the Egyptians for 4,477 days, which is twelve years and 97 days. For at that time neither the Egyptians nor anyone else knew how to calculate the number <of years>; rather, some counted the cycles of the moon as years, and others counted the cycles of the days as years. For the terms of twelve months were discovered afterward, from the time when a name was given to men being subject to the taxation of kings. This Helios, the son of Hephaistos, was honor-loving and mighty. He was informed by someone that a certain Egyptian woman, one of those who lived among them in wealth and good repute, was in love with a certain man and had committed adultery with him. When Helios heard this, he sought to catch her because of the legislation of his father Hephaistos, so that it might not be annulled. So, taking some soldiers from his army and having learned the time of night when her adulterous assignations occurred, he threw himself upon her when her husband wasn't there and found her sleeping with another man, the one with whom she was in love. He led her at once in a triumphal procession through the whole land of Egypt. And he executed that adulterer as well, and he was thanked for it. The poet Homer gives an account of this in poetic fashion, saying that Helios exposed Aphrodite consorting by night with Ares; he called the yearning after fornication brought to light by King Helios "Aphrodite." The truth, as has been written above, was recorded by Palaephatus, the exceeding wise chronographer.

10 After the death of King Helios, the son of Hephaistos, Sosis reigned over the Egyptians, and after his reign Osiris reigned, and after Osiris Horus reigned, and after Horus Thoulis reigned, who with a great force conquered the whole earth as far as the Ocean. And as he was returning, he came to the land of Africa, in arrogance he came to the oracle. He performed a sacrifice and enquired [of the oracle], saying, "Tell me, thou mighty with fire, unlying, blessed, who movest about the ethereal course, who before my reign was able to subdue all things, or who shall after me?" And this oracular response was given to him: "First God, thereafter Word, and Spirit with them; all things born together and going to One, whose might is eternal. Traipse on swift feet, thou mortal, and bring a paltry life to an end." And as soon as he left the oracle, he fell victim to a plot by his companions and was slain in Africa. Manetho prepared a record of these ancient and primeval kingdoms of the Egyptians; in his records it is intimated that the names

πέντε πλανητῶν ἀστέρων. τὸν γὰρ λεγόμενον Κρόνον ἀστέρα ἐκάλουν τὸν λάμποντα, τὸν δὲ Διὸς τὸν φαέθοντα, τὸν δὲ Ἄρεος τὸν πυρώδη, τὸν δὲ Ἀφροδίτης τὸν κάλλιστον, τὸν δὲ Ἑρμοῦ τὸν στίλβοντα· ἅτινα μετὰ ταῦτα Σωτάτης ὁ σοφώτατος ἑρμήνευσεν.

(3) καὶ λοιπὸν ἐν τοῖς μετὰ ταῦτα χρόνοις ἐβασίλευσεν Αἰγυπτίων πρῶτος ἐκ τῆς φυλῆς τοῦ Χὰμ Σῶστρις· κτλ.

2 ~ *Excerpta Latina Barbari* 1.6.1–3 (Garstad, *Apocalypse/ Alexandrian World Chronicle*, 186–90)

1 Temporibus vero iudicum recensuimus dicendo in ipsis fuerunt qui ec Diu dipinguntur; unde: Picus ille Cronu pronepus partibus occasu ipsis temporibus imperavit. Cronus quidem propater eius in divisione terrae fuit occidentales partes tenens, sicut sine urbes et sine reges essent: de quo multus est sermo et sine interpretatione sunt.

Post Cronis autem perditionem secundum successiones annorum Picus pronepus eius per tempora regnavit in Italia primus, quem et Serafin quidam interpretaverunt, alii autem Dia Olympium, ceteri autem Plutea Aidonium, et alii Chthonium Posidona. Istorum autem nominum ei pertinuit pro eo quod ille multa potuisset super omnes. Iste autem in Assyrios in iuventute regnans Ninus ibi vocabatur et condidit Ninivem civitatem Assyriorum. Uxor autem eius Semiramis mulier fuit maligna et praesumens et inpudica, quem Ream vocaverunt, alii autem Iram Zygiam, et alii Nemesim multiformem, ceteri autem Ecatin Chtonicam propter innumeram eius atrocitatem. Iste quidem relinquens uxori imperium occidentis partibus veniens imperavit. Erant enim omnes partes illas sine urbes et sine regem secundum quod narrat historia. In illis vero temporibus Picus Croni pronepus inveniens terram illam spaciosam manentem imperavit in illam annos LXXX patrias possidens. Et illas nobillissimas feminas per magicas et ingenia maligna convertens et avortivos faciebat, et sic mulieres, quae ab ipso deludebantur, domos et sedes praeparabant ei et sculptilia multa multa illi configebant sicut placebat eis, et quasi deo eas conmiscuisset et in deum eum esse gloriabantur.

2 (2) Post istius autem perditionem Faunus filius eius regnavit in Italiam annos XXXV. Hic factus est vir impius et strenuus valde. Tunc descendit in Egyptum et ibidem demoratus est inperialem vestem indutus. Et sapiens videbatur ab

of the five planets were called otherwise. For the star called Cronos they name the Bright One, that of Zeus the Shining One, that of Ares the Fiery One, that of Aphrodite the Fairest, and that of Hermes the Glistening One, which things the exceeding wise Sotates explained afterward.

Thereafter in the times after these events Sostris was the first from the tribe of Ham to reign over the Egyptians . . .

1 In the time of the Judges, we have mentioned, were those who are portrayed as the children of Zeus. So [we include here this narrative of him]: Picus, the son of Cronus, ruled in the regions of the West in those times. Cronus, his father, obtained the western regions in the division of the earth, as they were without cities and without kings (much is said concerning this, and it is not translated).

After the death of Cronus according to the passing of years Picus his son ruled, through time, the first in Italy, whom some have understood as Serapis, but others as Olympian Zeus, and still others as Pluto lord of Hades, and others as Chthonian Poseidon. But these names were his because he had great power over all. He reigned among the Assyrians in his youth, and was there called Ninus, and founded Nineveh, the city of the Assyrians. His wife, Semiramis, was a spiteful and brazen and shameless woman, whom they called Rhea, and some Hera patroness of marriage, and others Nemesis of many forms, still others Chthonian Hecate because of her numberless outrages. Picus surrendered his kingdom to his wife, and going to the regions of the West, ruled there. For those parts were without cities and without a king according to what the history says. In those times Picus, the son of Cronus, finding that land still open and broad, ruled there and occupied the land for eighty years. He also turned the heads of the most noble women through magic arts and great evils and corrupted them. So, the women who were enchanted by him prepared houses and seats for him and made many, many statuettes of him since he was pleased with these things. And as a god he had sexual relations with them, and they honored him as if he were a god.

2 After his death Faunus his son reigned in Italy for thirty-five years. He became an impious and cunningly wicked man. Then he went down to Egypt and stayed there and put on a royal robe. And he seemed wise to the Egyptians; he deceived

Egyptios, per magicas et maleficia eos decipiebat, et suspitiones et divinationes illos dicebat, avium narrationes et opupas adnuntiationes et equorum hinnos discebat et mortuorum divinationes et alia plura mala. Et dum conputatorem illum cernerent et valde loquacem sapientes Aegyptiorum, Hermem terbeatissimum illum glorificabant pro eo quod linguas eorum bene novisset ubique, simul autem et polyolbum et multoditatum et deorum illum ministrum suspicabant. Regnavit autem ibi annos XXXV. Fiunt autem ab Adam usque ad initium regni Picu qui interpraetatur Serapidus pronepus Croni anni quattuor milia C.

3 (3) Tunc Eraclius ab Spanorum partibus rediens arma sua posuit in Roma, in Boarium forum, in templo clausit. Dicunt enim Eraclium in Latothibis fuisse ec Dius et Alminius. Et fugiens Erysthea, regem Thibeorum, cum omnia sua navigavit et regnavit occidentis partibus: unde immagines auro vestitos sibi conposuit in novissimis occidentales partibus, qui et usque hodie stant: pro quo et Eurypidus ille poeta memoravit.

Fecit autem et filium ex ipsa neocorum Aleu filia Telefonum et Latinum eum vocauit. Regnavit autem Eraclius annos XXXVIII.

Post mortem autem Eraclii Telefus filius eius qui et Latinus vocatus est regnavit in ipsa provincia annos XVIII, et de eius nomine Romeos, qui et Cittei vocantur, Latinos nominavit, qui et usque hodiernum diem Latini vocantur.

3 ~ MALALAS 6.16B (THURN, *IOANNIS MALALAE CHRONOGRAPHIA*, 125)

ἦν δὲ Ἡρακλῆς γεννηθεὶς ἐν τοῖς προειρημένοις ἀνωτέρω χρόνοις ἐν Λατῷ τῆς Θηβαΐδος, ἐκ γένους ὑπάρχων τοῦ Ἡρακλέος τοῦ ἐκ τῆς Ἀλκμήνης καὶ τοῦ Πίκου Διός· ὅστις ἀνετράφη ἐν τῇ Ἱσπανίᾳ χώρᾳ, καὶ ἀνδρεῖος γενόμενος ἦλθεν τότε ἀπὸ τῆς Ἱσπανίας ἐπὶ Ἰταλίαν, φυγὼν τὸν Εὐρυσθέα βασιλέα· καὶ ἐβασίλευσεν ἔτη λη′. ὅστις ἔλαβεν γυναῖκα τὴν Αὔγην, τὴν Ἀλέου θυγατέρα βασιλέως, ἐβασίλευσεν δὲ ὡς ἐκ τοῦ γένους καταγόμενος τοῦ Πίκου Διός· ὅθεν καὶ στήλας αὐτῷ χρυσᾶς καὶ πορφυρᾶς ἀνέστησαν οἱ Ἰταλοὶ καὶ βασιλεῖς, ἤτοι ῥῆγες, ἐκ τοῦ γένους αὐτοῦ βασιλεύσαντες ἐν τοῖς ἐσχάτοις τῆς δύσεως μέρεσιν· αἵτινες στῆλαι ἕως τοῦ παρόντος ἵστανται.

them through magic arts and evil deeds. He spoke his suspicions and prophecies to them and taught them the speech of birds and the pronouncements of the hoopoe and the neighing of horses and the divination of the dead and many other evils. And since the wise men of the Egyptians perceived him to be a mathematician and very well-spoken they honored him as Hermes Trismegistus, because he knew their languages everywhere so well; they also admired him as a rich man and a servant of the gods. He reigned there for thirty-five years. There are from Adam up to the beginning of the reign of Picus, who is understood to be Serapis, the son of Cronus, 4,100 [*or* 4,200] years.

3 Then Heracles, coming back from Spain, set up his arms in Rome, in the Forum Boarium, and shut them in a temple. For they say that Heracles was born in Latus of the Thebaid, the child of Zeus and Alcmene. Fleeing Eurystheus, the king of Thebes, he sailed away with his household[?] and reigned in the regions of the West. So, he made images of himself clothed in gold in the furthest western regions, which stand even to this day, which Euripides the poet also recalls.

He also had a son by Auge, the daughter of Aleus the temple servant [?], Telephus, whom he also called Latinus. Heracles reigned for thirty-eight years.

After the death of Heracles, Telephus his son, who was also called Latinus, reigned in this province for eighteen years. From his name he named the Romans (who are also called Cittaeans) Latins, and they are called Latins to this very day.

In the aforementioned times Heracles was born in Latos of the Thebaid; he was of the family of Heracles, the son of Alcmene and Picus-Zeus. He was raised in the country of Spain, and when he reached a man's estate he went from Spain to Italy, fleeing Eurystheus, the king. And he reigned for thirty-eight years. He took to wife Auge, the daughter of King Aleus. He himself ruled as king because he came from the line of Picus-Zeus. For this reason, the Italian kings, or *reges*, of his family who ruled in the furthest regions of the West also set up gold and porphyry monuments to him; these monuments stand up to the present day.

4 ~ Malalas 6.18 (Thurn, *Ioannis Malalae Chronographia*, 125)

Τῆς δὲ Ἰταλίας ἐβασίλευσεν ὁ υἱὸς τοῦ Ἡρακλέος ὁ ἀπὸ τῆς Αὔγης, ὁ Τήλεφος. καὶ μετ᾽ αὐτὸν ἐβασίλευσεν ὁμοίως ὁ υἱὸς αὐτοῦ, ὅντινα Λατῖνον ἐκάλεσεν· ἐβασίλευσεν δὲ ἐν τῇ χώρᾳ ἐκείνῃ ὁ αὐτὸς Λατῖνος ἔτη ιη′, καὶ ἐκ τοῦ ἰδίου ὀνόματος τοὺς Κιτιαίους καλουμένους ἐπωνόμασε Λατίνους.

5 ~ Malalas 7.1a (Thurn, *Ioannis Malalae Chronographia*, 132)

Καὶ λοιπὸν ἐβασίλευσεν Ῥῶμος ὁ κτίστης τῆς Ῥώμης καὶ Ῥῆμος ὁ ἀδελφὸς αὐτοῦ· ὅθεν μετεκλήθησαν Ῥωμαῖοι. οἵτινες καὶ τὰ ὅπλα τοῦ Ἡρακλέος τοῦ ἐκ τοὺ γένους τοῦ Πίκου Διός εὑρηκότες ἀπέθεντο ἐν τῇ παρ᾽ αὐτῶν κτισθείσῃ πόλει Ῥώμῃ τῇ πρῴην λεγομένῃ κώμῃ Βαλεντίᾳ ἐν τῷ Βοαρίῳ φόρῳ εἰς τὸν ναὸν τοῦ Πίκου Διός, ἀποκλείσαντες αὐτὰ ἐκεῖ ἕως ἄρτι.

6 ~ Malalas 2.7b (Thurn, *Ioannis Malalae Chronographia*, 22–23)

τὴν δὲ Εὐρώπην οἱ ποιηταὶ ἐξέθεντο θυγατέρα εἶναι τοῦ Φοίνικος, τοῦ υἱοῦ Ἀγήνορος βασιλέως, μὴ ὁμοφωνήσαντες τοῖς χρονογράφοις. ἐπιρρίψας δὲ τῇ πόλει Τύρῳ Ταῦρος ὁ τῆς Κρήτης βασιλεύς, ναυμαχίᾳ πολεμήσας παρέλαβε τὴν αὐτὴν Τύρον πόλιν ἑσπέρας· καὶ πραιδεύσας ἔλαβεν αἰχμαλώτους ἐκ τῆς πόλεως πολλούς· ἐν οἷς ἔλαβε καὶ τὴν Εὐρώπην, θυγατέρα τοῦ Ἀγήνορος βασιλέως. ὁ δὲ Ἀγήνωρ καὶ οἱ υἱοὶ αὐτοῦ ἐπολέμουν ἐπὶ τὸ λίμιτον· [καὶ γνοὺς] τοῦτο Ταῦρος ὁ τῆς Κρήτης βασιλεὺς ἐξαίφνης ἐπέρριψε τῇ χώρᾳ διὰ θαλάττης· ἧστινος ἑσπέρας μνήμην ποιοῦνται οἱ Τύριοι ἕως τῆς νῦν, λέγοντες· «κακὴν ὀψινήν». ἀπήγαγε δὲ τὴν Εὐρώπην εἰς τὴν ἰδίαν πατρίδα ὁ Ταῦρος, ἥντινα καὶ γυναῖκα ἔλαβε, παρθένον οὖσαν καὶ εὐπρεπῆ· καὶ ἐκάλεσεν τὰ μέρη ἐκεῖνα εἰς ὄνομα αὐτῆς Εὐρώπεια. ἐξ ἧς ἔσχεν υἱὸν τὸν Μίνω, καθὼς καὶ Εὐριπίδης ὁ σοφώτατος ποιητικῶς συνεγράψατο, ὅς φησι, Ζεὺς μεταβληθεὶς εἰς Ταῦρον τὴν Εὐρώπην ἥρπασεν. ἔκτισεν δὲ ἐν τῇ αὐτῇ Κρήτῃ νήσῳ ὁ αὐτὸς Ταῦρος βασιλεὺς πόλιν μεγάλην, ἣν ἐκάλεσεν Γόρτυναν εἰς ὄνομα τῆς αὐτοῦ μητρὸς τῆς ἐκ γένους Πίκου Διός· τὴν δὲ τῆς αὐτῆς πόλεως τύχην ἐκαλεσεν Καλλινίκην εἰς ὄνομα τῆς σφαγιασθείσης παρ᾽ αὐτοῦ κόρης.

Telephus, the son of Heracles from Auge, ruled the land of Italy. And after him his son, whom they called Latinus, likewise ruled as king. This Latinus reigned in that land for eighteen years, and the people called Cittaeans were named Latins after his name.

And thereafter Romus, the founder of Rome, and Remus his brother ruled, for which reason they were renamed Romans. These men found the arms of Heracles of the family of Picus-Zeus and put them away in the city founded by them, Rome, which was formerly called the village of Valentia, in the Forum Boarium near the temple of Picus-Zeus, shutting them up there until the present.

The poets set out that Europa was the daughter of Phoenix, the son of King Agenor, not agreeing with the chroniclers. Tauros the king of Crete attacked the city of Tyre and making war in a sea battle he took this city of Tyre as evening fell; and in his plundering he took many prisoners from the city, among whom he even took Europa, the daughter of Agenor the king. Agenor and his sons were fighting on the frontier, [and learning] this Tauros suddenly attacked the country by sea. The Tyrians make a memorial of this evening up to the present, saying, "Bad evening!" Tauros carried Europa off to his own fatherland and took her as his wife, since she was a virgin and good-looking; and he called those parts Europe after her name. He had from her a son, Minos, just as the exceeding wise Euripides wrote poetically, who said, "Zeus turned himself into a bull (*tauros*) and seized Europa." This King Tauros established a great city on the island of Crete, which he called Gortyna after the name of his mother from the family of Picus-Zeus; he called the tyche of this city Callinice after the name of the maiden sacrificed by himself.

7 ~ MALALAS 2.11, 13 (THURN, *IOANNIS MALALAE CHRONOGRAPHIA*, 25–29)

1 Ὁ δὲ προειρημένος Πῖκος ὁ καὶ Ζεὺς ἐν τοῖς ἀνωτέροις χρόνοις ἔσχεν μετὰ τὸν Ἑρμῆν καὶ τὸν Ἡρακλέα καὶ ἄλλον υἱόν, τὸν Περσέα ἀπὸ εὐπρεποῦς γυναικὸς ὀνόματι Δανάης, θυγατρὸς τοῦ Ἀκρισίου τοῦ καταγομένου ἐκ τῆς Ἀργείων χώρας· περὶ ἧς ἐμυθολόγησεν Εὐριπίδης ὁ σοφώτατος ἐν τῇ συντάξει τοῦ αὐτοῦ δράματος ἐν κιβωτίῳ τινὶ βληθεῖσαν καὶ ῥιφεῖσαν κατὰ θάλασσαν τὴν Δανάην, ὡς φθαρεῖσαν ὑπὸ Διὸς μεταβληθέντος εἰς χρυσόν. ὁ δὲ σοφώτατος Βούττιος, ἱστορικὸς χρονογράφος, ἐξέθετο ὡς ὁ αὐτὸς Πῖκος ὁ καὶ Ζεὺς οὖσαν ταύτην ἐν κουβουκλείῳ παρακειμένῳ τῇ θαλάσσῃ πολλῷ χρυσῷ πείσας ἠδυνήθη προτρεψάμενος· ἥντινα ἁρπάσας ὡς πάνυ εὐπρεπῆ ἔφθειρεν, καὶ ἐξ αὐτῆς ἔσχεν υἱὸν ὀνόματι Περσέα, τὸν προειρημένον. ὅντινα πτερωτὸν γράφουσιν διὰ τὸ ἐκ παιδόθεν περίγοργον εἶναι τὸν παῖδα· ὅθεν καὶ ὁ τούτου πατὴρ Πῖκος ὁ καὶ Ζεὺς ἐδίδαξεν αὐτὸν πράττειν καὶ τελεῖν τὴν μαγγανείαν τοῦ μυσεροῦ σκύφους, διδάξας αὐτὸν πάντα τὰ περὶ αὐτοῦ μυστικὰ καὶ δυσσεβῆ πλανήματα, καὶ λέγων αὐτῷ, ὅτι· «νικᾷς πάντας τοὺς πολεμίους ἐξ αὐτοῦ καὶ τοὺς ἐχθρούς σου καὶ πάντα ἄνθρωπον ἐναντίον καὶ πάντας τοὺς βλέποντας ἐν αὐτῷ τῷ προσώπῳ τῆς Γοργόνης τυφλουμένους καὶ μένοντας ὡσεὶ νεκροὺς καὶ κατασφαζομένους ὑπὸ σου».

2 καὶ λοιπὸν ὁ Περσεὺς πεισθεὶς τῷ ἰδιῷ πατρὶ Πίκῳ τῷ καὶ Διί, εἰς τὸν μετὰ ταῦτα χρόνον μετὰ τελευτὴν τοῦ αὐτοῦ πατρὸς Πίκου τελείας ἡλικίας γενόμενος ἐπεθύμησεν τῆς τῶν Ἀσσυρίων βασιλείας, διαφθονούμενος τοῖς τέκνοῖς τοῦ Νίνου, τοῦ θείου αὐτοῦ, τοῦ ἀδελφοῦ τοῦ πατρὸς αὐτοῦ καὶ χρηματισθεὶς ἀπῆλθεν ἐν τῇ χώρᾳ τῆς Λιβύης· καὶ κατὰ τὴν ὁδὸν ὑπήντησεν τῷ αὐτῷ Περσεῖ μία παρθένος, κόρη χωρική, ἀγρίας ἔχουσα τὰς τρίχας καὶ ὀφθαλμούς. καὶ στήσας ἐπερώτησεν αὐτὴν λέγων· «τί σου τὸ ὄνομα;» ἡ δὲ εἶπεν μετὰ παρρησίας· «Μέδουσα». καὶ κρατήσας αὐτῆς τὰς τρίχας ᾧ ἐβάσταζεν λογχοδρεπάνῳ ξίφει ἀπέτεμεν αὐτῆς τὴν κάραν. καὶ λάβων ὁ Περσεὺς εὐθέως ἐτέλεσεν τὴν αὐτὴν κάραν μυστικῶς, καθὼς ἐδιδάχθη ὑπὸ τοῦ ἰδίου πατρὸς Πίκου τῆς μυσερᾶς μαγγανείας τὴν πλάνην· ἥντινα ἐβάσταζεν εἰς ἰδίαν βοήθειαν πρὸς πάντας ἐχθροὺς καὶ πολεμίους εἰς τὸ ὑποτάσσειν καὶ ἀναιρεῖν. τὴν δὲ κάραν ἐκάλεσεν Γοργόνα διὰ τὸ ὀξὺ τοῦ Βοηθήματος καὶ διὰ τὸ ἐνεργὲς πρὸς τοὺς ὑπεναντίους. κἀκεῖθεν περάσας ἦλθεν ἐπὶ τὴν τῆς Αἰθιοπίας χώραν, ἥτις ἐβασιλεύετο ὑπὸ τοῦ Κηφέως, καὶ εὑρηκὼς ἐκεῖ ἱερὸν Ποσειδῶνος εἰσῆλθεν ἐν αὐτῷ καὶ εἶδεν ἐν τῷ ἱερῷ

1 The aforementioned Picus, who is also Zeus, in earlier times had after Hermes and Heracles another son as well, Perseus, from a beautiful woman by the name of Danae, the daughter of Acrisius, who came down from the land of the Argives. The exceeding wise Euripides told the tale concerning her in the narrative of his drama, that Danae was thrown into a little chest and cast upon the sea, since she had been ravished by Zeus after he was changed into gold. The exceeding wise Bouttios, the historical chronographer, however, set out that this Picus, who is also Zeus, prevailed upon her with a great deal of money when she was in a chamber beside the sea and managed to "change" her mind. He seized this woman and ravished her because she was very beautiful, and he had out of her a son by the name of Perseus, who was mentioned above. They write that he had wings because from childhood he was a very fierce [*or* swift] youngster, for which reason his father, Picus, who is also Zeus, taught him to practice and perform the sorcery of the abominable *skyphos*, teaching him all the mystical and impious errors to do with it, and saying to him, "You will conquer all of your adversaries with it and your enemies and every man who stands opposed to you and all who look upon this face of the Gorgon will be blinded and remain like corpses and be slaughtered by you."

2 And thereafter Perseus obeyed his own father Picus, who is also Zeus, up to the time afterward, and after the death of his father Picus, having become a mature man he coveted the kingdom of the Assyrians and envied the children of Ninus, his uncle, the brother of his father. And he consulted an oracle and then went off to the country of Libya. And along the road a maiden on her own met Perseus, a country girl who had wild hair and eyes. He stood and questioned her, saying, "What is your name?" And she boldly said, "Medusa." And he grabbed her by the hair and cut off her head with the sickle-pointed sword that he bore. And taking hold of it Perseus at once performed mystical rites over the head, just as he had been taught the deceit of abominable sorcery by his own father, Picus. He carried this object as an aid for himself against all his enemies and adversaries to subdue and destroy them. He called the head Gorgon because of the swiftness of its help and because of its efficaciousness against his opponents. And from there he crossed over and came to the land of Ethiopia, which was ruled by Cepheus, and there he happened upon a temple of Poseidon and went into it and saw a girl

παραμένουσαν κόρην, κατὰ τάγμα τοῦ ἰδίου αὐτῆς πατρὸς τοῦ Κηφέως ἐκδοθεῖσαν, τὴν λεγομένην Ἀνδρομέδαν παρθένον. καὶ ταύτην ἀπέσπασεν ἐκ τοῦ ἱεροῦ, καὶ φθείρας αὐτὴν ὡς εὐπρεπῆ ἔλαβεν εἰς γυναῖκα.

3 καὶ καταπλεύσας ἀνεχώρησεν ἐκ τῆς χώρας ἐκείνης· ἐρχόμενος κατὰ τὴν Ἀσσυρίων χώραν κατήντησεν ἐν τῇ χώρᾳ τῆς Λυκαονίας· καὶ γνόντες οἱ Λυκάονες εὐθέως ἀντιστάντες ἐπολέμησαν αὐτῷ· καὶ χρησάμενος τῇ βοηθείᾳ τῆς κάρας τῆς Γοργόνης ἐνίκησε τοὺς Λυκάονας. καὶ εὑρηκὼς κώμην λεγομένην Ἄμανδραν ἐποίησεν αὐτὴν πόλιν, καὶ ἔστησεν ἑαυτῷ στήλην ἔξω τῶν πυλῶν, βαστάξουσαν τὸ ἀντεικόνισμα τῆς Γοργόνος, καὶ θυσίαν ποιήσας ἐκάλεσεν τὴν τύχην τῆς πόλεως Περσίδα εἰς τὸ ἴδιον αὐτοῦ ὄνομα· ἥτις στήλη ἕως τοῦ παρόντος ἵσταται ἐκεῖ. ἥντινα πόλιν ἐκάλεσεν τὸ Εἰκόνιον, διότι πρώτης νίκης εἰκόνα σὺν τῇ Γοργόνῃ ἐκεῖ ἔλαβεν. ὑπέταξε δὲ καὶ τὰς ἄλλας χώρας μηδενὸς ἀνθισταμένου. ἐρχόμενος δὲ ἐπὶ τὴν Ἰσαυρίαν καὶ Κιλικίαν, καὶ ἀντιστάσεις αὐτοῦ πολεμίων ὑπομένοντος, ἐχρηματίσθη ταῦτα, ὅτι· «ἀπὸ τοῦ ἰδίου ἵππου ἀποβὰς τὸν σὸν ταρσὸν τοῦ ποδὸς εἰς τὴν χθόνα πήξας νίκην λάβοις». καί κατελθὼν ἐκ τοῦ ἰδίου ἵππου ἐν τῇ λεγομένῃ κώμῃ Ἀνδρασῷ ἐκεῖ τὸν ταρσὸν τοῦ ποδὸς ἔπηξεν· καὶ νικήσας τῇ χρήσει τῆς Γοργόνος ἐποίησεν τὴν αὐτὴν κώμην πόλιν, ἥντινα ἐκάλεσεν Ταρσὸν ἐκ τοῦ χρησμοῦ τοῦ ἰδίου αὐτοῦ ποδὸς, θυσιάσας κόρην ἀδαῆ ὀνόματι Παρθενόπην εἰς ἀποκαθαρισμὸν τῆς πόλεως.

4 καὶ εὐχαριστήσας ὥρμησεν ἐκεῖθεν διὰ τοῦ Ἀργαίου ὄρους κατὰ Ἀσσυρίων· καὶ νικήσας αὐτοὺς καὶ φονεύσας τὸν Σαρδανάπολον, βασιλέα αὐτῶν, τὸν ἐκ τοῦ γένους αὐτοῦ καταγόμενον, ὑπέταξεν αὐτοὺς, καὶ ἐβασίλευσεν αὐτῶν ἔτη νγʹ, καὶ ἐπ᾽ ὀνόματι αὐτοῦ ἐκάλεσεν αὐτοὺς Πέρσας, ἀφελόμενος ἀπὸ Ἀσσυρίων τὴν βασιλείαν καὶ τὸ ὄνομα. καί ἐφύτευσε δένδρα, καὶ ἐκάλεσεν περσέας· οὐ μόνον δὲ ἐκεῖ, ἀλλὰ καὶ ἐν τοῖς Αἰγυπτίοις μέρεσιν ἐφύτευσεν τὰς περσέας εἰς μνήμην ἑαυτοῦ. ἐδίδαξεν δὲ καὶ τοὺς Πέρσας τὴν τελετὴν τοῦ μυσεροῦ καὶ ἀθέου σκύφους τῆς Μεδούσης· ὤντινων ἐκάλεσεν τὴν χώραν Μήδων διὰ τὸ μάθημα.

[(12) Ὁ δὲ αὐτὸς Περσεὺς μετὰ τὸ βασιλεῦσαι τῆς Περσικῆς χώρας ἔτη πολλά, κτλ.]

5 (13) Καὶ μετὰ καιρὸν ἐλθὼν ὁ Κηφεὺς βασιλεὺς κατ᾽ αὐτοῦ ἐκ τῆς Αἰθιοπίας, ὁ πατὴρ τῆς Ἀνδρομέδας, ἐπολέμησεν αὐτῷ· ἦν δὲ ὁ Κηφεὺς ἐκ τοῦ γήρους μὴ βλέπων. καὶ ἀκούσας ὁ Περσεύς, ὅτι πολεμεῖ αὐτῷ, ὀργισθεὶς πάνυ ἐξῆλθεν κατ᾽ αὐτοῦ βαστάζων τὴν κάραν, καὶ ὑπέδειξεν αὐτῷ αὐτήν. καὶ ὁ

staying in the temple, who had been devoted according to the command of her own father Cepheus, a maiden called Andromeda. And he dragged her out of the temple, and after he ravished her because she was beautiful, he took her to wife.

3 And he sailed back and returned out of that country. Going toward the land of the Assyrians he arrived in the country of Lycaonia. When the Lycaonians learned of it, they at once stood against him and made war on him. And he employed the aid of the head of the Gorgon and won a victory over the Lycaonians. And he came upon a village called Amandra and made it a city, and he set up a monument to himself outside of the gates, which bore a likeness of the Gorgon, and after he made a sacrifice, he called the tyche of the city Persis after his own name. This monument stands there up to the present. He called this city Iconium because there he seized upon the form (*icon*) of his first victory with the Gorgon. And so, he subjected the other lands with no one resisting him. He went to Isauria and Cilicia, and as he awaited the assaults of his enemies, he received an oracular response to the effect that "dismounting from your horse and fixing the flat [*tarsos*] of your foot on the earth you may seize the victory." And getting down off his horse in a village called Andrasus he fixed the flat of his foot there. And he won the victory by the use of the Gorgon and made this village a city, which he called Tarsus after the oracle of his foot, and he sacrificed an innocent girl by the name of Parthenope for the purification of the city.

4 And he gave thanks and proceeded from there by Mount Argaeus against the Assyrians. And after he conquered them and slew Sardanapalus their king, who was descended from his own family, he made them his subjects and ruled as their king for fifty-three years, and he called them Persians after his own name, depriving the Assyrians of the kingdom and their name for his own sake. And he planted trees and called them perseas; not only there, but also in the Egyptian regions he planted perseas as a memorial to himself. And he taught the Persians the initiatory rite of the abominable and godless *skyphos* of Medusa, and he called their land the land of the Medes because of this teaching.

[This Perseus, after he had ruled the Persian country for many years, . . .]

5 And after a time King Cepheus, the father of Andromeda, came against him out of Ethiopia and made war on him. Cepheus was blind on account of old age. And when Perseus heard that he was making war on him he became very angry and went out against him bearing the head, and he showed it to him. And since Cepheus

Κηφεὺς μὴ βλέπων ἐπέβαινεν αὐτῷ ἔφιππος· ὁ δὲ Περσεὺς ἀγνοῶν, ὅτι οὐ καθορᾷ, ἐλογίσατο μηκέτι ἐνεργεῖν τὴν κάραν ἧς κατεῖχεν Γοργόνος· καὶ στρέψας αὐτὴν πρὸς ἑαυτὸν προσέσχεν αὐτῇ· καὶ τυφλωθεὶς ἔμεινεν ὡσεὶ νεκρὸς καὶ ἀνῃρέθη. καὶ λοιπὸν ἐβασίλευσεν Περσῶν ὁ υἱὸς τοῦ Περσέως καὶ τῆς Ἀνδρομέδας Μέρρος, προβληθεὶς ἐκ τοῦ ἰδίου αὐτοῦ πάππου τοῦ Κηφέως, τοῦ βασιλέως τῆς Αἰθιοπίας· ὅστις ἐκέλευσεν, καὶ ἐκαύθη ἡ μυσερὰ κεφαλὴ τῆς Γοργόνος, καὶ ἀνεχώρησεν ἐπὶ τὴν ἰδίαν αὐτοῦ χώραν. καὶ ἔμεινε λοιπὸν τὸ γένος τοῦ Περσέως βασιλεῦον τῆς Βαβυλωνίας χώρας.

8 ~ Malalas 5.32b–36 (Thurn, *Ioannis Malalae Chronographia*, 104–9)

1 καὶ τοῦτο χρησμοδοτηθεὶς ὁ Ὀρέστης ἐσημειώσατο· καὶ εὐθέως καταπλεύσας ἅμα τῷ Πυλάδῃ κατέφθασεν ἐπὶ τὴν Αὐλίδα χώραν τῆς Σκυθίας. καὶ ἀνελθόντων αὐτῶν ἐκ τοῦ πλοίου προσέσχεν ὁ Ὀρέστης ἱερὸν ἑστὼς ὡς ἀπὸ μιλίων δύο τῆς θαλάττης καὶ θανόντων ἀνθρώπων ἐρριμμένα ὀστέα. καὶ λέγει Πυλάδῃ [ὁ Ὀρέστης]· «δοκεῖ σοι θεᾶς εἶναι τάδε μέλαθρα, ἔνθα σὺν νηυσὶν ἥκαμεν; ὁρῶ δὲ καὶ τῶν θανόντων ξένων τὰ ὀστέα». καὶ προσεσχηκὼς Πυλάδης λέγει τῷ Ὀρέστῃ· «φύγωμεν, ἐὰν σωθησόμεθα». ὁ δὲ Ὀρέστης ἔφη· «οὐ φεύγομεν· οὔτε γὰρ φεύγειν εἰώθαμεν οὐδὲ τὸν χρησμὸν τοῦ θεοῦ κακιστεύσομεν».

2 (33) Τούτους δὲ ἑωρακότες βουκόλοι ἔδραμον πρὸς τὴν Ἰφιγένειαν, λέγοντες αὐτῇ· «Ἀγαμέμνονος καὶ Κλυταιμνήστρης κόρη, ἥκασι δύο νεανίσκοι παρὰ τὴν κυανέαν». ἡ δὲ πρὸς αὐτούς· «ποταποί; τίνος γῆς; τί τοὔνομα ἔχουσιν οἱ ξένοι;» ἐπερώτα γὰρ πάντας ἡ Ἰφιγένεια τοὺς συλλαμβανομένους καὶ ἀγομένους εἰς θυσίαν, ἀπὸ οἵας εἰσὶ χώρας, καὶ τότε αὐτοὺς ἔσφαζε, βουλομένη μαθεῖν περὶ τοῦ ἰδίου πατρὸς αὐτῆς Ἀγαμέμνονος καὶ τῶν αὐτοῦ καὶ περὶ τοῦ κατὰ Φρυγῶν πολέμου τί ἐγένετο. οἱ δὲ βουκόλοι λέγουσιν αὐτῇ· «ἕτερος πρὸς τὸν ἕτερον ἔφη, Πυλάδη· τοῦ δὲ συζύγου τὸ ὄνομα οὐκ ἴσμεν· οὐδὲ γὰρ ἔφη». ἡ δὲ πρὸς αὐτούς· «τί γὰρ κοινὸν βουκόλοις ἐν θαλάττῃ;» οἱ δὲ εἶπον· «βοῦς ἥκαμεν νίψαι ἐν ἁλίᾳ δρόσῳ». καὶ πέμψασα Σκύθας συνέσχεν αὐτούς· καὶ ἤχθησαν εἰς θυσίαν δέσμιοι· καθὼς ὁ σοφώτατος Εὐριπίδης ἐξέθετο δρᾶμα ποιητικῶς, ὧν μέρος ὀλίγον ἐστὶ ταῦτα.

3 (34) καὶ δεσμευθέντων αὐτῶν ἐκέλευσεν ἀφορισθῆναι τὸν ἕνα, καὶ ἀχθῆναι τὸν ἄλλον εἰς θυσίαν. καὶ ἀφώρισαν παρὰ μίαν οἱ Σκύθαι τὸν Ὀρέστην· τὸν

was blind, he charged against him on horseback. Now Perseus did not know that Cepheus could not see, so he surmised that the head of the Gorgon which he held up was no longer effective. And he turned it toward himself and stared at it. And he was blinded and remained like a corpse and was killed. And thereafter the son of Perseus and Andromeda, Merros, ruled the Persians, as he was put forward by his grandfather, Cepheus, the king of Ethiopia. This man gave the command, and the abominable head of the Gorgon was burnt, and he withdrew to his own country. And thereafter the family of Perseus continued to rule the Babylonian country.

---

1 And after he received this oracle Orestes interpreted the portent; and he immediately set sail along with Pylades and came unawares to the land of Aulis in Scythia. And once they had disembarked from the vessel Orestes noticed a temple that stood about two miles from the sea, with the bones of dead men strewn all around. And [Orestes] said to Pylades, "Does this seem to you to be the house of the goddess where we have come by ship? I see the bones of dead wayfarers." And looking at him Pylades said to Orestes, "Let us flee, if we would save ourselves!" But Orestes said, "We are not fleeing, for neither have we been accustomed to flee, nor shall we abuse the oracle of the god."

2 Some herdsmen saw them and ran to Iphigenia, saying to her, "Maiden daughter of Agamemnon and Clytemnestra, two young men have arrived along the dark blue of the sea." She said to them, "From where? From what land? Do the strangers have names?" For Iphigenia asked all those who were captured and brought to sacrifice what country they were from, and then sacrificed them, since she wanted to learn about her own father Agamemnon and his family and about the war against the Phrygians and what had happened. The herdsmen said to her, "The one addressed the other as Pylades, but we don't know the name of his companion, for he did not say it." She asked them, "What do herdsmen have to do with the sea?" They said, "We came to wash our cattle in the sea water." And she sent Scythians to capture them, and they were brought bound for sacrifice, just as the exceeding wise Euripides set out the drama poetically, of which these things are a small part.

3 And once they were bound, she ordered the one to be set apart, and the other to be brought for sacrifice. And the Scythians set Orestes aside for the moment and

δὲ Πυλάδην ἤγαγον πρὸς θυσίαν παρὰ τὸν βωμὸν τῆς Ἀρτέμιδος. καὶ ἐπηρώτησεν αὐτὸν ἡ Ἰφιγένεια, ποίας ἂν εἴη χώρας. ὁ δὲ ἔφη· «χώρας μὲν Ἑλλάδος, πόλεως δὲ Μυκήνης ὁ δυστυχὴς πάρειμι». ἡ δὲ ἀκούσασα τὴν χώραν καὶ τὴν πόλιν, ἔνθα ἐβασίλευσεν ὁ αὐτῆς πατήρ, ἐδάκρυσεν. νομίσασα δέ, ὅτι ὑπὸ τῶν βουκόλων ἐδιδάχθησαν, λέγει αὐτῷ· «εἰ ἐκ Μυκήνης παρεγένου, οἶδας καὶ τίς ἐν αὐτῇ βασιλεύς». ὁ δὲ εἶπεν· «Ἀγαμέμνων ἦν πρῴην». ἡ δὲ πάλιν πρὸς αὐτόν· «εἰ τὸν Ἀγαμέμνονα ἠκρίβωσαι, τίς ἡ τούτου γυνή, καὶ τίνας ἐξ αὐτῆς παῖδας ἔσχεν;» ὁ δὲ εἶπεν· «ἔσχεν ἐκ Κλυταιμνήσρας Ὀρέστην καὶ Ἠλέκτραν καὶ Ἰφιγένειαν, ἥτις, ὡς λέγουσι, θυσία προσήχθη Ἀρτέμιδι, καὶ ἡ θεὸς ἐρρύσατο αὐτήν· καὶ οὐκ ἐγνώσθη, ποῦ ὑπάρχει. ἔσχεν δὲ καὶ Χρυσόθεμιν καὶ Λαοδίκην θυγατέρας». ἡ δὲ ἀκούσασα ταῦτα ἐκέλευσεν αὐτὸν λυθῆναι τῶν δεσμῶν· καὶ γράψασα εἰς δίπτυχον ἐπέδωκεν αὐτῷ, εἰποῦσα· «ἰδοὺ τὸ ζῆν ἡ θεός σοι παρέσχεν δι' ἐμοῦ. ἐπόμοσαι κατ' αὐτῆς, ὅτι τὸ δίπτυχον τοῦτο ἐπιδίδως τῷ Ὀρέστῃ καὶ κομίζεις μοι παρ' αὐτοῦ γράμματα». ὁ δὲ ἐπωμόσατο αὐτῇ ὅτι· «εἰς τὰς χεῖρας αὐτοῦ δίδωμι αὐτὸ καὶ πρὸς σὲ αὐτὸν φέρω». καὶ λαβὼν τὸ δίπτυχον ἐξῆλθε πρὸ τοῦ ἱεροῦ, ὅπου ἐφυλάττετο ὁ Ὀρέστης, καὶ ᾔτησε τοὺς Σκύθας λαλῆσαι αὐτῷ. καὶ ἐπιδέδωκεν αὐτῷ τὸ δίπτυχον, εἰπὼν αὐτῷ· «ἐλθὲ πρὸς τὴν σὴν ἀδελφήν». καὶ ἔμειναν οἱ Σκύθαι θαυμάζοντες τὸ συμβάν· καὶ εἰσήγαγον αὐτὸν ἅμα τῷ Πυλάδῃ πρὸς τὴν Ἰφιγένειαν. καὶ λέγει αὐτῇ ὁ Πυλάδης· «ἴδε, ὁ Ὀρέστης·» καὶ οὐκ ἐγνώρισεν αὐτόν. νομίσασα δέ, ὅτι οὐκ ἔστιν αὐτός, λέγει ὅτι· «ὁ ἐμὸς ἀδελφὸς τοῦ Πελοπείου γένους σήμαντρον ἔχει ἐλαίαν ἐν τῷ ὤμῳ». προσεσχηκυῖα δὲ ἐπὶ τὸν ὠμοπλάτην αὐτοῦ τὸν δεξιὸν εἶδε τὸ Πελόπειον σύσσημον ἔχοντα αὐτόν· καὶ περιεπτύξατο τὸν Ὀρέστην καὶ ἐκέλευσεν ἀνενεχθῆναι τὰ πλοῖα εἰς τὴν γῆν καὶ τοὺς ἐν αὐτοῖς ναύτας· καὶ νεωλκήσαντες αὐτὰ ἔμειναν ἐκεῖ τὸν χειμῶνα.

4 (35) Τοῦ δὲ θέρους καταφθάσαντος τὴν Ἰφιγένειαν καὶ τὸ ὁλόχρυσον ἄγαλμα τῆς Ἀρτέμιδος λάθρᾳ λαβὼν ὁ Ὀρέστης καὶ ὁ Πυλάδης ἔφυγον διὰ τῶν ὧν εἶχον ἰδίων πλοίων· καὶ ἀντεπέρασαν ἐπὶ τὴν χώραν τῶν Ἀδιαβηνῶν. κἀκεῖθεν ἦλθον εἰς τὴν ἀνατολὴν εἰς τὸ Σαρακηνικὸν λίμιτον· καὶ ἀνῆλθον εἰς τὴν χώραν τῆς Παλαιστίνης ἐπὶ τὴν Τρικωμίαν. καὶ προσεσχηκότες οἱ τῆς Τρικωμίας τὸ ἱερατικὸν τῆς Ἰφιγενείας σχῆμα ἐδέξαντο αὐτὴν ἐν τιμῇ· καὶ διέτριβον ἐκεῖ, τοῦ Ὀρέστου ληφθέντος ἐκεῖ καὶ μαινομένου. κτίσαντες δὲ οἱ Τρικωμῖται ἱερὸν Ἀρτέμιδος μέγα παρεκάλεσαν τὴν Ἰφιγένειαν θυσιάσαι Ἀρτέμιδι κόρην παρθένον καὶ τὸ ὄνομα αὐτῆς ἐπιθεῖναι τῇ κώμῃ· ἥντινα κόρην ὀνόματι Νύσσαν προσαγαγόντες αὐτῇ ἐποίησαν θυσίαν Ἀρτέμιδι. καὶ ποιήσαντες τῆς σφαγιασθείσης κόρης

brought Pylades for sacrifice by the altar of Artemis. And Iphigenia asked him what country he might be from. He said, "From the land of Greece and from the city of Mycenae I have come, unlucky me, to this pass." When she heard the country and the city where her father was king, she wept. Believing that they had been instructed by the herdsmen, she said to him, "If you have come from Mycenae, you know who is king there." He said, "It was till very lately Agamemnon." Again, she said to him, "If you know Agamemnon so well, who was his wife, and what children did he have from her?" He said, "He had from Clytemnestra Orestes and Electra and Iphigenia, who, as they say, was offered as a sacrifice to Artemis, and the goddess rescued her; and it is not known where she is. He also had Chrysothemis and Laodice as daughters." When she heard these things, she ordered that he be loosed from his bonds; and she wrote on a pair of tablets and gave it to him, saying, "Behold, the goddess has allowed you to live through me. Swear by her that you will give this pair of tablets to Orestes and convey to me a letter from him." He took an oath for her that "I will deliver this into his hands, and I will bring him to you." And taking the pair of tablets he went out in front of the temple, where Orestes was under guard, and asked the Scythians to speak with him. And he gave the pair of tablets to him, saying to him, "Come to your sister." The Scythians were struck with wonder at the coincidence, and they brought him in, along with Pylades, to Iphigenia. And Pylades said to her, "Look, it's Orestes," but she didn't recognize him. Thinking that it wasn't him, she said that, "My brother bears the mark of the family of Pelops, a birthmark on the shoulder." Once she inspected his right shoulder blade, however, she saw that he had the sign of Pelops, and she folded her arms around Orestes and ordered the ships and the men in them to be brought up on shore; and once they had hauled the ships up on land they remained there for the winter.

4 When summer arrived Orestes stealthily took Iphigenia and the solid gold statue of Artemis and he and Pylades fled in their own ships which they had; and they crossed over to the land of the Adiabenians. From there they went to the East, to the Saracen frontier; and they went up to the land of Palestine, to Tricomia. And when the inhabitants of Tricomia regarded the sacred mien of Iphigenia they received her with honor; and they delayed there, since Orestes was seized by his madness there. The Tricomitans, though, established a great shrine of Artemis and they called upon Iphigenia to sacrifice a virgin girl to Artemis and apply her name to the village. They brought forward a certain girl by the name of Nyssa for her and made a sacrifice to Artemis. And after they made

στήλην χαλκῆν τυχαίας, ἐκάλεσε τὴν πόλιν τὴν πρῴτην οὖσαν κώμην πόλιν Νύσσαν ἡ Ἰφιγένεια εἰς ὄνομα τῆς ὑπ᾽ αὐτῆς σφαγιασθείσης κόρης, ποιήσασα αὐτῇ καὶ βωμόν, ἐν ᾧ ἐπέγραψεν ταῦτα· «τοὺς ἐκ Σκυθίης φεύγοντας δέχνυσο, θεὰ πόα Νύσσα». ἅτινα ἕως νῦν ἐγγέγραπται.

Τοῦ δὲ Ὀρέστου ἀναλαβόντος τὰς ἰδίας φρένας ἡ Ἰφιγένεια εἶδεν ἐν ὁράματι ἔλαφον λέγουσαν αὐτῇ· «φεῦγε ἐκ τῆς χώρας ἐκείνης». καὶ ἀναστᾶσα τῷ πρωὶ ἅμα τῷ Ὀρέστῃ καὶ τῷ Πυλάδῃ ἔφυγεν ἐπὶ τὴν πάραλον τῆς Παλαιστίνης· κἀκεῖθεν ἀποπλεύσαντες ἦλθον ἐπὶ τὴν Συρίαν κατὰ τὸν χρησμόν.

5 (36) Ὁ δὲ βασιλεὺς τῆς Σκυθίας ὀνόματι Θόας ἀκούσας, ὅτι τὸ ἄγαλμα τῆς Ἀρτέμιδος τὸ ὁλόχρυσον ἔλαβεν ἡ Ἰφιγένεια καὶ ἔφυγεν, ἐξέπεμψεν Σκύθας πολλοὺς καταδιώκοντας αὐτήν, εἰρηκὼς αὐτοῖς, ὅτι· «μὴ ὑποστρέψητε εἰς τὴν Σκυθίαν, εἰ μὴ τὸ ἄγαλμα τὸ ὁλόχρυσον τῆς Ἀρτέμιδος ἀγάγητέ μοι μεθ᾽ ἑαυτῶν». οἱ δὲ καταδιώκοντες καὶ ἐπιζητήσαντες πανταχῇ ἔφθασαν τὴν Παλαιστίνην χώραν καὶ τὴν πρῴην λεγομένην Τρικωμίαν πόλιν Νύσσαν. καὶ μαθόντες, ὅτι κατῆλθον οἱ περὶ τὴν Ἰφιγένειαν καὶ τὸν Ὀρέστην ἐπὶ τὴν πάραλον [καὶ] εὐθέως ἀπέπλευσαν, τερφθέντες τῆς τοποθεσίας καὶ τῆς πόλεως Νύσσης καὶ τοῦ ἱεροῦ τῆς Ἀρτέμιδος, καὶ τὸν βασιλέα δὲ αὐτῶν φοβούμενοι, ἔμειναν αὐτοὶ ἐκεῖ οἰκοῦντες, μετακαλέσαντες τὴν πόλιν εἰς ἴδιον ὄνομα Σκυθῶν πόλιν.

9 ~ *Excerpta Latina Barbari* 1.6.6 (Garstad, *Apocalypse/Alexandrian World Chronicle*, 194)

Post haec tradidit dominus deus regnum terrae Romanorum in manus Assyriorum, Chaldaeorum, et Persarum, et Midorum. Et tributaria facta est terra illa Assyriis, et mansit Roma sine regnum, usque dum suscitavit deus Alexandrum Macedonem et conditorem. Iste quidem pugnavit contra regem Persarum et superavit eum. Et tradidit dominus in manum eius regnum Assyriorum, et introivit in potestate regnum eorum, et concussit civitates Persarum et Medorum, et liberavit omnem terram Romanorum et Grecorum et Egyptiorum de servitute Chaldeorum, et leges posuit mundo.

a bronze memorial of the slaughtered girl as a tyche, Iphigenia called the city, which had formerly been a village, the city of Nyssa after the name of the girl who had been sacrificed by her. She also raised an altar to her and wrote on it these words: "Receive those who flee from Scythia, Goddess Poa Nyssa." This inscription is there up to the present.

Once Orestes recovered his right mind Iphigenia saw in a vision a hind saying to her, "Flee from this land!" And arising early in the morning she fled along with Orestes and Pylades to the coast of Palestine. From there they sailed away and came to Syria, according to the oracle.

5 When the king of Scythia, Thoas by name, heard that Iphigenia had taken the solid gold image of Artemis and fled, he sent out many Scythians to pursue her, after telling them, "Do not return to Scythia if you do not bring the solid gold image of Artemis to me with you!" After chasing and searching everywhere they came to the land of Palestine and the city of Nyssa, formerly called Tricomia. And learning that those in the company of Iphigenia and Orestes had gone down to the coast [and] sailed straight away, since they were delighted with the situation of the city of Nyssa and the temple of Artemis and they were afraid of their king, they remained there as settlers, renaming the city after their own name Scythians' City [Scythopolis].

After these things the Lord God delivered the kingdom of the land of the Romans into the hands of the Assyrians, Chaldeans, and Persians, and Medes. And that land was made tributary to the Assyrians, and Rome remained without dominion until the time when God raised up Alexander of Macedon, the Founder. He fought against the king of the Persians and defeated him. And the Lord delivered into his hand the kingdom of the Assyrians, and he entered into power over their kingdom, and he overthrew the cities of the Persians and the Medes, and he freed the whole country of the Romans and the Greeks and the Egyptians from slavery to the Chaldeans, and he gave laws to the world.

10 ~ Malalas 6.1a (Thurn, *Ioannis Malalae Chronographia*, 117)

Ἐπὶ οὖν τῆς βασιλείας Ἰωακεὶμ βασιλέως ὁπλισάμενος κατὰ Ἰουδαίων ἀνῆλθεν Ναβουχοδονόσορ, βασιλεὺς Ἀσσυρίων· καὶ παρέλαβε τὴν Ἱερουσαλὴμ καὶ πᾶσαν τὴν γῆν τῆς Ἰουδαίας, καθὼς οἱ προφῆται προέλεγον τῷ Ἰσραήλ. καὶ ἀπήγαγε τὸν Ἰωακείμ, βασιλέα τῶν Ἰουδαίων, αἰχμάλωτον καὶ πάντα τὰ βασιλικὰ σεύη καὶ πάντας δοριαλώτους ἐποίησεν, καὶ οὐκέτι ἐβασίλευσε τῶν Ἰουδαίων οὔτε Ἱερουσαλήμ, πόλις τῆς Ἰουδαίας, οὔτε Σαμάρεια. καὶ λοιπὸν παρεδόθη ἡ βασιλεία τῶν Ἰουδαίων εἰς χεῖρας Ἀσσυρίων, καὶ ἐκυρίευσαν αὐτῶν.

11 ~ *Excerpta Latina Barbari* 1.8.1a (Garstad, *Apocalypse/Alexandrian World Chronicle*, 208)

Illi vero reges qui in Israhel et in Iudea et in Samaria finierunt, et tunc tradedit dominus deus regnum terrae in manus Assyriorum et Chaldeorum et Persarum et Midorum, et tributaria facta est eis omnis terra.

Vixit vero Nabuchodonosor iudicans omnem terram a Caspianas portas usque in Eracliae finibus et Aegyptum et omnem Iudeam, subiectos sibi faciens Pontum et totam Asiam et omnem terram Romanorum annos XVIIII.

12 ~ Malalas 7.17 (Thurn, *Ioannis Malalae Chronographia*, 144)

Μετὰ δὲ τὸ τὸν εἰρημένον Ἀρταξέρξην, βασιλέα Περσῶν, ἀποθανεῖν ἐβασίλευσεν Ὦχος, υἱὸς αὐτοῦ· ὅστις ἐπολέμησεν Αἰγυπτίοις καὶ παρέλαβε πᾶσαν τὴν γῆν Αἰγύπτου καὶ ἀπώλεσεν αὐτήν, βασιλεύοντος τῶν Αἰγυπτίων τότε τοῦ Νεκταναβώ, τοῦ ποιήσαντος λεκανομαντείαν καὶ γνόντος, ὅτι δεῖ τὸν Ὦχον, βασιλέα Περσῶν, παραλαβεῖν τὴν Αἴγυπτον. ὃς καὶ κουρευσάμενος τὴν ἰδίαν κόρην τῆς κεφαλῆς αὐτοῦ καὶ ἀλλάξας αὐτοῦ τὰ βασιλικὰ ἱμάτια ἔφυγε διὰ τοῦ Πηλουσίου ὁ αὐτος Νεκταναβώ, καὶ εἰς Πέλλην, πόλιν τῆς Μακεδονίας, διέτριβεν.

Ἐν τῷ χρόνῳ οὖν τῷ αὐτῷ ἦν τὰ κατὰ τὴν Ὀλυμπιάδα καὶ τὸν αὐτὸν Νεκταναβὼ θρυλλούμενα, ὡς διὰ χλεύης τινὸς ἐπορνεύθη ὑπ' αὐτοῦ καὶ συνέλαβε τὸν Ἀλέξανδρον, ὃν λέγουσιν ὑπὸ Διὸς Ἄμμωνος συλληφθῆναι. κατέσχεν οὖν ἡ βασιλεία τῶν Αἰγυπτίων καὶ Θηβαίων ἡ πρώτη ἔτη ͵αυϟγʹ. ταῦτα δὲ Εἰρηναῖος ὁ σοφὸς χρονογράφος ἐξέθετο.

In the reign of King Joachim, Nebuchadnezzar, the king of the Assyrians, armed himself and rose up against the Jews. And he took Jerusalem and the whole land of Judea, just as the prophets foretold to Israel. And he carried off Joachim, king of the Jews, as a prisoner and all the royal vessels and made everyone captive of his spear, and no longer did Jerusalem, the city of Judea, nor Samaria rule over the Jews. And thereafter the kingdom of the Jews was delivered into the hands of the Assyrians and they lorded it over them.

These kings who were in Israel and Judea and Samaria came to an end, and then the Lord God delivered the kingdom of the earth into the hands of the Assyrians and Chaldeans and Persians and Medes, and the whole earth was made tributary to them.

While Nebuchadnezzar lived he judged the whole earth from the Caspian Gates up to the Pillars of Hercules and Egypt and all of Judea, and made subject to himself Pontus and the whole of Asia and all the land of the Romans for nineteen years.

After the aforementioned Artaxerxes, king of the Persians, died, Ochus, his son, reigned. He made war on the Egyptians and gained possession of the whole land of Egypt and laid it waste, and Nectanebo, who then ruled the Egyptians, performed a bowl divination and learned that Ochus, king of the Persians, was bound to take possession of Egypt. And he, after he shaved the hair from his head and changed out of his kingly garments, this Nectanebo fled through Pelusium and he stayed in Pella, a city of Macedonia.

It was in that time, then, that those matters of gossip occurred in regard to Olympias and this same Nectanebo, how through a certain derisive trick she was seduced by him and conceived Alexander, who they say was conceived by Zeus Ammon. So, the first kingdom of the Egyptians and Thebans lasted for 1463 years. The wise chronographer Irenaeus explained these things.

13 ~ MALALAS 7.18B (THURN, *IOANNIS MALALAE CHRONOGRAPHIA*, 145)

. . . τότε δὲ οἱ ἀρχιερεῖς τῶν Ἰουδαίων καὶ τὸ ἔθνος ὅλον φόρους ἐδίδουν Ἀσσυρίοις. ὑπτιώθησαν δὲ τότε οἱ Ἀσσύριοι καὶ ὁ Ὦχος, βασιλεὺς αὐτῶν· καὶ ἐτυράννησαν πᾶσαν τὴν γῆν καὶ παρεδόθη ἡ βασιλεία εἰς χεῖρας Ἀσσυρίων καὶ Περσῶν καὶ Μήδων καὶ Πάρθων.

14 ~ [DUBIUM] MALALAS 7.19A (THURN, *IOANNIS MALALAE CHRONOGRAPHIA*, 145)

[Dub.] Τῆς δὲ Μακεδονίας ἐβασίλευσε Φίλιππος ἔτη κʹ. ὅστις νικήσας ὑπέταξε τὴν Θεσσαλίαν, καὶ κτίζει πόλιν εἰς τὴν Μακεδονίαν, ἣν ἐκάλεσεν Θεσσαλονίκην, τὴν πρῴην λεγομένην κώμην Θέρμας. Διονύσιος δὲ ἐξέθετο, ὅτι εἰς ὄνομα βασιλίσσης μιᾶς τοῦ γένους Φιλίππου μετὰ ταῦτα ἐκλήθη Θεσσαλονίκη. . . .

15 ~ MALALAS 7.19B (THURN, *IOANNIS MALALAE CHRONOGRAPHIA*, 145)

Καὶ μετὰ Φίλιππον ἐβασίλευσε τῆς Μακεδονίας Ἀλέξανδρος ὁ Φιλίππου. τῶν δὲ Βαβυλωνίων μετὰ τὸν Ὦχον ἐβασίλευσε Δαρεῖος ὁ Μῆδος ὁ Ἀσσαλάμου· καὶ κατεκυρίευσε πάντων.

16 ~ MALALAS 8.1–5A (THURN, *IOANNIS MALALAE CHRONOGRAPHIA*, 146–48)

1 τῷ δὲ τετάρτῳ ἔτει τῆς βασιλείας Δαρείου τοῦ Μήδου τοῦ Ἀσσαλάμου ἐξανέστησεν ὁ θεὸς τοῖς Ἀσσυρίοις καὶ Πέρσαις καὶ Πάρθοις καὶ Μήδοις Ἀλέξανδρον τὸν τῆς Μακεδονίας τοπάρχην, ἤτοι βασιλέα, τὸν Φιλίππου. ὅστις καὶ τὴν μεγάλην Ἀλεξάνδρειαν ἔκτισεν, τὴν πρῴην λεγομένην κώμην Ῥακοῦστιν· ἣν αὐτὸς ἐκάλεσεν εἰς ἴδιον ὄνομα Ἀλεξάνδρειαν, θυσιάσας κόρην παρθένον, Μακεδονίαν παρ' αὐτοῦ κληθεῖσαν. ἔκτισε δὲ καὶ ἱερὸν τῷ Σεράπι Ἡλίῳ, καὶ δημόσιον, ὃ καλεῖται ὁ Ἵππος, καὶ ἄλλα ἱερά. ὅστις βασιλεὺς Ἀλέξανδρος προτρεψάμενος ὁμόφρονας γενναίους στρατηγούς, κατὰ τῆς ἀπονοίας τῶν Ἀσσυρίων ὀργισθείς, πρῶτος παρετάξατο Δαρείῳ τῷ βασιλεῖ Περσῶν. καὶ ἐλθὼν εἰς Βυζούπολιν τῆς Εὐρώπης ἔκτισεν ἐκεῖ τόπον, ὅνπερ ἐκάλεσε

At that time the high priests of the Jews and the whole people paid tribute to the Assyrians. The Assyrians and Ochus, their king, were laid back in their haughtiness then, and they exercised a tyranny over the whole earth and the kingdom was delivered into the hands of the Assyrians and Persians and Medes and Parthians.

[Dub.] Philip reigned over Macedonia for twenty years. He conquered (*nikesas*) and subjected Thessaly and founded a city in Macedonia, which was called Thessalonica, up until then the village known as Thermae. Dionysius explained that it was called Thessalonica afterward, after the name of one of the queens from Philip's family. . . .

And after Philip, Alexander, the son of Philip, reigned over Macedonia. Darius the Mede, the son of Assalam, reigned over the Babylonians after Ochus; and he lorded it over all.

1 In the fourth year of the reign of Darius the Mede, the son of Assalam, God raised up against the Assyrians and Persians and Parthians and Medes Alexander the "toparch" of Macedonia, that is the king, the son of Philip. It was he who founded Alexandria the Great, which had previously been a village named Rhakoustis. He called it Alexandria after his own name, and sacrificed a virgin girl, called Macedonia by him. And he founded a temple to Serapis the Sun, and a *demosion*, which is called "the Horse," and other temples. This King Alexander, having persuaded a number of like-minded noble generals, because he was angered at the madness of the Assyrians, first marshaled his army against Darius, the king of the Persians. And he came to the city of Byzas [Byzantium] in Europe

τὸ Στρατήγιον· ἐκεῖ γὰρ στρατηγήσας τὰ τοῦ πολὲμου μετὰ τοῦ ἰδίου στρατοῦ καὶ τῶν συμμάχων αὐτοῦ ἐπέρασεν ἐκεῖθεν σὺν τῷ ἰδίῳ πλήθει ἄντικρυς εἰς ἐμπόριον τῆς Βιθυνίας λεγόμενον Δίσκοι. βουλόμενος δὲ προτρέψασθαι τὸ ἴδιον στράτευμα ἐρρόγευσεν αὐτοῖς ἐκεῖ πολὺν χρυσόν, καὶ μετεκάλεσε τὸ αὐτὸ ἐμπόριον Χρυσόπολιν· ὅπερ οὕτως καλεῖται ἕως τῆς νῦν. καὶ ἐξορμήσας ἐκεῖθεν ἐν τῇ Τροίᾳ ἦλθεν· καὶ ποιήσας θυσίαν εἰς τὸν τύμβον τοῦ Ἀχιλλέως ὡς ἐκ γένους αὐτοῦ καταγόμενος, ᾔτησε τὸ πνεῦμα αὐτοῦ συμμαχεῖν αὐτῷ ἐν τῷ πολέμῳ. ἐκ τοῦ γὰρ Μολοσσοῦ τοῦ υἱοῦ Πύρρου καὶ τῆς Ἀνδρομάχης κατήχθη ἡ Ὀλυμπιὰς ἡ μήτηρ τοῦ αὐτοῦ Ἀλεξάνδρου τοῦ Μακεδόνος. καὶ εὐθέως ὡς πάρδαλις ἐκεῖθεν ὁρμήσας ὁ Ἀλέξανδρος, ἅμα τοῖς σὺν αὐτῷ στρατηγοῖς παρέλαβε πάσας τὰς χώρας. καὶ νικήσας τὸν Δαρεῖον, βασιλέα Περσῶν, τὸν Ἀσσαλάμου, παρέλαβεν αὐτὸν καὶ πᾶσαν τὴν βασιλείαν αὐτοῦ καὶ πᾶσαν τὴν χώραν Ἀσσυρίων καὶ Μήδων καὶ Πάρθων καὶ Βαβυλωνίων καὶ Περσῶν καὶ πάσας τὰς βασιλείας τῆς γῆς, καθὼς Βόττιος ὁ σοφώτατος συνεγράψατο, ἐλευθερώσας ὁ αὐτὸς Ἀλέξανδρος καὶ τὰς πόλεις καὶ τὰς χώρας καὶ πᾶσαν τὴν γῆν τῶν Ῥωμαίων καὶ Ἑλλήνων καὶ Αἰγυπτίων ἐκ τῆς Ἀσσυρίων καὶ Περσῶν καὶ Πάρθων καὶ Μήδων ὑποταγῆς καὶ δουλείας, ἀποδοὺς Ῥωμαίοις πάντα ἃ ἀπώλεσαν.

[(2) γίνεται οὖν ἀπὸ Ἀδὰμ ἕως τῆς Ἀλεξάνδρου τοῦ Μακεδόνος νίκης ἔτη ͵εφνζʹ. ἦν δὲ τοτε ἀρχιερεὺς τῶν Ἰουδαίων ὁ Ἀδδούς.]

2 (3) ἐλύθη δὲ τότε τὰ Περσικὰ μέρη καὶ τὰ βασίλεια αὐτῆς καὶ κατεδυνάστευσαν οἱ Μακεδόνες καὶ Ἀλέξανδρος μετὰ τῶν ἅμα αὐτῷ συμμάχων τῆς γῆς Χαλδαίων καὶ Μήδων καὶ Περσῶν καὶ Πάρθων· καὶ νικήσαντες καὶ φονεύσαντες τὸν Δαρεῖον εἰσῆλθον εἰς τὰ βασίλεια τοῦ αὐτοῦ Δαρείου. καὶ ἐνομοθέτησεν ὁ αὐτὸς Ἀλέξανδρος τὴν χώραν αὐτῶν καὶ ἐβασίλευσεν αὐτῶν· καὶ ἤγειραν αὐτῷ οἱ Πέρσαι στήλην ἔφιππον χαλκῆν εἰς Βαβυλῶνα, ἥτις ἵσταται ἕως τῆς νῦν.

Ὁ δὲ αὐτὸς Ἀλέξανδρος τὴν θυγατέρα Δαρείου τοῦ βασιλέως Περσῶν Ῥωξάνην λαβὼν αἰχμάλωτον, παρθένον οὖσαν, ἠγάγετο εἰς γυναῖκα. παρέλαβεν δὲ καὶ πάντα τὰ Ἰνδικὰ μέρη καὶ τὰ βασίλεια αὐτῶν ὁ αὐτὸς Ἀλέξανδρος, λαβὼν καὶ Πῶρον τὸν βασιλέα Ἰνδῶν αἰχμάλωτον· καὶ τὰ ἄλλα πάντα τὰ τῶν ἐθνῶν βασίλεια δίχα τῆς βασιλείας τῆς Κανδάκης τῆς χήρας τῆς βασιλευούσης τῶν ἐνδοτέρων Ἰνδῶν· ἥτις συνελάβετο τὸν αὐτὸν Ἀλέξανδρον τῷ τρόπῳ τούτῳ.

3 Ἔθος εἶχεν ὁ αὐτὸς Ἀλέξανδρος μετὰ τῶν πεμπομένων παρ᾽ αὐτοῦ πρεσβευτῶν πρὸς τοὺς ἐναντίους βασιλεῖς εἰσέρχεσθαι ἐν σχήματι στρατιώτου καὶ ὁρᾶν

and established a place there which he called the Strategion; for there, after he had marshaled (*strategesas*) his preparations for war with his own army and his comrades [*or* allies], he crossed from there with his host straight to the trading station of Bithynia named Diskoi. Wishing to encourage his army he issued to them there a great deal of gold, and this same trading station was renamed Chrysopolis; which it is called up to the present. And he set out from there and came to Troy. And he made a sacrifice at the tomb of Achilles, since he was descended from his line, by which he sought his spirit to fight alongside him in the war. For Olympias, the mother of this Alexander of Macedon, was descended from Molossus the son of Pyrrhus and Andromache. And at once Alexander rushed forth from that place like a leopard, he and his generals along with him, and captured all the countries. Once he had defeated Darius, the king of the Persians, the son of Assalam, he captured him and his whole kingdom and the whole territory of the Assyrians and Medes and Parthians and Babylonians and Persians and all the kingdoms of the earth, as the most learned Bouttios has written, and this Alexander freed the cities and the territories and the whole country of the Romans and the Greeks and the Egyptians from subjection and slavery to the Assyrians and Persians and Parthians and Medes, returning to the Romans all that they had lost.

[So, there were from Adam up to the victory of Alexander of Macedon 5557 years. The high priest of the Jews was at that time Addous.]

2 At that time the Persian realms and their kingdoms were undone and the Macedonians and Alexander, together with his comrades, dominated the land of the Chaldaeans and Medes and Persians and Parthians. And when they had defeated and killed Darius they came into the kingdom of this Darius. And this Alexander bestowed laws upon their land and ruled over them. And the Persians raised to him an equestrian monument in bronze at Babylon, which still stands to the present.

This Alexander took the daughter of Darius the king of the Persians, Roxane, prisoner, and, as she was a virgin, took her to wife. This same Alexander came into possession of all the regions of India and their kingdoms, and took Porus, the king of the Indians, prisoner, and all of the other kingdoms of the nations, with the exception of the kingdom of the widow Candace, who reigned over the Inner Indians. This woman took Alexander himself captive in the following manner.

3 This Alexander had a habit of going along with the ambassadors he sent to opposing kings in the guise of a private soldier and seeing what kind of man

ὁποῖός ἐστιν ὁ βασιλεὺς ἐκεῖνος. ἡ δὲ Κανδάκη βασίλισσα μαθοῦσα τοῦτο περιειργάσατο ὁποίας ἐστὶ θέας καὶ τί ἔχει σύσσημον. καὶ ἐρρέθη αὐτῇ, ὅτι ἐστὶ χθαμαλός, ὀδόντας ἔχων μεγάλους καὶ φαινομένους, ἔχων δὲ ὀφθαλμὸν γλαυκὸν ἕνα καὶ ἕνα μέλανα. καὶ ἐσημειώσατο καθ᾽ ἑαυτὴν ταῦτα· καὶ εἰσελθόντα πρὸς αὐτὴν ἅμα τοῖς πεμφθεῖσι παρ᾽ αὐτοῦ πρεσβευταῖς γνωρίσασα οὖν αὐτὸν ἐκ τῶν συσσημάτων, συνέσχεν αὐτὸν καὶ εἶπεν αὐτῷ· «Ἀλέξανδρε βασιλεῦ, τὸν κόσμον ὅλον παρέλαβες· καὶ γυνή σε μία παρέλαβεν». ὁ δὲ Ἀλέξανδρος εἶπεν αὐτῇ· «διὰ τὸ σπουδαῖον καὶ περίεργον τῆς φρονήσεώς σου ἀβλαβῆ σε φυλάξω καὶ τὴν σὴν γῆν καὶ τοὺς σοὺς υἱεῖς, ἀγάγωμαι δέ σε καὶ εἰς γυναῖκα». ἥτις Κανδάκη ἀκούσασα δέδωκεν ἑαυτήν· ὁ δὲ Ἀλέξανδρος εὐθέως ἔλαβεν αὐτὴν μεθ᾽ ἑαυτοῦ καὶ εἰσῆλθεν ἐπὶ τὴν Αἰθιοπίαν καὶ εἰς ἄλλας χώρας.

4 Μέλλων δὲ τελευτᾶν ὁ αὐτὸς Ἀλέξανδρος διετάξατο, ὥστε πάντας τοὺς σὺν αὐτῷ ὑπερασπιστὰς καὶ συμμάχους βασιλεύειν τῆς αὐτῆς χώρας ὅπου ἦν αὐτοὺς ἐάσας καὶ κρατεῖν τῶν ἐκεῖσε τόπων. ἔζησεν δὲ ὁ αὐτὸς Ἀλέξανδρος ἔτη λς′, ἐβασίλευσε δὲ ὑποτάξας τὰ πάντα ἔτη ιζ′, ὁ δὲ πόλεμος αὐτοῦ ἐκράτησεν ἔτη θ′, ὑπέταξε δὲ βαρβάρων ἔθνη κβ′, Ἑλλήνων φυλὰς ιγ′, καὶ ἔκτισε πόλεις αὐτὸς καὶ οἱ μετ᾽ αὐτοῦ πολλάς.

[(4) Ἔστιν οὖν ἀπὸ Ἀδὰμ ἕως τῆς τελευτῆς Ἀλεξάνδρου τοῦ Μακεδόνος ἔτη ͵εφϟγ′, καθὼς συνεγράψατο Θεόφιλος ὁ χρονογράφος.]

(5) Μετὰ οὖν τὴν τελευτὴν Ἀλεξάνδρου τοῦ Μακεδόνος ἐμερίσθησαν εἰς τέσσαρας τοπαρχίας, ἤτοι βασιλείας, αἱ χῶραι ἃς ὑπέταξεν ὁ αὐτὸς Ἀλέξανδρος ἅμα τοῖς συμμάχοις αὐτοῦ· καὶ ἐβασίλευσαν αὐτῶν οἱ Μακεδόνες οἱ συνασπισταὶ τοῦ αὐτοῦ Ἀλεξάνδρου καθὼς διετάξατο οὕτως.

17 ~ *Excerpta Latina Barbari* 1.8.4a (Garstad, *Apocalypse/Alexandrian World Chronicle*, 214)

In his temporibus Ochus rex Persarum et Midorum proeliavit in Egyptum. <. . . Nectabo>[1] novissumus Farao regni Egypti, et cognoscens quia cessavit fortitudo Egyptiorum, capud suum radens et mutans vestimenta sua alio specie fugiit per Piluseum, et relinquens proprium regnum in Macedonia moratus ibidem astrologica arte didicebatur.

1 There is a lacuna before *novissimus.*

that king was. When Queen Candace learned of this, she concerned herself with what sort of appearance he had and what recognizable features he had. And it was reported to her that he was short, had large and noticeable teeth, and had one gray eye and one black. And she made a note of these things for herself, and when he came to her along with the ambassadors he sent, she knew him by his features and arrested him, and she said to him, "King Alexander, you have captured the whole world, but a single woman has captured you." And Alexander said to her, "Because your intelligence has been earnest and exceedingly careful, I shall keep you unmolested, as well as your people and your sons, and I shall take you to wife." When Candace heard this, she surrendered herself; and Alexander immediately took her with him and entered Ethiopia and other countries.

4 When he was about to die, this Alexander commanded all the champions and comrades who accompanied him to reign over the countries where he left them and to rule the places there. This Alexander lived for thirty-six years, and reigned, conquering all things, for seventeen years, and his conflict lasted for nine years; he conquered twenty-two barbarian nations and thirteen Greek tribes, and he founded many cities, he and those with him.

[So there are from Adam up to the death of Alexander the Macedonian 5,593 years, as the chronographer Theophilus has written.]

After the death of Alexander the Macedonian the lands which this Alexander, together with his comrades, made subject were divided into four toparchies, or kingdoms; and the Macedonians that had been the shield-fellows of this Alexander reigned over them thus, just as he commanded.

In these times Ochus the king of the Persians and Medes made war on Egypt. . . . [Nectanebo], the last Pharaoh of the kingdom of Egypt, and recognizing that the strength of the Egyptians had failed, he shaved his head and changed his clothes to take on a different appearance and fled through Pelusium, and abandoning his own kingdom he dwelt in Macedonia, and there he taught the art of astrology.

18 ~ *Excerpta Latina Barbari* 1.8.4c (Garstad, *Apocalypse/ Alexandrian World Chronicle*, 214–16)

[Post hunc autem regnavit in Babyloniam Darius Midus ille Alsami annos VI: fiunt simul anni V milia CXXVIIII. Istum deposuit Alexander Macedo et conditor. Fuit autem princeps sacerdotum Iaddus.]

Tunc Alexander Macedo et conditor, postquam legem poneret in Ellada et omnem Romanorum terram Syriam quoque et Egyptum et partes Lybiae, tunc venit in partes orientales et expugnans omnes civitates et oppida gentium obsedit regem Persarum Darium. Et tradidit dominus deus in manus eius Darium et omnem fortitudinem eius disperdit et omnem domum eius scrutavit.

Et dominavit Alexander Macedo et conditor omnem terram Chaldeorum et introivit in omnem fortitudinem Darii et legem posuit in omnes civitates eius, et tributarii facti sunt ei sicut proprio regi.

Ut enim condidit Alexander Alexandriam contra Egyptum, veniens in Hierusolima domino deo adoravit dicens: Gloria tibi, deus solus omnia tenens, qui vivis in saecula. Fuit autem tunc in Hierusalem princeps sacerdotum Iaddus.

19 ~ *Excerpta Latina Barbari* 2.6.4 (Garstad, *Apocalypse/ Alexandrian World Chronicle*, 264)

VI. Post hunc Iaddus filius Iohanni.

Quo tempore Alexander Macedo et conditor Alexandriam condidit. Et veniens in Hierusalem domino deo adoravit dicens: Gloria tibi, deus, qui vivis in secula, solus princeps.

20 ~ *Excerpta Latina Barbari* 1.8.4d–6 (Garstad, *Apocalypse/ Alexandrian World Chronicle*, 216–20)

1 [Regnavit autem Alexander Macedo et conditor post Darium Midorum Alsami filium annos VIII: fiunt simul ab Adam usque ad finem Alexandri conditori anni V milia CXXXVII, et tunc Ptolemei.]

(8.5) In diebus vero quibus regnavit Alexander Macedo et conditor, postquam superavit Darium regem Persarum, et Porum regem Indorum et omnes gentes

[After him Darius the Mede, the son of Arsames, reigned in Babylon for 6 years: altogether this makes 5,129 years. Alexander the Macedonian, the Founder, deposed him. The high priest was Jaddua.]

Then Alexander the Macedonian, the Founder, after he bestowed law upon Greece and all the land of the Romans and Syria as well and Egypt and parts of Libya, then went into the eastern regions and storming all the cities and towns of the nations he besieged Darius, the king of the Persians. And the Lord God delivered Darius into his hands and wrecked all his strength and searched out his whole house.

And Alexander the Macedonian, the Founder, dominated all the land of the Chaldaeans and entered into the whole strength of Darius and imposed law in all his cities, and they were made tributary to him as to their rightful king.

For once Alexander founded Alexandria over against Egypt he came to Jerusalem and worshipped the Lord God, saying, "Glory to you, Only God, grasping all things, who liveth unto the ages." The high priest in Jerusalem was Jaddus.

6. After him Jaddus the son of John,

In which time Alexander the Macedonian, the Founder, founded Alexandria. And he came to Jerusalem and worshipped the Lord God, saying, "Glory to you, God, who liveth unto the ages, Only Prince."

1 [Alexander the Macedonian, the Founder, reigned after Darius the Mede, the son of Arsames, for 8 years: altogether this makes from Adam up to the end of Alexander the Founder 5,137 years, and then there were the Ptolemies.]

In the days when Alexander the Macedonian, the Founder, reigned, after he defeated Darius the king of the Persians he conquered Porus the king of the

subiugavit a Caspiacas portas quae sunt in ortu solis usque in exteriores terminos Eraclii qui iacent in exteriores occidentis partibus contra Garirum.

2 Veniens ad mortem Alexander testamentum scripsit, ut unusquisque principum Alexandri regnarent singuli in proprias eorum provincias, sicut imperavit eis Alexander, sic.

Macedonia quidem Arideum quem et Filippum praecepit regnare.

Ponton autem Leona dixit regnare.

Paflagonia autem et Cappadocia Eumenium scriba memoratum praeordinavit regnare.

Insulanos autem dimisit liberos, et procuratores ac dispensatores eorum esse Rodios.

Pamphilia et Lucya Antigonum ordinavit regnare.

Frigiam autem et illam magnam Caesariam Deasandro tradidit.

Cilicia autem et Isauria et omnia circuita eius Filone ordinavit.

Syriam autem usque Mesopotamiam dedit Tapithone ut regnaret.

Syriam vero Cylem vocatum, Fynicem autem interpraetatam, Meleagrom ordinavit dominare.

Babylonia autem Seleucum praecepit regnare.

Egyptum autem et quae circa eum usque superiore Lybia Filippo qui vocabatur Ptolomeus donavit.

Quae autem de superiore Babylone usque Caspiacas portas, principes quidem in ea et satrapes, archistratigum autem eorum Perdicum ordinavit.

(8.6) India autem qui extendit circa Ydastem fluvium Taxio dedit regnare.

India autem qui dicitur sub Indo et usque Ydastem fluvium extendens Pythonae dominare praecepit.

Super Parapannisodum autem Oxydarcum ordinavit regnare.

Arachusia autem et Cedrusia Sybartum ordinavit regnare.

Arabiam autem totam Stasanoro donavit.

Et Ogdianiam Filippo minori dedit dominare.

Illam autem qui circuit contra aquilonis partes et illam qui habet Yrcaniam Antigono donavit regnare.

Germaniam autem totam Tripolemo donavit.

Persidam autem totam Perco donavit.

Indians and all the peoples from the Caspian Gates, which are at the rising of the sun, all the way to the outer Pillars of Hercules, which are in the outer regions of the West opposite Gadeira.

2 As he was approaching death Alexander wrote his will, so that every one of the captains of Alexander should rule, each in his own separate province, just as Alexander commanded them, thus:

He ordered Arrhidaeus, who is also called Philip, to rule Macedonia.

He told Leon [Leonnatus] to rule Pontus.

He arranged beforehand for Eumenes, the famous scribe [*or* his secretary], to rule Paphlagonia and Cappadocia.

He released the islanders as free men, and [ordered] the Rhodians to be their managers and stewards.

He appointed Antigonus to rule Pamphylia and Lycia.

He handed Phrygia and Great Caesarea [Caria] over to Asander.

He disposed of Cilicia and Isauria and all the surrounding territory to Philo.

Syria as far as Mesopotamia he gave to Pithon, that he might rule it.

He appointed Meleager to be lord of Syria, which is called Coele ["Hollow"], which is understood as Phoenicia.

He ordered Seleucus to rule Babylon.

Egypt and the surrounding regions as far as upper Libya he gave to Philip who was called Ptolemy.

The regions from upper Babylon as far as the Caspian Gates, the chief men in them and the satraps, he appointed Perdiccas their general.

He gave India which stretches to the river Hydaspes to Taxiles to rule.

He ordered Pytho to be lord of India which is called "under the Indus" and stretches as far as the river Hydaspes.

He commanded Oxydraces to rule over Paropanisadae.

He commanded Sibyrtius to rule Arachosia and Cedrosia.

He gave the whole of Arabia to Stasanor.

And he gave Sogdiana to Philip the Less to govern.

The region which encloses the parts to the North and the region which contains Hyrcania he granted to Antigonus to rule.

He gave the whole of Germany [Carmania] to Tlepolemus.

He gave the whole of Persia to Percus [Peucestas].

Spaniam autem usque Alyo fluvio et Eracleoticum terminum Antipalum ordinavit regnare.

Sic uero statuit et donavit Alexander suis principibus, et unusquisque eorum sic regnaverunt, sicut ipse disposuerat.

3 Vixit autem Alexander annos XXXVI. Regnavit quidem annos XVII sic: pugnavit enim annos VIIII usque dum factus est annorum XXVIII, illos autem alios octo annos vixit in pace et securitate. Subiugavit autem gentes barbaras XXII et Grecorum tribus XIII. Condidit autem Alexander civitates XII, qui usque nunc inhabitantur:

Alexander qui in Pentapolim, Alexandriam qui in Aegyptum, Alexandriam qui ad Arpam, Alexandriam qui Cabosium, Alexandriam Scythiam in Egeis, Alexandriam qui in Poro, Alexandriam qui super Cypridum fluvium, Alexandriam qui in Troada, Alexandriam qui in Babylonia, Alexandriam qui in Mesasgyges, Alexandriam qui in Persida, Alexandriam fortissimam, et mortuus est.

21 ~ Malalas 8.12 (Thurn, *Ioannis Malalae Chronographia*, 151–52)

Καὶ ἐν τῇ πόλει ἐλθὼν Ἀντιγονίᾳ τῇ κτισθείσῃ ὑπὸ Ἀντιγόνου τοῦ Πολιορκητοῦ (ἀπὸ γὰρ τῆς λίμνης ἐξερχομένου ἄλλου ποταμοῦ Ἀρκευθᾶ τοῦ καὶ Ἰάφθα ἐμεσάζετο ἡ πόλις Ἀντιγονία καὶ ἐν ἀσφαλείᾳ ἐκαθέζετο) καὶ ποιήσας ἐκεῖ θυσίαν τῷ Διὶ εἰς τοὺς βωμοὺς τοὺς ἀπὸ Ἀντιγόνου κτισθέντας ἔκοψε τὰ κρέα· καὶ ηὔξατο ἅμα τῷ ἱερεῖ Ἀμφίονι μαθεῖν διαδιδομένου σημείου, εἰ τὴν αὐτὴν ὀφείλει οἰκῆσαι πόλιν Ἀντιγονίαν μετονομάζων ἢ οὐκ ὀφείλει αὐτὴν οἰκῆσαι, ἀλλὰ κτίσαι πόλιν ἄλλην ἐν ἄλλῳ τόπῳ. καὶ ἐξαίφνης ἐκ τοῦ ἀέρος κατῆλθεν ἀετὸς μέγας καὶ ἐπῆρεν ἐκ τοῦ βωμοῦ τοῦ πυρὸς τῆς ὁλοκαυτώσεως κρέα καὶ ἀπῆλθεν παρὰ τὸ ὄρος τὸ Σίλπιον. καὶ καταδιώξας ἅμα τοῖς αὐτοῦ εὗρε τὸ κρέας τὸ ἱερατικὸν καὶ τὸν ἀετὸν ἐπάνω ἑστῶτα. τοῦ δὲ ἱερέως καὶ τῶν ὀρνεοσκόπων καὶ τοῦ αὐτοῦ Σελεύκου ἑωρακότων τὸ θαῦμα εἶπον ὅτι· «ἐνταῦθα δεῖ ἡμᾶς οἰκῆσαι, ἐν τῇ δὲ Ἀντιγονίᾳ οὐ δεῖ ἡμᾶς οἰκῆσαι οὔτε δὲ γενέσθαι αὐτὴν πόλιν, ὅτι οὐ βούλονται τὰ θεῖα». καὶ λοιπὸν ἐβουλεύετο ἅμα αὐτοῖς, ἐν ποίῳ τόπῳ ἀσφαλῆ ποιήσει τὴν πόλιν. καὶ φοβηθεὶς τὰς ῥύσεις τοῦ Σιλπίου ὄρους καὶ τοὺς κατερχομένους ἐξ αὐτοῦ χειμάρρους ἐν τῇ πεδιάδι τοῦ αὐλῶνος κατέναντι τοῦ ὄρους πλησίον τοῦ Δράκοντος ποταμοῦ τοῦ μεγάλου τοῦ μετακληθέντος Ὀρόντου, ὅπου ἦν ἡ κώμη ἡ καλουμένη Βωττία ἄντιρκυς τῆς Ἰωπόλεως,

He ordered Antipater to rule Spain as far as the river Halys and the boundary of Hercules.

Thus indeed did Alexander decide and grant gifts to his captains, and each of them ruled just as he had arranged.

3 Alexander lived for thirty-six years. He ruled for seventeen years in this way: he fought for nine years until he came to the age of twenty-eight years, and he lived the other eight years in peace and security. He subdued twenty-two barbarian peoples and thirteen tribes of the Greeks. Alexander founded twelve cities, which are inhabited up to the present:

Alexandria in Pentapolis, Alexandria in Egypt, Alexandria near Harpas, Alexandria Cabiosa, Scythian Alexandria among the Aegaeans, Alexandria in Porus, Alexandria on the river Cypris, Alexandria in the Troad, Alexandria in Babylonia, Alexandria among the Messagetae, Alexandria in Persia, Alexandria the Strongest, and he died.

And he [Seleucus Nicator] came to the city of Antigonia, founded by Antigonos the Besieger (for the city of Antigonia occupies a place in the midst of another river, the Arceuthas, or Iaphtha, and is securely situated) and made there a sacrifice to Zeus at the altars established by Antigonus and cut the meat into pieces; and along with the priest Amphion he prayed to learn by a sign granted whether he was bound to rename the city of Antigonia and settle there or not bound to settle there, but to found another city in another place. And suddenly a great eagle came down out of the air and snatched up some of the meat of the burnt offering from out of the altar fire and went away to Mount Silpius. And giving chase along with his attendants he found the consecrated meat and the eagle standing above it. Once the priest and the bird augurs and Seleucus himself had seen the marvel they said, "We ought to settle here, we should not settle in Antigonia nor should it be made a city, since the divine powers do not wish it." And furthermore, he took counsel with them as to in what sort of place he might make the city secure. And wary of the streams of Mount Silpius and the winter torrents coming down from it, on the level ground of the glen opposite the mountain by the mighty River Dracon, renamed the Orontes, where the village of Bottia was, across from

ἐκεῖ διεχάραξαν τὰ θεμέλια τοῦ τείχους, θυσιάσας δι' Ἀμφίονος ἀρχιερέως καὶ τελεστοῦ κόρην παρθένον ὀνόματι Αἰμάθην κατὰ μέσου τῆς πόλεως καὶ τοῦ ποταμοῦ μηνὶ ἀρτεμισίῳ τῷ καὶ μαΐῳ κβ', ὥρᾳ ἡμερινῇ α', τοῦ ἡλίου ἀνατέλλοντος, καλέσας αὐτὴν Ἀντιόχειαν εἰς ὄνομα τοῦ ἰδίου αὐτοῦ υἱοῦ τοῦ λεγομένου Ἀντιόχου Σωτῆρος, κτίσας εὐθέως καὶ ἱερόν, ὃ ἐκάλεσε Βωττίου Διός, ἀνεγείρας καὶ τὰ τείχη σπουδαίως φοβερὰ διὰ Ξεναρίου ἀρχιτέτονος, στήσας ἀνδριάντος στήλην χαλκῆν τῆς σφαγιασθείσης κόρης τύχην τῇ πόλει ὑπεράνω τοῦ ποταμοῦ, εὐθέως ποιήσας αὐτῇ τῇ τύχῃ θυσίαν.

22 ~ [Dubium] Malalas 8.13 (Thurn, *Ioannis Malalae Chronographia*, 152)

[Dub.] Καὶ ἀπελθὼν κατέστρεψεν τὴν Ἀντιγονίαν πόλιν πᾶσαν ἕως ἐδάφους, μετενεγκὼν καὶ τὰς ὕλας ἐκεῖθεν διὰ τοῦ ποταμοῦ καὶ ποιήσας καὶ τῇ τύχῃ Ἀντιγονίᾳ ἀνδριάντα στήλης χαλκῆς ἐχούσης Ἀμαλθείας κέρας ἔμπροσθεν αὐτῆς. καὶ ποιήσας ἐκεῖ τετρακιονιν ἐν ὕψει ἔστησεν αὐτὴν τὴν τύχην, καταστήσας ἔμπροσθεν αὐτῆς βωμὸν ὑψηλόν· ἥντινα στήλην τῆς τύχης μετὰ τελευτὴν Σελεύκου Δημήτριος ὁ υἱὸς Ἀντιγόνου τοῦ Πολιορκητοῦ ἀπήγαγεν ἐν Ῥώσῳ ἐν τῇ πόλει τῆς Κιλικίας. ἡ δὲ αὐτὴ πόλις Ῥῶσος ἐκτίσθη ὑπὸ Κίλικος τοῦ υἱοῦ Ἀγήνορος.

23 ~ Malalas 8.17 (Thurn, *Ioannis Malalae Chronographia*, 153)

Ἔκτισε δὲ ὁ αὐτὸς Σέλευκος ὁ Νικάτωρ καὶ ἄλλην παραλίαν πόλιν ἐν τῇ Συρίᾳ ὀνόματι Λαοδίκειαν εἰς ὄνομα τῆς αὐτοῦ θυγατρός, πρῴην οὖσαν κώμην ὀνόματι Μαζαβδάν, ποιήσας κατὰ τὸ ἔθος θυσίαν τῷ Διὶ καὶ αἰτησάμενος ποῦ κτίσει τὴν πόλιν ἦλθεν ἀετὸς πάλιν καὶ ἥρπασεν ἀπὸ τῆς θυσίας· καὶ ἐν τῷ καταδιώκειν αὐτὸν τὸν ἀετὸν ὑπήντησεν αὐτῷ σύαγρος μέγας ἐξελθὼν ἀπὸ καλαμῶνος, ὅντινα ἀνεῖλεν ᾧτινι κατεῖχε δόρατι· καὶ φονεύσας τὸν σύαγρον

Iopolis, there he[2] staked out the foundations of the wall, and through the agency of Amphion the high priest and officiant of the mysteries he sacrificed a virgin girl by the name of Aimathe in the space between the city and the river on the 22nd of Artemisios, or May, at the first hour of the day, as the sun was rising. He called [the city] after the name of his own son who was called Antiochus Soter. And he straightway established a temple, which he called that of Zeus Bottios. And he swiftly raised the tremendous walls through the agency of Xenarios the architect. He set up a bronze monument in the form of a statue of the maiden who had been offered as a sacrifice as the tyche of the city above the river, and at once he made a sacrifice to her as the tyche.

....

[Dub.] And he went off and demolished the whole city of Antigonia right down to its foundations, transporting the materials from there by river, and made a statue for the tyche of Antigonia, a bronze memorial having a horn of Amaltheia before it. And he made a shrine with four pillars there and set the tyche on a height and placed a high altar in front of her. After the death of Seleucus, Demetrius the son of Antigonus the Besieger carried off this memorial of the tyche to Rhosus, the city of Cilicia. This city of Rhosus was founded by Cilix the son of Agenor.

....

This same Seleucus Nicator founded another coastal city in Syria by the name of Laodicea after the name of his daughter, which had formerly been a village by the name of Mazabda; while he was according to custom making a sacrifice to Zeus and enquiring where he should found the city an eagle came again and grabbed some of the sacrifice; and in the pursuit of this eagle a great wild boar met him as it was breaking from a reed bed, and he killed it with the spear which he was

2 Here I have followed Jacoby's emendation of διεχάραξαν to διεχάραξεν noted by Thurn, *Ioannis Malalae Chronographia*, 151; otherwise there is no main verb for the singular participles.

καὶ σύρας τὸ λείψανον αὐτοῦ ἐκ τοῦ αἵματος αὐτοῦ διεχάραξε τὰ τείχη, ἐάσας τὸν ἀετόν· καὶ οὕτως τὴν αὐτὴν πόλιν ἔκτισεν ἐπάνω τοῦ αἵματος τοῦ συάγρου, θυσιάσας κόρην ἀδαῆ ὀνόματι Ἀγαύην, ποιήσας αὐτῇ στήλην χαλκῆν εἰς τύχην τῆς αὐτῆς πόλεως.

24 ~ Malalas 8.18a (Thurn, *Ioannis Malalae Chronographia*, 154)

Ἔκτισε δὲ ὁ αὐτὸς Σέλευκος ὁ Νικάτωρ καὶ ἄλλην πόλιν εἰς τὴν Συρίαν μεγάλην εἴς ὄνομα τῆς αὐτοῦ θυγατρὸς Ἀπάμας, εὑρηκὼς κώμην πρῴην λεγομένην Φαρνάκην· καὶ τειχίσας αὐτὴν ὁ αὐτὸς Σέλευκος ἐπωνόμασε πόλιν, καλέσας αὐτὴν Ἀπάμειαν, θυσίαν ποιήσας <κόρην,>[3] ἣν αὐτὸς μετεκάλεσεν ὀνόματι Πέλλαν διὰ τὸ ἔχειν τὴν τύχην τῆς αὐτῆς Ἀπαμείας πόλεως τὸ ὄνομα τοῦτο· ἦν γὰρ αὐτὸς Σέλευκος ἀπὸ Πέλλης τῆς πόλεως Μακεδονίας. ἐποίησε δὲ θυσίαν ταῦρον καὶ τράγον· καὶ ἐλθὼν πάλιν ὁ ἀετὸς ἐπῆρεν τὰς κεφαλὰς τοῦ ταύρου καὶ τοῦ τράγου· καὶ περιεχάραξεν ἐκ τοῦ αἵματος τὰ τείχη.

3 I have modified the punctuation and added the word κόρην to Thurn's text, which reads: θυσίαν ποιήσας· ἣν αὐτὸς. This makes the founding of Apamea another instance of tyche sacrifice. While most accounts of tyche sacrifice indicate this event itself with some form of the verb θυσιάζω taking κόρην as its object, in the story of Zarbas sacrificing a girl at the refoundation of Diocaesarea as Anazarbus (**F 30**) the phrase ποιήσας δὲ θυσίαν κόρην is employed, which provides a parallel for the emendation here. The emendation does away with the inexplicable sense of the received text, which seems to have Seleucus rename a city Pella that he has only just renamed Apamea. The revised reading has him rename the sacrificed girl, the tyche of the city, Pella, not the city of Apamea. The girl sacrificed to be the tyche of Alexandria, whom Alexander called Macedonia (**F 16.1**), offers a parallel to Seleucus naming the girl Pella, inasmuch as in both cases the sacrificing founder gives the victim a name derived from his own country of origin, the land of Macedonia. Cf. Ogden, *Legend of Seleucus*, 113–14, 135.

carrying. Once he had slain the boar, he trailed its remains after him and marked out the walls with its blood, and he left the eagle. In this way he founded this city over the blood of the boar, and he sacrificed an innocent girl by the name of Agave, making a bronze memorial to her as the tyche of the city.

This same Seleucus Nicator founded another city in Great Syria named after his daughter Apama, when he came upon the village formerly known as Pharnace. Seleucus walled it and named the city, calling it Apamea, and he made a sacrifice <of a maiden,> whom he renamed with the name of Pella, because the tyche of this city of Apamea had this name; for this Seleucus was from the Macedonian city of Pella. He also made a sacrifice of a bull and a billygoat; and again, the eagle came and snatched the heads of the bull and the billygoat and marked about the walls with the blood.

25 ⁓ Malalas 9.13a (Thurn, *Ioannis Malalae Chronographia*, 168)

Τὴν δὲ Γαλατίαν ὑπέταξεν ὁ αὐτὸς Αὔγουστος ὁ καὶ Ὀκταουϊανὸς νικήσας Δηιόταρον, τετράρχην αὐτῆς· καὶ τειχίσας κώμην τὴν λεγομένην Ἀρσίνην ἐποίησε πόλιν, ἥντινα ἐκάλεσεν Ἄγκυραν διὰ τὸ μέσην αὐτὴν εἶναι δύο θαλασσῶν, τῆς τε Ποντικῆς καὶ τῆς Ἀσιανῆς θαλάσσης. θυσιάσας δὲ κόρην παρθένον ὀνόματι Γρηγορίαν εἰς ἀποκαθαρισμόν, ποιήσας αὐτὴν ἐπαρχίαν, ἐάσας ἐκεῖ Γάλλους στρατιώτας διὰ τὸ φυλάττειν τὴν χώραν καὶ τὴν πόλιν, καλέσας εἰς ὄνομα αὐτῶν καὶ τὴν ἐπαρχίαν καὶ τὸν ποταμὸν Γάλλον.

26 ⁓ Malalas 10.10b (Thurn, *Ioannis Malalae Chronographia*, 178)

ὁ αὐτὸς Τιβέριος καὶ τὸν ποταμὸν τῆς πόλεως τὸν πρῴην λεγόμενον Δράκοντα μετεκάλεσεν Ὀρόντην τῇ Ῥωμαϊκῇ λέξει, ὅπερ ἑρμηνεύεται ἀνατολικός. ἔκτισεν δὲ καὶ τὸ θέατρον προσθεὶς ἄλλην ζώνην πρὸς τῷ ὄρει καὶ θυσιάσας κόρην παρθένον Ἀντιγόνην ὀνόματι· ὅπερ θέατρον οὐκ ἐπλήρωσεν εἶς τέλειον. ἔστησεν δὲ ἐπάνω τῆς ἀνατολικῆς πόρτας, ἧς αὐτὸς ἔκτισεν, στήλην λιθίνην τῇ λυκαίνῃ τρεφούσῃ τὸν Ῥῶμον καὶ τὸν Ῥῆμον, σημαίνων Ῥωμαῖον εἶναι τὸ κτίσμα τοῦ προστεθέντος τείχους τῇ αὐτῇ Ἀντιόχου πόλει. ἔκτισεν δὲ καὶ ὄπισθεν τοῦ θεάτρου ἱερὸν τοῦ Πανός. ταῦτα δὲ Δομνῖνος ὁ σοφὸς χρονογράφος ἐξέθετο.

27 ⁓ Malalas 10.48 (Thurn, *Ioannis Malalae Chronographia*, 198–99)

[Μετὰ δὲ τὴν βασιλείαν Τίτου ἐβασίλευσεν ὁ θειότατος Δομετιανὸς ἔτη ιεʹ καὶ μῆνας βʹ. ἦν δὲ μακρός, λεπτός, λευκός, ξανθός, κονδόθριξ, γλαυκός, ὑπόκυρτος,] φιλόσοφος ἄκρος. ἐπὶ δὲ τῆς αὐτοῦ βασιλείας διωγμὸς χριστιανῶν ἐγένετο· ὅστις καὶ τὸν ἅγιον Ἰωάννην τὸν θεολόγον ἀνήνεγκεν ἐν τῇ Ῥώμῃ καὶ ἐξήτασεν αὐτόν. καὶ θαυμάσας τοῦ αὐτοῦ ἀποστόλου τὴν σοφίαν ἀπέλυσεν αὐτὸν λάθρᾳ

This Augustus who is also Octavian conquered Galatia after he had defeated Deiotarus, the tetrarch of the region. And he walled a village known as Arsine and made it a city, which he called Ancyra [Anchor], because it is in the midst of two seas, the Pontic and the Asian sea. He sacrificed a virgin girl by the name of Gregoria for the purpose of a purification, and he created this province and left some Gallic troops there to guard the region and the city, calling the province and the river Gallos after their name.

This same Tiberius renamed the river of the city, formerly known as Dracon, the Orontes in the Roman tongue, which is interpreted as "eastern." He also built the theater, adding another tier by the mountain, and sacrificed a virgin girl by the name of Antigone; he did not completely finish this theater. He set up above the eastern gate, which he himself built, a stone memorial to the she-wolf nursing Romus and Remus, indicating that the construction of the wall added to the city of Antioch was Roman. He also founded a temple of Pan behind the theater. Domninos the wise chronographer set out these things.

[After the reign of Titus, the most godly Domitian was emperor for fifteen years and two months. He was tall, slender, fair, blonde, short-haired, slightly stooped,] a sharp philosopher. In his reign there arose a persecution of the Christians. He it was who brought Saint John the Theologian up to Rome and examined him. He was amazed at the wisdom of this apostle and released him to secretly return to

ἀπελθεῖν εἰς Ἔφεσον, εἰπὼν αὐτῷ· «ἄπελθε καὶ ἡσύχασον, ὅθεν ἦλθες».[4] καὶ ἐλοιδορήθη· καὶ ἐξώρισεν αὐτὸν εἰς Πάτμον. Πολλοὺς δὲ ἄλλους χριστιανοὺς ἐτιμωρήσατο, ὥστε φυγεῖν ἐξ αὐτῶν πλῆθος ἐπὶ τὸν Πόντον, καθὼς Βώττιος ὁ σοφὸς χρονογράφος συνεγράψατο κατ' αὐτῶν.

28 ~ Jerome, *Chron.*: *ann. Abr.* 2112 (Fotheringham, *Evsebii Pamphili Chronici Canones*, 274)

scribit Bruttius plurimos Christianorum sub Domitiano fecisse martyrium, inter quos et Flaviam Domitillam Flavii Clementis consulis ex sorore neptem in insulam Pontiam relegatam quia se Christianam esse testata sit.

29 ~ George Syncellus, *Chron.* 650 (Mosshammer, *Ecloga chronographica*, 419)

πολλοὶ δὲ Χριστιανῶν ἐμαρτύρησαν κατὰ Δομετιανόν, ὡς ὁ Βρέττιος ἱστορεῖ, ἐν οἷς καὶ Φλαυία Δομετίλλα ἐξαδελφὴ Κλήμεντος Φλαυίου ὑπατικοῦ ὡς Χριστιανὴ εἰς νῆσον Ποντίαν φυγαδεύεται· αὐτός τε Κλήμης ὑπὲρ Χριστοῦ ἀναιρεῖται.

4 Thurn prefers the reading suggested by Fitton, "Domitian and Saint John," on the basis of the Sophia Slavonic text (Gos. publičn. Biblioteka, Sofijsk. sobr. nr. 1454): ὅτι ὁ θεὸς ἦλθε, which changes the sense of the whole phrase ἄπελθε καὶ ἡσύχασον ὅτι ὁ θεὸς ἦλθε to "Go away and keep silent that God has come" and assumes that in response to this injunction Domitian was reviled (ἐλοιδορήθη) by St. John himself (rather than by unnamed detractors for his leniency to St. John) and Domitian banished him to Patmos as a consequence of his scorn, but I have retained the simpler, if more perfunctory, reading of the Oxford Greek text (Cod. Barocc. 182): ὅθεν ἦλθες.

Ephesus, saying to him, "Go back and live at peace where you have come from." But he was reviled and banished him to Patmos. He nevertheless punished many other Christians, so that a great number of them fled to Pontus, just as the wise chronographer Bottios has written concerning them.

Bruttius writes that very many Christians bore witness [were martyred] under Domitian, among whom Flavia Domitilla, the niece from his sister of the consul Flavius Clemens, was banished to the island of Pontia because she confessed that she was a Christian.

Many Christians bore witness [were martyred] under Domitian, as Brettios records, among whom also Flavia Domitilla, the niece of the consul Clemens Flavius, was banished as a Christian to the island of Pontia; this Clemens himself was slain for Christ's sake.

30 ⁓ Malalas 10.53–54 (Thurn, *Ioannis Malalae Chronographia*, 202–3)

[Μετὰ δὲ τὴν βασιλείαν Δομετιανοῦ ἐβασίλευσεν Νερβᾶς Αὔγουστος ἔτος α′ καὶ μῆνα α′. . . .] ἐπὶ δὲ τῆς αὐτοῦ βασιλείας ἔπαθεν ὑπὸ θεομηνίας τὸ τρίτον αὐτῆς πάθος Διοκαισάρεια, πόλις τῆς Κιλικίας, καὶ Νικόπολις καὶ ἡ χώρα αὐτῆς. καὶ εὐθέως ἔπεμψέν τινα ἐκεῖ ὁ αὐτὸς βασιλεὺς συγκλητικὸν Ῥωμαῖον ὀνόματι Ζάρβον εἰς τὸ κτίσαι αὐτήν, παρασχὼν αὐτῷ ὀκτὼ κεντηνάρια. καὶ καταλαβὼν τὴν Κιλικίαν ὁ αὐτὸς Ζάρβος ὁ συγκλητικὸς καὶ ἑωρακὼς τὰ πεπτωκότα πολλὴν σπουδὴν θέμενος ἀνενέωσε τὴν πόλιν, βελτίων αὐτὴν ποιήσας. ὅθεν καὶ εἰς τὸ αὐτοῦ ὄνομα ἐκλήθη ἡ πόλις, τῶν πολιτῶν εὐχαριστούντων αὐτῷ. ὁ γὰρ συνγκλητικὸς εἰς ὄνομα βασιλέως Νερβᾶ ἐκάλεσεν αὐτὴν πόλιν Νερβάν. συνέβη δὲ τελευτῆσαι τὸν Βασιλέα πρὸ τοῦ πληρωθῆναι αὐτήν· καὶ μετεκάλεσαν αὐτὴν Ἀνάξαρβον, ἐπιτρέψαντες τοῖς συμβολαιογράφοις οὕτως αὐτὴν χρηματίζειν. ἐλέγετο γὰρ ἐξ ἀρχῆς ἡ αὐτὴ πόλις Κύινδα· καὶ ἔπαθεν πρῶτον πάθος ἐπὶ τῶν ὑπάτων Ῥώμης, καὶ ἀνενεώθη καὶ μετεκλήθη Κίσκος πόλις. καὶ πάλιν ἔπαθεν ἐπὶ τοῦ Καίσαρος Ἰουλίου τὸ β′ αὐτῆς πάθος· καὶ ἀνενεώθη καὶ μετεκλήθη Διοκαισάρεια· καὶ παθοῦσα, ὡς προείρηται, ἐπὶ Νερβᾶ βασιλέως μετωνομάσθη Ἀνάζαρβος. ποιήσας δὲ θυσίαν κόρην ὁ Ζάρβος ὀνόματι Κηπάραν χωρικήν, ἐποίησεν αὐτῇ στήλην χαλκῆν εἰς τύχην τῆς πόλεως. ἐμήνυσεν δὲ τῷ αὐτῷ βασιλεῖ ὁ Ζάρβος περὶ τῶν πολιτῶν καὶ τοῖς σωσθεῖσι πολίταις ἐχαρίσατο, ὡς φιλότιμος, πολλὰ ὁ αὐτὸς βασιλεύς.

(54) Ὅστις Νερβᾶς ἀνεκαλέσατο τὸν ἀπόστολον τὸν ἅγιον Ἰωάννην· καὶ ἦλθεν ἐν Ἐφέσῳ πάλιν ἀπὸ Πάτμον.

31 ⁓ Malalas 11.9 (Thurn, *Ioannis Malalae Chronographia*, 208)

ὁ δὲ αὐτὸς εὐσεβέστατος Τραϊανὸς ἔκτισεν ἐν Ἀντιοχείᾳ τῇ μεγάλῃ ἀρξάμενος πρῶτον κτίσμα τὴν λεγομένον μέσην πύλην πλησίον τοῦ ἱεροῦ τοῦ Ἄρεως, ὅπου ὁ Παρμένιος χείμαρρος κατέρχεται, ἔγγιστα τοῦ νυνὶ λεγομένου Μακέλλου, γλύψας ἄνω ἄγαλμα λυκαίνης τρεφούσας τὸν Ῥῶμον καὶ τὸν Ῥῆμον, διὰ τὸ γινώσκεσθαι, ὅτι Ῥωμαῖόν ἐστι τὸ κτίσμα, θυσιάσας ἐκεῖ παρθένον κόρην εὐπρεπῆ πολίτιδα ὀνόματι Καλλιόπην ὑπὲρ λύτρου καὶ ἀποκαθαρισμοῦ τῆς πόλεως, νυμφαγωγίαν αὐτῇ ποιήσας. καὶ εὐθέως ἀνήγειρε τοὺς δύο ἐμβόλους τοὺς μεγάλους, καὶ ἄλλα δὲ πολλὰ ἔκτισεν ἐν τῇ αὐτῇ Ἀντιόχου πόλει καὶ δημόσιον καὶ ἀγωγὸν,

[After the reign of Domitian, Nerva Augustus ruled for one year and one month. . . .] In his reign Diocaesarea, a city of Cilicia, underwent its third disaster from the wrath of God, along with Nicopolis and its countryside. And immediately this emperor sent there a certain Roman senator by the name of Zarbus to rebuild it, granting him eight *centenaria*. Once this senator Zarbus had arrived in Cilicia and saw the destruction he took great pains to restore the city, making it better. And it is for this reason that the city was called after his name, since the citizens were grateful to him. For the senator called this city Nerva after the name of the emperor Nerva. But it happened that the emperor died before the city was completed, and they renamed it Anazarbus, commissioning the notaries that it be so called. For at first this city was known as Cuinda, and it suffered its first disaster under the consuls of Rome and was restored and renamed the city of Ciscus. And again, it suffered its second disaster under the Caesar Julius, and it was restored and renamed Diocaesarea. And after it suffered, as has been related above, under Emperor Nerva it was renamed Anazarbus. Zarbus made a sacrifice of a girl by the name of Cepara, a rustic maid, and made a bronze memorial to her as the tyche of the city. Zarbus reported to the emperor concerning the citizens and, as he was generous, this emperor freely gave a great deal to the surviving citizens.

This Nerva recalled the Apostle Saint John; and he went again to Ephesus from Patmos.

And this most pious Trajan made foundations in Antioch the Great, beginning with his first foundation, the gate called the Middle Gate near the temple of Ares, where the torrent of the Parmenios flows down, close to what is now called the Macellum. He carved above an image of the she-wolf nursing Romus and Remus, by which it would be recognized that this was a Roman foundation. There he sacrificed a comely virgin girl of the city by the name of Calliope for the sake of the redemption and cleansing of the city, and he held a bridal procession for her. And he immediately repaired the two great porticoes and established many other

ἀποστρέψας τὸ ὕδωρ τὸ ἀπὸ τῶν πηγῶν Δάφνης ἐκχεόμενον εἰς τὰς λεγομένας Ἀγρίας, ἐπιθήσας καὶ τῷ δημοσίῳ καὶ τῷ ἀγωγῷ εἰς τὸ ἴδιον ὄνομα, καὶ τὸ θέατρον δὲ τῆς αὐτῆς ἀντιοχείας ἀνεπλήρωσεν ἀτελὲς ὄν, στήσας ἐν αὐτῷ ὑπεράνω τεσσάρων κιόνων ἐν μέσῳ τοῦ νυμφαίου τοῦ προσκηνίου τῆς σφαθιασθείσης ὑπ‹ αὐτοῦ κόρης στήλην χαλκῆν κεχρυσωμένην, καθημένην ἐπάνω τοῦ Ὀρόντου ποταμοῦ εἰς λόγον τύχης τῆς αὐτῆς πόλεως, στεφομένην ὑπὸ Σελεύκου καὶ Ἀντιόχου βασιλέων.

32 ~ Malalas 11.10 (Thurn, *Ioannis Malalae Chronographia*, 208–9)

Ἐμαρτύρησε δὲ ἐπὶ αὐτοῦ τότε ὁ ἅγιος Ἰγνάτιος ὁ ἐπίσκοπος τῆς πόλεως Ἀντιοχείας· ἠγανάκτησε γὰρ κατ' αὐτοῦ, ὅτι ἐλοιδόρει αὐτόν. συνέσχεν δὲ τότε καὶ πέντε ὀνόματα χριστιανῶν γυναικῶν Ἀντιοχισσῶν καὶ ἐξέτασεν αὐτὰς λέγων· «τίς ἐστιν ἡ ἐλπὶς ὑμῶν, ὅτι οὕτως ἐκδίδοτε ἑαυτὰς εἰς θάνατον;» αἱ δὲ ἀπεκρίθησαν λέγουσαι, «ὅτι φονευομένας ἡμᾶς παρ' ὑμῶν ἀνίστασθαι ἡμᾶς πάλιν ὡς ἔχομεν σώματι εἰς αἰωνίαν ζωήν». καὶ ἐκέλευσεν αὐτὰς πυρικαύστους γενέσθαι καὶ τὸν χοῦν τῶν ὀστέων αὐτῶν συνέμιξε χαλκῷ καὶ ἐποίησε τὸν χαλκὸν εἰς ὃ ἐποίησε δημόσιον χαλκία τοῦ θερμοῦ. καὶ ὅτε ἤρξατο παρέχειν τὸ δημόσιον, εἴ τις ἐὰν ἐλούετο εἰς αὐτὸ τὸ δημόσιον, ἐσκοτοῦτο καὶ ἔπιπτεν καὶ ἐξήρχετο βασταγμῷ. καὶ μαθὼν ὁ βασιλεὺς Τραϊανὸς τοῦτο, ἤλλαξε τὰ αὐτὰ χαλκία καὶ ἐποίησεν ἄλλα ἀπὸ καθαροῦ χαλκοῦ, λέγων ὅτι· «οὐ καλῶς ἐποίησα χοῦν σωμάτων συμμίξας αὐτοῖς καὶ κοινώσας τὰ θερμὰ ὕδατα». ταῦτα δὲ ἔλεγεν, ἐπειδὴ οἱ χριστιανοὶ ὑπώξιζον τοῖς Ἕλλησι καυχώμενοι. τὰ δὲ πρῶτα χαλκία ἀναχωνεύσας ἐποίησε στήλας χαλκᾶς πέντε ταῖς αὐταῖς γυναιξί, λέγων ὅτι· «ἰδοὺ ἐγὼ αὐτὰς ἀνέστησα καθὼς εἶπον καὶ οὐχὶ ὁ θεὸς αὐτῶν». αἵτινες στῆλαι εἰς αὐτὸ τὸ δημόσιον λουτρὸν ἵστανται ἕως ἄρτι. ἐποίησε δὲ καὶ κάμινον πυρός, καὶ ἐκέλευσε τοὺς βουλομένους χριστιανοὺς βάλλειν ἑαυτοὺς ἐν προθέσει. καὶ πολλοὶ ἔβαλλον ἑαυτοὺς καὶ ἐμαρτύρησαν. ἐμαρτύρησε δὲ τότε ἡ ἁγία Δροσινὴ καὶ ἄλλαι παρθένοι πολλαί.

public works in the city of Antioch, among them the baths and the aqueduct, diverting the water which flowed from the springs of Daphne to the [ravines] called "the Wilds" (*Agriai*),[5] and gave his name to the baths and the aqueduct. And he completed the theater of Antioch, which was unfinished, setting up in it, on top of four small pillars in the middle of the nymphaeum of the proscenium, a gilded bronze monument of the maiden sacrificed by him. She was sitting over the river Orontes, depicted as the tyche of the city being crowned by the kings Seleucus and Antiochus.

Under him at that time Saint Ignatius the bishop of the city of Antioch was martyred; for he was vexed with him because he reviled him. At that time also he arrested five individuals, Christian women of Antioch, and interrogated them, saying, "What is your hope that you thus give yourselves over to death?" They replied, saying, "That even if we are slain by you, we are to be raised up again as we are in the body unto eternal life." And he ordered them to be burnt with fire and mixed the ashes of their bones with bronze and made the bronze into the vessels of hot water for the public bath he built. And when the bath began to be used, if anyone washed at this bath, he became dizzy and fell over and left on a stretcher. And when the emperor Trajan learned of it, he replaced the vessels and made others from pure bronze, saying, "I did not do well mixing the ashes of bones with them and contaminating the hot water." He said these things, since the Christians were acerbic in their boasting against the pagans. He recast the original vessels and made bronze memorials to those five women, saying, "Look, I myself have raised them up, just as they said, not their God." These memorials stand at the public bath up to the present. He also made a fiery furnace and called on those Christians who wished to publicly throw themselves in. And many threw themselves in and were martyred. At that time Saint Drosine was martyred, as well as many other virgins.

5 For this interpretation of the passage I depend on Downey, *History of Antioch*, 221.

33 ⁓ Malalas 13.7a (Thurn, *Ioannis Malalae Chronographia*, 245)

Καὶ ἐπὶ τῆς αὐτοῦ βασιλείας ἀνεκαινίσθη τό ποτε Βυζάντιον ἐπὶ τῆς ὑπατείας Γαλλικανοῦ καὶ Συμμάχου, τοῦ αὐτοῦ δὲ βασιλέως Κωνσταντίνου ποιήσαντος πρόκεσσον ἐπὶ πολὺν χρόνον, ἀπὸ Ῥώμης ἐλθόντος ἐν τῷ Βυζαντίῳ· ὅστις καὶ τὸ πρῴην τεῖχος τῆς αὐτῆς πόλεως ἀνενέωσε τὸ Βύζου καὶ προσθεὶς ἄλλο διάστημα πολὺ τῷ τείχει, καὶ συνάψας τῷ παλαιῷ τειχει τῆς αὐτῆς πόλεως, ἐκέλευσεν αὐτὴν Κωνσταντινούπολιν λέγεσθαι, . . .

34 ⁓ Malalas 13.7c (Thurn, *Ioannis Malalae Chronographia*, 246)

τὴν δὲ τύχην τῆς πόλεως τῆς ὑπ᾽ αὐτοῦ ἀνανεωθείσης καὶ εἰς ὄνομα αὐτοῦ κτισθείσης ποιήσας τῷ θεῷ θυσίαν ἀναίμακτον ἐκάλεσεν Ἄνθουσαν. ἥτις πόλις ἐκτίσθη ἐξ ἀρχῆς ὑπὸ Φιδαλίας· καὶ ἐκάλεσεν τότε τὴν τύχην αὐτῆς Κερόην. τὴν δὲ αὐτὴν Φιδαλίαν ἠγάγετο Βύζας ὁ τῆς Θρᾴκης βασιλεὺς μετὰ τὴν τελευτὴν Βαρβυσίου τοῦ πατρὸς αὐτῆς, τοῦ τοπάρχου καὶ φύλακος τοῦ αὐτοῦ ἐμπορίου. ὅστις Βαρβύσιος μέλλων τελευτᾶν ἐκέλευσε τὴν Φιδαλίαν ποιῆσαι τεῖχος τῷ τόπῳ ἕως θαλάσσης. ὁ δὲ Βύζας εἰς τὸ ἑαυτοῦ ὄνομα καλέσας τὴν χώραν ἐβασίλευσεν ἐν τῇ αὐτῇ πόλει.

35 ⁓ Malalas 13.8b (Thurn, *Ioannis Malalae Chronographia*, 247)

καὶ ἐπετέλεσεν ἑορτὴν μεγάλην μηνὶ μαΐῳ τῷ καὶ ἀρτεμισίῳ ια′, ἔτους κατὰ Ἀντιόχειαν τὴν μεγάλην χρηματίζοντος τοη′, κελεύσας διὰ θείου αὐτοῦ τύπου τῇ αὐτῇ ἡμέρᾳ ἐπιτελεῖσθαι τὴν ἑορτὴν τοῦ γενεθλίου τῆς πόλεως αὐτοῦ καὶ ἀνοίγειν τῇ αὐτῇ ια′ τοῦ μαΐου μηνὸς τὸ δημόσιον λουτρὸν τὸ Ζεύξιππον, πλησίον ὂν τοῦ Ἱππικοῦ καὶ τῆς Ῥηγίας καὶ τοῦ παλατίου, ποιήσας ἑαυτῷ ἄλλην στήλην ξοάνου κεχρυσωμένην βαστάζουσαν τῇ δεξιᾷ αὐτοῦ χειρὶ τὴν τύχην τῆς αὐτῆς πόλεως καὶ αὐτὴν κεχρυσωμένην, <ἣν> ἐκάλεσεν Ἄνθουσαν, κελεύσας κατὰ τὴν αὐτὴν ἡμέραν τοῦ γενεθλιακοῦ ἱππικοῦ εἰσιέναι τὴν αὐτὴν τοῦ ξοάνου στήλην διριγευομένην ὑπὸ τῶν στρατιωτῶν μετὰ χλαμύδων καὶ καμπαγίων, πάντων κατεχόντων κηρούς, καὶ περιέρχεσθαι τὸ ὄχημα τὸν ἄνω καμπτὸν καὶ ἔρχεσθαι εἰς τὸ σκάμμα κατέναντι τοῦ βασιλικοῦ καθίσματος, καὶ ἐγείρεσθαι τὸν κατὰ καιρὸν βασιλέα καὶ προσκυνεῖν, ὡς θεωρεῖ τὴν αὐτὴν στήλην Κωνσταντίνου καὶ τῆς τύχης τῆς πόλεως. καὶ πεφύλακται τοῦτο τὸ ἔθος ἕως τοῦ νῦν.

And in his reign the former Byzantium was renewed in the consulship of Gallicanus and Symmachus, when this emperor Constantine made a ceremonial progress of great duration, coming from Rome to Byzantium. He also restored the earlier wall of this city, that of Byzas, and added a further lengthy extension to the wall and connected it to the old wall of this city, which he commanded be known as Constantinople.

Making a bloodless sacrifice to God he called the tyche of the city restored by himself and established in his own name Anthousa. This city had at first been founded by Phidalia, and at that time she called its tyche Ceroe. Byzas, the king of Thrace, married this Phidalia after the death of Barbysios, her father, the toparch and protector of this trading post. When he was about to die this Barbysios ordered Phidalia to build a wall for the place up to the sea. But Byzas called the region after his own name and ruled it in this city.

And he celebrated a great festival on the eleventh of the month of May, that is Artemisios, in the year calculated according to the era of Antioch the Great 378, commanding under his sacred seal that the festival of the birthday of his city be celebrated on this day and that on the same eleventh of the month of May they open the public bath, the Zeuxippos, near the Hippodrome and the Regia, that is, the palace. He made another memorial statue of himself made of wood and gilded, holding in his right hand the tyche of this city, also gilded, <whom> he called Anthousa, and commanded that on the day of the anniversary horse race this wooden statue come in conducted by soldiers with mantles and boots, all holding wax tapers, and that the car come around the upper turning and come to the pit opposite the imperial box and that the emperor at the time rouse himself and make obeisance when he sees this memorial statue of Constantine and the tyche of the city. And this custom is observed up to the present.

ABBREVIATIONS

AHR	*American Historical Review*
AJA	*American Journal of Archaeology*
AJP	*American Journal of Philology*
AntCl	*L'antiquité Classique*
ByzAus	Byzantina Australiensia
BZ	*Byzantinische Zeitschrift*
CCSL	Corpus christianorum, Series Latina
CFHB	Corpus fontium historiae byzantinae
ChHist	*Church History*
CPh	*Classical Philology*
CQ	*Classical Quarterly*
CR	*Classical Review*
DOML	Dumbarton Oaks Medieval Library
EHR	*English Historical Review*
ELB	*Excerpta Latina Barbari*
EME	*Early Medieval Europe*
EO	*Échos d'Orient*
FGrHist	*Die Fragmente der griechischen Historiker*, ed. F. Jacoby (1923–58)
FHG	*Fragmenta historicorum graecorum*, ed. C. Müller (Paris, 1870–78)
GCS	Die griechischen christlichen Schriftsteller der ersten [drei] Jahrhunderte
GRBS	*Greek, Roman, and Byzantine Studies*
HSCPh	*Harvard Studies in Classical Philology*
HTR	*Harvard Theological Review*
HUkSt	*Harvard Ukrainian Studies*

ICS	*Illinois Classical Studies*
JAOS	*Journal of the American Oriental Society*
JBL	*Journal of Biblical Literature*
JEA	*Journal of Egyptian Archaeology*
JHS	*Journal of Hellenic Studies*
JIAN	*Journal international d'archéologie numismatique*
JJS	*Journal of Jewish Studies*
JLA	*Journal of Late Antiquity*
JMedHist	*Journal of Medieval History*
JNES	*Journal of Near Eastern Studies*
JQR	*Jewish Quarterly Review*
JR	*Journal of Religion*
JRS	*Journal of Roman Studies*
JTS	*Journal of Theological Studies*
LisFil	*Listy filologické*
MGH AuctAnt	Monumenta Germaniae historica, Auctores antiquissimi
OLP	*Orientalia Lovaniensia periodica*
PG	Patrologia cursus completus, Series graeca, ed. J.-P. Migne (Paris, 1857–66)
RBPH	*Revue belge de philologie et d'histoire*
RHR	*Revue de l'histoire des religions*
SC	Sources chrétiennes
SHA	Scriptores Historiae Augustae
SLA	*Studies in Late Antiquity*
StP	*Studia patristica*
TAPA	*Transactions [and Proceedings] of the American Philological Association*
TheolSt	*Theological Studies*
TM	*Travaux et mémoires*
TU	Texte und Untersuchungen zur Geschichte der altchristlichen Literatur (Leipzig-Berlin, 1882–)
VChr	*Vigiliae Christianae*
WSt	*Wiener Studien*
YCS	*Yale Classical Studies*
ZPapEpig	*Zeitschrift für Papyrologie und Epigraphik*

BIBLIOGRAPHY

Primary Sources

Aelius Aristides. *Aelii Aristidis Smyrnaei Quae Supersunt Omnia: Volumen 2 Orationes 17–53 Continens*. Edited by B. Keil. Berlin, 1898 (repr. 1958).

Alexander Romance. *Historia Alexandri Magni (Vol. 1, Recensio vetusta)*. Edited by W. Kroll. Berlin, 1926 (repr. 2005).

Anthologia Palatina. *Antologia Palatina*. Edited by F. M. Pontani. 4 vols. Turin, 1978–81.

Aphrahat. *Aphraate le sage persan, Les exposés*. Translated by M.-J. Pierre. SC 349, 359. Paris, 1988–89.

Arnobius. *Arnobii adversus nationes libri vii*. Edited by C. Marchesi. Corpus Scriptorum Latinorum Paravianum 62. Turin, 1934.

Athanasius. *Athanasius: Contra Gentes and De Incarnatione*. Edited by R. W. Thomson. Oxford, 1971.

Athenagoras. *Athenagoras: Legatio pro Christianis*. Edited by M. Marcovich. Berlin, 1990.

Ausonius. *Decimi Magni Ausonii Opera*. Edited by R. P. H. Green. Oxford, 1999.

Cedrenus, George. *Georgii Cedreni Historiarum Compendium*. Edited by L. Tartaglia. Bollettino dei Classici, suppl. 30. 2 vols. Rome, 2016.

Chronicon Paschale. Edited by L. Dindorf. 2 vols. Bonn, 1832.

Diodorus Siculus. *Diodore de Sicile, Bibliothèque historique: Fragments, livres VI–X*. Edited and translated by A. Cohen-Skalli. Paris, 2012.

———. *Diodori Bibliotheca Historica*. Edited by F. Vogel. 5 vols. Leipzig, 1888–1906.

———. *Diodori Siculi Bibliothecae Historicae quae supersunt*. Edited by L. Dindorf and C. Müller. 2 vols. Paris, 1842.

———. *Diodorus Siculus, The Library of History*. Edited and translated by C. H. Oldfather, et al. 12 vols. Cambridge, MA, 1933–67.

Dionysius of Tel Mahre. *Eusebii Canonum Epitome ex Dionysii Telmharensis chronico petita*. Edited by C. Siegfried and H. Gelzer. Leipzig, 1884.

Euripides. *Euripidis Fabulae*. Edited by G. Murray. 3 vols. Oxford, 1902–1909.

———. *Tragicorum graecorum fragmenta*. Edited by A. Nauck. Leipzig, 1889.

Eusebius. *Armenian Chronicle. Die Chronik aus dem Armenischen übersetzt mit textkritischem Commentar*. Edited by J. Karst. Eusebius Werke, Band 5. Leipzig, 1911.

———. *Commentaria in Isaiam. Der Jesajakommentar*. Edited by J. Ziegler. Eusebius Werke, Band 9. Berlin, 1975.

———. *Historia Ecclesiastica. Die Kirchengeschichte*. Edited by E. Schwartz. Eusebius Werke, Band 2, Teil 1. Leipzig, 1903.

———. *Laus Constantini: Kritische Beiträge zu den Constantin-Schriften des Eusebius*. Edited by I. A. Heikel. Eusebius Werke, Band 1. Leipzig, 1911.

———. *Vita Constantini. Kritische Beiträge zu den Constantin-Schriften des Eusebius: Über das leben des Kaisers Konstantin*. Edited by F. Winkelman. Eusebius Werke, Band 1, Teil 1. Berlin, 1975.

Excerpta Latina Barbari. *Apocalypse of Pseudo-Methodius. An Alexandrian World Chronicle*. Edited and translated by B. Garstad. DOML 14. Cambridge, MA, 2012.

George Hamartolos (Georgius Monachus). *Georgii Monachi Chronicon*. Edited by C. de Boor. 2 vols. Leipzig, 1904.

George the Syncellus (Georgius Syncellus). *Ecloga chronographica*. Edited by A. A. Mosshammer. Leipzig, 1984.

Gregory Nazianzenus. *Grégoire de Nazianze, Discours 4–5: Contre Julien*. Edited by J. Bernardi. SC 309. Paris, 1983.

Hippolytus. *Commentaria in Danielem. Kommentar zu Daniel*. Edited by G. N. Bonwetsch, revised by M. Richard. Hippolyt Werke, 1.1. GCS 7. Berlin, 2000.

Homer. *Homeri Opera*, 2nd ed. Edited by T. W. Allen. Oxford, 1917.

Jerome. *Chronicle. Eusebii Pamphili Chronici Canones Latine vertit, adauxit, ad sua tempora produxit S. Eusebius Hieronymus*. Edited by J. K. Fotheringham. London, 1923.

———. *Commentariorum in Danielem libri III <IV>*. F. Glorie. S. Hieronymi Presbyteri Opera, 1.5. CCSL 75A. Turnhout, 1964.

———. *In Hieremiam prophetam libri sex*. Edited by S. Reiter. S. Hieronymi Presbyteri Opera, 1.3. CCSL 74. Turnhout, 1960.

John Malalas. *Ioannis Malalae Chronographia*. Edited by J. Thurn. CFHB 35. Berlin, 2000.

John of Antioch. *Ioannis Antiocheni Fragmenta ex Historia chronica*. Edited by U. Roberto. TU 154. Berlin, 2005.

———. *Ioannis Antiocheni Fragmenta quae supersunt omnia*. Edited by S. Mariev. CFHB 47. Berlin, 2008.

John of Nikiu. *The Chronicle of John, Bishop of Nikiu, Translated from Zotenberg's Ethiopic Text*. Translated by R. H. Charles. London, 1916.

Julian, *Epistulae*. *Flavii Claudii Iuliani epistulae leges poematia fragmenta varia*. Edited by J. Bidez and F. Cumont. Paris, 1922.

Justin Martyr. *Justin, Philosopher and Martyr: Apologies*. Edited by D. Minns and P. Parvis. Oxford, 2009.

Lactantius Caecilius Firmianus. *Lactance, Institutions divines, Livre II*. Edited by P. Monat. SC 337. Paris, 1987.

Libanius. *Libanii Opera*. Edited by R. Foerster. 12 vols. Leipzig, 1903–27.

Orosius. *Orose, Histoires (Contre les Païens): Tome 2, Livres 4–6*. Edited by M.-P. Arnaud-Lindet. Paris, 2003.

Parastaseis Syntomoi Chronikai. See Av. Cameron and Herrin, *Constantinople in the Early Eighth Century*.

Patria Constantinopoleos. Edited by T. Preger. In *Scriptores Originum Constantinopolitanarum*, 2:135–289. 2 vols. Leipzig, 1901–1907.

———. *Accounts of Medieval Constantinople: The* Patria. Edited and translated by A. Berger. DOML 24. Cambridge, MA, 2013.

Plutarch, *Moralia*. *Plutarchi Chaeronensis Moralia*. Edited by G. Bernardakis. 7 vols. Leipzig, 1888–96.

Proclus, *Chrestomathia*. *Homeri Opera*, vol. 5, *Hymni Cyclus Pragmenta Margites Batrachomyomachia Vita*, 99–109. Edited by T. W. Allen. Oxford, 1912.

Suda. *Suidae Lexicon*. Edited by A. Adler. 5 vols. Leipzig, 1928–38.

Sozomen. *Sozomenos Historia Ecclesiastica / Kirchengeschichte*. Introduced and translated by G. C. Hansen. Fontes Christiani 73.1–4. Turnhout, 2004.

Stephanus of Byzantium. *Stephani Byzantii Ethnica*. Edited by Margarethe Billerbeck et al. 5 vols. CFHB 43.1–5. Berlin, 2006–2017.

Symeon Logothetes. *Symeonis Magistri et Logothetae Chronicon*. Edited by S. Wahlgren. CFHB 44. Berlin, 2006.

Theodoret of Cyrrhus. *Théodoret de Cyr, Thérapeutique des maladies helléniques*. Edited by P. Canivet. SC 57, 359. Paris, 1958.

———. *Theodoret of Cyrus: Commentary on Daniel*. Translated by R. C. Hill. Atlanta, 2006.

Secondary Sources

Aaronovitch, D. *Voodoo Histories: The Role of Conspiracy Theory in Shaping Modern History*. New York, 2010.

Abrahamson, E. L. "Euripides' Tragedy of Hecuba." *TAPA* 83 (1952): 120–29.

Acton, Lord, J. E. E. Dalberg-Acton, First Baron Acton. *Essays in Religion, Politics, and Morality*. Edited by J. R. Fears. 3 vols. Indianapolis, 1985–88.

Adler, M. "The Emperor Julian and the Jews." *JQR* 5 (1893): 591–651.

Agnosini, M. "Rome in Constantinople: The Hippodrome in John Lydus' *De mensibus*." *RBPH* 96 (2018): 925–45.

Aiello, V. "Costantino, la lebbra e il battesimo di Silvestro." In Bonamente and Fusco, *Costantino il Grande*, 1:17–58.

Aland, K. "The Relation between Church and State in Early Times: A Reinterpretation." *JTS* 19 (1968): 115–27.

Alexander, P. J. *The Oracle of Baalbek: The Tiburtine Sibyl in Greek Dress*. Washington, DC, 1967.

Alföldi, A. *The Conversion of Constantine and Pagan Rome*. Translated by H. Mattingly. Oxford, 1948.

———. *Die Kontorniaten: Ein verkanntes Propagandamittel der stadtrömischen heidnischen Aristokratie in ihrem Kampfe gegen das christliche Kaisertum*. Budapest, 1943.

———. "On the Foundation of Constantinople: A Few Notes." *JRS* 37 (1947): 10–16.

Allen, D. *Frederic Remington and the Spanish-American War*. New York, 1971.

Allen, P., and E. Jeffreys, eds. *The Sixth Century: End or Beginning?* ByzAus 10. Brisbane, 1996.

Allison, J. W. "Dissimulatio: Tiberius or Tacitus?" In *Conflict, Antithesis, and the Ancient Historian*, ed. J. W. Allison, 133–55. Columbus, 1990.

Amitay, O. *From Alexander to Jesus*. Berkeley, 2010.

Anderson, M. "Christianizing the Planetary Week and Globalizing the Seven-Day Cycle." *SLA* 3 (2019): 128–91.

Ando, C. *The Matter of the Gods: Religion and the Roman Empire*. Berkeley, 2008.

Andrade, N. J. *Syrian Identity in the Greco-Roman World*. Cambridge, 2013.

Anonymous. *A True and Faithful Narrative of Oliver Cromwell's Compact with the Devil for Seven Years*. London, 1720.

Anwander, A. "'Schicksal'-Wörter in Antike und Christentum." *Zeitschrift für Religions- und Geistesgeschichte* 1 (1948) 315–27.

Armstrong, A. H., ed. *The Cambridge History of Later Greek and Early Medieval Philosophy*. Cambridge, 1970.

Asirvatham, S. "Classicism and *Romanitas* in Plutarch's *De Alexandri Fortuna aut Virtute*." *AJP* 126 (2005): 107–25.

Athanassiadi-Fowden, P. *Julian and Hellenism: An Intellectual Biography*. Oxford, 1981.

Atkinson, J. E. *A Commentary on Q. Curtius Rufus'* Historiae Alexandri Magni, *Books 3 and 4*. Amsterdam, 1980.

Attridge, H. W., and G. Hata, eds. *Eusebius, Christianity, and Judaism*. Leiden, 1992.

Aubin, Melissa. "Reversing Romance? The Acts of Thecla and the Ancient Novel." In *Ancient Fiction and Early Christian Narrative*, ed. R. F. Hock, J. B. Chance, and J. Perkins, 257–72. Atlanta, 1998.

Badian, E. "Darius III." *HSCPh* 100 (2000): 241–67.

Bagnall, R. S., and K. Worp. *Chronological Systems of Byzantine Egypt*. 2nd ed. Leiden, 2004.

Bailey, C. *P. Ovidi Nasonis Fastorum Liber 3*. Oxford, 1921.

Baldwin, B. "The *Caesares* of Julian." *Klio* 60 (1978): 449–66.

Balsdon, J. P. V. D. *Romans and Aliens*. Chapel Hill, 1979.

———. *Roman Women: Their History and Habits*. New York, 1962.

Bammel, E. "Der Zeuge des Judentums." In Will and Heinrichs, *Zu Alexander d. Gr.*, 1:279–87.

Bardill, J. *Constantine, Divine Emperor of the Christian Golden Age*. Cambridge, 2012.

Barkun, M. *A Culture of Conspiracy: Apocalyptic Visions in Contemporary America*. Berkeley, 2003.

Barnes, T. *Constantine and Eusebius*. Cambridge, MA, 1981.

———. "Constantine and the Christians of Persia." *JRS* 75 (1985): 126–36.

———. *Constantine: Dynasty, Religion and Power in the Later Roman Empire*. Oxford, 2011.

———. "Constantine's Prohibition of Pagan Sacrifice." *AJP* 105 (1984): 69–72.

———. "The Editions of Eusebius' Ecclesiastical History." *GRBS* 21 (1980): 191–201.

Barnes, T., and J. Vander Spoel. "Julian and Themistius." *GRBS* 22 (1981): 187–89.

Baron, C. A. *Timaeus of Tauromenium and Hellenistic Historiography*. Cambridge, 2013.

Barton, T. "The *inventio* of Nero: Suetonius." In Elsner and Masters, *Reflections of Nero*, 48–63.

Bartsch, S. *Decoding the Ancient Novel: The Reader and the Role of Description in Heliodorus and Achilles Tatius*. Princeton, 1989.

Baumgarten, A. I. "Euhemerus' Eternal Gods: or How Not to Be Embarrassed by Greek Mythology." In *Classical Studies in Honor of David Sohlberg*, ed. R. Katzoff, 91–103. Ramat Gan, 1996.

Baynes, L. "The Watchers Traditions in *1 Enoch's Book of Parables*." In Harkins, Bautch, and Endres, *Watchers*, 151–63.

Baynes, N. H. "The Death of Julian the Apostate in a Christian Legend." *JRS* 27 (1937): 22–29.

———. "Review of Otto Seeck, *Geschichte des Untergangs der antiken Welt*." *EHR* 27 (1912): 755–60. [759–60 = *Byzantine Studies and Other Essays*. London, 1955. 346–47.]

Baynham, E. "'Joining the Gods': Alexander at the Euphrates; Arrian 7.27.3, *Metz Epitome* 101–102 and the *Alexander Romance*." In Stoneman, Nawotka, and Wojciechowska, *The* Alexander Romance*: History and Literature*, 189–98.

Beatrice, P. F. Anonymi Monophysitae Theosophia: *An Attempt at Reconstruction*. Leiden, 2001.

Becchi, F. "ΤΥΧΗ: Storia di un Nome." In *ΠΟΙΚΙΛΜΑ: Studi in onore di Michele R. Cataudella in occasione del 60° compleanno*, ed. S. Bianchetti and M. R. Cataudella, 1:111–27. 2 vols. La Spezia, 2001.

Becker, A. H. "The Ancient Near East in the Late Antique Near East: Syriac Christian Appropriation of the Biblical East." In *Antiquity in Antiquity: Jewish and Christian Pasts in the Greco-Roman World*, ed. G. Gardner and K. L. Osterloh, 394–415. Tübingen, 2008.

Bell, H. I. "Antinoopolis: A Hadrianic Foundation in Egypt." *JRS* 30 (1940): 133–47.

Bentley, R. *Epistola ad Joannem Millium*. 1691. Repr. Toronto, 1962.

———. *The Works of Richard Bentley, D.D.* Edited by A. Dyce. 3 vols. London, 1836.

Berger, A., trans. *Accounts of Medieval Constantinople: The Patria*. Cambridge, MA, 2013.

Betty, J. "The Cerne Giant Revisited." In Darvill et al., *The Cerne Giant*, 75–87.

Bidez, J., and F. Cumont. *Les mages hellénisés: Zoroastre, Ostanès et Hystaspe d'après la tradition grecque*. Paris, 1938.

Blanchetière, F. "Julien Philhellène, Philosémite, Antichrétien: L'affaire du Temple de Jerusalem (363)." *JJS* 31 (1980): 61–81.

Blass, F., and A. Debrunner. *A Greek Grammar of the New Testament and Other Early Christian Literature*. Translated by R. W. Funk. Chicago, 1961.

Bleckmann, B. "*Constantinus tyrannus*: Das negative Konstantinsbild in der paganen Historiographie und seine Nuancen." In Turner, Chong-Gossard, and Vervaet, *Private and Public Lies*, 343–54.

———. "Pagane Visionen Konstantins in der Chronik des Johannes Zonaras." In Bonamente and Fusco, *Costantino il Grande*, 1:151–70.

Bloch, H. "The Pagan Revival in the West at the End of the Fourth Century." In Momigliano, *Conflict between Paganism and Christianity*, 193–218.

Blockley, R. C. *The Fragmentary Classicizing Historians of the Later Roman Empire: Eunapius, Olympiodorus, Priscus and Malchus*. 2 vols. Liverpool, 1981–83.

Blum, G. "Numismatique d'Antinoos." *JIAN* 16 (1914): 33–70.

Boatwright, M. T. *Hadrian and the Cities of the Roman Empire*. Princeton, 2000.

———. *Hadrian and the City of Rome*. Princeton, 1987.

Bonamente, G., and F. Fusco, eds. *Costantino il Grande dall'Antichità all'Umanesimo: Colloquio sul Cristianesimo nel mondo antioc, Macerata 18–20 Dicembre 1990*. 2 vols. Macerata, Italy, 1992–93.

Boncquet, J. "Ctesias' Assyrian King-List and His Chronology of Mesopotamian History." *Ancient Society* 21 (1990): 5–16.

Bonnechere, P. "La Notion d' 'Act Collectif' dans le Sacrifice Humain Grec." *Phoenix* 52 (1998): 191–215.

———. *Le sacrifice humain en Grèce ancienne*. Athens/Liège, 1994.

Bosch, C. *Die kleinasiatischen Münzen der römischen Kaiserzeit*, vol. 2, *Einzeluntersuchungen*, part 1, *Bithynien. 1. Hälfte*. Stuttgart, 1935.

Bosworth, A. B. "The Historical Setting of Megasthenes' *Indica*." *CPh* 91 (1996): 113–27.

Bourier, H. *Über die Quellen der ersten vierzehn Bücher des Johannes Malalas*. 2 vols. Augsburg, 1899.

Bowersock, G. W. "The Emperor Julian on His Predecessors." *YCS* 27 (1982): 159–72.

———. *Julian the Apostate*. Cambridge, MA, 1978.

———. *Mosaics as History: The Near East from Late Antiquity to Islam*. Cambridge, MA, 2006.

Bowra, C. M. "Palladas on Tyche." *CQ* 10 (1960): 118–28.

Braccesi, L. *L'Alessandro occidentale: Il Macedone e Roma*. Rome, 2006.

Braccini, T. *Bisanzio prima di Bisanzio: Miti fondazioni della nuova Roma*. Rome, 2019.

Bradbury, S. "The Date of Julian's *Letter to Themistius*." *GRBS* 28 (1987): 235–51.

———. "Julian's Pagan Revival and the Decline of Blood Sacrifice." *Phoenix* 49 (1995): 331–56.

Brakke, D. *Athanasius and Asceticism*. Baltimore, 1995.

Bremmer, J. "Religious Violence and Its Roots: A View from Antiquity." In Mayer and de Wet, *Reconceiving Religious Conflict*, 30–42.

Brennan, B. “The Image of the Frankish Kings in the Poetry of Venantius Fortunatus.” *JMedHist* 10 (1984): 1–11.

Brisson, L. *How Philosophers Saved Myths: Allegorical Interpretation and Classical Mythology*. Translated by C. Tihanyi. Chicago, 2004.

———. *Plato the Myth Maker*. Translated by G. Naddaf. Chicago, 1998.

Brock, S. P. “Christians in the Sasanian Empire: A Case of Divided Loyalties.” *Studies in Church History* 18 (1982): 1–19.

Bromley, D. G. “Satanism: The New Cult Scare.” In *The Satanism Scare*, ed. J. T. Richardson, J. Best, and D. G. Bromley, 49–72. New York, 1991.

———. “The Satanism Scare in the United States.” In *Le Défi magique, volume 2: Satanisme, sorcellerie*, ed. J.-B. Martin, 49–64. Lyon, 1994.

Brown, A. “Justinian, Procopius, and Deception: Literary Lies, Imperial Politics, and the Archaeology of Sixth-century Greece.” In Turner, Chong-Gossard, and Vervaet, *Private and Public Lies*, 355–69.

Brown, C. H. *The Correspondents' War: Journalists in the Spanish-American War*. New York, 1967.

Brown, P. *Authority and the Sacred: Aspects of the Christianization of the Roman World*. Cambridge, 1995.

———. *Power and Persuasion in Late Antiquity: Towards a Christian Empire*. Madison, 1992.

Brown, P., and R. Lizzi Testa, eds. *Pagans and Christians in the Roman Empire: The Breaking of a Dialogue (4th–6th Century A.D.)*. Vienna, 2011.

Brown, S. *Late Carthaginian Child Sacrifice and Sacrificial Monuments in Their Mediterranean Context*. Sheffield, 1991.

Brown, T. S. “Hieronymus of Cardia.” *AHR* 52 (1947): 684–96.

———. *Timaeus of Tauromenium*. Berkeley, 1958.

Buck, R. J. “Mycenaean Human Sacrifice.” *Minos* 24 (1989): 131–37.

Burch, V. *Myth and Constantine the Great*. Oxford, 1927.

Burgess, R. W. “The Dates and Editions of Eusebius' *Chronici canones* and *Historia ecclesiastica*.” *JTS* 48 (1997): 471–504.

———. *Studies in Eusebian and Post-Eusebian Chronography*. Historia Einzelschriften 135. Stuttgart, 1999.

Burghardt, W. J. “On Early Christian Exegesis.” *TheolSt* 11 (1950): 78–116.

Buriks, A. A. “The Source of Plutarch's ΠΕΡΙ ΤΥΧΗΣ.” *Phoenix* 4 (1950): 59–69.

Burkert, W. *Greek Religion*. Translated by J. Raffan. Oxford, 1985.

———. *Homo Necans: The Anthropology of Ancient Greek Sacrificial Ritual and Myth*. Translated by P. Bing. Berkeley, 1983.

———. *The Orientalizing Revolution: Near Eastern Influence on Greek Culture in the Early Archaic Age*. Translated by M. E. Pinder and W. Burkert. Cambridge, MA, 1992.

Burstein, S. M. *Agatharchides of Cnidus:* On the Erythraean Sea. London, 1989.

Burton, A. *Diodorus Siculus, Book 1: A Commentary.* Leiden, 1972.

Butterfield, H. *The Whig Interpretation of History.* London, 1931.

Butts, A. M. "Assyrian Christians." In Frahm, *A Companion to Assyria*, 599–612.

Buxton, R., ed. *From Myth to Reason? Studies in the Development of Greek Thought.* Oxford, 1999.

Calandra, E. "La città e il nome: Progetto politico e utopia nella fondazione di Antinoe." In *Utiopia e utopie nel pensiero storico antico*, ed. C. Carsana and M. T. Schettino, 133–59. Rome, 2008.

———. "Villa Adriana scenario del potere." In Rizzi, *Hadrian and the Christians*, 21–50.

Calderini, R. "Ricerche sul doppio nome personale nell'Egitto greco-romano." *Aegyptus* 21 (1941): 221–60.

———. "Ricerche sul doppio nome personale nell'Egitto greco-romano II." *Aegyptus* 22 (1942): 3–45.

Camelot, P. T., ed. *Athanase d'Alexandrie, Contre les Païens*. 2nd ed. SC 18 bis. Paris, 1977.

Cameron, Alan. *The Last Pagans of Rome*. Oxford, 2011.

Cameron, Averil. *Christianity and the Rhetoric of Empire: The Development of Christian Discourse.* Berkeley, 1991.

———. "Eusebius of Caesarea and the Rethinking of History." In *Tria Corda: Scritti in onore di Arnaldo Momigliano*, ed. E. Gabba, 71–88. Biblioteca di Athenaeum 1. Como, 1983.

———. "Form and Meaning: The *Vita Constantini* and the *Vita Antonii*." In *Greek Biography and Panegyric in Late Antiquity*, ed. T. Hägg and P. Rousseau, 72–88. Berkeley, 2000.

———. "Virginity as Metaphor: Women and the Rhetoric of Early Christianity." In *History as Text: The Writing of Ancient History*, ed. Av. Cameron, 181–205. Chapel Hill, 1989.

Cameron, Averil, and S. G. Hall. *Eusebius,* Life of Constantine: *Translation, Introduction, and Commentary.* Oxford, 1999.

Cameron, Averil, and J. Herrin, in conjunction with Alan Cameron, R. Cormack, and C. Roueché. *Constantinople in the Early Eighth Century: The* Parastaseis Syntomoi Chronikai. Leiden, 1984.

Campbell, W. J. *The Year That Defined American Journalism: 1897 and the Clash of Paradigms*. London, 2006.

———. "Yellow Journalism: Why So Maligned and Misunderstood?" In *Sensationalism: Murder, Mayhem, Mudslinging, Scandals, and Disasters in 19th-Century Reporting*, ed. D. B. Sachsman and D. W. Bulla, 3–18. New Brunswick, 2013.

Cannadine, D. *The Undivided Past: Humanity beyond Our Differences*. New York, 2013.

Carlyle, T. *On Heroes, Hero-Worship, and the Heroic in History*. Notes and introduction by M. K. Goldberg. Berkeley, 1993.

Carrara, L., and O. Gengler. "Zu den Quellen der Chronik des Johannes Malalas: Eine Einleitung." In Carrara, Meier, and Radtki-Jansen, *Die Weltchronik des Johannes Malalas*, 9–24.

Carrara, L., M. Meier, and C. Radtki-Jansen, eds. *Die Weltchronik des Johannes Malalas: Quellenfragen*. Stuttgart, 2017.

Chadwick, H. *Early Christian Thought and the Classical Tradition: Studies in Justin, Clement, and Origen*. Oxford, 1966.

Champeaux, J. *Fortuna: Recherches sur le culte de la Fortune à Rome et dans le monde romain des origines à la mort de César*. 2 vols. Rome, 1982–87.

Chesnut, G. F. "Eusebius, Augustine, Orosius, and the Later Patristic and Medieval Christian Historians." In Attridge and Hata, *Eusebius, Christianity, and Judaism*, 687–713.

———. *The First Christian Histories: Eusebius, Socrates, Sozomen, Theodoret, and Evagrius*. 2nd ed. Macon, 1986.

Chesnutt, R. D. "The Descent of the Watchers and Its Aftermath According to Justin Martyr." In Harkins, Bautch, and Endres, *Watchers*, 167–80.

Chong-Gossard, J. H. K. O. "Who Slept with Whom in the Roman Empire? Women, Sex, and Scandal in Suetonius' *Caesares*." In Turner, Chong-Gossard, and Vervaet, *Private and Public Lies*, 295–327.

Chuvin, P. *A Chronicle of the Last Pagans*. Translated by B. A. Archer. Cambridge, MA, 1990.

———. "Les fondations syriennes de Séleucos Nicator dans la Chronique de Jean Malalas." In *Géographie historique au Proche-orient (Syrie, Phénicie, Arabie, grecques, romaines, byzantines)*, ed. P.-L. Gatier, B. Helly, and J.-P. Rey-Coquais, 99–110. Paris, 1988.

———. *Mythologie et géographie dionysiaques: Recherches sur l'oeuvre de Nonnos de Panopolis*. Clermont-Ferrand, 1991.

Clark, E. A. *Reading Renunciation: Asceticism and Scripture in Early Christianity.* Princeton, 1999.

Clover, C. J. *Men, Women, and Chain Saws: Gender in the Modern Horror Film.* Princeton, 1992.

Cohen, S. J. D. "Alexander the Great and Jaddus the High Priest According to Josephus." *AJS Review* 7 (1982): 41–68.

Cole, T. *Democritus and the Sources of Greek Anthropology.* Atlanta, 1990.

Connor, S. *Dumbstruck: A Cultural History of Ventriloquism.* Oxford, 2000.

Cook, A. B. *Zeus: A Study in Ancient Religion.* 3 vols. Cambridge, 1914–40.

———. "Zeus, Jupiter and the Oak." *CR* 17 (1903): 403–21.

Cooper, C. "Making Irrational Myth Plausible History: Polybian Intertextuality in Plutarch's *Theseus.*" *Phoenix* 61 (2007): 212–33.

Cooper, K. *The Virgin and the Bride: Idealized Womanhood in Late Antiquity.* Cambridge, MA, 1996.

Corley, J. "The Enochic Watchers Traditions and Deuterocanonical Literature." In Harkins, Bautch, and Endres, *Watchers*, 51–68.

Cornell, T., ed. *The Fragments of the Roman Historians.* 3 vols. Oxford, 2013.

Courcelle, P. *Late Latin Writers and Their Greek Sources.* Translated by H. E. Wedeck. Cambridge, MA, 1969.

———. *Les lettres grecques en Occident de Macrobe a Cassiodore.* Paris, 1948.

Cowan, D. E. *Bearing False Witness? An Introduction to the Christian Countercult.* Westport, 2003.

Cracco Ruggini, L. *Il paganesimo romano tra religione e politica (384–394 d.C.): Per una reinterpretazione del Carmen contra paganos.* Atti della Accademia nazionale dei Lincei: Memorie, Classe di Scienze morali, storiche e filologiche, ser. 8, vol. 23, fasc. 1. Rome, 1979.

Cranz, F. E. "Kingdom and Polity in Eusebius of Caesarea." *HTR* 45 (1952): 47–66.

Cribiore, R. *Libanius the Sophist: Rhetoric, Reality, and Religion in the Fourth Century.* Ithaca, 2013.

Croce, B. *History as the Story of Liberty.* Translated by S. Sprigge, revised by F. Leander and C. Ryn. Indianapolis, 2000.

———. *La storia come pensiero e come azione.* 7th ed. Bari, 1965.

Croke, B. "Byzantine Chronicle Writing, 1: The Early Development of Byzantine Chronicles." In E. Jeffreys, Croke, and Scott, *Studies in John Malalas*, 27–38.

———. "Malalas, the Man and His Work." In E. Jeffreys, Croke, and Scott, *Studies in John Malalas*, 1–25.

Croke, B., and J. Harries. *Religious Conflict in Fourth-Century Rome: A Documentary Study.* Sydney, 1982.

Cumont, F. "Les noms des planètes et l'astrolatrie chez les Grecs." *AntCl* 4 (1935): 5–43.

Currie, B. "Euthymos of Locri: A Case Study in Heroization in the Classical Period." *JHS* 122 (2002): 24–44.

Dagron, G. *Naissance d'une capitale: Constantinople et ses institutions de 330 à 451.* 2nd ed. Paris, 1984.

Dahmen, K. *The Legend of Alexander the Great on Greek and Roman Coins.* London, 2007.

D'Alfonso, F. *Euripide in Giovanni Malala.* Alessandria, 2006.

Damgaard, F. "Propaganda against Propaganda: Revisiting Eusebius' Use of the Figure of Moses in the *Life of Constantine.*" In *Eusebius of Caesarea: Tradition and Innovations*, ed. A. P. Johnson and J. Schott, 1:115–29. 2 vols. Washington, DC, 2013.

Darvill, T., K. Barker, B. Bender, and R. Hutton, eds. *The Cerne Giant: An Antiquity on Trial. Three Cases Presented to an Enquiry Convened to Consider the Origin of the Cerne Giant, Held in Cerne Abbas Village Hall, Dorset, on 23rd March 1996.* Oxford, 1999.

Datema, C. "New Evidence for the Encounter between Constantinople and 'India.'" In *After Chalcedon: Studies in Theology and Church History Offered to Professor Albert van Roey for his Seventieth Birthday*, ed. C. Laga, J. A. Munitiz, and L. van Rompay, 56–65. Leuven, 1985.

Davies, M. *The Greek Epic Cycle.* London, 1989.

Davies, N. *Human Sacrifice in History and Today.* New York, 1991.

Davis, D. B. "Some Themes of Counter-Subversion: An Analysis of Anti-Masonic, Anti-Catholic, and Anti-Mormon Literature." *Mississippi Valley Historical Review* 47 (1960): 205–24.

Davis, J. C. *Oliver Cromwell.* London, 2001.

De Leo, P. *Ricerche sui falsi medioevali 1, Il* Constitutum Constantini: *Compilazione agiografica del sec. VIII.* Reggio Calabria, 1974.

De Lubac, H. "'Typologie' et 'allégorisme.'" *Recherches de science religieuse* 34 (1947): 180–226.

De Meulenaere, H. "Les monuments du culte des rois Nectanébo." *Chronique d'Egypte* 35 (1960): 92–107.

Decrept, E. "Une persécution oubliée: la persécution d'Antioche sous Trajan." In *Antioche de Syrie: Histoires, images et traces de la ville antique* (*Topoi* Supplément 5), ed. B. Cabouret, P.-L. Gatier, and C. Saliou, 417–25. Lyon, 2004.

Delling, G. "Alexander der Grosse als Bekenner des jüdischen Gottesglaubens." *Journal for the Study of Judaism in the Persian, Hellenistic and Roman Period* 12 (1981): 1–51.

Demoen, K., and D. Praet, eds. *Theios Sophistes: Essays on Flavius Philostratus'* Vita Apolonii. Leiden, 2009.

den Hengst, D. *Emperors and Historiography: Collected Essays on the Literature of the Roman Empire by Daniël den Hengst*. Edited by D. W. P. Burgersdijk and J. A. van Waarden. Leiden, 2010.

Detienne, M. *The Creation of Mythology*. Translated by M. Cook. Chicago, 1986.

Diels, H., and W. Kranz. *Die Fragmente der Vorsokratiker*. 6th ed. Berlin, 1952.

Dillery, J. *Clio's Other Sons: Berossus and Manetho*. Ann Arbor, 2015.

———. "The First Egyptian Narrative History: Manetho and Greek Historiography." *ZPapEpig* 127 (1999): 93–116.

Di Serio, C. "La dimensione mitica di Alessandro nel *De Alexandri Magni fortuna aut virtute*." In Mythologica Plutarchea*: Estudios sobre los mitos en Plutarco. XIII Simposio Internacional de la Sociedad Española de Plutarquistas (Universidad de Lleida, 4–5–6 de octubre de 2018)*, ed. J. A. Clúa, 137–46. Madrid, 2020.

Djurslev, C. T. *Alexander the Great in the Early Christian Tradition: Classical Reception and Patristic Literature*. London, 2020.

Dodds, E. R. *Pagan and Christian in an Age of Anxiety: Some Aspects of Religious Experience from Marcus Aurelius to Constantine*. Cambridge, 1965.

Dohrn, T. *Die Tyche von Antiochia*. Berlin, 1960.

Dölger, F. J. "'*Sacramentum infanticidii*': Die Schlachtung eines Kindes und der Genuss seines Fleisches und Blutes als vermeintlicher Einweihungsakt im ältesten Christentum." *Antike und Christentum* 4 (1934): 188–228.

Downey, G. *A History of Antioch in Syria from Seleucus to the Arab Conquest*. Princeton, 1961.

———. "Julian the Apostate at Antioch." *ChHist* 8 (1939): 303–15.

———. "Libanius' Oration in Praise of Antioch." *TAPA* 103 (1959): 652–86.

———. "Strabo on Antioch: Notes on His Method." *TAPA* 72 (1941): 85–95.

Drake, H. A. "Fourth-Century Christianity and the 'Paranoid Style.'" In Hillard et al., *Ancient History in a Modern University*, 357–68.

———. In Praise of Constantine*: A Historical Study and New Translation of Eusebius' Tricennial Orations*. Berkeley, 1976.

Drews, R. "The Fall of Astyages and Herodotus' Chronology of the Eastern Kingdoms." *Historia* (1969): 1–11.

Drijvers, J. W. "Religious Conflict in the Syriac *Julian Romance*." In Brown and Lizzi Testa, *Pagans and Christians*, 131–62.

Droge, A. J. *Homer or Moses? Early Christian Interpretations of the History of Culture*. Tübingen, 1989.

Ducrey, P. *Le traitement des prisonniers de guerre dans la Grèce antique des origines a la conquête romaine*. Paris, 1968.

Dundes, A., ed. *The Walled-Up Wife: A Casebook*. Madison, 1996.

Dunning, B. *Conspiracies Declassified: The* Skeptoid® *Guide to the Truth behind the Theories*. New York, 2018.

Dvornik, F. *Early Christian and Byzantine Political Philosophy: Origins and Background*. Washington, DC, 1966.

Eckhardt, B. "'Bloodless Sacrifice': A Note on Greek Cultic Language in the Imperial Era." *GRBS* 54 (2014): 255–73.

Eco, U. *Il Cimitero di Praga*. Milan, 2010.

———. *Numero Zero*. Milan, 2015.

Edelstein, L., and I. G. Kidd. *Posidonius*. 2nd ed. Cambridge, 1989.

Edwards, M. *Religions of the Constantinian Empire*. Oxford, 2015.

———. "Some Theories on the Dating of Arnobius." *Ephemerides Theologicae Lovanienses* 94 (2016): 671–84.

Ehlert, T. "Alexander und die Frauen in spätantiken und mittelalterlichen Alexander-Erzählungen." In *Kontinuität und Transformation der Antike im Mittelalter*, ed. W. Erzgräber, 81–103. Sigmaringen, 1989.

Elm, S. "Gregory of Nazianzus' Life of Julian Revisited (*Or.* 4 and 5): The Art of Governance by Invective." In McGill, Sogno, and Watts, *From the Tetrarchs to the Theodosians*, 171–82.

———. "Gregory's Women: Creating a Philosopher's Family." In *Gregory of Nazianzus: Images and Reflections*, ed. J. Børtnes and T. Hägg, 171–91. Copenhagen, 2006.

———. "Hellenism and Historiography: Gregory of Nazianzus and Julian in Dialogue." In *The Cultural Turn in Late Ancient Studies: Gender, Asceticism, and Historiography*, ed. D. B. Martin and P. C. Miller, 258–77. Durham, 2005.

———. *Sons of Hellenism, Fathers of the Church: Emperor Julian, Gregory of Nazianzus, and the Vision of Rome*. Berkeley, 2012.

———. *Virgins of God: The Making of Asceticism in Late Antiquity*. Oxford, 1994.

Else, G. F. *Aristotle's Poetics: The Argument*. Cambridge, MA, 1957.

Elsner, J. "Describing Self in the Language of Other: Pseudo (?) Lucian at the Temple of Hierapolis." In Goldhill, *Being Greek under Rome*, 123–53.

Elsner, J., and J. Masters, eds. *Reflections of Nero: Culture, History, and Representation*. Chapel Hill, 1994.

Enslin, M. S. "Cain and Prometheus." *JBL* 86 (1966): 88–90.

Evans, D. M. "Eighteenth-century Descriptions of the Cerne Abbas Giant." In Darvill et al., *The Cerne Giant*, 108–15.

Fairbairn, D. "Patristic Exegesis and Theology: The Cart and the Horse." *Westminster Theological Journal* 69 (2007): 1–19.

Fatti, F. "Il principe, la *Tyche*, i cristiani: Giuliano a Cesarea." In P. Brown and Lizzi Testa, *Pagans and Christians*, 121–29.

Fauth, W. *Helios Megistos: Zur synkretistischen Theologie der Spätantike*. Leiden, 1995.

Felton, D. *Haunted Greece and Rome: Ghost Stories from Classical Antiquity*. Austin, 1999.

Ferguson, J. *Among the Gods: An Archaeological Exploration of Ancient Greek Religion*. London, 1989.

———. *The Religions of the Roman Empire*. Ithaca, 1970.

Festugière, A. J. *Antioch païenne et chrétienne: Libanius, Chrysostome et les moines de Syrie*. Paris, 1959.

Fitton, J. "Domitian and Saint John in Malalas." *Byzantion* 44 (1974): 143–44.

Fitzmyer, J. A. "Some Notes on Aramaic Epistolography." *JBL* 93 (1974): 201–25.

Flamant, J. *Macrobe et le Néo-Platonisme latin, à la fin du IVe siècle*. Leiden, 1977.

Foley, H. P. *Euripides: Hecuba*. London, 2015.

Fontenrose, J. "The Hero as Athlete." *California Studies in Classical Antiquity* 1 (1968): 73–104.

———. *Python: A Study of Delphic Myth and Its Origins*. Berkeley, 1959.

Fortenbaugh, W. W. *Quellen zur Ethik Theophrasts*. Amsterdam, 1984.

———. *Theophrastus of Eresus: Sources for His Life, Writings, Thought and Influence*. 2 vols. Leiden, 1993.

Fowden, G. *Empire to Commonwealth: Consequences of Monotheism in Late Antiquity*. Princeton, 1993.

Fowler, D. "Virgil on Killing Virgins." In *Homo Viator: Classical Essays for John Bramble*, ed. M. Whitby, P. R. Hardie, and M. Whitby, 185–98. Bristol, 1987.

Fox, M. *Roman Historical Myths: The Regal Period in Augustan Literature*. Oxford, 1996.

Frahm, E., ed. *A Companion to Assyria*. Hoboken, 2017.

Frankfurter, D. *Evil Incarnate: Rumors of Demonic Conspiracy and Satanic Abuse in History*. Princeton, 2006.

Franklin, S. "Malalas in Slavonic." In E. Jeffreys, Croke, and Scott, *Studies in John Malalas*, 276–87.

Fraser, A. *Cromwell, Our Chief of Men*. London, 1985.

Fraser, P. M. *Cities of Alexander the Great*. Oxford, 1996.

———. *Ptolemaic Alexandria*. 3 vols. Oxford, 1972.

Frazer, J. G. *The Golden Bough*. 3rd ed. 13 vols. London, 1911.

———. *Pausanias' Description of Greece*. 6 vols. London, 1898.

Freudenthal, J. *Alexander Polyhistor und die von ihm erhaltenen Reste judäischer und samaritanischer Geschichtswerke*. Breslau, 1875.

Froehlich, K. *Biblical Interpretation in the Early Church*. Philadelphia, 1984.

Fröhlich, I. "Mesopotamian Elements and the Watchers Traditions." In Harkins, Bautch, and Endres, *Watchers*, 11–24.

Frolow, A. "La dédicace de Constantinople dans la tradition byzantine." *RHR* 127 (1944): 61–127.

Frye, R. N. "Assyria and Syria: Synonyms." *JNES* 51 (1992): 281–85.

Gabba, E. "True History and False History in Classical Antiquity." *JRS* 71 (1981): 50–62.

Gabriel, J. "Die Kainitengenealogie, Gn 4, 17–24." *Biblica* 40 (1959): 409–27.

Gage, W. A. *The Gospel of Genesis: Studies in Protology and Eschatology*. Winona Lake, IN, 1984.

Gager, J. G. *The Origins of Anti-Semitism: Attitudes toward Judaism in Pagan and Christian Antiquity*. Oxford, 1983.

Galimberti, A. *Adriano e l'ideologia del principato*. Rome, 2007.

Gallardo, M. D. "Los *simposios* de Luciano, Ateneo, Metodio y Juliano." *Cuadernos de filología clasica* 4 (1972): 239–96.

Galli, M. "La *paideia* di Adriano: Alcune osservazioni sulla valenza politica del culto eroico." In Rizzi, *Hadrian and the Christians*, 51–69.

Garsoïan, N. G. *The Epic Histories Attributed to P'awstos Buzand (*Buzandaran Patmut'iwnk'*)*. Cambridge, MA, 1989.

Garstad, B. "The Account of Thoulis, King of Egypt, in the *Chronographia* of John Malalas." *BZ* 107 (2014): 51–76.

———. "Alexander's Circuit of the Mediterranean in the *Alexander Romance*." In Stoneman, Nawotka, and Wojciechowska, *The* Alexander Romance*: History and Literature*, 129–57.

———. "Alexander's Comrades in the *Chronicle* of John Malalas." *SLA* 4 (2020): 452–85.

———. "Alexander the Great's Liberation of Rome and an Idiosyncratic Model of World History in the *Chronicle* of John Malalas, the *Excerpta Latina Barbari*, and Fulgentius' *De aetatibus*." *WSt* 131 (2018): 179–205.

———. "The Assyrian Hero's Romantic Interlude in Libya: A *Topos* from Virgil in Pisander of Laranda, the Picus-Zeus narrative, and Nonnus of Panopolis." *Eranos* 101 (2003): 6–16.

———. "Barbarian Interest in the *Excerpta Latina Barbari*." *EME* 19 (2011): 3–42.

———. "Belus in the *Sacred History* of Euhemerus." *CPh* 99 (2004): 246–57.

———. "Deification in Euhemerus of Messene: Charisma or Contrivance?" In *Das Charisma des Herrschers*, ed. D. Boschung and J. Hammerstaedt, 151–72. Morphomata 29. Paderborn, 2015.

———. "Euhemerus and the *Chronicle* of John Malalas." *International History Review* 38 (2016): 900–929.

———. "The Excerpta Latina Barbari and the 'Picus-Zeus Narrative.'" *Jahrbuch für Internationale Germanistik* 34 (2002): 259–313.

———. "Joseph as a Model for Faunus-Hermes: Myth, History, and Fiction in the Fourth Century." *VChr* 63 (2009): 493–521.

———. "The Origins of Paganism and the Contemporary Persians in John Malalas' *Chronicle*." Forthcoming in *Johannes Malalas: Der Chronist als Zeithistoriker*, ed. O. Gengler and M. Meier. Malalas Studien 4. Stuttgart, 2021.

———. "Pausanias of Antioch: Introduction, Translation, and Commentary." *Aram* 23 (2011): 669–91.

———. "Perseus and the Foundation of Tarsus in the *Chronicle* of John Malalas: Sources and Allusions." *Byzantion* 84 (2014): 171–83.

———. "Rome in the *Alexander Romance*." *HSCPh* 108 (2015): 467–507.

———. "The Tyche Sacrifices in John Malalas: Virgin Sacrifice and Fourth-century Polemical History." *ICS* 30 (2005): 83–135.

Gastgeber, C. "Die *Osterchronik* und Johannes Malalas: Aspekte der Rezeption." In Meier, Radtki-Jansen, and Schulz, *Die Weltchronik des Johannes Malalas*, 187–224.

Gelzer, H. *Sextus Julius Africanus und die byzantinische Chronographie*. 2 vols. Leipzig, 1880–89.

Gengler, O. "Johannes Malalas und seine Quellen: Überlegungen zum Fall Philostratos (Malalas XII 26)." In *Byzanz und das Abendland 4. Studia Byzantino-Occidentalia*, 175–85. Budapest, 2016.

Genna, G. *Nel nome di Ishmael*. Milan, 2001.

Gilbert, M. *La critique des dieux dans le Livre de la Sagesse (Sg 13–15)*. Rome, 1973.

Gill, C. "The Genre of the Atlantis Story." *CPh* 72 (1977): 287–304.

———. "Plato on Falsehood—Not Fiction." In Gill and Wiseman, *Lies and Fiction*, 38–87.

———. *Plato's Atlantis Story: Text, Translation and Commentary*. Liverpool, 2017.

Gill, C. and T. Wiseman, eds. *Lies and Fiction in the Ancient World*. Austin, 1993.

Ginsborg, P. *A History of Contemporary Italy: Society and Politics, 1943–1988*. London, 1990.

Ginzburg, C. *The Judge and the Historian: Marginal Notes on a Late-Twentieth-Century Miscarriage of Justice*. Translated by A. Shugaar. London, 1999.

Gleason, M. W. "Festive Satire: Julian's *Misopogon* and the New Year at Antioch." *JRS* 76 (1986): 106–19.

———. "Identity Theft: Doubles and Masquerades in Cassius Dio's Contemporary History." *Classical Antiquity* 30 (2011): 33–86.

Goldhill, S., ed. *Being Greek under Rome: Cultural Identity, the Second Sophistic and the Development of Empire*. Cambridge, 2001.

Goldstein, J. A. "Alexander and the Jews." *Proceedings of the American Academy for Jewish Records* 59 (1993): 59–101.

Gollancz, H. *Julian the Apostate, Now Translated for the First Time from the Syriac Original*. London, 1928.

Gomme, A. W. *A Historical Commentary on Thucydides*. 5 vols. Oxford, 1956–66.

Gowen, H. H. "The Cainite and Sethite Genealogies in Gen. 4 & 5." *Anglican Theological Review* 2 (1924): 326–27.

Grabar, A. *Christian Iconography: A Study of Its Origins*. Trans. T. Grabar. Princeton, 1968.

———. *L'empereur dans l'art byzantin: Recherches sur l'art officiel de l'Empire d'Orient*. Paris, 1936.

Graf, F. *Greek Mythology: An Introduction*. Translated by T. Marier. Baltimore, 1993.

———. *Magic in the Ancient World*. Translated by F. Philip. Cambridge, MA, 1997.

Grant, M. *Greek and Roman Historians: Information and Misinformation*. London, 1995.

Grant, R. M. "Five Apologists and Marcus Aurelius." *VChr* 42 (1988): 1–17.

Graves, M. *Biblical Interpretation in the Early Church*. Minneapolis, 2017.

Gray, J. *Black Mass: Apocalyptic Religion and the Death of Utopia*. London, 2007.

Greatrex, G. "Roman Frontiers and Foreign Policy in the East." In *Aspects of the Roman East: Papers in Honour of Professor Fergus Millar FBA*, ed. R. Alston and S. Lieu, 103–73. Turnhout, 2007.

Green, P. "'These fragments have I shored against my ruins': Apollonios Rhodios and the Social Revalidation of Myth for a New Age." In *Hellenistic Constructs: Essays in Culture, History, and Historiography*, ed. P. Cartledge, P. Garnsey, and E. Gruen, 35–71. Berkeley, 1997.

Green, R. P. H. *The Works of Ausonius*. Oxford, 1991.

Green, T. M. *The City of the Moon God: Religious Traditions of Harran*. Leiden, 1992.

Griffith, S. H. "Ephraem the Syrian's Hymns 'Against Julian': Meditations on History and Imperial Power." *VChr* 41 (1987): 238–66.

Grünewald, T. "Der letzte Kampf des Heidentums in Rom? Zur postumen Rehabilitation des Virius Nicomachus Flavianus." *Historia* 41 (1992): 462–87.

Guillet, J. "Les exégètes d'Alexandrie et d'Antioche. Conflit ou malentendu?" *Recherches de science religieuse* 34 (1947): 257–302.

Guyot, P. "Antinous als Eunuch: Zur christlichen Polemik gegen das Heidentum." *Historia* 30 (1981): 250–54.

Gyselinck, W., and K. Demoen. "Author and Narrator: Fiction and Metafiction in Philosotratus' *Vita Apollonii*." In Demoen and Praet, *Theios Sophistes*, 95–127.

Hadley, R. A. "Hieronymus of Cardia and Early Seleucid Mythology." *Historia* 18 (1969): 142–52.

Hägg, T. *The Novel in Antiquity*. Berkeley, 1983.

Halfmann, H. "Kaiser Trajan und die Grenzen des Imperium Romanum im Osten." In *Stuttgarter Kolloquium zur historischen Geographie des Altertums: 4, 1990*, ed. E. Olshausen and H. Sonnabend, 577–88. Amsterdam, 1994.

Halkin, F. *Bibliotheca Hagiographica Graeca*. 3rd ed. Bruxelles, 1957.

Halliday, W. R. "Picus-Who-Is-Also-Zeus." *CR* 36 (1922): 110–12.

Hamilton, V. P. *The Book of Genesis: Chapters 1–17*. Grand Rapids, 1990.

Harkins, A. K., K. C. Bautch, and J. C. Endres, eds. *The Watchers in Jewish and Christian Traditions*. Minneapolis, 2014.

Harl, K. W. "Sacrifice and Pagan Belief in Fifth- and Sixth-Century Byzantium." *Past & Present* 128 (1990): 7–27.

Harlan, E. C. "The Description of Paintings as a Literary Device and Its Application in Achilles Tatius." Phd diss., Columbia University, 1965.

Harrer, G. A. "Saul Who Also Is Called Paul." *HTR* 33 (1940): 19–33.

Harris, J. R. *Boanerges*. Cambridge, 1913.

———. *Picus Who Is Also Zeus*. Cambridge, 1916.

Harrison, J. E. *Themis: A Study of the Social Origins of Greek Religion*. Cambridge, 1912.

Hassrick, P. H., and M. W. Speidel. *Frederic Remington: A Catalogue Raisonne of Paintings, Watercolors, and Drawings*. 2 vols. Cody, WY/Seattle, 1996.

Hauser, A. J., and D. F. Watson, eds. *A History of Biblical Interpretation, Volume 1: The Ancient Period*. Grand Rapids, 2003.

———. "Introduction and Overview." In Hauser and Watson, *History of Biblical Interpretation, 1*, 1–54.

Hawes, G. *Rationalizing Myth in Antiquity*. Oxford, 2014.

Hays, G. "A World without Letters: Fulgentius and the *De aetatibus mundi et hominis*." *Journal of Medieval Latin* 29 (2019): 303–39.

Heckel, W. *The Last Days and Testament of Alexander the Great: A Prosopographic Study*. Historia Einzelschriften 56. Stuttgart, 1988.

Hedrick, C. W., Jr. *History and Silence: Purge and Rehabilitation of Memory in Late Antiquity*. Austin, 2000.

Hengel, M. *Jews, Greeks and Barbarians: Aspects of the Hellenization of Judaism in the Pre-Christian Period*. Translated by J. Bowden. Philadelphia, 1980.

Henrichs, A. "Demythologizing the Past, Mythicizing the Present: Myth, History, and the Supernatural at the Dawn of the Hellenistic Period." In Buxton, *From Myth to Reason?*, 223–48.

———. "Pagan Ritual and the Alleged Crimes of the Early Christians: A Reconsideration." In *Kyriakon: Festschrift Johannes Quasten*, ed. P. Granfield and J. A. Jungmann, 1:18–35. 2 vols. Münster, 1970.

———. "The Sophists and Hellenistic Religion: Prodicus as the Spiritual Father of the Isis Aretalogies." *HSCPh* 88 (1984): 139–58.

———. "Two Doxographical Notes: Democritus and Prodicus on Religion." *HSCPh* 79 (1975): 93–123.

Hermann, A. "Antinous infelix: Zur Typologie des Heiligen-Unheiligen in der Spätantike." In *Mullus: Festschrift Theodor Klauser*, ed. A. Stuiber and A. Hermann, 155–67. Münster, 1964.

Hershbell, J. P. "Plutarch's Concept of History: Philosophy from Examples." *Ancient Society* 28 (1997): 225–43.

Heyman, G. *The Power of Sacrifice: Roman and Christian Discourses in Conflict*. Washington, DC, 2007.

Hidal, S. "Exegesis of the Old Testament in the Antiochene School with its Prevalent Literal and Historical Method." In *Hebrew Bible / Old Testament: The History of Its Interpretation. Volume 1: From the Beginnings to the Middle Ages (Until 1300), Part 1: Antiquity*, ed. M. Sæbø, 543–68. Göttingen, 1996.

Hillard, T. W., R. A. Kearsley, C. E. V. Nixon, and A. M. Nobbs, eds. *Ancient History in a Modern University, Volume 2: Early Christianity, Late Antiquity, and Beyond*. Grand Rapids, 1988.

Hilton, J. "Myth and Narrative Fiction in the Works of the Roman Emperor Julian." *LisFil* 140 (2017): 39–70.

Hjort, Ø. "Augustus Christianus—Livia Christiana: *Sphragis* and Roman Portrait Sculpture." In Rydén and Rosenqvist, *Aspects of Late Antiquity*, 99–112.

Hofstadter, R. *The Paranoid Style in American Politics and Other Essays*. New York, 1966.

Hogarth, D. G. "Nectanebo, Pharaoh and Magician." *EHR* 11 (1896): 1–12.

Hollerich, M. J. "Religion and Politics in the Writings of Eusebius: Reassessing the First 'Court Theologian.'" *ChHist* 59 (1990): 309–25.

Horak, U. "Πινουτίων μουσικός und Βίκτωρ Τάραξ." *Tyche* 4 (1989): 101–7.

Hornblower, J. *Hieronymus of Cardia*. Oxford, 1981.

Ho Tai, H.-T. "Remembered Realms: Pierre Nora and French National Memory." *AHR* 106 (2001): 906–22.

Hughes, D. D. *Human Sacrifice in Ancient Greece*. London, 1991.

Hunger, H. *Die hochsprachliche profane Literatur der Byzantiner*. 2 vols. Munich, 1978.

Hunter, R. "The *Aithiopika* of Heliodorus: Beyond Interpretation?" In *Studies in Heliodorus*, ed. R. Hunter, 40–59. Cambridge, 1998.

Huxley, G. "Fulgentius on the Cretan Hecatomphonia." *CPh* 68 (1973): 124–27.

Ibsen, H. *Emperor and Galilean: A World-Historic Drama*. Translated by W. Archer. New York, 1923.

———. *Samlede verker*. Oslo, 1968.

Instinsky, H. U. *Alexander der Grosse am Hellespont*. Godesberg, 1949.

Iricinschi, E. "Good Hebrew, Bad Hebrew: Christians as *Triton Genos* in Eusebius' Apologetic Writings." In *Reconsidering Eusebius: Collected Papers on Literary, Historical, and Theological Issues*, ed. S. Inowlocki and C. Zamagni, 69–86. Leiden, 2011.

Isaac, B. *The Invention of Racism in Classical Antiquity*. Princeton, 2004.

Istrin, V. M. "Khronika Ioanna Malaly v slavyanskom perevode, kniga II," *Letopis' istoriko-filologisheskogo obshchestva pri Imp. Novorossiyskom universitete* 10 (1902): 437–86.

———. "Khronika Ioanna Malaly v slavyanskom perevode, kniga X," *Letopis' istoriko-filologisheskogo obshchestva pri Imp. Novorossiyskom universitete* 17 (1912): 3–44.

———. *Khronika Ioanna Malaly*. Repr. Moscow, 1994.

Jaeger, W. *Paideia: The Ideals of Greek Culture*. Translated by G. Highet. 3 vols. New York, 1944.

Janiszewski, P. *The Missing Link: Greek Pagan Historiography in the Second Half of the Third Century and in the Fourth Century AD*. Translated by D. Dzierzbicka. Warsaw, 2006.

Jeffreys, E. "The *Chronicle* of John Malalas: A Commentary." In P. Allen and Jeffreys, *The Sixth Century*, 52–74.

———. "Malalas' Sources." In E. Jeffreys, Croke, and Scott, *Studies in John Malalas*, 167–216.

Jeffreys, E., with B. Croke and R. Scott, eds. *Studies in John Malalas*. ByzAus 6. Sydney, 1990.

Jeffreys, E., and M. Jeffreys. "Language of Malalas, 3: Portraits." In E. Jeffreys, Croke, and Scott, *Studies in John Malalas*, 231–44.

Jeffreys, E., with M. Jeffreys and R. Scott, et al. *The Chronicle of John Malalas: A Translation*. ByzAus 4. Melbourne, 1986.

Jeffreys, M. "Language of Malalas, 2: Formulaic Phraseology." In E. Jeffreys, Croke, and Scott, *Studies in John Malalas*, 225–30.

Johansen, T. K. "Myth and Logos in Aristotle." In Buxton, *From Myth to Reason?*, 279–91.

Johnson, A. P. *Ethnicity and Argument in Eusebius'* Praeparatio Evangelica. Oxford, 2006.

———. "Greek Ethnicity in Eusebius' *Praeparatio Evangelica*." *AJP* 128 (2007): 95–118.

———. "Hellenism and Its Discontents." In *The Oxford Handbook of Late Antiquity*, ed. S. F. Johnson, 437–66. Oxford, 2012.

Jones, B. W. *The Emperor Domitian*. London, 1992.

Jones, C. P. *New Heroes in Antiquity: From Achilles to Antinoos*. Cambridge, MA, 2010.

Jones, T. *The Dark Heart of Italy*. London, 2003.

Jouanno, C. "Alexandre à Jérusalem: Variations byzantines sur une thème hérité de Flavius Josephus." *Anabases* 23 (2016): 75–95.

———. "Du roman grec au roman byzantin: Réflexions sur le rôle de la *tyché*." In *Les Hommes et les Dieux dans l'ancien roman: Actes du colloque de Tours, 22–24 octobre 2009*, ed. C. Bost-Pouderon and B. Pouderon, 287–304. Lyon, 2012.

———. *Naissance et métamorphoses du Roman d'Alexandre: Domaine grec*. Paris, 2002.

Juhász, E. "Die Indiktionsangaben bei Johannes Malalas und in der *Osterchronik*." In Meier, Radtki-Jansen, and Schulz, *Die Weltchronik des Johannes Malalas*, 225–37.

Jürgens, H. *Pompa diaboli: Die lateinischen Kirchenväter und das antike Theater.* Stuttgart, 1972.

Kaldellis, A. "The Historical and Religious Views of Agathias: A Reinterpretation." *Byzantion* 69 (1999): 206–52.

———. *Procopius of Caesarea: Tyranny, History, and Philosophy at the End of Antiquity*. Philadelphia, 2004.

———, ed. and trans. *Prokopios, The Secret History, with Related Texts.* Indianapolis, 2010.

Kannengiesser, C. "Eusebius of Caesarea, Origenist." In Attridge and Hata, *Eusebius, Christianity, and Judaism*, 435–66.

Kastely, J. L. "Violence and Rhetoric in Euripides' *Hecuba*." *PMLA* 108 (1993): 1036–49.

Kazhdan, A. "'Constantin imaginaire': Byzantine Legends of the Ninth Century about Constantine the Great." *Byzantion* 57 (1987): 196–250.

Kebric, R. B. *In the Shadow of Macedon: Duris of Samos*. Historia Einzelschriften 29. Wiesbaden, 1977.

Kent, R. G. "The Oldest Old Persian Inscriptions." *JAOS* 66 (1946): 206–12.

Kerekes, D., and D. Slater. *Killing for Culture: An Illustrated History of Death Film from Mondo to Snuff*. London, 1995.

Keresztes, P. "The Jews, the Christians, and Emperor Domitian." *VChr* 27 (1973): 1–28.

Kiilerich, B. "Defacement and Replacement as Political Strategies in Ancient and Byzantine Ruler Images." In Kolrud and Prusac, *Iconoclasm*, 57–73.

———. *Late Fourth Century Classicism in the Plastic Arts: Studies in the So-called Theodosian Renaissance*. Odense, 1993.

———. "Sculpture in the Round in the Early Byzantine Period: Constantinople and the East." In Rydén and Rosenqvist, *Aspects of Late Antiquity*, 85–97.

Kilmer, M. F. *Greek Erotica on Red-Figure Vases.* London, 1993.

———. "Sexual Violence: Archaic Athens and the Recent Past." In *'Owls to Athens': Essays on Classical Subjects Presented to Sir Kenneth Dover*, ed. E. M. Craik, 261–77. Oxford, 1990.

King, S. *Danse Macabre*. New York, 2010.

Kirk, G. S. *The Iliad: A Commentary, Volume 1: Books 1–4*. Cambridge, 1985.

Klaffenbach, G., ed. *Inscriptiones Graeciae Septentrionalis, voluminibus VII et VIII non comprehensae*, part 1, *Inscriptiones Phocidis Locridis Aetoliae Acarnaniae insularum maris Ionii*, fasc. 3, *Inscriptiones Locridis occidentalis* (*Inscriptiones Graecae*, vol. 9, part 1, fasc. 3). Berlin, 1968.

Klein, R. "Das Bild des Augustus in der frühchristlichen Literatur." In von Haehling, *Rom und das himmlische Jerusalem*, 205–36.

———. "Zur Beurteilung Alexanders des Großen in der patristischen Literatur." In Will and Heinrichs, *Zu Alexander d. Gr.*, 2:925–89.

Kleingünther, A. *ΠΡΩΤΟΣ ΕΥΡΕΤΗΣ: Untersuchungen zur Geschichte einer Fragestellung*. Leipzig, 1933.

Klemm, P. "Kain und die Kainiten." *Zeitschrift für Theologie und Kirche* 78 (1981): 391–408.

Knights, M. "The Tory Interpretation of History in the Rage of the Parties." *Huntington Library Quarterly* 68 (2005): 353–73.

Koch, S. *Double Lives: Stalin, Willi Münzenberg and the Seduction of the Intellectuals*. 2nd ed. New York, 2004.

Koenen, L. "Review of Corpus Papyrorum Judaicarum, 2." *Gnomon* 40 (1968): 250–59.

Kofsky, A. *Eusebius of Caesarea against Paganism*. Leiden, 2000.

Kokoszko, M. *Descriptions of Personal Appearance in John Malalas' Chronicle*. Łódź, 1998.

Kolrud, K., and M. Prusac, eds. *Iconoclasm from Antiquity to Modernity*. Farnham, Surrey, 2014.

Konstan, D. "The Alexander Romance: The Cunning of the Open Text." *Lexis* 16 (1998): 123–38.

Korteweg, T. "Justin Martyr and His Demon-ridden Universe." In *Demons and the Devil in Ancient and Medieval Christianity*, ed. N. Vos and W. Otten, 145–58. Leiden, 2011.

Krappe, A. H. "Picus Who Is Also Zeus." *Mnemosyne* 9 (1941): 241–57.

Krautheimer, R. "The Ecclesiastical Building Policy of Constantine." In Bonamente and Fusco, *Costantino il Grande*, 2:509–52.

Kristensen, T. M. "Embodied Images: Christian Response and Destruction in Late Antique Egypt." *JLA* 2 (2009): 224–50.

Lacombrade, C., ed. and trans. *L'empereur Julien: Oeuvres complètes, Tome 2—2e partie: Les Césars—Sur Hélios-Roi—Le Misopogon*. Paris, 1964.

Lambert, R. *Beloved and God: The Story of Hadrian and Antinous*. New York, 1984.

Lambertz, M. "Zur Ausbreitung des Supernomen oder Signum im römischen Reiche, 2." *Glotta* 5 (1913): 99–170.

Lane Fox, R. J. "The Itinerary of Alexander: Contantius to Julian." *CQ* 47 (1997): 239–52.

Lathoud, D. "La consécration et la dédicace de Constantinople." *EO* 23 (1924): 289–314.

———. "La consécration et la dédicace de Constantinople (Suite [I].)." *EO* 24 (1925): 180–201.

Latte, K. *Römische Religionsgeschichte*. Munich, 1960.

Laws, P. *The Frighteners: A Journey through our Cultural Fascination with the Macabre*. New York, 2018.

Leclerq, H. "Note concernant les noms doubles en Egypte ptolémaïque." *Aegyptus* 43 (1963): 192–94.

———. "Note de grammaire sur les doubles noms dans le Nouveau Testament grec." *OLP* 6/7 (1975/76): 361–72.

Lefkowitz, M. R. "'Impiety' and 'Atheism' in Euripides' Dramas." *CQ* 39 (1989): 70–82.

Lenfant, D. *Ctésias de Cnide: La Perse, L'Inde, Autres Fragments*. Paris, 2004.

Lenski, N. *Constantine and the Cities: Imperial Authority and Civic Politics*. Philadelphia, 2016.

Lerat, L. *Les Locriens de l'Ouest*. 2 vols. Bibliothèque des Écoles françaises d'Athènes et de Rome 176. Paris, 1952.

Lesher, J. H. *Xenophanes of Colophon, Fragments: A Text and Translation with Commentary*. Toronto, 1992.

Levick, B., and J. Rich. "Bruttius." In Cornell, *Fragments of the Roman Historians*, 1:593–95, 2:1089–95, 3:629–31.

Levison, W. "Konstantinische Schenkung und Silvester-Legende." In *Miscellanea Francesco Ehrle: Scritti di Storia e Paleografia, Vol. 2: Per la storia di Roma*, 159–247. Studi i Testi 38. Roma, 1924.

Levy, R. S. Introduction to *A Lie and a Libel: The History of the* Protocols of the Elders of Zion, by B. W. Segel, 1–47. Translated and edited by Levy. Lincoln, 1995.

Liebeschuetz, W. *East and West in Late Antiquity: Invasion, Settlement, Ethnogenesis and Conflicts of Religion*. Leiden, 2015.

———. "Libanius and Late Antique Autobiography." In *Mélanges A. F. Norman*, Topoi: Orient-Occident, Suppl. 7, ed. Á. González Gálvez and P.-L. Malosse, 263–76. Paris, 2006.

———. "The Significance of the Speech of Praetextatus." In *Pagan Monotheism in Late Antiquity*, ed. P. Athanassiadi and M. Frede, 185–205. Oxford, 1999.

———. "The Use of Pagan Mythology in the Christian Empire with Particular Reference to the *Dionysiaca* of Nonnus." In P. Allen and Jeffreys, *The Sixth Century*, 75–91.

———. "The View from Antioch: From Libanius via John Chrysostom to John Malalas and Beyond." In P. Brown and Lizzi Testa, *Pagans and Christians*, 309–37.

Lieu, S. N. C. "From History to Legend and Legend to History: The Medieval and Byzantine Transformation of Constantine's *Vita*." In *Constantine: History, Historiography and Legend*, ed. S. Lieu and D. Montserrat, 136–76. London, 1998.

———. "Constantine in Legendary Literature." In *The Cambridge Companion to the Age of Constantine*, ed. N. Lenski, 298–321. Rev. ed. Cambridge, 2012.

Lieu, S. N. C., and D. Montserrat, eds. *From Constantine to Julian: Pagan and Byzantine Views. A Source History*. London, 1996.

Lightfoot, J. L. *Lucian, On the Syrian Goddess*. Oxford, 2003.

Linder, A. "Ecclesia and Synagoga in the Medieval Myth of Constantine the Great." *RBPH* 54 (1976): 1019–60.

Lippold, A. "The Ideal of the Ruler and Attachment to Tradition in Pacatus' Panegyric." In *Latin Panegyric*, ed. R. Rees, 360–86. Oxford, 2012.

Llewellyn-Jones, L., and J. Robson. *Ctesias' History of Persia: Tales of the Orient*. London, 2010.

Lloyd, A. B. *Herodotus, Book II*. 3 vols. Leiden, 1975–88.

Lloyd, M. "Paris/Alexandros in Homer and Euripides." *Mnemosyne* 42 (1989): 76–79.

Loraux, N. *Tragic Ways of Killing a Woman*. Translated by A. Forster. Cambridge, MA, 1987.

Lubow, A. *The Reporter Who Would Be King: A Biography of Richard Harding Davis*. New York, 1992.

MacDonald, D. R. *The Acts of Andrew and the Acts of Andrew and Matthias in the City of the Cannibals*. Atlanta, 1990.

MacMullen, R. *Christianizing the Roman Empire (A.D. 100–400)*. New Haven, 1984.

———. *Enemies of the Roman Order*. Oxford, 1966.

Malley, W. J. *Hellenism and Christianity: The Conflict between Hellenic and Christian Wisdom in the* Contra Galilaeos *of Julian the Apostate and the* Contra Julianum *of St. Cyril of Alexandria*. Rome, 1978.

Manganaro, G. "Il poemetto anonimo contra paganos: testo tradizione e commento." *Nuovo Didaskalion* 11 (1961): 23–45.

———. "La reazione pagana a Roma nel 408–9 d.c. e il poemetto anonimo 'Contra Paganos.'" *Giornale italiano di filologia* 13 (1960): 210–24.

Mango, C. "The Tradition of Byzantine Chronography." *HUkSt* 12/13 (1988/1989): 360–72.

Marasco, G. "Sacrifici umani e cospirazioni politiche." *Sileno* 7 (1981): 167–78.

Marcone, A. *Giuliano: L'Imperatore filosofo e sacerdote che tentò la restaurazione del paganesimo*. Rome, 2019.

Markus, R. A. "The Roman Empire in Early Christian Historiography." *Downside Review* 81 (1963): 340–54.

Marsch, E. *Biblische Prophetie und chronographische Dichtung: Stoff- und Wirkungsgeschichte der Vision des Propheten Daniel nach Dan. 7*. Berlin, 1972.

Martin, D. B. *Inventing Superstition: From the Hippocratics to the Christians*. Cambridge, MA, 2004.

Matthews, J. F. "The Historical Setting of the 'Carmen contra paganos' (cod. Par. Lat. 8084)." *Historia* 19 (1970): 464–79.

Mayer, W. "Re-Theorizing Religious Conflict: Early Christianity to Late Antiquity and Beyond." In Mayer and de Wet, *Reconceiving Religious Conflict*, 3–29.

Mayer, W., and C. L. de Wet, eds. *Reconceiving Religious Conflict: New Views from the Formative Centuries of Christianity*. Abingdon, 2018.

Mayer, W., with B. Neil. *Saint John Chrysostom: The Cult of the Saints*. Crestwood, NY, 2006.

McConnachie, J., and R. Tudge. *The Rough Guide to Conspiracy Theories*. London, 2005.

McGill, S., C. Sogno, and E. J. Watts, eds. *From the Tetrarchs to the Theodosians: Later Roman History and Culture, 284–450 CE*. *YCS* 34. Cambridge, 2010.

Meier, M. "Nero, Traian und die Christen in die *Weltchronik* des Johannes Malalas." In *Dalla storiografia ellenistica alla storiografia tardoantica: Aspetti, problemi, prospettive*, ed. U. Roberto and L. Mecella, 239–63. Soveria Mannelli, Italy, 2010.

Meier, M., C. Radtki-Jansen, and F. Schulz, eds. *Die Weltchronik des Johannes Malalas: Autor—Werk—Überlieferung*. Stuttgart, 2016.

Meijering, E. P. *Athanasius: Contra Gentes. Introduction, Translation and Commentary*. Leiden, 1984.

Merrill, E. T. *Essays in Early Christian History*. London, 1924.

Millar, F. "The Jews of the Graeco-Roman Diaspora between Paganism and Christianity, AD 312–438." In *The Jews among Pagans and Christians in the Roman Empire*, ed. J. Lieu, J. North, and T. Rajak, 97–123. London, 1992.

———. "P. Herennius Dexippus: The Greek World and the Third-Century Invasions." *JRS* 59 (1969): 12–29.

———. "Porphyry: Ethnicity, Language, and Alien Wisdom." In *Rome, the Greek World, and the East, volume 3: The Greek World, the Jews, and the East*, ed. F. Millar, H. M. Cotton, and G. M. Rogers, 331–50. Chapel Hill, 2006. [= *Philosophia Togata 2: Plato and Aristotle at Rome*, ed. J. Barnes and M. T. Griffin, 241–62. Oxford, 1997.]

———. *The Roman Near East, 31 BC–AD 337*. Cambridge, MA, 1993.

———. *A Study of Cassius Dio*. Oxford, 1964.

———. "Theodoret of Cyrrhus: A Syrian in Greek Dress?" In *From Rome to Constantinople: Studies in Honour of Averil Cameron*, ed. H. Amirav and B. Haar Romeny, 105–25. Leuven, 2007.

Miller, B. M. *From Liberation to Conquest: The Visual and Popular Cultures of the Spanish-American War of 1898*. Amherst, 2011.

Miller, J. M. "The Descendents of Cain: Notes on Genesis 4." *Zeitschrift für die alttestamentliche Wissenschaft* 86 (1974): 164–74.

Mitchell, M. M. "Patristic Rhetoric on Allegory: Origen and Eustathius Put 1 Samuel 28 on Trial." *JR* 85 (2005): 414–45.

Moffatt, A. "A Record of Public Buildings and Monuments." In Jeffreys, Croke, and Scott, *Studies in John Malalas*, 87–109.

Mombritius, B. *Sanctuarium seu Vitae Sanctorum*. 2 vols. Paris, 1910 (repr. 1978).

Momigliano, A., ed. *The Conflict between Paganism and Christianity in the Fourth Century*. Oxford, 1963.

———. "Flavius Josephus and Alexander's Visit to Jerusalem." *Athenaeum* 57 (1979): 442–48.

———. "Pagan and Christian Historiography in the Fourth Century A.D." In Momigliano, *Conflict between Paganism and Christianity*, 79–99.

Mommsen, T. "Carmen codicis Parisini 8084." *Hermes* 4 (1870): 350–63.

Moore, G. F. *A Critical and Exegetical Commentary on Judges*. Edinburgh, 1895.

Moorton, R. "The Genealogy of Latinus in Vergil's *Aeneid*." *TAPA* 118 (1988): 253–59.

Moreau, J. "Zum Problem der Vita Constantini." *Historia* 4 (1955): 234–45.

Morello, R. "Livy's Alexander Digression (9.17–19): Counterfactuals and Apologetics." *JRS* 92 (2002): 62–85.

Morgan, K. A. *Myth and Philosophy from the Presocratics to Plato*. Cambridge, 2000.

Morlet, S. *La Démonstration Évangélique d'Eusèbe de Césarée: Étude sur l'apologétique chrétienne à l'époque de Constantin*. Paris, 2009.

Moscovich, M. J. "Cassius Dio's Palace Sources for the Reign of Septimius Severus." *Historia* 53 (2004): 356–68.

Mosshammer, A. A. *The* Chronicle *of Eusebius and Greek Chronographic Tradition.* Lewisburg, PA, 1979.

Most, G. W., ed. *Collecting Fragments/Fragmente sammeln.* Göttingen, 1997.

Müller-Karpe, H. *Handbuch der Vorgeschichte.* 3 vols. Munich, 1966–74.

Muntz, C. E. *Diodorus Siculus and the World of the Late Roman Republic.* Oxford, 2017.

Murray, O. "Greek Historians." In *The Oxford History of Greece and the Hellenistic World*, ed. J. Boardman, J. Griffin, and O. Murray, 214–39. Oxford, 1986.

———. "Hecataeus of Abdera and Pharaonic Kingship." *JEA* 56 (1970): 141–71.

Murray, P. "What Is a *Muthos* for Plato?" In Buxton, *From Myth to Reason?*, 251–62.

Naddaff, R. A. *Exiling the Poets: The Production of Censorship in Plato's* Republic. Chicago, 2002.

Nadich, J. *Jewish Legends of the Second Commonwealth.* Philadelphia, 1983.

Nadig, P. "Antinoos—Ein Paradigma der heidnisch-christlichen Auseinandersetzung." In von Haehling, *Rom und das himmlische Jerusalem*, 237–56.

Nassif, B. "The 'Spiritual Exegesis' of Scripture: The School of Antioch Revisited." *Anglican Theological Review* 75 (1993): 437–70.

Nilsson, M. P. *Geschichte der griechischen Religion.* 3 vols. Munich, 1955–67.

———. "The Origin of Belief among the Greeks in the Divinity of the Heavenly Bodies." *HTR* 33 (1940): 1–8.

Nock, A. D. *Conversion: The Old and the New in Religion from Alexander the Great to Augustine of Hippo.* Oxford, 1933.

———. "The Praises of Antioch." *JEA* 40 (1954): 76–82.

———. *Sallustius, Concerning the Gods and the Universe.* London, 1926.

———. "A Vision of Mandulis Aion." *HTR* 27 (1934): 53–104.

Nöldeke, T. "ΑΣΣΥΡΙΟΣ ΣΥΡΙΟΣ ΣΥΡΟΣ." *Hermes* 5 (1871): 443–68.

Nora, P. "Between Memory and History: *Les Lieux de Mémoire.*" Translated by M. Roudebush. *Representations* 26 (1989): 7–24.

Norman, A. F. *Libanius, Autobiography and Selected Letters.* 2 vols. Cambridge, MA, 1992.

Oakley, F. *Kingship: The Politics of Enchantment.* Oxford, 2006.

Obbink, D. "The Origin of Greek Sacrifice: Theophrastus on Religion and Cultural History." In *Theophrastean Studies: On Natural Science, Physics and Metaphysics, Ethics, Religion, and Rhetoric*, ed. W. W. Fortenbaugh and R. W. Sharples, 272–95. New Brunswick, 1988.

Ogden, Daniel. *The Legend of Seleucus: Kingship, Narrative and Mythmaking in the Ancient World.* Cambridge, 2017.

———. *Perseus*. London, 2008.

O'Keefe, J. J. "Christianizing Malachi: Fifth-Century Insights from Cyril of Alexandria." *VChr* 50 (1996): 136–58.

———. "Impassible Suffering? Divine Passion and Fifth-Century Christology." *TheolSt* 58 (1997): 39–60.

O'Toole, G. J. A. *The Spanish War: An American Epic—1898*. New York, 1984.

Pack, R. "Notes on the *Caesars* of Julian." *TAPA* 77 (1946): 151–57.

Papademetriou, N. D. "Οἱ 'Σοφοὶ Χρονογράφοι' τοῦ Μαλάλα." *Θεολογια* 60 (1989): 672–700.

Parpola, S. "National and Ethnic Identity in the Neo-Assyrian Empire and Assyrian Identity in Post-Empire Times." *Journal of Assyrian Academic Studies* 18 (2004): 5–22.

Partenie, C. *Plato, Selected Myths*. Oxford, 2004.

Parvis, P. "Justin, Philosopher and Martyr: The Posthumous Creation of the *Second Apology*." In *Justin Martyr and His Worlds*, ed. S. Parvis and P. Foster, 22–37. Minneapolis, 2007.

Paschoud, F. *Cinq études sur Zosime*. Paris, 1975.

Patzig, E. "Die Abhängigkeit des Jo. Antiochenus von Jo. Malalas." *BZ* 10 (1901): 40–53.

Pazdernik, C. "'Our Most Pious Consort Given Us by God': Dissident Reactions to the Partnership of Justinian and Theodora, A.D. 525–548." *Classical Antiquity* 13 (1994): 256–81.

Pearson, L. "Credulity and Scepticism in Herodotus." *TAPA* 72 (1941): 335–55.

———. "Thucydides as Reporter and Critic." *TAPA* 78 (1947): 37–60.

Pease, A. S. *M. Tulli Ciceronis De Natura Deorum*. 2 vols. Cambridge, MA, 1955–58.

Pekáry, T. *Das römische Kaiserbildnis in Staat, Kult und Gesellschaft: Dargestellt anhand der Schriftquellen*. Berlin, 1985.

Pelling, C. *Plutarch and History: Eighteen Studies*. Swansea, 2002.

Perry, A. "Killing for 'Mother' Kali." *Time Asia*, 22 July 2002, http://content.time.com/time/subscriber/article/0,33009,322673,00.html.

Perry, B. E. "The Egyptian Legend of Nectanebus." *TAPA* 97 (1966): 327–33.

Peter, H. *Historicorum Romanorum Reliquiae*. 2 vols. Leipzig, 1870–1906.

Pfaff, W. *The Bullet's Song: Romantic Violence and Utopia*. New York, 2004.

Pietri, C. "Les temps de la semaine à Rome et dans l'Italie chrétienne (4–5ᵉ s.)." In *Le Temps chrétien de la fin de l'Antiquité au Moyen Âge, 3ᵉ–13ᵉ siècles: Paris, 9–12 mars 1981*, ed. J.-M. Leroux, 63–97. Paris, 1984.

Popham, M. R. "The Hero of Lefkandi." *Antiquity* 56 (1982): 169–74.

Popović, M. "Zum Bild des römischen Kaisers Trajan in der byzantinischen Literatur." In *Wiener Byzantinistik und Neogräzistik: Beitrage zum Symposion Vierzig Jahre Institut für Byzantinistik und Neogräzistik der Universität Wien in Gedenken an Herbert Hunger (Wien, 4.–7. Dezember 2002)*, ed. W. Hörandner, J. Koder, and M. A. Stassinopoulou, 337–47. Byzantina et Neograeca Vindobonensia 24. Vienna, 2004.

Portmann, W. *Geschichte in der spätantiken Panegyrik*. Frankfurt am Main, 1988.

Potter, D. *Constantine the Emperor*. Oxford, 2013.

Powell, J. E. "The Sources of Plutarch's *Alexander*." *JHS* 59 (1939): 229–40.

Praet, D. "Pythagoreanism and the Planetary Deities: The Philosophical and Literary Master-structure of the *Vita Apollonii*." In Demoen and Praet, *Theios Sophistes*, 283–320.

Preston, R. "Roman Questions, Greek Answers: Plutarch and the Construction of Identity." In Goldhill, *Being Greek under Rome*, 86–119.

Price, S. R. F. *Rituals and Power: The Roman Imperial Cult in Asia Minor*. Cambridge, 1984.

Prusac, M. "*Presence* and the Image Controversies in the Third and Fourth Centuries AD." In Kolrud and Prusac, *Iconoclasm*, 41–56.

Quaegebeur, J. "Les appellations grecques des temples de Karnak." *OLP* 6/7 (1975/76): 463–78.

———. "Greco-Egyptian Double Names as a Feature of a Bi-cultural Society: The Case of Ψοσνευς ὁ καὶ Τριάδελφος." In *Life in a Multi-cultural Society: Egypt from Cambyses to Constantine and Beyond*, ed. J. H. Johnson, 265–72. Chicago, 1992.

Rea, G. B. *Facts and Fakes about Cuba: A Review of Various Stories Circulated in the United States Concerning the Present Insurrection*. New York, 1897.

Redford, D. B. *Pharaonic King-Lists, Annals and Day-Books: A Contribution to the Study of the Egyptian Sense of History*. Mississauga, ON, 1986.

Reed, A. Y. *Fallen Angels and the History of Judaism and Christianity: The Reception of Enochic Literature*. Cambridge, 2005.

Rehm, R. *Marriage to Death: The Conflation of Wedding and Funeral Rituals in Greek Tragedy*. Princeton, 1994.

Reimitz, H. *History, Frankish Identity and the Framing of Western Ethnicity, 550–850*. Cambridge, 2015.

Ridings, D. *The Attic Moses: The Dependency Theme in Some Early Christian Writers*. Göteborg, 1995.

Riemer, U. "Domitian—(k)ein Christenverfolger?" *Zeitschrift für Religions- und Geistesgeschichte* 52 (2000): 75–80.

Rives, J. B. "Human Sacrifice among Pagans and Christians." *JRS* 85 (1995): 65–85.

———. "Phrygian Tales." *GRBS* 45 (2005): 223–44.

Rizzi, M., ed. *Hadrian and the Christians*. Berlin, 2010.

Roberto, U. "Julius Africanus und die Tradition der hellenistischen Universalgeschichte." In Wallraff, *Julius Africanus und die christliche Weltchronistik*, 3–16.

Robertson Smith, W. *Lectures on the Religion of the Semites*. New York, 1927.

Roisman, J. "Hieronymus of Cardia: Causation and Bias from Alexander to His Successors." In *Philip II and Alexander the Great: Father and Son, Lives and Afterlives*, ed. E. D. Carney and D. Ogden, 135–48. Oxford, 2010.

———. *The Rhetoric of Conspiracy in Ancient Athens*. Berkeley, 2006.

Rollinger, R. "Assyria in Classical Sources." In Frahm, *A Companion to Assyria*, 570–82.

———. "Assyrios, Syrios, Syros und Leukosyros." *Die Welt des Orients* 36 (2006): 72–82.

———. "The Terms 'Assyria' and 'Syria' Again." *JNES* 65 (2006): 283–87.

Rosivach, V. J. "Latinus' Genealogy and the Palace of Picus (*Aeneid* 7.45–9, 170–91)." *CQ* (1980): 140–52.

Roubekas, N. P. *An Ancient Theory of Religion: Euhemerism from Antiquity to the Present*. London, 2017.

Routh, M. J. "Julius Africanus, ex libris quinque de temporibus seu chronico." In *Reliquiae Sacrae*, ed. M. J. Routh, 2:238–309, 357–509. 5 vols. Oxford, 1846–48.

Rowe, C. "Myth, History, and Dialectic in Plato's *Republic* and *Timaeus-Critias*." In Buxton, *From Myth to Reason?*, 263–78.

Rowley, H. H. *Darius the Mede and the Four World Empires in the Book of Daniel: A Historical Study of Contemporary Theories*. Cardiff, 1964.

Rubiés, J.-P. "Nero in Tacitus and Nero in Tacitism: The Historian's Craft." In Elsner and Masters, *Reflections of Nero*, 29–47.

Rusten, J. S. *Dionysius Scytobrachion*. Opladen, 1982.

Ruzicka, S. *Trouble in the West: Egypt and the Persian Empire, 525–332 BCE*. Oxford, 2012.

Ryberg, I. S. "Tacitus' Art of Innuendo." *TAPA* 73 (1942): 383–404.

Rydén, L., and J. O. Rosenqvist, eds. *Aspects of Late Antiquity and Early Byzantium*. Swedish Research Institute in Istanbul, Transactions, vol. 4. Stockholm, 1993.

Sacks, K. S. "Diodorus and His Sources: Conformity and Creativity." In *Greek Historiography*, ed. S. Hornblower, 213–32. Oxford, 1994.

———. *Diodorus Siculus and the First Century*. Princeton, 1990.

———. *Polybius on the Writing of History*. Berkeley, 1981.

Sagan, E. *The Honey and the Hemlock: Democracy and Paranoia in Ancient Athens and Modern America*. New York, 1991.

Saliou, Catherine. "Les lieux du polythéisme dans l'espace urbain et le paysage mémoriel d'Antioche-sur-l'Oronte, de Libanios à Malalas (4e–6e s.)." In *Religious Practices and Christianization of the Late Antique City (4th–7th cent.)*, ed. A. Busine, 38–70. Leiden, 2015.

———. "Statues d'Antioche de Syrie dans la Chronographie de Malalas." In *Recherches sur la Chronique de Jean Malalas* 2, ed. S. Agusta-Boularot et al., 69–95. Paris, 2006.

Samuel, A. E. "The Ptolemies and the Ideology of Kingship." In *Hellenistic History and Culture*, ed. P. Green, 168–92. Berkeley, 1993.

Samuels, H., and P. Samuels. *Frederic Remington: A Biography*. Garden City, 1982.

Sartori, P. "Über das Bauopfer." *Zeitschrift für Ethnologie* 30 (1898): 1–54.

Sauer, E. W. "Disabling Demonic Images: Regional Diversity in Ancient Iconoclasts' Motives and Targets." In Kolrud and Prusac, *Iconoclasm*, 15–40.

Schäublin, C. *Untersuchungen zu Methode und Herkunft der antiochenischen Exegese*. Cologne, 1974.

Schmidt, P. L. "Zu den Quellen der römischen Mythistorie bei den frühen lateinischen Apologeten." *StP* 19 (1989): 99–105.

Schnusenberg, C. *The Relationship between the Church and the Theatre: Exemplified by Selected Writings of the Church Fathers and by Liturgical Texts until Amalarius of Metz, 75–852 AD*. Lanham, MD, 1988.

Schoene, A., ed. *Eusebi Chronicorum libri duo*. 2 vols. Berlin, 1866–75.

Scott, A. *Origen and the Life of the Stars: A History of an Idea*. Oxford, 1991.

Scott, R. "Malalas' View of the Classical Past." In *Reading the Past in Late Antiquity*, ed. G. Clarke, with B. Croke, R. Mortley, and A. E. Nobbs, 147–64. Rushcutters Bay, New South Wales, 1990.

Segal, Charles. "Golden Armor and Servile Robes: Heroism and Metamorphosis in *Hecuba* of Euripides." *AJP* 111 (1990): 304–17.

Setton, K. M. *Christian Attitude towards the Emperor in the Fourth Century, Especially as Shown in Addresses to the Emperor*. New York, 1941.

Shanzer, D. *A Philosophical and Literary Commentary on Martianus Capella's* De Nuptiis Philologiae et Mercurii *Book 1*. Berkeley, 1986.

Shatzman, I. "Tacitean Rumours." *Latomus* 33 (1974): 549–78.

Shelton, K. J. "Imperial Tyches." *Gesta* 18 (1979): 27–38.

Shepardson, C. "Rewriting Julian's Legacy: John Chrysostom's *On Babylas* and Libanius' *Oration* 24." *JLA* 2 (2009): 99–115.

Sherwin-White, S. "Aristeas Ardibelteios: Some Aspects of the Use of Double Names in Seleucid Babylonia." *ZPapEpig* 50 (1983): 209–24.

Simmons, M. B. *Arnobius of Sicca: Religious Conflict and Competition in the Age of Diocletian*. Oxford, 1995.

Simon, M. *Verus Israel: Étude sur les relations entre les chrétiens et juifs dans l'empire romain (135–425)*. Paris, 1964.

Simonetti, M. *Biblical Interpretation in the Early Church: An Historical Introduction to Patristic Exegesis*. Translated by J. A. Hughes, edited by A. Bergquist and M. Bockmuehl. Edinburgh, 1994.

Simpson, R. H. "Abbreviation of Hieronymus in Diodorus." *AJP* 80 (1959): 370–79.

Skinner, J. *A Critical and Exegetical Commentary on Genesis*. 2nd ed. Edinburgh, 1930.

Smalley, B. *The Study of the Bible in the Middle Ages*. 3rd ed. Oxford, 1983.

Smelik, K. A. D. "My Servant Nebuchadnezzar: The Use of the Epithet 'My Servant' for the Babylonian King Nebuchadnezzar in the Book of Jeremiah." *Vetus Testamentum* 64 (2014): 109–34.

Smith, A. "The Image of Cromwell in Folklore and Tradition." *Folklore* 79 (1968): 17–39.

Smith, C. "C. Sempronius Tuditanus." In Cornell, *Fragments of the Roman Historians*, 1:240–42, 2:336–43, 3:222–24.

Smith, R. B. E. "The Casting of Julian the Apostate 'in the Likeness' of Alexander the Great: A Topos in Antique Historiography and its Modern Echoes." *Histos* 5 (2011): 44–106.

———. *Julian's Gods: Religion and Philosophy in the Thought and Action of Julian the Apostate*. London, 1995.

———. "A Lost Historian of Alexander 'Descended from Alexander', and Read by Julian? Praxagoras of Athens Reviewed in the Light of Attic Epigraphy." *Historia* 56 (2007): 356–80.

Smith, W. R. *The Religion of the Semites: The Fundamental Institutions*. New York, 1956.

Sokoloff, M. *The Julian Romance: A New English Translation, revised edition*. Piscataway, 2017.

Soraci, R. "La figura di Alessandro Magno nell'opera di Ammiano Marcellino." In Will and Heinrichs, *Zu Alexander d. Gr.*, 2:1006–22.

Southern, P. *Augustus*. London, 1998.

Spalinger, A. "The Date of the Dream of Nectanebo." *Studien zur Altägyptischen Kultur* 19 (1992): 295–304.

Spencer, Diana. *The Roman Alexander: Reading a Cultural Myth*. Exeter Press, 2002.

Spencer, David R. *The Yellow Journalism: The Press and America's Emergence as a World Power*. Evanston, IL, 2007.

Ste. Croix, G. E. M. de. "Aristotle on History and Poetry (*Poetics*, 9, 1451a36–b11)." In *Essays on Aristotle's* Poetics, ed. A. O. Rorty, 23–32. Princeton, 1992.

Stein, E. *Histoire du Bas-Empire*. 2 vols. Paris, 1949–59.

Stoneman, R. *Alexander the Great: A Life in Legend*. Yale, 2008.

———. "Jewish Traditions on Alexander the Great." *Studia Philonica Annual* 6 (1994): 37–53.

———. "The Latin Alexander." In *Latin Fiction: The Latin Novel in Context*, ed. H. Hofmann, 167–86. London, 1999.

Stoneman, R., K. Nawotka, and A. Wojciechowska, eds. *The* Alexander Romance: *History and Literature*. Groningen, 2018.

Strait, D. J. "The Wisdom of Solomon, Ruler Cults, and Paul's Polemic against Idols in the Areopagus Speech." *JBL* 136 (2017): 609–32.

Stroumsa, G. G. *The End of Sacrifice: Religious Transformations in Late Antiquity*. Translated by S. Emanuel. Chicago, 2009.

Stuart, M. "How Were Imperial Portraits Distributed throughout the Roman Empire?" *AJA* 43 (1939): 601–17.

Sulimani, I. *Diodorus' Mythistory and the Pagan Mission: Historiography and Culture-Heroes in the First Pentad of the* Bibliotheke. Leiden, 2011.

Sullivan, K. "The Watchers Traditions in *1 Enoch* 6–16: The Fall of Angels and the Rise of Demons." In Harkins, Bautch, and Endres, *Watchers*, 91–103.

Sunstein, C. R. *Conspiracy Theories and Other Dangerous Ideas*. New York, 2014.

Svoray, Y., with T. Hughes. *Gods of Death*. New York, 1997.

Swain, S. *Hellenism and Empire: Language, Classicism, and Power in the Greek World AD 50–250*. Oxford, 1996.

———. "Plutarch: Chance, Providence, and History." *AJP* 110 (1989): 272–302.

———. "Plutarch's *De Fortuna Romanorum*." *CQ* 39 (1989): 504–16.

Swerdlow, N. M. "On the Cosmical Mysteries of Mithras." *CPh* 86 (1991): 48–63.

Swift, E. H. "Imagines in Imperial Portraiture." *AJA* 27 (1923): 286–301.

Syme, R. *Emperors and Biography: Studies in the Historia Augusta*. Oxford, 1971.

———. "Praesens the Friend of Hadrian." In *Studia in Honorem Iiro Kajanto*, 273–91. *Arctos*, suppl. 11. Helsinki, 1985.

———. *Tacitus*. 2 vols. Oxford, 1958.

Sypherd, W. O. *Jephthah and His Daughter: A Study in Comparative Literature.* Newark, DE, 1948.

Szalc, A. "Kandake, Meroe and India—India and the Alexander Romance." In *Alexander the Great and Egypt: History, Art, Tradition*, ed. V. Grieb, K. Nawotka, and A. Wojciechowska, 377–90. Wiesbaden, 2014.

Szidat, J. "*Alexandrum Imitatus* (Amm. 24,4,27): Die Beziehung Iulians zu Alexander in der Sicht Ammians." In Will and Heinrichs, *Zu Alexander d. Gr.*, 2:1023–35.

Tcherikover, V. A. *Hellenistic Civilization and the Jews.* Translated by S. Applebaum. Philadelphia, 1959.

Thompson, D. *Counterknowledge: How We Surrendered to Conspiracy Theories, Quack Medicine, Bogus Science, and Fake History.* Toronto, 2008.

Tierney, P. *The Highest Altar: Unveiling the Mystery of Human Sacrifice.* New York, 1989.

Timpe, D. "Domitian als Christenfeind und die Tradition der Verfolgerkaiser." In *Heil und Geshichte: Die Geschichtsbezogenheit des Heils und das Problem der Heilsgeschichte in der biblischen Tradition und in der theologischen Deutung*, ed. J. Frey, S. Krauter, and H. Lichtenberger, 213–42. Tübingen, 2009.

Torrance, A. "Barsanuphius, John, and Dorotheos on Scripture: Voices from the Desert in Sixth-Century Gaza." In *What Is the Bible? The Patristic Doctrine of Scripture*, ed. M. Baker and M. Mourachian, 67–81. Minneapolis, 2016.

Toynbee, J. M. C. "Roma and Constantinopolis in Late Antique Art from 312 to 365." *JRS* 37 (1947): 135–44.

Treadgold, W. T. "Byzantine Historiography and the Supposedly Lost Books of Ammianus Marcellinus." In *Armenia between Byzantium and the Orient: Celebrating the Memory of Karen Yuzbashyan (1927–2009)*, ed. B. Outtier, C. B. Horn, B. Lourié, and A. Ostrovsky, 530–79. Leiden, 2020.

———. "The Byzantine World Histories of John Malalas and Eustathius of Epiphania." *International History Review* 29 (2007): 709–45.

———. *The Early Byzantine Historians.* Basingstoke, 2007.

———. *The Middle Byzantine Historians.* Basingstoke, 2013.

———. *The Nature of the* Bibliotheca *of Photius.* Washington, DC, 1980.

———. "Review of Roberto and Mariev." *Speculum* 85 (2010): 689–91.

Trigg, J. W. "Eustathius of Antioch's Attack on Origen: What Is at Issue in an Ancient Controversy?" *JR* 75 (1995): 219–38.

Turcan, R. *The Cults of the Roman Empire.* Translated by A. Nevill. Oxford, 1996.

Turner, A. J., J. H. K. O. Chong-Gossard, and F. Vervaet, eds. *Private and Public Lies: The Discourse of Despotism and Deceit in the Graeco-Roman World*. Leiden, 2010.

Tuzlak, A. "The Magician and the Heretic: The Case of Simon Magus." In *Magic and Ritual in the Ancient World*, ed. P. Mirecki and M. Meyer, 416–26. Leiden, 2002.

Ulansey, D. "Mithras and Perseus." *Society of Biblical Literature Seminar Papers* 21 (1982): 535–39.

———. *The Origins of the Mithraic Mysteries: Cosmology and Salvation in the Ancient World*. Oxford, 1989.

Ulrich, J. "Euseb, HistEccl III, 14–20 und die Frage nach der Christenverfolgung unter Domitian." *Zeitschrift für die neutestamentliche Wissenschaft* 87 (1996): 269–89.

Urbainczyk, T. *Socrates of Constantinople: Historian of Church and State*. Ann Arbor, 1997.

Vale, V. "Churchwardens and the Other God." In Darvill et al., *The Cerne Giant*, 71–75.

Van Dam, R. *The Roman Revolution of Constantine*. Cambridge, 2007.

———. *Rome and Constantinople: Rewriting Roman History during Late Antiquity*. Waco, TX, 2010.

Van Hoof, L., and P. Van Nuffelen. *The Fragmentary Latin Histories of Late Antiquity (AD 300–600): Edition, Translation and Commentary*. Cambridge, 2020.

van Minnen, P. "A Change of Names in Roman Egypt after A.D. 202? A Note on P. Amst. I 72." *ZPapEpig* 62 (1986): 87–92.

Van Nuffelen, P. "Malalas and the Chronographic Tradition." In Carrara, Meier, and Radtki-Jansen, *Die Weltchronik des Johannes Malalas*, 261–72.

Van Nuffelen, P., and L. Van Hoof. *Clavis Historicorum Antiquitatis Posterioris: An Inventory of Late Antique Historiography (A.D. 300–800)*. Turnhout, 2020.

Verbrugghe, G. P., and J. M. Wickersham. *Berossos and Manetho, Introduced and Translated: Native Traditions in Ancient Mesopotamia and Egypt*. Ann Arbor, 1996.

Vermeule, E., and S. Chapman. "A Protoattic Human Sacrifice?" *AJA* 75 (1971): 285–93.

Vessey, M. "Reinventing History: Jerome's *Chronicle* and the Writing of the Post-Roman West." In McGill, Sogno, and Watts, *From the Tetrarchs to the Theodosians*, 265–89.

Vidal-Naquet, P. *The Atlantis Story: A Short History of Plato's Myth*. Translated by J. Lloyd. Exeter, 2007.

Visintin, M. *La vergine e l'eroe: Temesa e la leggenda di Euthymos di Locri*. Bari, 1992.

Vogt, J. *Kaiser Julian und das Judentum: Studien zum Weltanschauungskampf der Spätantike*. Leipzig, 1939.

Vogt-Spira, G. *Dramaturgie des Zufalls: Tyche und Handeln in der Komödie Menanders*. Munich, 1992.

von Fritz, K. "Tacitus, Agricola, Domitian, and the Problem of the Principate." *CPh* 52 (1957): 73–97.

von Haehling, R., ed. *Rom und das himmlische Jerusalem: Die frühen Christen zwischen Anpassung und Ablehung*. Darmstadt, 2000.

von Stauffenberg, A. S. Graf. *Die römische Kaisergeschichte bei Malalas: Griechischer Text der Bücher IX–XII und Untersuchungen*. Stuttgart, 1931.

Vout, C. "Biography as Fantasy, History as Image." In *Antinous: The Face of the Antique*, ed. P. Curtis, 23–39. Leeds, 2006.

Walbank, F. W. *A Historical Commentary on Polybius*. 3 vols. Oxford, 1957–79.

———. *Polybius*. Berkeley, 1972.

Wallace-Hadrill, D. S. *Christian Antioch: A Study of Early Christian Thought in the East*. Cambridge, 1982.

Wallraff, M. *Iulius Africanus, Chronographiae: The Extant Fragments*. Berlin, 2007.

———, ed. *Julius Africanus und die christliche Weltchronistik*. Berlin, 2006.

———. "Die neue Fragmentensammlung der Chronographie des Julius Africanus. Bemerkungen zur Methodik anhand einiger Dubia vel Spuria." In Wallraff, *Julius Africanus und die christliche Weltchronistik*, 45–59.

Walsh, D. *The Cult of Mithras in Late Antiquity: Development, Decline and Demise, ca. AD 270–430*. Leiden, 2019.

Wardman, A. E. "Plutarch and Alexander." *CQ* (1955): 96–107.

Warmington, B. H. "Aspects of Constantinian Propaganda in the Panegyrici Latini." *TAPA* 104 (1974): 371–84.

———. "Eusebius of Caesarea and the Governance of Constantine." In Hillard et al., *Ancient History in a Modern University*, 266–79.

Watts, E. J. *The Final Pagan Generation*. Oakland, 2015.

West, M. L., ed. *Delectus ex Iambis et Elegis Graecis*. Oxford, 1980.

———. *Hesiod, Theogony*. Oxford, 1966.

Westermann, C. *Genesis 1–11: A Commentary*. Translated by J. J. Scullion. Minneapolis, 1984.

Whitby, Michael. "Religious Views of Procopius and Agathias." *Electrum* 13 (2007): 73–93.

———, and Mary Whitby. *Chronicon Paschale 284–628 AD*. Liverpool, 1989.

White, L. "Between Gluckman and Foucault: Historicizing Rumour and Gossip." *Social Dynamics* 20 (1994): 75–92.

———. *Speaking with Vampires: Rumor and History in Colonial Africa*. Berkeley, 2000.

Whitehead, J. D. "Some Distinctive Features of the Language of the Aramaic Arsames Correspondence." *JNES* 37 (1978): 119–40.

Whitmarsh, T. "Alexander's Hellenism and Plutarch's Textualism." *CQ* 52 (2002): 174–92.

Whittaker, C. R. *Frontiers of the Roman Empire: A Social and Economic Study*. Baltimore, 1994.

Wiles, M. F. "Theodore of Mopsuestia as Representative of the Antiochene School." In *The Cambridge History of the Bible, Volume 1: From the Beginnings to Jerome*, ed. P. R. Ackroyd and C. F. Evans, 489–510. Cambridge, 1970.

Wilken, R. L. *John Chrysostom and the Jews: Rhetoric and Reality in the Late 4th Century*. Berkeley, 1983.

Wilkinson, K. W. "Palladas and the Age of Constantine." *JRS* 99 (2009): 36–60.

———. "Palladas and the Foundation of Constantinople." *JRS* 100 (2010): 179–94.

Will, W., and J. Heinrichs, eds. *Zu Alexander d. Gr.: Festschrift G. Wirth zum 60. Geburtstag am 9.12.86*. 2 vols. Amsterdam, 1987–88.

Williams, C. *Roman Homosexuality: Ideologies of Masculinity in Classical Antiquity*. Oxford, 1999.

Williams, J. "From Jerusalem to the Ends of the Earth: The Meaning of Paul's Two Names at Acts 13.9." In *Fame and Infamy: Essays for Christopher Pelling on Characterization in Greek and Roman Biography and Historiography*, ed. R. Ash, J. M. Mossman, and F. B. Titchener, 327–34. Oxford, 2015.

Wilmanns, W. "Alexander und Candace." *Zeitschrift für deutsches Altertum und deutsche Literatur* 45 (1901): 229–44.

Winiarczyk, M. *Euhemeros von Messene: Leben, Werk und Nachwirkung*. Munich, 2002.

———. *The* Sacred History *of Euhemerus of Messene*. Translated by W. Zbirohowski-Kościa. Berlin, 2013.

Winkelmann, F. "Historiography in the Age of Constantine." In *Greek and Roman Historiography in Late Antiquity: Fourth to Sixth Century AD*, ed. G. Marasco, 3–41. Leiden, 2003.

Winkler, J. J. "Lollianos and the Desperadoes." *JHS* 100 (1980): 155–81.

———. "The Mendacity of Kalasiris and the Narrative Strategy of Heliodoros' *Aithiopika*." In *Oxford Readings in the Greek Novel*, ed. S. Swain, 286–350. Oxford, 1999. [= *YCS* 27 [(1982): 109–35.]

Wirth, G. *Der Weg in die Vergessenheit: Zum Schicksal des antiken Alexanderbildes*. Vienna, 1993.

Wisan, J. E. *The Cuban Crisis as Reflected in the New York Press (1895–1898)*. New York, 1934.

Wiseman, T. P. "Lying Historians: Seven Types of Mendacity." In Gill and Wiseman, *Lies and Fiction*, 122–46.

———. "Monuments and the Roman Annalists." In *Past Perspectives: Studies in Greek and Roman Historical Writing*, ed. I. S. Moxon, J. D. Smart, and A. J. Woodman, 87–100. Cambridge, 1986.

———. *Remus: A Roman Myth*. Cambridge, 1995.

Wood, G. S. "Conspiracy and the Paranoid Style: Causality and Deceit in the Eighteenth Century." *William and Mary Quarterly* 39 (1982): 401–41.

Wood, I. "Incest, Law and the Bible in Sixth-Century Gaul." *EME* 7 (1998): 291–304.

Wood, P. "Multiple Voices in Chronicle Sources: The Reign of Leo I (457–474) in Book Fourteen of Malalas." *JLA* 4 (2011): 298–314.

———. *"We Have No King but Christ": Christian Political Thought in Greater Syria on the Eve of the Arab Conquest (c. 400–585)*. Oxford, 2010.

Woodford, S. *The Trojan War in Ancient Art*. Ithaca, 1993.

Woodhouse, W. J. *Aetolia, Its Geography, Topography, and Antiquities*. Oxford, 1897.

Woodward, J. M. *Perseus: A Study in Greek Art and Legend*. Cambridge, 1937.

Wooten, C. W. "The Nature of Form in Demosthenes' *De corona*." *Classical World* 72 (1979): 321–27.

Wylie, A. B. "The Exegesis of History in John Chrysostom's *Homilies on Acts*." In *Biblical Hermeneutics in Historical Perspective: Studies in Honor of Karlfried Froehlich on His Sixtieth Birthday*, ed. M. S. Burrows and P. Rorem, 59–72. Grand Rapids, 1991.

Yarrow, L. M. *Historiography at the End of the Republic: Provincial Perspectives on Roman Rule*. Oxford, 2006.

Young, F. M. "Alexandrian and Antiochene Exegesis." In Hauser and Watson, *A History of Biblical Interpretation*, 1, 334–54.

———. *Biblical Exegesis and the Formation of Christian Culture*. Cambridge, 1997.

———. "The Rhetorical Schools and Their Influence on Patristic Exegesis." In *The Making of Orthodoxy: Essays in Honour of Henry Chadwick*, ed. R. Williams, 182–99. Cambridge, 1989.

———. "Traditions of Exegesis." In *The New Cambridge History of the Bible, Volume 1: From the Beginnings to 600*, ed. J. C. Paget and J. Schaper, 734–51. Cambridge, 2013.

Zanker, P. "Prinzipat und Herrscherbild." *Gymnasium* 86 (1979): 353–68 (plates I–XII).

Ziegler, R. "Der Perseus-Mythos im Prestigedenken kaiserzeitlicher städtischer Eliten Kilikiens." In *Griechische Mythologie und frühes Christentum: Die antiken Götter und der eine Gott*, ed. R. von Haehling, 85–105. Darmstadt, 2005.

Zuckerman, C. "Heraclius and the Return of the Holy Cross." In *Constructing the Seventh Century* (*TM* 17), ed. C. Zuckerman, 197–218. Paris, 2013.

INDEX OF FRAGMENTS

INDEX LOCORUM

BIBLICAL PASSAGES

GENERAL INDEX

Page numbers in *italics* indicate illustrative material. Titles of authored works will be found under the name of the author.